# Oracle Linux Cookbook

Embrace Oracle Linux and master Linux Server Management

**Erik Benner**

**Erik B. Thomsen**

**Jonathan Spindel**

BIRMINGHAM—MUMBAI

# Oracle Linux Cookbook

**Group Product Manager**: Pavan Ramchandani
**Publishing Product Manager**: Neha Sharma
**Book Project Manager**: Neil Dmello
**Senior Editor**: Romy Dias
**Technical Editor**: Rajat Sharma
**Copy Editor**: Safis Editing
**Language Support Editor**: Safis Editing
**Proofreader**: Safis Editing
**Indexer**: Subalakshmi Govindhan
**Production Designer**: Nilesh Mohite
**DevRel Marketing Coordinator**: Marylou Dmello

First published: January 2024
Production reference: 1221223

Published by Packt Publishing Ltd.
Grosvenor House
11 St Paul's Square
Birmingham
B3 1RB, UK

ISBN 978-1-80324-928-5
www.packtpub.com

*To Wim Coekaerts, Robert Shimp, Jim Wright, and the Oracle Product Management team, which works to keep Oracle Linux free to download, free to distribute, and free to use.*

# Foreword

This book is for systems administrators who are either interested in, looking to switch to, or have chosen Oracle Linux for their IT infrastructure. Welcome!

*Oracle Linux Cookbook* brings together two great technologists (Erik Benner and Erik Thomsen) serving up a generous helping of Linux know-how that will have you hungry for more. The Eriks share their combined knowledge and experience through easy-to-follow steps, troubleshooting tips, and tested best practices that can help you master adopting and managing your Oracle Linux systems.

I've had the pleasure of knowing Erik Benner for many years, as we've both worked with (or in my case, at) Oracle since the mid-late 1990s. Erik is well versed in core Oracle technologies, including Oracle Linux, Oracle Cloud, and Oracle Database. His experience in creating, delivering, and managing Oracle-based solutions spans government and commercial customers of all sizes, which means he's dealt with nearly everything imaginable when it comes to technology implementations—from those that deserved a Michelin star rating to those he's had to save from being undercooked catastrophes.

A member of the Oracle Linux team, Erik B. Thomsen started his software career while on active duty in the US Air Force. There, he sought creative, out-of-the-box ways to solve problems, including using database technology. He sharpened his skills at a global aerospace company where his passion for Linux and open source software took hold. He has held positions including as a DBA, product manager, and DevOps engineer. Erik is passionate about delivering finely assembled technological solutions and writing thorough procedural documentation, akin to a masterful recipe. He has proved his mettle helping customers streamline processes and achieve outstanding results.

Jonathan Spindel is a seasoned technologist and an Oracle subject matter expert, with more than 23 years of experience providing end-to-end management and delivering turnkey cloud solutions. This, coupled with his expertise in automation leads to high quality processes and satisfied customers.

*Oracle Linux Cookbook* covers a wide range of topics: from installation and upgrades to software management and security to storage and containers. Several Oracle Linux ingredients are detailed, such as the Unbreakable Enterprise Kernel, Red Hat Compatible Kernel, Btrfs, Leapp, and Podman. A chapter is dedicated to the use of Oracle Ksplice to help you improve system security. Guides to building an operational **Preboot Execution Environment** (**PXE**) are provided and Application Streams are described in depth. You will also discover how to automate tasks with Ansible and Terraform and build RPM packages for custom applications.

After reading this book, you'll have a solid understanding of Oracle Linux and how to use it to optimize server performance, availability, and security—in addition to getting a taste of what makes it unique among Enterprise Linux distributions. In my decades of working with our customers, they consistently say that performance, stability, and security are the key reasons they've become Oracle Linux connoisseurs. I hope you'll join them.

Whether you're new to Oracle Linux or an experienced systems administrator continuing to sharpen your skills, this is an excellent reference book and one that should become an indispensable addition to your bookshelf.

It's time to get cooking with Oracle Linux.

*Robert G. Shimp,*

*Senior Vice President,*

*Infrastructure Software Product Management, Oracle*

# Contributors

## About the authors

**Erik Benner** is the VP of Enterprise Transformation and an Oracle ACE director. He is an expert strategist for customers across the United States. His customer engagements range from enterprise cloud transformations to data center consolidation and modernization. He frequently presents at conferences such as Oracle CloudWorld, ASCEND, BLUEPRINT 4D, and FOSSY. Having worked with Oracle and Sun Systems since the mid-90s, Erik is well-versed in most of the core Oracle technologies, including Oracle Cloud, Oracle Linux, and Oracle Database. When not flying to far points of the country from the Metro Atlanta area, he enjoys spending time with his family at their observatory, where the telescopes outnumber the people.

*This book is for all the family members who felt left out when the last one was dedicated to someone from work. I also want to thank Sloan Frey for supporting my after-hours efforts.* ☺

**Erik B. Thomsen** is a principal sales consultant passionate about Linux, cloud-native technologies, and "Everything as Code." He is an innovative strategist with extensive experience working in multiple facets of IT, including DevSecOps, product management for databases and Linux, and platform engineering, where he led the development of an enterprise Kubernetes container platform. He has many years of consulting experience working for numerous Fortune 500 companies. Often described as a "visionary" or "thought leader" by his peers, Erik leverages his expertise in technology with his creative development and automation skills to help customers design, deploy, and manage cutting-edge IT solutions.

*I dedicate this book to my parents, wife, and children. To my parents, thank you for always believing in me and teaching me there are no limits if we have the right mindset. To my wife, for all your support in proofreading my work and letting me geek out on my hobbies. To my children, for giving me some of the most joyous moments of my life that I will forever cherish. I love you all.*

**Jonathan Spindel** is a highly skilled and experienced technology leader and evangelist with a strong emphasis on Oracle ecosystems cloud infrastructure and automation. With over 23 years in the industry, he possesses a comprehensive understanding of managing, designing, and deploying multi-tenant enterprise systems and cloud solutions to address business needs and enhance operational processes. Jonathan excels in providing end-to-end management and technical turnkey cloud solutions that drive increased business productivity and reduce operational costs, ultimately delivering timely returns on investment. His hands-on approach and deep expertise in Oracle and mainstream infrastructure and cloud technologies enable him to optimize performance and streamline operations, while his proficiency in automation ensures efficient and error-free processes.

*To my amazing parents, whose love and sacrifice have been the foundation of my life. Your unwavering support and belief in me have fueled my aspirations. To my loving wife, your unwavering presence, love, and encouragement have been my anchor in the stormy seas of life. To my wonderful children, you are my greatest joy and inspiration. Every word I write, every accomplishment I achieve, is dedicated to you. This book is a tribute to the immeasurable love and gratitude I hold in my heart for each of you. Thank you for being my rock, my light, and my reason to dream.*

# About the reviewers

For nearly a decade, **Avi Miller** was one of the Oracle Linux product managers at Oracle. His experience spans the operating system, virtualization, and application stacks, having worked at both small development houses and large enterprise hardware and software vendors. These days, he does open source things for Oracle Cloud Infrastructure. At night and on weekends, his love for technology extends to annoying his husband with smart home upgrades as well as more useful stuff such as volunteering for community-based organizations.

**Satishbabu Gunukula** has over 23 years of experience in a wide range of technologies and specializes in highly available solutions such as databases (Oracle, MS SQL Server, SAP HANA, MySQL, etc.), data analytics, and visualization (Tableau, SAP, Microsoft, etc.), middleware, the cloud (OCI, AWS, Azure), business apps (ERP, Hyperion, Agile, etc.) and systems administration. He has implemented business-critical systems for Fortune 500 companies. He has been honored with the prestigious Oracle ACE Pro Award and World Innovation Day Hack 2023 Honorable and Finalist Mentor awards. He has done a master's degree in computer applications, written articles for major publications, spoken at Oracle-related events, and technical reviews for five books with PACKT Publishing.

*I am grateful to my whole family for providing me with support, tolerating my busy schedule, and still standing by my side.*

# Table of Contents

# 3

# Exploring the Various Boot Options and Kernels in Oracle Linux          65

# 4

# Creating and Managing Single-Instance Filesystems          95

# 5

# Software Management with DNF                                           127

# 6

# Eliminating All the SPOFs! An Exercise in Redundancy          161

# 9

## Keeping the Data Safe – Securing a System    279

# 10

## Revisiting Modules and AppStreams    313

# 11

## Lions, Tigers, and Containers – Oh My! Podman and Friends    331

# 12

# Navigating Ansible Waters                                359

# 13

# Let's All Go to the Cloud                                429

# Preface

Enterprise Linux stands out as the premier choice for organizations seeking a robust, secure, and reliable operating system. In the realm of Linux distributions, Enterprise Linux, exemplified by distributions such as Oracle Linux and Rocky Linux, has earned its reputation as the go-to solution for businesses worldwide. This book explores the key reasons why Oracle Linux is considered the best distribution for enterprise environments and explores several technologies, including Oracle's distribution, through a series of easy-to-follow, step-by-step examples called recipes. These recipes will teach you how to use technologies in several key areas.

Security is paramount in enterprise environments, and Oracle Linux has set the standard for robust security features. Features such as **Security-Enhanced Linux (SELinux)**, mandatory access control, and a proactive security patching system for no-downtime patching contribute to creating a secure environment. Regular security audits and prompt zero-downtime patching help mitigate vulnerabilities, making Oracle Linux a trusted choice for handling sensitive and mission-critical data.

Enterprise Linux distributions are designed to scale seamlessly, whether on a single server or in a large-scale, clustered environment. The performance optimizations integrated into these distributions ensure that they can handle the demands of modern enterprise applications. Oracle Linux is the leader in performance, with the option to use the Oracle **Unbreakable Enterprise Kernel (UEK)**. This book covers how to install this option and shows several of the key features it brings to the table, such as the Btrfs filesystem. We also cover availability, with more easy-to-follow recipes that cover highly available storage and application clustering.

Oracle Linux benefits from a vast ecosystem of software and applications that are certified and optimized for compatibility. This ecosystem includes database management systems, development tools, middleware, and enterprise applications, making it easier for organizations to build, deploy, and manage their software stacks. This book highlights some of these technologies that support DevOps and DevSecOps teams, such as Ansible and Podman.

Oracle Linux stands tall as the best distribution for enterprise environments due to its rock-solid stability, robust security features, scalability, comprehensive support, compliance with industry standards, and a rich ecosystem. Whether managing critical workloads, securing sensitive data, or ensuring high-performance computing, Enterprise Linux continues to be the top choice for organizations aiming for a reliable and secure operating system.

# Who this book is for

This book is for Enterprise Linux admins, specifically admins that manage Oracle Enterprise Linux. Whether you are migrating from CentOS or building a new system, this book is full of useful tricks and tips. The author's goal is to help you be a more productive admin, adding new technologies to your bag of tricks to make you stand out from the rest.

This book is for Linux system administrators and developers of applications that run on Oracle Linux 8, so you should have a basic understanding of Linux administration and be comfortable with editing configuration files.

# What this book covers

*Chapter 1*, *Oracle Linux 8 – Get It? Got It? Good!*, covers how you can get Oracle Linux, upgrade Oracle Linux versions, and run them on ARM systems and the cloud!

*Chapter 2*, *Installing with and without Automation Magic*, is where we will automate the installation of Oracle Linux with PXE and kickstart the process.

*Chapter 3*, *Exploring the Various Boot Options and Kernels in Oracle Linux*, explores what a kernel is and how UEK is different.

*Chapter 4*, *Creating and Managing Single-Instance Filesystems*, provides tricks and tips to better manage Btrfs, xfs, and RAID.

*Chapter 5*, *Software Management with DNF*, we will look at how to build local reops, make custom RPMs, and better leverage DNF.

*Chapter 6*, *Eliminate All the SPOFs! An Exercise in Redundancy*, covers eliminating single points of failure through load balancing, proxies, clusters, cluster filesystems, and network redundancy options.

*Chapter 7*, *Oracle Linux 8 – Patching Doesn't Have to Mean Rebooting*, covers how to patch without rebooting. We will also look at what Ksplice is and why you should be using it.

*Chapter 8*, *DevOps Automation Tools – Terraform, Ansible, Packer, and More*, looks at automating the management with Terraform, Vagrant, and Packer.

*Chapter 9*, *Keeping the Data Safe – Securing a System*, looks at how to keep out of the news by securing your systems. We will cover encrypting your data, using SELinux, scanning systems for vulnerabilities, and managing GPG keys for signing things.

*Chapter 10*, *Revisiting Modules and AppStreams*, looks at how AppStreams has changed software deployment and modernizing application deployments.

*Chapter 11*, *Lions, Tigers, and Containers – Oh My! Podman and Friends*, looks at what Podman is, how to use it as a Docker replacement, and how to use Podman, Buildah, and Skopeo to facilitate all your containerized needs.

*Chapter 12, Navigating Ansible Waters*, covers everything Ansible, from deploying Ansible at the enterprise level with **Oracle Linux Automation Manager (OLAM)** to writing playbooks.

*Chapter 13, Let's All Go to the Cloud*, moves us to the cloud, where we will look at building custom images for AWS and OCI, as well as how to build new VMs in the cloud.

## To get the most out of this book

Many of the recipes in this book can be carried out on your desktop system, leveraging Oracle VM VirtualBox to run some complex systems as VMs. We are assuming you are familiar with the basic Linux installation process and admin skills such as becoming the root user.

| Software/hardware covered in the book | OS requirements |
| --- | --- |
| Oracle Linux 8 | Oracle Linux 8 |

Many of these recipes assume you are the root user, and most admin tasks require this access.

**If you are using the digital version of this book, we advise you to type the code yourself or access the code via the GitHub repository (link available in the next section). Doing so will help you avoid any potential errors related to the copying and pasting of code.**

## Download the example code files

You can download the example code files for this book from GitHub at `https://github.com/PacktPublishing/Oracle-Linux-Cookbook`. In case there's an update to the code, it will be updated on the existing GitHub repository.

We also have other code bundles from our rich catalog of books and videos available at `https://github.com/PacktPublishing/`. Check them out!

## Conventions used

There are a number of text conventions used throughout this book.

`Code in text`: Indicates code words in text, database table names, folder names, filenames, file extensions, pathnames, dummy URLs, user input, and Twitter handles. Here is an example: "Using the `.efi` file gives a user more control of the boot process, including the ability to take advantage of new security features."

A block of code is set as follows:

```
[ req ]
default_bits = 4096
distinguished_name = req_distinguished_name
prompt = no
string_mask = utf8only
x509_extensions = extensions
```

When we wish to draw your attention to a particular part of a code block, the relevant lines or items are set in bold:

```
        </Directory>
        RewriteEngine On
        RewriteCond %{REQUEST_URI} !^/.well-known/acme-challenge [NC]
        RewriteCond %{HTTPS} off
        RewriteRule (.*) https://%{HTTP_HOST}%{REQUEST_URI} [R=301,L]
    </VirtualHost>
```

Any command-line input or output is written as follows:

```
[root@ol8 # grubby --info=/boot/vmlinuz-0-rescue-c32316cc4b5241b8adb3
12707ae46458
```

**Bold**: Indicates a new term, an important word, or words that you see onscreen. For example, words in menus or dialog boxes appear in the text like this. Here is an example: "Select **Enroll MOK** from the menu."

> **Tips or important notes**
> Appear like this.

# Sections

In this book, you will find several headings that appear frequently (*Getting ready*, *How to do it...*, *How it works...*, *There's more...*, and *See also*).

To give clear instructions on how to complete a recipe, use these sections as follows:

## Getting ready

This section tells you what to expect in the recipe and describes how to set up any software or any preliminary settings required for the recipe.

## How to do it...

This section contains the steps required to follow the recipe.

## How it works...

This section usually consists of a detailed explanation of what happened in the previous section.

## There's more...

This section consists of additional information about the recipe in order to make you more knowledgeable about the recipe.

## See also

This section provides helpful links to other useful information for the recipe.

# Get in touch

Feedback from our readers is always welcome.

**General feedback**: If you have questions about any aspect of this book, mention the book title in the subject of your message and email us at customercare@packtpub.com.

**Errata**: Although we have taken every care to ensure the accuracy of our content, mistakes do happen. If you have found a mistake in this book, we would be grateful if you would report this to us. Please visit www.packtpub.com/support/errata, selecting your book, clicking on the Errata Submission Form link, and entering the details.

**Piracy**: If you come across any illegal copies of our works in any form on the Internet, we would be grateful if you would provide us with the location address or website name. Please contact us at copyright@packt.com with a link to the material.

**If you are interested in becoming an author**: If there is a topic that you have expertise in and you are interested in either writing or contributing to a book, please visit authors.packtpub.com.

# Reviews

Please leave a review. Once you have read and used this book, why not leave a review on the site that you purchased it from? Potential readers can then see and use your unbiased opinion to make purchase decisions, we at Packt can understand what you think about our products, and our authors can see your feedback on their book. Thank you!

For more information about Packt, please visit packt.com.

## Share Your Thoughts

Once you've read *Oracle Linux Cookbook*, we'd love to hear your thoughts! Scan the QR code below to go straight to the Amazon review page for this book and share your feedback.

https://packt.link/r/1803249285

Your review is important to us and the tech community and will help us make sure we're delivering excellent quality content.

# Download a free PDF copy of this book

Thanks for purchasing this book!

Do you like to read on the go but are unable to carry your print books everywhere?

Is your eBook purchase not compatible with the device of your choice?

Don't worry, now with every Packt book you get a DRM-free PDF version of that book at no cost.

Read anywhere, any place, on any device. Search, copy, and paste code from your favorite technical books directly into your application.

The perks don't stop there, you can get exclusive access to discounts, newsletters, and great free content in your inbox daily

Follow these simple steps to get the benefits:

1.  Scan the QR code or visit the link below

    https://packt.link/free-ebook/978-1-80324-928-5

2.  Submit your proof of purchase

3.  That's it! We'll send your free PDF and other benefits to your email directly

# Oracle Linux 8 – Get It? Got It? Good!

You finally made the choice to upgrade to the most secure and reliable free Linux distribution and now need to learn a few tricks. What's next? How do you get started? It's time to go back to the basics and answer the question *How do you install Oracle Linux?*

Back in the old days, installing a Linux distribution was a simple task; you simply ordered a CD-ROM, popped it into your computer, and booted from the disk. *Simple… effective…* and a *pain* for many system administrators. Who wants to order a CD-ROM, or for that matter, who even uses CD-ROMs or DVDs, or even Blu-ray disks, anymore? Do you even need media? Can't you just boot from the network to install? To make it more complicated, what happens when you are in the cloud? Doesn't the cloud do it all for you? What about the CPU type, such as Arm or x86? How can you automate things?

We also need to consider that there is more than just x86-64, with Arm becoming more and more popular due to its advantages. What about older systems; do you have to install Oracle Linux 8 from scratch, or can you just upgrade an Oracle Linux 7 system? Speaking of upgrades, what about RHEL and CentOS system? Can they be migrated to Oracle Linux? After all, they are both Fedora-based, just like Oracle Linux.

This chapter will provide insights into these questions and help you learn a few tricks to automate installing Oracle Linux, as well as some helpful troubleshooting tips if the installation does not go as planned.

We will cover the following main recipes in this chapter:

- Oracle Linux 8 – which ISO is right? USB? Does anyone use DVDs?
- Burning an ISO so it's bootable
- Two for the price of one – running Oracle Linux on **Windows Subsystem for Linux (WSL)**
- Arm'ing for the future of IT – it's not just a slice of Raspberry Pi
- Leapping from Oracle Linux 7 to 8
- Migrating from CentOS to Oracle Linux

# Technical requirements

The related configuration files for many of the recipes in this book are available on GitHub, at `https://github.com/PacktPublishing/Oracle-Linux-Cookbook`.

# Oracle Linux 8 – which ISO is right? USB? Does anyone use DVDs?

Before we start anything else, let's look at installing Oracle Linux.

## Getting ready

When installing Oracle Linux, you must first decide how to do the installation. There are a variety of options, from booting a new computer to an installable image, cloning a drive from another system, or even booting from the network. For all of these options, you need to have the right media. Trying to install using the source code **Red Hat Package Manager** (**RPM**) or the wrong CPU architecture is not going to cut it. Before you download anything, you will need internet access and enough free disk space to save the ISO file. Usually, at least 10 GB is recommended to download the ISO. Additional space will also be needed if you are going to use Oracle VM VirtualBox to run VMs based on the ISO. It's common to allocate 100 GB or more per VM, as this allows you to quickly grow a filesystem without having to add another disk to the volume group. That being said, 50 GB is the default for Oracle's cloud images and can work for many users. In the cloud, the advantage of using a smaller disk is reduced costs, as the smaller disk equates to lower expenses.

> **Note**
> RPM is also defined as RPM Package Manager, but that's recursive and confusing to many folks.

## How to do it...

You also need to understand the hardware you are using for the installation. Burning an ISO to a DVD (or other optical formats) might be great for older systems that have these drives, but modern systems more often than not install via USB boot. Enterprise-grade servers take this to an even higher level, enabling you to boot from an ISO file mounted over the network or virtual console. You can also boot most systems from a **Preboot eXecution Environment** (**PXE**) server, for a more automated network-based installation. The choice of what method you use is really based on your hardware, and then how much automation you need.

> **Note**
>
> Be careful of the automation trap. Often, you can spend significantly more time automating an installation than doing it by hand. In smaller environments, while automation is nice, it can take significantly more time to build and maintain the automation compared to doing 3-4 manual builds a year.

> **Note**
>
> Though disk images are commonly called an ISO, the actual format of the ISO file is ISO 9660 Joliet, which is a format for optical disk media. **ISO** is actually an acronym for the **International Organization for Standardization** (`https://www.iso.org/home.html`). The ISO organization was formed in 1947 and has standards for everything from quality management (ISO 9001) to food safety (ISO 22000).

The easiest way to get the media is to download the ISO files from `https://yum.oracle.com/oracle-linux-isos.html`.

On the site, there are four types of ISOs:

- **Full ISO**: This is the full installation for Oracle Linux. The ISO file contains everything needed to install Oracle Linux and is bootable. You can boot a system with this ISO by burning the file to a USB stick, or even a DVD. Also, on many servers, you can boot a system by virtually mounting the ISO via the lights-out management software. There are many types of remote control options on systems, including the generic **Intelligent Platform Management Interface** (**IPMI**), which has basic functionality, and the open source **Baseboard Management Controller** (**BMC**), which adds additional features. Most major hardware vendors also offer specific technologies, such as Oracle **Integrated Lights Out Manager** (**ILOM**), Dell's **integrated Dell Remote Access Controller** (**iDRAC**), and HP's **Integrated Lights Out** (**ILO**).

- **Boot ISO**: This ISO is bootable using the Red Hat-compatible kernel for the installation process. It does not include all the files required to install. While this is a much smaller file, you will need the remainder of the installed RPM on your network or a local device. You can access the files via HTTP, enabling sourcing the files from `https://yum.oracle.com/` or a local HTTP server on your network.

> **Note**
>
> The **Unbreakable Enterprise Kernel** (**UEK**) for Oracle Linux has many advantages, such as enabling the BTFS filesystem for root, or a more modern kernel that matches the mainstream Linux kernel and includes better support for modern devices.

- **UEK boot ISO**: This ISO is bootable to the more modern UEK, but just like the boot ISO, it does not include all the files required to install. Installing using the more modern UEK is helpful, especially on systems that can't install correctly on the older **Red Hat-Compatible Kernel (RHCK)**. While this is a much smaller file, you will need the remainder of the installed RPMs on your network. UEK the only option for installation on the Arm architecture.

- **Source ISO**: This ISO is *not* bootable, but it's helpful as it contains all the source RPMs, enabling you to audit the source code.

> **Note**
>
> With both boot ISO options, the media must be available on the network on an FTP server, an HTTP/HTTPS server, or an NFS server.

Additionally, there are two CPU families available. Make sure you pick the correct architecture for the installation. Let's look at what they are:

- **x86_64**: This is the most common architecture and is used on most Intel and AMD systems. This includes Intel X-series processors and the i9, i7, i5, and i3 processors. For AMD systems, this includes the AMD EPYC processors, Ryzen processors, and the Athlon line. This is the most common option, but it's being challenged in the industry by the Arm option. The full list of options from the download site for x86 can be seen in the following figure:

Oracle Linux ISO images available to download for x86_64

| Release | Full ISO | Boot ISO | UEK boot ISO | Source ISO |
| --- | --- | --- | --- | --- |
| 8.5 | OracleLinux-R8-U5-x86_64-dvd.iso | OL8U5 x86_64-boot.iso | OL8U5 x86_64-boot-uek.iso | OracleLinux-R8-U5-src-dvd.iso |
| 8.4 | OracleLinux-R8-U4-x86_64-dvd.iso | OL8U4 x86_64-boot.iso | OL8U4 x86_64-boot-uek.iso | OracleLinux-R8-U4-src-dvd.iso |
| 8.3 | OracleLinux-R8-U3-x86_64-dvd.iso | OL8U3 x86_64-boot.iso | OL8U3 x86_64-boot-uek.iso | OracleLinux-R8-U3-src-dvd.iso |
| 7.9 | OracleLinux-R7-U9-Server-x86_64-dvd.iso | OL7U9 x86_64-boot.iso | OL7U9 x86_64-boot-uek.iso | OracleLinux-R7-U9-src-dvd1.iso<br>OracleLinux-R7-U9-src-dvd2.iso |
| 7.8 | OracleLinux-R7-U8-Server-x86_64-dvd.iso | OL7U8 x86_64-boot.iso | OL7U8 x86_64-boot-uek.iso | OracleLinux-R7-U8-src-dvd1.iso<br>OracleLinux-R7-U8-src-dvd2.iso |
| 7.7 | OracleLinux-R7-U7-Server-x86_64-dvd.iso | OL7U7 x86_64-boot.iso | OL7U7 x86_64-boot-uek.iso | OracleLinux-R7-U7-src-dvd1.iso<br>OracleLinux-R7-U7-src-dvd2.iso |
| 6.10 | OracleLinux-R6-U10-Server-x86_64-dvd.iso | OL6U10 x86_64-boot.iso | OL6U10 x86_64-boot-uek.iso | OracleLinux-R6-U10-src-dvd1.iso<br>OracleLinux-R6-U10-src-dvd2.iso |
| 6.9 | OracleLinux-R6-U9-Server-x86_64-dvd.iso | OL6U9 x86_64-boot.iso | OL6U9 x86_64-boot-uek.iso | OracleLinux-R6-U9-src-dvd1.iso<br>OracleLinux-R6-U9-src-dvd2.iso |
| 6.8 | OracleLinux-R6-U8-Server-x86_64-dvd.iso | OL6U8 x86_64-boot.iso | OL6U8 x86_64-boot-uek.iso | OracleLinux-R6-U8-src-dvd1.iso<br>OracleLinux-R6-U8-src-dvd2.iso |

Figure 1.1 – x86_64 ISOs

- **AArch64**: This is what you need when using Oracle Linux on Arm servers, such as Raspberry Pi, or Ampere's high-performance *cloud-native processor* CPUs. A cloud-native processor is a term for a CPU specifically designed for running cloud-native applications, optimized for lower power consumption with a more scalable architecture.

Running Oracle Linux on Arm is a very interesting option, as the application building blocks such as Java, Apache, Python, and Podman run using the same software versions that the x86 architectures use. All of these building blocks run almost identically to how they do on the x86 architecture, making the switch to Arm using Oracle Linux really easy for the applications. The advantage of Arm is it runs at a lower cost and higher density, offering a very attractive cost/performance story, enabling organizations to easily lower costs while improving performance. The currently available matrix of options for downloading Arm ISOs from the download site can be found in the following figure:

| Oracle Linux ISO images available to download for aarch64 | | | |
|---|---|---|---|
| Release | Full ISO | UEK boot ISO | Source ISO |
| 8.5 | OracleLinux-R8-U5-Server-aarch64-dvd.iso | OL8U5 aarch64-boot-uek.iso | OracleLinux-R8-U5-src-dvd.iso |
| 8.4 | OracleLinux-R8-U4-Server-aarch64-dvd.iso | OL8U4 aarch64-boot-uek.iso | OracleLinux-R8-U4-src-dvd.iso |
| 8.3 | OracleLinux-R8-U3-Server-aarch64-dvd.iso | OL8U3 aarch64-boot-uek.iso | OracleLinux-R8-U3-src-dvd.iso |
| 7.9 | OracleLinux-R7-U9-Server-aarch64-dvd.iso | OL7U9 aarch64-boot-uek.iso | OracleLinux-R7-U9-src-dvd1.iso<br>OracleLinux-R7-U9-src-dvd2.iso |
| 7.8 | OracleLinux-R7-U8-Server-aarch64-dvd.iso | OL7U8 aarch64-boot-uek.iso | OracleLinux-R7-U8-src-dvd1.iso<br>OracleLinux-R7-U8-src-dvd2.iso |
| 7.7 | OracleLinux-R7-U7-Server-aarch64-dvd.iso | OL7U7 aarch-boot-uek-20190809.iso | OracleLinux-R7-U7-src-dvd1.iso<br>OracleLinux-R7-U7-src-dvd2.iso |

Figure 1.2 – Arm ISOs

Once we understand the platform, we also need to make another decision as to what version to use. Sometimes you may be able to download older versions and you may want to verify that the release will be supported. At the time of writing, while release 6 can be downloaded, support is available if you have purchased *Extended Support*, which is only available until June 2024.

> **Note**
>
> Extended Support from Oracle allows you to pay a fee in order to get support, including patches and fixes for critical security issues and select high-impact critical bugs. This support does not cover all RPMs. Given this, you may want to reconsider downloading and using older versions of Linux and avoid delaying upgrading the OS past the point of it being generally available. The value of Extended Support is that it can give you additional time to upgrade applications that require older versions of Oracle Linux.

Before you pick a release, check with your application team to verify the version is supported. There are differences between the major number (7 versus 8, etc.) and some software may not be available on all major release numbers. An example is **Oracle Linux Automation Manager** (this gives you centralized Ansible control, based on the AWX project, and is almost identical to Ansible Tower from Red Hat), which requires Oracle Linux 8. Another example is Oracle Linux Manager (aka Spacewalk), which requires Oracle Linux 7 for the server.

> **Note**
>
> Since Oracle Linux tracks Red Hat Enterprise Linux, the major and minor numbers are identical. Oracle Linux 7.10 is the same as Red Hat Enterprise Linux 7.10.

# Burning an ISO so it's bootable

Once you have the ISO downloaded, you may need to do some additional preparations. If you are installing using a USB device, simply copying the file to a flash drive will not work, as the ISO is not actually unpacked on the media. If the ISO is not correctly unpacked and the media is not made bootable, you will be unable to boot and install from the media. The process of burning the ISO file to media correctly unpacks the media into individual files and directories as well as making the media bootable. If this is not done, all the media will have is a copy of the single ISO file.

There are several tools available to do this. With most systems no longer using optical media, the most common way is to boot a server from a flash drive or a virtual disk.

## Getting ready

Before you start, you will first need to download an ISO image. You also will need a USB flash drive, ideally with more than 16 GB of space. As the distro grows, 8 GB drives are no longer large enough for a full media installation ISO.

## How to do it...

Before you can boot from a flash drive, you must first burn the ISO file to the flash drive. In Windows systems, a commonly used free tool is **balenaEtcher**, which can be downloaded from `https://www.balena.io/etcher/`. Take the following steps:

1.  Once **Etcher** is installed, you will need to run it (make sure you right-click on it and run it as an administrator) and select the image file as the source and the flash drive as the destination.

2.  In the following screenshot, the source is the **Oracle Linux 8.7 ISO** for **x64**, and the destination is a flash drive:

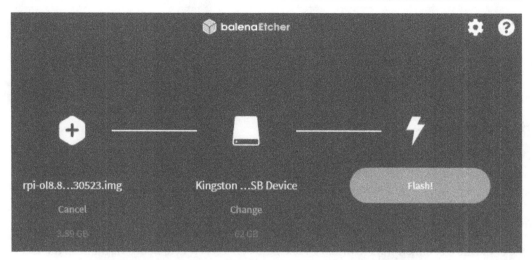

Figure 1.3 – Selecting the source and destination with Etcher

3.  Etcher can automatically work with the compressed file, so in a few minutes (as seen in the following screenshot), you should have a flash drive with the image installed and ready to boot:

Figure 1.4 – balenaEtcher burning an ISO

> **Note**
>
> When using flash devices , be careful of discount brands. Often, off-brand cards can have significantly slower performance than name-brand cards. Also, when buying online, be careful of fake cards. Always buy flash devices from reputable vendors.

## How it works...

Once you have the ISO file burned to a USB device, you can boot a server from the media. How you can boot from a USB device is based on the make and model of the system. Arm x86 systems have a setting in their **basic input/output system (BIOS)** that will allow you to boot from the freshly burned media. Arm systems usually use the **Unified Extensible Firmware Interface (UEFI)** firmware to boot from an ISO or USB stick.

One of the most common ways to install Oracle Linux on a server is to boot straight from the ISO file. Enterprise-grade servers, such as Ampere Arm systems, can allow you to boot from the ISO file by mounting the ISO as a virtual drive. Additionally, you can boot using a network boot technology called PXE, which is pronounced *pixie*.

# Two for the price of one – running Oracle Linux on Windows Subsystem for Linux (WSL)

There is one last way to install Oracle Linux on Microsoft Windows desktops, with WSL.

WSL lets you easily install Oracle Linux directly on Windows without the need to install a traditional VM such as VirtualBox. WSL includes an integrated VM, preconfigured for Windows, hiding the hypervisor from the user. WSL also has the advantage of enabling Linux commands straight from Windows, including Linux services such as Apache, MySQL, SSHD, Nginx, and PostgreSQL.

## Getting ready

Before you start, you will need a Windows 10 or Windows 11 system with internet access. You will also need local admin privileges on the system. This is not a difficult recipe and is well worth the time.

## How to do it...

Installing WSL is fairly straightforward. You will need to take the following steps:

1.  Start Command Prompt as an administrator. Don't forget to right-click on **Command Prompt** to run this as an administrator, as shown in the following screenshot:

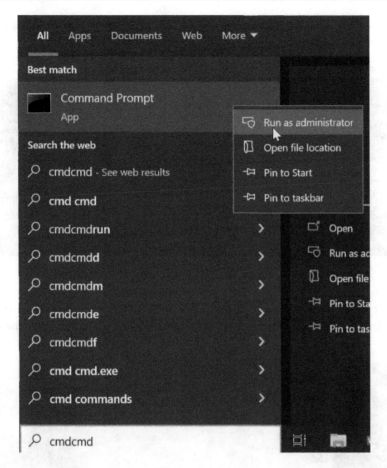

Figure 1.5 – Running Command Prompt as an administrator

**Note**

While these instructions are for WSL, please note that it's really covering **WSL2**. There was an earlier release of WSL, also known as **WSL1**, that works slightly differently and is no longer used or deployed. Older versions of WSL should normally be avoided. This also goes for the OS version; use the latest 8.X version when possible.

2.  From Command Prompt, run the `wsl.exe -install` command. This will start several tasks off, including installing the Microsoft VM platform that enables WSL under the covers, installing the WSL subsystem itself, and installing an Ubuntu Linux distro.

Once the installation is complete, as seen in the following screenshot, Windows will need to be rebooted:

```
Administrator: Command Prompt

Microsoft Windows [Version 10.0.19043.1526]
(c) Microsoft Corporation. All rights reserved.

C:\windows\system32>wsl.exe --install
Installing: Virtual Machine Platform
Virtual Machine Platform has been installed.
Installing: Windows Subsystem for Linux
Windows Subsystem for Linux has been installed.
Downloading: WSL Kernel
Installing: WSL Kernel
WSL Kernel has been installed.
Downloading: Ubuntu
The requested operation is successful. Changes will not be effective until the system is rebooted.

C:\windows\system32>_
```

Figure 1.6 – WSL installation

3.  Once your system is backed up, we will install Oracle Linux 8.5 as the Linux OS used by WSL. To do this, start the **Microsoft Store** application and search for `Oracle Linux` in the search bar:

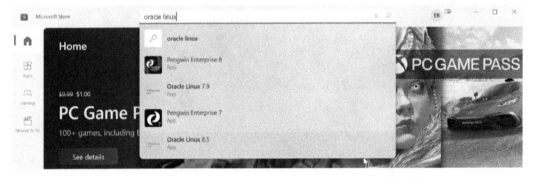

Figure 1.7 – Microsoft Store searching for Oracle Linux 8.5

4.  In the search results, select the **Oracle Linux 8.5** app. This will take you to the screen where you can download and install Oracle Linux 8.5 under WSL:

Figure 1.8 – Oracle Linux 8.5 in the Microsoft Store

5.　Click on the **Get** button. This will start the download and installation of Oracle Linux 8.5 for the Windows system. The download should only take a few minutes, and once completed, you can run Oracle Linux 8.5. However, in the future, you will need to run the Oracle Linux 8.5 subsystem by searching for it in the program list, by hitting the *Windows* key and then typing in `Oracle Linux`. This not only finds the subsystem but also gives you the option to pin the subsystem to your taskbar or Start menu, as shown in the following screenshot:

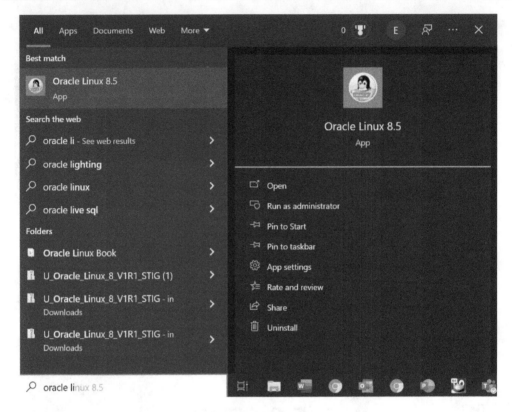

Figure 1.9 – Oracle Linux 8.5 subsystem app options

6.   When you run the WSL subsystem, it works almost identically to any other Oracle Linux 8.5 system. You can easily run Oracle Linux commands under Windows now. This includes checking storage capacity, using dnf to install programs, editing files, and SSHing to other hosts:

```
[erik@NOT-A-DELL ~]$ uptime
 23:18:34 up 0 min,  0 users,  load average: 0.00, 0.00, 0.00
[erik@NOT-A-DELL ~]$ df -h
Filesystem     Size  Used Avail Use% Mounted on
/dev/sdb       251G  573M  238G   1% /
tmpfs           25G     0   25G   0% /mnt/wsl
tools          1.9T  1.1T  756G  60% /init
none            25G     0   25G   0% /dev
none            25G  4.0K   25G   1% /run
none            25G     0   25G   0% /run/lock
none            25G     0   25G   0% /run/shm
none            25G     0   25G   0% /run/user
tmpfs           25G     0   25G   0% /sys/fs/cgroup
drivers        1.9T  1.1T  756G  60% /usr/lib/wsl/drivers
lib            1.9T  1.1T  756G  60% /usr/lib/wsl/lib
C:\            1.9T  1.1T  756G  60% /mnt/c
E:\            1.9T  533G  1.4T  28% /mnt/e
[erik@NOT-A-DELL ~]$ uname -a
Linux NOT-A-DELL 5.10.16.3-microsoft-standard-WSL2 #1 SMP Fri Apr 2 22:23:49 UTC 2021 x86_64 x86_64 x86_64 GNU/Linux
[erik@NOT-A-DELL ~]$ _
```

Figure 1.10 – WLS OS commands

You can also install new software with dnf. An example of installing nmap is shown in the following figure:

```
[root@NOT-A-DELL ~]# exit
logout
[erik@NOT-A-DELL ~]$ clear
[erik@NOT-A-DELL ~]$ sudo su -
Last login: Sat Mar  5 23:50:16 EST 2022 on pts/0
[root@NOT-A-DELL ~]# dnf install nmap -y
Last metadata expiration check: 0:00:32 ago on Sat Mar  5 23:50:30 2022.
Dependencies resolved.
===============================================================================================
 Package              Architecture     Version             Repository            Size
===============================================================================================
Installing:
 nmap                 x86_64           2:7.70-6.el8         ol8_appstream         5.8 M
Installing dependencies:
 hwdata               noarch           0.314-8.10.el8       ol8_baseos_latest     1.7 M
 libibverbs           x86_64           35.0-1.el8           ol8_baseos_latest     335 k
 libnl3               x86_64           3.5.0-1.el8          ol8_baseos_latest     323 k
 libpcap              x86_64           14:1.9.1-5.el8        ol8_baseos_latest     169 k
 nmap-ncat            x86_64           2:7.70-6.el8         ol8_appstream         237 k
 pciutils             x86_64           3.7.0-1.el8          ol8_baseos_latest     105 k
 pciutils-libs        x86_64           3.7.0-1.el8          ol8_baseos_latest      54 k
 rdma-core            x86_64           35.0-1.el8           ol8_baseos_latest      59 k

Transaction Summary
===============================================================================================
```

Figure 1.11 – WSL installing nmap with dnf

You can also access your Windows drives from WLS. They will each be presented under the /mtn/DRIVE location, where the C: drive is /mnt/c. The Windows system can also access the Linux directory under the \\wsl$\OracleLinux_8_5 path:

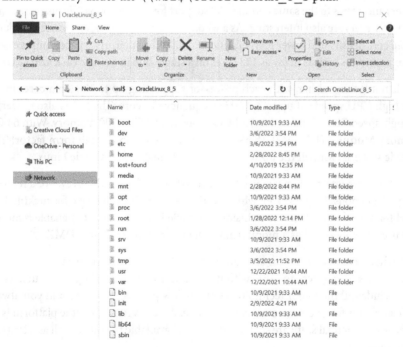

Figure 1.12 – Windows File Explorer and WSL

> **Caution**
>
> As a note of caution, be careful when you're editing files. Windows and Linux format text differently, and you can easily accidentally corrupt files if you are not careful. It is recommended that Windows files are stored and accessed using Windows, and Linux files are edited and stored on the WSL image.

Running Oracle 8.5 as a Windows subsystem is a great tool for system administrators and developers. Its integration with Windows makes for a quick and easy installation while enabling transparent access to a Linux system on your personal system.

## Arm'ing for the future of IT – it's not just a slice of Raspberry Pi

First, let's chat about Oracle Linux on **advanced RISC machines**, more commonly known as Arm CPUs. This newer architecture has many advantages over the older x86_64 architecture that Intel and AMD use. This includes lower power consumption; lower latency, enabling better performance; and a simplified architecture that enables higher-density systems. Leveraging Oracle Linux on an Arm system is a popular option for both cloud-scale operators such as Oracle and Microsoft as well as smaller organizations that are looking at reducing their compute power and cooling needs.

Having a single *enterprise OS* on all Linux systems has several advantages, such as using the same tools across all servers and access to the same commercial support for your systems. The use cases for Arm in your inventory of servers are also interesting. As a whole, Arm processors offer a lower cost due to their higher *potential* core density and lower *power consumption*. In the enterprise space, **Ampere** dominates and offers Arm processors with as many as 128 cores on a single chip in a single **rack unit** (**RU**) of space.

Performance is not lacking either, with each processor supporting up to 128 Arm cores in two RUs of space with high CPU speeds of up to 3.0 GHz frequency per core. The I/O is also powerful, with 128 lanes of high-speed PCIe Gen4 and 8×72 ECC-protected DDR4 3200 memory. With 64 GB **Dual In-Line Memory Modules** (**DIMMs**), that's *4 terabytes* of RAM in a small form factor! These are enterprise-grade systems, with all the power, security, and reliability of Oracle Linux.

Arm is not just for data centers; when you need a small system, such as a DNS server or a remote access device, there is the famous Raspberry Pi, which works well with it's small size for tucking it away in a wiring closet for a backup DNS server or inside an Oracle Exadata cabinet to enable remote access. You can even use a Raspberry Pi as a monitoring system or a web server in a DMZ.

Regardless of what Arm platform you are running on (Ampere or Raspberry Pi), when running Oracle Linux, you also get access to UEK with its enhancements, including tools such as Ansible. Oracle Linux includes all the major technologies at one low price for support, and you always have the option of using it for free; you can even patch for free. As far as Arm goes, the platform is also not limited. You have commercial software such as MySQL 8.0 available to you, as well as a large amount of open source software.

It's not just the Raspberry Pi use cases that are powerful. When you get to the larger Arm-based services, you open up a huge number of use cases for edge computing. Edge computing needs the application to bring data from the cloud into the locations that need low-latency access to the data. With MySQL 8.0 replication features, you can easily replicate data from the cloud to the edge, maintaining performance while, at the same time, leveraging the high core counts and low-power requirements of Arm systems made by companies such as Ampere, which offers an 80-core CPU with a low 210w of power consumption. The high core counts combined with container technologies such as Docker and Kata containers enable a distributed microservices architecture, with centrally maintained applications that take advantage of the cloud's automation but still provide the performance of a traditional on-premises solution. This is the future of IT.

## Getting ready

Before you start, you will need a Raspberry Pi with a Micro SD slot. You also will need a Micro SD card that can be used to install the OS. If you are using a Raspberry Pi compute module, or an enterprise Arm server such as an Ampere system, jump to *Chapter 2* and PXE boot the system.

## How to do it...

That being said, let's get Oracle Linux on a Raspberry Pi. While I've been using Oracle Linux on Arm and installing it the hard way, there is now a much easier way to install it. Oracle offers free images for the Raspberry Pi, with the OS already installed.

Let's take the following steps:

1.  Download the Oracle image at the following link: `https://www.oracle.com/linux/downloads/linux-arm-downloads.html`.

2.  Next, you will need to write the image to an SD card. The easiest way to do this from a Windows system is to use **balenaEtcher**, which is a free utility that makes it easy to write images to SD cards and USB drives. You can download it from `https://www.balena.io/etcher/`.

> **Note**
> While balenaEtcher is used for the example, there are many other ways to write the file to a flash drive, such as Raspberry Pi Imager, or just using the dd command to write the file to a flash drive in Linux.

3.  Run Etcher (make sure you right-click on it and run as administrator) and select the image file as the *source* and the SD card as the *destination*:

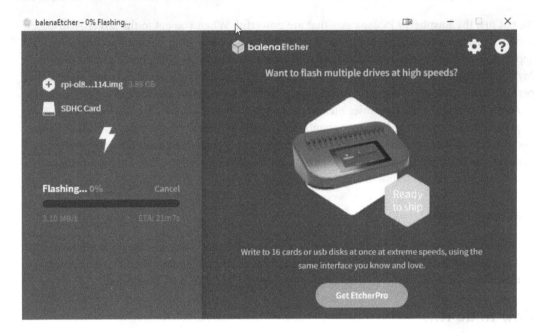

Figure 1.13 – Burning the Pi SD card

Etcher can automatically work with the compressed file, so in a minute or two, you should have an SD card with the image installed.

4.   Next, pop the card into your Pi and boot the Pi. The normal GRUB loader will start, and you should have a login prompt.

```
Oracle Linux Server 8 (5.15.0-3.60.5.1.el8uek.aarch64)
System setup
```

Figure 1.14 – Booting the Pi

Yup, it's that easy!

5.   Once it's booted, log in as root, with the password oracle. The system will require you to change the password.

```
Oracle Linux Server 8.7
Kernel 5.15.0-3.60.5.1.el8uek.aarch64 on an aarch64

rpi login: root
Password:
You are required to change your password immediately (administrator enforced)
Current password:
New password:
Retype new password:
[root@rpi ~]# uname -a
Linux rpi 5.15.0-3.60.5.1.el8uek.aarch64 #2 SMP Wed Oct 19 20:17:59 PDT 2022 aarch64 aarch64 aarch64 GNU/Linux
[root@rpi ~]#
```

Figure 1.15 – First login

6. Now it's up to you what you want to install. By default, it has access to the free Oracle public **yum** server, so yum works out of the box.

7. For Oracle Linux 8, you have access to the following repos:

   - **BaseOS Latest**: The basic OS and utilities.

   - **AppStream Latest**: This includes user-space applications, such as bind, Corosync, Evolution, Firefox, FreeRADIUS, Perl libraries, PHP, and X11.

   - **EPEL: Extra Packages for Enterprise Linux**, better known as **EPEL**, contains applications such as Ansible, HWiNFO, Cacti, Nagios, and strongSwan (for VPN). EPEL can be added manually by adding an EPEL.repo file with the following text in the /etc/yum/repos.d directory:

```
[ol8_EPEL]
name=Oracle Linux 8 EPEL ($basearch)
baseurl=https://yum$ociregion.oracle.com/repo/OracleLinux/OL8/
developer/EPEL/$basearch/
gpgkey=file:///etc/pki/rpm-gpg/RPM-GPG-KEY-oracle
gpgcheck=1
enabled=1
```

   The EPEL library can also be added using dnf with the following command:

```
dnf install oracle-epel-release-el8
```

Take a few minutes to play around with an Arm system. They are versatile, low cost, and very flexible. You should find plenty of uses for Oracle Linux on Arm.

# Leapping from Oracle Linux 7 to 8

A challenge system admins often face is what to do when you have an older OS deployed and it's about to reach the date when support ends. It happens, and it's not fun. This will put you in a position to reinstall the newer OS on new systems, and then migrate your workload over. For many systems, there is a better way known as **Leapp**.

Leapp allows you to upgrade your OS from Oracle Linux 7 to Oracle Linux 8. There is no need to reinstall everything on new systems. **Leapping** consists of two phases:

- A pre-upgrade phase that checks the system to determine whether the software can be upgraded

- A second phase that actually performs the upgrade

Sounds good. But there are a few things you need to know.

## Getting ready

First, Leapping from 7 to 8 is not supported for all use cases. *Table 1.1* shows what Oracle will support when performing the operation. Leapp does not always work well with complex applications, such as database systems that have specific installation options based on the underlying *OS version*. It also may break some applications that are not included with the OS:

| Supported by Leapp | Unsupported by Leapp |
|---|---|
| Platforms (latest shipping updates):<br><br>• x86_64<br>• Arm (AArch64)<br><br>Operating systems:<br><br>• Current Oracle Linux 7 version only<br><br>Profiles:<br><br>• Minimal installation<br>• Virtualization host<br>• Server with GUI<br>• Basic web server<br>• Infrastructure server<br>• File and print server | Systems installed with the following:<br><br>• ISV applications, including Oracle Database and middleware<br><br>Note<br><br>ISVs must provide and validate Leapp actors to coordinate their application upgrades:<br><br>• Oracle Linux Manager or Spacewalk for Oracle Linux<br>• Installations that did not use ISO images such as Ceph and GlusterFS<br>• Migration of disks that are encrypted with LUKS<br>• Systems that are registered with ULN<br>• Systems in FIPS mode or running Secure Boot<br>• Systems configured with Docker containers |

Table 1.1 – Leapp support matrix from Oracle

Next, Leapp also has some limitations when upgrading the kernel. This matrix from Oracle is seen in the following table:

| Platform Notes | Starting Kernel (Oracle Linux 7) | Ending Kernel (Oracle Linux 8) | Supported |
|---|---|---|---|
| x86_64 not using Btrfs filesystem | RHCK | RHCK | Yes |
| | RHCK | UEK | No |
| | UEK | UEK | Yes |
| | UEK | RHCK | No |
| x86_64 using Btrfs filesystem | RHCK | RHCK | No |
| | RHCK | UEK | Yes |
| | UEK | UEK | Yes |
| | UEK | RHCK | No |
| AArch64 | UEK | UEK | Yes |

Table 1.2 – Supported kernel upgrade from Oracle

## Always look before you Leapp

Before Leapping from 7 to 8, you need to check a few things, as follows:

- Make sure you have a solid backup. Snapshots of the system work best in case things don't go well.
- If Secure Boot is running, disable it with `mokutil --sb-state`. You can check the status by running the `bootctl status` command.
- Make sure you have console access, just in case you need to troubleshoot issues.
- Disable any network mounts, such as NFS mounts, Samba mounts, GlusterFS mounts, and so on. Disable them in your `/etc/fstab` file.
- If you are using `yum-plugin-versionlock`, clear any locks with the `yum versionlock clear` command.
- If you are running *any KVM VMs*, stop them all. You can do this with `virsh shutdown $VM_NAME`. If you're not sure whether you are running any VMs, the `virsh list --all` command will list them all for you.
- If you are using Spacewalk, Oracle Linux Manager, Unbreakable Linux Network, or any other centralized yum manager, unregister the system from it. You must Leapp against the `yum.oracle.com` repos.

- If you need an HTTP proxy to access the yum.oracle.com repos, make sure it's added to your /etc/yum.conf file.

- Verify that you are using en_US.UTF-8 in /etc/locale.conf. You can switch via the localectl set-locale LANG=en_US.UTF-8 command.

- In your /etc/ssh/sshd_config file, verify that you can log in as root. PermitRootLogin yes should be in the config file.

Once you've verified this list, patch your system against yum.oracle.com with yum update -y, and then reboot.

Finally, you can add the *Leapp* repo with the following command:

```
yum install -y leapp --enablerepo=ol7_leapp,ol7_latest
```

Next, do another sanity reboot, and maybe grab a second backup. After the reboot, if you are using a proxy to access them, then you need to add the proxy server for each repository entry in /etc/yum.repos.d/leapp-upgrade-repos-ol8.repo. You can do this with a simple sed command: sed -I '/^enabled=0.*/a proxy=http://proxy-host:proxy-port' /etc/yum.repos.d/eap-upgrade-repos-ol8.repo.

Congratulations, you are now ready to analyze the system!

## How to do it...

You will need to take the following steps:

1. If you are running anywhere but on Oracle's cloud (known as OCI), you can run the report with the following command:

   ```
   leapp preupgrade --oraclelinux
   ```

2. If you are on OCI, run this command:

   ```
   leapp preupgrade --oci
   ```

Both commands will run many checks and will give an alert if there are major issues. But you need to dig deeper into these:

Figure 1.16 – Leapp pre-upgrade results

3.  Now, you should have some interesting output. The `/var/log/leapp/leapp-report.txt` file will identify any risks with the upgrade. They are classified in three rankings, with the highest being a *show stopper*. Address any of the risks, rerun the analyzer, and check the report again. Once you are comfortable with the results, you can continue.

4.  The next step is to look at `/var/log/leapp/answerfile`. The file consists of specific checks that Leapp performs on the system. Each check contains information about the system and also prompts you for confirmation on the action to be performed:

```
[root@ol7 leapp]# more answerfile
[remove_pam_pkcs11_module_check]
# Title:            None
# Reason:           Confirmation
# ================== remove_pam_pkcs11_module_check.confirm ==================
# Label:            Disable pam_pkcs11 module in PAM configuration? If no, the upgrade process will be interrupted.
# Description:      PAM module pam_pkcs11 is no longer available in OL-8 since it was replaced by SSSD.
# Type:             bool
# Default:          None
# Available choices: True/False
# Unanswered question. Uncomment the following line with your answer
# confirm =

[root@ol7 leapp]#
```

Figure 1.17 – Leapp answerfile

In this example, there is only one answer to confirm. To accept an item in the file, add `confirm = True` in the section. Optionally, you can use the `leapp` command to confirm the line item, making sure the section matches:

```
leapp answer --section remove_pam_pkcs11_module_check.confirm=true
```

### Time to take the Leapp and start phase two

Now that we're set, it's time to make the jump forward! As with the *Leapp pre-upgrade*, how you Leapp in OCI is slightly different than other environments:

1.  For non-OCI environments (as seen in the following screenshot), run `leapp upgrade --oraclelinux`. For OCI environments, run `leapp upgrade --oci`:

```
[root@ol7 ~]# leapp upgrade --oraclelinux
==> Processing phase `configuration_phase`
====> * ipu_workflow_config
        IPU workflow config actor
==> Processing phase `FactsCollection`
====> * udevadm_info
        Produces data exported by the "udevadm info" command.
====> * scanmemory
        Scan Memory of the machine.
====> * removed_pam_modules_scanner
        Scan PAM configuration for modules that are not available in OL-8.
====> * tcp_wrappers_config_read
        Parse tcp_wrappers configuration files /etc/hosts.{allow,deny}.
====> * firewalld_facts_actor
        Provide data about firewalld
====> * scan_sap_hana
        Gathers information related to SAP HANA instances on the system.
====> * scan_subscription_manager_info
        Scans the current system for subscription manager information
====> * authselect_scanner
        Detect what authselect configuration should be suggested to administrator.
====> * network_manager_read_config
        Provides data about NetworkManager configuration.
====> * scan_custom_repofile
        Scan the custom /etc/leapp/files/leapp_upgrade_repositories.repo repo file.
====> * transaction_workarounds
        Provides additional RPM transaction tasks based on bundled RPM packages.
====> * common_leapp_dracut_modules
        Influences the generation of the initram disk
====> * read_openssh_config
        Collect information about the OpenSSH configuration.
====> * storage_scanner
        Provides data about storage settings.
====> * system_facts
        Provides data about many facts from system.
```

Figure 1.18 – Leapp upgrade starting

2.  Leapp will take some time. Did you remember to make your backup? As Leapp runs, it will download all the Oracle Linux 8 packages, downloading about 600 MB for a small system and 1 GB for larger installations:

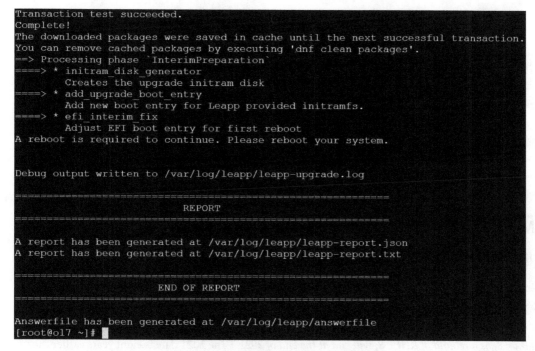

```
Transaction test succeeded.
Complete!
The downloaded packages were saved in cache until the next successful transaction.
You can remove cached packages by executing 'dnf clean packages'.
==> Processing phase `InterimPreparation`
====> * initram_disk_generator
        Creates the upgrade initram disk
====> * add_upgrade_boot_entry
        Add new boot entry for Leapp provided initramfs.
====> * efi_interim_fix
        Adjust EFI boot entry for first reboot
A reboot is required to continue. Please reboot your system.


Debug output written to /var/log/leapp/leapp-upgrade.log

=====================================================================
                          REPORT
=====================================================================

A report has been generated at /var/log/leapp/leapp-report.json
A report has been generated at /var/log/leapp/leapp-report.txt

=====================================================================
                       END OF REPORT
=====================================================================

Answerfile has been generated at /var/log/leapp/answerfile
[root@ol7 ~]#
```

Figure 1.19 – Leapp upgrade completed

When the Leapp process is done (as seen in the preceding screenshot), reboot.

## How it works...

Leapp performs the in-place upgrade, installing or upgrading the new RPMs and reconfiguring the boot loader to the upgraded OS version. This process upgrades the Oracle Linux-supported applications, as well as migrating configurations and preferences to the new version.

## There's more...

When you've done the reboot, you should see /etc/oracle-release updates for Oracle Linux 8. You can also check the kernel with uname -r. After the upgrade, you will also need to do a few other tasks:

1. If you disabled **Secure Boot**, you will need to re-enable it in the system's firmware.
2. Re-enable the firewall, as it was disabled during the upgrade:

    ```
    sytemctl start firewalld
    systemctl enable firewalld
    ```

3.  If you use *SELinux*, you will need to set it back to enforcing by using the `setenforce enforcing` command to do this. You can also check the current state of SELinux with the `getenforce` command.

4.  If you have KVM VMs running, you will need to restart them with the `virsh start $VMNAME` command.

5.  You can remove the `/root/tmp_leapp_py3` directory. This is optional but will free up disk space.

6.  You can reconnect the system to your normal patch and management systems. They should be added back as Oracle Linux 8 systems. Please verify that your management software reflects the new version; not all management systems will update the major release correctly.

## Migrating from CentOS to Oracle Linux

The first question is *why?* Why are we talking about moving from **CentOS** to Oracle Linux?

Before we explain this, let's chat a little bit about the surprise that IBM Red Hat dropped on the Linux community on December 8, 2020. CentOS as we know it is *dead!* It is `> /dev/null`.

On December 8th, 2020, CentOS (which is controlled by IBM Red Hat) announced the news: "*CentOS Linux 8, as a rebuild of RHEL 8, will end at the end of 2021.*" The 2021 date is eight years earlier than planned, with 2029 being the original published date for the end of development on the CentOS 8 distribution. This means if you have CentOS 8 and you want to continue using a stable and predictable release, then you need to make a change.

The CentOS team is "*shifting focus from CentOS Linux, the rebuild of Red Hat Enterprise Linux (RHEL), to CentOS Stream, which tracks just ahead of a current RHEL release.*" Remember Fedora, where new technology is constantly being introduced and withdrawn, where change is normal and expected? That is basically how the community looks at CentOS Stream. This one change basically destroyed the ability for **enterprise system administrators** to use CentOS 8 and beyond in production, and dev, test, and **quality assurance (QA)** environments.

So, *what's next?* There are already several projects that have forked or cloned the CentOS model to replicate the effort and provide a stable distro that tracks RHEL, with a predictable release schedule and a stable organization to back up the project. A concern you should have with the multitude of projects that have started is picking the right one. You have no idea what new distros will fail or succeed. Some of these forks will take years to stabilize, and users need a solution now. As an admin, you do not need a fork or immature distribution that may change direction. You need a stable distribution that has the goal of maintaining compatibility with RHEL. Oracle Linux provides both, the proven stability and is actively investing in maintaining compatibility with RHEL though the **Open Enterprise Linux Association (OpenELA.rg)**

OpenELA was founded by Oracle, SUSE and CIQ, the company that is behind RockyLinux.OpenELA is a trade association that builds a compatible code base that is a drop in replacement for RHEL. This allows the open source community to combine their efforts to prove a stable replacement for CentOS.

## CentOS is dead as we know it, have you looked at Oracle Linux yet?

Oracle Linux tracks RHEL, using OpenELA as their base code going forward, so Oracle Linux 8.3 is basically the same as RHEL 8.3 or CentOS 8.3 or even RockyLinux 8.3. It's used by over 86% of the Fortune Global 100, making it one of the most popular Linux options in the Enterprise. Since Oracle runs its business and Oracle Cloud on Oracle Linux, you know it will be supported regardless of what other bombshells IBM Red Hat drops on the users.

Did I mention Oracle Linux is free? It's free to download, free to distribute, and free to patch! To distribute, I can give you a copy for free and no lawyers are required. To patch, there's no need to register your system or pay any fees, and it would also be free to download. There is no license fee to get it!

Yes, Oracle has a paid support offering that is a lot less expensive than RHEL, and due to the free model to download and patch, you can easily use Oracle Linux for free in your non-production systems and still have paid support for your production systems on the same distribution. It is also very stable as it has been available since 2006. They even support Arm these days (Raspberry Pi, anyone?), and have several public mirrors where you can download it in case you don't want to download it from `http://yum.oracle.com/oracle-linux-isos.html`.

There are several cool things you can get if you pay for support, but all of these are well above and beyond what RHEL offers with their support. This includes a few technologies such as the following:

- **Ksplice**: This lets you patch kernel and user space libraries while running
- **DTrace**: This came over from Solaris and gives you a real-time view into kernel and application internals
- **Enterprise Manager**: To manage and monitor the OS, logs, and more

If you are on CentOS, it's really easy to move to Oracle Linux. Best of all is that when you move, you keep everything the same, so all your apps continue to run. Remember, Oracle Linux tracks RHEL, making it an easy drop-in replacement. Oracle has made the migration script free for anyone to use, and you can access it from the following GitHub URL: `https://github.com/oracle/centos2ol`.

## Getting ready

Before you start, you will need a system running Scientific Linux 7.x and 8.x, Rocky 8.x, and CentOS 7.x and 8.X. If your CentOS system is CentOS Stream, the script will not work. There are a few other things to think about before running the Oracle script, as follows:

- Make sure you have a solid backup. Snapshots of the system work best in case things don't go well.
- If Secure Boot is running, disable it with `mokutil --sb-state`. You can check the status by running the `bootctl status` command.

- Make sure you have console access, just in case you need to troubleshoot issues.

- Disable any network mounts, such as NFS mounts, Samba mounts, and GlusterFS mounts. Disable them in your `/etc/fstab` file.

- If you are using `yum-plugin-versionlock`, clear any locks with the `yum versionlock clear` command.

- If you are running *any KVM VMs*, stop them all. You can do this with `virsh shutdown $VM_NAME=`. If you're not sure whether you're running any VMs, the `virsh list --all` command will list them all out for you.

- If you are using Spacewalk, Oracle Linux Manager, Unbreakable Linux Network, or any other centralized *yum* manager, make sure the `yum` command works. Unlike Leapp, you can run the script against a private repo.

- If you need an HTTP proxy to access your yum server, make sure it is added to your `/etc/yum.conf` file.

- If you are using any third-party *yum repos*, please validate that their packages will not conflict with what you are running. It's best to disable these repos while doing the switch.

- Check for stale repos. If the repo isn't working, disable it.

- Make sure you have at least 5 GB of free space in `/var/cache`.

- Disable all automatic *yum* updates.

## How to do it...

Now that you have checked and prepared the system to be migrated from CentOS, the actual migration from CentOS 8.x is fairly straightforward. You'll now need to follow these steps:

1. The easy way to do the upgrade is to use `wget` to download the script from GitHub as a raw file: `https://raw.githubusercontent.com/oracle/centos2ol/main/centos2ol.sh`.

2. Next, you will need to perform the `chmod +x` operation the script with the following:

   ```
   chmod +x centos2ol.sh
   ```

3. Remember how CentOS 8 hit EOL really early? This also means that the CentOS *yum repos* for version 8 are gone. There is a workaround to this small problem, though. For now, you can use a copy located at `vault.centos.org`, but each of the repo files will need to be updated. That can be done with this command:

   ```
   sed -i 's/mirrorlist/#mirrorlist/g' /etc/yum.repos.d/CentOS-*
   ```

You can also use this one:

```
sed -i 's|#baseurl=http://mirror.centos.org|baseurl=http://
vault.centos.org|g' /etc/yum.repos.d/CentOS-*
```

4.  Next, run the script using `./centos2ol.sh`:

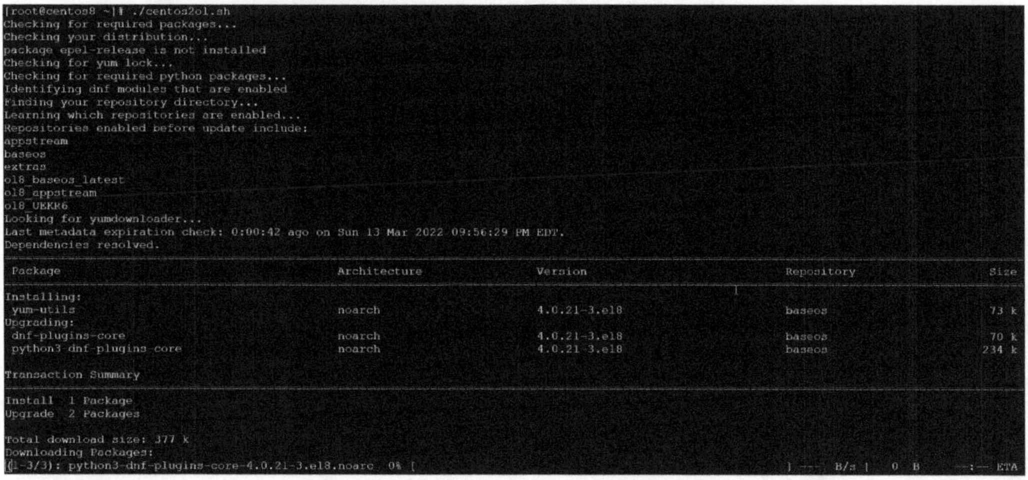

Figure 1.20 – CentOS to Oracle Linux process starting

This will run for about 5 minutes on a fast system with 1GB/s internet speeds. Other systems can take as long as 45 minutes. When the script is done, reboot. As with Leapp, you can check the upgrade by looking at `/etc/oracle-release` and checking the kernel version with `uname -r`:

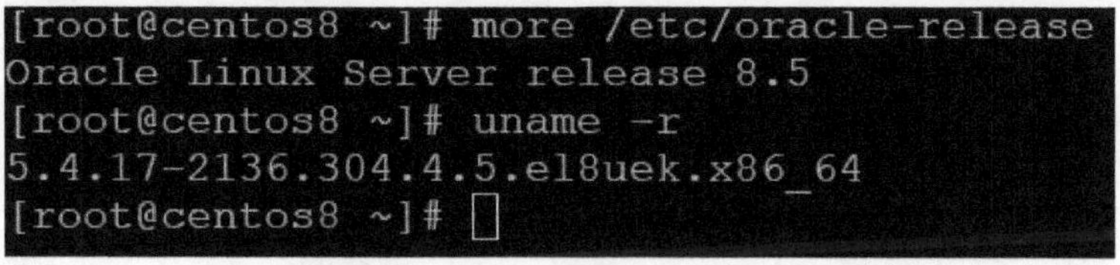

Figure 1.21 – Migration from CentOS 8 completed

Once the reboot has finished and the server is up, `/etc/oracle-release` should correctly show Oracle Linux.

## How it works...

The script will connect your system to new patch repositories, and then basically perform an extended patch process against the Oracle repos. Old RPMs will be replaced with RPMs from Oracle. The script can also upgrade you from the older Linux 4.x kernel to UEK, where you can benefit from the performance advantages of the newer Linux 5 kernel.

# 2
# Installing with and without Automation Magic

While you can manually install Oracle Linux from a USB or an ISO image, at an enterprise level, it is more common to automate the installation. The *Appendix – kickstart options* at the end of this chapter covers the manual installation, which is easier to do when you have occasional installs.

Most data center installs use an automated method, as this allows you to scale quickly.

This chapter provides different recipes to help build an operational **Preboot Execution** (**PXE**; pronounced *pixie*) system.

PXE booting is a technology developed by Intel. It allows systems with the appropriate ISO (or OS RPMs) to boot from the network, downloading all the required files from a server. While there are older methods, such as the **bootstrap protocol** (**BOOTP**), the industry has rapidly adopted **PXE boot** as the most common standard. While PXE booting started with Intel systems, ARM systems can also boot using TFTP. For the PXE boot process to work, you would normally have a DHCP server and a PXE server on the network. A high-level summary of the process can be seen in the following diagram:

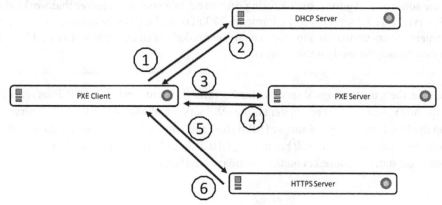

Figure 2.1 – PXE boot process

The following are each of the steps described at a high level:

1. The **PXE client** will request an IP address from an available **DHCP server**.

2. The first DHCP server on the network to respond to the client will provide it with an IP address, network mask, DNS information, default route, and other required network parameters.

3. The **PXE client** will do a boot service discovery, looking for a **PXE server**. Optionally, the DHCP server can be configured to point to the PXE server to boot from.

4. The PXE server sends the client the network bootstrap program and IP information on where to download the files. This enables the client to boot from the network to install an OS.

5. The PXE client requests media (RPMs and control files) as needed from an **HTTPS server**. HTTPS is not the only protocol required; NFS and FTP servers can also be used, although HTTPS is the most common method. The PXE system also sends the *kickstart* parameters to the client via the kickstart file. These parameters contain the specifics to configure the system's storage, network, and packages to be installed.

6. The media server sends the files requested to the PXE client, allowing an OS to be installed.

When configuring the PXE server in this example, there are three components required:

- **DHCP server**: This assigns not only IP addresses to servers as they boot but also important parameters that enable PXE boot.

- **Trivial File Transfer Protocol Daemon** (**TFTPD**): This service works as a TFTP server, allowing the bootloader to run on the client, starting the OS installation.

- **HyperText Transfer Protocol Daemon** (**HTTPD**): This is a web server and is used to host config files and RPMs used for the installation.

---

**Note**

There are some other options, such as using `dnsmasq` as a combined server that works as a DHCP server, a TFTP server (most commonly TFTPD), and a DNS forwarder. However, in many enterprise environments, separate systems are needed. As an example, a Microsoft DHCP server may already be used on the network.

---

In this example, there are two logical servers running three different services, a DHCP server, a TFTP server on the first system. The second system is the PXE server and will also be the HTTP server used to serve up the **Red Hat Package Manager** (**RPM**) files and control files required for the installation. Both systems are multihomed and will be running DHCP and PXE on their secondary interface. The systems also have static IP addresses on the secondary interfaces.

We will cover the following main recipes, which make up the PXE feast, in this chapter:

- Automating the OS install options with kickstart

- DHCP server – more than just IPs

- Setting up a web server – HTTPD

- Serving up the boot – TFTPD

- Back in the day – a manual installation

> **Note**
>
> A multihomed server is a system that is connected to multiple networks at the same time. This is often done in enterprise data centers to isolate systems, while at the same time allowing a controlled system that allows some data to pass. It is possible to set up a PXE server on a single network.

# Technical requirements

The easy way to create a new kickstart file requires building a new OS, as this process will automatically create the file, which can later be modified as needed. A PXE environment also requires additional systems or VMs for a DHCP server and HTTPS server. Before you start, you will first need to download an ISO image. Using a desktop virtualization product such as Oracle VM VirtualBox is recommended.

The related configuration files for many of the recipes in this book are available on GitHub, at https:// github.com/PacktPublishing/Oracle-Linux-Cookbook.

# Automating the OS install options with kickstart

The **kickstart** file is one of the most important parts of the automated install process. This file contains all the information required to automatically install and configure the OS. The kickstart file is a simple text file that contains the directions to allow an unattended installation.

## Getting ready

In order to work with kickstart files, you will need somewhere to build the system, such as Oracle VM VirtualBox. This system can be used to create your first kickstart file, as well as testing new kickstart files before moving them into the PXE environment.

> **Note**
>
> Anaconda is the Oracle Linux installer. It can operate via an automated install using a kickstart file, or interactively via a graphic or text install interface.

## How to do it...

While you can manually create a file from scratch, it is much easier to start with the file that Anaconda creates on installation. This kickstart file is created automatically when a manual is installed and saved on the new system in /root/anaconda-ks.cfg. This file can be easily edited and reused for future builds. Let's look at the file by breaking it down into smaller sections. This system is a graphical installation. Other options are text or cmdline:

> **Note**
>
> There are many options for kickstart, and they are listed in *Appendix – kickstart options*.

```
#version=OL8
# Use graphical install
graphical
```

The repo used to install Oracle Linux was a directory that was loopback mounted from an ISO file. baseurl can also be an HTTPS server, an NFS location, or an FTP server. For example, --baseurl=https://pxe.m57.local/ol8 will tell kickstart to pull the RPMs from a web server:

```
repo --name="AppStream" --baseurl=file:///run/install/sources/mount-
0000-cdrom/AppStream
```

The packages are the software packages selected. Names starting with an @ sign are package groups, and lines without @ are individual packages. Also, the ^ symbol is used to enable the installation of only the required packages in a group. If ^ is not set, all packages in the group are installed. In this example, the graphical-server-environment package group RPMs are installed as well as the kexec-tools package:

```
%packages
@^graphical-server-environment
kexec-tools

%end
```

This is where the default keyboard and language are selected:

```
# Keyboard layouts
keyboard --xlayouts='us'
# System language
lang en_US.UTF-8
```

This is the hostname for the new server. Ideally, it should be the **Fully Qualified Domain Name (FQDN)** for the system:

```
# Network information
network  --hostname=ol802.lab.m57.local
```

This is used to select a CD-ROM or a CD-ROM mounted on a filesystem as the installation media:

```
# Use CDROM installation media
cdrom
```

This is used to run the setup agent on the first boot:

```
# Run the Setup Agent on first boot
firstboot --enable
```

Here, the install disk is selected, as well as the configuration of the logical volume manager and filesystems:

```
ignoredisk --only-use=sda
# Partition clearing information
clearpart --none --initlabel
# Disk partitioning information
part /boot --fstype="xfs" --ondisk=sda --size=1024
part pv.116 --fstype="lvmpv" --ondisk=sda --size=80868
volgroup ol --pesize=4096 pv.116
logvol /home --fstype="xfs" --size=5120 --name=home --vgname=ol
logvol / --fstype="xfs" --size=51200 --name=root --vgname=ol
logvol /u01 --fstype="xfs" --size=10240 --name=u01 --vgname=ol
logvol /var --fstype="xfs" --size=5120 --name=var --vgname=ol
logvol swap --fstype="swap" --size=4056 --name=swap --vgname=ol
logvol /var/log --fstype="xfs" --size=5120 --name=var_log --vgname=ol
```

This is the time zone for the server:

```
# System timezone
timezone America/New_York --isUtc
```

An encrypted root password can be set on the new system. Normally, the password is encrypted, but optionally, you can use the `--plaintext` option with a plaintext password. You can also generate an encrypted password using the `python3 -c 'import crypt,getpass;pw=getpass.getpass();print(crypt.crypt(pw) if (pw==getpass.getpass("Confirm: ")) else exit())'` Python command:

```
# Root password
rootpw --iscrypted $6$W5fC.GDUSIVXPDS7$zQFm49tGCtRbfyAd/0f57QcuPZYtOB/
gobgN2oKNG
zqrseiNtm7QqkthCcdiNxGJhzLSIQpNyxRQXEPJPuaYM.
```

This enables kdump, allowing the kernel to save a crash dump to a device for troubleshooting:

```
%addon com_redhat_kdump --enable --reserve-mb='auto'
%end
```

This is the password policy for root, users, and **Linux Unified Key Setup (LUKS)** passphrases:

```
%anaconda
pwpolicy root --minlen=6 --minquality=1 --notstrict --nochanges
--notempty
pwpolicy user --minlen=6 --minquality=1 --notstrict --nochanges
--emptyok
pwpolicy luks --minlen=6 --minquality=1 --notstrict --nochanges
--notempty
%end
```

You can edit the file as needed. Before using a new file, it can be tested with the `ksvalidator` command. This command is part of the `pykickstart` package, installed via `dnf install -y pykickstart`.

Once the package is installed, test a new kickstart file by running `ksvalidator $FILE`. A sample with an error will look like the following, where line 3 defines the install as `xgraphical`, which is an unknown option:

```
[root@localhost ~]# ksvalidator anaconda-ks.cfg
The following problem occurred on line 3 of the kickstart file:
Unknown command: xgraphical
```

Resolve the error and rerun the validation. In this example, `graphical` is the correct parameter to use. A clean validation returns nothing and will look as follows:

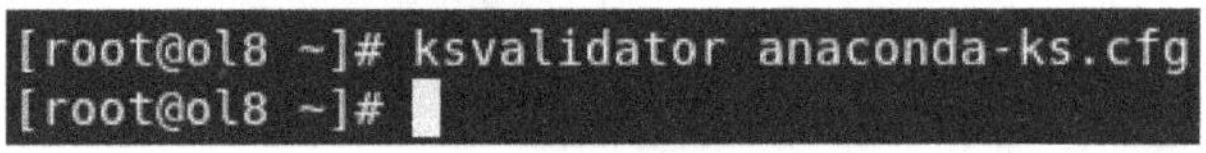

Figure 2.2 – Clean ksvalidator

### Kickstart options!

Now that you have a basic understanding of the kickstart file, you can start adding new options. These options allow you to automate the installation and also grant you more control. The options are covered in *Appendix – kickstart options*.

## How it works...

You can boot any system with kickstart manually by adding the `ks` parameter to the **GRand Unified Bootloader (GRUB)** entry. The format is `ks=PATH_TO_FILE`, where `PATH_TO_FILE` is a URL where the kickstart file can be read from. This is usually placed on an HTTP server that is accessible to clients.

# DHCP server – more than just IPs

The DHCP server will be running a standard DHCP server that is available with Oracle Linux 8. Installation of DHCP is straightforward.

## Getting ready

To set up a DHCP server, you will need an Oracle Linux 8 VM running on the same subnet that VMs that will be installed are using.

## How to do it...

Install the DHCP server with the `dnf install -y dhcp-sever` command. The following screenshot shows the full process:

```
[root@dhcp ~]# dnf install -y dhcp-server
Last metadata expiration check: 0:14:50 ago on Sun 06 Mar 2022 11:48:32 PM EST.
Dependencies resolved.
================================================================================
 Package              Arch       Version              Repository         Size
================================================================================
Installing:
 dhcp-server          x86_64     12:4.3.6-45.el8      ol8_baseos_latest  530 k
Installing dependencies:
 bind-export-libs     x86_64     32:9.11.26-6.el8     ol8_baseos_latest  1.1 M
 dhcp-common          noarch     12:4.3.6-45.el8      ol8_baseos_latest  207 k
 dhcp-libs            x86_64     12:4.3.6-45.el8      ol8_baseos_latest  148 k

Transaction Summary
================================================================================
Install  4 Packages

Total download size: 2.0 M
Installed size: 4.6 M
Downloading Packages:
(1/4): dhcp-libs-4.3.6-45.el8.x86_64.rpm           44 kB/s | 148 kB     00:03
(2/4): dhcp-common-4.3.6-45.el8.noarch.rpm         62 kB/s | 207 kB     00:03
(3/4): bind-export-libs-9.11.26-6.el8.x86_64.rp   348 kB/s | 1.1 MB     00:03
(4/4): dhcp-server-4.3.6-45.el8.x86_64.rpm         24 MB/s | 530 kB     00:00
--------------------------------------------------------------------------------
Total                                             609 kB/s | 2.0 MB     00:03
Running transaction check
Transaction check succeeded.
Running transaction test
Transaction test succeeded.
Running transaction
  Preparing        :                                                       1/1
  Installing       : dhcp-libs-12:4.3.6-45.el8.x86_64                      1/4
  Installing       : dhcp-common-12:4.3.6-45.el8.noarch                    2/4
  Installing       : bind-export-libs-32:9.11.26-6.el8.x86_64              3/4
  Running scriptlet: bind-export-libs-32:9.11.26-6.el8.x86_64              3/4
  Running scriptlet: dhcp-server-12:4.3.6-45.el8.x86_64                    4/4
  Installing       : dhcp-server-12:4.3.6-45.el8.x86_64                    4/4
  Running scriptlet: dhcp-server-12:4.3.6-45.el8.x86_64                    4/4
  Verifying        : bind-export-libs-32:9.11.26-6.el8.x86_64              1/4
  Verifying        : dhcp-common-12:4.3.6-45.el8.noarch                    2/4
  Verifying        : dhcp-libs-12:4.3.6-45.el8.x86_64                      3/4
  Verifying        : dhcp-server-12:4.3.6-45.el8.x86_64                    4/4

Installed:
  bind-export-libs-32:9.11.26-6.el8.x86_64   dhcp-common-12:4.3.6-45.el8.noarch
  dhcp-libs-12:4.3.6-45.el8.x86_64           dhcp-server-12:4.3.6-45.el8.x86_64

Complete!
```

Figure 2.3 – DHCP server installation

Once installed, enable DHCP traffic through the firewall (as seen in the following screenshot) with the `firewall-cmd --add-service=dhcp --permanent` and `firewall-cmd --reload` commands:

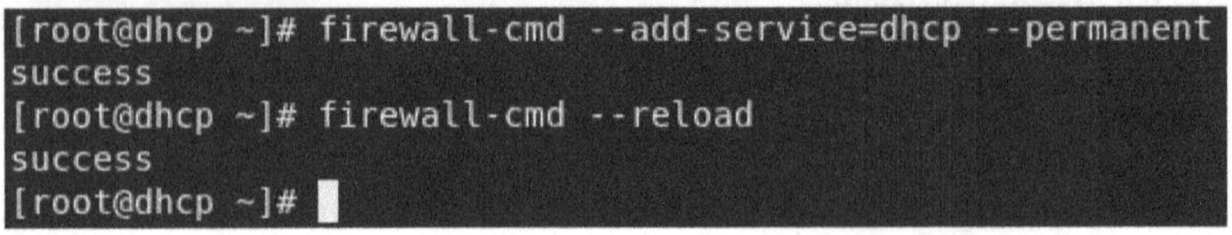

```
[root@dhcp ~]# firewall-cmd --add-service=dhcp --permanent
success
[root@dhcp ~]# firewall-cmd --reload
success
[root@dhcp ~]#
```

Figure 2.4 – DHCP firewall commands

The DHCP server has a sample DHCP config file installed in `/usr/share/doc/dhcp-server`. This has sample config files for both IPv4 in `/usr/share/doc/dhcp-server/dhcpd.conf.example` and IPv6 in `/usr/share/doc/dhcp-server/dhcpd6.conf.example`. For this DHCP server, we will use IPv4 and copy the sample config file to `/etc/dhcp/dhcpd.conf`. There is an existing config file, but by default, it is mostly empty with no configuration and can be replaced as in the following screenshot:

```
[root@dhcp ~]# cp /usr/share/doc/dhcp-server/dhcpd.conf.example /etc/dhcp/dhcpd.conf
cp: overwrite '/etc/dhcp/dhcpd.conf'? y
[root@dhcp ~]#
```

Figure 2.5 – Copy dhcp.conf

Next, the config file will need to be updated, changing the IP address range, as well as adding an NTP server to the configuration with the option of `option ntp-servers 192.168.200.1`, which sets the NTP server to `192.168.200.1`. While configuring a NTP server is optional, it is highly recommended. Additionally, when the PXE server is *not* the DHCP server, you will need to add the next server parameter to the subnet. This will point DHCP clients to the TFTP boot from the PXE server.

> **Note**
>
> If you are using an existing DHCP server, make sure you add the `next-server` parameter to point to the PXE server that has the TFTP server.

Since the TFTP server is running on the PXE server, the DHCP server will need the next server option to be set to the IP address of the PXE server. A complete sample config file is shown here:

```
# dhcpd.conf
#
# These options are common to all networks
option domain-name "lab.m57.local";
option domain-name-servers 192.168.56.10;

default-lease-time 600;
```

```
max-lease-time 7200;
# If the DHCP server is the main server for the network, this should
be set authoritative;

# This sets where logs are sent. By default they are sent to syslog.
You can reconfigure sysylog to send to a different location as needed.
log-facility local7;

subnet 192.168.56.0 netmask 255.255.255.0 {
  range dynamic-bootp 192.168.56.100 192.168.56.150 ;
  option broadcast-address  192.168.56.255;
  option routers 192.168.56.1;
  option domain-name-servers 192.168.56.10 ;
  option domain-name "lab.m57.local";
  option ntp-servers 192.168.200.1;
   next-server pxe.lab.m57.local;


}


# Hosts which require special configuration options can be listed
here, with the host details. This could be used to hard-code an IP
address to a host, or define host-specific parameters like a non-
0standard vmunix filename or a fixed IP address.

host fixedhost {
  hardware ethernet 0:0:aa:bb:cc:dd;
  filename "vmunix.fixedhost";
  server-name "fixedhost.m57.local;
}

# When using a fixed IP address, it is more common to assign the host
an IP address outside of the DHCP managed IP address range. set.
host fantasia {
  hardware ethernet 08:01:02:03:04:05;
  fixed-address fixedhost2.m57.local;
}
```

Next, we need to test the DHCP server. To do this, install the nmap program with dnf install -y nmap.

Nmap is a powerful utility and can be used for many things. It is most well known as a port scanning tool, letting the user scan networks looking for servers that respond to a ping with nmap -sP 192.168.200.1/28, as seen in the following screenshot:

```
[root@dhcp dhcp]# nmap -sP 192.168.200.1/28
Starting Nmap 7.70 ( https://nmap.org ) at 2022-03-06 00:00 EST
Nmap scan report for 192.168.200.1
Host is up (0.00014s latency).
MAC Address: 76:AC:B9:45:E1:62 (Unknown)
Nmap scan report for 192.168.200.3
Host is up (0.0021s latency).
MAC Address: 00:21:9B:B3:94:D0 (Dell)
Nmap scan report for nas.m57.local (192.168.200.10)
Host is up (0.00025s latency).
MAC Address: 24:5E:BE:4B:41:3F (Qnap Systems)
Nmap done: 16 IP addresses (3 hosts up) scanned in 641616.25 seconds
```

Figure 2.6 – Nmap ping scan

It can also be used to identify the OS and open ports of a specific server, with `nmap 192.168.200.34 -O`:

```
[root@dhcp dhcp]# nmap 192.168.200.34 -O
Starting Nmap 7.70 ( https://nmap.org ) at 2022-03-06 00:00 EST
Nmap scan report for 192.168.200.34
Host is up (0.00096s latency).
Not shown: 995 filtered ports
PORT     STATE SERVICE
22/tcp   open  ssh
80/tcp   open  http
443/tcp  open  https
5120/tcp open  barracuda-bbs
5555/tcp open  freeciv
MAC Address: 00:10:E0:3C:E9:28 (Oracle)
Warning: OSScan results may be unreliable because we could not find at least 1 open and 1 closed port
Device type: general purpose|phone
Running: Linux 2.6.X
OS CPE: cpe:/o:linux:linux_kernel:2.6.24
OS details: Linux 2.6.24, Linux 2.6.9 - 2.6.33, Linux 2.6.24 (Palm Pre mobile phone)
Network Distance: 1 hop

OS detection performed. Please report any incorrect results at https://nmap.org/submit/ .
Nmap done: 1 IP address (1 host up) scanned in 641501.25 seconds
```

Figure 2.7 – Nmap ID server

While Nmap is a powerful tool for scanning networks, it can also be used for many additional tasks, including checking that a DHCP server is replying correctly. This is done with the `broadcast-dhcp-discover` script and is used via the `nmnap --script` option. Additionally, if your system has multiple interfaces, you can specify the network interface used by the scan with the `-e` option. In this environment, the DHCP server is verified with the `nmap --script broadcast-dhcp-discover -e enp0s8` command:

```
[root@dhcp dhcp]# nmap --script broadcast-dhcp-discover -e enp0s8
Starting Nmap 7.70 ( https://nmap.org ) at 2022-03-06 00:00 EST
Pre-scan script results:
| broadcast-dhcp-discover:
|   Response 1 of 1:
|     IP Offered: 192.168.56.101
|     DHCP Message Type: DHCPOFFER
|     Server Identifier: 192.168.56.10
|     IP Address Lease Time: 5m00s
|     Subnet Mask: 255.255.255.0
|     Router: 192.168.56.1
|     Domain Name Server: 192.168.56.10
|     Domain Name: lab.m57.local
|     Broadcast Address: 192.168.56.255
|_    NTP Servers: 192.168.200.1
WARNING: No targets were specified, so 0 hosts scanned.
Nmap done: 0 IP addresses (0 hosts up) scanned in 0.36 seconds
```

Figure 2.8 – Nmap DHCP discovery

We now know how the DHCP server works, so next is the Apache HTTPD server.

# Setting up the web server – HTTPD

The next step for the PXE server is to install a web server. In this example, we will use Apache. Other web servers will also work, but Apache is one of the most common.

## Getting ready

To set up an HTTP server, you will need an Oracle Linux 8 VM running in your environment. The server's IP address should be routable to the subnets the VMs are using, and the firewall ports should allow HTTP/HTTPS traffic. Ideally, you should also have enough space for several ISO files. Normally, 20-30 GB is enough data space.

## How to do it...

Starting the install of the Apache HTTPD server is simple; just run `yum install -y httpd`.

Once the web server is installed, copy the full ISO file to the server into a directory of your choice. In our example, `OracleLinux-R8-U5-x86_64-dvd.iso` is copied into `/root`, as seen in *Figure 2.9*.

```
[root@pxe ~]# ls
anaconda-ks.cfg  initial-setup-ks.cfg  OracleLinux-R8-U5-x86_64-dvd.iso
[root@pxe ~]#
```

Figure 2.9 – Oracle Linux ISO in /root

The next step is to mount the ISO file in a directory under `docroot`. With the standard install of Apache, `docroot` is in `/var/www/html`, so a directory named `OL8` is created. When the ISO is mounted, it is more efficient to use a loopback mount method. This allows an ISO file to be mounted as a normal filesystem. Next, using a loopback mount, mount the ISO file using `/var/www/html/OL8` as the mount point using the following command:

```
mount -o ro,loop /root/OracleLinux-R8-U5-x86_64-dvd.iso /var/www/html/
OL8
```

Once mounted, a `df` command will show the mounted filesystem. The entire chain of commands can be seen in the following screenshot, *Figure 2.10*.

```
[root@pxe html]# mkdir /var/www/html/OL8
[root@pxe html]# mount -o ro,loop /root/OracleLinux-R8-U5-x86_64-dvd.iso /var/www/html/OL8
[root@pxe html]# df -h
Filesystem              Size    Used  Avail  Use%  Mounted on
devtmpfs                316M      0   316M    0%  /dev
tmpfs                   344M      0   344M    0%  /dev/shm
tmpfs                   344M   5.4M   339M    2%  /run
tmpfs                   344M      0   344M    0%  /sys/fs/cgroup
/dev/mapper/ol-root      50G    17G    34G   33%  /
/dev/mapper/ol-home      10G   118M   9.9G    2%  /home
/dev/sda1              1014M   468M   547M   47%  /boot
tmpfs                    69M    12K    69M    1%  /run/user/42
tmpfs                    69M      0    69M    0%  /run/user/0
/dev/loop0               10G    10G      0  100%  /var/www/html/OL8
[root@pxe html]#
```

Figure 2.10 – ISO mounted

Now that the filesystem is mounted, let's open up ports `80` and `443` in the firewall. This is easily done with `firewall-cmd`, adding both the `http` and `https` ports opened and saved as permanent changes to the firewall. Once the ports are opened, the firewall rules are reloaded. The following three commands are run to perform these tasks:

```
firewall-cmd --add-service=http --permanent
firewall-cmd --add-service=https --permanent
firewall-cmd --reload
```

Now that the firewall is opened, Apache is installed, and the ISO is mounted via a loopback, we can start the Apache server with the `systemctl start httpd` command.

You can verify that all is working as expected by pointing your browser to the server's IP address and the `OL8` directory, as seen in the following screenshot. This will show the contents of the ISO, including the release notes and the RPMs under the `BaseOS` directory, as seen in *Figure 2.11*.

Figure 2.11 – ISO file accessible via httpd

## Serving up the boot – TFTPD

**TFTP** is used for simple file transfers over the network. This is most often used to load the initial bootloader for an OS, or some firmware updates for embedded devices and older hardware. In the context of the PXE server, the TFTP system is used for the initial bootloader.

### Getting ready

To set up a TFTP server, you will need an Oracle Linux 8 VM running in your environment. The server should be on the same network subnet that the systems being built are using. Ideally, you should also have enough space for several boot files. Normally, 5 GB is enough data space.

## How to do it...

Installing TFTP is simple. Run the `dnf install -y tftp-server` command, as seen in *Figure 2.12.*

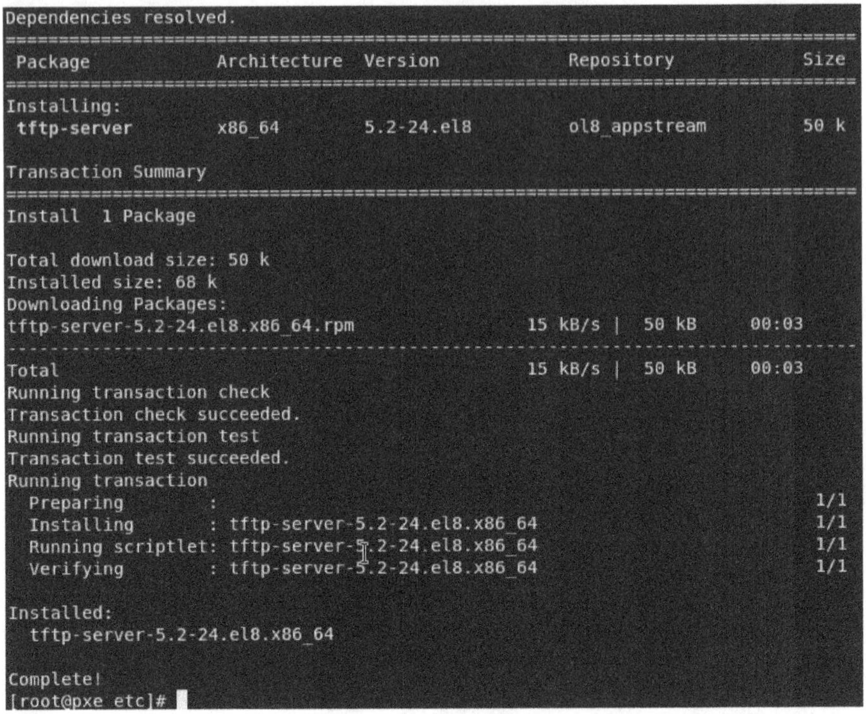

```
Dependencies resolved.
================================================================================
 Package          Architecture   Version           Repository          Size
================================================================================
Installing:
 tftp-server      x86_64         5.2-24.el8        ol8_appstream        50 k

Transaction Summary
================================================================================
Install  1 Package

Total download size: 50 k
Installed size: 68 k
Downloading Packages:
tftp-server-5.2-24.el8.x86_64.rpm                  15 kB/s |  50 kB     00:03
--------------------------------------------------------------------------------
Total                                              15 kB/s |  50 kB     00:03
Running transaction check
Transaction check succeeded.
Running transaction test
Transaction test succeeded.
Running transaction
  Preparing        :                                                        1/1
  Installing       : tftp-server-5.2-24.el8.x86_64                          1/1
  Running scriptlet: tftp-server-5.2-24.el8.x86_64                          1/1
  Verifying        : tftp-server-5.2-24.el8.x86_64                          1/1

Installed:
  tftp-server-5.2-24.el8.x86_64

Complete!
[root@pxe etc]#
```

Figure 2.12 – TFTP installation

Once the installation is complete, we need to open up the firewall for TFTP and reload it:

```
firewall-cmd --add-service-tftp --permanent
firewall-cmd --reload
```

The output of these commands is as shown in the following screenshot:

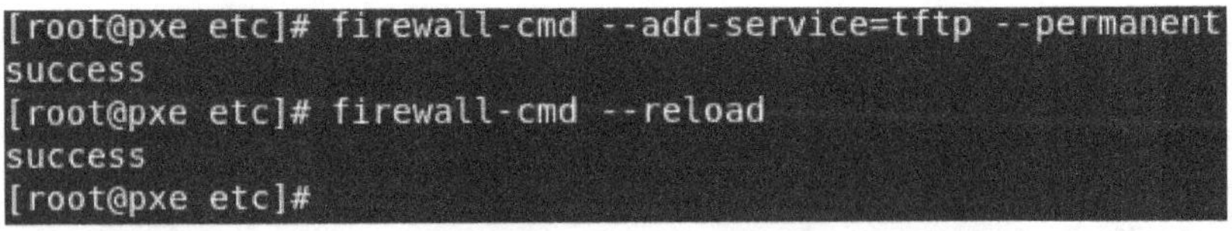

```
[root@pxe etc]# firewall-cmd --add-service=tftp --permanent
success
[root@pxe etc]# firewall-cmd --reload
success
[root@pxe etc]#
```

Figure 2.13 – TFTP firewall

After installation and the firewall has opened, we need to prepare the system by installing the bootloaders, preparing an Oracle Linux 8 TFTP location, and creating a boot menu.

> **Note**
>
> This example is using a BIOS-based host. If you want to use a UEFI host, you will need to install `grub2-efi` and configure UEFI-specific parameters. The Oracle docs for this can be found at `https://docs.oracle.com/en/operating-systems/oracle-linux/8/install/install-CreatingaNetworkInstallationSetup.html#uefi-clients`.

To install the bootloaders for BIOS-based installs, we will install the `syslinux` package. The `syslinux` package includes bootloaders for network booting (`PXELINUX`), Linux (`ext2/ext3/ext4`) or `btrfs` filesystems (`EXTLINUX`), MS-DOS FAT filesystems (`SYSLINUX`), and bootable El Torito CD-ROMs (`ISOLINUX`). For network booting, we will be using `PXELINUX`:

```
Dependencies resolved.
================================================================================
 Package               Architecture   Version        Repository          Size
================================================================================
Installing:
 syslinux              x86_64         6.04-5.el8     ol8_baseos_latest   578 k
Installing dependencies:
 syslinux-nonlinux     noarch         6.04-5.el8     ol8_baseos_latest   553 k

Transaction Summary
================================================================================
Install  2 Packages

Total download size: 1.1 M
Installed size: 2.6 M
Downloading Packages:
(1/2): syslinux-6.04-5.el8.x86_64.rpm              168 kB/s | 578 kB   00:03
(2/2): syslinux-nonlinux-6.04-5.el8.noarch.rpm     161 kB/s | 553 kB   00:03
--------------------------------------------------------------------------------
Total                                              328 kB/s | 1.1 MB   00:03
Running transaction check
Transaction check succeeded.
Running transaction test
Transaction test succeeded.
Running transaction
  Preparing        :                                                       1/1
  Installing       : syslinux-nonlinux-6.04-5.el8.noarch                   1/2
  Installing       : syslinux-6.04-5.el8.x86_64                            2/2
  Running scriptlet: syslinux-6.04-5.el8.x86_64                            2/2
  Verifying        : syslinux-6.04-5.el8.x86_64                            1/2
  Verifying        : syslinux-nonlinux-6.04-5.el8.noarch                   2/2

Installed:
  syslinux-6.04-5.el8.x86_64              syslinux-nonlinux-6.04-5.el8.noarch

Complete!
[root@pxe etc]#
```

Figure 2.14 – Syslinux installation

Next, we will copy the boot image file, `pxelinux.0`, and copy the file into `/var/lib/tftpboot`:

```
cp /usr/share/syslinux/pxelinux.0 /var/lib/tftpboot/
```

Then, we will create an Oracle Linux 8 boot directory under `tftpboot`:

```
mkdir /var/lib/tftpboot/ol8
```

Now, we need to copy over the PXE boot files from the ISO we previously mounted when installing the HTTP server to the new Oracle Linux 8 boot directory:

```
cp /var/www/html/OL8/images/pxeboot/* /var/lib/tftpboot/ol8/
```

Next, we need a boot menu. Luckily, we can copy over the samples and get things moving quickly. We only need the menu files, so using the following command to copy things works just fine:

```
cp -v /usr/share/syslinux/{ldlinux.c32,libcom32.c32,libutil.c32,menu.
c32,vesamenu.c32} /var/lib/tftpboot/
```

Almost done here. To make a directory for the PXS config files and build the default menu, use the following:

```
mkdir /var/lib/tftpboot/pxelinux.cfg
```

We can finally install a config file. Copy this sample configuration file into `/var/lib/tftpboot/pxelinux.cfg/default`:

```
default linux-auto
prompt 1
timeout 60

display boot.msg

label linux-auto
  menu label ^Install OL8 in Graphical Mode using the kickstart file
  menu default
  kernel ol8/vmlinuz
  append initrd=ol8/initrd.img ip=dhcp inst.repo=http://pxe.lab.m57.
local/ol8 ks=http://pxe.lab.m57.local/ks_files/ol8ks.cfg

label linux-manual
  menu label ^Install OL8 in Graphical Mode with manual input
  menu default
  kernel ol8/vmlinuz
  append initrd=ol8/initrd.img ip=dhcp inst.repo=http://pxe.lab.m57.
local/ol8
```

```
label rescue
  menu label ^Rescue installed system
  kernel ol8/vmlinuz
  append initrd=ol8/initrd.img rescue
label local
  menu label Boot from ^local drive
  localboot 0xffff
```

In this sample, the default install will be `linux-auto`, and that will start in 60 seconds unless the user manually selects one of the following options:

- `linux-auto`: This is the default and will install Oracle Linux using the kickstart parameters

- `linux-manual`: This will kick off a traditional install or Oracle Linux, prompting the user to select all the options from Anaconda manually

- `rescue`: This will boot in rescue mode

- `local`: This will boot from the existing local disk

You can easily modify the menus as needed to meet your specific needs. PXE booting, while daunting at first, provides a powerful tool to manage your Linux installations.

## How it works...

When systems boot, they will load the bootloader based on the DHCP server config. This will then have the system boot from the TFTP server, starting the PXE process.

# Back in the day – a manual installation

Automated installations are great, but for some admins, the complexity of configuring and maintaining the infrastructure to support an automated installation is more effort than doing a manual installation. This recipe will go over how the manual installation works.

## Getting ready

To do this, you will need a system to install from. In the example, Oracle VM VirtualBox will be used, but it could just as easily be on a bare-metal server or a different hypervisor. You will also need installation media. Normally, an ISO works fine, but you can also use a boot ISO and an HTTP server, an FTP server, or even a network file share.

## How to do it...

Regardless of whether you boot from an ISO, a USB stick, or even a kickstart file with a graphical installation option set, the process is the same!

If you are booting from a boot-only image, you will need to enable the network and then point to an installation source. This is shown in the next few steps. If you are installing from an ISO or USB, skip to the *How it works…* section:

1.  When booting from a boot image, you will need to select **Install Oracle Linux X** to start the process. When possible, use the latest version of Oracle Linux. When doing an installation you will get the first screen where you can test the boot image or continue:

Figure 2.15 – Linux installer boot

2.  Next, pick your language:

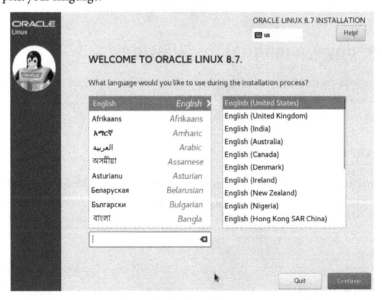

Figure 2.16 – Install language

3. Click on **Continue** once you have picked your language. Next, you should see the **INSTALLATION SUMMARY** section:

Figure 2.17 – Installation Summary

For now, we need to do two tasks:

- Enable the network

- Set **Installation Source** to Oracle's yum repo

To enable the network, click on the **Network & Host Name** option.

4. Here, you will need to switch Ethernet on, and also update the hostname with the name of the server. The network will automatically use DHCP to configure the boot image. You can optionally manually configure the IP stack by clicking the **Configure** option.

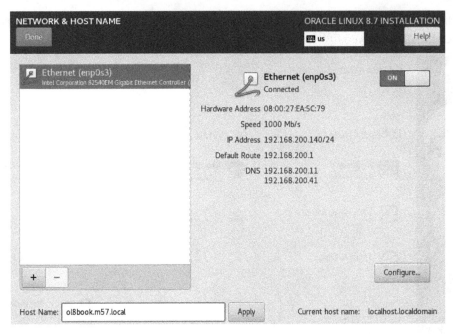

Figure 2.18 – Network & Host Name

5.  Next, click **Apply** and then **Done**. This will take you back to the **INSTALLATION SUMMARY** page. From there, we will need to select **Installation Source** to set where we will get the install files.

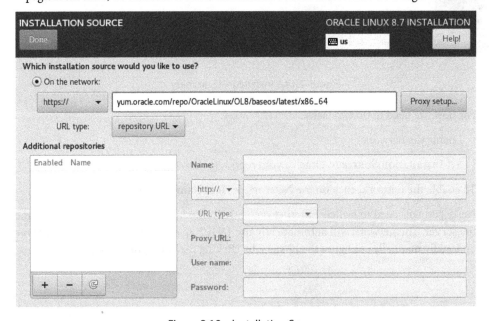

Figure 2.19 – Installation Source

In this example, we are using the Oracle Public YUM server as the installation source. You can optionally add additional repositories if needed, as well as set any proxy settings if required. You can also set an FTP : / / patch for an NFS server path. Once you have a path, select **Done**.

6.  This will take you back to the **INSTALLATION SUMMARY** page. Wait a few minutes for the repo index to load. Once it loads, you should see the **Installation Source** option, as well as the option for **Software Selection**.

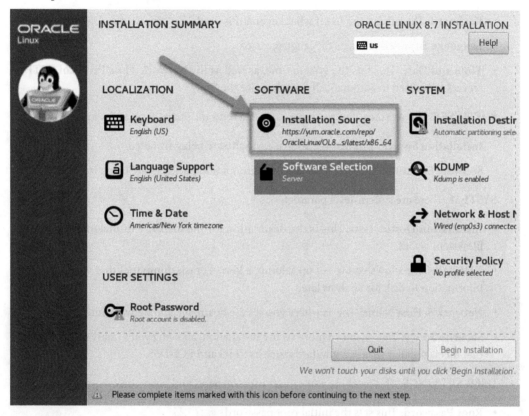

Figure 2.20 – Selecting Installation Source

Manually network booting is otherwise the same as an ISO or USB boot.

## How it works...

A manual boot process is fairly simple to do. Once booted, on the **INSTALLATION SUMMARY** screen, you have many options:

- **LOCALIZATION**: This is where you can set settings for country-specific options language, keyboard type, time, and more:

  - **Keyboard**: This allows you to set what keyboard is used. You can use non-US keyboards.

  - **Language Support**: This sets the language used.

  - **Time and Date**: This sets the system time, as well as the **Network Time Protocol** (**NTP**) servers to be used to automatically synchronize the time.

- **SOFTWARE**: This sets the software sources and what software groups or packages will be installed:

  - **Installation Source**: This sets the source and software being installed

  - **Software Selection**: This sets what software groups and packages are being installed

- **SYSTEM**: These are system-level parameters:

  - **Installation Destination**: This is the destination for the install. This includes the initial filesystem layout.

  - **KDUMP**: This allows you to set up kdump, a kernel crash dump tool that writes system information to disk for analysis later.

  - **Network & Host Name**: This is where you set the hostname and network information.

  - **Security Policy**: This enables a more secure installation, allowing you to start with a system that meets popular security standards such as STIG and PCI-DSS.

- **USER SETTINGS**: This is where you can set users, groups, and passwords:

  - **Root Password**: This sets the initial root password

Generally, the first setting that is set is the network. This is key for not only network installations but also setting up NTP for time synchronization:

1.  To set up the network, select **Network & Host Name**:

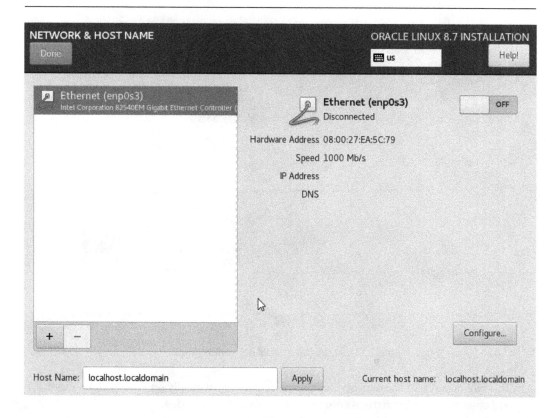

Figure 2.21 – Setting hostname and IP info

By default, the network port is not enabled and the hostname is not set. You can manually set the hostname. Don't forget to use an FQDN when setting the hostname. This should include the name and the domain name. When you enable the network, the system will automatically grab DHCP IP info. If you want to manually configure this, click on **Configure…**:

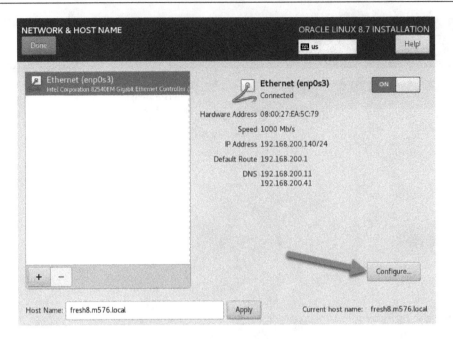

Figure 2.22 – Accessing manual network settings

2.  This will take you to the network details, where you can manually set the MTU, IP address, and other NIC-specific settings. You can also disable IPv6 if needed.

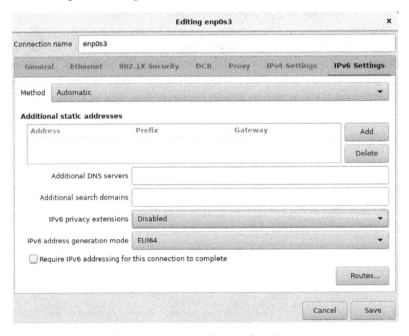

Figure 2.23 – Manual network settings

3.  Once the network is set, you can use network resources such as NTP servers to synchronize the clock. To do this, under **TIME & DATE**, click on the gears:

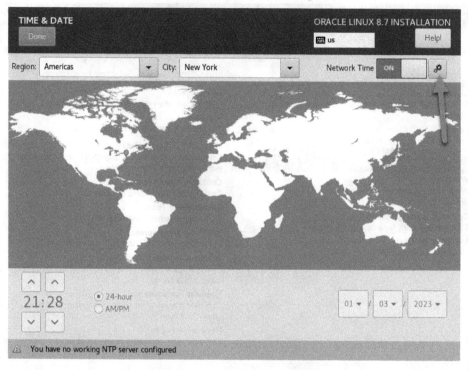

Figure 2.24 – Accessing NTP settings

4.  Then, you can add NTP servers. By default, a public server is used, but if you run local NTP servers, make sure you add those here.

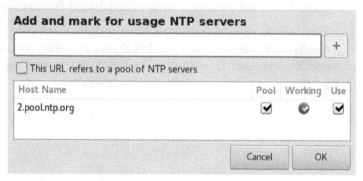

Figure 2.25 – NTP settings

5.  Next, additional software sources can be added under **Installation Source** as needed. This was done previously when doing a network install.

You can also set what RPM groups are installed, along with any additional software. This is done under **SOFTWARE SELECTION**:

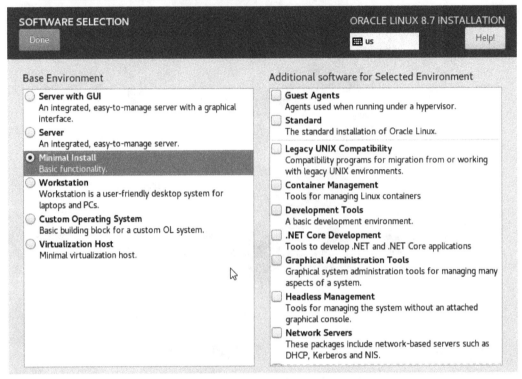

Figure 2.26 – Software Selection

6.  After setting **Base Environment** and adding any additional software, the next task is to set up the installation destination. This is done by clicking on **Installation Destination**.

    From here, you should see the physical and logical drives available to the system. The default is to set **Storage Configuration** as **Automatic**, but let's explore a different boot disk structure by selecting a custom configuration. Once **Custom** is selected, click on the **Done** button.

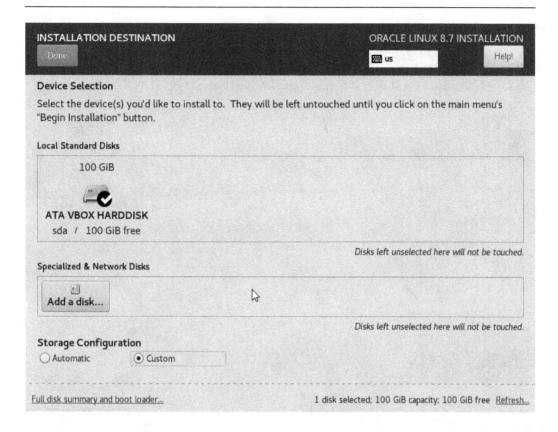

INSTALLATION DESTINATION

Figure 2.27 – Installation Destination

7.   From here, you can pick the default volume management strategy, as well as manually creating a new layout. Most systems will use an LVM install, as this gives you the flexibility to resize partitions down the road.

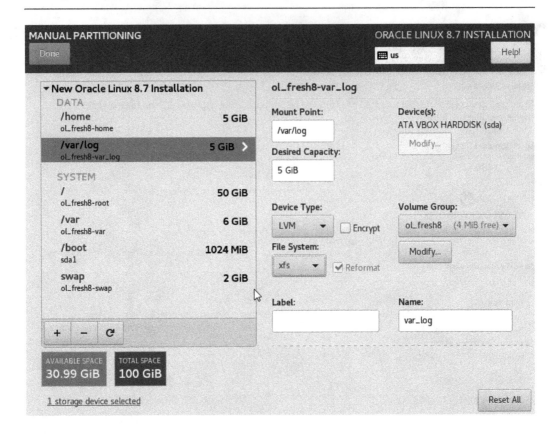

Figure 2.28 – Manual Partitioning

Don't forget to click **Done** and accept all the changes to the layout.

8.  As a note, if you boot from a UEK-based install, you now have the option to use Btrfs as the root filesystem.

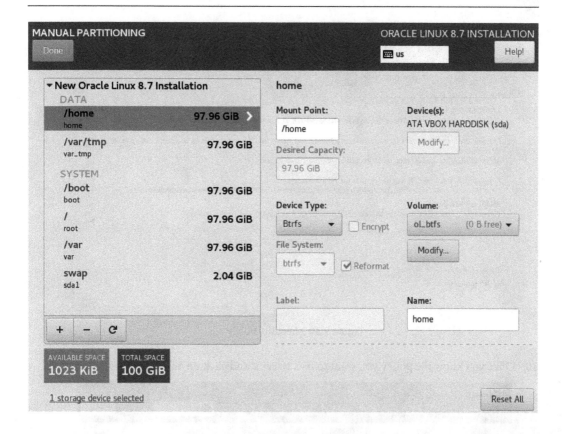

Figure 2.29 – Btfrs partitioning

Btrfs will look a little different, as the system combines the role of volume manager and filesystem into one system. This means at the time of installation, all of the filesystems will show all the space available. This can be updated after the OS is installed and a quota is set for each directory that needs to be limited. This is covered in the Btrfs recipes in *Chapter 4*.

You could finish up now by just giving root a password… but there is one more basic task, and that is to apply a security policy to the system. The security policy allows the installer to preconfigure the system to follow the policy set. This is very helpful when installing systems that support workloads such as HIPPA, PCI DSS for credit card processing, or STIG for public sector workloads.

9. To set a policy, select **Security Policy** from **Installation Summary**:

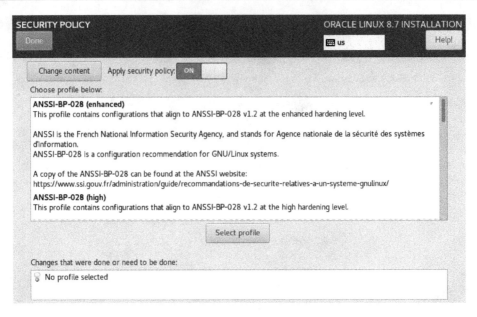

Figure 2.30 – Security Policy

10. Once you know the policy you want to use, select it and click on **Select profile**:

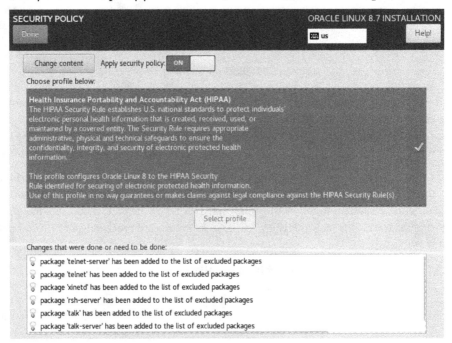

Figure 2.31 – Applying a security policy

You will now see the policy and a list of all the changes being made to the system. You will also see some changes that may need to be made to the filesystem layout. This is seen in policies such as STIG, where /var and /var/log need to be separate filesystems.

Once done, from the **Installation Summary**, click on **Begin Installation** to start the install.

## Appendix – kickstart options

The following table covers the most popular options that control the installation and their syntax:

| | | | |
|---|---|---|---|
| **Option Name** | `authselect` | | |
| **Description** | It configures the authentication options for the system using the `authselect` command. `authselect` options are the same as the `authselect` command. They are passed directly to the command. | | |
| **Options** | See the `authselect` command. | | |
| **Option Name** | `autostep` | | |
| **Description** | This option is not recommended for production use. It is more of a troubleshooting command that makes the installer step through every screen, displaying them for a short amount of time. | | |
| **Options** | `--autoscreenshot` will take an automated screenshot of every install screen. The images are stored in /tmp/anaconda-screenshots/ during the installation and then moved over to /root/anaconda-screenshots when the installation completes. This is helpful for troubleshooting because if you missed a required kickstart option and the installation does not automatically run, you will be at the screen with missing data, and can manually enter the missing configuration data. Then, when you click to continue, the screen is automatically captured with the data you entered. | | |
| **Option Name** | `cmdline` | | |
| **Description** | When used, the install runs in a non-interactive command-line mode. Any prompt from Anaconda for input stops the installation. Make sure to test with the `autostep` option first. | | |
| **Options** | None | | |

| Option Name | eula | | |
|---|---|---|---|
| **Description** | If used, the `--agreed` option is required. This option allows you to automatically accept the **End User License Agreement (EULA)**. When this option is used, the installer will not prompt for acceptance of the EULA on the first reboot of the system. This is very useful for environments that use a PXE boot as part of the auto-scaling strategy. | | |
| **Options** | `--agreed` forces the EULA to be accepted and must be used. If the option is not used, the EULA parameter is ignored. | | |
| **Option Name** | firewall | | |
| **Description** | This configures the firewall on the installed system. | | |
| **Options** | <ul><li>`--enabled` or `–enable` is required. It enables or disables the firewall.</li><li>`--disabled` or `–disable` is required. If disabled, `iptables` rules are not configured.</li><li>`--trust` sets a trusted network device, allowing all traffic to pass through the firewall. To configure multiple devices, list each one as its own entry with no commas, such as `–trust eth0 –trust eth8`.</li><li>`--incoming` adds each of the following tags to allow incoming traffic for these common services:<ul><li>`–ssh`</li><li>`–smtp`</li><li>`–http`</li><li>`–ftp`</li></ul></li><li>`--port=` specifies a specific port to allow access to the server. You can use ports from `/etc/service` for specific `port:protocol` combinations. Multiple ports are comma delimited. An example is `ldap:tcp, 1521:tcp`.</li><li>`--service=` allows an easy way to enable specific services, such as CUPS, or services that require multiple UDP/TCP ports to be opened. This enables an easy way to open these ports in a readable format.</li><li>`--use-system-defaults` does not configure the firewall. If other options are specified, they are ignored.</li></ul> | | |

| Option Name | `firstboot` | | |
|---|---|---|---|
| Description | This option can disable the running of the setup application when the system boots. If enabled, make sure you have `initial-setup.rpm` (`initial-setup-gui.rpm` if a GUI is required) installed. This option is disabled by default. | | |
| Options | <ul><li>`--enable` or `–enabled` starts the setup the first time the system boots.</li><li>`--disable` or `–disabled` does not start the setup the first time the system boots.</li><li>`--reconfig` enables the setup to start at boot time in reconfiguration mode. This enables the networking configuration, root password, time zone, language, mouse, and keyboard options to be set in addition to the default options.</li></ul> | | |

| Option Name | `graphical` | | |
|---|---|---|---|
| Description | The `graphical` command is the default, if not set. The installation continues with a fully graphical install. | | |
| Options | `--non-interactive` performs the installation in a completely non-interactive mode. This mode will terminate the installation when user interaction is required. | | |
| Option Name | `group` | | |
| Description | This option creates a user group on the system. | | |
| Options | <ul><li>`--name=` is required and sets the name of the group.</li><li>`--gid=` is an optional parameter and will set the GID of the group.</li></ul> | | |

| Option Name | `halt` | | |
|---|---|---|---|
| Description | If used, the system with halt after the installation is completed. This is the default completion method if no other method is set. Other completion methods are `poweroff`, `reboot`, and `shutdown`. | | |
| Options | None | | |

| Option Name | `logging` | | |
|---|---|---|---|
| Description | This is useful for troubleshooting PXE installs. It controls the logging from the installer during the installation. It does not configure logging on the system being installed. | | |

| Options | • `--host=` is the syslog host logs are sent to.<br><br>• `--port=` is the port used for syslog on the remote syslog host. If not set, the default port (UDP 514) is used.<br><br>• `--level=` specifies the minimum level of messages sent to device `tty3`. Regardless of this level, all messages are still sent to the log host and file. Valid values are `critical`, `debug`, `error`, `info`, and `warning`. |
| --- | --- |
| Syntax | `logging [--host=host] [--port=port] [--level=critical|debug|error|info]` |

| Option Name | poweroff | | |
| --- | --- | --- | --- |
| Description | When used, a shutdown and power-off are performed on the system after the installation completes. | | |
| Options | None | | |

| Option Name | reboot | | |
| --- | --- | --- | --- |
| Description | It reboots the system after the install completes. | | |
| Options | `--eject` ejects bootable media (DVD, USB, etc.) before rebooting the system. | | |

| Option Name | repo | | |
| --- | --- | --- | --- |
| Description | Enables additional DNF/YUM repos as installation sources. Each repo will need its own line. | | |
| Options | • `--name=` is required and sets both the repo name and URL. If a name conflicts with an existing repo, it will be ignored. The format is `--name=repoid [--baseurl=url|--mirrorlist=url|--metalink=url] [options]`. The following additional options can be added to the URL. As a warning, variables that can be used in yum repository config files are not supported. However, you can use `$releasever` and `$basearch`:<br><br> ▪ `--baseurl`: This is the URL of the repo<br><br> ▪ `--mirrorlist`: This is a list of mirrors for a repo<br><br> ▪ `--metalink`: This is the URL with `metalink` for the repo<br><br>• `--proxy=[protocol://][username[:password]@]host[:port]` sets the proxy for the repo.<br><br>• `--noverifyssl` disables SSL verification of an HTTPS server. | | |

| Option Name | `selinux` | | |
| --- | --- | --- | --- |
| Description | Used to configure the initial policy and state of `selinux`. The default policy is enforcing. | | |
| Options | <ul><li>`--enforcing` enables SELinux with the policy set to enforcing. This is the default setting.</li><li>`--permissive` enables SELinux with the policy set to permissive. This allows warnings to output to console of syslog without enforcing the policy.</li><li>`--disabled` disables SELinux.</li></ul> | | |

| Option Name | `shutdown` | | |
| --- | --- | --- | --- |
| Description | Runs the `shutdown` command on the system after the installation has completed. | | |
| Options | None | | |

| Option Name | `sshkey` | | |
| --- | --- | --- | --- |
| Description | This adds an SSH key to the authorized keys files for the specified user. | | |
| Options | `--username` is mandatory. It is used with the following syntax:<br><br>`sshkey --username=user KEY` | | |
| Option Name | `text` | | |
| Description | When used, the installation runs in text mode. By default, the installer runs the GUI install method. Only one of the text/graphical options can be used. | | |
| Options | `--non-interactive` does the install in a non-interactive mode. If a user action is required, the mode will terminate the install. | | |

| Option Name | url | | |
|---|---|---|---|
| Description | When used, it will use the URL specified for the install files from an ISO. URLs can be formatted for FTP, HTTP, or HTTPS. | | |
| Options | <ul><li>`--url` is required. This is the URL used for the source files. An example of the syntax is as follows:<br><br>`http://server/direcort ftp://username:password@server/path`</li><li>`--mirrorlist` is an optional parameter that sets the mirror URL to install from.</li><li>`--proxy` is an optional parameter that sets a proxy to use while performing the install from an HTTP/HTTPS or FTP server.</li><li>`--noverifyssl` is an optional parameter that disables SSL verification when using an HTTPS server.</li><li>`--metalink` is an optional parameter that sets the ULN/metalink URL to install from. Variable substitution is done for `$releasever` and `$basearch`.</li></ul> | | |
| Option Name | user | | |
| Description | Creates a new user on the system | | |
| Options | <ul><li>`--name` is a required parameter and is the username.</li><li>`--uid` is the user's **User ID (UID)**.</li><li>`--gid` the user's **Group ID (GID)**.</li><li>`--groups` is a comma-separated list of group names the user should belong to.</li><li>`--homedir` is the home directory for the user.</li><li>`--lock` will, if used, lock a new user's account by default.</li><li>`--password` is the password for the new user.</li><li>`--iscrypted`, if used, means that the password argument is the encrypted password. You can get this from the `/etc/shadow` file on a running system.</li><li>`--plaintext`, if used, means that the password argument is the plain text password.</li><li>`--shell` is the path to the user's default shell.</li></ul> | | |

Table 2.1 – Kickstart options

# 3

# Exploring the Various Boot Options and Kernels in Oracle Linux

This chapter will teach you about **boot** and its options, kernels, and more. You will also learn about many exciting opportunities, tools, and applications to make your life easier and more enjoyable. For example, you will learn how to change your booting kernel and remove and reinstall a kernel on your system. You will even learn how to use the boot process to switch between Linux kernels.

Booting involves more than just loading the operating system; it also helps secure the system using Secure Boot or TrenchBoot.

This chapter has the following recipes:

- Kernel basics – UEK and RHCK
- Playing with UEFI
- Playing with Secure Boot
- TrenchBoot – improving boot security and integrity
- Removing the RHCK

## Kernel basics – UEK and RHCK

Before we get started with UEK and RHCK, let's understand what is a Linux kernel. A Linux kernel release refers to an updated version of the core component of the Linux operating system. Its main function is to act as a bridge between the hardware and software layers of a computer system. The Linux kernel is a collaborative development effort by a large community of developers worldwide, with Linus Torvalds as the original creator and official maintainer of the mainline kernel. These kernel updates are introduced periodically to provide new features, improvements, bug fixes, security patches, and hardware support.

Linux kernel releases are assigned a version number that consists of three components: major version, minor version, and patch level. For instance, a kernel version is represented as X.Y.Z, where X represents the major version, Y is the minor version, and Z is the patch level. The major version is usually incremented for significant changes that may affect compatibility, while the minor version and patch level represent incremental updates and bug fixes.

Linux kernel releases are distributed as source code, and various distributions or operating systems based on Linux typically package and distribute their own versions of the kernel, incorporating it into their respective releases. In addition, users who want to compile and install the kernel directly on their systems can access the source code. The following table shows the Linux kernel mainline releases for Linux 7, 8, and 9.

| OS Version | RHCK Release | Latest UEK Release |
|---|---|---|
| Linux 7 | Linux 3.x | UEK 6/Linux 5.4 |
| Linux 8 | Linux 4.x | UEK 7/Linux 5.15 |
| Linux 9 | Linux 5.14 | UEK 7/Linux 5.15 |

Table 3.1 – Available Kernel options by release

## Kernel basics – UEK and RHCK

With a fresh installation of Oracle Linux, the **Unbreakable Enterprise Kernel** (**UEK**) is the default. However, in some cases, you may want to switch to the **Red Hat Compatible Kernel** (**RHCK**).

The default kernel might not be the correct version to use in some scenarios:

- UEK releases are based on newer kernel releases than the **RHCK** version, which is the standard for Red Hat servers. With Oracle Linux, you have the option to use the UEK, which provides a more up-to-date kernel release.

- The current kernel version might be incompatible with your particular hardware. A UEK system will boot on new hardware, while the older RHCK will not. An example of this is UEK 7, which supports the **Microsoft Azure Network Adapter** (**MANA**), whereas UEK 6 does not.

- Suppose a UEK beta or technical preview release is installed on the system. In that case, UEK needs to be demoted to ensure that the kernel is used only if intentionally and manually selected as the boot kernel by an administrator.

- The UEK for Oracle Linux provides many advantages, such as significant performance improvements and new features. The Linux operating system is a modular system in which the kernel interacts with the hardware and controls and schedules access to resources on behalf of applications. Most applications run in what is called user space and call only a stable set of system libraries to ask for kernel services. The exceptions are applications that directly access the kernel, most commonly security applications.

- Installing the UEK does not change system libraries such as glibc, which is the interface that nearly all applications, including Oracle Database, use. The glibc version is the same whether you run Oracle Linux with the UEK or with the RHCK. This is not limited to just gloc, but is the case for all system libraries, such as libssl, libcurl, and libcrypt.

---

**Note**

Multiple versions of the UEK may be available for any baseline operating system release. Choosing the version of the UEK is up to the application team and must reflect any compatibility requirements.

---

These examples and similar cases require you to switch between kernel types. In older releases, managing the default kernel was performed by configuring the GRUB boot loader. However, with Oracle Linux 8 and later, you should use the `grubby` command to control and manage the configuration for booting the kernel. `grubby` is part of the **Grand Unified Bootloader version 2 (GRUB 2)** boot loader, which is available from the GNU project. GRUB is the default bootloader for many Linux distributions on the market. After loading it into memory, it transfers control to the operating system kernel.

GRUB 2 is the default bootloader program used on Oracle Linux, and it can load many different operating systems, including Microsoft Windows.

## Getting ready

Let's start by looking deeper at the boot process to better understand it.

### The boot process

You have an understanding of how Oracle Linux boot options help you troubleshoot problems encountered when booting the system. This knowledge is beneficial when using new hardware or cloud environments.

As an Oracle Linux system boots, it performs many tasks that may change depending on the type of firmware your hardware uses to handle the system boot. It could be **Unified Extensible Firmware Interface (UEFI)** firmware or legacy BIOS firmware. The legacy **Basic Input/Output System (BIOS)** firmware is a legacy boot process that uses BIOS firmware. The BIOS maintains a list of bootable devices and the order of devices from which a boot is attempted. This data is stored in a **Complementary Metal-Oxide Semiconductor (CMOS)** chip on the system, requiring a battery to keep the settings when the system is not powered. Systems using a BIOS boot process are generally old systems, although even a modern system may still use a BIOS. A more popular option on modern servers is UEFI-based firmware. It also manages the boot process on a server but stores the boot process (initialization and startup) in a boot loader executable `.efi` file in a particular partition on the system's drive. Using the

.efi file gives a user more control of the boot process, including the ability to take advantage of new security features. An example of a new security feature is Secure Boot, which is covered in this chapter.

### The UEFI-based booting sequence

The following sequence order is used by UEFI-based booting hardware:

1.  The system first performs a **power-on self-test** (**POST**), which identifies the system's configuration and all possible boot identifiers.

2.  UEFI searches for a **GUID Partition Table** (**GPT**) partition with a specific **Globally Unique Identifier** (**GUID**) that identifies it as the **EFI System Partition** (**ESP**), containing **Extensible Firmware Interface** (**EFI**) applications such as booters. If there are multiple boot devices, the UEFI boot manager determines the appropriate ESP based on the order defined in the boot manager. With the **efibootmgr** tool, you can specify a different order if you do not use the default definition.

3.  The UEFI boot manager checks whether Secure Boot is enabled. If Secure Boot is not enabled, the boot manager runs the GRUB 2 boot loader on the ESP. Otherwise, the boot manager requests a certificate from the boot loader and validates this against keys stored in the UEFI Secure Boot key database. The environment is configured to perform a two-stage boot process, and the shim to handle the certificate validation process.efi application that is responsible for the certification is loaded first before loading the GRUB 2 boot loader. If the certificate is valid, the boot loader runs and, in turn, validates the kernel that it is configured to load.

    The boot loader first loads the vmlinuz kernel image into memory and then creates a temporary RAM-based filesystem called tmpfs. This is then used to extract the contents of the initramfs image file. vmlinuz is the name of the bootable compressed Linux kernel executable. The root filesystem embedded into the Linux kernel and loaded early in the boot process is called initramfs.

4.  Driver modules are then loaded from the initramfs filesystem. These are needed to allow the kernel to access the root filesystem.

5.  The system then starts with the first process, systemd. All future processes spawn from this process. The systemd process will always have a process ID of 1.

6.  The systemd process will run any additional processes defined for it. You can specify any other actions to be processed during the boot process by defining your systemd unit. This method is advised to be used instead of the /etc/rc.local file approach.

## The legacy BIOS sequence

Legacy BIOS booting hardware uses the following sequence order:

1.  The system first performs a POST, which identifies the configuration of the system, tests memory, and identifies all possible boot devices.

2.  Once the BIOS has identified the boot device, it reads the first sector of the device, which is the **Master Boot Record (MBR)**. The MBR contains the boot loader, which is a small program that is responsible for loading the operating system. The MBR reads the partition table, to determine the boot partition. Additionally, the MBR includes the pointer to the boot loader program called GRUB 2. GRUB can then run a boot on the same device that GRUB is installed on or a separate device. This is helpful when multi-booting the same system with both Linux and Windows.

3.  The boot loader first loads the `vmlinuz` kernel image into memory and then creates a temporary RAM-based filesystem called `tmpfs`. This is then used to extract the contents of the `initramfs` image file. `vmlinuz` is the name of the bootable compressed Linux kernel executable. The root filesystem embedded in the Linux kernel and loaded early in the boot process is called initramfs.

4.  Driver modules are then loaded from the initramfs filesystem. These modules are needed to allow the kernel to access the root filesystem.

5.  The kernel then starts the systemd process.

6.  The systemd process runs any other processes defined for it. You can specify any additional actions to be processed during the boot process by defining your systemd unit. This method is recommended instead of the `/etc/rc. local` file approach.

## How to do it...

Now that we have discussed the basics, we can leave behind all the boring parts and get to the action. It is time to play and learn!

One of the first things we can do is determine the currently loaded kernel in our system. The following command will display all kernels that are installed and configured within our Linux system (please run as root):

```
# grubby --info=ALL
```

Here is one example of the output:

```
[root@arm1 ~]# grubby --info=ALL
index=0
kernel="/boot/vmlinuz-5.4.17-2136.315.5.el8uek.aarch64"
args="ro crashkernel=auto rd.lvm.lv=ol/root rd.lvm.lv=ol/swap $tuned_params"
root="/dev/mapper/ol-root"
initrd="/boot/initramfs-5.4.17-2136.315.5.el8uek.aarch64.img $tuned_initrd"
title="Oracle Linux Server 8 (5.4.17-2136.315.5.el8uek.aarch64) "
id="b1424363d09c42d68d4a3f69c70caa52-5.4.17-2136.315.5.el8uek.aarch64"
index=1
kernel="/boot/vmlinuz-5.4.17-2136.313.6.el8uek.aarch64"
args="ro crashkernel=auto rd.lvm.lv=ol/root rd.lvm.lv=ol/swap $tuned_params"
root="/dev/mapper/ol-root"
initrd="/boot/initramfs-5.4.17-2136.313.6.el8uek.aarch64.img $tuned_initrd"
title="Oracle Linux Server 8 (5.4.17-2136.313.6.el8uek.aarch64) "
id="b1424363d09c42d68d4a3f69c70caa52-5.4.17-2136.313.6.el8uek.aarch64"
index=2
kernel="/boot/vmlinuz-5.4.17-2136.300.7.el8uek.aarch64"
args="ro crashkernel=auto rd.lvm.lv=ol/root rd.lvm.lv=ol/swap $tuned_params"
root="/dev/mapper/ol-root"
initrd="/boot/initramfs-5.4.17-2136.300.7.el8uek.aarch64.img $tuned_initrd"
title="Oracle Linux Server 8 (5.4.17-2136.300.7.el8uek.aarch64) "
id="b1424363d09c42d68d4a3f69c70caa52-5.4.17-2136.300.7.el8uek.aarch64"
index=3
kernel="/boot/vmlinuz-0-rescue-b1424363d09c42d68d4a3f69c70caa52"
args="ro crashkernel=auto rd.lvm.lv=ol/root rd.lvm.lv=ol/swap"
root="/dev/mapper/ol-root"
initrd="/boot/initramfs-0-rescue-b1424363d09c42d68d4a3f69c70caa52.img"
title="Oracle Linux Server 8 (0-rescue-b1424363d09c42d68d4a3f69c70caa52) "
id="b1424363d09c42d68d4a3f69c70caa52-0-rescue"
[root@arm1 ~]#
```

Figure 3.1 – grubby output

> **Note**
> The sample is done using an Arm system, hence the `aarch64` suffix. x86_64 systems will show `x86_64` suffixes.

We can also determine the default kernel in use by executing the following command:

```
#grubby --info=DEFAULT
```

Here is one example of an output:

```
[root@arm1 ~]# grubby --info=DEFAULT
index=0
kernel="/boot/vmlinuz-5.4.17-2136.315.5.el8uek.aarch64"
args="ro crashkernel=auto rd.lvm.lv=ol/root rd.lvm.lv=ol/swap $tuned_params"
root="/dev/mapper/ol-root"
initrd="/boot/initramfs-5.4.17-2136.315.5.el8uek.aarch64.img $tuned_initrd"
title="Oracle Linux Server 8 (5.4.17-2136.315.5.el8uek.aarch64) "
id="b1424363d09c42d68d4a3f69c70caa52-5.4.17-2136.315.5.el8uek.aarch64"
[root@arm1 ~]#
```

Figure 3.2 – grubby default kernel

We can configure a specific kernel to be used as the default boot kernel by running the following command:

```
#grubby --set-default <Kernel>
```

Here is one example of using the preceding command to change the default kernel in use. Knowing that RHCK is going to be a version 4 kernel, we will use 4.18.0-425.13.1.el8_7.x86_64. Next, we need to point to the file in /boot, adding vmlinuz- to the name.

```
[root@ol8 ~]# grubby --set-default /boot/vmlinuz-4.18.0-425.13.1.el8_7.x86_64
The default is /boot/loader/entries/3f1be2edc0d247d9b6bb392429792aa1-4.18.0-425.13.1.
el8_7.x86_64.conf with index 2 and kernel /boot/vmlinuz-4.18.0-425.13.1.el8_7.x86_64
[root@ol8 ~]# grubby --info=DEFAULT
index=2
kernel="/boot/vmlinuz-4.18.0-425.13.1.el8_7.x86_64"
args="ro crashkernel=auto resume=/dev/mapper/ol-swap rd.lvm.lv=ol/root rd.lvm.lv=ol/s
wap rhgb quiet $tuned_params"
root="/dev/mapper/ol-root"
initrd="/boot/initramfs-4.18.0-425.13.1.el8_7.x86_64.img $tuned_initrd"
title="Oracle Linux Server (4.18.0-425.13.1.el8_7.x86_64) 8.7"
id="3f1be2edc0d247d9b6bb392429792aa1-4.18.0-425.13.1.el8_7.x86_64"
[root@ol8 ~]#
```

Figure 3.3 – Changing the default kernel with grubby

Another possible use of the grubby command is to use it to update a kernel configuration entry or to add or remove boot arguments that should be passed to the kernel by default; the following is one example of it. But first, we will show all the information about a specific kernel in the system:

```
[root@ol8 # grubby --info=/boot/vmlinuz-0-rescue-c32316cc4b5241b8adb3
12707ae46458
```

This will show the details for the specified kernel, including the patch to the kernel and any arguments:

```
[root@ol8 ~]# grubby --info=/boot/vmlinuz-0-rescue-3f1be2edc0d247d9b6bb392429792aa1
index=4
kernel="/boot/vmlinuz-0-rescue-3f1be2edc0d247d9b6bb392429792aa1"
args="ro crashkernel=auto resume=/dev/mapper/ol-swap rd.lvm.lv=ol/root rd.lvm.lv=ol/s
wap rhgb quiet $tuned_params"
root="/dev/mapper/ol-root"
initrd="/boot/initramfs-0-rescue-3f1be2edc0d247d9b6bb392429792aa1.img $tuned_initrd"
title="Oracle Linux Server 8 (0-rescue-3f1be2edc0d247d9b6bb392429792aa1) "
id="3f1be2edc0d247d9b6bb392429792aa1-0-rescue"
[root@ol8 ~]#
```

Figure 3.4 – grubby kernel info

With these kernel details, we remove the rhgb quiet configuration from the kernel arguments and add a new test by using the following command:

```
grubby --remove-args="rhgb quiet" --args=test --update-kernel /boot/
vmlinuz-0-rescue-3f1be2edc0d247d9b6bb392429792aa1
```

As you can see, we used the kernel name to update the arguments on that kernel (we used the `--remove-args` attribute to remove an argument configuration and the `--args` attribute to add a new one). Now, we can check whether the argument's structure changed by running the `grubby --info=$BOOTENV` command with the boot environment as seen in the following figure.

Note that you can always use the `man grubby` command to review all the options available within the `grubby` command:

```
[root@ol8 ~]# grubby --info=/boot/vmlinuz-0-rescue-3f1be2edc0d247d9b6bb392429792aa1
index=4
kernel="/boot/vmlinuz-0-rescue-3f1be2edc0d247d9b6bb392429792aa1"
args="ro crashkernel=auto resume=/dev/mapper/ol-swap rd.lvm.lv=ol/root rd.lvm.lv=ol/s
wap $tuned_params test"
root="/dev/mapper/ol-root"
initrd="/boot/initramfs-0-rescue-3f1be2edc0d247d9b6bb392429792aa1.img $tuned_initrd"
title="Oracle Linux Server 8 (0-rescue-3f1be2edc0d247d9b6bb392429792aa1) "
id="3f1be2edc0d247d9b6bb392429792aa1-0-rescue"
```

Figure 3.5 – grubby info after making the change

## How it works...

As mentioned before, Oracle Linux comes with two flavors of kernels: the UEK, which is Oracle's default flavor of Linux kernel, and the RHCK, which is compatible with the RHEL kernel. Regardless of what kernel is used, the rest of the operating system is the same; that is, it has the same applications, libraries, and file locations.

This section will teach you how to switch the default kernel (UEK) to the RHCK and vice versa. So, let's get started.

First, once again, we will use the `grubby` command to check the default kernel in use and, again, to check all kernels available within your system by using the `grubby --info=DEFAULT` and `grubby --info=ALL` commands. The difference between the two commands is with the DEFAULT option, only the booting info is shown. With the ALL option, all available kernels are shown:

```
[root@ol8 ~]# grubby --info=ALL
index=0
kernel="/boot/vmlinuz-5.15.0-8.91.4.1.el8uek.x86_64"
args="ro crashkernel=auto resume=/dev/mapper/ol-swap rd.lvm.lv=ol/root rd.lvm.lv=ol/s
wap rhgb quiet $tuned_params"
root="/dev/mapper/ol-root"
initrd="/boot/initramfs-5.15.0-8.91.4.1.el8uek.x86_64.img $tuned_initrd"
title="Oracle Linux Server 8 (5.15.0-8.91.4.1.el8uek.x86_64) "
id="3f1be2edc0d247d9b6bb392429792aa1-5.15.0-8.91.4.1.el8uek.x86_64"
index=1
kernel="/boot/vmlinuz-5.15.0-3.60.5.1.el8uek.x86_64"
args="ro crashkernel=auto resume=/dev/mapper/ol-swap rd.lvm.lv=ol/root rd.lvm.lv=ol/s
wap rhgb quiet $tuned_params"
root="/dev/mapper/ol-root"
initrd="/boot/initramfs-5.15.0-3.60.5.1.el8uek.x86_64.img $tuned_initrd"
title="Oracle Linux Server 8 (5.15.0-3.60.5.1.el8uek.x86_64) "
id="3f1be2edc0d247d9b6bb392429792aa1-5.15.0-3.60.5.1.el8uek.x86_64"
index=2
kernel="/boot/vmlinuz-4.18.0-425.13.1.el8_7.x86_64"
args="ro crashkernel=auto resume=/dev/mapper/ol-swap rd.lvm.lv=ol/root rd.lvm.lv=ol/s
wap rhgb quiet $tuned_params"
root="/dev/mapper/ol-root"
initrd="/boot/initramfs-4.18.0-425.13.1.el8_7.x86_64.img $tuned_initrd"
title="Oracle Linux Server (4.18.0-425.13.1.el8_7.x86_64) 8.7"
id="3f1be2edc0d247d9b6bb392429792aa1-4.18.0-425.13.1.el8_7.x86_64"
index=3
kernel="/boot/vmlinuz-4.18.0-425.3.1.el8.x86_64"
args="ro crashkernel=auto resume=/dev/mapper/ol-swap rd.lvm.lv=ol/root rd.lvm.lv=ol/s
wap rhgb quiet $tuned_params"
root="/dev/mapper/ol-root"
initrd="/boot/initramfs-4.18.0-425.3.1.el8.x86_64.img $tuned_initrd"
title="Oracle Linux Server (4.18.0-425.3.1.el8.x86_64) 8.7"
id="3f1be2edc0d247d9b6bb392429792aa1-4.18.0-425.3.1.el8.x86_64"
index=4
kernel="/boot/vmlinuz-0-rescue-3f1be2edc0d247d9b6bb392429792aa1"
args="ro crashkernel=auto resume=/dev/mapper/ol-swap rd.lvm.lv=ol/root rd.lvm.lv=ol/s
wap $tuned_params test"
root="/dev/mapper/ol-root"
initrd="/boot/initramfs-0-rescue-3f1be2edc0d247d9b6bb392429792aa1.img $tuned_initrd"
title="Oracle Linux Server 8 (0-rescue-3f1be2edc0d247d9b6bb392429792aa1) "
id="3f1be2edc0d247d9b6bb392429792aa1-0-rescue"
[root@ol8 ~]# grubby --info=DEFAULT
index=0
kernel="/boot/vmlinuz-5.15.0-8.91.4.1.el8uek.x86_64"
args="ro crashkernel=auto resume=/dev/mapper/ol-swap rd.lvm.lv=ol/root rd.lvm.lv=ol/s
wap rhgb quiet $tuned_params"
root="/dev/mapper/ol-root"
initrd="/boot/initramfs-5.15.0-8.91.4.1.el8uek.x86_64.img $tuned_initrd"
title="Oracle Linux Server 8 (5.15.0-8.91.4.1.el8uek.x86_64) "
id="3f1be2edc0d247d9b6bb392429792aa1-5.15.0-8.91.4.1.el8uek.x86_64"
[root@ol8 ~]#
```

Figure 3.6 – Kernel version before swapping to RHCK

In the preceding example, you can see that, in this case, the default kernel in use is /boot/vmlinuz-5.15.0-8.91.4.1.el8uek.x86_64, which is a UEK flavor of the kernel. A UEK system should always have uek after el#. You can also check the current kernel using the uname -a command:

```
[root@ol8 ~]# uname -a
Linux ol8.m57.local 5.15.0-8.91.4.1.el8uek.x86_64 #2 SMP Tue Mar 7 18:28:34 PST 2023
x86_64 x86_64 x86_64 GNU/Linux
[root@ol8 ~]#
```

Figure 3.7 – uname -a before swapping to the RHCK

To check all the kernels available on the system, we could use the data from the previously run `grubby`
`-info` command, or use the `rpm -qa kernel*core*` command:

```
[root@ol8 ~]# rpm -qa kernel*core*
kernel-uek-core-5.15.0-8.91.4.1.el8uek.x86_64
kernel-uek-core-5.15.0-3.60.5.1.el8uek.x86_64
kernel-core-4.18.0-425.13.1.el8_7.x86_64
kernel-core-4.18.0-425.3.1.el8.x86_64
[root@ol8 ~]#
```

Figure 3.8 – Checking the kernels using the rpm command

When checking all available kernels, we can quickly identify two versions of the UEK and two versions
of the RHCK. For this example, we will use the RHCK version called `4.18.0-425.13.1.el8_7`,
which is found in boot at `/boot/vmlinuz-4.18.0-425.13.1.el8_7`. So now, let's use the
`grubby --set-default` command to make the selected RHCK the new default. We then check
the default kernel using the `grubby --info=DEFAULT` command:

```
[root@ol8 ~]# grubby --set-default /boot/vmlinuz-4.18.0-425.13.1.el8_7.x86_64
The default is /boot/loader/entries/3f1be2edc0d247d9b6bb392429792aa1-4.18.0-425.13.1.
el8_7.x86_64.conf with index 2 and kernel /boot/vmlinuz-4.18.0-425.13.1.el8_7.x86_64
[root@ol8 ~]#
[root@ol8 ~]# grubby --info=DEFAULT
index=2
kernel="/boot/vmlinuz-4.18.0-425.13.1.el8_7.x86_64"
args="ro crashkernel=auto resume=/dev/mapper/ol-swap rd.lvm.lv=ol/root rd.lvm.lv=ol/s
wap rhgb quiet $tuned_params"
root="/dev/mapper/ol-root"
initrd="/boot/initramfs-4.18.0-425.13.1.el8_7.x86_64.img $tuned_initrd"
title="Oracle Linux Server (4.18.0-425.13.1.el8_7.x86_64) 8.7"
id="3f1be2edc0d247d9b6bb392429792aa1-4.18.0-425.13.1.el8_7.x86_64"
```

Figure 3.9 – Switching to the RHCK

And that's it. Now all we need to do is reboot the system to reflect the kernel change. Then, if you want
to switch it back to the previous RHCK flavor of the kernel, all you need to do is run the `grubby`
`--set-default` command again, but this time specify the name of the RHCK version that you want.

# Playing with UEFI

One way hackers can compromise systems is by attacking the system before it boots. In order to prevent
this, you must secure the operating system by enabling security in UEFI. In other words, you cannot
run software if it cannot be trusted to execute code correctly because untrusted software can tamper

with your bootloader or, even worse, compromise your firmware. To solve this, a new, secure method is required to boot systems, called UEFI. UEFI is implemented in the firmware and has become the interface between your hardware and the operating system, replacing the legacy BIOS firmware that was previously the industry default. A feature of UEFI is Secure Boot, which ensures that your system boots by only using software trusted by the hardware manufacturer of your system. In addition, it provides a verification mechanism (by verifying each piece of boot software by using cryptographic checksums and signatures) to ensure that the code that is launched is trusted by validating the boot loader before executing it (even before loading the operating system). If the feature is available, UEFI systems can also boot in legacy BIOS mode via a compatibility support module.

## Getting ready

To boot in UEFI mode, Oracle Linux requires the UEFI firmware to be present during the system installation as it is detected at installation time. Next, a GPT is automatically set up, creating an ESP on the /boot/efi mount, which contains the files needed for the UEFI booting. GPT is a way of storing partitioning information on a drive that includes information such as where partitions begin and end on a physical disk. GPT is a new standard that gradually replaces the MBR standard previously widely used. GPT doesn't suffer from MBR's limits, such as the number of partitions and the drivers' size, with size limits depending on the operating system and its filesystems. Note that GPT is the type of partition table required by UEFI and was initiated by Intel.

### MBR versus GPT

When it comes to partitioning schemes on storage devices such as hard drives and solid-state drives, MBR and GPT are two distinct options. To help distinguish between the two, here are the primary differences to keep in mind.

- **Partitioning capacity**:

  - **MBR**: Your computer's MBR allows either four primary partitions or three primary partitions and one extended partition, which can be further divided into multiple logical partitions. However, it does have a capacity restriction of a maximum disk size of 2 TB.

  - **GPT**: By default, GPT can support up to 128 partitions and it is not limited in terms of partition count. Additionally, it can accommodate larger disk sizes of up to 9.4 ZB.

- **Compatibility**:

  - **MBR**: MBR provides improved compatibility with legacy systems and operating systems. It is widely supported by BIOS-based computers, as well as old versions of Windows and Linux.

  - **GPT**: Modern systems, especially those utilizing UEFI instead of BIOS, exhibit better compatibility with GPT. This partitioning scheme is backed by most contemporary operating systems, such as Windows, macOS, and Linux.

When deciding whether to use MBR or GPT, it's important to take into account factors such as disk size, desired partition count, compatibility needs, and the specific system or operating system you plan to use. For large disks and new systems, GPT is usually the better choice, while MBR remains viable for old systems or small disks that require compatibility with the older booting partition.

## How to do it...

Let's run the df -h command to view the partitions in the system. Please notice that /boot/efi is mounted on the /dev/sda1 partition in this example:

```
[root@demo2 ~]# df -h
Filesystem                 Size  Used Avail Use% Mounted on
devtmpfs                    16G     0   16G   0% /dev
tmpfs                       16G     0   16G   0% /dev/shm
tmpfs                       16G   90M   16G   1% /run
tmpfs                       16G     0   16G   0% /sys/fs/cgroup
/dev/mapper/ol-root         50G   21G   30G  41% /
/dev/mapper/ol-u01         4.7G   66M  4.6G   2% /u01
/dev/mapper/ol-home         10G  244M  9.8G   3% /home
/dev/mapper/ol-var         4.7G  1.8G  2.9G  39% /var
/dev/sda2                 1014M  666M  349M  66% /boot
/dev/mapper/ol-var_log     4.7G  139M  4.6G   3% /var/log
/dev/sda1                  200M   10M  190M   5% /boot/efi
tmpfs                      3.2G   24K  3.2G   1% /run/user/1000
[root@demo2 ~]#
```

Figure 3.10 – df -h command

If you run the ls -l /boot/efi/EFI/redhat command, this directory contains a first-stage bootloader called shimx64.efi, a GRUB 2 bootloader called grubx64.efi, and a GRUB 2 configuration file called grub.cfg. The location of the grub.cfg file is different in BIOS mode as it resides in /boot/grub2:

```
[root@demo2 ~]# ls -l /boot/efi/EFI/redhat
total 4112
-rwx------. 1 root root     134 Aug 27 15:51 BOOTX64.CSV
drwx------. 2 root root    4096 Oct 15 19:59 fonts
-rwx------. 1 root root    6545 Feb 14 20:45 grub.cfg
-rwx------. 1 root root    1024 Feb 14 22:31 grubenv
-rwx------. 1 root root    1024 Feb 14 21:15 grubenvRvxfzJ
-rwx------. 1 root root 2288320 Oct 15 19:59 grubx64.efi
-rwx------. 1 root root  905400 Aug 27 15:51 mmx64.efi
-rwx------. 1 root root  984688 Aug 27 15:51 shimx64.efi
[root@localhost falvarez]#
```

The /etc/default/grub file is responsible for containing the user settings for the grub.cfg file. Note that this file is also located in the same location when in BIOS mode. Furthermore, if you make any changes to this file, the grub.cfg file will need to be rebuilt:

```
[root@demo2 ~]# cat /etc/default/grub
GRUB_TIMEOUT=5
GRUB_DISTRIBUTOR="$(sed 's, release .*$,,g' /etc/system-release)"
GRUB_DEFAULT=saved
GRUB_DISABLE_SUBMENU=true
GRUB_TERMINAL_OUTPUT="console"
GRUB_CMDLINE_LINUX="crashkernel=auto resume=/dev/mapper/ol-swap
rd.lvm.lv=ol/root rd.lvm.lv=ol/swap rhgb quiet"
GRUB_DISABLE_RECOVERY="true"
GRUB_ENABLE_BLSCFG=true
```

To rebuild the grub.cfg file, please use the grub2-mkconfig command specifying the output file, using the -o option, such as /boot/efi/EFI/redhat/grub.cfg:

```
[root@demo2 ~]# grub2-mkconfig -o /boot/efi/EFI/redhat/grub.cfg
Generating grub configuration file ...
Adding boot menu entry for EFI firmware configuration
done
```

The utility used to manage the UEFI boot process is called efibootmgr (it provides a boot menu showing the boot entries). It also allows us to manipulate boot entries by doing the following:

- Altering the boot order
- Creating boot entries
- Removing boot entries
- Specifying the boot entry for the next boot

## How it works...

You can view a summary of boot entries by running the efibootmgr command with no options. For more details, add the -v option to it:

```
[root@demo2 ~]# efibootmgr -v
BootCurrent: 0004
Timeout: 0 seconds
BootOrder: 0004,0000,0001,0002,0003
Boot0000* UiApp
Boot0001* UEFI VBOX CD-ROM VB2-01700376
Boot0002* UEFI VBOX HARDDISK VB2d5be0c5-80049c5d
```

```
Boot0003* EFI Internal Shell
Boot0004* Oracle Linux
[root@demo2 ~]# efibootmgr -v
BootCurrent: 0004
Timeout: 0 seconds
BootOrder: 0004,0000,0001,0002,0003
Boot0000* UiApp FvVol(7cb8bdc9-f8eb-4f34-aaea-3ee4af6516a1)/
FvFile(462caa21-7614-4503-836e-8ab6f4662331)
Boot0001* UEFI VBOX CD-ROM VB2-01700376        PciRoot(0x0)/
Pci(0x1,0x1)/Ata(1,0,0)N.....YM....R,Y.
Boot0002* UEFI VBOX HARDDISK VB2d5be0c5-80049c5d        PciRoot(0x0)/
Pci(0xd,0x0)/Sata(0,65535,0)N.....YM....R,Y.
Boot0003* EFI Internal Shell    FvVol(7cb8bdc9-f8eb-4f34-aaea-
3ee4af6516a1)/FvFile(7c04a583-9e3e-4f1c-ad65-e05268d0b4d1)
Boot0004* Oracle Linux    HD(1,GPT,dff50c5d-96ed-406c-9823-
212649b405bd,0x800,0x12c000)/File(\EFI\redhat\shimx64.efi)
```

As you can see in the preceding example, boot 0004 (Oracle Linux) is the boot entry used to start the currently running system, called BootCurrent. BootOrder is the boot order used in the boot manager; consequently, the boot manager will boot the first active entry in the list. If it's not successful, it will try the next entry, and so on. If you're using UEFI on your system, efibootmgr is a handy command-line tool that enables you to manage your EFI boot entries. With this utility, you can easily view, create, modify, and delete boot entries in the EFI boot manager.

If you want to delete a boot entry, you can use the -B option. In this case, we will delete the CDROM record (0001) option using the following command:

```
efibootmgr -b 0001 -B
```

You can also change the boot order with the -o option. In the following command, we will change the boot order to make the UFEI shell the default boot:

```
efibootmgr -o 0003,0004,0002,0003
```

Please use the man command to learn more about the efibootmgr command.

> **Warning**
> Be very careful when changing the config. Accidentally changing the boot order to a device that is not bootable can put you in a situation where you are recovering the system. This is even more important if you are running in an environment where you do not have access to the console.

# Playing with Secure Boot

**Secure Boot** is an additional optional feature implemented in UEFI intended to help prevent malware execution during a boot process. To enable or disable Secure Boot, you need to access your specific UEFI setup program. This is different for each system manufacturer. Check your system documentation to see how to access the UEFI configuration.

The Secure Boot steps are identical to the regular UEFI booting but an important exception is that it requires the components to be signed and authenticated to be loaded and executed (private and public key pairs are used for authentication). It consists of two launch **Roots of Trust (RoT)** to build the transitive trust chains:

- The verification RoT is responsible for the signature verification. The verification RoT is the launch RoT, which is what most are referring to when speaking about Secure Boot, and it will lie on the boot flash drive as the RoT for storage to protect the key database. Verify only after the **Driver eXecution Environment (DXE)** phase, not during the **SECurity (SEC)** phase.

- The measurement RoT is responsible for the measurement collection.

Secure Boot will establish a chain of trust by following this process:

1. First, the first-stage bootloader (shim) signed by Oracle and Microsoft is authenticated; then, it loads the GRUB 2 loader.

2. The GRUB 2 bootloader validates the kernel signature signed by Oracle and authenticates it before loading and executing the kernel.

3. The kernel signed by Oracle is authenticated and executed. Secure Boot loads signed/authenticated kernel modules only (for example, all kernel modules included with the kernel RPM and those used with Oracle Ksplice have the corresponding Oracle signatures and the signed/authenticated kernel module running validated, or they would not be loaded).

Now that we have covered some basics of Secure Boot, let's learn how to sign kernel modules with it. First, before you can sign a module, you will need to install several required packages, including the source for the kernel. Furthermore, you will need to create a signing certificate for a key pair. The private key is used to sign the kernel module, and a public key is added to Secure Boot to a kernel keyring to allow the system to verify the signature.

## Getting ready

The first step is to install the UEK development libraries. This is done with the following command:

```
[root@demo2 ~]# dnf -y  install kernel-uek-devel-`uname -r`
```

> **Note**
>
> While you can just run `dnf install kernel-uek-devel`, adding the uname option to the command makes sure that you install the `devel` packages for the kernel you are currently running. Also, don't forget to make sure your `devel` packages are updated after you patch.

As a good practice, it is always recommended to update the system to ensure that you have the most recent kernel and related packages available:

```
[root@@demo2 ~]# dnf  -y update
```

This update can take some time, depending on when you last patched the system.

If you are using the UEK, the kernel headers required to compile kernel modules are available in the `kernel-uek-devel` package. When using the UEFI Secure Boot functionality, Oracle recommends installing and using the UEK. When installing the UEK, also install the `devel` packages. `uname -r` is added to the command to make sure the correct headers are installed. This is important if you are not running on the latest kernel version. If you are using the RHCK, use `kernel-devel` instead of `kernel-uek-devel`.

It is time to install the utilities required to perform the module signing operations (`openssl`, `keyutils`, `mokutil`, and `pesign`):

```
[root@demo2 ~]# dnf -y  install openssl keyutils mokutil pesign
```

If you require building a module from a source, you can optionally install the `Development Tools` group to ensure the option to create tools is available:

```
[root@demo2 ~]# dnf -y  group install "Development Tools"
```

## How to do it...

1.  Create a configuration file that OpenSSL can use to obtain default values when generating your certificates. You can create this file at any location, but it is useful to keep it with the rest of your OpenSSL configuration in `/etc/ssl/x509.conf`. The file should look similar to the following:

    ```
    [ req ]
    default_bits = 4096
    distinguished_name = req_distinguished_name
    prompt = no
    string_mask = utf8only
    x509_extensions = extensions

    [ req_distinguished_name ]
    O = Module Signing Example
    ```

```
CN = Module Signing Example Key
emailAddress = first.last@example.com

[ extensions ]
basicConstraints=critical,CA:FALSE
keyUsage=digitalSignature
extendedKeyUsage = codeSigning
subjectKeyIdentifier=hash
authorityKeyIdentifier=keyid
```

You should edit the O, CN, and emailAddress fields to be more appropriate. Note that in the extensions section of the configuration, the keyUsage field is set as digitalSignature. Additionally, the extendedKeyUsage option is set to codeSigning for compatibility with key verification tools.

2. Generate a new key pair using this configuration file:

```
[root@demo2 ~]# openssl req -x509 -new -nodes -utf8 -sha512
-days 3650 -batch -config /etc/ssl/x509.conf -outform DER -out /
etc/ssl/certs/pubkey.der -keyout /etc/ssl/certs/priv.key
Generating a RSA private key
........++++
.......++++
writing new private key to '/etc/ssl/certs/priv.key'
-----
[root@demo2 ~]#
```

This signing certificate is valid for 10 years (3,650 days). Ensure that the keys are adequately protected. This can be done by copying the keys off the server and storing them in a secure location. Placing the keys on a USB stick and putting that in a desk drawer is *not* a secure location. Use a locked location, such as a safe.

3. Export the certificate in PEM format:

```
[root@demo2 ~]# openssl x509 -inform DER -in /etc/ssl/certs/
pubkey.der -out /etc/ssl/certs/pubkey.pem
[root@demo2 ~]#
```

## Signing the module

The sign-file utility ensures that the module is signed correctly for the kernel. This utility is provided within the kernel source. The following instructions assume that you are signing a module for the currently running kernel. If you intend to sign a module for a different kernel, you must provide the path to the sign-file utility within the correct kernel version source. If you do not use the right utility, the signature type for your module may not align correctly with the expected signature type.

To sign the module, run the `sign-file` utility for your currently running kernel and provide it with the path to your private key and the public key that you created for the purpose of signing your modules (for this example, I've used a public module called `hello`):

```
[root@demo2 ~]# sudo /usr/src/kernels/$(uname -r)/scripts/sign-file
sha512 /etc/ssl/certs/priv.key \
> /etc/ssl/certs/pubkey.der /lib/modules/$(uname -r)/extra/hello.ko
```

Note that the module should already be installed into `/lib/modules/`, and you need to provide the correct path to the module.

## Updating the Machine Owner Key database

**Machine Owner Key** (**MOK**) is a security feature designed to protect the boot process of a computer system from unauthorized modifications or attacks. It is typically used in systems that support **UEFI** and Secure Boot, which require all bootloaders and kernel modules to be signed by trusted entities.

The MOK database is stored in a non-volatile memory location within the system's firmware and contains a list of public keys that are allowed to sign the bootloaders and kernel modules. Each key in the MOK database is associated with a unique identifier and is used to verify the digital signature of the bootloaders and kernel modules. If a digital signature is valid, the boot process continues and the software is loaded. If a digital signature is not valid or the key used to sign the software is not in the MOK database, the boot process is halted and the system will not boot.

To enroll an MOK key, you must manually do so on each target system using the UEFI system console.

Because the key that you created is not included in the UEFI Secure Boot key database, you must enroll in the MOK database in the shim by using the `mokutil` command:

```
mokutil --import /etc/ssl/certs/pubkey.der
```

The previous command prompts you for a single-use password that you use when the MOK management service enrolls the key after you reboot the system.

### Reboot the system

1.  The UEFI shim should automatically start the shim UEFI key manager at boot, as shown in the following figure. If you do not hit any key within 10 seconds, you will be unable to enroll your MOK key:

Figure 3.11 – Shim utility

Press any key to continue.

2.  Then you should see the shim main menu. Select **Enroll MOK** from the menu.

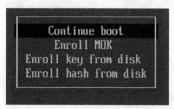

Figure 3.12 – Shim main menu

This will let you continue to enroll the key or view the key.

3.  Select **View key 0** from the menu (as shown in the following figure) to display the key details.

Figure 3.13 – View key

4. This will then display the key details. Verify that the values presented match the key you used to sign the module and that you inserted into the kernel image:

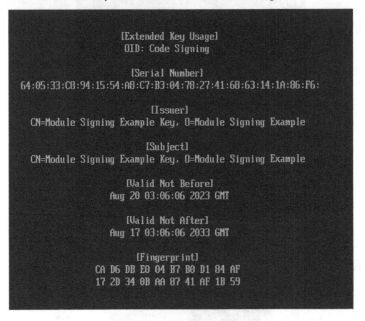

Figure 3.14 – Key details

Then press any key to return to the **Enroll MOK** menu.

5. Select **Continue** from the menu.

6. The **Enroll the key(s)?** screen is displayed, and you can now select **Yes** from the menu (as shown in the following figure).

Figure 3.15 – Enrolling the key

Select **Yes** to enroll the key.

7. You will then be prompted for a password. Enter the password you used when you imported the key using the mokutil command.

The key is enrolled within the UEFI Secure Boot key database.

8.  You are now redirected to the main menu. Select **Reboot** from the menu.

Figure 3.16 – Reboot when done

## How it works...

After booting the system, you can validate whether a key is included in the appropriate kernel keyring. Validation depends on the kernel version that you are running. Also, the keyring name that you need to check varies, as the implementation has changed across kernel versions.

If the key generated for signing custom modules is listed within the correct keyring, you can load modules signed with this key while in Secure Boot mode.

For RHCK on Oracle Linux 8 and UEK R6U3 kernels or later, keys within both the builtin_trusted_keys keyring and the platform keyring are trusted for both module signing and for the kexec tools, which means you can follow the standard procedure to sign a module and add it to the MOK database for the key to appear in the platform keyring, and it is automatically trusted.

Because a key can be loaded into the builtin_trusted_keys keyring, you should check both keyrings for the module signing key. Here's an example:

```
[root@demo2 ~]# keyctl show %:.builtin_trusted_keys
Keyring
 718980051 ---lswrv      0     0  keyring: .builtin_trusted_keys
 889527021 ---lswrv      0     0   \_ asymmetric: Oracle CA Server:
23652876a2ec7c7794eb905265a1145e5ad5b873
 643918572 ---lswrv      0     0   \_ asymmetric: Oracle IMA signing
CA: a2f28976a05984028f7d1a4904ae14e8e468e551
 668816900 ---lswrv      0     0   \_ asymmetric: Oracle
America, Inc.: Ksplice Kernel Module Signing Key:
09010ebef5545fa7c54b626ef518e077b5b1ee4c
  35441076 ---lswrv      0     0   \_ asymmetric: Oracle Linux Kernel
Module Signing Key: 2bb352412969a3653f0eb6021763408ebb9bb5ab
[root@demo2 ~]# keyctl show %:.platform
Keyring
 858046056 ---lswrv      0     0  keyring: .platform
 886150219 ---lswrv      0     0   \_ asymmetric: Oracle America,
Inc.: 430c85cb8b531c3d7b8c44adfafc2e5d49bb89d4
```

```
   698748825 ---lswrv       0       0   \_ asymmetric: Oracle America Inc.:
2e7c1720d1c5df5254cc93d6decaa75e49620cf8
   790695213 ---lswrv       0       0   \_ asymmetric: Oracle America,
Inc.: 795c5945e7cb2b6773b7797571413e3695062514
   227851788 ---lswrv       0       0   \_ asymmetric: Oracle America,
Inc.: f9aec43f7480c408d681db3d6f19f54d6e396ff4
```

# TrenchBoot – improving boot security and integrity

**TrenchBoot** is a GitHub cross-community and cross-platform framework integration that grew from an idea by Apertus Solutions that originated in 2014 to deal with the limitations of using tboot to launch Xen for the OpenXT project and other contributors, such as Oracle (Intel), 3mdep (AMD), and Citrix (https://github.com/TrenchBoot). Its primary purpose is to expand the mechanism of security and the integrity of the boot process by using a standard and unified approach (between Xen, KVM, Linux, BSDs, and potentially proprietary kernels). A common location where you will see this being used is Oracle Cloud's shielded instances.

## Getting ready

One of the main capabilities of TrenchBoot is securely launching Linux. This feature enables the Linux kernel to be dynamically launched by AMD and Intel by introducing an intermediate phase to the boot launch. Unlike traditional first-launch scenarios, such as the bootstrap phase used by open source dynamic launch tools such as XMHF, OSLO, OpenText Secure Boot, and tboot, TrenchBoot provides the ability to launch kernel upgrades through a key exec. You could then launch an integrity kernel that could dynamically inspect the system and establish the integrity of the platform before persisting everything to a diskless embedded environment during a shutdown. Note that the newly introduced **intermediate phase** includes an **intermediate loader** called **TrenchBoot Loader** that various bootstrap solutions can launch. TrenchBoot Loader contains the **TrenchBoot Security Engine**, which implements integrity processing. Please refer to the following diagram:

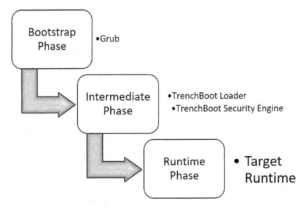

Figure 3.17 – TrenchBoot process overview

Oracle has added more TrenchBoot support to the Oracle Linux kernel to enable a Secure Boot protocol for the Linux kernel for multiple use cases, such as **two-factor authentication** (**2FA**) for laptops or crowdsourcing integrity handling; this option is the best choice.

> **Note**
>
> You can see some of Oracle's efforts by reading the kernel.org archive at `https://lore.kernel.org/lkml/20230504145023.835096-1-ross.philipson@oracle.com/`.

## How it works...

The TrenchBoot Loader is composed of well-known components such as Linux and u-root. Let's take a closer look at the main components within it:

- A TrenchBoot-enabled kernel with integrated TrenchBoot u-root initramfs
- Integrated TrenchBoot Security Engine as an extension to u-root
- A new image that can be launched by the boot loader

This build process is shown in the following diagram:

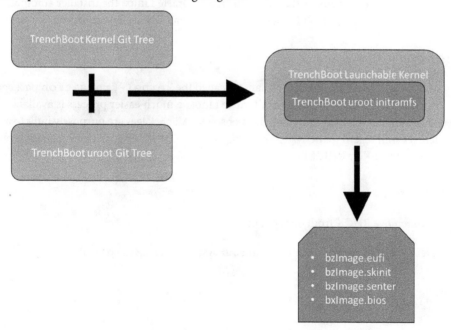

Figure 3.18 – TrenchBoot image process

The main benefits of using TrenchBoot are as follows:

- **Secure boot**: TrenchBoot provides a Secure Boot process that ensures that only trusted software is executed on the system. This prevents the execution of malicious software that could compromise the system.

- **Runtime integrity**: TrenchBoot ensures that the system remains secure even after booting by verifying the integrity of the software and data at runtime. It uses technologies such as Intel SGX and AMD SEV to provide hardware-based isolation and attestation.

- **Protection against attacks**: TrenchBoot provides protection against various types of attacks, including firmware attacks, malware, and kernel rootkits.

- **Platform-agnostic**: TrenchBoot is platform-agnostic and can be used on different hardware platforms, including x86, Arm, and RISC-V.

- **Open source**: TrenchBoot is an open source project, which means that anyone can inspect the code and contribute to its development. This makes TrenchBoot more transparent and trustworthy.

## Removing the RHCK

In this recipe, you will learn how to remove RHCK and its unique package dependencies while keeping all of UEK dependencies. Remember that when installing Oracle Linux, the installer automatically installs the Oracle UEK as the default kernel, but you can install RHCK for compatibility purposes.

### Getting ready

Old versions of Oracle Linux required a special tool called the `kernel-transition` package to manage dependencies. With new versions of Oracle Linux, a much easier process is available. For example, with Oracle Linux 8, this requirement is obsolete. All packages are purposely built to avoid any dependencies with regard to the system running on a UEK or RHCK. This makes it significantly easier to remove the UEK or RHCK from the system.

### How to do it...

Let's see how to remove RHCK from our system:

1.  First, let's check all kernels running within our system by using the `grubby` command:

```
[root@ol8 ~]# grubby --info=ALL
index=0
kernel="/boot/vmlinuz-5.15.0-8.91.4.1.el8uek.x86_64"
args="ro crashkernel=auto resume=/dev/mapper/ol-swap rd.lvm.lv=ol/root rd.lvm.lv=ol/s
wap rhgb quiet $tuned_params"
root="/dev/mapper/ol-root"
initrd="/boot/initramfs-5.15.0-8.91.4.1.el8uek.x86_64.img $tuned_initrd"
title="Oracle Linux Server 8 (5.15.0-8.91.4.1.el8uek.x86_64) "
id="3f1be2edc0d247d9b6bb392429792aa1-5.15.0-8.91.4.1.el8uek.x86_64"
index=1
kernel="/boot/vmlinuz-5.15.0-3.60.5.1.el8uek.x86_64"
args="ro crashkernel=auto resume=/dev/mapper/ol-swap rd.lvm.lv=ol/root rd.lvm.lv=ol/s
wap rhgb quiet $tuned_params"
root="/dev/mapper/ol-root"
initrd="/boot/initramfs-5.15.0-3.60.5.1.el8uek.x86_64.img $tuned_initrd"
title="Oracle Linux Server 8 (5.15.0-3.60.5.1.el8uek.x86_64) "
id="3f1be2edc0d247d9b6bb392429792aa1-5.15.0-3.60.5.1.el8uek.x86_64"
index=2
kernel="/boot/vmlinuz-4.18.0-425.13.1.el8_7.x86_64"
args="ro crashkernel=auto resume=/dev/mapper/ol-swap rd.lvm.lv=ol/root rd.lvm.lv=ol/s
wap rhgb quiet $tuned_params"
root="/dev/mapper/ol-root"
initrd="/boot/initramfs-4.18.0-425.13.1.el8_7.x86_64.img $tuned_initrd"
title="Oracle Linux Server (4.18.0-425.13.1.el8_7.x86_64) 8.7"
id="3f1be2edc0d247d9b6bb392429792aa1-4.18.0-425.13.1.el8_7.x86_64"
index=3
kernel="/boot/vmlinuz-4.18.0-425.3.1.el8.x86_64"
args="ro crashkernel=auto resume=/dev/mapper/ol-swap rd.lvm.lv=ol/root rd.lvm.lv=ol/s
wap rhgb quiet $tuned_params"
root="/dev/mapper/ol-root"
initrd="/boot/initramfs-4.18.0-425.3.1.el8.x86_64.img $tuned_initrd"
title="Oracle Linux Server (4.18.0-425.3.1.el8.x86_64) 8.7"
id="3f1be2edc0d247d9b6bb392429792aa1-4.18.0-425.3.1.el8.x86_64"
index=4
kernel="/boot/vmlinuz-0-rescue-3f1be2edc0d247d9b6bb392429792aa1"
args="ro crashkernel=auto resume=/dev/mapper/ol-swap rd.lvm.lv=ol/root rd.lvm.lv=ol/s
wap $tuned_params test"
root="/dev/mapper/ol-root"
initrd="/boot/initramfs-0-rescue-3f1be2edc0d247d9b6bb392429792aa1.img $tuned_initrd"
title="Oracle Linux Server 8 (0-rescue-3f1be2edc0d247d9b6bb392429792aa1) "
id="3f1be2edc0d247d9b6bb392429792aa1-0-rescue"
[root@ol8 ~]#
```

Figure 3.19 – Checking the kernels

We can see in the preceding output that the default kernel in use is /boot/vmlinuz-5.15.0-8.91.4.1.el8uek.x86_64, which is a UEK; also, we can see that we have a couple of RHCKs installed, /boot/vmlinuz-4.18.0-425.13.1.el8_7.x86_64 and /boot/vmlinuz-4.18.0-425.3.1.el8.x86_64, that we can safely remove.

2.  Now that we know that we are using a UEK, we can safely remove the desired RHCK using the dnf remove kernel command as recommended in the Oracle Linux manual. It will detect the unused kernels and show the dependencies within them.

```
[root@ol8 ~]# dnf remove kernel
Dependencies resolved.
================================================================================
 Package        Arch         Version                    Repository          Size
================================================================================
Removing:
 kernel         x86_64       4.18.0-425.3.1.el8         @anaconda              0
 kernel         x86_64       4.18.0-425.13.1.el8_7      @ol8_baseos_latest     0

Transaction Summary
================================================================================
Remove  2 Packages

Freed space: 0
Is this ok [y/N]: y
Running transaction check
Transaction check succeeded.
Running transaction test
Transaction test succeeded.
Running transaction
  Preparing        :                                                       1/1
  Erasing          : kernel-4.18.0-425.13.1.el8_7.x86_64                   1/2
  Running scriptlet: kernel-4.18.0-425.13.1.el8_7.x86_64                   1/2
  Erasing          : kernel-4.18.0-425.3.1.el8.x86_64                      2/2
  Running scriptlet: kernel-4.18.0-425.3.1.el8.x86_64                      2/2
  Verifying        : kernel-4.18.0-425.3.1.el8.x86_64                      1/2
  Verifying        : kernel-4.18.0-425.13.1.el8_7.x86_64                   2/2

Removed:
  kernel-4.18.0-425.3.1.el8.x86_64          kernel-4.18.0-425.13.1.el8_7.x86_64

Complete!
[root@ol8 ~]#
```

Figure 3.20 – dnf remove kernel

3.   As you can see in the preceding screenshot, both installed RHCKs were detected and deleted from the system. Now, let's run the grubby command again to see whether the RHCKs were really removed from our system boot options.

> **Warning**
>
> Do not run dnf remove kernel a second time. This may accidentally remove the booting kernel, resulting in a system that will no longer boot.

```
[root@ol8 ~]# grubby --info=ALL
index=0
kernel="/boot/vmlinuz-5.15.0-8.91.4.1.el8uek.x86_64"
args="ro crashkernel=auto resume=/dev/mapper/ol-swap rd.lvm.lv=ol/root rd.lvm.lv=ol/s
wap rhgb quiet $tuned_params"
root="/dev/mapper/ol-root"
initrd="/boot/initramfs-5.15.0-8.91.4.1.el8uek.x86_64.img $tuned_initrd"
title="Oracle Linux Server 8 (5.15.0-8.91.4.1.el8uek.x86_64) "
id="3f1be2edc0d247d9b6bb392429792aa1-5.15.0-8.91.4.1.el8uek.x86_64"
index=1
kernel="/boot/vmlinuz-5.15.0-3.60.5.1.el8uek.x86_64"
args="ro crashkernel=auto resume=/dev/mapper/ol-swap rd.lvm.lv=ol/root rd.lvm.lv=ol/s
wap rhgb quiet $tuned_params"
root="/dev/mapper/ol-root"
initrd="/boot/initramfs-5.15.0-3.60.5.1.el8uek.x86_64.img $tuned_initrd"
title="Oracle Linux Server 8 (5.15.0-3.60.5.1.el8uek.x86_64) "
id="3f1be2edc0d247d9b6bb392429792aa1-5.15.0-3.60.5.1.el8uek.x86_64"
index=2
kernel="/boot/vmlinuz-4.18.0-425.13.1.el8_7.x86_64"
args="ro crashkernel=auto resume=/dev/mapper/ol-swap rd.lvm.lv=ol/root rd.lvm.lv=ol/s
wap rhgb quiet $tuned_params"
root="/dev/mapper/ol-root"
initrd="/boot/initramfs-4.18.0-425.13.1.el8_7.x86_64.img $tuned_initrd"
title="Oracle Linux Server (4.18.0-425.13.1.el8_7.x86_64) 8.7"
id="3f1be2edc0d247d9b6bb392429792aa1-4.18.0-425.13.1.el8_7.x86_64"
index=3
kernel="/boot/vmlinuz-4.18.0-425.3.1.el8.x86_64"
args="ro crashkernel=auto resume=/dev/mapper/ol-swap rd.lvm.lv=ol/root rd.lvm.lv=ol/s
wap rhgb quiet $tuned_params"
root="/dev/mapper/ol-root"
initrd="/boot/initramfs-4.18.0-425.3.1.el8.x86_64.img $tuned_initrd"
title="Oracle Linux Server (4.18.0-425.3.1.el8.x86_64) 8.7"
id="3f1be2edc0d247d9b6bb392429792aa1-4.18.0-425.3.1.el8.x86_64"
index=4
kernel="/boot/vmlinuz-0-rescue-3f1be2edc0d247d9b6bb392429792aa1"
args="ro crashkernel=auto resume=/dev/mapper/ol-swap rd.lvm.lv=ol/root rd.lvm.lv=ol/s
wap $tuned_params test"
root="/dev/mapper/ol-root"
initrd="/boot/initramfs-0-rescue-3f1be2edc0d247d9b6bb392429792aa1.img $tuned_initrd"
title="Oracle Linux Server 8 (0-rescue-3f1be2edc0d247d9b6bb392429792aa1) "
id="3f1be2edc0d247d9b6bb392429792aa1-0-rescue"
```

Figure 3.21 – RHCK removed

Sadly, both kernels are still there. The RHCK `kernel-<version>` package is merely a metadata package containing no files. It is intended to ensure all dependent kernel packages are correctly installed. So, in other words, removing the `"kernel-<version>.el8"` RPM does not remove any of the kernel-subpackages, which includes the packages that update the `/boot` associated files and the boot loader entries.

To solve this situation, we need to remove the corresponding `kernel-core-<version>` packages containing the `/boot/` and all kernel-related files/directories.

4. As shown in the following screenshot, we will use the `dnf erase kernel-core` command to remove all related `kernel-core` packages:

```
[root@OL8 ~]# dnf erase kernel-core -y
Dependencies resolved.
============================================================================================
 Package                  Architecture   Version                  Repository              Size
============================================================================================
Removing:
 kernel-core              x86_64         4.18.0-425.3.1.el8        @anaconda               70 M
 kernel-core              x86_64         4.18.0-425.13.1.el8_7     @ol8_baseos_latest      70 M
Removing dependent packages:
 NetworkManager-wifi      x86_64         1:1.40.0-5.0.3.el8_7      @ol8_baseos_latest     167 k
 initial-setup-gui        x86_64         0.3.81.7-1.0.1.el8        @AppStream              26 k
 kernel-modules           x86_64         4.18.0-425.3.1.el8        @anaconda               24 M
 kmod-kvdo                x86_64         6.2.7.17-88.0.2.el8_7     @ol8_baseos_latest      1.7 M
 vdo                      x86_64         6.2.7.17-14.el8           @anaconda               3.3 M
Removing unused dependencies:
 anaconda-core            x86_64         33.16.7.12-1.0.2.el8      @AppStream              11 M
 anaconda-gui             x86_64         33.16.7.12-1.0.2.el8      @AppStream             2.4 M
 anaconda-tui             x86_64         33.16.7.12-1.0.2.el8      @AppStream             375 k
 anaconda-user-help       noarch         1:8.3.3-1.0.1.el8        @AppStream             115 k
 anaconda-widgets         x86_64         33.16.7.12-1.0.2.el8      @AppStream              94 k
 blivet-data              noarch         1:3.4.0-13.0.2.el8        @AppStream             402 k
 crda                     noarch         3.18_2020.04.29-1.el8     @anaconda              9.7 k
 cxl-libs                 x86_64         73-1.0.1.el8              @ol8_UEKR7              98 k
 daxctl-libs              x86_64         73-1.0.1.el8              @ol8_UEKR7              86 k
```

                              **EDITED FOR BEREVITY**

```
  NetworkManager-wifi-1:1.40.0-5.0.3.el8_7.x86_64        anaconda-core-33.16.7.12-1.0.2.el8.x86_64
  anaconda-gui-33.16.7.12-1.0.2.el8.x86_64               anaconda-tui-33.16.7.12-1.0.2.el8.x86_64
  anaconda-user-help-1:8.3.3-1.0.1.el8.noarch            anaconda-widgets-33.16.7.12-1.0.2.el8.x86_64
  blivet-data-1:3.4.0-13.0.2.el8.noarch                  crda-3.18_2020.04.29-1.el8.noarch
  cxl-libs-73-1.0.1.el8.x86_64                           daxctl-libs-73-1.0.1.el8.x86_64
  iniparser-4.1-5.el8.x86_64                             initial-setup-0.3.81.7-1.0.1.el8.x86_64
  initial-setup-gui-0.3.81.7-1.0.1.el8.x86_64            iw-4.14-5.el8.x86_64
  kernel-core-4.18.0-425.3.1.el8.x86_64                  kernel-core-4.18.0-425.13.1.el8_7.x86_64
  kernel-modules-4.18.0-425.3.1.el8.x86_64               kernel-modules-4.18.0-425.13.1.el8_7.x86_64
  keybinder3-0.3.2-4.el8.x86_64                          kmod-kvdo-6.2.7.17-88.0.2.el8_7.x86_64
  langtable-0.0.51-4.el8.noarch                          libblockdev-btrfs-2.24-11.0.1.el8.x86_64
  libblockdev-dm-2.24-11.0.1.el8.x86_64                  libblockdev-kbd-2.24-11.0.1.el8.x86_64
  libblockdev-mpath-2.24-11.0.1.el8.x86_64               libblockdev-nvdimm-2.24-11.0.1.el8.x86_64
  libreport-2.9.5-15.0.3.el8.x86_64                      libreport-anaconda-2.9.5-15.0.3.el8.x86_64
  libreport-cli-2.9.5-15.0.3.el8.x86_64                  libreport-gtk-2.9.5-15.0.3.el8.x86_64
  libreport-plugin-bugzilla-2.9.5-15.0.3.el8.x86_64      libreport-plugin-reportuploader-2.9.5-15.0.3.el8.x86_64
  libreport-web-2.9.5-15.0.3.el8.x86_64                  libtar-1.2.20-15.el8.x86_64
  libtimezonemap-0.4.5.1-4.el8.x86_64                    lz4-1.8.3-3.el8_4.x86_64
  metacity-3.28.0-1.el8.x86_64                           ndctl-73-1.0.1.el8.x86_64
  ndctl-libs-73-1.0.1.el8.x86_64                         python3-blivet-1:3.4.0-13.0.2.el8.noarch
  python3-blockdev-2.24-11.0.1.el8.x86_64                python3-bytesize-1.4-3.el8.x86_64
  python3-dasbus-1.2-2.el8.noarch                        python3-kickstart-3.16.15-1.0.1.el8.noarch
  python3-langtable-0.0.51-4.el8.noarch                  python3-libreport-2.9.5-15.0.3.el8.x86_64
  python3-meh-0.47.2-1.el8.noarch                        python3-meh-gui-0.47.2-1.el8.noarch
  python3-pid-2.1.1-7.el8.noarch                         python3-ordered-set-2.0.2-4.el8.noarch
  python3-pwquality-1.4.4-5.el8.x86_64                   python3-productmd-1.11-3.el8.noarch
  python3-pytz-2017.2-9.el8.noarch                       python3-pyparted-1:3.11.7-4.el8.x86_64
  python3-requests-ftp-0.3.1-11.el8.noarch               python3-requests-file-1.4.3-5.el8.noarch
  satyr-0.26-2.el8.x86_64                                python3-simpleline-1.1.1-3.el8.noarch
  tigervnc-server-minimal-1.12.0-9.el8_7.1.x86_64        tigervnc-license-1.12.0-9.el8_7.1.noarch
  wpa_supplicant-1:2.10-1.el8.x86_64                     vdo-6.2.7.17-14.el8.x86_64
  xmlrpc-c-client-1.51.0-8.el8.x86_64                    xmlrpc-c-1.51.0-8.el8.x86_64

Complete!
[root@OL8 ~]#
```

Figure 3.22 – dnf erase kernel-core

Now, let's rerun the grubby command to see whether the RHCKs were removed this time from our system:

```
[root@OL8 ~]# grubby --info=ALL
index=0
kernel="/boot/vmlinuz-5.15.0-8.91.4.1.el8uek.x86_64"
args="ro crashkernel=auto resume=/dev/mapper/ol-swap rd.lvm.lv=ol/root rd.lvm.lv=ol/swap rhgb quiet $tuned_params"
root="/dev/mapper/ol-root"
initrd="/boot/initramfs-5.15.0-8.91.4.1.el8uek.x86_64.img $tuned_initrd"
title="Oracle Linux Server 8 (5.15.0-8.91.4.1.el8uek.x86_64) "
id="dcac4c1fc2ff40c1bc068337acdf0c23-5.15.0-8.91.4.1.el8uek.x86_64"
index=1
kernel="/boot/vmlinuz-5.15.0-3.60.5.1.el8uek.x86_64"
args="ro crashkernel=auto resume=/dev/mapper/ol-swap rd.lvm.lv=ol/root rd.lvm.lv=ol/swap rhgb quiet $tuned_params"
root="/dev/mapper/ol-root"
initrd="/boot/initramfs-5.15.0-3.60.5.1.el8uek.x86_64.img $tuned_initrd"
title="Oracle Linux Server 8 (5.15.0-3.60.5.1.el8uek.x86_64) "
id="dcac4c1fc2ff40c1bc068337acdf0c23-5.15.0-3.60.5.1.el8uek.x86_64"
index=2
kernel="/boot/vmlinuz-0-rescue-dcac4c1fc2ff40c1bc068337acdf0c23"
args="ro crashkernel=auto resume=/dev/mapper/ol-swap rd.lvm.lv=ol/root rd.lvm.lv=ol/swap rhgb quiet $tuned_params"
root="/dev/mapper/ol-root"
initrd="/boot/initramfs-0-rescue-dcac4c1fc2ff40c1bc068337acdf0c23.img $tuned_initrd"
title="Oracle Linux Server 8 (0-rescue-dcac4c1fc2ff40c1bc068337acdf0c23) "
id="dcac4c1fc2ff40c1bc068337acdf0c23-0-rescue"
[root@OL8 ~]#
```

Figure 3.23 – grubby post RHCK removal

As you can now see, all RHCKs were removed from our system.

Furthermore, if you later decide to restore the deleted RHCKs, you can quickly restore them using the dnf install kernel command:

```
[root@OL8 ~]# dnf -y install kernel
Last metadata expiration check: 0:34:36 ago on Sun 19 Mar 2023 03:34:19 PM EDT.
Dependencies resolved.
================================================================================================
 Package            Architecture    Version                 Repository               Size
================================================================================================
Installing:
                    x86_64          4.18.0-425.13.1.el8_7    ol8_baseos_latest        8.8 M
Installing dependencies:
                    x86_64          4.18.0-425.13.1.el8_7    ol8_baseos_latest        41 M
                    x86_64          4.18.0-425.13.1.el8_7    ol8_baseos_latest        33 M

Transaction Summary
================================================================================================
Install  3 Packages

Total download size: 83 M
Installed size: 94 M
Downloading Packages:
(1/3): kernel-4.18.0-425.13.1.el8_7.x86_64.rpm                   23 MB/s | 8.8 MB  00:00
(2/3): kernel-modules-4.18.0-425.13.1.el8_7.x86_64.rpm           39 MB/s |  33 MB  00:00
(3/3): kernel-core-4.18.0-425.13.1.el8_7.x86_64.rpm              41 MB/s |  41 MB  00:00
------------------------------------------------------------------------------------------------
Total                              I                             83 MB/s |  83 MB  00:01
Running transaction check
Transaction check succeeded.
Running transaction test
Transaction test succeeded.
Running transaction
  Preparing        :                                                                    1/1
  Installing       : kernel-core-4.18.0-425.13.1.el8_7.x86_64                           1/3
  Running scriptlet: kernel-core-4.18.0-425.13.1.el8_7.x86_64                           1/3
```

Figure 3.24 – Reinstalling the RHCK

As you can see, with Oracle Linux, switching kernels is a simple task, as is removing kernels from the operating system. When you have a chance, compare the system performance between the RHCK and UEKs; you will be pleasantly surprised how much faster tasks such as I/O are with the more modern UEK.

# 4

# Creating and Managing Single-Instance Filesystems

Without data, there is no reason for a system to exist, and with that thought, the data has to live somewhere. In this chapter, we will cover the two most popular filesystems used to manage data that is local to the server: **B-Tree File System** (**Btrfs**, pronounced *Butter F S*) and **eXtended File System** (**XFS**, pronounced *X F S*).

These are single-instance filesystems, which are basically filesystems that are only mounted on a single server at any one time. There are also multi-instance filesystems that are mounted on multiple systems at the same time. Common examples are **Oracle Clustered File System version 2** (**OCFS2**) and **Global File System 2** (**GFS2**). All of these examples use shared block storage for the underlying storage.

Additionally, there is **Ceph**, which is not an acronym, but instead a reference to **cephalopod**. This is because Ceph is a distributed architecture that stores data on all nodes of a Ceph cluster. This allows Ceph to offer scalable storage with some additional complexity. **Gluster** is another example of a distributed filesystem.

> **Note**
>
> Why not **ZFS**? Because Btrfs and XFS are built into the Oracle Linux **Unbreakable Enterprise Kernel** (**UEK**), and ZFS is not available outside of third-party repositories.

We will cover the following recipes that will help you understand and manage local filesystems:

- What you need to know about local filesystems
- Btrfs – creating, resizing, and monitoring
- Btrfs – subvolumes, snapshots, quotas, and more
- Protecting data with mdadm – a software RAID solution
- Playing with logical volume management
- XFS – creating, modifying, and more

## Technical requirements

For this recipe, you will need an **Oracle Linux 8** system. As with most of these recipes, a VM on your desktop using a desktop virtualization product such as **Oracle VirtualBox** is recommended. A small VM with two cores, 2 GB RAM, and a few free gigabytes of disk space is fine. You will also need some additional disks assigned to the VM, ideally at least five equally sized disks. Ideally, before you start, patch your system to the latest packages available. This only takes a few minutes and can save a ton of time when troubleshooting issues caused by a bug.

Many of the recipes in this book have their related configuration files available on GitHub, located at `https://github.com/PacktPublishing/Oracle-Linux-Cookbook`.

## What you need to know about local filesystems

This recipe will discuss the differences between local and remote filesystems, as well as the core differences between Btrfs and ZFS.

The backbone of an **operating system** (**OS**) is the local filesystem. It enables efficient storage and management of files and directories on a computer or server using a hierarchical structure. This structure allows users and programs to easily create, modify, and access files on local storage devices such as hard disks, solid-state drives, and storage **logical unit numbers** (**LUNs**) from a local **storage area network** (**SAN**) or cloud provider. These filesystems are designed specifically for file and folder management efficiency, protecting files from accidental deletion or corruption. They come equipped with features such as file permissions, ownership, and access control, which provide users with utmost security and privacy. In comparison to remote filesystems, local filesystems offer superior performance, though files are not available on other systems unless paired with a remote filesystem technology. Notable examples of local Linux filesystems include Btrfs, XFS, ext4, fat32, and even ZFS.

> **Note**
> While ZFS is a local filesystem, it is not included in the kernel and needs to be added using software from `https://zfsonlinux.org`.

A remote filesystem allows you to access files and directories on a remote server through a network. This system provides the convenience of accessing and manipulating files on a remote machine as if they were stored locally, eliminating the need to transfer them physically. Remote filesystems are widely used in distributed computing environments where multiple computers or servers need to share data and resources. They are also valuable in cloud computing and web hosting environments where data is stored remotely and accessed over the internet. However, it's important to note that using remote filesystems can impact performance when sharing files between multiple servers over a network.

Examples of remote filesystems include **Network File System** (**NFS**), **Server Message Block** (**SMB**), and **Common Internet File System** (**CIFS**), which are widely used in Unix, Linux, and Windows environments, respectively. Other popular remote filesystems include **s3fs**, which allows users to access files securely over cloud-based object storage.

For optimal performance when managing MySQL, Postgres, and Oracle databases, it's highly recommended to utilize local filesystems instead of network filesystems. This strategy can also be effectively applied to the OS.

## Getting ready

You need to understand the core differences between the two filesystems. The XFS filesystem is surprisingly much older than many admins realize. It started back in 1993, as the filesystem for the **Silicon Graphics IRIX** OS, and was ported over to Linux in 2001. Btrfs is much newer, being developed in 2007 by Oracle (as an open source project) for Linux. Btrfs is also more than a filesystem, as it includes the volume manager, data redundancy, and filesystem functionality in one technology.

With XFS, you need to combine it with a logical volume manager for dynamic volumes and also **redundant array of inexpensive disks (RAID)** technology (most commonly configured with the mdadm command) to provide for fault tolerance.

With Btrfs, you have the choice of five types of RAID volumes. What you pick is based on your use case as it's a balance between performance, disk space required, and the usable capacity of the volume. The details are in the following table:

| Type | Description | Performance | Redundance | Capacity |
|------|-------------|-------------|------------|----------|
| RAID 0 | Striping across disks | Best | None | 100% |
| RAID 1 | Mirror two disks | Good | 1 drive failure | 50% |
| RAID 10 | Mirrored then striped, min of 4 disks | Almost the best | 1 drive failure | 50% |
| RAID1C3 | 3 copies of the metadata, min of 3 disks | Average | 2 drive failures | 66% |
| RAID1C4 | 4 copies of the metadata, min of 4 disks | Lowest | 3 drive failures | 75% |

Table 4.1 – Btrfs RAID options

Both systems have the same limitation for the maximum filesystem size of 8 exabytes! But Btrfs also adds features such as snapshots, transparent compression, integrated checksum-based data integrity, and rollback capabilities. XFS is not left out though, with higher performance through I/O threads and more bandwidth, though these advantages may not be realized once you integrate XFS with an LVM and RAID technology. One other major difference is that Btrfs requires that you use the UEK, though XFS works well with both UEKs and **Red Hat Compatible Kernels (RHCKs)**.

## How to do it...

Oracle Linux by default uses the XFS filesystem, but when doing the installation, you can use Btrfs as the root filesystem. If you want to use XFS as the boot filesystem, install it as you normally would. If you want to use Btrfs, then you should continue.

> **Note**
> Your boot filesystem can be different from the data filesystems on the server. You can easily have the root use XFS and the data filesystem use Btrfs, or vice versa.

The easiest way to run Btrfs is to pick it when doing an installation using the UEK boot disk. This will let you choose Btrfs as the destination filesystem. When running the install, select **Install Destination**, and then select a custom storage configuration. This will then give you the manual partitioning option where you can use the dropdown and select **Btrfs**, as seen in the following screenshot:

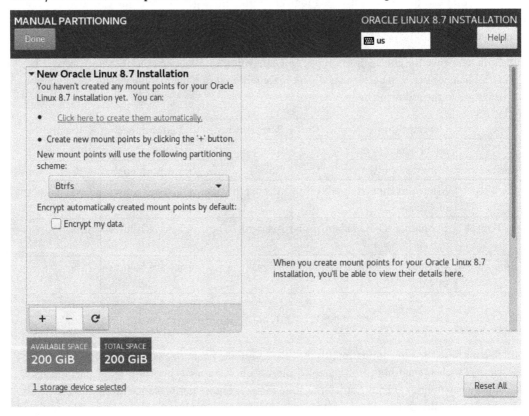

Figure 4.1 – Btrfs selection

When setting up the custom configuration, you can add additional directories for /var or /var/tmp (a **secure technical implementation guide** (**STIG**) requirement). These are actually not just directories, but subvolumes of the main volume. This is why they show the same available space:

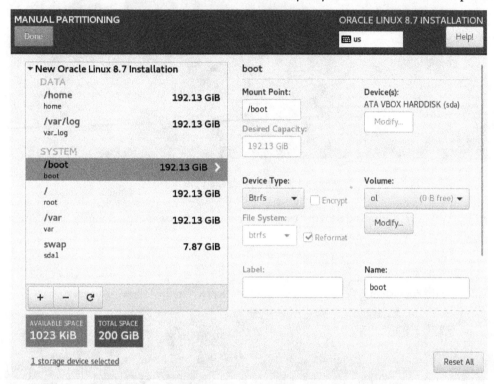

Figure 4.2 – Btrfs mountpoints

This is because with Btrfs, they all use the same volume and have the same usable disk space. We can limit this later using quotas.

Finish the install using your normal settings for network and software source, though as a note, you will likely need to set **Installation Source** as a URL or local network share. You will also need to add the UEK repository if running 8.7 or earlier.

Once the system is booted, you will see that it is now using Btrfs. This can be checked once the system is up.

## How it works...

You can check the filesystem in several ways, the easiest being by checking /etc/fstab to see how the filesystem was mounted. This is seen in the following screenshot:

```
[root@brtfs ~]# more /etc/fstab

#
# /etc/fstab
# Created by anaconda on Sun May 14 01:31:56 2023
#
# Accessible filesystems, by reference, are maintained under '/dev/disk/'.
# See man pages fstab(5), findfs(8), mount(8) and/or blkid(8) for more info.
#
# After editing this file, run 'systemctl daemon-reload' to update systemd
# units generated from this file.
#
UUID=f59eed86-86b5-4a98-948b-335cad68fa49 /                btrfs    subvol=root    0 0
UUID=f59eed86-86b5-4a98-948b-335cad68fa49 /boot            btrfs    subvol=boot    0 0
UUID=f59eed86-86b5-4a98-948b-335cad68fa49 /home            btrfs    subvol=home    0 0
UUID=f59eed86-86b5-4a98-948b-335cad68fa49 /var             btrfs    subvol=var     0 0
UUID=f59eed86-86b5-4a98-948b-335cad68fa49 /var/log         btrfs    subvol=var_log 0 0
UUID=1dac1d94-ab8f-4b60-9c8a-e6884ef02b69 none             swap     defaults       0 0
[root@brtfs ~]#
```

Figure 4.3 – Btrfs fstab example

You can also use the df command with the T option to show the filesystem type. Running the following command will show you this info:

```
df -T
```

This will show the filesystem type for each mounted file, as seen in the following figure:

```
[root@brtfs ~]# df -T
Filesystem     Type      1K-blocks      Used Available Use% Mounted on
devtmpfs       devtmpfs    3894356         0   3894356   0% /dev
tmpfs          tmpfs       3912864         0   3912864   0% /dev/shm
tmpfs          tmpfs       3912864     16888   3895976   1% /run
tmpfs          tmpfs       3912864         0   3912864   0% /sys/fs/cgroup
/dev/sda2      btrfs     201457664   2469816 196974536   2% /
/dev/sda2      btrfs     201457664   2469816 196974536   2% /var
/dev/sda2      btrfs     201457664   2469816 196974536   2% /home
/dev/sda2      btrfs     201457664   2469816 196974536   2% /boot
/dev/sda2      btrfs     201457664   2469816 196974536   2% /var/log
tmpfs          tmpfs        782572         0    782572   0% /run/user/0
[root@brtfs ~]#
```

Figure 4.4 – df -T with Btrfs filesystems

# Btrfs – creating, resizing, and monitoring

In this recipe, we will create a new RAIDed Btrfs volume and filesystem, using multiple disks for fault-tolerant storage. We will then add a new LUN, growing the filesystem. We will wrap up by modifying the filesystem to compress the data!

## Getting ready

To get started, I added five 10 GB drives to the OS. These will be used to build a new RAID1C4 volume. I can see these new devices by using the `fdisk -l` command, grepping for `GiB` using the following command:

```
fdisk -l | grep GiB
```

The output is seen in the following figure:

```
[root@brtfs ~]# fdisk -l | grep GiB
Disk /dev/sde: 10 GiB, 10737418240 bytes, 20971520 sectors
Disk /dev/sdc: 10 GiB, 10737418240 bytes, 20971520 sectors
Disk /dev/sdf: 10 GiB, 10737418240 bytes, 20971520 sectors
Disk /dev/sdd: 10 GiB, 10737418240 bytes, 20971520 sectors
Disk /dev/sdb: 10 GiB, 10737418240 bytes, 20971520 sectors
Disk /dev/sda: 200 GiB, 214748364800 bytes, 419430400 sectors
[root@brtfs ~]# _
```

Figure 4.5 – fdisk output

Here, we can see that the 10 GB devices are `sdb`, `sdc`, `sbd`, `sbe`, and `sbf`. We will need this info to make the Btrfs volume.

## How to do it...

Now that we know the devices, let's manually create a RAID1C3 volume. We will use all five devices in a RAID1C3 configuration and name the volume `data`.

We will then use the following command to make the volume:

```
mkfs.btrfs -L data -d raid1c3 -m raid1c3 /dev/sd[bcdef]
```

Please refer to the following figure to view the output:

```
[root@brtfs ~]# mkfs.btrfs -L data -d raid1c3 -m raid1c3 /dev/sd[bcdef]
btrfs-progs v5.15.1
See http://btrfs.wiki.kernel.org for more information.

NOTE: several default settings have changed in version 5.15, please make sure
      this does not affect your deployments:
      - DUP for metadata (-m dup)
      - enabled no-holes (-O no-holes)
      - enabled free-space-tree (-R free-space-tree)

Label:               data
UUID:                1114f133-19a0-4544-87a8-56d78ca3a54d
Node size:           16384
Sector size:         4096
Filesystem size:     50.00GiB
Block group profiles:
  Data:              RAID1C3              1.00GiB
  Metadata:          RAID1C3              256.00MiB
  System:            RAID1C3              8.00MiB
SSD detected:        no
Zoned device:        no
Incompat features:   extref, skinny-metadata, no-holes, raid1c34
Runtime features:    free-space-tree
Checksum:            crc32c
Number of devices:   5
Devices:
  ID          SIZE  PATH
   1      10.00GiB  /dev/sdb
   2      10.00GiB  /dev/sdc
   3      10.00GiB  /dev/sdd
   4      10.00GiB  /dev/sde
   5      10.00GiB  /dev/sdf
```

Figure 4.6 – mkfs.btrfs output

> **Note**
>
> When mounting a Btrfs volume, you normally use the first device in the volume or the UUID. The UUID is reported by mkfs.btrfs when the volume is created.

Next, let's mount this in /data. Make the /data directory, then mount it with the following commands:

```
mkdir /data
mount /dev/sdb /data
```

Optional, though highly recommended, is to add this to the fstab file. With this example, we are using the UUID of the volume, and since data has no subvolume, the subvol parameter is defined but left blank:

```
[root@brtfs ~]# more /etc/fstab


#
# /etc/fstab
# Created by anaconda on Sun May 14 01:31:56 2023
#
# Accessible filesystems, by reference, are maintained under '/dev/disk/'.
# See man pages fstab(5), findfs(8), mount(8) and/or blkid(8) for more info.
#
# After editing this file, run 'systemctl daemon-reload' to update systemd
# units generated from this file.
#
UUID=f59eed86-86b5-4a98-948b-335cad68fa49 /                     btrfs    subvol=root     0 0
UUID=f59eed86-86b5-4a98-948b-335cad68fa49 /boot                 btrfs    subvol=boot     0 0
UUID=f59eed86-86b5-4a98-948b-335cad68fa49 /home                 btrfs    subvol=home     0 0
UUID=f59eed86-86b5-4a98-948b-335cad68fa49 /var                  btrfs    subvol=var      0 0
UUID=f59eed86-86b5-4a98-948b-335cad68fa49 /var/log              btrfs    subvol=var_log  0 0
UUID=0c6bb93a-ffe4-4fd6-bd82-9cebf09de732 /data                 btrfs    subvol=         0 0
UUID=1dac1d94-ab8f-4b60-9c8a-e6884ef02b69 none                  swap     defaults        0 0
[root@brtfs ~]#
```

Figure 4.7 – Sample fstab using UUID

## How it works...

Now that we have a mounted volume, let's do a few things with it! First, we can use the `btrfs` command to check several things. The first is to check the device's health, which is useful to see whether the RAID has any failing devices. The `btrfs stats /$DEVICE` command is used to show the status. Don't forget to replace $DEVICE with the actual Btrfs device you are checking:

```
[root@brtfs ~]# btrfs device stats /data
[/dev/sdb].write_io_errs       0
[/dev/sdb].read_io_errs        0
[/dev/sdb].flush_io_errs       0
[/dev/sdb].corruption_errs     0
[/dev/sdb].generation_errs     0
[/dev/sdc].write_io_errs       0
[/dev/sdc].read_io_errs        0
[/dev/sdc].flush_io_errs       0
[/dev/sdc].corruption_errs     0
[/dev/sdc].generation_errs     0
[/dev/sdd].write_io_errs       0
[/dev/sdd].read_io_errs        0
[/dev/sdd].flush_io_errs       0
[/dev/sdd].corruption_errs     0
[/dev/sdd].generation_errs     0
[/dev/sde].write_io_errs       0
[/dev/sde].read_io_errs        0
[/dev/sde].flush_io_errs       0
[/dev/sde].corruption_errs     0
[/dev/sde].generation_errs     0
[/dev/sdf].write_io_errs       0
[/dev/sdf].read_io_errs        0
[/dev/sdf].flush_io_errs       0
[/dev/sdf].corruption_errs     0
[/dev/sdf].generation_errs     0
[root@brtfs ~]#
```

Figure 4.8 – Healthy devices

When a device starts to fail, you should start to see errors in this report.

Next up, we will add a few more devices to the volume. Four more 10 GB disks were added: `sdg`, `sdh`, `sdi`, and `sdj`.

Before we add the device, we can see that /data has 50 GB of usable raw space. This is seen using the following command:

```
btrfs filesystem usage /data
```

The output from the command is shown in the following screenshot:

```
[root@brtfs ~]# btrfs filesystem usage /data
Overall:
    Device size:                 50.00GiB
    Device allocated:             3.77GiB
    Device unallocated:          46.23GiB
    Device missing:               0.00B
    Used:                       576.00KiB
    Free (estimated):            16.41GiB        (min: 16.41GiB)
    Free (statfs, df):            9.74GiB
    Data ratio:                   3.00
    Metadata ratio:               3.00
    Global reserve:               3.25MiB        (used: 0.00B)
    Multiple profiles:            no

Data,RAID1C3: Size:1.00GiB, Used:0.00B (0.00%)
    /dev/sdd          1.00GiB
    /dev/sde          1.00GiB
    /dev/sdf          1.00GiB

Metadata,RAID1C3: Size:256.00MiB, Used:176.00KiB (0.07%)
    /dev/sdd        256.00MiB
    /dev/sde        256.00MiB
    /dev/sdf        256.00MiB

System,RAID1C3: Size:8.00MiB, Used:16.00KiB (0.20%)
    /dev/sdd          8.00MiB
    /dev/sde          8.00MiB
    /dev/sdf          8.00MiB

Unallocated:
    /dev/sdb         10.00GiB
    /dev/sdc         10.00GiB
    /dev/sdd          8.74GiB
    /dev/sde          8.74GiB
    /dev/sdf          8.74GiB
```

Figure 4.9 – Btrfs filesystem usage

Here we can see the stats, mainly the 50 GB of free raw space, as well as the other metrics, including the space allocated to each device in the volume and which devices have the metadata.

Next, let's add the four new devices. This is done with the `btrfs device add` command:

```
btrfs device add /dev/sdg /data
```

Do this for each device being added to the volume, or bulk add them with /dev/sd[a-z], replacing a and z with the appropriate range. When done, you can check using the usage option, as seen in the following sample:

```
[root@brtfs ~]# btrfs filesystem usage /data
Overall:
    Device size:                    90.00GiB
    Device allocated:                3.77GiB
    Device unallocated:             86.23GiB
    Device missing:                    0.00B
    Used:                          576.00KiB
    Free (estimated):               29.74GiB      (min: 29.74GiB)
    Free (statfs, df):              29.74GiB
    Data ratio:                         3.00
    Metadata ratio:                     3.00
    Global reserve:                  3.25MiB      (used: 0.00B)
    Multiple profiles:                    no

Data,RAID1C3: Size:1.00GiB, Used:0.00B (0.00%)
    /dev/sdd            1.00GiB
    /dev/sde            1.00GiB
    /dev/sdf            1.00GiB

Metadata,RAID1C3: Size:256.00MiB, Used:176.00KiB (0.07%)
    /dev/sdd          256.00MiB
    /dev/sde          256.00MiB
    /dev/sdf          256.00MiB

System,RAID1C3: Size:8.00MiB, Used:16.00KiB (0.20%)
    /dev/sdd            8.00MiB
    /dev/sde            8.00MiB
    /dev/sdf            8.00MiB

Unallocated:
    /dev/sdb           10.00GiB
    /dev/sdc           10.00GiB
    /dev/sdd            8.74GiB
    /dev/sde            8.74GiB
    /dev/sdf            8.74GiB
    /dev/sdg           10.00GiB
    /dev/sdh           10.00GiB
    /dev/sdi           10.00GiB
    /dev/sdj           10.00GiB
```

Figure 4.10 – Btrfs devices added

You will now see the device at 90 GB. Now, as space in /data gets consumed, you should start to see the available space go down, as well as the distribution of data against the individual disks:

```
[root@brtfs ~]# btrfs filesystem usage /data
Overall:
    Device size:                   72.00GiB
    Device allocated:              13.09GiB
    Device unallocated:            58.91GiB
    Device missing:                 0.00B
    Used:                           9.07GiB
    Free (estimated):              59.84GiB          (min: 20.57GiB)
    Free (statfs, df):             59.84GiB
    Data ratio:                     1.00
    Metadata ratio:                 3.00
    Global reserve:                 3.25MiB          (used: 0.00B)
    Multiple profiles:                 no

Data,single: Size:10.00GiB, Used:9.06GiB (90.62%)
    /dev/sdb          1.00GiB
    /dev/sdd          1.00GiB
    /dev/sde          1.00GiB
    /dev/sdf          1.00GiB
    /dev/sdg          1.00GiB
    /dev/sdh          1.00GiB
    /dev/sdi          2.00GiB
    /dev/sdj          2.00GiB

Metadata,RAID1C3: Size:1.00GiB, Used:2.77MiB (0.27%)
    /dev/sdd          1.00GiB
    /dev/sde          1.00GiB
    /dev/sdf          1.00GiB

System,RAID1C3: Size:32.00MiB, Used:16.00KiB (0.05%)
    /dev/sdd         32.00MiB
    /dev/sde         32.00MiB
    /dev/sdf         32.00MiB

Unallocated:
    /dev/sdb          1.00GiB
    /dev/sdd          7.97GiB
    /dev/sde          7.97GiB
    /dev/sdf          7.97GiB
    /dev/sdg          9.00GiB
    /dev/sdh          9.00GiB
    /dev/sdi          8.00GiB
    /dev/sdj          8.00GiB
[root@brtfs ~]#
```

Figure 4.11 – Btrfs space used

For the last example, we will be removing a device to free up space, and then rebalancing the data. To delete a physical device, use the `btrfs device delete` command, passing the device mountpoint:

```
btrfs device delete /dev/sdj /data
```

This will remove the device:

```
[root@brtfs ~]# btrfs device delete /dev/sdj /data
[ 1283.894195] BTRFS info (device sdi): relocating block group 11036262400 flags data
[ 1284.990885] BTRFS info (device sdi): found 2 extents, stage: move data extents
[ 1285.017431] BTRFS info (device sdi): found 2 extents, stage: update data pointers
[ 1285.037017] BTRFS info (device sdi): relocating block group 1372585984 flags data
[ 1286.580065] BTRFS info (device sdi): found 3 extents, stage: move data extents
[ 1286.608136] BTRFS info (device sdi): found 3 extents, stage: update data pointers
[ 1286.652004] BTRFS info (device sdi): device deleted: /dev/sdj
[root@brtfs ~]# _
```

Figure 4.12 – Device removal

Once the device is removed, rerun the usage report. What you will now see is the remaining devices, and which data is on which device:

```
[root@brtfs ~]# btrfs filesystem usage /data
Overall:
    Device size:                80.00GiB
    Device allocated:            3.77GiB
    Device unallocated:         76.23GiB
    Device missing:              0.00B
    Used:                      576.00KiB
    Free (estimated):           26.41GiB      (min: 26.41GiB)
    Free (statfs, df):          19.74GiB
    Data ratio:                     3.00
    Metadata ratio:                 3.00
    Global reserve:              3.25MiB      (used: 0.00B)
    Multiple profiles:                no

Data,RAID1C3: Size:1.00GiB, Used:0.00B (0.00%)
    /dev/sdd            1.00GiB
    /dev/sde            1.00GiB
    /dev/sdf            1.00GiB

Metadata,RAID1C3: Size:256.00MiB, Used:176.00KiB (0.07%)
    /dev/sdd          256.00MiB
    /dev/sde          256.00MiB
    /dev/sdf          256.00MiB

System,RAID1C3: Size:8.00MiB, Used:16.00KiB (0.20%)
    /dev/sdd            8.00MiB
    /dev/sde            8.00MiB
    /dev/sdf            8.00MiB

Unallocated:
    /dev/sdb           10.00GiB
    /dev/sdc           10.00GiB
    /dev/sdd            8.74GiB
    /dev/sde            8.74GiB
    /dev/sdf            8.74GiB
    /dev/sdg           10.00GiB
    /dev/sdh           10.00GiB
    /dev/sdi           10.00GiB
```

Figure 4.13 – Unbalanced usage

While it may appear to be a minor issue, it has the potential to cause complications down the line. Fortunately, the solution is simple – a system rebalance. This is done using the `balance` option in the `btrfs` command. The following command will be used to balance the /data filesystem:

```
btrfs filesystem balance /data
```

This command will then rebalance the data chunks, and when done, the usage will show the data balanced across the disks:

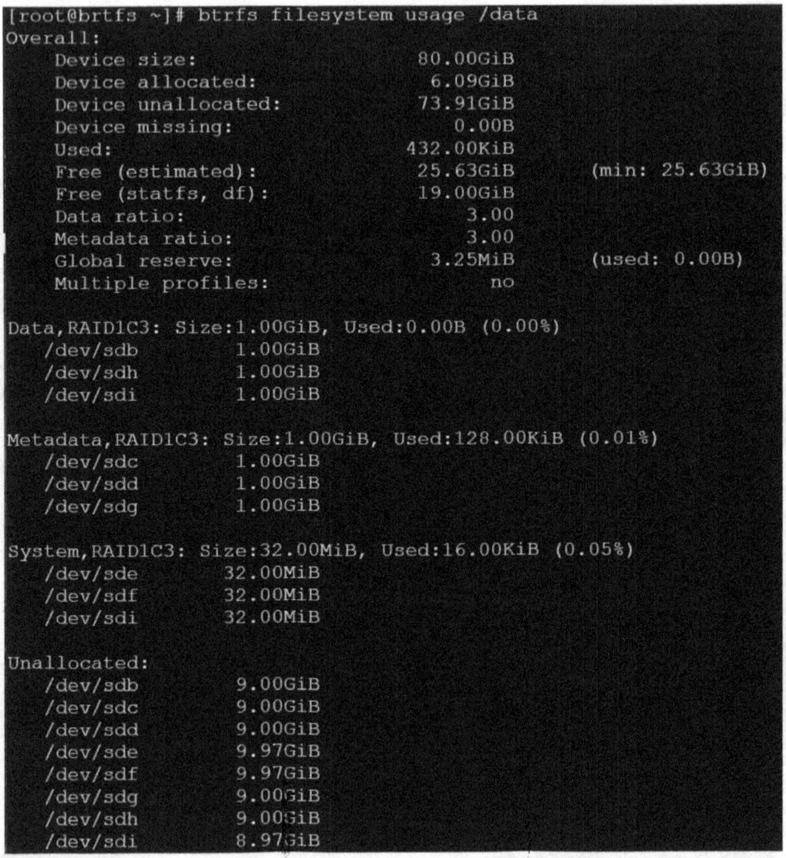

```
[root@brtfs ~]# btrfs filesystem usage /data
Overall:
    Device size:                     80.00GiB
    Device allocated:                 6.09GiB
    Device unallocated:              73.91GiB
    Device missing:                    0.00B
    Used:                           432.00KiB
    Free (estimated):                25.63GiB      (min: 25.63GiB)
    Free (statfs, df):               19.00GiB
    Data ratio:                          3.00
    Metadata ratio:                      3.00
    Global reserve:                   3.25MiB      (used: 0.00B)
    Multiple profiles:                     no

Data,RAID1C3: Size:1.00GiB, Used:0.00B (0.00%)
    /dev/sdb          1.00GiB
    /dev/sdh          1.00GiB
    /dev/sdi          1.00GiB

Metadata,RAID1C3: Size:1.00GiB, Used:128.00KiB (0.01%)
    /dev/sdc          1.00GiB
    /dev/sdd          1.00GiB
    /dev/sdg          1.00GiB

System,RAID1C3: Size:32.00MiB, Used:16.00KiB (0.05%)
    /dev/sde          32.00MiB
    /dev/sdf          32.00MiB
    /dev/sdi          32.00MiB

Unallocated:
    /dev/sdb          9.00GiB
    /dev/sdc          9.00GiB
    /dev/sdd          9.00GiB
    /dev/sde          9.97GiB
    /dev/sdf          9.97GiB
    /dev/sdg          9.00GiB
    /dev/sdh          9.00GiB
    /dev/sdi          8.97GiB
```

Figure 4.14 – Balanced usage

> **Note**
>
> To ensure a well-balanced distribution of data, it is recommended to always balance your system when adding or removing devices, even though there may be slight variations. This practice is essential for maintaining an optimally performing filesystem. The `btrfsmaintenance` package in the `ol8_developer` repo is a great tool for automating all the required Btrfs maintenance tasks.

# Btrfs – subvolumes, snapshots, quotas, and more

Btrfs can do so much more than the older XFS technology. This includes subvolumes, snapshots, and quotas. Btrfs subvolumes are an exceptional tool that allows users to create multiple snapshots or subfilesystems within a single Btrfs filesystem. These subvolumes are displayed as distinct directories in the filesystem hierarchy, but they utilize the same storage space and can be managed independently.

The flexibility and versatility of subvolumes make them ideal for various purposes, such as creating backups or isolating different parts of the filesystem for easier management. Snapshots are particularly useful since they offer read-only copies of the filesystem at a specific point in time. With snapshots, users can restore files or entire subvolumes to a previous state or easily create replicable backups that can be moved to another system.

Subvolumes also enable users to manage disk space more efficiently. For example, users can create a subvolume for a specific application or project and restrict its disk usage to a certain amount to prevent it from using up too much space on the filesystem. Additionally, subvolumes can be used to implement access controls by assigning different permissions to different subvolumes or creating separate subvolumes for different users or groups. This recipe will go over how to do all of this.

## Getting ready

This recipe will require a Btrfs filesystem, and will use the data filesystem created in the previous recipe for the examples.

## How to do it...

In this recipe, we will do the following:

1.  Create a subvolume in /data and mount it.
2.  Set a quota on the subvolume.
3.  Create a snapshot.
4.  Enable compression.

Creating a subvolume is straightforward and is done by using the btrfs command and specifying the full path to the subvolume:

```
btrfs subvolume create /data/vol1
```

Once created, simply add it to fstab, this time declaring the subvolume name in the fourth column. This is seen in the following screenshot, where /data/vol1 is mounted using subvolume vol1:

```
[root@brtfs ~]# more /etc/fstab

#
# /etc/fstab
# Created by anaconda on Sun May 14 01:31:56 2023
#
# Accessible filesystems, by reference, are maintained under '/dev/disk/'.
# See man pages fstab(5), findfs(8), mount(8) and/or blkid(8) for more info.
#
# After editing this file, run 'systemctl daemon-reload' to update systemd
# units generated from this file.
#
UUID=f59eed86-86b5-4a98-948b-335cad68fa49 /             btrfs  subvol=root     0 0
UUID=f59eed86-86b5-4a98-948b-335cad68fa49 /boot         btrfs  subvol=boot     0 0
UUID=f59eed86-86b5-4a98-948b-335cad68fa49 /home         btrfs  subvol=home     0 0
UUID=f59eed86-86b5-4a98-948b-335cad68fa49 /var          btrfs  subvol=var      0 0
UUID=f59eed86-86b5-4a98-948b-335cad68fa49 /var/log      btrfs  subvol=var_log  0 0
UUID=0c6bb93a-ffe4-4fd6-bd82-9cebf09de732 /data         btrfs  subvol=         0 0
UUID=0c6bb93a-ffe4-4fd6-bd82-9cebf09de732 /data/vol1    btrfs  subvol=vol1     0 0
UUID=1dac1d94-ab8f-4b60-9c8a-e6884ef02b69 none          swap   defaults        0 0
[root@brtfs ~]#
```

Figure 4.15 – Subvolume in fstab

Now that we have the subvolume mounted, let's add a quota to limit it to 5 GB. To do this, we first need to enable quotas for the volume. This is done with the following command:

```
btrfs quota enable /data
```

Next, we need to assign a quota-group limit to the subvolume. This will restrict the subvolume to the size defined. This is done using the limit option, as seen in the following command:

```
btrfs qgroup limit 5g /data/vol1
```

You can see what quotas are defined in a volume using the btrfs qgroup show command with the -reF option:

```
btrfs qgroup show -reF /data/vol1
```

The command and its output are shown in the following screenshot:

```
[root@brtfs ~]# btrfs qgroup show -reF /data/vol1
qgroupid          rfer          excl        max_rfer       max_excl
--------          ----          ----        --------       --------
0/256          16.00KiB      16.00KiB        5.00GiB          none
[root@brtfs ~]#
```

Figure 4.16 – Set quotas

Now that we have a quota set, let's create a snapshot for backups. We do need a place for the backups, so let's create a subvolume for the backups with the following command:

```
btrfs subvolume create /data/backup
```

Btrfs snapshots are highly useful copies of a Btrfs filesystem, capturing a specific point in time. Through a seamless copy-on-write process, these snapshots separate any changes made to the filesystem from the snapshot itself. This makes them ideal for different purposes, such as creating backups, testing software configurations, and providing an effortless way to undo system updates. Additionally, backups can be created rapidly and with minimal storage space, as the snapshots only store the differences between the current state of the filesystem and the state at the moment the snapshot was taken. To create a Btrfs snapshot, you can use the `btrfs subvolume snapshot` command, specifying the subvolume you want to snapshot and the name and location of the snapshot:

```
btrfs subvolume snapshot /data/vol1 /data/backup/vol1_backup1
```

This command creates a read-only snapshot of the `/data/vol1` subvolume and saves it as a separate subvolume in the `/data/backup` directory.

Don't worry if you've already taken a snapshot – you can easily revert the filesystem to its exact state at that time using the powerful Btrfs rollback feature. With Btrfs snapshot rollback, you can restore your Btrfs filesystem to a previous state by simply selecting a snapshot. Rolling back to a snapshot discards all changes made to the filesystem since the snapshot was taken and restores the filesystem to the exact state it was in when the snapshot was created.

To roll back a Btrfs snapshot, you can use the `btrfs subvolume snapshot` command with the `-r` option, which specifies that the snapshot should be used for a rollback:

```
btrfs subvolume snapshot -r /data/backups/vol1_backup1 /data/vol1
```

This command rolls back `/data/vol1` to the state it was in when the `/data/backup/vol1_backlup1` snapshot was created.

It is important to note that rolling back a snapshot will discard any changes made to the filesystem since the snapshot was taken. However, this feature is extremely useful when you want to fully revert the filesystem to a previous state. Btrfs snapshots provide a simple and effective solution for data management and protection, allowing for effortless backup creation and easy restoration of prior filesystem versions.

> **Note**
>
> Automatic snapshots can be enabled so a `dnf` transaction will create a snapshot. This is done by the `dnf-plugin-snapper` tool. More information can be found here: `https://docs.oracle.com/en/operating-systems/oracle-linux/8/fsadmin/fsadmin-ManagingtheBtrfsFileSystem.html#snapper-btrfs`.

This section will cover how to enable compression using the Btrfs filesystem. Btrfs compression is a powerful feature that allows you to compress data in real time while writing it to the filesystem. This feature can significantly reduce storage space, making it ideal for filesystems that store vast amounts of data, such as media archives and backup systems. Additionally, it's beneficial for systems with limited storage space, such as mobile devices and embedded systems.

Btrfs compression uses various compression algorithms to compress data while writing it to the filesystem. The compressed data is then stored on the disk and automatically decompressed on the fly when accessed. This process is seamless to the applications accessing the data, so there's no need for them to be aware of the compression process as Btrfs handles it. Btrfs supports three compression algorithms, zlib, lzo, and zstd, each with its own strengths and weaknesses:

- zlib: This is a widely used general-purpose compression algorithm that provides good compression ratios but can be relatively slow, especially at higher compression levels. It is suitable for compressing general-purpose data and text files.

- lzo: This is a lightweight compression algorithm that provides good compression ratios and is relatively fast. It is suitable for compressing data that is already compressed, such as media files and archives.

- zstd: This is a newer compression algorithm that provides a good balance between compression ratio and speed. It is suitable for compressing a wide range of data types, including text, media files, and archives.

The choice of compression algorithm depends on the specific use case and performance requirements.

To enable compression on a filesystem, you can use the btrfs property command to set the compression for the filesystem:

```
btrfs property set /data/vol1 compression zstd
```

When compression is enabled, only new data being written to the filesystem is compressed. However, you can also use the defragment command to compress the data that was on the filesystem before compression was enabled. To do this on a subvolume, you will also need to recursively run the command using the -r option along with the -c option to compress data:

```
btrfs filesystem defragment -rc /data/vol1
```

## There's more...

Compression efficiency will vary, depending on the data and algorithm used. Let's first check how much space we have, using the following command:

```
[root@btrfs vol1]# btrfs filesystem usage /data/vol1 | grep Data |
grep Used
Data,RAID1C3: Size:1.00GiB, Used:0.00B (0.00%)
```

Now, let's create a 2 GB file with random data:

```
head -c 2G </dev/urandom > /data/vol1/test1
```

Next, we can use the df and du commands to compare the space consumed and the space used:

```
df -h /data/vol1
du -hd0 /data/vol
```

The sample outputs for these commands are as follows:

```
[root@btrfs vol1]# df -h /data/vol1
Filesystem      Size  Used Avail Use% Mounted on
/dev/sdb         30G   2G    28G   1% /data/vol1
[root@brtfs vol1]# du -hd0 /data/vol1
2.0G    /data/vol1
[root@brtfs vol1]#
```

Here, we can see 2 GB is used (via the du command), and also 2 GB (via the df command) is actually consumed. So, for this random data file, we can see no benefit from the compression.

Let's delete the test1 file now:

```
rm /data/vol1/test1
```

To speed things up, let's defrag and rebalance the volume. This is needed to actually free up the space from the deleted file now, instead of waiting:

```
[root@btrfs vol1]# btrfs filesystem defragment -rc /data/vol1
[root@brtfs vol1]# btrfs filesystem balance /data
Done, had to relocate 4 out of 4 chunks
[root@btrfs vol1]#
```

Now, with a file with lots of repeating data, we will see more compression. To create a 2 GB file with repeating data, run the following command:

```
yes "repeating text" | head -c 2G >test2
```

Now, we repeat the same du and df commands as before, but we will see very different results:

```
[root@brtfs vol1]# df -h /data/vol1
Filesystem      Size  Used Avail Use% Mounted on
/dev/sdb         30G   62M    29G   1% /data/vol1
[root@brtfs vol1]# du -hd0 /data/vol1
2.0G    /data/vol1
[root@brtfs vol1]#
```

Here, we see 4 GB is allocated, but only 62 MB is actually used! That's a huge benefit from the compression.

# Protecting data with mdadm – a software RAID solution

Modern computing systems rely on RAID technology to ensure data integrity, availability, and performance. By distributing data across multiple disks in various configurations, RAID provides fault tolerance, allowing systems to continue functioning even if one or more disks fail. This redundancy is critical to prevent data loss and minimize downtime.

Moreover, RAID configurations such as striping and mirroring can significantly improve read and write performance by allowing data to be accessed in parallel from multiple disks. As data volume and importance continue to increase in today's digital world, RAID plays a vital role in protecting, optimizing, and maintaining storage system reliability. The easiest way to do this when not using Btrfs with Oracle Linux 8 is to use a tool called **mdadm**.

## Getting ready

mdadm is a software utility for managing and configuring software RAID arrays in Linux systems. It stands for **multiple device administration** and is commonly used to create, manage, monitor, and maintain RAID arrays. These arrays leverage a kernel driver called **multiple device** (**MD**). mdadm allows users to create various RAID levels, including RAID, RAID 0, RAID 1, RAID 5, RAID 6, RAID 0+1, and RAID 10, using a combination of multiple physical disks:

| Type | Description | Notes |
|------|-------------|-------|
| RAID | Spanning | No redundancy or performance advantages. |
| RAID-0 | Striping | No redundancy, but better performance versus RAID. |
| RAID-1 | Mirroring | Mirrored redundancy, but no performance advantage in write workloads. Read workloads may improve. |
| RAID-5 | Striping with double parity | Redundancy and good performance. Can lose one disk without data loss. Recommended to use at least four disks. |
| RAID-6 | Striping with tripple parity | Redundancy and good performance. Can lose two disks without data loss. Recommended to use at least five disks. |
| RAID 0+1 | Mirroring of striped disks | Great performance, but recovering a lost disk takes a long time. This requires at least four disks. |
| RAID 10 | Striping of mirrored disks | Most expensive option, but generally considered the best for redundancy, performance, and rebuild time. This requires at least four disks. |

Table 4.2 – MD RAID options

> **Note**
>
> It's not uncommon to confuse a **JBOD (just a box of disks)** enclosure with a RAID enclosure. JBOD is a simple disk enclosure with no hardware RAID. A RAID disk enclosure has a hardware controller that offloads all the RAID logic for the disks within the enclosure. For this example, hardware RAID is not being used, only JBOD. All the RAID logic is being performed by Oracle Linux.

mdadm is an essential tool for administrators to create, modify, and monitor RAID arrays. It allows users to add or remove disks from an existing array, perform data recovery operations, and configure various parameters such as RAID level and spare disks. With its command-line interface, mdadm provides flexibility in managing and maintaining disk redundancy and performance. It is a reliable and robust solution that optimizes storage performance, ensures data redundancy, and maintains high availability of data. mdadm is normally installed when Oracle Linux is installed.

## How to do it...

Creating an MD device is fairly simple. But before you create the device, you need to plan a few things in advance:

- What type of RAID will you be using? As mentioned previously, the MD kernel driver supports many types of RAID algorithms. You need to pick one before running the command. This maps to the -level option.

- How many drives will you be using in the device? Most RAID types use even numbers of disks, but you still need to know how many disks will be used for data. This maps to the -raid-devices option.

- Will you configure a hot spare device? Hot spares are a great option when systems need to automatically rebuild the data if a device fails. It's not uncommon in remote locations to have many hot spares. When picking hot spares, balance the required space versus how long it will take for a replacement to be installed. This maps to the -spare-devices option.

- What is the number of the MD device? Traditionally, you start with 0 and work your way up, but track the numbers so you do not accidentally use the wrong device. This maps to /dev/md#.

- What are the paths to the drives that you are going to use? They are normally /dev/sd#, /dev/nvme#, or even /dev/vd#.

In the following example, we will create a RAID-5 array with one hot spare. The device being used is /dev/sd[bcdef] and this will be the /dev/md0 device:

```
mdadm --create /dev/md0 --level=5 --raid-devices=4 --spare-devices=1 /
dev/sd[bcdef]
```

You can quickly check the status by cating the `/proc/mdstat` file:

```
[root@xfs ~]# cat /proc/mdstat
Personalities : [raid6] [raid5] [raid4]
md0 : active raid5 sde[5] sdf[4](S) sdd[2] sdc[1] sdb[0]
      62862336 blocks super 1.2 level 5, 512k chunk, algorithm 2 [4/3] [UUU_]
      [============>........]  recovery = 61.7% (12943096/20954112) finish=1.0mi
n speed=128242K/sec

unused devices: <none>
[root@xfs ~]# ~
```

Figure 4.17 – /proc/mdstat

The last step, while optional, is highly recommended. This will save the current config to the mdadm configuration file. This helps the kernel assemble the array at boot. This is done with the following command:

```
mdadm --examine --scan >> /etc/mdadm.conf
```

## How it works...

Now, let's look at a few things about the MD device. First, if we use the `lsblk` command, we will see that the disks used by md0 are now identified as having md0 as children. This is because md0 is a child of the actual disk:

```
[root@xfs ~]# lsblk
NAME            MAJ:MIN RM   SIZE RO TYPE MOUNTPOINT
sda               8:0    0   100G  0 disk
├─sda1            8:1    0     1G  0 part /boot
└─sda2            8:2    0  72.9G  0 part
  ├─ol-root     252:0    0    50G  0 lvm  /
  ├─ol-swap     252:1    0   7.9G  0 lvm  [SWAP]
  ├─ol-var      252:2    0     5G  0 lvm  /var
  ├─ol-home     252:3    0     5G  0 lvm  /home
  └─ol-var_log  252:4    0     5G  0 lvm  /var/log
sdb               8:16   0    20G  0 disk
└─md0             9:0    0    60G  0 raid5
sdc               8:32   0    20G  0 disk
└─md0             9:0    0    60G  0 raid5
sdd               8:48   0    20G  0 disk
└─md0             9:0    0    60G  0 raid5
sde               8:64   0    20G  0 disk
└─md0             9:0    0    60G  0 raid5
sdf               8:80   0    20G  0 disk
└─md0             9:0    0    60G  0 raid5
sr0              11:0    1  1024M  0 rom
[root@xfs ~]#
```

Figure 4.18 – lsblk command output

We can also check the device with the -Q option to the mdamd command. Simply pass the device as a parameter, and the command will give you a short summary:

```
mdadm -Q /dev/md0
```

The output is as follows:

```
[root@xfs ~]# mdadm -Q /dev/md0
/dev/md0: 59.95GiB raid5 4 devices, 1 spare. Use mdadm --detail for more detail.
[root@xfs ~]#
```

Figure 4.19 – mdadm -Q

Optionally, you can pass the --detail option to get significantly more information about the array:

```
[root@xfs ~]# mdadm --detail /dev/md0
/dev/md0:
           Version : 1.2
     Creation Time : Mon May 15 23:28:00 2023
        Raid Level : raid5
        Array Size : 62862336 (59.95 GiB 64.37 GB)
     Used Dev Size : 20954112 (19.98 GiB 21.46 GB)
      Raid Devices : 4
     Total Devices : 5
       Persistence : Superblock is persistent

       Update Time : Mon May 15 23:30:43 2023
             State : clean
    Active Devices : 4
   Working Devices : 5
    Failed Devices : 0
     Spare Devices : 1

            Layout : left-symmetric
        Chunk Size : 512K

Consistency Policy : resync

              Name : xfs.m57.local:0   (local to host xfs.m57.local)
              UUID : d8d0c13c:ec25be76:790eef52:1bb1f730
            Events : 18

    Number   Major   Minor   RaidDevice State
       0       8       16        0      active sync   /dev/sdb
       1       8       32        1      active sync   /dev/sdc
       2       8       48        2      active sync   /dev/sdd
       5       8       64        3      active sync   /dev/sde

       4       8       80        -      spare   /dev/sdf
[root@xfs ~]# 
```

Figure 4.20 – mdadm --detail

Here, we can see not only the health of the array but also its creation date and lower-level metrics such as block size and layout.

Once the volume is created, you can now use it for filesystems or as storage for a logical volume manager.

# Playing with logical volume management

When it comes to filesystems, one of the biggest issues is their inflexibility when it comes to storage. Creating a volume on a disk means the space is locked in for the volume, which also locks in the size of the filesystem. However, **Logical Volume Manager** (**LVM**) provides a solution to this problem. LVM is a widely used tool in the field of computer storage management that acts as a layer of abstraction between physical storage devices, such as hard drives or SSDs, and the OS. This enables the flexible and efficient management of storage resources. LVM is especially valuable for Linux systems, as it offers a flexible and scalable storage management solution.

With LVM, administrators can dynamically allocate and resize storage volumes without the need to repartition disks or disrupt the system. This flexibility is particularly useful in environments where storage requirements change frequently or where efficient resource allocation is needed. Additionally, LVM introduces the concept of volume groups, which act as logical containers for physical storage devices. By creating logical volumes within volume groups, administrators can easily allocate and manage storage space, simplifying the management of storage resources in Linux systems and making it easier to organize and utilize storage resources effectively.

With LVM, there are three core components of the storage:

- **Physical volumes** (**PVs**): These are the block-level disk devices that are used for storage. They can be physical disks, virtual disks (such as the MD devices created in the mdadm recipe), or other block-level devices.

- **Volume groups** (**VGs**): These are groups of PVs that are combined into a single logical device. They can be a single device to start with, with new devices added later to add capacity.

- **Logical volumes** (**LVs**): These are logical disks built into the VG. They are used to create filesystems and can be dynamically resized as needed.

LVM, a VG, is a central component that acts as a logical container for one or more PVs. A VG is created by combining physical storage devices, such as hard drives or SSDs, into a single storage pool.

In this recipe, we will show you how to initialize PVs, create a VG, and then add LVs for future use by a filesystem. We will also show some of the basic management commands.

## Getting ready

The examples in this recipe will use the /dev/md0 virtual disk created in the mdadm recipe, in addition to a few extra LUNs. The LVM RPMs are normally installed by default with a normal installation.

## How to do it...

The first step is to identify what disks we can use. This is done with the `lvmdiskscan` command:

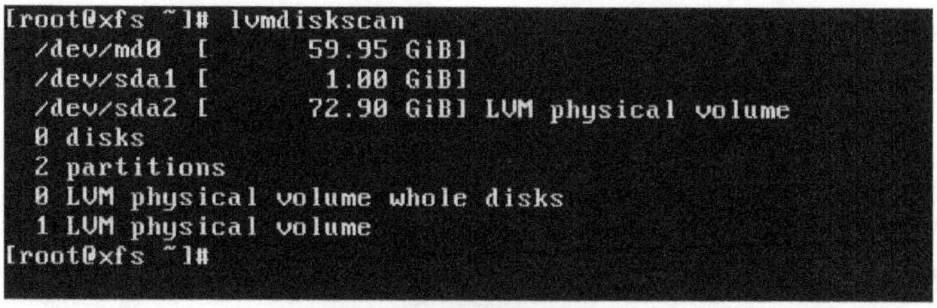

```
[root@xfs ~]# lvmdiskscan
  /dev/md0 [          59.95 GiB]
  /dev/sda1 [          1.00 GiB]
  /dev/sda2 [          72.90 GiB] LVM physical volume
  0 disks
  2 partitions
  0 LVM physical volume whole disks
  1 LVM physical volume
[root@xfs ~]#
```

Figure 4.21 – lvmdiskscan

Here, we can see three devices, `md0`, `sda1`, and `sda2`. We can also see that `sda2` is already initialized as a PV. We can use the `pvs` command to display the PVs on the system:

```
[root@xfs ~]# pvs
  PV           VG Fmt  Attr PSize   PFree
  /dev/sda2    ol lvm2 a--  <72.90g 4.00m
[root@xfs ~]#
```

Figure 4.22 – pvs

Here, we can see that the `/dev/sda2` device is used by the `ol` VG. Let's go ahead and use `pvcreat` to initialize `/dev/md0`. This is done with the following command:

```
pvcreate /dev/md0
```

Now that the device is initialized, we can create a VG. This is done with the `vgcreate` command. The command uses the first parameter as the name of the VG and then a list of devices. In this case, we will only use `/dev/md0` to create the DATA VG:

```
vgcreate DATA /dev/md0
```

## How it works...

We can see the list of VGs on a system using the `vgs` command:

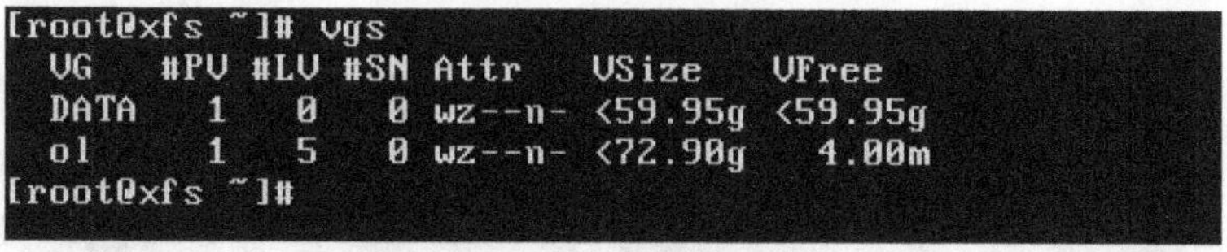

```
[root@xfs ~]# vgs
  VG   #PV #LV #SN Attr   VSize   VFree
  DATA   1   0   0 wz--n- <59.95g <59.95g
  ol     1   5   0 wz--n- <72.90g   4.00m
[root@xfs ~]#
```

Figure 4.23 – vgs

Here, we can see two VGs: the freshly created DATA VG and the existing ol VG where the OS is installed. We will then use the VG to create an LV. This is done with the lvcreate command. The lvcreate command takes a few parameters: -L to set the size of the volume, -n for the name, and then at the end, the VG where the volume will exist. Let's create a 3 GB volume named xfs1 in the DATA VG:

```
lvcreate -L 2G -n xfs1 DATA
```

We can also tell lvcreate to use all available space. This is done using a lowercase l and the special 100%FREE option:

```
lvcreate -l 100%FREE -n xfs2 DATA
```

The lvs command will show all the LVs on a server:

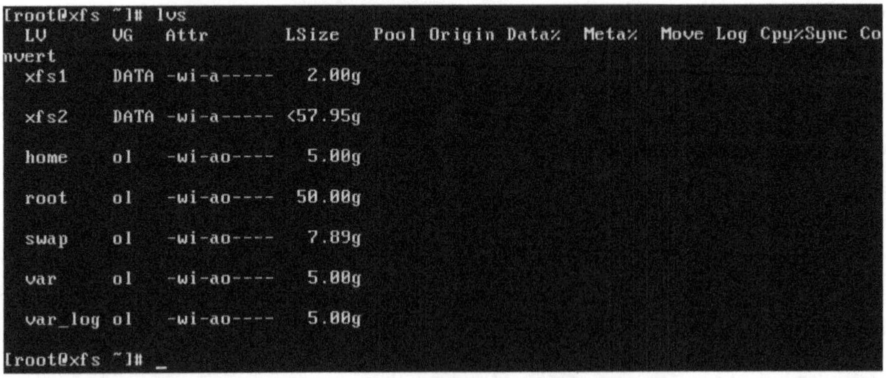

```
[root@xfs ~]# lvs
  LV       VG    Attr       LSize    Pool Origin Data%  Meta%  Move Log Cpy%Sync Co
nvert
  xfs1     DATA  -wi-a-----   2.00g
  xfs2     DATA  -wi-a-----  <57.95g
  home     ol    -wi-ao----   5.00g
  root     ol    -wi-ao----  50.00g
  swap     ol    -wi-ao----   7.89g
  var      ol    -wi-ao----   5.00g
  var_log  ol    -wi-ao----   5.00g
[root@xfs ~]# _
```

Figure 4.24 – lvs

Here, we can see the xfs1 and xfs2 volumes and their size. Additionally, we can see all the volumes in ol, where Linux was installed.

Let's go ahead and free up some space by deleting the xfs2 LV. This is done with the lvremove command. When using lvremove, use the VG/LV to identify the LV being deleted. The following command will remove the xfs2 LV:

```
lvremove DATA/xfs2
```

You will also need to acknowledge the removal:

```
[root@xfs ~]# lvremove DATA/xfs2
Do you really want to remove active logical volume DATA/xfs2? [y/n]: y
  Logical volume "xfs2" successfully removed.
[root@xfs ~]#
```

Figure 4.25 – lvremove

The last trick is to see the details of a specific LV. This is done with the lvdisplay command. You can run the command by itself, and this will show the details for all LVs on the server. Optionally, you can use the command to report on a single LV, in this case the xfs1 LV:

```
lvdisplay /dev/DATA/xfs1
```

The output is as follows:

```
[root@xfs ~]# lvdisplay /dev/DATA/xfs1
  --- Logical volume ---
  LV Path                /dev/DATA/xfs1
  LV Name                xfs1
  VG Name                DATA
  LV UUID                iwkYdN-Y91y-R8gZ-20eJ-NZJ1-Uvpe-90HPBj
  LV Write Access        read/write
  LV Creation host, time xfs.m57.local, 2023-05-16 20:31:57 -0400
  LV Status              available
  # open                 0
  LV Size                2.00 GiB
  Current LE             512
  Segments               1
  Allocation             inherit
  Read ahead sectors     auto
  - currently set to     8192
  Block device           252:5

[root@xfs ~]# _
```

Figure 4.26 – lvdisplay

Here, you can see the volume creation date, the UUID, and the size of the volume.

Once created, there are various ways to access LVs, but the most common method is by using their mapper addresses. In Linux, the /dev/mapper directory is utilized to access device mapper devices, which is a kernel-level framework that allows for the creation and management of virtual block devices. With a device mapper, advanced storage functionalities such as software RAID, encryption, and LVM can be achieved. By using LVM, a device mapper creates virtual devices that are represented as device mapper devices under the /dev/mapper directory, which act as abstractions and provide an interface for accessing and managing the underlying storage features.

For instance, logical volumes set up using LVM are mapped to device mapper devices located in the /dev/mapper directory. Each logical volume has a corresponding device mapper device entry that can be used to interact with the logical volume as if it were a regular block device. The path for accessing it is /dev/mapper followed by the VG-LV name. Thus, DATA/xfs1 would be /dev/mapper/DATA-xfs1. You can use the dmsetup ls command to show all of the mapped devices:

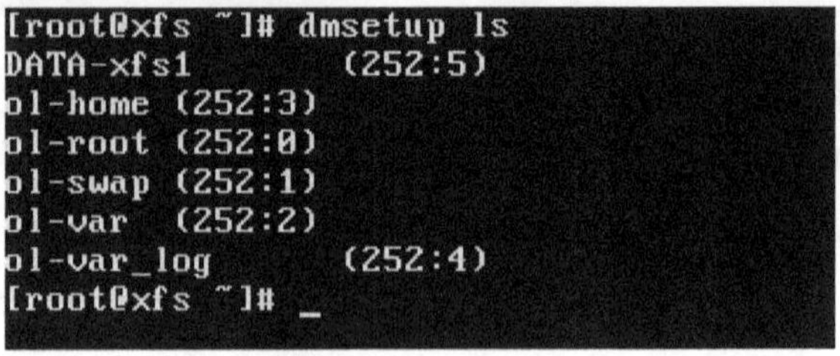

Figure 4.27 – dmsetup ls

# XFS – creating, modifying, and more

XFS is a highly advanced and established filesystem that boasts an array of benefits and features, making it an ideal option for a wide range of use cases. XFS is designed to handle vast storage capacities, making it suitable for environments with heavy data demands. It can support filesystems and files up to 8 exabytes in size, allowing for the management of vast amounts of data. This scalability makes XFS highly suitable for big data applications, enterprise storage systems, and large-scale storage deployments. XFS has exceptional performance capabilities. It employs advanced techniques such as allocation-group-based block mapping, delayed allocation, and asynchronous I/O, which optimize disk I/O operations and improve overall throughput. XFS is particularly effective at handling large files and performing tasks that involve intensive read and write operations.

XFS incorporates data protection features to safeguard against data corruption. It employs checksumming for both metadata and data, allowing the filesystem to detect and address potential data integrity issues. Additionally, XFS supports **copy-on-write (COW)** snapshots, enabling efficient point-in-time backups and data recovery options. XFS also uses a journaling mechanism that provides fast recovery in case of system crashes or power failures. The journaling feature records modifications to the filesystem metadata, ensuring the consistency and integrity of data. This results in faster boot times and improved reliability, as well as the reduction of time required for filesystem checks during system startup.

> **Note**
>
> Oracle actively contributes to many Linux technologies. The COW XFS feature was one example of an Oracle contribution to the community, keeping Linux free and open source. For more info, refer to `https://blogs.oracle.com/linux/post/xfs-data-block-sharing-reflink`.

With XFS, administrators can perform a broad range of filesystem operations while the filesystem is mounted and in use. This includes online resizing, enabling seamless expansion or contraction of filesystems without requiring unmounting or disruption of services. These online administration capabilities make XFS highly suitable for environments that demand continuous availability and minimal downtime. XFS also offers extensive support for extended attributes, **access-control lists (ACLs)**, and timestamps with nanosecond precision. These features provide flexibility in managing file metadata and enable the implementation of complex permission structures and custom metadata schemes.

XFS is natively supported by the Linux kernel, making it a well-integrated and widely adopted choice for Linux distributions. It is the default filesystem in Oracle Linux and continues to benefit from ongoing development and improvement by Oracle and the Linux community. Additionally, XFS comes with a comprehensive set of tools for filesystem management and administration, making it an all-around top-notch option.

## Getting ready

The examples in this recipe will use the previously created xfs1 LV. XFS filesystems can be created on any block device.

## How to do it...

The most common way to create an XFS filesystem is to use the mkfs.xfs command with a single block device. This will place both the data and the journal on the same device:

```
mkfs.xfs /dev/mapper/DATA-xfs1
```

Additionally, you can get more control using additional parameters:

| Option | Description | Samples |
|--------|-------------|---------|
| -L | This adds a label to the filesystem. | -L Test |
| -b | This sets the block size. | -b 8192 |
| -f | This is the force option. | -f |
| -l | This sets the location and size for the journal. This is commonly used to tune the  performance by enabling the journal to be on a fast device while the data is on a slower device.<br><br>Size=20m /dev/$DEVICE | -l 20m /dev/mapper/journal1 |

Table 4.3 – XFS options

Next, add in the /etc/fstab entry info. Make sure to verify whether the mountpoint exists, and that you're using the correct /dev/mapper path. The updated files are seen in the following screenshot:

```
#
# /etc/fstab
# Created by anaconda on Mon May 15 00:49:10 2023
#
# Accessible filesystems, by reference, are maintained under '/dev/disk/'.
# See man pages fstab(5), findfs(8), mount(8) and/or blkid(8) for more info.
#
# After editing this file, run 'systemctl daemon-reload' to update systemd
# units generated from this file.
#
/dev/mapper/ol-root          /                xfs      defaults        0 0
UUID=d3b7bd08-738d-44e2-a850-11f70e070ef7 /boot           xfs         defaul
ts      0 0
/dev/mapper/ol-home          /home            xfs      defaults        0 0
/dev/mapper/ol-var           /var             xfs      defaults        0 0
/dev/mapper/ol-var_log       /var/log         xfs      defaults        0 0
/dev/mapper/DATA-xfs1        /xfs1            xfs      defaults        0 0
/dev/mapper/ol-swap          none             swap     defaults        0 0
```

Figure 4.28 – /etc/fstab

We can now mount the filesystem with the following mount command:

```
mount /xfs1
```

We can clearly see the filesystem is mounted now, as seen in the output from the df command:

```
[root@xfs ~]# df     -h
Filesystem                 Size  Used Avail Use% Mounted on
devtmpfs                   3.8G     0  3.8G   0% /dev
tmpfs                      3.8G     0  3.8G   0% /dev/shm
tmpfs                      3.8G   12M  3.8G   1% /run
tmpfs                      3.8G     0  3.8G   0% /sys/fs/cgroup
/dev/mapper/ol-root         50G  5.3G   45G  11% /
/dev/mapper/ol-var         5.0G  1.7G  3.4G  33% /var
/dev/mapper/ol-var_log     5.0G   81M  5.0G   2% /var/log
/dev/mapper/ol-home        5.0G   83M  5.0G   2% /home
/dev/sda1                 1014M  495M  520M  49% /boot
tmpfs                      765M     0  765M   0% /run/user/0
/dev/mapper/DATA-xfs1      2.0G   47M  1.9G   3% /xfs1
[root@xfs ~]# _
```

Figure 4.29 – df -h

## How it works...

Now that the filesystem is mounted, we can do a few things to it. The first task is to grow the filesystem as 2 GB was a tad small for the application. This is done in a few steps. First, we grow the LV that holds the filesystem, and then we can grow the filesystem. Let's grow this to 10 GB.

To grow the volume, we will use the lvextend command, passing to it the + option to add an additional 8 GB:

```
lvextend -L +8G /dev/mapper/DATA-xfs1
```

The output is seen in the following screenshot:

```
[root@xfs ~]# lvextend -L +8G /dev/mapper/DATA-xfs1
  Size of logical volume DATA/xfs1 changed from 2.00 GiB (512 extents) to 10.00
GiB (2560 extents).
  Logical volume DATA/xfs1 successfully resized.
[root@xfs ~]#
```

Figure 4.30 – lvextend

Once the LV is grown, we need to extend the actual filesystem. This is done with the `xfs_growfs` command, passing the mapper path:

```
xfs_growfs /dev/mapper/DATA-xfs1
```

Depending on how much activity is on the filesystem, the growth can take a few minutes. The output from the `xfs_growfs` command will show the details of the filesystem when it completes:

```
[root@xfs ~]# xfs_growfs /dev/mapper/DATA-xfs1
meta-data=/dev/mapper/DATA-xfs1  isize=512      agcount=8, agsize=65536 blks
         =                       sectsz=512     attr=2, projid32bit=1
         =                       crc=1          finobt=1, sparse=1, rmapbt=0
         =                       reflink=1      bigtime=0 inobtcount=0
data     =                       bsize=4096     blocks=524288, imaxpct=25
         =                       sunit=128      swidth=384 blks
naming   =version 2              bsize=4096     ascii-ci=0, ftype=1
log      =internal log           bsize=4096     blocks=25600, version=2
         =                       sectsz=512     sunit=8 blks, lazy-count=1
realtime =none                   extsz=4096     blocks=0, rtextents=0
data blocks changed from 524288 to 2621440
[root@xfs ~]# _
```

Figure 4.31 – xfs_growfs

You can also see these details by using the `xfs_info` command, passing the mountpoint of the filesystem or the mapper path.

If you encounter problems mounting an `xfs` filesystem, you can use the `xfs_repair` command-line utility to repair and recover it. However, keep in mind that the command must be run on an unmounted filesystem. The main purpose of `xfs_repair` is to fix inconsistencies and repair filesystem corruption in XFS partitions caused by power failures, system crashes, or hardware issues. You can also use the `-n` option to check a filesystem without repairing it. For example, you can check the `xfs1` filesystem without repairing it by using the following command:

```
xfs_repair -n /dev/mapper/DATA-xfs1
```

# 5
# Software Management with DNF

Without packages, a fresh Linux installation is about as useful as a car with no tires! You need to be able to add software to the system to make it useful. This can be done in several ways. Back in the old days (hey, I am a true gray-bearded Unix/Linux guy), you used to download the source files and then build and install them manually. On occasion, you could get prebuilt packages but, often, the dependencies that were required would take hours to run down manually. Then, in 1997, along came **Red Hat Package Manager** (RPM) files. These really simplified the process, as all you needed to do was track down all the RPM files needed to install an application, and off you went.

Then, the applications started getting more complex; an example is the Apache HTTP server – all of its optional features went from 2-3 RPMs to a dozen, plus all the required dependencies. Tracking down all the RPMs and their dependencies became a chore... and due to mismatched versions, chaos quickly took control. This came to a screeching halt when **Yellowdog Updater, Modified** (YUM) was released in 2003. Now you could have a centralized location for all of the RPMs, with an easy way to install and patch the packages and all of the dependencies. **Red Hat Enterprise Linux** (RHEL) moved to YUM, and life was good.

> **Note**
>
> YUM replaced **Yellowdog Update Program** (YUP), which was the original tool used by Yellowdog Linux for the installer. Yellowdog Linux was a Linux distribution built for the POWER7 CPU used on the PlayStation 3 and IBM systems and was CentOS/RHEL based. While it died in 2012, it lives on with YUM.

Linux distributions (such as RHEL and Oracle Linux) maintained YUM servers specific to their distribution online, but what if you could build your own RPM packages and maintain your own RPM repositories? What if these custom RPMs could be used to deploy internally built applications, and also make the required configuration changes so they run as expected? This chapter covers the management of RPM files, from moving from the yum command to the dnf command to managing RPMs, creating private RPM repositories, and making new RPMs.

This chapter contains the following recipes:

- What have they done to YUM, moving to DNF?
- Using the DNF time machine
- Building a DNF/YUM mirror from ULN
- Creating a new RPM package

# What have they done to YUM, moving to DNF?

YUM was good – it worked and it allowed admins to easily install and patch software. You could even use it to roll back a bad installation. So, what happened to it? Why was DNF released? What is DNF and how hard will it be to learn a new tool?

First, **DNF** stands for **Dandified YUM** and is a rewrite of the YUM software. It was released in 2013 in Fedora 18 and was built to address many issues that YUM was starting to face.

The two most common problems with YUM were performance and RAM usage:

- **Poor performance**: YUM had performance issues. A lot of this was caused by dependency resolution, the process in which all the packages and their dependencies are put together. This process could take as long as 10 minutes. DNF moved to libsolv, which significantly decreased the time to resolve complex dependencies. This is now more common that ever, with some applications requiring 30+ RPMs.
- **High RAM usage**: YUM uses a lot of RAM; this really started to become an issue with RHEL/ CentOS 7, with smaller servers often running out of RAM while updating.

## Getting ready

DNF changes are not just in performance; there are also some key differences in its behavior. In order to test these changes, you will need an Oracle Linux 8 system and access to at least the free public repos, such as https://yum.oracle.com. You may also want to be running Oracle Linux in a virtualized environment where you can leverage snapshots to keep copies of the OS before and after a change. Oracle VM VirtualBox is a great way to do this.

## How to do it...

For the most part, DNF and YUM work the same: dnf install and yum install appear to work the same way, but with DNF being faster. The same applies to dnf upgrade and yum upgrade, so you probably already know the basics.

In YUM, `update` and `upgrade` have slightly different behaviors, with `yum update` removing the older packages from the system. With DNF, both `update` and `upgrade` will update the installed software but the `upgrade` option will also remove the obsolete packages. Additionally, the `auto-remove` option will remove packages that are no longer required on the system.

> **Note**
>
> Starting with Oracle Linux 8, the `yum` command is a **symbolic link (symlink)** to the `dnf` command.

At this point in the development of DNF, most of the commands are the same, but DNF does have a few tricks up its sleeve, such as automatically running an update.

## DNF automatic updates

You can set up DNS to run automatically. To do this, install the `dnf-automatic` package, and enable the service with the following commands:

```
yum install dnf-automatic
systemctl enable dnf-automatic.timer
systemctl start dnf-automatic.timer
```

Next, edit the `/etc/dnf/automatic.conf` file. There are a few tricks in this file. You can override whether patches are applied when downloaded by setting the `apply_updates` parameter to `yes`. This will force patches to be applied when the job runs.

Don't forget to set the `system_name` parameter so that emails and notifications will have the correct name.

You can also set up the system to email you a report of what was installed. Set up email in the `[email]` stanza. If using an email relay, make sure it does not require authentication, or add that to the configuration if needed.

As a final trick, you can change the `emit_via` parameter from `stdio` to `motd`. When set to `motd`, the system `motd` file is updated to reflect what patches were installed. When users log in to the system, they will see a complete list of what patches were installed and when, as shown in the following screenshot:

```
root@ol8splice2:~                                                              ⌐      —   □   ×
xorg-x11-server-Xorg x86_64 1.20.11-5.el8        ol8_x86_64_appstream    1.5 M
xorg-x11-server-Xwayland
                     x86_64 21.1.3-2.el8          ol8_x86_64_appstream    963 k
xorg-x11-server-common
                     x86_64 1.20.11-5.el8         ol8_x86_64_appstream     42 k
xz                   x86_64 5.2.4-4.el8_6         ol8_x86_64_baseos_latest 153 k
xz-libs              x86_64 5.2.4-4.el8_6         ol8_x86_64_baseos_latest  94 k
zlib                 x86_64 1.2.11-18.el8_5       ol8_x86_64_baseos_latest 102 k
Installing group/module packages:
kernel-uek           x86_64 5.4.17-2136.308.9.el8uek
                                                 ol8_x86_64_UEKR6         109 M
Installing dependencies:
NetworkManager-initscripts-updown
                     noarch 1:1.36.0-4.0.1.el8   ol8_x86_64_baseos_latest 137 k
autogen-libopts      x86_64 5.18.12-8.el8        ol8_x86_64_appstream      75 k
glibc-gconv-extra    x86_64 2:2.28-189.1.0.1.ksplice1.el8
                                                 ol8_x86_64_userspace_ksplice
                                                                          1.6 M
gnutls-dane          x86_64 3.6.16-4.el8         ol8_x86_64_appstream      52 k
gnutls-utils         x86_64 3.6.16-4.el8         ol8_x86_64_appstream     348 k
grub2-tools-efi      x86_64 1:2.02-123.0.3.el8   ol8_x86_64_baseos_latest 478 k
iwlax2xx-firmware    noarch 999:20220304-999.13.el8
                                                 ol8_x86_64_baseos_latest  14 M
kernel-core          x86_64 4.18.0-372.9.1.el8   ol8_x86_64_baseos_latest  39 M
kernel-modules       x86_64 4.18.0-372.9.1.el8   ol8_x86_64_baseos_latest  32 M
ksplice-helper       x86_64 1.0.56-1.el8         ol8_x86_64_userspace_ksplice
                                                                           26 k
libbpf               x86_64 0.4.0-3.el8          ol8_x86_64_baseos_latest 125 k
libfdt               x86_64 1.6.0-1.el8          ol8_x86_64_appstream      32 k
libtpms              x86_64 0.9.1-0.20211126git1ff6fe1f43.module+el8.6.0+20659+3dcf7c70
                                                 ol8_x86_64_appstream     184 k
linux-firmware-core  noarch 999:20220304-999.13.gitf011ccb4.el8
                                                 ol8_x86_64_baseos_latest 509 k
mdevctl              x86_64 1.1.0-2.el8          ol8_x86_64_appstream     745 k
qemu-kvm-docs        x86_64 15:6.2.0-11.module+el8.6.0+20659+3dcf7c70
                                                 ol8_x86_64_appstream     2.6 M
qemu-kvm-hw-usbredir x86_64 15:6.2.0-11.module+el8.6.0+20659+3dcf7c70
                                                 ol8_x86_64_appstream     184 k
qemu-kvm-ui-opengl   x86_64 15:6.2.0-11.module+el8.6.0+20659+3dcf7c70
                                                 ol8_x86_64_appstream     176 k
qemu-kvm-ui-spice    x86_64 15:6.2.0-11.module+el8.6.0+20659+3dcf7c70
                                                 ol8_x86_64_appstream     223 k
shadow-utils-subid   x86_64 2:4.6-16.el8         ol8_x86_64_baseos_latest 112 k
swtpm                x86_64 0.7.0-1.20211109gitb79fd91.module+el8.6.0+20659+3dcf7c70
                                                 ol8_x86_64_appstream      43 k
swtpm-libs           x86_64 0.7.0-1.20211109gitb79fd91.module+el8.6.0+20659+3dcf7c70
                                                 ol8_x86_64_appstream      49 k
swtpm-tools          x86_64 0.7.0-1.20211109gitb79fd91.module+el8.6.0+20659+3dcf7c70
                                                 ol8_x86_64_appstream     119 k

Transaction Summary
================================================================================
Install   26 Packages
Upgrade  621 Packages

Updates completed at Wed 22 Jun 2022 06:23:47 AM EDT
Activate the web console with: systemctl enable --now cockpit.socket

Last login: Wed Jun 22 12:25:01 2022 from 192.168.56.1
[root@ol8splice2 ~]# █
```

Figure 5.1 – MOTD on login

By default, the service checks for updates at 6 A.M. This can be changed by editing the /etc/systemd/system/timers.target.wants/dnf-automatic.timer file:

```
[root@ol8splice2 ~]# more /etc/systemd/system/timers.target.wants/dnf-automatic.timer
[Unit]
Description=dnf-automatic timer
# See comment in dnf-makecache.service
ConditionPathExists=!/run/ostree-booted
Wants=network-online.target

[Timer]
OnCalendar=*-*-* 6:00
RandomizedDelaySec=60m
Persistent=true

[Install]
WantedBy=timers.target
[root@ol8splice2 ~]# ▮
```

Figure 5.2 – The dnf-automatic.timer file

In this file, the [Timer] stanza controls the time, as well as a randomized delay. To change when this runs, replace 6:00 with whatever time you want, in a 24-hour format. For example, if you want the check to run at 10 P.M., the time should be 22:00.

Since this uses the standard OnCalendar function, you have other options. OnCalendar is a very flexible method; the following are some of the most commonly used examples:

| OnCalendar Example | Description |
|---|---|
| DOW YYYY-MM-DD HH:MM:SS | Generic time formatting methods. |
| *-*-* 2:00 | Runs every day at 2:00 A.M. |
| Weekly | Every Monday at midnight. |
| Sat *-*-* 2:00 | Every Saturday at 2:00 A.M. |
| Sat | Every Saturday at midnight. |
| Sun 2022-*-* | Every Sunday in 2022 at midnight. |
| *-*-1,15 22:15 | The 1st and 15th of every month at 10:15 P.M. |
| *-05-03/2 | Runs on the third day of the month in May, and then on the second day of every other month. Runs every year with the same cycle. This date format expression uses the dash for formatting. |

Table 5.1 – OnCalendar example date rules

RandomizedDelaySec is also an important setting. This will add a random delay to the clock, which is helpful in enterprise environments where large numbers of systems are running. Having 200 servers hitting a YUM repo at 6 A.M. can be a little overwhelming to the server. Adding a randomized delay in /etc/dnf/automatic.conf of maybe 600 seconds would spread the load across a few minutes.

DNF is an upgraded version of YUM, with a few enhancements. As seen in the recipe, it does have a few tricks up its sleeve, but it still does a great job of providing an easy way for admins to install and patch software on an Oracle Linux system.

# Using the DNF time machine

DNF has a time machine built into it! This isn't just a way to look back through the cosmos; it actually allows you to see the history of what was installed and also allows you to roll back a single change, or all changes up to a point.

## Getting ready

To do this, you will need a test system, running Oracle Linux 8, with access to an RPM repo.

## How to do it...

When DNF installs software, it keeps a history of all the actions performed. This includes upgrades to the software, installed software, and removal of the software. The dnf history command shows this history:

```
[root@arm2 ~]# dnf history
ID    | Command line                                                              | Date and time    | Action(s)   | Altered
-----------------------------------------------------------------------------------------------------------------------------
   39 | --disablerepo=* install -y /var/lib/oracle-cloud-agent/pool2/f084d28f-28e3-4b52-a382-fae8 | 2022-06-22 18:45 | Upgrade     |    1 EE
   38 | --disablerepo=* install -y /var/lib/oracle-cloud-agent/pool2/d9fafla0-01e7-4890-b4ff-7943 | 2022-05-17 20:45 | Upgrade     |    1 EE
   37 | update -y                                                                  | 2022-05-17 00:32 | ?, E, I, U  |   51 EE
   36 | --disablerepo=* --enablerepo=ol8_aarch64_userspace_ksplice update          | 2022-04-23 21:40 | I, U        |    8
   35 | update -y                                                                  | 2022-04-17 01:31 | ?, E, I, U  |  120 EE
   34 | install nmap                                                               | 2022-04-15 22:12 | Install     |    1
   33 | --disablerepo=* install -y /var/lib/oracle-cloud-agent/pool2/0bd33683-e751-4b0d-80f1-cfc6 | 2022-04-12 22:27 | Upgrade     |    1 EE
   32 | --disablerepo=* install -y /var/lib/oracle-cloud-agent/pool2/443410ee-621e-4901-bb39-34e7 | 2022-03-16 20:26 | Upgrade     |    1 EE
   31 | --disablerepo=* install -y /var/lib/oracle-cloud-agent/pool2/f503e428-9980-460a-b4a0-738e | 2022-02-15 20:24 | Upgrade     |    1 EE
   30 | update -y                                                                  | 2022-01-25 22:16 | I, O, U     |  335 EE
   29 | --disablerepo=* install -y /var/lib/oracle-cloud-agent/pool2/7910d8eb-84c3-4e12-aca5-5bf3 | 2022-01-21 00:23 | Upgrade     |    1 EE
   28 | --disablerepo=* install -y /var/lib/oracle-cloud-agent/pool2/554cf9d7-ff3c-4daa-b982-f5c1 | 2021-12-20 22:22 | Upgrade     |    1 EE
   27 | --disablerepo=* install -y /var/lib/oracle-cloud-agent/pool2/abf52ee4-c48f-46f8-b11f-1d13 | 2021-11-19 18:21 | Upgrade     |    1 EE
   26 | install snapd                                                              | 2021-11-09 22:44 | Install     |    4
   25 | install ImageMagick                                                        | 2021-11-01 21:06 | Install     |   82
   24 | update -y                                                                  | 2021-11-01 20:16 | I, U        |   20 EE
   23 | -y install oci-utils-0.12.6-1.el8.noarch.rpm                               | 2021-09-30 01:50 | Upgrade     |    1 EE
   22 | -y install iperf3                                                          | 2021-09-30 01:50 | Install     |    2
   21 | -y install perf                                                            | 2021-09-30 01:50 | Install     |    2
   20 | -y install trace-cmd                                                       | 2021-09-30 01:50 | Install     |    1 EE
   19 | -y install kernel-uek-devel                                                | 2021-09-30 01:49 | Install     |    1
   18 | -y install bcc                                                             | 2021-09-30 01:48 | Install     |    9
   17 | -y install ltrace                                                          | 2021-09-30 01:48 | Install     |    1
   16 | -y install dtrace                                                          | 2021-09-30 01:48 | Install     |    1
   15 | -y install oswatcher                                                       | 2021-09-30 01:48 | Install     |    3 EE
   14 | -y install systemtap                                                       | 2021-09-30 01:48 | Install     |   24
   13 | -y install oci-linux-config                                                | 2021-09-30 01:48 | Install     |    1 EE
   12 | -y install tuned-profiles-oci-recommend                                    | 2021-09-30 01:47 | Install     |    2
   11 | -y install ksplice --enablerepo ol8_codeready_builder                      | 2021-09-30 01:47 | Install     |    7
   10 | -y install uptrack                                                         | 2021-09-30 01:47 | Install     |   36 EE
    9 | -y install /tmp/oracle-cloud-agent.rpm                                     | 2021-09-30 01:47 | Install     |    1 EE
    8 | -y update --exclude=*12.6-0*                                               | 2021-09-30 01:46 | I, U        |   24 EE
    7 | -y install oci-utils --exclude=*12.6-0*                                    | 2021-09-30 01:45 | I, U        |   21 EE
    6 | -y install mysql-release-el8                                               | 2021-09-30 01:45 | Install     |    1
    5 | -y install oracle-epel-release-el8                                         | 2021-09-30 01:45 | Install     |    1
    4 | -y install ksplice-release-el8                                             | 2021-09-30 01:45 | Install     |    1
    3 | -y localinstall /tmp/oci-included-release-el8-1.0-3.0.1.el8.aarch64.rpm     | 2021-09-30 01:45 | Install     |    1
    2 | -y install oraclelinux-developer-release-el8                               | 2021-09-30 01:45 | Install     |    1
    1 |                                                                            | 2021-09-30 01:42 | Install     |  577 EE
[root@arm2 ~]#
```

Figure 5.3 – The dnf history command

There are five columns – ID, Command line, Date and time, Action(s), and Altered:

- ID: This is the identifier for the history, and is used in commands that will show info, roll back, undo, or store a transaction

- Command line: This is the option passed to DNF when the command was run that added to the transaction history

- Date and time: This is the timestamp of when the transaction was run

- Action(s): This is what actions were taken; multiple actions can performed in the same transaction:

  - (D) Downgrade: A package was downgraded

  - (E) Erase: A package was removed

  - (I) Installed: A package was installed

  - (R) Reinstall: A package was reinstalled

  - (O) Obsoleting: A package was flagged as obsolete

  - (U) Update: A package was updated

- Altered: This is the number of packages altered when the command was run, in addition to several exception flags:

  - E/EE: The transaction was completed but had an output generated. Not all outputs are errors!

  - P: The transaction was completed but problems exist in the rpm database.

  - s: The transaction was completed but since the --skip-broken parameter was enabled, some packages were skipped.

  - >: The rpm database was changed outside of DNF after the transaction ran.

  - <: The rpm database was changed outside of DNF before the transaction ran.

  - *: The transaction was aborted before completion.

  - #: The transaction was completed but returned a non-zero status.

When there are error codes, you can see the details with the dnf history info {ID} command, as seen in *Figure 5.4*:

```
[root@arm2 ~]# dnf history info 39
Transaction ID : 39
Begin time     : Wed 22 Jun 2022 06:45:47 PM GMT
Begin rpmdb    : 793:3aabcde3121251a5a0fab4fe55da80bd91bf0c5e
End time       : Wed 22 Jun 2022 06:45:55 PM GMT (8 seconds)
End rpmdb      : 793:87abfc551bb7ed4464f4df6c2e4bea27cd8086f7
User           : System <unset>
Return-Code    : Success
Releasever     : 8
Command Line   : --disablerepo=* install -y /var/lib/oracle-cloud-agent/pool2/f084d28f-28e3-4b52-a382-fae823c1cdf8/oracle-cloud-agent-1.24.0-1.e
18.aarch64.rpm          I
Comment        :
Packages Altered:
    Upgrade  oracle-cloud-agent-1.24.0-1.el8.aarch64 @@commandline
    Upgraded oracle-cloud-agent-1.23.0-2.el8.aarch64 @@System
Scriptlet output:
    1 Changing ownership of agent.yml* files to oracle-cloud-agent:oracle-cloud-agent
    2 Changing ownership of /var/log/oracle-cloud-agent/updater.log to oracle-cloud-agent-updater:adm
    3 Setting capabilities on bastions plugin
    4 2022/06/22 18:45:53 Capability set on filePath: /usr/libexec/oracle-cloud-agent/plugins/bastions = [1 0 0 10 11 0 0 0 0 0 0 0 0 0 0 0 0 0
0]
    5 2022/06/22 18:45:53 Capability set on filePath: 20 = [1 0 0 10 11 0 0 0 0 0 0 0 0 0 0 0 0 0 0]
    6 2022/06/22 18:45:53 Capability set properly : [1 0 0 10 11 0 0 0 0 0 0 0 0 0 0 0 0 0 0]
    7 Changing ownership of /var/lib/ocarun/db/runcommand.db to ocarun:oracle-cloud-agent
    8 post install upgrade: stop service
    9 post install upgrade : clean up old files if any
   10 post install: starting services
```

Figure 5.4 – The dnf history info command

In this example, the output is more informational, with no actual errors. This is not uncommon.

You can also use `dnf history` to uninstall a package. There are two ways to do this: `rollback` or `undo`. A `rollback` command attempts to reverse out all of the DNF transactions from the current point to the transaction ID specified. An `undo` command simply undoes the transactions in the ID identified.

On the test system, let's undo the installation of Nmap from 4/17/2022, which was ID 34, using the `dnf history undo 34` command:

```
[root@arm2 ~]# dnf history undo 34
Last metadata expiration check: 1:58:19 ago on Mon 04 Jul 2022 06:47:45 PM GMT.          I
Dependencies resolved.
==========================================================================================================================
 Package              Architecture            Version                  Repository                Size
==========================================================================================================================
Removing:
 nmap                 aarch64                 2:7.70-6.el8             @ol8_appstream           23 M

Transaction Summary
==========================================================================================================================
Remove  1 Package

Freed space: 23 M
Is this ok [y/N]: y
Running transaction check
Transaction check succeeded.
Running transaction test
Transaction test succeeded.
Running transaction
  Preparing        :                                                                              1/1
  Erasing          : nmap-2:7.70-6.el8.aarch64                                                    1/1
  Running scriptlet: nmap-2:7.70-6.el8.aarch64                                                    1/1
  Verifying        : nmap-2:7.70-6.el8.aarch64                                                    1/1

Removed:
  nmap-2:7.70-6.el8.aarch64

Complete!
```

Figure 5.5 – The dnf history undo command

This was a fairly simple undo, with Nmap being uninstalled. When the DNF history is looked at after the transaction, you will see a new ID of 40, showing the undo command:

```
[root@arm2 ~]# dnf history
ID    | Command line                                                                    | Date and time     | Action(s)   | Altered
-------------------------------------------------------------------------------------------------------------------------------------
40 | history undo 34                                                                    | 2022-07-04 20:46 | Removed     |     1
39 | --disablerepo=* install -y /var/lib/oracle-cloud-agent/pool2/f064d28f-28e3-4b52-a382-fae8 | 2022-06-22 18:45 | Upgrade     |     1 EE
38 | --disablerepo=* install -y /var/lib/oracle-cloud-agent/pool2/d9fafla0-01e7-4890-b4ff-7943 | 2022-05-17 20:45 | Upgrade     |     1 EE
37 | update -y                                                                          | 2022-05-17 00:32 | ?, E, I, U  |    51 EE
36 | --disablerepo=* --enablerepo=ol8_aarch64_userspace_ksplice update                 | 2022-04-23 21:40 | I, U        |     8
35 | update -y                                                                          | 2022-04-17 01:31 | ?, E, I, U  |   120 EE
34 | install nmap                                                                       | 2022-04-15 22:12 | Install     |     1
33 | --disablerepo=* install -y /var/lib/oracle-cloud-agent/pool2/0bd33603-e751-4b0d-80f1-cfc6 | 2022-04-12 22:27 | Upgrade     |     1 EE
32 | --disablerepo=* install -y /var/lib/oracle-cloud-agent/pool2/443410ee-621e-4901-bb39-34e7 | 2022-03-18 20:26 | Upgrade     |     1 EE
31 | --disablerepo=* install -y /var/lib/oracle-cloud-agent/pool2/f503e428-9980-460a-b4a0-738e | 2022-02-15 20:24 | Upgrade     |     1 EE
30 | update -y                                                                          | 2022-01-25 22:16 | I, O, U     |   335 EE
29 | --disablerepo=* install -y /var/lib/oracle-cloud-agent/pool2/7910d8eb-84c3-4e12-aca5-5bf3 | 2022-01-21 00:23 | Upgrade     |     1 EE
28 | --disablerepo=* install -y /var/lib/oracle-cloud-agent/pool2/554cf9d7-ff3c-4daa-b982-f5c1 | 2021-12-20 22:22 | Upgrade     |     1 EE
27 | --disablerepo=* install -y /var/lib/oracle-cloud-agent/pool2/abf52ee4-c48f-46f8-b11f-1d13 | 2021-11-19 18:21 | Upgrade     |     1 EE
26 | install snapd                                                                      | 2021-11-09 22:44 | Install     |     4
25 | install ImageMagick                                                                | 2021-11-01 21:06 | Install     |    82
24 | update -y                                                                          | 2021-11-01 20:16 | I, U        |    20 EE
23 | -y install oci-utils-0.12.6-1.el8.noarch.rpm                                       | 2021-09-30 01:50 | Upgrade     |     1 EE
22 | -y install iperf3                                                                  | 2021-09-30 01:50 | Install     |     2
21 | -y install perf                                                                    | 2021-09-30 01:50 | Install     |     2
20 | -y install trace-cmd                                                               | 2021-09-30 01:50 | Install     |     1 EE
19 | -y install kernel-uek-devel                                                        | 2021-09-30 01:49 | Install     |     1
18 | -y install bcc                                                                     | 2021-09-30 01:48 | Install     |     9
17 | -y install ltrace                                                                  | 2021-09-30 01:48 | Install     |     1
16 | -y install dtrace                                                                  | 2021-09-30 01:48 | Install     |     1
15 | -y install oswatcher                                                               | 2021-09-30 01:48 | Install     |     3 EE
14 | -y install systemtap                                                               | 2021-09-30 01:48 | Install     |    24
13 | -y install oci-linux-config                                                        | 2021-09-30 01:48 | Install     |     1 EE
12 | -y install tuned-profiles-oci-recommend                                            | 2021-09-30 01:47 | Install     |     2
11 | -y install ksplice --enablerepo ol8_codeready_builder                              | 2021-09-30 01:47 | Install     |     7
10 | -y install uptrack                                                                 | 2021-09-30 01:47 | Install     |    36 EE
 9 | -y install /tmp/oracle-cloud-agent.rpm                                             | 2021-09-30 01:47 | Install     |     1 EE
 8 | -y update --exclude=*12.6-0*                                                       | 2021-09-30 01:46 | I, U        |    24 EE
 7 | -y install oci-utils --exclude=*12.6-0*                                            | 2021-09-30 01:45 | I, U        |    21 EE
 6 | -y install mysql-release-el8                                                       | 2021-09-30 01:45 | Install     |     1
 5 | -y install oracle-epel-release-el8                                                 | 2021-09-30 01:45 | Install     |     1
 4 | -y install ksplice-release-el8                                                     | 2021-09-30 01:45 | Install     |     1
 3 | -y localinstall /tmp/oci-included-release-el8-1.0-3.0.1.el8.aarch64.rpm            | 2021-09-30 01:45 | Install     |     1
 2 | -y install oraclelinux-developer-release-el8                                       | 2021-09-30 01:45 | Install     |     1
 1 |                                                                                    | 2021-09-30 01:42 | Install     |   577 EE
[root@arm2 ~]# []
```

Figure 5.6 – DNF history after the undo

Now, if the goal was to roll back all of the changes, let's say to ID 37, the command would be dnf history rollback 37. This will roll back the system to match the state it was in when transaction 37 was completed.

```
[root@arm2 ~]# dnf history rollback 37
Last metadata expiration check: 2:04:13 ago on Mon 04 Jul 2022 06:47:45 PM GMT.
Dependencies resolved.
================================================================================
 Package            Architecture       Version           Repository        Size
================================================================================
Installing:
                    aarch64            2:7.70-6.el8       ol8_appstream     5.7 M
Downgrading:
                    aarch64        I    1.22.0-2.el8      ol8_oci_included   64 M

Transaction Summary
================================================================================
Install    1 Package
Downgrade  1 Package

Total download size: 69 M
Is this ok [y/N]: y
Downloading Packages:
(1/2): nmap-7.70-6.el8.aarch64.rpm                        25 MB/s | 5.7 MB  00:00
(2/2): oracle-cloud-agent-1.22.0-2.el8.aarch64.rpm        33 MB/s |  64 MB  00:01
--------------------------------------------------------------------------------
Total                                                     36 MB/s |  69 MB  00:01
Running transaction check
Transaction check succeeded.
Running transaction test
Transaction test succeeded.
Running transaction
  Preparing        :                                                        1/1
  Running scriptlet: nmap-2:7.70-6.el8.aarch64                              1/1
  Installing       : nmap-2:7.70-6.el8.aarch64                              1/3
  Running scriptlet: oracle-cloud-agent-1.22.0-2.el8.aarch64                2/3
  Downgrading      : oracle-cloud-agent-1.22.0-2.el8.aarch64                2/3
  Running scriptlet: oracle-cloud-agent-1.22.0-2.el8.aarch64                2/3
Changing ownership of agent.yml* files to oracle-cloud-agent:oracle-cloud-agent
Changing ownership of /var/log/oracle-cloud-agent/updater.log to oracle-cloud-agent-updater:adm
Setting capabilities on bastions plugin
2022/07/04 20:52:12 Capability set on filePath: /usr/libexec/oracle-cloud-agent/plugins/bastions = [1 0 0 10 10 0 0 0 0 0 0 0 0 0 0 0 0 0]
2022/07/04 20:52:12 Capability set on filePath: 20 = [1 0 0 10 10 0 0 0 0 0 0 0 0 0 0 0 0 0]
2022/07/04 20:52:12 Capability set properly : [1 0 0 10 10 0 0 0 0 0 0 0 0 0 0 0 0 0]
Changing ownership of /var/lib/ocarun/db/runcommand.db to ocarun:oracle-cloud-agent
post install upgrade: stop service
post install upgrade : clean up old files if any
post install: starting services

  Running scriptlet: oracle-cloud-agent-1.24.0-1.el8.aarch64                3/3
  Cleanup          : oracle-cloud-agent-1.24.0-1.el8.aarch64                3/3
  Running scriptlet: oracle-cloud-agent-1.24.0-1.el8.aarch64                3/3
  Verifying        : oracle-cloud-agent-1.22.0-2.el8.aarch64                1/3
  Verifying        : oracle-cloud-agent-1.24.0-1.el8.aarch64                2/3
  Verifying        : nmap-2:7.70-6.el8.aarch64                              3/3

Downgraded:
  oracle-cloud-agent-1.22.0-2.el8.aarch64
Installed:
  nmap-2:7.70-6.el8.aarch64

Complete!
```

Figure 5.7 – DNF rollback

The rollback command rolls back the transitions, so Nmap is actually reinstalled, and the oracle-cloud-agent RPM is downgraded. This is reflected in the new history summary as ID 41 (shown in the following screenshot) where we see the install and downgrade actions in ID 41:

```
[root@arm2 ~]# dnf history
ID   | Command line                                                              | Date and time      | Action(s)   | Altered
--------------------------------------------------------------------------------------------------------------------------------
    41 | history rollback 37                                                       | 2022-07-04 20:52   | D, I        |   2 EE
    40 | history undo 34                                                           | 2022-07-04 20:46   | Removed     |   1
    39 | --disablerepo=* install -y /var/lib/oracle-cloud-agent/pool2/f084d28f-28e3-4b52-a382-fae8 | 2022-06-22 18:45   | Upgrade     |   1 EE
    38 | --disablerepo=* install -y /var/lib/oracle-cloud-agent/pool2/d9fa1a0-01e7-4890-b4ff-7943 | 2022-05-17 20:45   | Upgrade     |   1 EE
    37 | update -y                                                                 | 2022-05-17 00:32   | ?, E, I, U  |  51 EE
```

Figure 5.8 – DNF history post rollback

> **Note**
>
> While the rollback and undo commands often work well, it is still good practice to keep OS snapshots using hypervisor or cloud-native tooling. You can also take snapshots using Btrfs. Sometimes, the rollback scripts in the RPMs do not undo all the changes to the system. When leveraging a storage-based snapshot, you reduce the risk of having issues due to this.

The DNF system maintains a database of all transactions, with the dnf history command and its options giving you access to the database to examine what happened, as well as the ability to undo a single transaction or roll back from the latest transaction to a specific ID in the history. This is a very helpful tool for admins when they need to back out of patches and software installation.

# Building a DNF/YUM mirror from ULN

It is very common for admins to not enable internet access for the systems running in a secure network, like banking of Government networks. A local mirror of Oracle's **Unbreakable Linux Network** (**ULN**) is a great way to allow systems to access patches without having to reach out across the internet to access them.

## Getting ready

To do this, you will need a YUM server system running Oracle Linux 8. The local system should have internet access to be able to reach the ULN servers via direct access or a proxy server. Only the system (often called a YUM server) synchronizing to ULN will require this access; all the systems using this system will not need access to the internet, they will use this system to access patches.

The system is not CPU- or RAM-intensive – 2 cores and 4 GB of RAM are often more than enough for the server, but the system will use a lot of disk space. You can check how much space is needed by running the dnf repolist -v command.

A terabyte can go quickly, depending on how many repos the server is subscribed to. The good news on space is that high-performance storage is not required. You will also need a valid support contract with Oracle, which is included with the hardware support contract if you are running on Oracle servers. On my local repos, I keep the repo in /var/www and mount it as a separate filesystem under **Logical Volume Management** (**LVM**). This way, additional space can easily be added when needed.

Additionally, an HTTP server should be installed and you must ensure that the firewall ports are opened. If you need help doing that, go back to *Chapter 2, Installing with and without Automation Magic*, where setting up a HTTP server is covered.

## How to do it...

To build the mirror, follow these steps:

1.  The first step is to validate that enough space is in /var/www. For even a small mirror, 600 GB is recommended as a starting point. Watch the disk space carefully, as more will be needed down the road. Larger mirrors can easily consume 2 TB.

2.  Next, install the uln-yum-mirror package using the dnf install uln-yum-mirror -y command. The uln-yum-mirror package includes the scripts that automate

the replication of the Oracle ULN repository to a local server. Make sure that the system has access to the `ol8_addons` repo:

```
[root@yum yum]# dnf install uln-yum-mirror -y
There was an error communicating with Unbreakable Linux Network or Spacewalk.
Unbreakable Linux Network or Spacewalk based repositories will be disabled.
rhn-plugin: Error communicating with server. The message was:
This system is not registered with this server
Last metadata expiration check: 0:02:34 ago on Mon 04 Jul 2022 06:19:25 PM EDT.
Dependencies resolved.
================================================================================
 Package              Architecture      Version          Repository       Size
================================================================================
Installing:
                      noarch            0.4.0-3.el8       ol8_addons       37 k

Transaction Summary
================================================================================
Install  1 Package

Total download size: 37 k
Installed size: 78 k
Downloading Packages:
uln-yum-mirror-0.4.0-3.el8.noarch.rpm            14 kB/s |  37 kB     00:02
--------------------------------------------------------------------------------
Total                                            14 kB/s |  37 kB     00:02
Running transaction check
Transaction check succeeded.
Running transaction test
Transaction test succeeded.
Running transaction
  Preparing        :                                                        1/1
  Installing       : uln-yum-mirror-0.4.0-3.el8.noarch                      1/1
  Verifying        : uln-yum-mirror-0.4.0-3.el8.noarch                      1/1

Installed:
  uln-yum-mirror-0.4.0-3.el8.noarch

Complete!
[root@yum yum]#
```

Figure 5.9 – The uln-yum-mirror install

3.  This will install the scripts from Oracle. Next, let's register the system with ULN. This is done using the `uln_register` command. You will need to know the **support identifier** (**SI**) you will be using for the system, as well as your Oracle **single sign-on** (**SSO**) credentials. As a note, SIs are also often called by an older term, **customer support identifier** (**CSI**). To start the process of registering the server, run the `uln_register` command. From there, you will get the main screen:

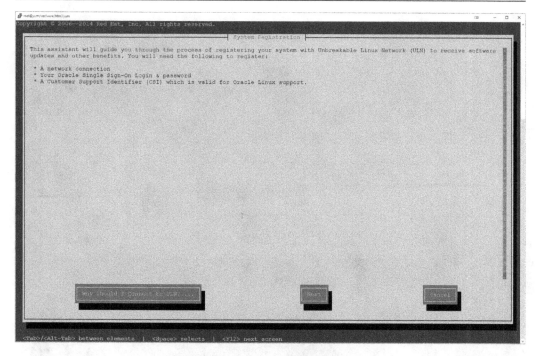

Figure 5.10 – The uln_register start screen

4.  Click **Next** to continue. On the next screen, you will be prompted to put in your Oracle SSO credentials. The CSI is the support identifier. Use the CSI assigned to you with your Premier hardware support, or your Oracle Linux subscription. Do *not* use a CSI for the Oracle database, WebLogic, E-Business Suite, and so on. The CSI should be for Oracle Linux.

> **Note**
>
> In production environments, you may want to consider creating a shared account to register all your servers using ULN directly. This makes it easier to manage the servers as staff members come and go.

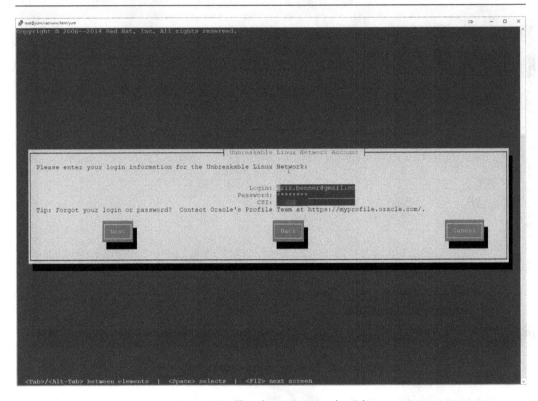

Figure 5.11 – The uln_register credentials

5.  Next, you will need to identify the server for ULN. Normally, you would use the **Fully Qualified Domain Name (FQDN)** of the server, but the choice is yours. You can also choose to upload the hardware details, but this is optional.

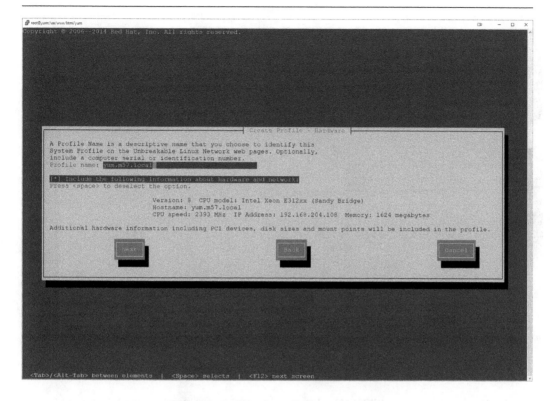

Figure 5.12 – The uln_register system name

6. Next, the system will update ULN with the software installed on the server, which will let you track installed RPMs via ULN but *only* for systems directly registered with ULN. When using a local repository, you may want to consider using a tool such as Oracle Linux Manager to track software installed on systems not registered with ULN:

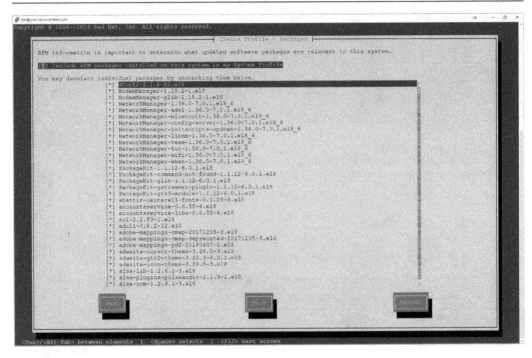

Figure 5.13 – The uln_register initial packages

7.  Registering the server with ULN is almost complete. The last step is to send the info to ULN to register the server, this is done automatically in the next step:

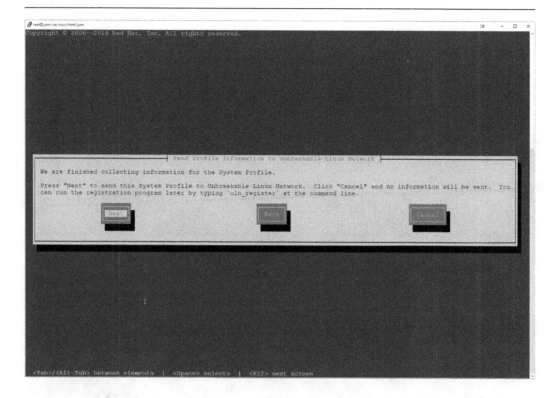

Figure 5.14 – uln_register send

The upload can take up to a minute, depending on your internet speed.

After the upload, the system is now registered in ULN. The next step is optional. It will set up Ksplice for the server. If you do not want to use Ksplice, you are done. Ksplice also requires that you have an Oracle Linux Premier Support subscription. This is included with Oracle hardware support and Oracle Cloud VMs. You can also purchase this for third-party systems, often at a cheaper price than other commercial Linux distributions.

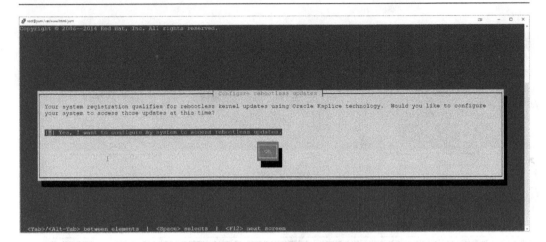

Figure 5.15 – uln_register ksplice

8.  Ksplice is a quick step; just review the settings, as seen in the following screenshot, and click **OK**:

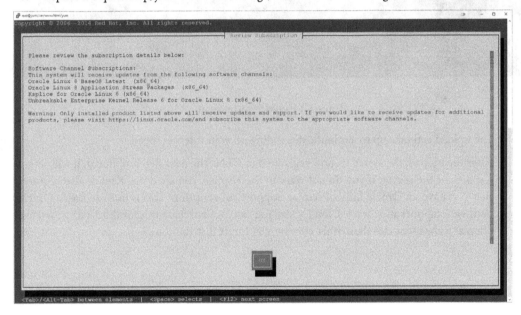

Figure 5.16 – The uln_register settings

9.  The registration is now complete. You should now patch the server with `dnf -y update` (as recommended in the tool) before continuing:

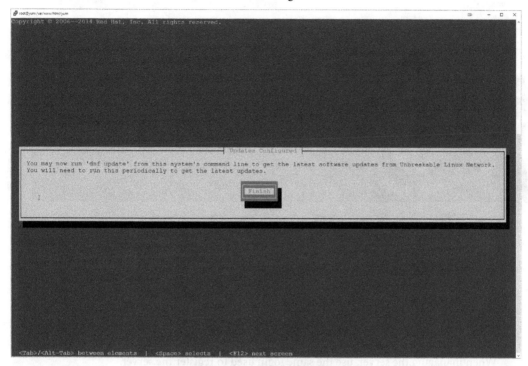

Figure 5.17 – Completed uln_register

10. Next, go ahead and patch the system with `dnf update -y` and reboot the system. As a note, the position of the `-y` option does not matter for the command. Once the system is back online, you need to log in to `https://linux.oracle.com/`. While this server is registered to ULN now, it is not a local repo yet! We need to tell ULN this is a local repo and select what repos we need to mirror.

To do this, head over to `https://linux.oracle.com` and click the **Sign In** button:

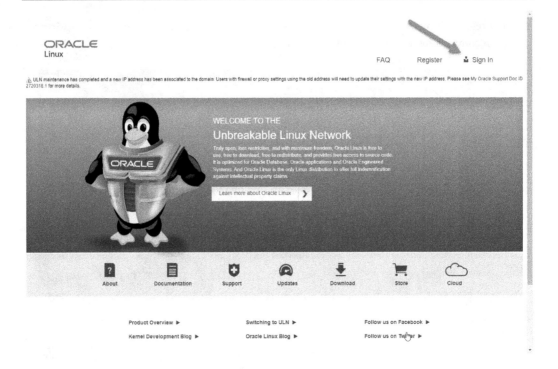

Figure 5.18 – ULN main page

When managing the server, use the same login used to register the server.

11. Once you are logged in to ULN, you will see all the servers registered to your account. You will also see what channels have been recently updated and added to the system:

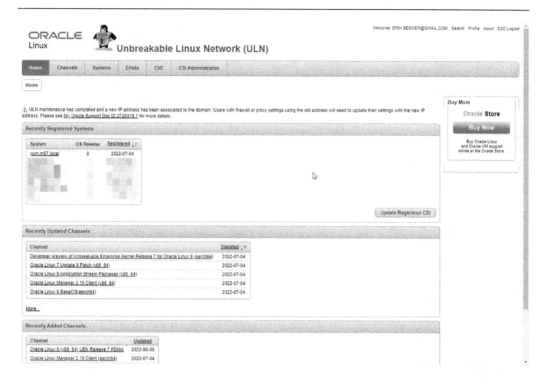

Figure 5.19 – Managed servers

12. From here, we need to promote a server to be a YUM repo. This will tell ULN to allow this server to have any channel assigned to it, allowing it to download RPMs not required by the specific servers. This includes patches for different major versions of Oracle Linux, different CPU architectures such as AArch64, and special patches for platforms such as Exadata. To do this, click on the server name, and then the **Edit** button:

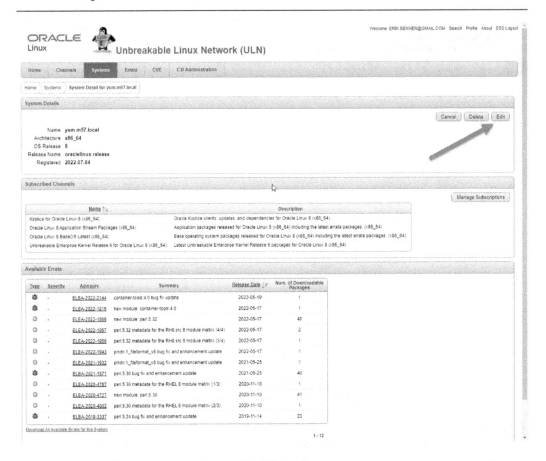

Figure 5.20 – Editing the server

13. On this page, we will update the server properties to make it a YUM server. Select the **Yum Server** checkbox and then click **Apply Changes**:

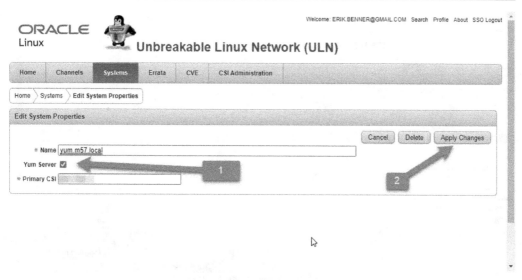

Figure 5.21 – Making it a repo

14. Next, we need to assign additional channels to the server. This will allow the server to serve up any channel it is subscribed to. To manage the RPM channels that contain a grouping of related RPMs, click the **Manage Subscriptions** button:

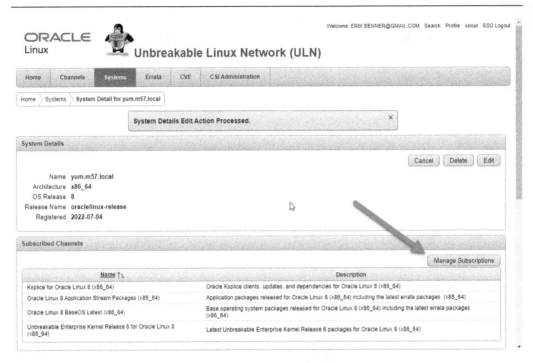

Figure 5.22 – Manage Subscriptions

15. Next, you will see all the available channels on the left and the channels assigned to the server on the right. While you can bulk-select all channels, it is better to only select the channels you need. In this example, **Oracle Linux 8 Addons x86_64** is being added. You can also add channels for a different major release number, such as Oracle Linux 7. When selecting a channel, make sure to select the < or > symbol to subscribe to or unsubscribe from the local server. This is seen in step 2 in the following figure. Also, once you are done with the selection, you must click on the **Save Subscriptions** option to update the subscription. Exiting without saving the subscription will cause any changes made to be lost.

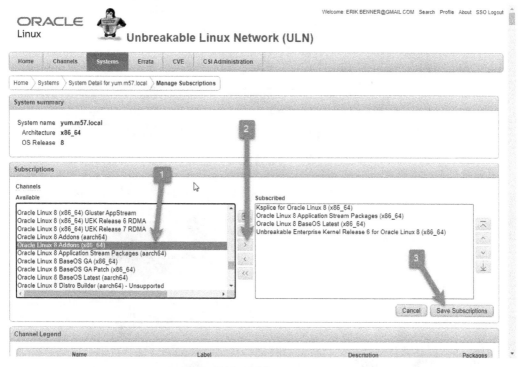

Figure 5.23 – Adding more repos

> **Note**
> When adding channels, only add what you need to conserve space and bandwidth. You can easily download a few terabytes if not careful. Also, the archived channels can be very large and are normally not needed for most sites, as they contain older releases. Expect multiple terabytes of disk space if you start using these channels locally.

16.  Make sure you see the **Subscriptions saved** message:

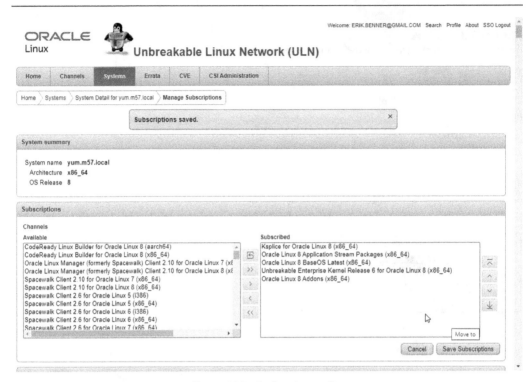

Figure 5.24 – Saving the config

Now, we finally have that local repo set. Next up is to run the `uln-yum-mirror` command as root, and the repo will start to sync. This process can take several hours, depending on your internet speed and how many channels you are subscribed to. The system will also run daily automatically, keeping your local copy current.

> **Note**
>
> When doing your first sync, watch your disk space closely. You may need to add more space quickly the first time. If this happens, add the space, and manually restart the `uln-yum-mirror` command.

When you finish a manual run, the script will let you know how much data was copied for each repo:

```
Directories           : 28
Regular files         : 50844
Comparisons           : 498
Hardlinked this run   : 497
Total hardlinks       : 497
Bytes saved this run  : 4388388721 (4.087 gibibytes)
Total bytes saved     : 4388388721 (4.087 gibibytes)
Total run time        : 28.1349639893 seconds
## 20220705132222 END HARDLINK PROCESSING ##                 I
[root@yum ~]#
```

Figure 5.25 – Completed mirror

Once configured, the system will automatically synchronize your local repository with ULN. As you add new channels, they will automatically be downloaded when the cron job runs.

# Creating a new RPM package

While Oracle provides a large number of RPMs, sometimes you just need to create a custom RPM package that allows you to easily deploy your own software. Creating an RPM file is easy to do!

## Getting ready

To do this, you will need a development system, running Oracle Linux 8, with access to the **Extra Packages for Enterprise Linux** (**EPEL**) channel. It is highly recommended to have a dedicated system to build RPMs on, and to not build RPMs on production systems. You will also need a system to test installing the RPM on.

> **Note**
>
> Depending on the package being built, you may need additional channels, such as CodeReady or Distro Builder.

There are a few things we need to do first – mainly, installing the RPM developer tools. In order to do this, we also need to add the EPEL repo to the system.

While most of the recipes in this book use the root user for most of the work, this recipe will only use root for the installation of the software. Perform the next few steps as root.

To add the EPEL repo, run the following command:

```
dnf install oracle-epel-release-el8
```

Next, run the following commands to enable EPEL and the `codeready` and `distro_builder` repos. Having all of these on your build system will make it easier down the road to take advantage of more advanced build tools such as Mock:

```
dnf config-manager --enable ol8_developer_EPEL
dnf config-manager --enable ol8_codeready_builder
dnf config-manager --enable ol8_distro_builder
```

Next, we will install the basic utilities to build `rpm` files. Run the following command to install these:

```
dnf install -y rpm-build yum-utils rpmdevtools
```

If you are pulling software from Git, you may need to install `git` and `git-lfs` (**Git Large File Storage**) software. The `gcc`, `make` and `python3-service-identity` RPMs are also common. You can install all of these with the following command:

```
dnf install -y git git-lfs make gcc python3-service-identity
```

## How to do it...

Now that we have all the tools installed, switch to your non-root user:

1.  Make a directory for the RPM. Here, we will have a source file for the software, plus all of the files and directories required to make it an RPM. In my case, I am putting everything in `/home/erik/`.

2.  Next, we need to make the RPM directory tree. This is done by running the `rpmdev-setuptree` command. Once you run the command, the tree is created in your `$HOME` under `rpmbuild`:

```
[erik@ol8 rpmbuild]$ pwd
/home/erik/rpmbuild
[erik@ol8 rpmbuild]$ ls
BUILD  RPMS  SOURCES  SPECS  SRPMS
[erik@ol8 rpmbuild]$ █
```

Figure 5.26 – The rpmbuild directories

Five directories are also built, each with a specific purpose:

*   `BUILD`: This is where binaries are saved after being compiled.

*   `RPMS`: RPMs are created here, with `rpm` files ready for use. There will be subdirectories for different CPU architectures.

*   `SOURCES`: This is where the source code is put, usually a tar file.

- SPECS: This is where the .spec files live.

- SRPMS: Source RPMs are built here – usually, packages containing the source code for the software.

3. Create a simple Bash shell script to distribute as an RPM. This will live in the xyzzy directory in the rpmbuild directory. A simple Bash script is also created:

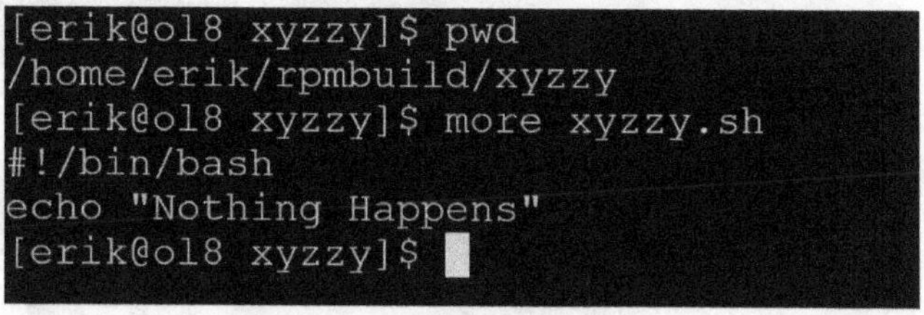

```
[erik@ol8 xyzzy]$ pwd
/home/erik/rpmbuild/xyzzy
[erik@ol8 xyzzy]$ more xyzzy.sh
#!/bin/bash
echo "Nothing Happens"
[erik@ol8 xyzzy]$
```

Figure 5.27 – The xyzzy.sh script

4. Next, create a compressed tar file with the contents of the xyzzy directory:

```
[erik@ol8 rpmbuild]$ tar -cvf SOURCES/xyzzy-1.0.tar.gz xyzzy
xyzzy/
xyzzy/xyzzy.sh
```

5. Now that we have our simple shell script, we need to create the .spec file. The .spec file contains the name of the program, a description of the program, licensing information, project URL, build architecture, and more. The following command will create a default .spec file in the SPECS directory:

```
rpmdev-newspec SPECS/xyzzy.spec
```

The skeleton is very sparse and will need information added.

The sample skeleton is seen as follows:

```
Name:            xyzzy
Version:
Release:         1%{?dist}
Summary:

License:
URL:
Source0:

BuildRequires:
Requires:

%description


            I

%prep
%autosetup


%build
%configure
%make_build


%install
rm -rf $RPM_BUILD_ROOT
%make_install


%files
%license add-license-file-here
%doc add-docs-here



%changelog
* Sun Jul 10 2022 Erik Benner
_
```

Figure 5.28 – Basic .spec file

Much has to be done to make this functional.

The Version and Summary sections need to be filled in, as well as the License details and a URL for the project. Additionally, set the build architecture to noarch, as this will install on both ARM and X64 systems. It is important to make sure that you include the **Name, Epoch, Version, Release, and Architecture (NEVRA)** information. This is used to help make sure the correct RPMs are installed on the system.

A description is set, and the %install section is updated to reflect the script being installed in the normal binary directory.

The %files section shows that /usr/bin/xyzzy.sh because all .sh files are added to the installer. Unused sections are also removed.

The final result is as follows:

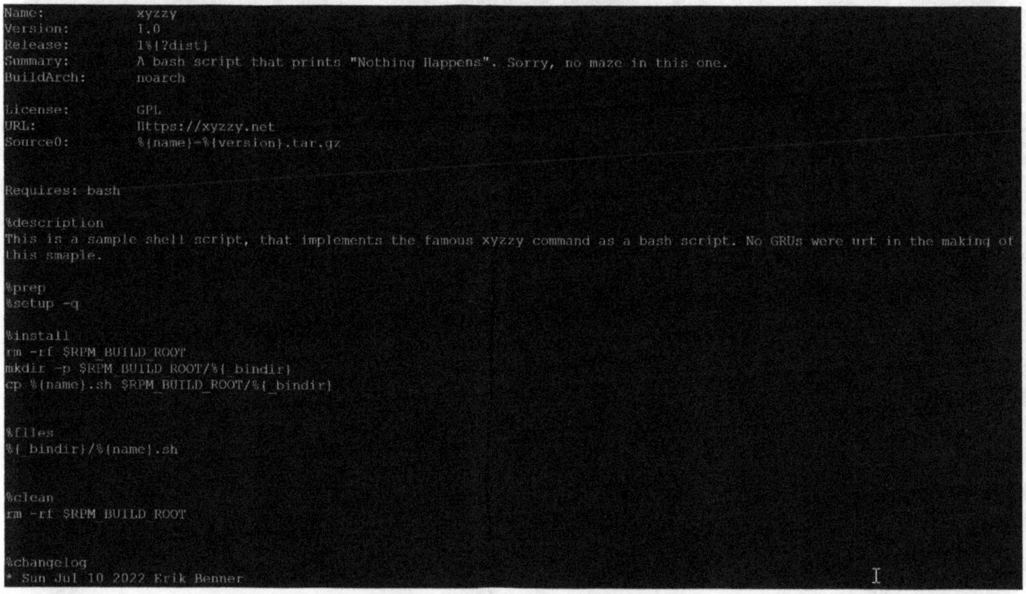

```
Name:           xyzzy
Version:        1.0
Release:        1%{?dist}
Summary:        A bash script that prints "Nothing Happens". Sorry, no maze in this one.
BuildArch:      noarch

License:        GPL
URL:            Https://xyzzy.net
Source0:        %{name}-%{version}.tar.gz


Requires: bash

%description
This is a sample shell script, that implements the famous xyzzy command as a bash script. No GRUs were urt in the making of
this smaple.

%prep
%setup -q

%install
rm -rf $RPM_BUILD_ROOT
mkdir -p $RPM_BUILD_ROOT/%{_bindir}
cp %{name}.sh $RPM_BUILD_ROOT/%{_bindir}


%files
%{_bindir}/%{name}.sh


%clean
rm -rf $RPM_BUILD_ROOT

%changelog
* Sun Jul 10 2022 Erik Benner
```

Figure 5.29 – Finished .spec file

6.  The rpm file will be built using the rpmbuild command, passing it the location of the .spec file. The rpmbuild -bb -v SPECS/xyzzy.spec command is used, with the following output:

```
[erik@ol8 rpmbuild]$ rpmbuild -bb -v SPECS/xyzzy.spec
Executing(%prep): /bin/sh -e /var/tmp/rpm-tmp.jrjHmN
+ umask 022
+ cd /home/erik/rpmbuild/BUILD
+ cd /home/erik/rpmbuild/BUILD
+ rm -rf xyzzy-1.0
+ /usr/bin/tar -xof /home/erik/rpmbuild/SOURCES/xyzzy-1.0.tar.gz
+ cd xyzzy-1.0
+ /usr/bin/chmod -Rf a+rX,u+w,g-w,o-w .
+ exit 0
Executing(%install): /bin/sh -e /var/tmp/rpm-tmp.8anyRn
+ umask 022
+ cd /home/erik/rpmbuild/BUILD
+ '[' /home/erik/rpmbuild/BUILDROOT/xyzzy-1.0-1.el8.x86_64 '!=' / ']'
+ rm -rf /home/erik/rpmbuild/BUILDROOT/xyzzy-1.0-1.el8.x86_64
++ dirname /home/erik/rpmbuild/BUILDROOT/xyzzy-1.0-1.el8.x86_64
+ mkdir -p /home/erik/rpmbuild/BUILDROOT
+ mkdir /home/erik/rpmbuild/BUILDROOT/xyzzy-1.0-1.el8.x86_64
+ cd xyzzy-1.0
+ rm -rf /home/erik/rpmbuild/BUILDROOT/xyzzy-1.0-1.el8.x86_64
+ mkdir -p /home/erik/rpmbuild/BUILDROOT/xyzzy-1.0-1.el8.x86_64//usr/bin
+ cp xyzzy.sh /home/erik/rpmbuild/BUILDROOT/xyzzy-1.0-1.el8.x86_64//usr/bin
+ '[' noarch = noarch ']'
+ case "${QA_CHECK_RPATHS:-}" in
+ /usr/lib/rpm/check-buildroot
+ /usr/lib/rpm/redhat/brp-ldconfig
/sbin/ldconfig: Warning: ignoring configuration file that cannot be opened: /etc/ld.so.conf: No such file or directory
+ /usr/lib/rpm/brp-compress
+ /usr/lib/rpm/brp-strip /usr/bin/strip
+ /usr/lib/rpm/brp-strip-comment-note /usr/bin/strip /usr/bin/objdump
+ /usr/lib/rpm/brp-strip-static-archive /usr/bin/strip
+ /usr/lib/rpm/brp-python-bytecompile '' 1
+ /usr/lib/rpm/brp-python-hardlink
+ PYTHON3=/usr/libexec/platform-python
+ /usr/lib/rpm/redhat/brp-mangle-shebangs
Processing files: xyzzy-1.0-1.el8.noarch
Provides: xyzzy = 1.0-1.el8
Requires(rpmlib): rpmlib(CompressedFileNames) <= 3.0.4-1 rpmlib(FileDigests) <= 4.6.0-1 rpmlib(PayloadFilesHavePrefix) <= 4.
0-1
Requires: /bin/bash
Checking for unpackaged file(s): /usr/lib/rpm/check-files /home/erik/rpmbuild/BUILDROOT/xyzzy-1.0-1.el8.x86_64
Wrote: /home/erik/rpmbuild/RPMS/noarch/xyzzy-1.0-1.el8.noarch.rpm
Executing(%clean): /bin/sh -e /var/tmp/rpm-tmp.ZcFokz
+ umask 022
+ cd /home/erik/rpmbuild/BUILD
+ cd xyzzy-1.0
+ rm -rf /home/erik/rpmbuild/BUILDROOT/xyzzy-1.0-1.el8.x86_64
+ exit 0
[erik@ol8 rpmbuild]$
```

Figure 5.30 – The output of rpmbuild

7.  The RPM file is now in the RPMS directory, under the noarch directory:

```
[erik@ol8 rpmbuild]$ ls -lart RPMS/noarch/
total 8
drwxrwxr-x. 3 erik erik   20 Jul 10 18:00 ..
drwxr-xr-x. 2 erik erik   40 Jul 10 18:00 .
-rw-rw-r--. 1 erik erik 6856 Jul 10 18:04 xyzzy-1.0-1.el8.noarch.rpm
[erik@ol8 rpmbuild]$
```

Figure 5.31 – The RPM file

This RPM file can now be copied over to systems to be manually installed, or it can be added to a YUM repo.

8.  Once installed, you can use the rpm -qi xyzzy-1.0 command to see the details from the .spec file for license, description, and so on:

```
[root@ol8 ~]# rpm -qi xyzzy-1.0
Name         : xyzzy
Version      : 1.0
Release      : 1.el8
Architecture: noarch
Install Date: Sun 10 Jul 2022 06:04:01 PM EDT
Group        : Unspecified
Size         : 35
License      : GPL
Signature    : (none)
Source RPM   : xyzzy-1.0-1.el8.src.rpm
Build Date   : Sun 10 Jul 2022 06:00:32 PM EDT
Build Host   : ol8.m57.local
Relocations  : (not relocatable)
URL          : Https://xyzzy.net
Summary      : A bash script that prints "Nothing Happens". Sorry, no maze in
 this one.
Description :
This is a sample shell script, that implements the famous xyzzy command as a
 bash script. No GRUs were urt in the making of this smaple.
[root@ol8 ~]#
```

Figure 5.32 – RPM file details

The RPM tool allows you to easily build custom RPM files for distribution. This is driven by the
.spec file, which contains all the dependencies, descriptions, file locations, and even build info to
create the RPM file.

6

# Eliminating All the SPOFs!
# An Exercise in Redundancy

It's crucial to have redundancy in your architecture to ensure smooth operations. Eliminating **Single Points of Failure (SPOFs)** is a common way to achieve this. Implementing **High-Availability (HA)** technology is one way to eliminate SPOFs. HA technology is crucial because it helps businesses maintain operational continuity, enhance performance, improve reliability, facilitate **Disaster Recovery (DR)**, build customer trust, and comply with regulations. With HA technology, minimizing downtime and ensuring continuous service availability is possible, contributing to overall success and competitiveness in today's technology-driven world.

> **Note**
>
> What about DR? We are not covering the failure of data centers in this chapter. That being said, the approach to implementing DR is very different than HA. When running in the cloud, look for services such as Oracle Full Stack Disaster Recovery Service that automate the DR process for the entire tech stack.

The recipes in this chapter will help you eliminate SPOFs in your environment. We'll start with a general overview of what HA is, as well as availability, and then get into several examples of how you can add redundancy to your application. The four most common technologies that are used to help eliminated SPOFs in applications are HAProxy, Corosync, Pacemaker, and GlusterFS. Each of these provides a specific set of features to help make an application highly available:

- **HAProxy**: This is a load balancer, and allows you to balance web workloads between servers
- **Corosync**: This is a communication system that enables communication to help implement HA within applications
- **Pacemaker**: Pacemaker is an open source resource manager that is used to build small and large clusters
- **GlusterFS**: This is a scalable network filesystem that allows multiple nodes to read and write data to the same storage at the same time

The following recipes will help you implement these common HA technologies. This includes everything from load-balancing applications and clustering application systems to clustered storage and redundant networking:

- Getting 99.999% availability and beyond

- Load balancing a website

- Making HAProxy highly available with Keepalived

- HA clustering for all with Corosync and Pacemaker

- Sharing a filesystem across multiple machines – cluster or distribute?

- Generating, configuring, and monitoring Ethernet traffic over bond

## Technical requirements

For most of these recipes, you will need a pair of Oracle Linux 8 systems. As with most of these recipes, a VM on your desktop using a desktop virtualization product such as Oracle VirtualBox is recommended. A small VM is fine, with two cores, 2 GB RAM, and a few free gigabytes of disk space. You will also need some additional disks assigned to the VM, ideally at least five equally sized disks. Before you start, patch your system to the latest packages available. This only takes a few minutes and can save a ton of time when troubleshooting issues that are caused by a bug.

Many of the recipes in this book have their related configuration files available on GitHub at `https://github.com/PacktPublishing/Oracle-Linux-Cookbook`.

## Getting 99.999% availability and beyond

This recipe will discuss the differences between DR and HA and how to architect HA solutions. Before we get into that, let's refine the definition of a few key terms:

- **High availability**, or **HA**: This means protecting from the failure of a single component. Think of this as protecting against the failure of a system.

- **Disaster recovery**, or **DR**: This is the failure of the data center or cloud region.

- **Availability nines**: When referring to *nines of availability*, it is a way to quantify the uptime or reliability of a system by specifying the number of nines in the uptime percentage. Each *nine* represents a decimal place in the uptime percentage.

Here's a breakdown of the most commonly used *nines* and their corresponding uptime percentages, assuming 24x7x365 operations:

| Nines | Downtime per Year | Downtime per Month |
|---|---|---|
| 99 | 3d 14h 56m 18s | 7h 14m 41s |
| 99.9 | 8h 41m 38s | 43m 28s |
| 99.99 | 52m 10s | 4m 21s |
| 99.999 | 5m 13s | 26s |
| 99.9999 | 31s | 2.6s |

Table 6.1 – Nines downtime

In the preceding table, each additional nine in the uptime percentage signifies a higher level of availability and a reduced tolerance for downtime. Achieving higher numbers of nines typically requires implementing redundant systems, failover mechanisms, and rigorous maintenance practices to minimize downtime and ensure continuous operation. In addition, when setting up a **Service-Level Agreement** (**SLA**), you can also define the uptime during business hours and exclude scheduled maintenance. As an example, using a working schedule of Monday through Friday with 12 working hours a day, and 10 holidays off per year, the matrix would look very different!

| Nines | Downtime per Year | Downtime per Month |
|---|---|---|
| 99 | 1d 7h 2m 58s | 2h 35m 14s |
| 99.9 | 3h 6m 18s | 15m 31s |
| 99.99 | 18m 38s | 1m 33s |
| 99.999 | 1m 52s | 9s |
| 99.9999 | 11s | 1s |

Table 6.2 – Business hours downtime

> **Note**
>
> When setting SLAs with the business, carefully understand the differences between including maintenance windows and operational hours within the SLA.

## Getting ready

When designing HA systems, there are several considerations that need to be taken into account to ensure the system is resilient and can handle failures. Here are some key considerations:

- **Redundancy**: Having redundancy in HA systems is essential. It requires replicating components or whole systems to eliminate potential SPOFs. Redundancy can be implemented at different levels, such as hardware, software, and network infrastructure. To minimize the impact of localized failures, it's crucial to distribute redundant components across different physical locations.

- **Failover and load balancing**: It is important for HA systems to be equipped with failover mechanisms that enable automatic switching to a backup system whenever a failure occurs. One way to achieve this is through replicating data and services across multiple servers, coupled with the use of load-balancing techniques that ensure the even distribution of workload. With load balancing, traffic can be easily redirected to available servers in the event of a server failure.

- **Scalability**: When designing HA systems, it is important to ensure that they can handle increased workloads and scale effortlessly. This can be achieved through horizontal scaling, which entails adding more servers to distribute the load, or vertical scaling, which involves adding resources to existing servers. Additionally, the system should be capable of dynamically adjusting resource allocation based on demand to prevent overloading.

- **Data replication and backup**: Maintaining data integrity and availability is crucial for HA systems. To ensure that data can still be accessed in case of a system failure, it is essential to replicate data across multiple storage systems or databases. Additionally, performing regular backups is vital to safeguard against potential data loss or corruption.

- **Fault tolerance**: Systems used for highly available architectures should have fault tolerance, which means they must be able to function even if specific components or subsystems malfunction. Achieving this requires creating a system that can manage errors with ease, recover automatically, and ensure continuity of service.

- **Disaster recovery**: Having a DR plan is crucial for HA systems to effectively deal with catastrophic events such as natural disasters or widespread outages. This plan entails generating off-site backups, setting up secondary data centers, and relying on cloud-based services to guarantee business continuity, even amid extreme situations.

- **Documentation and testing**: It is crucial to document the system architecture, configurations, and procedures to effectively troubleshoot and maintain the HA system. Regular testing, such as failover tests, load testing, and DR drills, plays a significant role in identifying potential issues and ensuring the system operates as intended in various scenarios.

- **Cost and complexity**: Designing, implementing, and maintaining HA systems can be both complex and costly. It is important to carefully consider the available budget, as well as the expertise and resources required to effectively manage and monitor the system.

By addressing these considerations, you can design a robust and resilient HA system that ensures HA, fault tolerance, and continuity of critical services.

## How to do it...

As a rule, you should pick the right technology for the right subsystem and application.

When aiming to achieve HA for a web application, the first step is to place a load balancer in front of the web servers. This enables scaling of the application while also offering some fault tolerance for these systems. However, attention should also be given to the data tier, which can be addressed by clustering the database or building a cluster capable of running the database, depending on the limitations of the database technology.

If you are utilizing a technology such as Oracle Database, you have the option to establish a database-specific cluster known as **Oracle Real Application Clusters** (**Oracle RAC**). This cluster allows for both scalability and availability. With RAC, the database remains accessible for queries as long as one node is online. While other databases may utilize their own exclusive clustering technology (such as MySQL Cluster), you may opt to utilize generic cluster technologies such as Pacemaker for cluster management and Corosync for inter-cluster communications. This approach presents the advantage of enabling almost any technology to be made highly available in a Linux environment.

You can achieve HA in storage by implementing filesystems across the entire cluster. Gluster allows you to mount a filesystem across multiple servers, while at the same time replicating the storage across servers. This provides both scalability and reliability at the filesystem level.

Finally, the network is a common point of failure, and using network bonding technologies can enable both HA as well as some scaling abilities. This works by combining at least two network ports into a single virtual port.

> **Note**
> The best HA architectures mix these approaches to cover the entire technology stack.

## Load balancing a website

Nowadays, most applications are web-based, whether it's a traditional web interface or a RESTful API. This first tier is typically set up for HA using a load balancer. A load balancer is a system that distributes incoming network traffic or workload across multiple servers or resources. Its main goal is to optimize resource utilization, improve performance, and ensure the reliability and availability of applications or services. When multiple servers are involved in serving a particular application or service, a load balancer acts as an intermediary between the client and the server pool. It receives incoming requests from clients and intelligently distributes them across the available servers based on various algorithms, such as round-robin, least connections, or weighted distribution.

The load balancer is responsible for ensuring the servers' optimal health and performance by redirecting traffic from overloaded or problematic servers. This distribution of workloads helps to prevent any one server from getting overwhelmed, thus enhancing response time and overall system capacity and scalability.

> **Note**
>
> While a load balancer can help distribute the workloads, the actual server load is based on other factors, so do not expect all servers to have the same utilization of CPU, RAM, networking, and so on.

Load balancers not only distribute traffic but also offer advanced features, such as SSL termination, session persistence, caching, and content routing. They are extensively used in web applications, cloud-based services, and other environments that demand HA and scalability.

One of the most popular load balancers is HAProxy.

HAProxy is a great open source load-balancer option. Standing for **High Availability Proxy**, **HAProxy** is widely used due to its excellent performance and ability to improve the availability and scalability of applications. Operating at the application layer (Layer 7) of the OSI model, this software is able to make routing decisions based on specific application-level information, such as HTTP headers and cookies. Compared to traditional network-level (Layer 4) load balancers, HAProxy allows for more advanced load-balancing and traffic-routing capabilities.

Some key features and capabilities of HAProxy include the following:

- **Load balancing**: With HAProxy, incoming traffic can be evenly distributed across multiple servers using various algorithms, such as round-robin, least connections, and source IP, among others.

- **High availability**: One of the beneficial features of HAProxy is its ability to support active-passive failover setups. In the event the active server becomes unavailable, a standby server will take over. Additionally, it also has the capability to monitor the health of servers and make automatic adjustments to the load-balancing pool by adding or removing servers.

- **Proxying**: One of HAProxy's primary functions is to act as a reverse proxy, which involves receiving client requests and directing them to the correct backend servers. Additionally, it can function as a forward proxy by intercepting client requests and directing them to external servers.

- **SSL/TLS termination**: With HAProxy, SSL/TLS encryption and decryption can be efficiently managed, taking the load off of the backend servers.

- **Session persistence**: HAProxy is capable of preserving session affinity by routing follow-up requests from a client to the same backend server, thus guaranteeing the proper operation of session-based applications.

- **Health checks and monitoring**: To guarantee the availability and optimal performance of backend servers, HAProxy conducts routine health checks. It has the ability to identify failed servers and promptly exclude them from the load-balancing pool.

- **Logging and statistics**: With HAProxy, administrators can effectively monitor and analyze traffic patterns, performance metrics, and error conditions. Its detailed logging and statistics feature makes this possible.

HAProxy can be deployed on various operating systems and is often used in high-traffic web environments, cloud infrastructure, and containerized deployments. Its versatility and extensive feature set make it a powerful tool for managing and optimizing application traffic and open source-based load balancers.

For this recipe, we will put HAProxy on one system (as the load balancer) and then two identical web servers to balance traffic to:

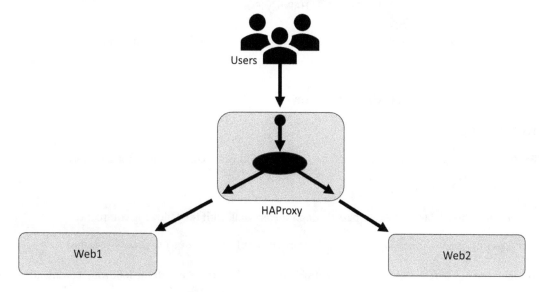

Figure 6.1 – HAProxy example diagram

## Getting ready

To get started, we first need three servers. For this exercise, we will call them lb1, web1, and web2. They are identical systems, each with 8 GB RAM, 4 vCPUs, and 100 GB of drive space. The filesystems have 50 GB in /, 5 GB in /home, and 8 GB in swap. The remaining disk space is unallocated. You will also need the IP address for each host. In this example, the following IP addresses were used:

| Host | IP |
| --- | --- |
| Web1 | 192.168.56.200 |
| Web2 | 192.168.56.201 |
| Lb1 | 192.168.56.202 |

Table 6.3 – HAProxy IP addresses

Once the server is built, patch it to the current software with the following command:

```
dnf update -y
```

Once the software is patched, reboot the systems.

### Web servers

For both web servers, we will install Apache, using the following commands as the root user:

```
dnf install httpd -y
```

We next need to enable port 80 to pass through the firewall, with the following command:

```
firewall-cmd --permanent --add-service=http; firewall-cmd --reload
```

We then need to start the server and make it start on boot. This is done with the following command:

```
systemctl enable --now httpd
```

We now need to put in a basic home page for this server.

> **Note**
>
> Depending on your environment, you may need to edit the Apache config file in /etc/httpd/conf/httpd.conf to specify your servername. In the config file, it will be a single entry on a single line, like the following:
>
> `ServerName server.m57.local:80`

This needs to go into `/var/www/html/index.html`. The following is an example file. Adjust the text as needed so each server is unique. This way, you can see what server is being hit:

```
<!DOCTYPE html>
<html>
<body>
<h1> Running on web1</h1>
</body>
</html>
```

Next, point your browser to the system to test it:

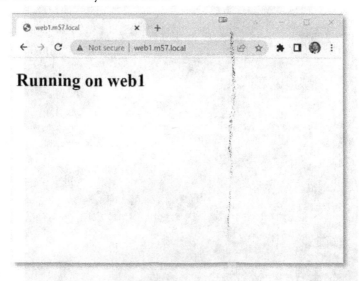

Figure 6.2 – Simple website

Next, repeat the process on the other web server. Once that system is up, we will set up the load balancer.

> **Note**
> If you are using `httpd` (TLS/SSL) on your server, don't forget to enable `https` in your local firewalls as well.

## Load balancer

For the single load-balancer system, we will need to install HAProxy. This is done using the `dnf` command as root:

```
dnf install -y haproxy
```

We next need to open up port 80 in the firewall with the following command:

```
firewall-cmd --permanent --add-service=http; firewall-cmd --reload
```

Next, we will need to edit the config file. The config file is located in /etc/haproxy/haproxy.cfg.

The config file has two main sections, global and defaults. There can only be a single global section in the config file. This is where TLS/SSL config data, the logging configuration, and the user and group settings go for the user running haproxy. By default, haproxy runs as the user haproxy with the group haproxy. For most use cases, the global section should not need to be changed. An example is seen in the following figure:

```
#---------------------------------------------------------------------
# Global settings
#---------------------------------------------------------------------
global
    # to have these messages end up in /var/log/haproxy.log you will
    # need to:
    #
    # 1) configure syslog to accept network log events.  This is done
    #    by adding the '-r' option to the SYSLOGD_OPTIONS in
    #    /etc/sysconfig/syslog
    #
    # 2) configure local2 events to go to the /var/log/haproxy.log
    #    file. A line like the following can be added to
    #    /etc/sysconfig/syslog
    #
    #    local2.*                       /var/log/haproxy.log
    #
    log         127.0.0.1 local2

    chroot      /var/lib/haproxy
    pidfile     /var/run/haproxy.pid
    maxconn     4000
    user        haproxy
    group       haproxy
    daemon

    # turn on stats unix socket
    stats socket /var/lib/haproxy/stats

    # utilize system-wide crypto-policies
    ssl-default-bind-ciphers PROFILE=SYSTEM
    ssl-default-server-ciphers PROFILE=SYSTEM
```

Figure 6.3 – HAProxy global settings

The next section, called the defaults section, is where you will make most of your edits. This is built using three subsections: frontend, backend, and listen.

The frontend section listens on all IP addresses and ports that are defined. This is what users will connect to. A HAProxy server can have multiple frontend sections, though each one needs a unique name and IP/port combination.

The backend section defines the servers being load balanced to, defining the load-balancing method as well as the servers and ports where traffic is being sent to. A HAProxy server can have multiple backend sections, though each one needs a unique name.

The `listen` section is used to define how you can monitor the load balancer, with the port, URI, and authentication information needed to monitor HAProxy. Normally, you will only have one `listen` section.

For the same frontend, we will be listening on port `80` of the `lb1` system, called www_app, and will define this IP/port combination to use the www_servers backend.

### frontend

The `frontend` section of the HAProxy configuration file offers various options to manage incoming traffic behavior. These options can be used to control the traffic on a frontend. Here are some commonly used frontend options:

- `bind`: Defines the IP address and port on which the frontend will listen for incoming traffic. For example, `bind *:80` listens on all IP addresses on port `80`.

- `mode`: Specifies the mode of the frontend, such as `http`, `tcp`, or `ssl`. For HTTP traffic, use `mode http`. If you want to load balance a generic TCP port, use `mode tcp`.

- `option`: Enables or disables specific options for the frontend. Some commonly used options are as follows:

  - `option httplog`: Enables HTTP request/response logging

  - `option dontlognull`: Prevents logging of requests with missing or empty user-agent strings

  - `option forwardfor`: Adds the client's IP address to the HTTP request headers when using HTTP proxy mode

  - `option http-server-close`: Forces the server connection to close after processing a request, rather than using keep-alive

- `timeout`: Configures various timeouts for the frontend:

  - `timeout client`: Sets the maximum allowed time for the client to establish a connection and send data

  - `timeout server`: Sets the maximum allowed time for the server to respond to a request

  - `timeout connect`: Sets the maximum time to wait for a connection to the backend server

- `acl`: Defines rules for matching specific conditions. ACLs are used in conjunction with backend configurations to control traffic routing based on various criteria.

- `use_backend`: Specifies which backend to use for handling traffic that matches specific ACL conditions. It allows you to direct traffic to different backend servers based on certain conditions.

- `default_backend`: Defines the default backend to use if no ACL conditions match the incoming traffic.

- `redirect`: Performs a URL redirection for specific conditions. For example, you can use the `https://example.com` redirect location to redirect HTTP traffic to HTTPS.

- `http-request` and `http-response`: These are used to add custom HTTP request/response headers or to perform specific actions based on HTTP request/response data.

- `capture`: Captures parts of the request or response headers and saves them into variables.

For the sample frontend, we will define the frontend as www_app binding to all IPs on the load-balancer system on port 80. This looks like the following figure:

```
frontend www_app
    bind *:80
    default_backend                    www_servers
```

Figure 6.4 – Example frontend

## backend

When using HAProxy, the backend options play a crucial role in configuring the behavior of backend servers and the routing of traffic toward them. These options are specifically designated within the backend section of the HAProxy configuration file. Here are some frequently utilized backend options:

- `mode`: Specifies the mode of the backend, such as `http`, `tcp`, or `ssl`. For HTTP traffic, use `http` mode.

- `balance`: Defines the load-balancing algorithm to distribute traffic across backend servers. Common options include the following:

  - `balance roundrobin`: Requests are distributed in a round-robin fashion to each server in sequence

  - `balance leastconn`: Traffic is sent to the server with the lowest number of active connections

  - `balance source`: Based on a hash of the client's IP address, traffic is directed to a specific server consistently

- `server`: Defines the backend servers and their addresses, ports, and optional parameters.

- `timeout`: Configures various timeouts for the backend:

  - `timeout server`: Sets the maximum allowed time for the server to respond to a request

  - `timeout tunnel`: Configures the maximum time allowed to establish a tunnel (used in TCP mode)

- `http-request` and `http-response`: Similar to frontend options, these are used to add custom HTTP request/response headers or perform specific actions based on HTTP request/response data.

- `cookie`: Configures sticky session persistence using cookies. It allows the backend server to be selected based on a specific cookie value from the client.

- `check`: Enables health checks for backend servers to determine their availability. If a server fails the health check, HAProxy will stop sending traffic to it until it recovers.

- `option`: Enables or disables specific options for the backend. Some commonly used options include the following:

  - `option httpchk`: Enables HTTP health checks instead of TCP health checks

  - `option redispatch`: Allows HAProxy to reselect a server if the connection to the selected server fails

- `errorfile`: Specifies a file to use as a custom error page for backend server errors.

In the sample backend, it is defined as `www_servers` and will use `roundrobin` load balancing against the `web1` and `web2` servers:

```
backend www_servers
    balance     roundrobin
    server      web1 192.168.56.200:80 check
    server      web2 192.168.56.201:80 check
```

Figure 6.5 – HAProxy sample backend

> **Note**
> It is highly recommended to always use the `check` option for your servers. If you do not run the checks, the system will still send traffic to the server!

## listen

In HAProxy, the `listen` section is used to define a frontend and backend configuration together in one block, making it a convenient way to combine both. The `listen` section allows you to define options specific to the listening socket and how the incoming traffic is handled. The following are some commonly used options in the `listen` section:

- `bind`: Defines the IP address and port on which HAProxy will listen for incoming traffic. For example, `bind *:80` listens on all IP addresses on port `80`.

- `stats`: Enables the HAProxy statistics page for monitoring and managing HAProxy.

- `stats enable`: Enables statistics monitoring for HAProxy.

- `stats uri`: Specifies the URI path for accessing the statistics page. For example, `stats uri /haproxy_stats` sets the statistics page to be accessible at `http://your-haproxy-ip/haproxy_stats`.

- `stats realm`: Sets the realm (authentication realm) for HTTP basic authentication when accessing the statistics page. This adds a layer of security to prevent unauthorized access.

- `stats auth`: Configures the username and password for HTTP basic authentication when accessing the statistics page. The format is `stats auth username:password`.

- `stats hide-version`: Hides the HAProxy version number from the statistics page to enhance security.

- `stats show-node`: Displays the server node names on the statistics page. This is useful when using dynamic server templates.

- `stats refresh`: Sets the interval (in milliseconds) for automatic refresh of the statistics page. For example, `stats refresh 10s` refreshes the page every 10 seconds.

- `stats admin`: Specifies the IP address and port for allowing administrative access to HAProxy statistics. It allows remote management of HAProxy using the statistics page. For example, stats admin if `localhost` permits access only from the local machine.

- `stats maxconn`: Limits the number of connections allowed to the statistics page. It helps to prevent overload and potential denial-of-service attacks.

- `errorfile`: Specifies a file to use as a custom error page for frontend errors.

For the sample `listen` section, we will define it as metrics, allowing admin access from `192.168.56.1`. The user will use the username as `admin` and the password `passw0rd` to log in. This is seen in the following figure:

```
listen metrics
        mode http
        bind *:8080
        stats enable
        stats uri /stats
        stats auth admin:passw0rd
```

Figure 6.6 – HAProxy listen sample

Since the status page is running on port `8080`, don't forget to add the port to the firewall and reload the firewall. This can be done with the following command;

```
firewall-cmd --permanent --add-port=8080/tcp; firewall-cmd --reload
```

## How it works...

Now that we have our two web servers, and the load balancer configured, we need to start the load balancer. This is done using `systemctl`:

- Use the following to start HAProxy:

  ```
  systemctl start haproxy
  ```

- Use the following to check the status:

  ```
  systemctl status haproxy
  ```

- If you edit the config file, do not forget to reload HAProxy with the following command:

  ```
  systemctl reload haproxy
  ```

Now, point your browser to the load balancer IP. You will get the web server page. This is seen in the following figure:

# Running on web2

Figure 6.7 – Working HAProxy

Since the rule is `roundrobin`, and we configured the timeout at one minute, wait a minute and then reload the page. You will see a new server.

# Running on web1

Figure 6.8 – Working load balancing

As an admin, you will also want to check on the health of your resources. Point your browser to the stats URL, and enter the username and password configured. This will show the stats page. In the case of this example, the URL is `http://lb1.m57.local:8080/stats`. You will see a sample in the following figure:

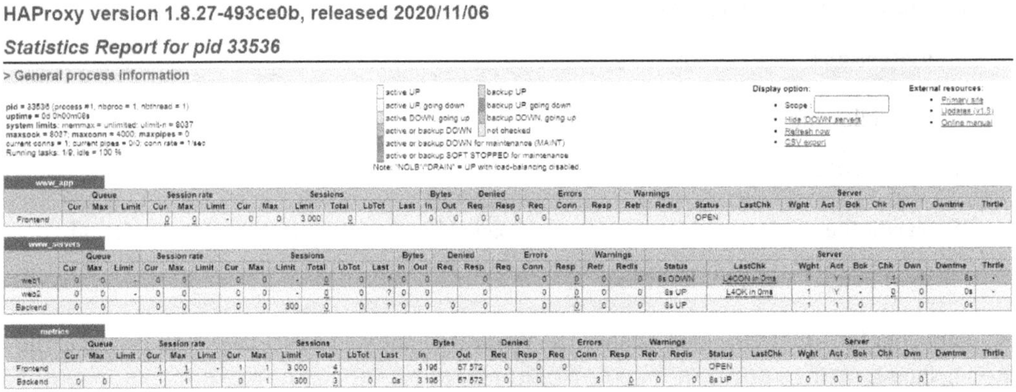

Figure 6.9 – HAProxy status page

On the sample page, you will see that `web1` is offline. You can also see how much traffic each frontend and backend rule has processed, and to what servers.

## Making HAProxy highly available with Keepalived

In the previous recipe, we used HAProxy to give our web servers some redundancy. The challenge with that solution is we now have a failure point in the load balancer itself. When architecting for HA, you need to cover all points of failure to make sure there is redundancy and that there is no SPOF. In this recipe, we will use Keepalived to add some HA to our configuration. Keepalived is a software application that is open source and designed for Linux-based systems. Its main function is to manage network load balancing and failover, ensuring the HA of web services. Keepalived is often used alongside HAProxy. The software primarily uses the **Virtual Router Redundancy Protocol** (**VRRP**) to achieve fault tolerance and evenly distribute the load. Keepalived uses the following features to provide its redundancy:

- **High availability**: With Keepalived, you can establish a cluster of backup servers that utilize a shared **Virtual IP** (**VIP**) address. This setup ensures that even if the primary server experiences a failure, a secondary server will automatically take over and handle incoming traffic, resulting in minimal downtime.

- **VRRP**: VRRP is a commonly used protocol that enables automatic router failover in IP networks. Keepalived utilizes VRRP to keep a VIP address operational, which can be assigned to any node within the cluster as needed.

- **Health checking**: The monitoring system of Keepalived regularly checks the health of active servers. If a server becomes unresponsive, Keepalived will remove it from the pool and redirect traffic to the healthy servers.

- **Notification mechanisms**: With Keepalived, it's possible to set up notifications for failover events or when certain thresholds are exceeded. These notifications are useful for keeping an eye on the overall health of the cluster.

In a cluster, Keepalived designates one node as the master and the others as backups. The master node handles incoming traffic and responds to ARP requests for the VIP address, while the backups act as standby routers and monitor the master's status. The nodes communicate using the VRRP protocol, with the master periodically sending VRRP advertisements to show its functioning. Often, a VIP is used to allow a single IP address for end user access. This normal operation is seen in the following figure, where we have Keepalived managing two HAProxy systems.

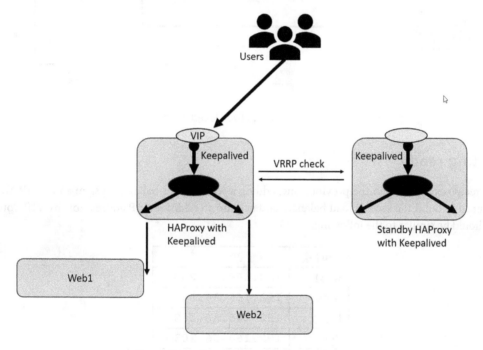

Figure 6.10 – Keepalived normal operations

If the backups stop receiving advertisements or detect any issues with the master, one backup node will take over as the new master. Keepalived checks the servers' health using mechanisms such as ICMP (ping) checks or Layer 4 checks (e.g., checking whether a specific port is open) and removes failed servers from the pool. The VRRP priority is adjusted to ensure a healthy backup server takes over. This is seen in the following figure, where the VIP that users connect to has migrated over to the second node, and that node is now using HAProxy to manage the workload.

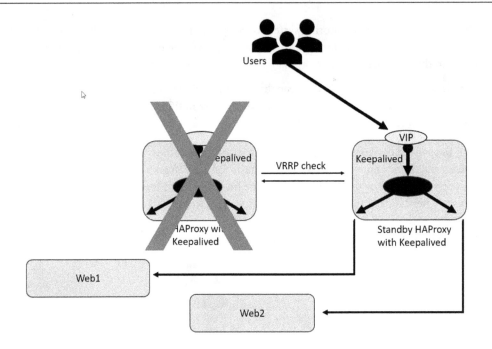

Figure 6.11 – Keepalived failed node

## Getting ready

This recipe expands upon the previous one, adding a second load-balancer system and a VIP. You will need to build the second load balancer and acquire an additional IP address for the VIP. Your IPs should be similar to the following:

| Host | IP |
|------|-----|
| web1 | 192.168.56.200 |
| web2 | 192.168.56.201 |
| lb1 | 192.168.56.202 |
| lb2 | 192.168.56.203 |
| vip | 192.168.56.204 |

Table 6.4 – Keepalived IP addresses

## How to do it...

Before you start configuring Keepalived, you need to configure HAProxy on the second server. You can easily install HAProxy, open up the firewall ports, and copy over the config file from the existing system.

You can test this by simply pointing your browser to the second load balancer and seeing the app server.

Next, we will start to configure Keepalived.

For each load balancer, you will need to install Keepalived as the root user:

```
dnf -y install keepalived
```

Next, we will need to edit the Keepalived config file. This is found in /etc/keepalived/keepalived.conf. There are two major sections to edit, global_defs and vrpp_instance.

global_defs is the global definition used by Keepalived. These settings are used by all vrrp_instance types configured in the system.

There are several parameters that you will need to update:

- notification_email: This is a list of email addresses that will be emailed when there is an event
- notification_email_from_user: This is the sending email address
- smtp_server: This is the SMTP relay server
- router_id: This is a unique name for this Keepalived cluster

For the sample, this section looks like the following:

```
global_defs {
    notification_email {
     admins@company.com
     appteam@company.com
    }
    notification_email_from user@company.com
    smtp_server smtp.company.com
    smtp_connect_timeout 30
    router_id ORACLE_LINUX8
    vrrp_skip_check_adv_addr
    vrrp_strict
    vrrp_garp_interval 0
    vrrp_gna_interval 0
}
```

Figure 6.12 – Keepalived globals

The next section is vrrp_instance. You can have multiple vrrp_instance types in the cluster, each supporting different VIPs.

For `vrrp_instance`, you need to give each one a unique name. Additionally, there are several parameters that will need to be updated:

- `state`: The state of the instance, usually master for the primary node and backup for the secondary node.

- `interface`: The Ethernet interface used for this host in the cluster.

- `virtual_router_id`: A unique number for this instance. No other instances should use the same ID.

- `authentication`: This section defines how members are authenticated:

  - `auth_type`: Normally sent to PASS, to allow nodes to authenticate as members of this instance. There is a second support type called **Authentication Header (AH)**, but it is not recommended for use.

  - `auth_pass`: The password for the instance.

- `virtual_ipaddress`: A list of VIPs managed by this instance.

In our example, the section will look as follows;

```
vrrp_instance VIP1 {
    state MASTER
    interface eth0
    virtual_router_id 10
    priority 100
    advert_int 1
    authentication {
        auth_type PASS
        auth_pass 1234
    }
    virtual_ipaddress {
        192.168.56.204
    }

}
```

Figure 6.13 – Keepalived vrrp_instance

Once the config file is built, copy it over to the second load balancer. Do not forget to change the state to BACKUP on the second system, and also update the interface if it is different on that system.

Next, start Keepalived on both nodes with the following command as the root user:

```
systemctl enable --now keepalived
```

You can now point your browser to the VIP! This is seen in the following example.

Figure 6.14 – Keepalived VIP in use

You can check the status by looking at the journal entries for the daemon, using the following command:

```
journalctl -u keepalived
```

This will show all the activity of the daemon. You should see `Sending gratuitous ARP` messages, as this is the system checking the health. You will also see messages about the state, such as `Entering MASTER STATE` or `Entering BACKUP STATE`, as the system switches between MASTER and BACKUP.

## HA clustering for all with Corosync and Pacemaker

In the previous recipes, we addressed HA by distributing traffic between two active application servers. However, this method is only effective for stateless applications where the server or browser doesn't contain specific user or session data. For applications that are not stateless or run on a complex server, a different approach to HA is necessary. The solution is to start and stop the application components on different servers, using the combination of Pacemaker and Corosync. These two open source software projects work together to provide HA clustering for Linux-based systems. They coordinate and manage multiple nodes in a cluster, ensuring that critical services remain available even during hardware or software failures.

Corosync serves as the communication layer for the HA cluster stack, allowing for dependable communication between nodes. It utilizes a membership and quorum system to monitor the cluster's active nodes and guarantee that only one node operates as the primary (or master) at a given time. The messaging layer is essential for sharing data regarding the cluster's state, node status, and resource conditions. Corosync plays a vital role in the cluster's functionality, providing key features such as the following:

- **Cluster communication**: Corosync enables nodes to exchange messages reliably and efficiently, allowing them to coordinate and synchronize their actions.

- **Membership and quorum**: Corosync is a tool that keeps track of active nodes in a cluster and uses a quorum algorithm to ensure that there are enough nodes available to make decisions. This helps avoid split-brain scenarios and makes sure that only one node is active. It's crucial to avoid split-brain clusters because they can cause data inconsistencies, corruption, and service disruptions. A split-brain scenario occurs when nodes in a cluster lose communication with each other. As a result, each node thinks it's the only active one in the cluster. This can happen because of network issues, communication failures, or misconfigurations.

> **Note**
>
> When there is a split-brain scenario, several nodes within the cluster may begin running services or using shared resources on their own, thinking that they are the only active node. This can cause conflicts and data inconsistencies since each node operates independently without any coordination. When possible, use an odd number of nodes in a cluster, or enable some protection using quorum.

Pacemaker is a cluster resource manager that utilizes Corosync's messaging and membership features to manage cluster resources and handle resource failover. It determines which node in the cluster should run specific services (resources) based on established policies and constraints. Pacemaker brings the following features to the cluster:

- **Resource management**: With Pacemaker, administrators can set up resources that require strong availability, such as IP addresses, services, databases, and applications

- **Resource monitoring**: Pacemaker continuously monitors the status of resources and nodes to detect failures or changes in the cluster

- **Resource failover**: If a node fails or there are resource problems, Pacemaker will begin a failover process, transferring resources to functioning nodes to guarantee uninterrupted availability

- **Resource constraints**: Administrators can set constraints and rules for resource placement and failover, defining which nodes are preferred or prohibited for specific resources

- **Colocation and order constraints**: Pacemaker allows defining relationships between resources, specifying which resources must run together on the same node or in a specific order

- **Cluster management**: Pacemaker provides various command-line utilities and graphical interfaces (such as Hawk) for managing and configuring the cluster

## Getting ready

For this recipe, you will need two VMs, each with at least two vCPUs, 8 GB of RAM, and 50 GB of disk space. You should have Oracle Linux 8 installed, and also a third IP address for a floating VIP to be managed by the cluster. Both of the web servers will be patched to the latest software. For this example, the following IPs will be used:

| Host | IP |
|------|-----|
| Web1 | 192.168.56.200 |
| Web2 | 192.168.56.201 |
| vip | 192.168.56.204 |

Table 6.5 – HA cluster IPs

Before we start with the cluster, you will also need to set up an httpd (Apache 2.4) server on each host. This is similar to other hosts set up in other recipes.

First, on both servers, as root, install the Apache web server:

```
dnf -y install httpd
```

We do need to enable the status page for Apache. This is one way the resource will be checked. To do this, copy the following lines into /etc/httpd/conf.d/status.conf:

```
<Location /server-status>
    SetHandler server-status
    Order Deny,Allow
    Deny from all
    Allow from 127.0.0.1
</Location>
```

We also need a simple web page. For testing purposes, put the following into /var/www/html/index.html on both servers.

> **Note**
>
> When setting up an application such as a web server, putting your content directory (such as /var/www/html) on a Gluster filesystem makes it easier to manage updating your content. This also works for other data that the application uses, such as temporary state data.

Next, on both servers, add port 80 to the local firewall with the following command:

```
firewall-cmd --permanent --add-service=http; firewall-cmd --reload
```

Now, for testing purposes, manually start the server on both nodes. Do not enable the service to automatically start. This will be done later when Pacemaker is configured:

```
systemctl start httpd
```

You should now see a basic page on both servers, as shown in the following screenshot:

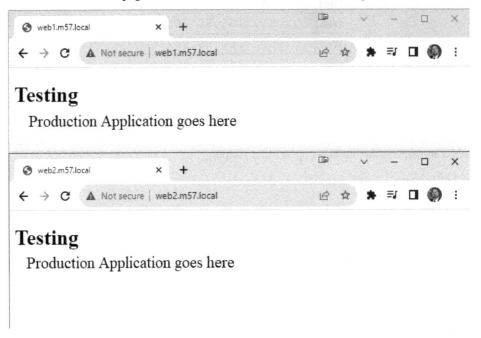

Figure 6.15 – httpd server test

You can also test the `server-status` page using the `wget` command:

```
wget localhost4/server-status
```

Sample output of a success is seen in the following screenshot.

```
[root@web1 conf.d]# wget localhost4/server-status
--2023-07-29 18:53:47--  http://localhost4/server-status
Resolving localhost4 (localhost4)... 127.0.0.1
Connecting to localhost4 (localhost4)|127.0.0.1|:80... connected.
HTTP request sent, awaiting response... 200 OK
Length: 6040 (5.9K) [text/html]
Saving to: 'server-status.1'

server-status.1           100%[===================================================================>]   5.90K  --.-KB/s    in 0s

2023-07-29 18:53:47 (677 MB/s) - 'server-status.1' saved [6040/6040]

[root@web1 conf.d]#
```

Figure 6.16 – Successful server-status

You are now ready to install and configure Pacemaker and Corosync.

# How to do it...

Now that you have installed the Apache httpd server that we will cluster, let's start by installing the software. First, we need to enable the addons repo. This is done with the following commands on both servers as root.

First, on both nodes, enable the repo with the following commands as root:

```
dnf config-manager --enable  ol8_addons
```

Then, you will install the software:

```
dnf install -y pacemaker pcs
```

Once the installation of these packages is complete, a new user named hacluster will be added to your system. Please note that remote login will be disabled for this user after installation. To carry out tasks such as synchronizing the configuration or starting services on other nodes, it is necessary to set the same password for the hacluster user on both nodes. We can use the passwd command to set the password:

```
passwd hacluster
```

Next, we need to enable the pcs service and start it:

```
systemctl enable --now pcsd.service
```

Next, we need to open up the firewall for the cluster port. This is done with the following command:

```
firewall-cmd --permanent --add-service=high-availability ; firewall-cmd --reload
```

Now we're done with both nodes for a bit. The next few commands can be done on either of the nodes, but note, you still should be root.

Next, we need to add both nodes to the cluster:

```
pcs host auth web1 web2 -u hacluster
```

> **Note**
>
> If your nodes are not resolvable in DNS or the /etc/hosts file, you can optionally add addr=$IPADDR for each host after the hostname. But it's highly recommended to make sure all hosts are resolvable. This option, if used, would look as follows:
>
> ```
> pcs host auth web1 addr=192.168.56.200 node2 addr=192.168.56.201 -u hacluster
> ```

Next, we will create the cluster:

```
pcs cluster setup webapp web1 web2
```

Now, we can start the cluster:

```
pcs cluster start --all
```

To verify that the cluster is running, we can check with the `pcs` command:

```
pcs cluster status
```

A healthy new cluster should return a similar output as the following example:

```
[root@web1 conf.d]# pcs cluster status
Cluster Status:
 Status of pacemakerd: 'Pacemaker is running' (last updated 2023-07-29 21:04:38 -04:00)
 Cluster Summary:
   * Stack: corosync
   * Current DC: web2 (version 2.1.5-8.0.1.el8-a3f44794f94) - partition with quorum
   * Last updated: Sat Jul 29 21:04:38 2023
   * Last change:  Sat Jul 29 21:03:33 2023 by hacluster via crmd on web2
   * 2 nodes configured
   * 0 resource instances configured
 Node List:
   * Online: [ web1 web2 ]

PCSD Status:
  web1: Online
  web2: Online
```

Figure 6.17 – Cluster status

In a cluster consisting of only two nodes, the quorum operates differently than in clusters with more nodes. In such a cluster, the quorum value is set to 1 to ensure that the primary node is always considered in quorum. If both nodes go offline due to a network outage, they compete to fence each other, and the first to succeed wins the quorum. To increase the chances of a preferred node winning the quorum, the fencing agent can be configured to give it priority. This is done with the following command:

```
pcs resource defaults update
```

The last step is to disable **STONITH**, which stands for **Shoot The Other Node In The Head**. This is an advanced fencing tool that requires configuration specific to your environment. If you want to experiment with this technology then check out the official Oracle docs here – `https://docs.oracle.com/en/operating-systems/oracle-linux/8/availability/availability-ConfiguringFencingstonith.html#ol-pacemaker-stonith`:

```
pcs property set stonith-enabled=false
```

To set up a cluster, we'll need to create resources. A resource agent name has two or three fields separated by a colon. The first field is the resource class that indicates the standard followed by the resource agent and helps Pacemaker locate the script. For example, the IPaddr2 resource agent follows the

**Open Cluster Framework** (OCF) standard. The second field varies based on the standard used, and OCF resources use it for the OCF namespace. The third field denotes the name of the resource agent.

Meta-attributes and instance attributes are available for resources. Meta-attributes are not resource-type dependent, while instance attributes are specific to each resource agent.

In a cluster, resource operations refer to the actions that can be taken on a specific resource, such as starting, stopping, or monitoring it. These operations are identified by the op keyword. To ensure the resource remains healthy, we will add a monitor operation with a 15-second interval. The criteria for determining whether the resource is healthy depends on the resource agent being used. This is also why we enabled the server-status page on the httpd server, as the httpd agent uses that page to help determine the health of the system.

So, let's add the VIP address:

```
pcs resource create AppIP ocf:heartbeat:IPaddr2 ip=192.168.56.204 \
  cidr_netmask=24 op monitor interval=15s
```

Next up, we will add the httpd server:

```
pcs resource create AppWebServer ocf:heartbeat:apache \
configfile=/etc/httpd/conf/httpd.conf \
statusurl=http://127.0.0.1/server-status \
  op monitor interval=15s
```

Now that we have two resources, we also will need to tie them together as a group. With most applications, multiple resources need to be on the same physical server at the same time. This could be IP addresses, Tomcat servers, httpd servers, and so on. We are going to call this group WebApp and add both the VIP and https servers to it. Each resource is added individually, so two commands will need to be run:

```
pcs resource group add WebApp AppIP
pcs resource group add WebApp AppWebServer
```

Now, we will use the pcs status command to check the configuration:

```
pcs status
```

The output is as follows:

```
[root@web2 ~]# pcs status
Cluster name: webapp

WARNINGS:
No stonith devices and stonith-enabled is not false

Status of pacemakerd: 'Pacemaker is running' (last updated 2023-07-29 21:32:12 -04:00)
Cluster Summary:
  * Stack: corosync
  * Current DC: web2 (version 2.1.5-8.0.1.el8-a3f44794f94) - partition with quorum
  * Last updated: Sat Jul 29 21:32:13 2023
  * Last change:  Sat Jul 29 21:30:28 2023 by root via cibadmin on web2
  * 2 nodes configured
  * 2 resource instances configured

Node List:
  * Online: [ web1 web2 ]

Full List of Resources:
  * Resource Group: WebApp:
    * AppIP      (ocf::heartbeat:IPaddr2):          Stopped
    * AppWebServer      (ocf::heartbeat:apache):          Stopped

Daemon Status:
  corosync: active/disabled
  pacemaker: active/disabled
  pcsd: active/enabled
[root@web2 ~]#
```

Figure 6.18 – pcs status

We can now see the cluster, with its resource group, `WebApp`, with both the server VIPs.

## How it works...

Now that everything is configured, let's start up the resources and manage them. We can first start the entire cluster. This will online all nodes in the cluster:

```
pcs cluster start --all
```

We can also set up the cluster to start on boot with the following commands:

```
systemctl enable --now corosync
systemctl enable --now pacemaker
```

You will need to run both of these commands as root on both nodes.

Next up, let's look at a few useful commands.

Sometimes a resource gets broken; maybe it was a bad config file, or maybe you started a resource outside of the cluster control, confusing the cluster. Once you fix the issues, you will likely need to refresh the resource. This will tell the cluster to forget about the failure and restart the service clear of any errors:

```
pcs resource refresh AppWebServer
```

You also can check the details of a resource, using the `config` option. This is helpful if you forget how the resource was configured. An example is seen in the following figure:

```
[root@web1 conf.d]# pcs resource config  AppIP
Resource: AppIP (class=ocf provider=heartbeat type=IPaddr2)
  Attributes: AppIP-instance_attributes
    cidr_netmask=24
    ip=192.168.56.204
  Operations:
    monitor: AppIP-monitor-interval-15s
      interval=15s
    start: AppIP-start-interval-0s
      interval=0s
      timeout=20s
    stop: AppIP-stop-interval-0s
      interval=0s
      timeout=20s
[root@web1 conf.d]# 
```

Figure 6.19 – Resource configuration

Next, let's move WebApp to server web2:

```
pcs resource move WebApp web2
```

When you run `move`, you can also monitor the move by checking the constraints. This is a little cleaner than using the `pcs status` command:

```
pcs constraint
```

The output is as follows:

```
[root@web1 ~]# pcs constraint
Location Constraints:
  Resource: WebApp
    Enabled on:
      Node: web2 (score:INFINITY) (role:Started)
Ordering Constraints:
Colocation Constraints:
Ticket Constraints:
[root@web1 ~]# 
```

Figure 6.20 – Cluster constraints

The power of the Pacemaker/Corosync technology is its flexibility. You can cluster just about anything with it, making it a powerful tool for the sysadmin.

# Sharing a filesystem across multiple machines – cluster or distribute?

When you start using technologies such as load balancers and clustering software, you often end up in a situation where you need the same files on multiple servers. While you could simply copy the files, what if you could mount the files on each of the servers, sharing the filesystem across the systems without the SPOF that an NFS server introduces? One of the easiest ways to do this is to use Gluster.

**Gluster**, also known as **GlusterFS**, is an open source distributed filesystem that provides scalable and flexible storage for large volumes of data. Initially developed by Gluster Inc., it is now maintained by the open source community. Gluster uses a distributed architecture to create a single and unified filesystem that can span across multiple servers and storage devices. This approach allows you to aggregate the storage capacity of multiple servers and present it as a single, well-structured filesystem to users and applications. It has a wide range of applications, such as data storage, backup, and content delivery.

Key features and concepts of Gluster include the following:

- **Scalability**: Adding more storage servers to the cluster allows Gluster to easily accommodate growing data storage needs while scaling horizontally.

- **Redundancy**: Gluster ensures data availability by replicating data across multiple nodes for redundancy and fault tolerance.

- **Flexibility**: Gluster supports various storage options, including local disks, NAS, and cloud storage. It can be customized to fit specific use cases and technologies.

- **Filesystem abstraction**: It provides users and applications with a standard filesystem interface, making integration into existing systems relatively easy.

- **Data distribution**: Data is distributed across the cluster in a way that improves both performance and reliability. Data can be distributed evenly or based on specific criteria.

- **Automatic healing**: Gluster has a self-healing feature that automatically detects and repairs data inconsistencies or corrupted files.

Gluster is often used in environments where large-scale, distributed storage is required, such as web servers, cloud computing, big data analytics, and media streaming services. It provides a cost-effective and flexible solution for managing data across a network of servers and storage devices.

## Getting ready

For this recipe, you will need two Oracle Linux 8 systems, each with access to YUM repos. For this exercise, we will call them `gluster1` and `gluster2`. They are identical systems, each with 8 GB RAM, 4 vCPUs, and 100 GB of drive space. The filesystems have 50 GB in `/`, 5 GB in `/home`, and 8 GB in swap. The remaining disk space is unallocated. Additionally, for this example, each node will have a 100 GB LUN used for storing Gluster data.

> **Warning**
>
> Having at least three nodes in a cluster is highly recommended to avoid split-brain clusters. Although a two-node cluster is possible, it poses a risk of corrupt data if the system ever splits its brain. Split-brain clusters are undesirable in distributed computing environments because they can result in data inconsistency, corruption, and operational issues. Split brain occurs when the nodes in a cluster lose connectivity or communication with each other, leading to the cluster's division into multiple isolated nodes. Each node thinks it is the active or primary cluster, resulting in the potential for conflicts and data discrepancies.

On each server, you will need to perform the following prep work:

1. Create an XFS filesystem on the 100 GB LUN. This space will be used to store the Gluster data, known as **bricks**. In the context of Gluster, a *brick* refers to a basic storage unit within the storage cluster. A cluster is made up of multiple bricks, which are essentially directories on storage servers or devices where data is stored. Each brick represents a portion of the overall storage capacity of the cluster.

2. Since we will be using Gluster to manage the storage, we will not be using LVM on the filesystem. On these systems, /dev/sdb is the 100 GB LUN. The following commands are used to create and mount the filesystem:

```
mkfs.xfs -f -i size=512 -L glusterfs /dev/sdb
mkdir -p /data/glusterfs/volumes/bricks
echo 'LABEL=glusterfs /data/glusterfs/volumes/bricks xfs
defaults  0 0' |sudo tee -a /etc/fstab
mount -a
```

3. When completed, check with a df command to verify that the filesystem is mounted, as seen in the following example:

```
[root@gluster2 ~]# df -h
Filesystem                  Size  Used Avail Use% Mounted on
devtmpfs                    3.8G     0  3.8G   0% /dev
tmpfs                       3.8G     0  3.8G   0% /dev/shm
tmpfs                       3.8G  9.0M  3.8G   1% /run
tmpfs                       3.8G     0  3.8G   0% /sys/fs/cgroup
/dev/mapper/ol-root          50G  5.5G   45G  11% /
/dev/sdb                    100G  746M  100G   1% /data/glusterfs/volumes/bricks
/dev/mapper/ol-var          5.0G  781M  4.3G  16% /var
/dev/mapper/ol-home         5.0G   83M  5.0G   2% /home
/dev/mapper/ol-var_tmp      5.0G   69M  5.0G   2% /var/tmp
/dev/sda1                  1014M  496M  519M  49% /boot
tmpfs                       765M     0  765M   0% /run/user/0
```

Figure 6.21 – Bricks mounted

4.  Next, we need to make sure that all the nodes are in the `/etc/hosts` file. In this example, `gluster1`, `gluster2`, and `gluster3` are in the file, using both the short name and the **Fully Qualified Doman Name (FQDN)**. This is seen in the following code snippet:

```
[root@gluster3 ~]# more /etc/hosts
127.0.0.1    localhost localhost.localdomain localhost4
localhost4.localdomain4
::1          localhost localhost.localdomain localhost6
localhost6.localdomain6
192.168.200.110 gluster1.m57.local      gluster1
192.168.200.125 gluster2.m57.local      gluster2
[root@gluster3 ~]#
```

5.  In order to install the software, we need to enable the Gluster repo. Then, the `glusterfs` and Gluster server software can be installed and started. This is done with the following commands:

```
dnf -y install oracle-gluster-release-el8
dnf -y config-manager --enable ol8_gluster_appstream ol8_baseos_
latest ol8_appstream
dnf -y module enable glusterfs
dnf -y install @glusterfs/server
systemctl enable --now glusterd
```

6.  Once running, you can verify that the Gluster daemon is running with the `systemctl status glusterd` command. Verify that the service is active and running, as seen in the following example:

```
[root@gluster1 ~]# systemctl status glusterd
• glusterd.service - GlusterFS, a clustered file-system server
   Loaded: loaded (/usr/lib/systemd/system/glusterd.service; enabled; vendor preset: disabled)
   Active: active (running) since Sat 2023-09-02 11:25:07 EDT; 1min 46s ago
     Docs: man:glusterd(8)
  Process: 4404 ExecStart=/usr/sbin/glusterd -p /var/run/glusterd.pid --log-level $LOG_LEVEL $GLUST>
 Main PID: 4405 (glusterd)
    Tasks: 9 (limit: 48530)
   Memory: 3.6M
   CGroup: /system.slice/glusterd.service
           └─4405 /usr/sbin/glusterd -p /var/run/glusterd.pid --log-level INFO

Sep 02 11:25:06 gluster1 systemd[1]: Starting GlusterFS, a clustered file-system server...
Sep 02 11:25:07 gluster1 systemd[1]: Started GlusterFS, a clustered file-system server.
[root@gluster1 ~]#
```

Figure 6.22 – Gluster daemon is running

7.  Next, let's configure the firewall to allow the `glusterfs` port with the following commands:

```
firewall-cmd --permanent --add-service=glusterfs
firewall-cmd --reload
```

8.  Additionally, to improve security, let's create a self-signed key, to encrypt the communication between the nodes:

```
openssl genrsa -out /etc/ssl/glusterfs.key 2048
openssl req -new -x509 -days 365 -key /etc/ssl/glusterfs.key
-out /etc/ssl/glusterfs.pem
```

When generating the `.pem` file, since this is a self-signed certificate, you will need to enter your contact info into the certificate; however, it will work with the defaults!

> **Note**
>
> In this example, we are using a self-signed certificate. In a secure production environment, you will want to consider using a commercially signed certificate.

We will use these files later to encrypt the communication.

## How to do it...

Now that all the prep work has been completed on each of the nodes, we will create the trusted storage pools and encrypt the communications. This will have everything ready to create volumes, where data is stored and shared.

A trusted storage pool in Gluster pertains to a setup where a cluster of Gluster servers, referred to as storage nodes or peers, have established trust among themselves to work together within a storage cluster. This trust is established through a trusted storage pool configuration that typically involves the following steps:

- **Authentication**: Various methods, such as SSH keys, certificates, or shared secrets, can be used to authenticate nodes in the trusted storage pool. This ensures that only authorized servers are part of the storage cluster.

- **Authorization**: After nodes are authenticated, they authorize each other to access and manipulate specific data within the Gluster storage cluster. The authorization settings determine which nodes have read and write access to particular volumes or bricks within the cluster.

- **Communication**: Members of the trusted storage pool communicate over a secure network to replicate data, synchronize metadata, and perform other cluster-related operations, ensuring that the storage cluster functions cohesively.

- **Data integrity**: Trusted storage pools ensure data integrity and redundancy via distributed replication across multiple nodes.

- **Scalability**: It is possible to add more storage nodes to the trusted pool, which enhances storage capacity and performance. The trusted nature of the pool makes it easy for new nodes to join the cluster and contribute to its resources.

In Gluster, a trusted storage pool is a crucial element as it lays the foundation for the fault-tolerant and distributed nature of the filesystem. It guarantees that all nodes within the cluster can work seamlessly and securely in collaboration with each other. The following steps will walk you through how to create a GlusterFS on two hosts.

1.  To create the pool, we need to probe the other nodes in the cluster. In this example, we will probe from gluster1 to gluster2 using the gluster peer probe gluster2 command:

    ```
    [root@gluster1 etc]# gluster peer probe gluster2
    peer probe: success
    ```

2.  You can then use the gluster pool list command to see what nodes are peered with the node where you ran the command from; in the following example, the command was run on gluster2:

    ```
    [root@gluster2 etc]#  gluster pool list
    UUID                              Hostname        State
    b13801f3-dcbd-487b-b3f3-
    2e95afa8b632                      gluster1        Connected
    bc003cd0-f733-4a25-85fb-
    40a7c387d667                      localhost       Connected
    ```

3.  Here, it shows gluster1 and localhost connected as this was run on gluster2. If you run the same command from gluster1, you will see gluster2 as the remote host:

    ```
    [root@gluster1 ~]# gluster pool list
    UUID                              Hostname        State
    bc003cd0-f733-4a25-85fb-
    40a7c387d667                      gluster2        Connected
    b13801f3-dcbd-487b-b3f3-
    2e95afa8b632                      localhost       Connected
    ```

4.  Now that we have the cluster, let's create a replicated volume. This volume will re-write the bricks across the cluster, enabling protection against failed storage or a failed node.

    The following command will create the volume:

    ```
    gluster volume create data1 replica 2 gluster{1,2}:/data/
    glusterfs/volumes/bricks/data1
    ```

    Once the volume is created, we need to start it:

    ```
    gluster volume start data1
    ```

5.  We now can mount it. For now, we will use the Gluster native client, and mount it on the /mnt mount point:

    ```
    mount -t glusterfs gluster2:data1 /mnt
    ```

6. We can now see the storage mounted using the `df` command:

```
[root@gluster2 ~]# df -h
Filesystem              Size  Used Avail Use% Mounted on
devtmpfs                3.8G     0  3.8G   0% /dev
tmpfs                   3.8G   84K  3.8G   1% /dev/shm
tmpfs                   3.8G  9.0M  3.8G   1% /run
tmpfs                   3.8G     0  3.8G   0% /sys/fs/cgroup
/dev/mapper/ol-root      50G  5.5G   45G  11% /
/dev/sdb                100G  746M  100G   1% /data/glusterfs/volumes/bricks
/dev/mapper/ol-var      5.0G  785M  4.3G  16% /var
/dev/mapper/ol-home     5.0G   83M  5.0G   2% /home
/dev/sda1              1014M  496M  519M  49% /boot
/dev/mapper/ol-var_tmp  5.0G   84M  5.0G   2% /var/tmp
tmpfs                   765M  4.0K  765M   1% /run/user/0
gluster2:data1          100G  1.8G   99G   2% /mnt
[root@gluster2 ~]#
```

Figure 6.23 – data1 mounted on /mnt

7. If you want to mount this on other nodes, you will need to repeat the command on each node, updating the node name as needed. The following example shows mounting on `gluster1`:

```
mount -t glusterfs gluster1:data1 /mnt
```

8. Next, we need to set up the encryption using the keys we previously created. The first step is to take the `.pem` files previously created and concatenate them into the `/etc/ssl/glusterfs.ca` file. This file should be placed on all nodes of the cluster.

9. Now, we need to enable the encryption. This is done by touching the secure-access file on each node using the following command:

```
touch /var/lib/glusterd/secure-access
```

10. Now, for each volume, we will need to enable SSL for both the client and the server. In the example command, we will enable this for the `data1` volume that was just created:

```
gluster volume set data1 client.ssl on
gluster volume set data1  server.ssl on
```

Now, restart `glusterd`:

```
systemctl restart glusterd
```

Gluster communication is now encrypted for this volume.

## How it works...

There is more you can do with Gluster. First, volumes have multiple options when you create them, each offering options for replication and distribution:

- **Distributed**: When using distributed volumes, files are randomly distributed across the bricks in the volume. This type of volume is useful when the need is to scale storage, and redundancy is not necessary or is already provided by other hardware or software layers. However, it is important to note that disk or server failures can result in significant data loss, as the data is spread randomly across the bricks in the volume. An example command to build a distributed volume is the following:

```
gluster volume create data1  gluster{1,2}:/data/glusterfs/
volumes/bricks/data1
```

- **Replicated**: Files are copied across bricks for HA in replicated volumes. An example command to build a replicated volume is the following:

```
gluster volume create data1 replica 2 gluster{1,2}:/data/
glusterfs/volumes/bricks/data1
```

- **Distributed replicated**: Distributed files across replicated bricks in the volume for improved read performance, HA, and reliability. When creating a distributed replicated volume, the number of nodes should be a multiple of the number of bricks. An example command to build a distributed replicated volume is the following:

```
gluster volume create data1 replica 2 cluster{1,2,3,4}:/data/
glusterfs/volumes/bricks/data1
```

- **Dispersed**: This volume type utilizes erasure codes to efficiently protect against disk or server failures. It works by striping the encoded data of files across multiple bricks in the volume while adding redundancy to ensure reliability. Dispersed volumes allow for customizable reliability levels with minimal space waste. A dispersed volume must have at least three bricks. An example command to build a dispersed volume is the following:

```
gluster volume create data1 disperse 3 redundancy 1 \
cluster{1,2,3}:/data/glusterfs/volumes/bricks/data1
```

- **Distributed dispersed**: Distributes data across dispersed bricks, providing the same benefits of distributed replicated volumes but using dispersed storage. A dispersed volume must have at least six bricks. An example command to build a distributed dispersed volume is the following:

```
gluster volume create data1 disperse 3 redundancy 1 \
cluster{1,2,3,4,5,6}:/data/glusterfs/volumes/bricks/data1
```

When adding bricks to any volume, you can put more than one brick on a Gluster node. Simply define the additional brick in the command. In this example, a distributed dispersed volume is created, by putting two bricks on each node:

```
gluster volume create data1 disperse 3 redundancy 1 \ cluster{1,2,3}:/
data/glusterfs/volumes/bricks/data1 \ cluster{1,2,3}:/data/glusterfs/
volumes/bricks/data2
```

Volumes can be stopped with the `gluster stop volume volumename` command. An example to stop the `data1` volume is the following:

```
gluster stop volume data1
```

You can also add bricks to a volume to grow it. This can be done after a new node is added to the cluster. In the following example, `gluster3` was added to the cluster with the `gluster node probe gluster3` command first. Then, `data1` was grown with the following command:

```
gluster volume add-brick data1 gluster3:/data/glusterfs/volumes/
bricks/data1
```

> **Note**
>
> When adding bricks to a volume, make sure you add the required number of bricks. Volume types such as distributed replicated volumes will need more than a single brick added.

You can also check the status of all volumes with the following command:

```
gluster volume status
```

An example is seen in the following screenshot:

```
[root@gluster1 ~]#
[root@gluster1 ~]# gluster volume status
Status of volume: data1
Gluster process                              TCP Port  RDMA Port  Online  Pid
------------------------------------------------------------------------------
Brick gluster1:/data/glusterfs/volumes/bric
ks/data1                                     49152     0          Y       19239
Brick gluster2:/data/glusterfs/volumes/bric
ks/data1                                     49152     0          Y       18656
Self-heal Daemon on localhost                N/A       N/A        Y       19741
Self-heal Daemon on gluster2                 N/A       N/A        Y       19259

Task Status of Volume data1
------------------------------------------------------------------------------
There are no active volume tasks
```

Figure 6.24 – volume status

You can see the summary for a single volume by adding the volume name to the command. You can also see more details by adding the `detail` option. These can be combined, as seen in the following screenshot:

```
[root@gluster1 ~]# gluster volume status data1 detail
Status of volume: data1
------------------------------------------------------------------------------
Brick                   : Brick gluster1:/data/glusterfs/volumes/bricks/data1
TCP Port                : 49152
RDMA Port               : 0
Online                  : Y
Pid                     : 19239
File System             : xfs
Device                  : /dev/sdb
Mount Options           : rw,seclabel,relatime,attr2,inode64,logbufs=8,logbsize=32k,noquota
Inode Size              : 512
Disk Space Free         : 99.2GB
Total Disk Space        : 99.9GB
Inode Count             : 52428800
Free Inodes             : 52428525
------------------------------------------------------------------------------
Brick                   : Brick gluster2:/data/glusterfs/volumes/bricks/data1
TCP Port                : 49152
RDMA Port               : 0
Online                  : Y
Pid                     : 18656
File System             : xfs
Device                  : /dev/sdb
Mount Options           : rw,seclabel,relatime,attr2,inode64,logbufs=8,logbsize=32k,noquota
Inode Size              : 512
Disk Space Free         : 99.2GB
Total Disk Space        : 99.9GB
Inode Count             : 52428800
Free Inodes             : 52428525
```

Figure 6.25 – Volume details

If you want to see performance information about a volume, the `top` option can be used. This will show what bricks are being used for read/write activity as well as I/O throughput to each brick. The basic command is `gluster volume top volume_name option`, with `volume_name` being the name of the volume and the options being as follows:

- `read`: This shows the highest read calls for each brick, as well as the counts.

- `write`: This shows the highest write calls for each brick, as well as the counts.

- `open`: This shows what bricks have open file descriptors.

- `opendir`: This shows what bricks have open calls on each directory, as well as the counts.

- `read-perf`: This shows read-performance throughput by brick. Run using the options `bs` (for block size) `1024` and `count` `1024`.

- `write-perf`: This shows read-performance throughput by brick. Run using the options `bs` (for block size) `1024` and `count` `1024`.

Several examples are seen in the following figure:

```
[root@gluster1 ~]# gluster volume top data1 write-perf bs 1024 count 1024
Brick: gluster1:/data/glusterfs/volumes/bricks/data1
Throughput 624.52 MBps time 0.0017 secs
MBps Filename                                         Time
==== ========                                         ====
   0 /test2                                           2023-09-03 15:13:18.975213
Brick: gluster2:/data/glusterfs/volumes/bricks/data1
Throughput 765.38 MBps time 0.0014 secs
MBps Filename                                         Time
==== ========                                         ====
   0 /test2                                           2023-09-03 15:13:18.977800
[root@gluster1 ~]# gluster volume top data1 read-perf bs 1024 count 1024
Brick: gluster1:/data/glusterfs/volumes/bricks/data1
Throughput 2595.49 MBps time 0.0004 secs
Brick: gluster2:/data/glusterfs/volumes/bricks/data1
Throughput 2608.40 MBps time 0.0004 secs
[root@gluster1 ~]# gluster volume top data1 write
Brick: gluster1:/data/glusterfs/volumes/bricks/data1
Count          filename
=======================
812406         /test2
Brick: gluster2:/data/glusterfs/volumes/bricks/data1
Count          filename
=======================
812407         /test2
[root@gluster1 ~]#
```

Figure 6.26 – volume top examples

Volumes can also be deleted. This is done with the `gluster volume delete volume_name` command, where `volume_name` is the volume being deleted. As a note, when deleting volumes, don't forget to use the `rm` command to delete the bricks from storage.

# Generating, configuring, and monitoring Ethernet traffic over bond

When using bare-metal servers as dedicated hosts or Linux systems that host virtual machines using the KVM hypervisor, the network can be a weak point. Fortunately, this issue can be resolved by implementing Ethernet bonding, also known as network bonding, or **Network Interface Card (NIC)** bonding. It is a technology in Linux that allows you to combine multiple NICs into a single logical interface. This logical interface, known as a bond or bonded interface, provides increased network bandwidth, fault tolerance, and load balancing. These are summarized as follows:

- **Load balancing**: Bonding distributes network traffic across multiple NICs, increasing bandwidth. Various algorithms, such as round-robin, active-backup, and XOR, can be used depending on specific requirements.

- **Fault tolerance**: In the event of an NIC or network link failure, Ethernet bonding can automatically switch traffic to another active NIC. This provides redundancy and fault tolerance, ensuring network connectivity remains available even if one NIC becomes unavailable.

- **Link aggregation**: Bonding can be used to create **link aggregation groups (LAGs)** or NIC teams, which enhance bandwidth and redundancy in HA setups.

In this recipe, we will configure bonding, and then show some common tools that will allow you to both monitor and generate Ethernet traffic over the bond.

Additionally, there are a few technologies you need to be familiar with.

## MAC

A **Media Access Control (MAC)** address is a hardware identifier assigned to network interfaces such as Ethernet cards and Wi-Fi adapters for communication on a local network. It is hardcoded into the network hardware during manufacturing and is used at the data link layer (Layer 2) of the OSI model. One of the most important features of MAC addresses is that they must be unique. Each MAC address is meant to be globally unique, and manufacturers bear the responsibility of ensuring that no two network interfaces have the same MAC address, though this can be a challenging task to accomplish in practice, especially in virtualized environments. This can be an issue with networking, as duplicate MAC addresses on any network will cause issues. Additionally, many of the bonding modes rely on MAC addresses to load balance traffic.

## Bonding modes

Bonding modes refer to the various strategies or algorithms used to determine how network traffic is distributed across the physical network interfaces that have been aggregated into a bonded interface using the Linux bonding driver. These modes control the load-balancing and failover behavior of the bonded interface. The choice of bonding mode depends on your specific network requirements and goals. Here are some common Linux bonding modes:

- `balance-rr`: In this mode, outgoing network traffic is distributed evenly across the available network interfaces in a round-robin fashion. It's a simple load-balancing mode that provides improved outbound traffic performance but does not consider the state of the interfaces, which can lead to uneven inbound traffic distribution. Occasionally, this mode does not work well with some switching systems.

- `active-backup`: A commonly used mode, which is often referred to as failover mode, this mode has a primary interface, while the others remain on standby. If the primary interface fails, the next available interface is automatically activated to ensure continuity. This mode provides redundancy and is one of the easiest modes to get working in any environment.

- `balance-xor`: This mode utilizes a straightforward XOR operation to maintain a balance between the transmission and reception of data. The process involves distributing traffic based on the MAC addresses of the source and destination. This guarantees that packets between the same endpoints will always take the same path. The primary purpose of this mode is to ensure fault tolerance. Occasionally, this mode does not work well with some switching systems.

- `balance-tlb`: When operating in this mode, the outgoing traffic is distributed among all available interfaces based on their current load. However, incoming traffic is not actively balanced, and it is only received by the active interface. This mode is particularly useful when the switch does not support **Link Aggregation Control Protocol** (**LACP**). Occasionally, this mode does not work well with some switching systems.

- `balance-alb`: This mode actively balances both incoming and outgoing traffic by considering the availability and load of each interface. Occasionally, this mode does not work well with some switching systems.

## LACP

All of the preceding modes can operate without any changes to the switches that the server is connected to. However, there is another mode that is more commonly used, called LACP. LACP is the most complex mode used to aggregate multiple network connections, usually Ethernet, into a single high-bandwidth link. This process is commonly known as link aggregation, NIC teaming, or bonding. LACP is defined by the IEEE 802.3ad standard and is frequently used in enterprise and data center environments to enhance network performance, redundancy, and fault tolerance.

However, to utilize LACP, switches must be configured to use it. As an administrator, it is essential to communicate your configuration requirements to ensure that the switch is configured in a compatible mode. The configuration must match on both ends for LACP to work correctly. Most enterprise-grade network switches and server NICs provide LACP support. Key characteristics and features of LACP include the following:

- **Aggregated links**: LACP enables the aggregation of multiple physical network links into a single logical link, which appears as a single interface to network devices.

- **Increased bandwidth**: Aggregating multiple links with LACP can boost network bandwidth for bandwidth-intensive applications and server-to-switch connections. However, each MAC-to-MAC connection is usually limited to the speed of a single member of the aggregated link. If you have a host with two 1 Gb/s ports in the link, you will likely be unable to get more than 1 Gb/s of communication between the host and a client.

- **Load balancing**: LACP can distribute network traffic across aggregated links using various load-balancing algorithms, preventing network congestion on a single link while optimizing network utilization.

- **Fault tolerance**: In addition to providing increased bandwidth, LACP also offers redundancy and fault-tolerance capabilities. If one physical link fails, LACP can automatically redirect traffic to the remaining active links, minimizing downtime and ensuring network availability.

- **Dynamic protocol**: LACP is a dynamic protocol that dynamically negotiates and establishes link aggregations between network devices using LACP frames.

- **Modes**: LACP supports two modes of operation:

  - **Active mode**: In this mode, the device actively sends LACP frames to negotiate and establish link aggregations.

  - **Passive mode**: In passive mode, the device listens for LACP frames but does not actively send them. It relies on the other end configured in active mode to initiate the aggregation.

LACP is commonly used in scenarios where HA and network performance are critical, such as server-to-switch connections, inter-switch links, and connections to **Storage Area Networks** (**SANs**). It allows organizations to make efficient use of available network resources and improve network reliability.

## Getting ready

For this recipe, you will need three Oracle Linux 8 systems, each with access to yum repos. For this exercise, we will call them `networking`, `client1`, and `client2`. They are mostly identical systems, each with 8 GB RAM, 4 vCPUs, and 100 GB of drive space. The difference is that networking should have two network interfaces on the same network. The filesystems have 50 GB in `/`, 5 GB in `/home`, and 8 GB in swap. The remaining disk space is unallocated.

## How to do it...

While this can be done from the GUI, this recipe will cover doing this from the command line. As a note, when working on the main network connection to the server, you will want to be on the system console. Doing this via a remote connection such as SSH can leave you in a situation where you lose access to the server. Following are the steps to configure a redundant connection.

1. The first thing you will need to do is create the bond. In this example, we will create it using the `balance-alb` mode to best balance both incoming and outgoing traffic:

   ```
   nmcli connection add type bond con-name "Bond 0" ifname bond0
   bond.options "mode=balance-alb"
   ```

2. Next, we will configure the bond to use DHCP. On production servers, you would normally use a manually configured IP address:

   ```
   nmcli connection modify "Bond 0" ipv4.method auto
   ```

3. Add the adapters that will be members of the bond. In this case, we will be using `enp0s3` and `enp0s8`:

> **Note**
>
> If you are adding a port into a bond that is already in use, you should delete that port now. In this case, enp0s3 was in use, so it was deleted with the following command:
>
> ```
> nmcli connection del enp0s3
> ```

```
nmcli connection add type ethernet slave-type bond con-name
bond0-if1 ifname enp0s3 master bond0

nmcli connection add type ethernet slave-type bond con-name
bond0-if2 ifname enp0s8 master bond0
```

4.  Now, we will start the connection and check the status:

```
nmcli connection up "Bond 0"
nmcli device
```

When completed, the output of the nmcli device command should look like the following:

```
[root@networking ~]# nmcli device
DEVICE   TYPE       STATE       CONNECTION
bond0    bond       connected   Bond0
enp0s3   ethernet   connected   bond0-if1
enp0s8   ethernet   connected   bond0-if2
lo       loopback   unmanaged   --
[root@networking ~]#
```

Figure 6.27 – nmcli device output with a working bind

You can see bond0 as the device, with members enp0s3 and enp0s8.

5.  When you look at the IP address, you will see that that is now on the bond0 device. This can be checked with the ifconfig bond0 command, with the output as follows:

```
[root@networking ~]# ifconfig bond0
bond0: flags=5187<UP,BROADCAST,RUNNING,MASTER,MULTICAST>  mtu 1500
        inet 192.168.200.179  netmask 255.255.255.0  broadcast 192.168.200.255
        inet6 fe80::a843:503e:3b0d:968b  prefixlen 64  scopeid 0x20<link>
        ether 08:00:27:9e:be:ed  txqueuelen 1000  (Ethernet)
        RX packets 2595  bytes 169235 (165.2 KiB)
        RX errors 0  dropped 0  overruns 0  frame 0
        TX packets 1093  bytes 72219 (70.5 KiB)
        TX errors 0  dropped 0 overruns 0  carrier 0  collisions 0

[root@networking ~]#
```

Figure 6.28 – Output from ifconfig bond0

You can continue to use the system normally now, but with bond0 being the network device.

## How it works...

Now that we have a working bond, let's look at the traffic going in and out. To do this, we need to install the `iptraf-ng` command:

```
dnf -y install iptraf-ng
```

This tool allows you to monitor Ethernet traffic on a server. For this example, we will run the `iptraf-ng` command. This will launch the program, and you will be on the main screen, as seen in the following screenshot:

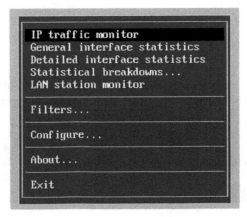

Figure 6.29 – iptraf main menu

From here, we will look at the **General interface statistics** by hitting the *S* key. This will then show a real-time flow of traffic on each interface:

```
iptraf-ng 1.2.1
┌ Iface ───── Total ─── IPv4 ─── IPv6 ─── NonIP ── BadIP ───── Activity ──
  bond0         63816       63816        0        0        0      1349.38 Mbps
  emp0s3        18938       18938        0        0        0    463928.71 kbps
  emp0s8        44898       44898        0        0        0       885.45 Mbps
  lo                0           0        0        0        0         0.00 kbps
```

Figure 6.30 – General interface statistics

You can see that both in and out traffic is balanced between the two physical interfaces. This is because the bond was built using the `balance-alb` mode. To generate this traffic, a simple flood ping was used from the `client2` system. This was done with the following command:

```
ping -f 192.168.200.179
```

> **Note**
>
> Be careful using the `-f` option, as this will flood the network with traffic, and it is generally not acceptable to do so on production networks without coordinating with the network and security teams. It can cause performance issues for systems using the network.

There is a better way to really stress the network, though. That is to use a tool that will generate the maximum levels of packets the interface will support.

### iperf – network stress tool

We will use a tool called `iperf`. It will generate the maximum amount of traffic that the interface can support. To install `iperf`, run the following command on all systems:

```
dnf -y install iperf3
```

We also will need to open up a TCP port for the system to use and reload the firewall. Each instance of the server can only handle a single client connection. We will add multiple ports to enable running multiple servers, each with a different port. This is done with the following commands:

```
firewall-cmd --permanent --add-port=8000-8010/tcp
firewall-cmd --reload
```

`iperf` works using a client-server model. In order to use it, we first need to start an `iperf` server on the networking system. With this example, we will set up the server to listen on port `8001` using TCP. This is started with the following command:

```
[root@networking ~]# iperf3 -s -p 8001
-----------------------------------------------------------
Server listening on 8001
-----------------------------------------------------------
```

We will repeat the same command in a different window, running on port `8002` instead:

```
[root@networking ~]# iperf3 -s -p 8002
-----------------------------------------------------------
Server listening on 8002
-----------------------------------------------------------
```

Now, with two servers running, we can run a test from `client1`.

The test is run with the following command:

```
iperf -c 192.168.200.179 -p 8001
```

The test will kick off and for a few seconds run the maximum traffic possible, as seen in the following output:

```
[root@client1 ~]# iperf3 -c 192.168.200.179 -p 8001
Connecting to host 192.168.200.179, port 8001
[  5] local 192.168.200.143 port 55624 connected to 192.168.200.179 port 8001
[ ID] Interval           Transfer     Bitrate         Retr  Cwnd
[  5]   0.00-1.00   sec   359 MBytes   3.01 Gbits/sec  315   492 KBytes
[  5]   1.00-2.00   sec   360 MBytes   3.02 Gbits/sec  180   349 KBytes
[  5]   2.00-3.00   sec   356 MBytes   2.99 Gbits/sec  225   469 KBytes
[  5]   3.00-4.00   sec   329 MBytes   2.76 Gbits/sec  180   513 KBytes
[  5]   4.00-5.00   sec   359 MBytes   3.01 Gbits/sec  135   508 KBytes
[  5]   5.00-6.00   sec   342 MBytes   2.87 Gbits/sec  225   397 KBytes
[  5]   6.00-7.00   sec   335 MBytes   2.81 Gbits/sec  135   479 KBytes
[  5]   7.00-8.00   sec   346 MBytes   2.90 Gbits/sec  135   431 KBytes
[  5]   8.00-9.00   sec   349 MBytes   2.93 Gbits/sec  135   467 KBytes
[  5]   9.00-10.00  sec   335 MBytes   2.81 Gbits/sec  180   400 KBytes
- - - - - - - - - - - - - - - - - - - - - - - - -
[ ID] Interval           Transfer     Bitrate         Retr
[  5]   0.00-10.00  sec   3.39 GBytes  2.91 Gbits/sec  1845             sender
[  5]   0.00-10.04  sec   3.39 GBytes  2.90 Gbits/sec                   receiver

iperf Done.
```

Figure 6.31 – iperf client output

While the test runs, we can monitor the performance from the iptraf command, and we will see most of the traffic is hitting a single interface. This is seen in the following screenshot:

```
iptraf-ng 1.2.1
 Iface ──────── Total ──────── IPv4 ──────── IPv6 ──────── NonIP ── BadIP ──────── Activity ──────
 bond0          890132         890132        0             0        0              2866.94 Mbps
 enp0s3         248514         248514        0             0        0                 2.15 kbps
 enp0s8         641991         641991        0             0        0              2866.94 Mbps
 lo             0              0             0             0        0                 0.00 kbps
```

Figure 6.32 – Single-client traffic

This traffic is all on the enp0s8 interface. This is because the load-balancing algorithm uses the MAC address of the client. This limits the traffic to a single interface in the bond.

Next up, can run a test from client1 and client2 simultaneously. The difference is that client2 will use port 8002. The results are seen in the following screenshot:

```
iptraf-ng 1.2.1
 Iface ──────── Total ──────── IPv4 ──────── IPv6 ──────── NonIP ── BadIP ──────── Activity ──────
 bond0          446477         446477        0             0        0              1821.63 Mbps
 enp0s3         175566         175566        0             0        0              1820.39 Mbps
 enp0s8         271241         271241        0             0        0              1237.58 kbps
 lo             0              0             0             0        0                 0.00 kbps
```

Figure 6.33 – Test with two different clients

Here, we can see that both interfaces are being used for heavy network loads. This is happening because each client is using a different MAC address. If a third client were used, we would then see it competing for traffic for one of the interfaces, potentially causing issues.

This is an important factor to consider when bonding in environments where heavy network performance is required from multiple clients. When using bonds, and you have random performance latency issues, monitor the ports. You might face some contention. One way to address this is to add additional ports to the bond. You can also upgrade the interfaces to units that can support more bandwidth.

# 7

# Oracle Linux 8 – Patching Doesn't Have to Mean Rebooting

I've rebooted when patching for my entire life, why change now?

Since Linux was released back in 1991, when the kernel was patched, you had to reboot the system. At the time, even the IBM mainframes that dominated corporate IT needed to be rebooted when patched, so it was considered normal for all other systems to be rebooted when patched. This process appeared to work fine for almost the next 20 years, but the seeds of change were planted in 2005 when a **Massachusetts Institute of Technology (MIT)** student came up with a simple question. *What if you could patch without rebooting the system?* His team came up with an answer in 2009 when Ksplice was released, enabling the ability to patch a Linux kernel while the system was running.

In this chapter, we will cover why you should start using Ksplice and how it is used to improve the security of your system.

This chapter contains the following recipes:

- Setting up Ksplice with internet access
- Using Ksplice with no internet access
- Installing and enabling Known Exploit Detection

## Setting up Ksplice with internet access

Before we get into the recipe, let's understand what's all the fuss around Ksplice.

## What's all the fuss about Ksplice?

The first question is, *Why is this important to IT, and more importantly, to defending the applications running on the servers?* Before we get to that, you first need to understand the process that hackers use to compromise systems.

The basic process includes three main stages: reconnaissance, gaining access, and then maintaining access. Once a system is compromised, the process is repeated on other systems on the network:

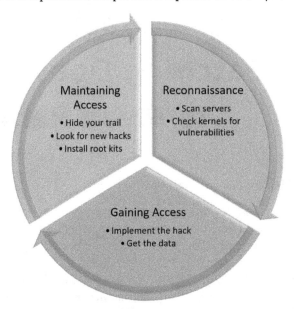

Figure 7.1 – Security life cycle

In the first phase, **reconnaissance**, hackers use a variety of methods to scan the system for vulnerabilities. Often, this attacking phase against servers starts after hackers have gained access to a low-level support account that has access to the server. Once there, it is a trivial task to look at the kernel version and identify what vulnerabilities the kernel is susceptible to. Oracle offers a free site (`https://ksplice.oracle.com/inspector`) that lets you easily check the vulnerabilities of the kernel. The results of such a check are shown in *Figure 7.2*:

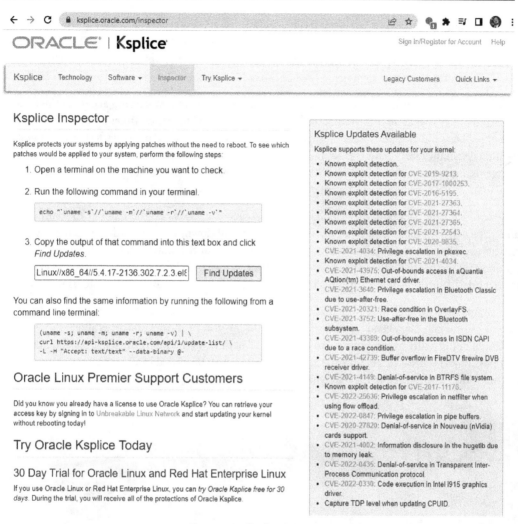

Figure 7.2 – Ksplice Inspector

> **Note**
>
> The MITRE Corporation is a non-profit company funded by the US federal government that researches ways to improve safety across multiple industries, including aviation, healthcare, homeland security, defense, and cybersecurity. The **Common Vulnerabilities and Exposures (CVE)** program was launched in 1999 and quickly became the go-to location to track cybersecurity vulnerabilities. More information about the CVE program can be found at `https://cve.org`.

Not only will the system identify the CVE that the kernel is susceptible to but it also links to the MITRE site with the CVE details. In the example report, you can see the kernel is susceptible to several CVEs, including a few that would allow the attacker to gain root access. Surprisingly, unlike other similar technologies, Ksplice also helps defend against this phase with its ability to detect attacks against the running kernel, seeking to gain privileged escalation using the **Known Exploit Detection** technology. This effectively turns every system using Ksplice into a free intrusion detection system for the kernel.

In the next phase, gaining access, the hacker exploits the vulnerability, gaining access to the data. This is often done weeks after the initial discovery phase. Hackers take their time; they do this to run under the radar, and they know that most environments are only patched on a quarterly basis at best. Additionally, many attacks come from inside the organization, from people who have limited access to systems as part of their normal role. Ksplice disrupts this pattern, enabling the system admin to easily patch daily, closing the window of opportunity for the hacker.

In the last phase, the hackers work to maintain access, often using the same vulnerability to continually mine the system for data. Ksplice allows this to also be shut down, as it closes the vulnerability not only for exploits post-patch but also shuts down the exploit for the attack while in progress. This is an important feature of Ksplice: the ability to patch the kernel and close the exploit while the exploit is being used. This shuts down the exploit mid-flight, significantly enhancing the system's security.

Now, about that patching effort – once a quarter at best? Kernel patches are released almost daily, yet systems can remain unpatched for almost a quarter of the year or more. This gives attackers a huge window of opportunity to compromise your systems. Not only is scheduling the patch a challenge for most mission-critical systems but the patch process itself is very time- and labor-intensive. Let's look at why this is the case. As seen in the following diagram, there are many steps required to patch a server:

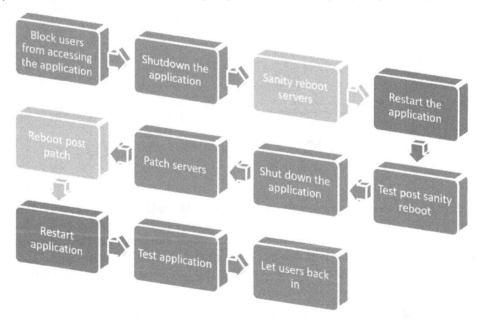

Figure 7.3 – Legacy patch process

The following list provides a short description of each of these steps:

1. **Block users from accessing the application**: Disable load balancers or disable user logins to the application so users do not accidentally corrupt data.

2. **Shut down the application**: Shut down the databases, application servers, schedulers, load balancers, and so on. This is to prepare for the operating system reboot.

3. **Sanity reboot the servers**: Perform a reboot of the servers, with no other changes made. This is to verify that the servers can perform a clean reboot. Often in this step, a snapshot is made of the app servers.

4. **Restart the application**: Start the application back up to verify that it is working. This is to verify the sanity reboot.

5. **Test post sanity reboot**: Often, some changes get made to the application and/or its infrastructure that can cause issues with the application. This step verifies that there is a good system before the patches are applied.

6. **Shut down the application**: Shut everything down again to prepare for the patching.

7. **Patch the servers**: Apply the operating system patches.

8. **Reboot post patch**: Reboot so the patches take effect.

9. **Restart the application**: Restart the application again.

10. **Test the application**: Test the application, and verify all is good.

11. **Let users back in**: Allow users back into the application.

> **Note**
>
> Not every organization follows the full path process, skipping steps to save some time. While this can save some time in the short term, all it takes is one bad patch cycle where changes were made to the application and/or its infrastructure between patch cycles to make for a very bad, long night, or worse, long days.

As you can see, properly patching takes a lot of time, and the more complex the application, the more people and time are required for each patch cycle. Most of this time and effort is caused due to the reboots required.

When you avoid the reboot, the patch process is significantly simplified; as shown in the following diagram, there are only two steps!

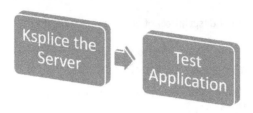

Figure 7.4 – Ksplice patching process

The following list provides a short description of these two steps:

- **Ksplice the servers**: Apply the kernel and user space patches with ksplice.

- **Testing**: Test the application

By using Ksplice, your team can save a ton of time, reduce late nights, and improve security. Best of all, it's easy to set up and use!

### Discovering Ksplice

Ksplice is easy to configure. There are a few concepts and points you need to understand before Ksplicing your servers:

- If your servers are running on **Oracle Cloud Infrastructure** (**OCI**), using Oracle's default platform images, all the Ksplice preparation work and access to the Ksplice repo is already performed to support online Ksplice usage. Systems will also need a route (usually done with a NAT gateway) to the Ksplice endpoint. This is automatically set up when using the **Virtual Cloud Network** (**VCN**) wizard.

- If you are using Autonomous Linux on OCI, your systems are already being Kspliced automatically.

- There are two Ksplice clients: the legacy Uptrack client and the Enhanced client.

- You do not need internet access to use Ksplice; you can use specially built Ksplice .rpm files using the offline mode. This will require that you mirror the ULN Ksplice repos on a local YUM server. This was covered in *Chapter 5*.

Both the Enhanced client and the Uptrack client allow you to Ksplice the kernel, but the Enhanced client also offers the ability to Ksplice user space libraries, KVM hypervisors, and Arm-based systems and offers Known Exploit Detection on x86_64 platforms. Most new users should use the Enhanced client.

The older Uptrack client does not offer the advantages the Enhanced client offers, but it does support the ability to patch some non-Oracle Linux systems.

Ksplice offers two different modes: the online mode and the offline mode. The online mode requires that each system registers to the Oracle ULN but offers a Ksplice web interface, the Ksplice Uptrack API, for advanced automation and the ability to patch a Xen hypervisor. However, since this requires every system to not only register with ULN but also for internet access, many system administrators use the offline mode.

The offline mode allows the system to use Ksplice without internet access. This is most often used by Enterprise and Government environments where all servers do not have internet access. In these use cases, the most common method is to set up a ULN mirror, giving that system access to the internet, and the local Oracle Linux servers will pull from that mirror to use Ksplice:

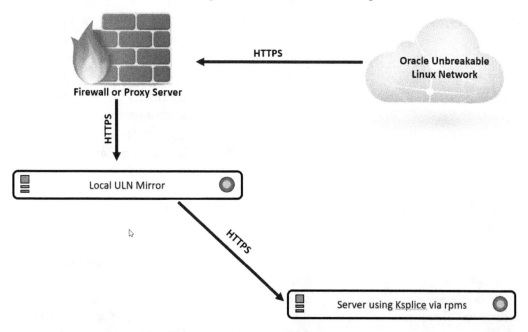

Figure 7.5 – Ksplice offline mode using RPMs

With the offline mode, only the local ULN mirror needs to be able to access the Oracle ULN, via the HTTPS protocol. This can be done via a basic firewall rule or a more advanced proxy server. Once the ULN mirror is registered and synced from the ULN, the servers behind the firewall can pull their RPMs via HTTP/HTTPS from the ULN mirror. There are a couple of advantages to the offline mode: less bandwidth is used for the internet and not every client needs to be registered. Of course, having no API, there are some limitations with more advanced automation.

Regardless of what mode is used, the clients must have access to a few specific Ksplice channels. The following table describes the channels that are available for Ksplice in Oracle Linux:

| Channel Name | Enhanced Client | Channel Label | Description |
| --- | --- | --- | --- |
| Ksplice for Oracle Linux 7 (x86_64) | Optional | `ol7_x86_64_ksplice` | Ksplice RPMs for Oracle Linux 7 on x86_64 systems |
| Ksplice for Oracle Linux 7 (aarch64) | Optional | `ol7_aarch64_ksplice` | Ksplice RPMs for Oracle Linux 7 on aarch64 systems |
| Ksplice for Oracle Linux 8 (x86_64) | Optional | `ol8_x86_64_ksplice` | Ksplice RPMs for Oracle Linux 8 on x86_64 systems |
| Ksplice for Oracle Linux 8 (aarch64) | Optional | `ol8_aarch64_ksplice` | Ksplice RPMs for Linux 8 on aarch64 systems |
| Ksplice-aware user space packages for Oracle Linux 7 (x86_64) | Required | `ol7_x86_64_userspace_ksplice` | Latest RPMs for Ksplice-aware user space packages for Oracle Linux 7 (x86_64) |
| Ksplice-aware user space packages for Oracle Linux 7 (aarch64) | Required | `ol7_aarch64_userspace_ksplice` | Latest RPMs for Ksplice-aware user space packages for Oracle Linux 7 (aarch64) |
| Ksplice-aware user space packages for Oracle Linux 8 (x86_64) | Required | `ol8_x86_64_userspace_ksplice` | Latest RPMs for Ksplice-aware user space packages for Oracle Linux 8 (x86_64) |
| Ksplice-aware user space packages for Oracle Linux 8 (aarch64) | Optional | `ol8_aarch64_userspace_ksplice` | Latest RPMs for Ksplice-aware user space packages for Oracle Linux 8 (aarch64) |

Table 7.1 – Ksplice channels

> **Note**
>
> If `prelink` is installed, revert the pre-linked binaries to their original state (`prelink -au`) and then uninstall `prelink` (`dnf remove prelink -y`). While not often used, `prelink` is not compatible with Ksplice.

Now that you have an understanding of why you need to use Ksplice and the basics of how it works, let's get to the recipe.

The easiest way to use Ksplice is to allow each system to access the Oracle Ksplice service directly. This is called online mode. This can be done via an internet proxy, direct access, or by running the systems in OCI.

## Getting ready

To do this, you will need a test system, running Oracle Linux 8, with access to the internet.

## How to do it…

When using Ksplice, make sure you match each system for both the operating system version, and the user-space libraries. Do not use an Oracle Linux 9 repo for an Oracle Linux 8 system. An example of what a system should look like can be seen in the following screenshot:

Figure 7.6 – Required channels

If you are using an internet proxy server, you will need to export some environmental variables to set the proxy servers:

```
sudo http_proxy=http://proxy_server_URL:http_port
sudo https_proxy=http://proxy_server_URL:https_port
sudo export http_proxy https_proxy
```

Set `proxy_server_URL` to the proxy server, and `http_port` to the port the proxy server uses.

Next, Ksplice will be installed using `dnf`. Both the `ksplice` and `uptrack` packages are needed:

```
dnf install -y ksplice uptrack
```

When the installation is complete, please verify that your system is seen in the ULN and that an access key has been populated in `/etc/uptrack/uptrack.conf`.

The access key should be in the [Auth] section and should look similar to this:

```
[Auth]
accesskey =
b3ag33k1746d141edb377f6f643344e23ad9638ae4d896ead4dcdddbb350a058b
```

Once done, perform a normal dnf update and then reboot the system. This dnf update is required so the Ksplice-aware user space libraries are loaded; it is only required the first time Ksplice is used.

Once the server is rebooted, Ksplice can now be used to patch user space libraries and the kernel.

To see what updates are available for the kernel, you can run the Ksplice kernel upgrade command, passing -n for no action:

```
ksplice -n kernel upgrade
```

The output from this command is seen in the following screenshot:

```
[root@arm2 ~]#  ksplice -n kernel upgrade
Effective kernel version is 5.4.17-2136.306.1.3.el8uek
The following steps will be taken:
Install [juh9olc4] CVE-2021-4034: Privilege escalation in pkexec.
[root@arm2 ~]#
[root@arm2 ~]#
[root@arm2 ~]#
```

Figure 7.7 – Ksplice available upgrades

In this system, only one update is available, patching CVE-2021-4034. To splice the system, run the same command, replacing -n with -y to say yes to applying the kernel path:

```
[root@arm2 ~]#  ksplice -y kernel upgrade
The following steps will be taken:
Install [juh9olc4] CVE-2021-4034: Privilege escalation in pkexec.
Installing [juh9olc4] CVE-2021-4034: Privilege escalation in pkexec.
Your kernel is fully up to date.
Effective kernel version is 5.4.17-2136.306.1.3.el8uek
[root@arm2 ~]#
```

Figure 7.8 – Ksplice updating the kernel

From here, you can see that the CVE patch has now taken place without a reboot!

The kernel that has been patched is referred to as the effective kernel. When you use the ksplice kernel uname -r command in Ksplice, it displays the effective kernel version, which indicates the current security status of the kernel based on the applied patches. This version typically varies from the initially booted kernel version and is meant to reflect the present condition of the kernel regarding any potential security threats or major issues.

You can now validate what your effective kernel is by using the following Ksplice command:

```
ksplice kernel show
```

Note that the version of the running kernel and the installed kernel will not match! This is because when Ksplice splices the kernel, it splices the RAM of the running kernel with the new code. This patches the kernel (and selected user space libraries) but has the effect of uname no longer matching the effective kernel:

```
Effective kernel version is 5.4.17-2136.306.1.3.el8uek
[root@arm3 ~]# uname -a
Linux arm3 5.4.17-2136.302.7.2.1.el8uek.aarch64 #2 SMP Tue Jan 18 12:11:39 PST 2022 aarch64 aarch64 aarch64 GNU/Linux
[root@arm3 ~]#
```

Figure 7.9 – Ksplice uname

Here, the installed kernel is 5.4.17-2136.302.7.2.1.el8uek.aarch64, but the effective kernel that has been Kspliced is a newer kernel at version 5.4.17-2136.306.1.3.el8uek. This is normal behavior with Ksplice.

User space libraries can be patched in the same way, replacing the kernel with the user. As a note, if the Ksplice user space libraries are *not* installed, the first time the command is run, you will be prompted to upgrade the user libraries to a Ksplice-compatible version:

```
[root@arm2 ~]# ksplice -n user upgrade
Updating on-disk packages for new processes
Ksplice aware userspace packages for Oracle Linux 8 (aarch64)                    5.3 MB/s | 1.0 MB    00:00
Dependencies resolved.
================================================================================================================
 Package             Architecture     Version                              Repository                      Size
================================================================================================================
Upgrading:
 glibc               aarch64          2:2.28-164.0.5.ksplice2.el8_5.3      ol8_aarch64_userspace_ksplice   3.6 M
 glibc-common        aarch64          2:2.28-164.0.5.ksplice2.el8_5.3      ol8_aarch64_userspace_ksplice   1.3 M
 glibc-devel         aarch64          2:2.28-164.0.5.ksplice2.el8_5.3      ol8_aarch64_userspace_ksplice   1.0 M
 glibc-headers       aarch64          2:2.28-164.0.5.ksplice2.el8_5.3      ol8_aarch64_userspace_ksplice   473 k
 glibc-langpack-en   aarch64          2:2.28-164.0.5.ksplice2.el8_5.3      ol8_aarch64_userspace_ksplice   831 k
 openssl             aarch64          2:1.1.1k-6.ksplice1.el8_5            ol8_aarch64_userspace_ksplice   690 k
 openssl-libs        aarch64          2:1.1.1k-6.ksplice1.el8_5            ol8_aarch64_userspace_ksplice   1.3 M
Installing dependencies:
 ksplice-helper      aarch64          1.0.55-1.el8                         ol8_aarch64_userspace_ksplice    23 k

Transaction Summary
================================================================================================================
Install  1 Package
Upgrade  7 Packages

Total download size: 9.2 M
Is this ok [y/N]:
```

Figure 7.10 – Installing Ksplice user libraries for the first time

> **Note**
>
> You can also check user space available packages to Ksplice with the ksplice user show --available command but if you did not install the Ksplice-aware packages, you will get this error:
>
> ```
> No active user-space Ksplice targets
> Have you installed Ksplice-aware libraries and rebooted?
> ```

You can also check what user space targets are currently running and can be patched. This is done with the following command:

```
ksplice all list-targets
```

The sample output is shown in the following screenshot:

```
[root@arm3 ~]# ksplice all list-targets
100% |###################################################################################################################
User-space targets:

glibc-libnss_files-2.28.164.0.5.ksplice2.el8_5.3-aarch64:
 - crond (37487)
 - ksplice (67241)

glibc-libpthread-2.28.164.0.5.ksplice2.el8_5.3-aarch64:
 - crond (37487)
 - ksplice (67241)

glibc-libc-2.28.164.0.5.ksplice2.el8_5.3-aarch64:
 - crond (37487)
 - sleep (67182)
 - ksplice (67241)
 - less (67245)

glibc-libdl-2.28.164.0.5.ksplice2.el8_5.3-aarch64:
 - crond (37487)
 - ksplice (67241)

glibc-librt-2.28.164.0.5.ksplice2.el8_5.3-aarch64:
 - ksplice (67241)

openssl-libssl-1.1.1k.6.ksplice1.el8_5-aarch64:
 - ksplice (67241)

glibc-libm-2.28.164.0.5.ksplice2.el8_5.3-aarch64:
 - ksplice (67241)

glibc-libutil-2.28.164.0.5.ksplice2.el8_5.3-aarch64:
 - ksplice (67241)

openssl-libcrypto-1.1.1k.6.ksplice1.el8_5-aarch64:
 - ksplice (67241)

Kernel version: Linux/aarch64/5.4.17-2136.302.7.2.1.el8uek.aarch64/#2 SMP Tue Jan 18 12:11:39 PST 2022
[root@arm3 ~]#
```

Figure 7.11 – Ksplice targets

The Ksplice command can also be used to roll back a splice. By using the `ksplice kernel show` command, you can see all the splices currently installed:

```
[root@arm3 ~]# ksplice kernel show
Installed updates:
[ien9pqdn] CVE-2021-4034: Privilege escalation in pkexec.
[33t3hakz] Delays in realtime scheduling or network traffic handling tasks.
[h26cy11t] CVE-2022-0492: Privilege escalation in Control Groups feature.
[ep86xik8] CVE-2021-43975: Out-of-bounds access in aQuantia AQtion(tm) Ethernet card driver.
[oozzmvxm] CVE-2021-20321: Race condition in OverlayFS.
[8f6yhp9u] CVE-2021-3752: Use-after-free in the Bluetooth subsystem.
[qd1g4vxd] CVE-2021-4149: Denial-of-service in BTRFS file system.
[mm2nv40d] CVE-2021-3640: Privilege escalation in Bluetooth Classic due to use-after-free.
[2v0kh9y6] CVE-2022-25636: Privilege escalation in netfilter when using flow offload.
[lrav84fj] CVE-2022-0847: Privilege escalation in pipe buffers.
[7w408xbj] CVE-2020-27820: Denial-of-service in Nouveau (nVidia) cards support.
[16a8704b] CVE-2021-4002: Information disclosure in the hugetlb due to memory leak.
[p6mb2n44] CVE-2022-0435: Denial-of-service in Transparent Inter-Process Communication protocol.
[gmsooca9] CVE-2022-24448: Information leak when NFSv4 directory lookup fails.
[qogt9cqb] CVE-2021-22600: Privilege escalation in Packet protocol subsystem due to double-free.
[owhqpfck] CVE-2022-0617: NULL-pointer dereference when processing UDF metadata.
[d9kvweqx] CVE-2022-26966: Information disclosure in CoreChip SR9700 USB 10/100 Ethernet adapter.
[obt12e91] CVE-2020-36516: Multiple vulnerabilities in TCP/IP protocol.
[a084mvfp] CVE-2022-1016: Information leak in the netfilter subsystem.

Effective kernel version is 5.4.17-2136.306.1.3.el8uek
[root@arm3 ~]#
```

Figure 7.12 – Installed kernel patches

Each Ksplice patch has a unique **Ksplice identifier** (**KID**). The KID is also unique to the specific kernel build and patch, so when comparing KIDs across different kernels, be careful. If using automation to leverage the KID, make sure that you limit the automation to systems with the same kernel build and architecture.

This is the first column in the list of installed patches. If you need to uninstall a specific patch, it is possible. In this example, KID qd1g4vxd (CVE-2021-4149: denial-of-service in the BTRFS filesystem) will be uninstalled using the Ksplice undo command, passing the specific KID. You can also pass -v for verbose. Once uninstalled, check the list of installed KIDs to verify the removal of the single KID:

```
[root@arm3 ~]# ksplice -v kernel undo qd1g4vxd
We are an OCI system. Determining region.
OCI host running in us-ashburn-1 (domain oraclecloud.com)
Region-local remote root set to https://updates.ksplice.us-ashburn-1.oci.oraclecloud.com/ksplice/request
Running kernel undo.
removing qd1g4vxd from the kernel
[root@arm3 ~]# ksplice kernel show
Installed updates:
[ien9pqdn] CVE-2021-4034: Privilege escalation in pkexec.
[33t3hakz] Delays in realtime scheduling or network traffic handling tasks.
[h26cy11t] CVE-2022-0492: Privilege escalation in Control Groups feature.
[ep86xik8] CVE-2021-43975: Out-of-bounds access in aQuantia AQtion(tm) Ethernet card driver.
[oozzmvxm] CVE-2021-20321: Race condition in OverlayFS.
[8f6yhp9u] CVE-2021-3752: Use-after-free in the Bluetooth subsystem.
[mm2nv40d] CVE-2021-3640: Privilege escalation in Bluetooth Classic due to use-after-free.
[2v0kh9y6] CVE-2022-25636: Privilege escalation in netfilter when using flow offload.
[lrav84fj] CVE-2022-0847: Privilege escalation in pipe buffers.
[7w408xbj] CVE-2020-27820: Denial-of-service in Nouveau (nVidia) cards support.
[16a8704b] CVE-2021-4002: Information disclosure in the hugetlb due to memory leak.
[p6mb2n44] CVE-2022-0435: Denial-of-service in Transparent Inter-Process Communication protocol.
[gmsooca9] CVE-2022-24448: Information leak when NFSv4 directory lookup fails.
[qogt9cqb] CVE-2021-22600: Privilege escalation in Packet protocol subsystem due to double-free.
[owhqpfck] CVE-2022-0617: NULL-pointer dereference when processing UDF metadata.
[d9kvweqx] CVE-2022-26966: Information disclosure in CoreChip SR9700 USB 10/100 Ethernet adapter.
[obt12e91] CVE-2020-36516: Multiple vulnerabilities in TCP/IP protocol.
[a084mvfp] CVE-2022-1016: Information leak in the netfilter subsystem.
[root@arm3 ~]#
```

Figure 7.13 – Ksplice undo

Optionally, all installed KIDs can be removed from a running system by using the following command:

```
ksplice kernel remove --all
```

This will remove all the KIDs from the running kernel in memory:

```
[root@arm3 ~]# ksplice kernel remove --all
The following steps will be taken:
Remove [a084mvfp] CVE-2022-1016: Information leak in the netfilter subsystem.
Remove [obt12e9l] CVE-2020-36516: Multiple vulnerabilities in TCP/IP protocol.
Remove [d9kvweqx] CVE-2022-26966: Information disclosure in CoreChip SR9700 USB 10/100 Ethernet adapter.
Remove [owhqpfck] CVE-2022-0617: NULL-pointer dereference when processing UDF metadata.
Remove [qogt9cqb] CVE-2021-22600: Privilege escalation in Packet protocol subsystem due to double-free.
Remove [gmsooca9] CVE-2022-24448: Information leak when NFSv4 directory lookup fails.
Remove [p6mb2n44] CVE-2022-0435: Denial-of-service in Transparent Inter-Process Communication protocol.
Remove [16a8704b] CVE-2021-4002: Information disclosure in the hugetlb due to memory leak.
Remove [7w408xbj] CVE-2020-27820: Denial-of-service in Nouveau (nVidia) cards support.
Remove [lrav84fj] CVE-2022-0847: Privilege escalation in pipe buffers.
Remove [2v0kh9y6] CVE-2022-25636: Privilege escalation in netfilter when using flow offload.
Remove [mm2nv40d] CVE-2021-3640: Privilege escalation in Bluetooth Classic due to use-after-free.
Remove [8f6yhp9u] CVE-2021-3752: Use-after-free in the Bluetooth subsystem.
Remove [oozzmvxm] CVE-2021-20321: Race condition in OverlayFS.
Remove [ep86xik8] CVE-2021-43975: Out-of-bounds access in aQuantia AQtion(tm) Ethernet card driver.
Remove [h26cy1lt] CVE-2022-0492: Privilege escalation in Control Groups feature.
Remove [33t3hakz] Delays in realtime scheduling or network traffic handling tasks.
Remove [ien9pqdn] CVE-2021-4034: Privilege escalation in pkexec.

Go ahead [y/N]? y
Removing [a084mvfp] CVE-2022-1016: Information leak in the netfilter subsystem.
Removing [obt12e9l] CVE-2020-36516: Multiple vulnerabilities in TCP/IP protocol.
Removing [d9kvweqx] CVE-2022-26966: Information disclosure in CoreChip SR9700 USB 10/100 Ethernet adapter.
Removing [owhqpfck] CVE-2022-0617: NULL-pointer dereference when processing UDF metadata.
Removing [qogt9cqb] CVE-2021-22600: Privilege escalation in Packet protocol subsystem due to double-free.
Removing [gmsooca9] CVE-2022-24448: Information leak when NFSv4 directory lookup fails.
Removing [p6mb2n44] CVE-2022-0435: Denial-of-service in Transparent Inter-Process Communication protocol.
Removing [16a8704b] CVE-2021-4002: Information disclosure in the hugetlb due to memory leak.
Removing [7w408xbj] CVE-2020-27820: Denial-of-service in Nouveau (nVidia) cards support.
Removing [lrav84fj] CVE-2022-0847: Privilege escalation in pipe buffers.
Removing [2v0kh9y6] CVE-2022-25636: Privilege escalation in netfilter when using flow offload.
Removing [mm2nv40d] CVE-2021-3640: Privilege escalation in Bluetooth Classic due to use-after-free.
Removing [8f6yhp9u] CVE-2021-3752: Use-after-free in the Bluetooth subsystem.
Removing [oozzmvxm] CVE-2021-20321: Race condition in OverlayFS.
Removing [ep86xik8] CVE-2021-43975: Out-of-bounds access in aQuantia AQtion(tm) Ethernet card driver.
Removing [h26cy1lt] CVE-2022-0492: Privilege escalation in Control Groups feature.
Removing [33t3hakz] Delays in realtime scheduling or network traffic handling tasks.
Removing [ien9pqdn] CVE-2021-4034: Privilege escalation in pkexec.
Effective kernel version is 5.4.17-2136.302.7.2.1.el8uek
[root@arm3 ~]#
```

Figure 7.14 – Ksplice remove

Ksplice also allows for automatic updates. They can be enabled or disabled by simply touching a file, or removing a file. If the /etc/uptrack/disable file exists, Ksplice will not automatically update the system when you reboot. If the file is not there, then Ksplice will check on reboot for any new KIDs and apply them. You can also modify this behavior by updating the uptrack.conf file. This is covered later in this chapter.

## How it works...

When you are using Ksplice with internet access, the Ksplice client connects to the Oracle ULN Ksplice system, and downloads and applies the required splices.

# Using Ksplice with no internet access

Not all systems have internet access. That is fine, as it's possible to use Ksplice against a local patch repository.

## Getting ready

To do this, you will need a test system running Oracle Linux 8, with access to a local YUM repository on the network.

## How to do it...

To install the client, make sure that your server is using an RPM repo that is mirrored locally. To install Ksplice, you must decide on either the online or offline client. As a reminder, the online client requires that the system be registered with ULN, and the offline client will use a local RPM repository.

To install the online client, run the following command:

```
dnf install -y ksplice uptrack
```

To install the offline client, run the following command:

```
dnf install -y ksplice ksplice-offline uptrack-offline
```

The output from this command is shown in the following screenshot:

```
Running transaction check
Transaction check succeeded.
Running transaction test
Transaction test succeeded.
Running transaction
  Preparing          :                                                    1/1
  Installing         : uptrack-offline-1.2.75.offline-0.el8.noarch        1/7
  Running scriptlet: uptrack-offline-1.2.75.offline-0.el8.noarch          1/7
There are no existing modules on disk that need basename migration.
Now run 'uptrack-upgrade' to protect your kernel

  Installing         : boost-filesystem-1.66.0-10.el8.x86_64              2/7
  Running scriptlet: boost-filesystem-1.66.0-10.el8.x86_64                2/7
  Installing         : boost-python3-1.66.0-6.el8.x86_64                  3/7
  Running scriptlet: boost-python3-1.66.0-6.el8.x86_64                    3/7
  Installing         : ksplice-core0-1.0.55-1.el8.x86_64                  4/7
  Installing         : ksplice-tools-1.0.55-1.el8.x86_64                  5/7
  Running scriptlet: ksplice-tools-1.0.55-1.el8.x86_64                    5/7
  Installing         : ksplice-1.0.55-1.el8.x86_64                        6/7
  Running scriptlet: ksplice-1.0.55-1.el8.x86_64                          6/7
  Installing         : ksplice-offline-1.0.55-1.el8.x86_64                7/7
  Running scriptlet: ksplice-offline-1.0.55-1.el8.x86_64                  7/7
  Verifying          : boost-python3-1.66.0-6.el8.x86_64                  1/7
  Verifying          : ksplice-1.0.55-1.el8.x86_64                        2/7
  Verifying          : ksplice-core0-1.0.55-1.el8.x86_64                  3/7
  Verifying          : ksplice-offline-1.0.55-1.el8.x86_64                4/7
  Verifying          : ksplice-tools-1.0.55-1.el8.x86_64                  5/7
  Verifying          : uptrack-offline-1.2.75.offline-0.el8.noarch        6/7
  Verifying          : boost-filesystem-1.66.0-10.el8.x86_64              7/7

Installed:
  boost-filesystem-1.66.0-10.el8.x86_64        boost-python3-1.66.0-6.el8.x86_64
  ksplice-1.0.55-1.el8.x86_64                  ksplice-core0-1.0.55-1.el8.x86_64
  ksplice-offline-1.0.55-1.el8.x86_64          ksplice-tools-1.0.55-1.el8.x86_64
  uptrack-offline-1.2.75.offline-0.el8.noarch

Complete!
[root@ol8 /]#
```

Figure 7.15 – Offline Ksplice installation

Once Ksplice is installed, you can now splice the server.

> **Note**
>
> Since the Uptrack client has no advantages over the new client with Oracle Linux 8 (or Oracle Linux 7 for that matter), we will focus on the Enhanced client. If you are using an older operating system, you may need to use the older Uptrack client.

Ksplice with the offline method is really easy; simply use `dnf` to patch the system:

```
dnf -y update
```

This will patch in both the normal way and then with Ksplice for the kernel and user libraries. If you want to disable this behavior, you can set `skip_apply_after_pkg_install` to `true` in `/etc/uptrack/uptrack.conf`.

Before you patch, make sure you have added a Ksplice entry in `/etc/yum.repos.d`. A sample Ksplice entry may look like the following:

```
[root@ol8 ~]# more /etc/yum.repos.d/Ksplice.repo
[Ksplice_ol8_local]
name=Ksplice for OL8
baseurl=http://yum.m57.local/yum/OracleLinux/OL8/Ksplice/x86_64/ol8_
x86_64_Ksplice/
gpgkey=file:///etc/pki/rpm-gpg/RPM-GPG-KEY
gpgcheck=1
enabled=1

[Ksplice_ol8_userspace]
name=Ksplice OL8 userspace
baseurl=http://yum.m57.local/yum/OracleLinux/OL8/userspace/Ksplice/
x86_64/ol8_x86_64_userspace_Ksplice/
gpgkey=file:///etc/pki/rpm-gpg/RPM-GPG-KEY
gpgcheck=1
enabled=1
```

## How it works...

Ksplice is a tool that allows Linux systems to stay current with security fixes and vital updates without requiring system reboots. This is especially beneficial for servers and settings that need to stay up and running with little downtime. It's worth noting that while Ksplice can handle many patches, some changes may be too intricate to apply in a live environment and will require a traditional reboot-based update.

# Installing and enabling Known Exploit Detection

One of the most critical things to do to secure your system (and, more importantly, the data in the system) is to implement the ability to detect when the bad guys are trying to break in. Ksplice has a unique feature called **Known Exploit Detection (KED)** that will report on known attacks against the kernel. Normally, only exploits that allow the hacker to access additional privileges are instrumented for KED and, for these to trigger, the kernel should already have been spliced for the vulnerability.

## Getting ready

To do this, you will need a test system running Oracle Linux 8, with Ksplice set up.

## How to do it...

This is done via tripwire code, which is triggered when specific events are detected. Normally, only events that enable the attacker to gain privileged access are monitored. This package is available on both x86 and ARM systems.

To enable this, the pack must first be installed by using the following command:

```
dnf install -y ksplice-known-exploit-detection
```

Regardless of whether the installation is on an ARM or x64 server, the installation is almost identical, with the major differences being more about the software already installed on each system. This brings a point to mind: regardless of whether ARM or x64, the admin tasks are the same.

> **Note**
> When KED is installed, `postfix` is also installed to enable sending emails as part of the notification system.

The output from installing this on an ARM-based system is shown in the following screenshot:

```
[root@arm3 ~]# dnf -y  install ksplice-known-exploit-detection
Last metadata expiration check: 1:23:34 ago on Sun 24 Apr 2022 02:00:29 PM GMT.
Dependencies resolved.
================================================================================================
 Package                   Architecture        Version            Repository              Size
================================================================================================
Installing:
                           aarch64             1.0.55-1.el8       ol8_ksplice             16 k
Installing dependencies:
                           aarch64             2:3.5.8-2.el8      ol8_baseos_latest        1.5 M

Transaction Summary
================================================================================================
Install  2 Packages

Total download size: 1.5 M
Installed size: 6.2 M
Downloading Packages:
(1/2): postfix-3.5.8-2.el8.aarch64.rpm                         11 MB/s | 1.5 MB      00:00
(2/2): ksplice-known-exploit-detection-1.0.55-1.el8.aarch64.rpm  30 kB/s |  16 kB    00:00
------------------------------------------------------------------------------------------------
Total                                                          2.8 MB/s | 1.5 MB     00:00
Running transaction check
Transaction check succeeded.
Running transaction test                                                   I
Transaction test succeeded.
Running transaction
  Preparing        :                                                                   1/1
  Running scriptlet: postfix-2:3.5.8-2.el8.aarch64                                     1/2
  Installing       : postfix-2:3.5.8-2.el8.aarch64                                     1/2
  Running scriptlet: postfix-2:3.5.8-2.el8.aarch64                                     1/2
  Installing       : ksplice-known-exploit-detection-1.0.55-1.el8.aarch64             2/2
  Running scriptlet: ksplice-known-exploit-detection-1.0.55-1.el8.aarch64             2/2
  Verifying        : ksplice-known-exploit-detection-1.0.55-1.el8.aarch64             1/2
  Verifying        : postfix-2:3.5.8-2.el8.aarch64                                     2/2

Installed:
  ksplice-known-exploit-detection-1.0.55-1.el8.aarch64         postfix-2:3.5.8-2.el8.aarch64

Complete!
[root@arm3 ~]# 
```

Figure 7.16 – KED installation on ARM

The output from installing this on an x86_64-based system is shown in the following screenshot:

```
[root@ol8splice2 ~]# dnf install -y ksplice-known-exploit-detection
This system is receiving updates from Unbreakable Linux Network or Spacewalk.
Last metadata expiration check: 3:01:04 ago on Sun 24 Apr 2022 08:24:43 AM EDT.
Dependencies resolved.
================================================================================================
 Package                   Architecture        Version            Repository              Size
================================================================================================
Installing:
                           x86_64              1.0.55-1.el8       ol8_x86_64_ksplice      16 k
Installing dependencies:
                           x86_64              1.2-15.el8         ol8_x86_64_developer_EPEL  58 k
                           x86_64              1.0.6-18.el8       ol8_x86_64_developer_EPEL  71 k
                           x86_64              1.14-1.el8         ol8_x86_64_appstream    32 k

Transaction Summary
================================================================================================
Install  4 Packages

Total download size: 177 k
Installed size: 469 k
Downloading Packages:
(1/4): liblockfile-1.14-1.el8.x86_64.rpm                       179 kB/s |  32 kB      00:00
(2/4): ksplice-known-exploit-detection-1.0.55-1.el8.x86_64.rpm  91 kB/s |  16 kB     00:00
(3/4): esmtp-1.2-15.el8.x86_64.rpm                             278 kB/s |  58 kB      00:00
(4/4): libesmtp-1.0.6-18.el8.x86_64.rpm                        955 kB/s |  71 kB      00:00
------------------------------------------------------------------------------------------------
Total                                                          697 kB/s | 177 kB     00:00
Running transaction check
Transaction check succeeded.
Running transaction test
Transaction test succeeded.
Running transaction
  Preparing        :                                                                   1/1
  Installing       : libesmtp-1.0.6-18.el8.x86_64                                      1/4
  Installing       : liblockfile-1.14-1.el8.x86_64                                     2/4
  Running scriptlet: liblockfile-1.14-1.el8.x86_64                                     2/4
/sbin/ldconfig: /etc/ld.so.conf.d/kernel-5.4.17-2102.201.3.el8uek.x86_64.conf:6: hwcap directive ignored

  Installing       : esmtp-1.2-15.el8.x86_64                                           3/4
  Running scriptlet: esmtp-1.2-15.el8.x86_64                                           3/4
  Installing       : ksplice-known-exploit-detection-1.0.55-1.el8.x86_64              4/4
  Running scriptlet: ksplice-known-exploit-detection-1.0.55-1.el8.x86_64              4/4
/sbin/ldconfig: /etc/ld.so.conf.d/kernel-5.4.17-2102.201.3.el8uek.x86_64.conf:6: hwcap directive ignored

  Verifying        : liblockfile-1.14-1.el8.x86_64                                     1/4
  Verifying        : ksplice-known-exploit-detection-1.0.55-1.el8.x86_64              2/4
  Verifying        : esmtp-1.2-15.el8.x86_64                                           3/4
  Verifying        : libesmtp-1.0.6-18.el8.x86_64                                      4/4

Installed:
  esmtp-1.2-15.el8.x86_64    ksplice-known-exploit-detection-1.0.55-1.el8.x86_64    libesmtp-1.0.6-18.el8.x86_64    liblockfile-1.14-1.el8.x86_64

Complete!
[root@ol8splice2 ~]# 
```

Figure 7.17 – KED installation on x64

Once KED is installed, the feature needs to be enabled. This is done by adding the following lines to `/etc/uptrack/uptrack.conf`:

```
[Known-Exploit-Detection]
enabled = yes
```

Next, you will need to Ksplice the kernel to enable the feature in the running kernel:

```
ksplice --yes  kernel upgrade
```

The output for this is shown in the following screenshot:

```
[root@arm3 ~]# ksplice kernel upgrade
Nothing to be done.
Your kernel is fully up to date.
Effective kernel version is 5.4.17-2136.306.1.3.el8uek
[root@arm3 ~]#
```

Figure 7.18 – Enabling KED in a running kernel

As a note, if no Ksplice patches are available, you will get a notification that the kernel is up to date, as shown in the preceding screenshot. But if the system requires patches, Ksplice will patch the kernel at this time while enabling KED.

To verify that KED is enabled, cat `/proc/sys/kernel/known_exploit_detection` and look for an output of 1. If the file is missing or there is a zero there, KED is not enabled so won't be monitoring your system:

```
[root@ol8splice2 ~]# cat /proc/sys/kernel/known_exploit_detection
1
[root@ol8splice2 ~]#
```

Figure 7.19 – Checking whether KED is enabled

Notifications from KED are controlled from the `/etc/log-known-exploit.conf` configuration file. A sample configuration file is shown in the following screenshot:

```
[root@ol8splice2 ~]# more  /etc/log-known-exploit.conf
[syslog]
enabled: 1

[email]
enabled: 1
recipients: erik@talesfromthedatacenter.com

[actions]
# You can use this section to set specific actions to be taken for specific
# tripwires.
#
# Currently valid actions are:
#  - report
#  - ignore
#
# Ignoring specific tripwires could be useful in the rare case that a
# legitimate user/application actually causes a false positive report.
# In this case, you can do e.g.:
#
#     [actions]
#     CVE-2017-1234: ignore
#
# You can specify a default action using the 'default' entry. So if you
# wanted to ignore everything and enable only one specific tripwire, you
# could do:
#
#     [actions]
#     default: ignore
#     CVE-2017-1234: report
[root@ol8splice2 ~]# █
```

Figure 7.20 – KED notifications configuration

In the config file, you can control the following actions:

- [syslog]: Most admins log events to syslog for capture and analysis using log analytics tools such as OCI Log Analytics or Splunk. The enabled:  0 setting will disable logging to syslog.

- [email]: This section allows you to enable emails to be sent when a tripwire is triggered. Add email addresses for recipients as needed. This will also require that the system can send emails, either through a cloud service such as the OCI Email Delivery Service or your own **Simple Mail Transport Protocol (SMTP)** relay.

- [actions]: You can specifically disable notifications for a specific CVE. This is helpful if you have an accidental false positive on a system. To disable a CVE, add a line with the CVE and ignore. The default: parameter sets the default behavior for all CVE.

> **Note**
>
> If you enable email notification, make sure your email subsystem is configured before enabling emails from KED.

You can also test the system with the `log-known-exploit` command. This will log a test message in the kernel:

```
/usr/sbin/log-known-exploit -f -d ; tail /var/log/messages
```

The test event will look like the following in `/var/log/messages`:

```
Apr 22 23:01:02 ol8splice2 /log-known-exploit[4192]: exploit attempt
detected; id=CVE-2012-1234 pid=1337 uid=1000 comm=./dummy-exploit
lost=0
```

In the log, you will see the time, the CVE that was triggered, and also the **Process ID (PID)** and **User ID (UID)** of the process and user that triggered the event.

## How it works...

Ksplice installs a piece of tripwire code in the kernel for specific exploits, detecting when something tries to exploit the exploit. These triggers then kick off the notification subsystem, letting you know when an attack happens.

# 8

# DevOps Automation Tools – Terraform, Ansible, Packer, and More

What good is an operating system if it doesn't cater to developers? After all, an operating system that's easy to develop on tends to enjoy a much stronger ecosystem than one that does not. You'll be happy to learn that Oracle Linux plays very nicely with developers, and this chapter is all about common development tools that will make your life easier when setting out to work on your next project.

There are countless development tools that work well on Oracle Linux, but the ones we're focusing on in this chapter are all about automation. We'll be talking about automating cloud infrastructure, automating the operating system build cycle, automating system administrators' tasks, and automating the launching of virtual machines for development purposes.

In this chapter, we're going to cover the following recipes:

- Do it once manually – rinse and repeat with Terraform
- Creating portable roles for Ansible
- Managing secrets with Ansible Vault
- Cooking up the perfect lab environment with Vagrant
- Using Packer to modify source images
- Pack it up, pack it in, let me begin, err, umm… build

## Technical requirements

We're covering a lot of technologies in this chapter. Let's prepare your machine so that you can conveniently follow along with the recipes.

## Ansible

For Oracle Linux 8, we can install Ansible by leveraging the **Oracle Linux Automation Manager** repository, so let's install the repository first, and then we'll install Ansible:

```
$ sudo dnf install -y oraclelinux-automation-manager-release-el8
$ sudo dnf install -y ansible
```

## Packer, Vagrant, and Terraform

Packer is a tool used for automating the creation of machine images, Vagrant is used for managing the lifecycle of virtual machines, and Terraform is an infrastructure-as-code tool. Packer, Vagrant, and Terraform are all products of HashiCorp, but they work well on Oracle Linux.

We're going to install Packer, Vagrant, and Terraform directly from HashiCorp:

```
$ sudo dnf install -y dnf-plugins-core
$ sudo dnf config-manager --add-repo https://rpm.releases.hashicorp.
com/RHEL/hashicorp.repo
$ sudo dnf install -y packer vagrant terraform
```

Once that's finished, let's go ahead and install **Oracle VM VirtualBox**, as we'll be using VirtualBox with **Packer** and **Vagrant**:

```
$ sudo dnf install -y oraclelinux-developer-release-el8
$ sudo dnf install -y VirtualBox-7.0
```

Finally, along with Terraform, we'll also want to create an **Oracle Cloud Infrastructure** (**OCI**) account. If you prefer, you may opt to use a different cloud, but use OCI if you want to follow this tutorial directly.

> **Important note**
> Be sure to remember your Cloud Account Name as this is an important detail required in order to access your OCI account.

## Downloading the source code

The source code for the recipes in this chapter can be found at `https://github.com/PacktPublishing/Oracle-Linux-Cookbook/tree/main/ch8`.

# Do it once manually – rinse and repeat with Terraform

Terraform is an **infrastructure-as-code** (**IaC**) tool that lets you build, change, and version infrastructure safely and efficiently. This recipe will provide a general overview of a good technique for automating the *ugly* with **Terraform**. What do I mean by *ugly*? Well, it's anything that's being done manually. We want to cut out the manual steps and automate as much as possible. In the case of Terraform specifically, this means we're going to automate the deployment of cloud infrastructure. Thanks to Terraform, we no longer need to click around through a hundred different menu settings. Instead, we're going to define our **infrastructure as code**. This results in faster and more consistent deployments. Additionally, it's also much easier to make changes to your infrastructure since it can all be edited via code.

## Getting started

You will need the following for this recipe:

- Oracle Linux

- Terraform

Refer to the *Technical requirements* section at the beginning of this chapter if you need help installing Terraform.

## How to do it...

Any time you set out to automate something, it's always a good idea to have a solid grasp on what needs to be done under the hood. Can you guess what that means? Yep, you've got to perform all the manual steps at least once before trying to automate it.

### First, do it once manually...

The goal for this recipe is to use Terraform to deploy a simple VM in the cloud. It's an easy enough task, but before we jump into how this can be done using code, it's generally best to do it manually first. So, with that being said, let's go ahead and deploy a virtual machine using the OCI web GUI:

1.  Log in to the Oracle Cloud Infrastructure Console (`https://cloud.oracle.com/`).

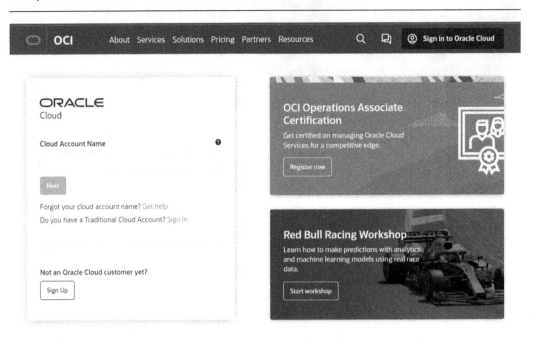

Figure 8.1 – OCI Console Login Page

2.    Click on the hamburger menu icon at the top left:

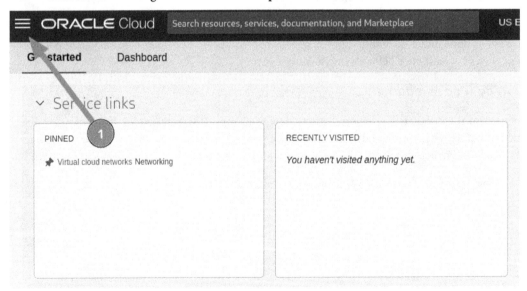

Figure 8.2 – OCI Console main screen

Then click on **Compute | Instances**:

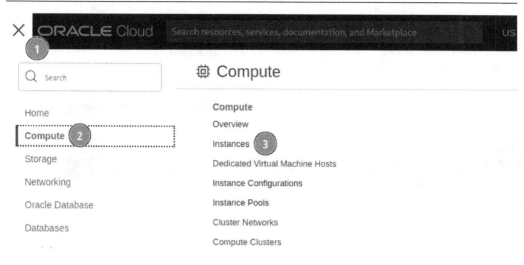

Figure 8.3 – OCI Cloud Compute menu

Verify you are in the desired **Compartment**, and finally, click on **Create instance**:

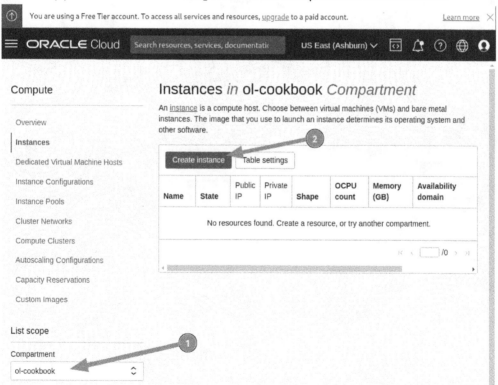

Figure 8.4 – OCI Cloud Compute Instances

> **Info**
>
> For brevity, when multiple menu items need to be clicked, the pipe symbol (|) indicates the sequence in which to click buttons/links.

3.  We're going to use the default Oracle Linux image, but if you want to change this, you can go to **Image and shape** and click on **Edit**.

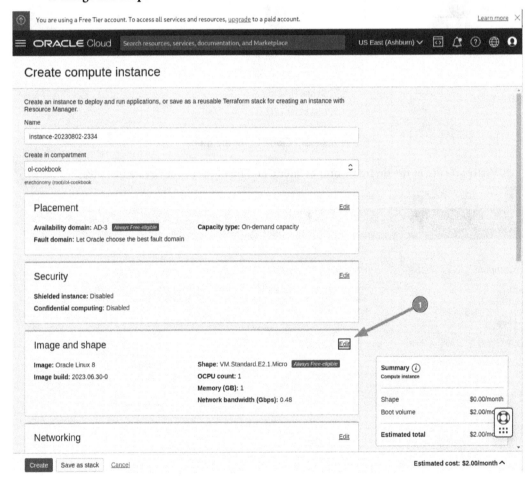

Figure 8.5 – OCI Console Compute Image and shape

> **Note**
>
> There's no cost as long as you stick to all **Always Free-eligible** resources; however, at the time of writing, there is a bug that falsely shows a $2.00 per month charge for the boot volume. This is a bug as the boot volume uses block storage and OCI gives you up to 200 GB of block storage for free.
>
> At the time of writing, the latest version is *Oracle Linux 8* (image build: 2023.06.30-0).

4.  Under **Add SSH Keys**, select **Generate a key pair for me** and then click on **Save Private Key** and **Save Public Key**.

> **Tip**
>
> Choose a place that is easy for you to remember, as you'll need this later when you seek to SSH into your VM.

5.  Finally, click on **Create**.

> **Note**
>
> Feel free to grab a coffee while waiting for the image to build.

Now, let's use SSH to connect to the instance:

1.  On the **Instance information** tab, click on **Copy** next to the **Public IP address** entry.

2.  Open up a terminal application and use the ssh command to connect. We'll use -i (where i stands for identify file) to reference the private key we saved in the previous steps. The default username for official Oracle Linux instances hosted in the OCI is opc, so we'll instruct ssh to connect as opc. Finally, input the **Public IP address** you obtained in the previous step. Your command should look a bit like this:

```
[vagrant@localhost ol8-cookbook]$ ssh -i ssh-key-2023-08-03.key opc@129.80.70.82
The authenticity of host '129.80.70.82 (129.80.70.82)' can't be established.
ECDSA key fingerprint is SHA256:IZz/L8HMm8ZopD6on7aMN3VwLcAcqkal6f25QlMQ9FM.
Are you sure you want to continue connecting (yes/no/[fingerprint])? yes
Warning: Permanently added '129.80.70.82' (ECDSA) to the list of known hosts.
@@@@@@@@@@@@@@@@@@@@@@@@@@@@@@@@@@@@@@@@@@@@@@@@@@@@@@@@@@@@@@@@@@@
@       WARNING: UNPROTECTED PRIVATE KEY FILE!          @
@@@@@@@@@@@@@@@@@@@@@@@@@@@@@@@@@@@@@@@@@@@@@@@@@@@@@@@@@@@@@@@@@@@
Permissions 0644 for 'ssh-key-2023-08-03.key' are too open.
It is required that your private key files are NOT accessible by others.
This private key will be ignored.
Load key "ssh-key-2023-08-03.key": bad permissions
opc@129.80.70.82's password: 
```

Figure 8.6 – SSH into compute instance (failure)

3. Uh oh! Did you notice the big warning, as well as that last message? We were denied access because of bad permissions. Let's fix that using chmod to give only the owner permission to access the key file:

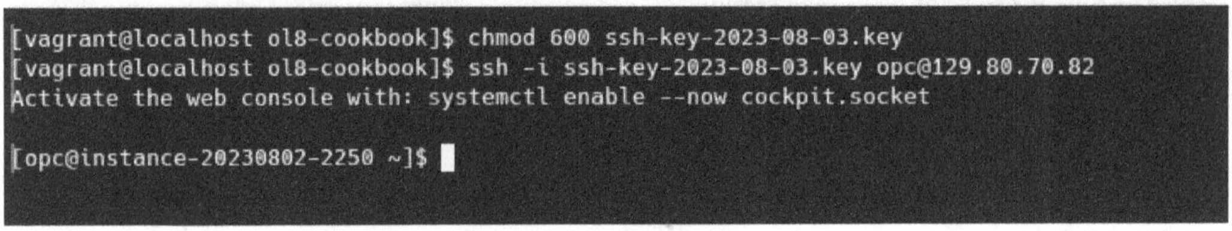

```
[vagrant@localhost ol8-cookbook]$ chmod 600 ssh-key-2023-08-03.key
[vagrant@localhost ol8-cookbook]$ ssh -i ssh-key-2023-08-03.key opc@129.80.70.82
Activate the web console with: systemctl enable --now cockpit.socket

[opc@instance-20230802-2250 ~]$ 
```

Figure 8.7 – SSH into compute instance (success)

Great! We've connected to the machine via SSH.

Now I do realize that this wasn't all that difficult, but imagine if you had to do this a hundred times? Why not automate the process with Terraform?

### Now it's time to rinse and repeat with Terraform

This time around, we're going to accomplish the exact same thing that was described earlier – that is, we're going to create another virtual machine in OCI. However, this time around, we're going to define our IaC using Terraform:

1. First, let's create three new files within the root of your project directory (I'm naming this one terraform) using your favorite code editor, and name them as follows:

    A. main.tf

    B. variables.tf

    C. terraform.tfvars

2. Next, let's head to the Terraform Registry (https://registry.terraform.io/) to find the provider for **Oracle Cloud Infrastructure (OCI)**.

3. On the Terraform Registry, search for either oci or oracle cloud infrastructure and select **oracle/oci**.

> **Note**
>
> Alternatively, you can click on **Browse Providers** and then click on the **Oracle Cloud Infrastructure** button.

4. Click on **USE PROVIDER**, and copy and paste the code displayed into your main.tf file:

```
terraform {
  required_providers {
    oci = {
      source = "oracle/oci"
      version = "5.7.0"
    }
  }
}

provider "oci" {
  # Configuration options
}
```

Figure 8.8 – Terraform OCI provider

5.  Notice the comment for # Configuration options under the provider "oci".
    This tells us we may need to supply some configuration options in order to use the provider.

    Let's take a look at how to do this:

    A.  Click on the **Documentation** tab (it's right next to **USE PROVIDER**), then find the link
        on **How to configure the provider**.

    B.  You'll find that the OCI Terraform provider supports four authentication methods:

        • **API Key Authentication** (default)

        • **Instance Principal Authorization**

        • **Resource Principal Authentication**

        • **Security Token Authentication**

    C.  For this recipe, I'll be using the default authentication method; that is, **API Key Authentication**.
        This method has the fewest limitations, but depending on your use case, you can choose
        the one that best meets your needs.

    > **Important note**
    > There's no shortcut to providing the authentication details; however, for some helpful guidance,
    > you may want to reference the oci-provider-conf.md file in the GitHub repository
    > associated with this recipe. If you want greater details, I recommend working through the
    > documentation described in the **How to configure the provider** section referenced earlier.

    D.  If you decided to use **API Key Authentication** for your authentication method, go ahead
        and add the following configuration options to provider "oci" in the main.tf file:

```
...
...
...
provider "oci" {
  # API Key Authentication
  tenancy_ocid     = var.tenancy_ocid
  user_ocid        = var.user_ocid
  fingerprint      = var.fingerprint
  private_key_path = var.private_key_path
  region           = var.region
}
```

Figure 8.9 – API key authentication details

In order to keep things clean, we're going to reference variables for these values. I will provide more details on how to define/declare variables later in this recipe.

> **Note**
>
> To illustrate that we're adding to a file, I am using three series of three dots. This is meant to represent a continuation of what we did in the previous steps.
>
> Here's an example:
>
> . . .
>
> . . .
>
> . . .

6.  Now that we've got our provider set up, it's not going to do much unless we add a resource. In this case, we want to add an `oci_core_instance`.

    Do you recall when we generated an SSH key pair during the manual process? Well, now we need to figure out a way to do this dynamically using code. The following instruction is how we can do this using Terraform. We'll create a `tls_private_key` resource, and reference that as our `ssh_authorized_keys` under the metadata for the `oci_core_instance` resource.

    Let's start with the SSH key pair, which is created with the `tls_private_key` resource. Details on this resource can be found under the `hashicorp/tls` provider on the Terraform registry. Continue to edit the `main.tf` file, and add the following:

```
...
...
...
# Generate SSH Key Pair for access
resource "tls_private_key" "ssh" {
  algorithm = "RSA"
}
resource "local_sensitive_file" "ssh_private_key" {
  filename        = "${path.module}/instances/${var.instance_name}/id_rsa"
  file_permission = "600"
  content = tls_private_key.ssh.private_key_pem
}
```

Figure 8.10 – Defining SSH key pair with Terraform

7.  You'll need to define a valid availability domain. One way to do this is by using Terraform to query a list of availability domains and reference one of the items from that list, so let's add the following code to the `main.tf` file:

```
...
...
...
# Get a list of Availability Domains
data "oci_identity_availability_domains" "ads" {
  compartment_id = var.compartment_ocid
}
```

Figure 8.11 – Getting a list of availability domains using Terraform

8.  Finally, we're going to add a resource for `oci_core_instance`. If you review the `oci_core_instance` resource from the `oracle/oci` provider on the Terraform registry, you'll see a long list of parameters that can be used to define the `oci_core_instance` resource; however, not everything from this list is required as many of the parameters are preceded with `#Optional`. For this recipe, we're going to use the bare minimum that is required for this resource – so that should look something like this:

```
...
...
...
# Create an OCI core instance
resource "oci_core_instance" "ol_instance" {
  depends_on = [
    tls_private_key.ssh
  ]
  display_name       = var.instance_name
  availability_domain = data.oci_identity_availability_domains.ads.availability_domains[2].name
  compartment_id     = var.compartment_ocid
  shape              = "VM.Standard.E2.1.Micro"

  source_details {
    source_id   = var.os_image_ocid
    source_type = "image"
  }
  create_vnic_details {
    assign_public_ip = true
    subnet_id        = var.subnet_ocid
    nsg_ids          = [var.nsg_ocid]
  }
  metadata = {
    ssh_authorized_keys = tls_private_key.ssh.public_key_openssh
  }
}
```

Figure 8.12 – OCI Core instance resource details

9.  Once you are finished with the `oci_core_instance` resource, your entire `main.tf` file should look something like this:

```
terraform {
  required_providers {
    oci = {
      source  = "oracle/oci"
      version = "5.7.0"
    }
  }
}

provider "oci" {
  # API Key Authentication
  tenancy_ocid     = var.tenancy_ocid
  user_ocid        = var.user_ocid
  fingerprint      = var.fingerprint
  private_key_path = var.private_key_path
  region           = var.region
}

# Generate SSH Key Pair for access
resource "tls_private_key" "ssh" {
  algorithm = "RSA"
}
resource "local_sensitive_file" "ssh_private_key" {
  filename        = "${path.module}/instances/${var.instance_name}/id_rsa"
  file_permission = "600"
  content = tls_private_key.ssh.private_key_pem
}

# Get a list of Availability Domains
data "oci_identity_availability_domains" "ads" {
  compartment_id = var.compartment_ocid
}

# Create an OCI core instance
resource "oci_core_instance" "ol_instance" {
  depends_on = [
    tls_private_key.ssh
  ]
  display_name        = var.instance_name
  availability_domain = data.oci_identity_availability_domains.ads.availability_domains[2].name
  compartment_id      = var.compartment_ocid
  shape               = "VM.Standard.E2.1.Micro"

  source_details {
    source_id   = var.os_image_ocid
    source_type = "image"
  }
  create_vnic_details {
    assign_public_ip = true
    subnet_id        = var.subnet_ocid
  }
  metadata = {
    ssh_authorized_keys = tls_private_key.ssh.public_key_openssh
  }
}
```

Figure 8.13 – Contents of main.tf file

10. Now we need to declare all of those variables we referenced throughout the `main.tf` file. In order to keep things organized, let's put them in the `variables.tf` file. Each variable should, at a minimum, contain a type; however, we'll also add a description to explain the purpose of the variable.

Input the following into your `variables.tf` file:

```
variable "instance_name" {
  description = "A user-friendly name. Does not have to be unique, and it's changeable."
  type        = string
  default     = "My first IaC instance"
}

variable "region" {
  description = "An OCI region"
  type        = string
}

variable "tenancy_ocid" {
  description = "OCID of your tenancy"
  type        = string
}

variable "compartment_ocid" {
  description = "The OCID for your compartment"
  type        = string
}

variable "user_ocid" {
  description = "OCID of the user calling the API"
  type        = string
}

variable "subnet_ocid" {
  description = "The OCID of the subnet to create the VNIC in"
  type        = string
}

variable "os_image_ocid" {
  description = "The OCID for the OS image."
  type        = string
  default     = "ocid1.image.oc1.iad.aaaaaaaa3xkkahj6owvlxqpfsbn7zfhcz5bovin3dpst7ywmlphnrjgmb4ca"
}

variable "private_key_path" {
  description = "The path to the private key file"
  type        = string
}

variable "fingerprint" {
  description = "Fingerprint for the key pair being used"
  type        = string
}
```

Figure 8.14 – Declaration of variables in the variables.tf file

11. Finally, we would want to assign values to the variables. For this, you can use the `terraform.tfvars` file. It should look something like this:

```
instance_name    = "instance1"
region           = "us-ashburn-1"
tenancy_ocid     = "ocid1.tenancy.oc1..aaaaaaaa******"
compartment_ocid = "ocid1.compartment.oc1..aaaaaaaa******"
user_ocid        = "ocid1.user.oc1..aaaaaaaa******"
subnet_ocid      = "ocid1.subnet.oc1.iad.aaaaaaaa******"
os_image_ocid    = "ocid1.image.oc1.iad.aaaaaaaa******"
private_key_path = "./.oci/oci_api_key.pem"
fingerprint      = "12:34:56:78:90:ab:cd:ef:12:34:56:78:90:ab:cd:ef"
```

Figure 8.15 – Content of terraform.tfvars file

**Note**

Reference the following guide to find the *ocid* for `tenancy_ocid`, `compartment_ocid`, `user_ocid`, `fingerprint`, `subnet_ocid`, and `private_key_path`: https://docs.oracle.com/en-us/iaas/Content/API/SDKDocs/terraformproviderconfiguration.htm.

To get the OCID for Oracle Linux 8, visit the following link: https://docs.oracle.com/en-us/iaas/images/oracle-linux-8x/. This is region specific as well as architecture specific, so you'll want to find the latest Oracle Linux 8 image for x86 (or in other words, look for one without the `aarch64` text in the image name).

**Warning**

Just be sure to add the `terraform.tfvars` file to your `.gitignore` list to avoid checking any sensitive information into version control.

12. Next, let's run Terraform to see if we did everything correctly:

```
$ terraform init
$ terraform plan
$ terraform apply
```

The `terraform init` command initializes the working directory containing your Terraform project files and this should always be the first command that you run after you write a new Terraform configuration. After this, it is a good idea to run `terraform plan` as this will give you a chance to preview/verify the plan. During this command, Terraform will compare your real infrastructure against your configuration. Finally, running `terraform apply` will display the plan again, but it will additionally give you the chance to enter `yes` to perform any actions proposed by the plan.

When you see the prompt that asks you to Enter a value, go ahead and type yes, and then press *Enter*.

> **Important note**
>
> If you get a 401-NotAuthenticated error, make sure you've added your public key to the OCI console. This is the public key that pairs with private_key_path under the *API Key Authentication* method.
>
> For help with adding your public key to the OCI console, visit https://docs.oracle.com/en-us/iaas/Content/API/Concepts/apisigningkey.htm#three.

13. If all goes well, you should be able to watch as your resources are created. Once this is complete, you'll see a message like this:

```
Apply complete! Resources: 3 added, 0 changed, 0 destroyed.
```

14. If you check the OCI console, you will see your newly created instance and you will be able to connect to it via the SSH key pair the Terraform code generated and stuffed inside the instances folder within your Terraform project.

    This is easy enough to do, but why not automate a bit more so we don't need to check the OCI console for the public IP address? All we need to do is add a bit more code to our main.tf file and we can really start to take things to the next level.

    Go ahead and add the following code to your main.tf file:

```
...
...
...
output "connection_details" {
  value       = format("ssh -i ./instances/${var.instance_name}/id_rsa opc@%s", oci_core_instance.ol_instance.public_ip)
  description = "Details how to connect using the public IP address of the instance."
}

resource "local_file" "readme" {
  filename = "${path.module}/instances/${var.instance_name}/README.md"
  content  = oci_core_instance.ol_instance.public_ip
}
```

Figure 8.16 – Terraform code that outputs connection details

15. Now that we have that in place, save your file and run terraform apply once more to see what this does:

```
$ terraform apply
```

Terraform will again compare your real infrastructure with your configuration, but this time, since most of our infrastructure is in place, it's only going to propose adding one resource. When you see the Enter a value prompt, go ahead and type yes, and then press *Enter*.

16. Terraform will do its thing, and at the end, you'll see output that provides instructions on how to SSH into the newly created instance. That should look a bit like this:

```
Apply complete! Resources: 1 added, 0 changed, 0 destroyed.

Outputs:

connection_details = "ssh -i ./instances/instance1/id_rsa opc@129.213.122.14"
```

Figure 8.17 – Output of "terraform apply"

I realize that what we have just covered seems like a lot of information, but let's consider what we've done here. We automated the deployment of an instance into the cloud. Every parameter is easily configurable within our `terraform.tfvars` file. Finally, trivial steps including generating SSH keys are also automated, and we even print a statement at the end that clearly instructs how to connect to the newly deployed instance. I hope you enjoyed this recipe and are starting to see the true value of **IaC**!

The source code for this recipe can be found at `https://github.com/PacktPublishing/ Oracle-Linux-Cookbook/tree/main/ch8/terraform`.

## Creating portable roles for Ansible

Before attempting to follow this recipe, I recommend having some basic knowledge of Ansible and how to write an Ansible playbook. If you've never written an Ansible playbook, I recommend following the *Creating a playbook* guide from the official Ansible documentation. That can be found here: `https://docs.ansible.com/ansible/latest/getting_started/get_ started_playbook.html`.

In this recipe, you will learn how easy it is to move things around when using **Ansible roles**. When I first started using Ansible, I wrote my playbooks using *tasks* only. This to me seemed like a logical approach at the time and was more akin to traditional scripting since everything happened in chronological order.

The problem with writing playbooks in this way is there are no clear dependencies, and the tasks are defined along with the hosts, all in the same file. If you wanted to move things to another playbook, you'd have to be careful to grab the correct dependencies with each task, and you may be repeating yourself unnecessarily since tasks on their own are not reusable. As your playbooks become more complex and/or increase in size, you'll eventually want something more portable for the sake of manageability.

According to Red Hat, roles are designed to be *self-contained portable units of automation.*

Organizing your tasks into roles will allow you to easily reuse them and share them with others. In fact, if you visit Ansible Galaxy (`https://galaxy.ansible.com/`) you will find plenty of content in the form of *pre-packaged units of work referred to in Ansible as roles and collections*. It's much easier to reuse and share Ansible roles as organized units of automation because they are decoupled from the rest of the Ansible playbook framework.

If you're a programmer, you can think of roles as functions or methods. Easy enough? Let's get cooking!

## Getting started

For this recipe, you will need the following:

- Oracle Linux
- Ansible

Refer to the *Technical requirements* section at the beginning of this chapter if you need help installing Ansible.

## How to do it...

It's not difficult to convert a series of tasks into roles. It's really just a matter of stripping out the tasks and organizing them into categories that represent a role. This recipe aims to describe that process, and hopefully by the end, you will have a good understanding of how to do the same with your playbooks.

### Original playbook

To kick things off, let's first take a look at a playbook that doesn't leverage roles so we can dive into what needs to be done.

A typical playbook that does not leverage roles looks something like this:

```yaml
---
- name: Applies the standard configuration
  hosts: [ localhost ]
  become: yes
  vars:
    - ansible_python_interpreter: /usr/bin/python3

  tasks:
    - name: Get hostname
      debug:
        msg: '{{ ansible_hostname }}'
      tags:
        - always

    - name: Ensure groups exists
      ansible.builtin.group:
        name: admins
        state: present

    - name: Ensure groups exists
      ansible.builtin.group:
        name: developers
        state: present

    - name: Create standard user and add to specific groups
      ansible.builtin.user:
        name: user1
        shell: /bin/bash
        groups: admins,developers
        append: yes

    - name: Create a 2048-bit SSH key for user 'user1'
      ansible.builtin.user:
        name: user1
        generate_ssh_key: yes
        ssh_key_bits: 2048
        ssh_key_file: .ssh/id_rsa

    - name: Install Podman and related tools
      ansible.builtin.dnf:
        name: '@container-tools:ol8'
        state: present

    - name: Configure Podman to use netavark as network backend
      ansible.builtin.replace:
        path: /usr/share/containers/containers.conf
        regexp: 'network_backend = "cni"'
        replace: 'network_backend = "netavark"'

    - name: Run NGINX container image
      containers.podman.podman_container:
        name: my-ol9
        image: ghcr.io/oracle/oraclelinux9-nginx:1.20
        state: started
        detach: yes
```

Figure 8.18 – Long playbook without roles

> **Note**
>
> The screenshot fades out at the end because it's a long playbook and the entire contents of the playbook are not important.

This playbook automates several tasks. First, it creates a standard user if they do not already exist, then it installs Podman via the container-tools AppStream module, after which it launches an NGINX container, and then eventually it proceeds to upgrading all the packages on the system and checking whether the system needs to be rebooted.

As you can see from this example, if you write all your tasks directly into a playbook, it doesn't take long for that file to become massive and unwieldy. Before long, you will find yourself repeating preparatory tasks throughout, and you'll most likely add hash marks at the beginning of each line for unnecessary tasks, which will make the automation engine see it as a comment rather than code – you might even find yourself toggling between disabling and enabling tasks in order to target a specific task when running the playbook. This can become overwhelming, and if you're not careful, you might end up removing bits of code when you don't need them (even though sometimes, you might need them). Roles offer a better way to organize your playbooks. In fact, you can write as many roles as you want, and neatly call them in the playbook – this makes the playbook far easier to read and maintain over time.

### Creating a role

In Ansible, roles are organized under the `roles` directory. You create a folder under `roles`, and whatever you name the folder will become the name of the role. Then within that folder, you create a minimum of one folder called `tasks`, which should contain a `main.yml` file defining the primary tasks that the role will perform:

1. Let's break things up and create a role for our users by creating a `users` folder in the `roles` directory.

   Your directory structure should look a bit like this:

   ```
   ├── playbook.yml
   └── roles
       └── users
           ├── files
           │   └── wallpaper.jpg
           └── tasks
               └── main.yml
   ```

2. Now, create a `main.yml` file in the `tasks` directory, and let's port our user-related tasks over into that file.

```
- name: Create standard user and add to specific groups
  ansible.builtin.user:
    name: user1
    shell: /bin/bash
    groups: admins,developers # depends on
    append: yes

- name: Create a 2048-bit SSH key for user 'user1'
  ansible.builtin.user:
    name: user1
    generate_ssh_key: yes
    ssh_key_bits: 2048
    ssh_key_file: .ssh/id_rsa

- name: Copy Wallpaper
  copy:
    src: files/
    dest: /home/user1/Documents/Wallpaper
```

Figure 8.19 – Ansible role for provisioning users

3.  Now we have the beginnings of a role. We can take advantage of other features to facilitate pre-configuration operations. Here are two features that I tend to use most often – `files` and `meta`:

    • First, you'll notice we are referencing a `files` directory. That is a special directory that belongs to a role, and contains files related to that role.

    • The other is a `meta` directory that acts as a way to declare dependencies. For example, since the `users` role depends on certain groups to exist, it may be a good idea to make this role dependent on the `groups` role first. To do this, we can simply create a role for `groups` and then call this role from the `meta` directory.

4.  The `groups` role may look like the following. Notice the directory structure, along with the accompanying files – all of which are elements that make up a role. Your directory structure should look like this:

```
├── playbook.yml
└── roles
    └── groups
        └── tasks
            └── main.yml
```

5.  The actual task should be written in the main.yml file with the following content:

```
- name: Ensure groups exists
  ansible.builtin.group:
    name: admins
    state: present

- name: Ensure groups exists
  ansible.builtin.group:
    name: developers
    state: present
```

Figure 8.20 – Ansible role for user groups

6.  Now, in the meta/main.yml file for the users role, we just need to call the groups role as a dependency:

```
---

dependencies:
  - role: groups
```

7.  Finally, run the playbook with the following command:

```
$ ansible-playbook playbook.yml
```

You have successfully created a role within Ansible.

8.  Next, repeat this process until you have everything organized into roles. For me, I ended up with the following directory structure:

```
├── playbook.yml
└── roles
    ├── base_software
    │   └── tasks
    │       └── main.yml
    ├── containers
    │   └── tasks
    │       └── main.yml
    ├── get_hostname
    │   └── tasks
    │       └── main.yml
    ├── groups
    │   └── tasks
    │       └── main.yml
    ├── update_packages
    │   ├── meta
    │   │   └── main.yml
```

```
|       └── tasks
|           └── main.yml
├── uptime
|   └── tasks
|       └── main.yml
└── users
    ├── files
    |   └── wallpaper.jpg
    ├── meta
    |   └── main.yml
    └── tasks
        └── main.yml
```

## New and improved playbook

As for the actual playbook itself, it can now be simplified to just the following:

```
---
- name: Applies the standard configuration
  hosts: [ localhost ]
  become: yes
  vars:
    - ansible_python_interpreter: /usr/bin/python3

  roles:
    - get_hostname
    - users
    - containers
    - uptime
    - update_packages
```

Figure 8.21 – Ansible playbook leveraging roles

> **Note**
> Notice that we are not listing out the base_software and groups roles in the playbook as these are dependencies we have defined under the meta directories.

As you can see, instead of tasks, we are now simply referencing roles. It is very neat and organized, and much easier to understand what the playbook is set out to do. If you want to understand what a specific role does, all you need to do is look into the roles directory for the name of the respective role and examine the main.yml file in the role's tasks folder.

When you're ready, run the playbook just as you normally would:

```
$ ansible-playbook playbook.yml
```

If all went well, it should have accomplished everything that was being done in our original playbook; however, this time around we are using Ansible roles, and thus our playbook will be far easier to maintain going forward.

The source code for this recipe can be found at `https://github.com/PacktPublishing/Oracle-Linux-Cookbook/tree/main/ch8/ansible-roles`.

# Managing secrets with Ansible Vault

This recipe aims to provide guidance on leveraging **Ansible Vault** for *secrets management*.

There are multiple ways to store secrets in Ansible. When starting out, you may be inclined to encrypt the entire `hosts` file. This works and keeps everything secure in the context of using a version control system without compromising your secrets/passwords; however, it is not manageable, nor does it provide any useful information in version control systems because all you're left with is a long nonsensical string of encrypted characters.

## Getting started

You will need the following for this recipe:

- Oracle Linux
- Ansible

Refer to the *Technical requirements* section at the beginning of this chapter if you need help installing Ansible.

## How to do it...

First, let's take a look at whole-file encryption. To begin, we'll first need to define our Ansible host file in plain text.

### Whole-file encryption

Typically, an Ansible hosts file will look something like this:

```
# hosts
[host1]
192.168.2.70
[host1:vars]
```

```
ansible_user=admin
ansible_password=B@by-Y0dA
ansible_connection=ssh
ansible_shell_type=powershell

[host2]
192.168.2.71
[host2:vars]
ansible_user=admin
ansible_password=B@by-Y0dA
ansible_connection=ssh
ansible_shell_type=powershell
```

You can encrypt the file by running the following into the terminal/console:

```
$ ansible-vault encrypt hosts --ask-vault-pass
New Vault password:
Confirm New Vault password:
Encryption successful
```

I am using a randomly generated string as my vault password.

Another way to encrypt the file is to use a **vault password file** so you don't have to input the password every time you need to encrypt/decrypt something. To do this, create a file named `vault_password` and paste only the vault password into it.

> **Note**
>
> It's a good idea to set the permissions to `0600` on the `vault_password` file (this can be done by running `chmod 0600 ./vault_password`) so it's protected from other users.

Now, instead of using `--ask-vault-pass`, you can use the following:

```
$ ansible-vault encrypt hosts --vault-password-file vault_password
Encryption successful
```

Cool! Just be sure to add the `vault_password` file to your `.gitignore` list to avoid checking that into version control.

Now if you `cat` your `hosts` file, you will see the contents are encrypted:

```
) cat hosts
$ANSIBLE_VAULT;1.1;AES256
37633932393061646166393161353133376531613765633132666566646137616366393132616366
30313136333932653732636632346664386264313239363630a34313361386661613034323839663 8
61323363316238663937356131643464643965663935396165396137643139333734323939333434
65356163396638303 00a63313333336316565383062616333336326232306564323 96539303862633 8
35366636666566386565663539393130373262 6132 6137613 23333 33643 5636637393 63 461386362
66323 5646566316639393 0613365323 46232393 53 23 0636238365363 3656565663 4643531383030
636630633732303 03562383439633 063353235306562326232539396237326535362 6664323 03 76132
36393 0303 966383539313437303 0376333666336 65373233363135386331 656366643 3626336356 1
31393 4306336613 335346464366 364323638323738326133 303 537393 9353 566534646261323 735
646266613165563 6436323 036313 063627336434326464363 33 6333665663766623 5396233313830
3861623 96434613 2643 5306231636463656136313333 06536353366376134343 8 643 4376630643334
6664386435613833656637613131313135353 9306233 63 62633335646664353832316430666333 6465
303 93 96565633 06335363161633163396335 65353 4633766373132623 7323435646263393 93 06634
346137626366313 23964366363133 34343636 4663639316 43032 6162343333 4326464663438623163
626632356466333 03 3393166373 961633262396461613065333623 76631616637 386461396564303 2
623 2313631623 564626539346533 653 761 6562626664383864383935316335353 8396 56239663634
6666633133 34343 6633131333762 33 6337303664333362 3 9396631633 83936 346 4 63
```

Figure 8.22 – Contents of encrypted "hosts" file

This is great, but anytime you need to make changes to the `hosts` file, you are faced with two options:

- Decrypt the `hosts` file, make your changes, then encrypt it again
- Use `ansible-vault edit hosts` to leverage ansible-vault's *vim* mode to edit the file

These aren't terrible options, but in practice this can become cumbersome. I propose a better way, which is to use the `encrypt_string` method within Ansible Vault to encrypt only the sensitive data, and use variables in place of passwords/secrets to reference those encrypted strings.

## *Hiding passwords in plain sight*

Hiding passwords in plain sight is in direct contrast to the whole-file encryption we described previously. We're still going to encrypt our sensitive data, but this time around we'll encrypt *only* the sensitive data, and leave everything else in plain, unencrypted text:

1.  We will use the `encrypt_string` method. In this example, the password we want to encrypt is `B@by-Y0dA` and we will name the variable that identifies this password as `admin_password`.

    ```
    $ ansible-vault encrypt_string --vault-password-file vault_
    password 'B@by-Y0dA' --name 'admin_password'
    ```

    In the terminal/console, once you press *Enter* you will see what `'B@by-Y0dA'` looks like once encrypted:

```
) ansible-vault encrypt_string --vault-password-file vault_password 'B@by-Y0dA' --name 'admin_password'
admin_password: !vault |
          $ANSIBLE_VAULT;1.1;AES256
          3735326630616163316465626632613763623832303562366433623734343062626438343030306430
          6132383830303964353131343034353262363633333461620a3433346263335636356363623463613166
          3138373962313066656546632383466613837643330353376332626134346639643864656664613036
          3433376337323630650a35616466363731633335636346635353538366362633131356330663939316463
          3332
Encryption successful
```

Figure 8.23 – Encrypting secrets

2. Next, we need to copy the output of that into a `secrets.yml` file (you could just append `>> secrets.yml` to the command entered previously to automatically copy the output to the file). Here's an example:

```
$ ansible-vault encrypt_string --vault-password-file vault_
password 'B@by-Y0dA' --name 'admin_password' >> secrets.yml
```

Your `secrets.yml` file should look something like this:

```
) cat secrets.yml
admin_password: !vault |
          $ANSIBLE_VAULT;1.1;AES256
          6636306235306262613766643863336366436346637383561353634353632316632653063306663730
          3531303839613062373538613631316535339653737636363390a61663838643462313430306464623065
          66636238346637316430363666636132663765346330373934343362386336306232656362333237
          3134373662623035310a623639303535316432336237393333062633634313135393836643265333163
          6234
```

Figure 8.24 – Contents of secrets.yml file

> **Important note**
>
> You may notice the encrypted value is different every time you run the command, even when you encrypt the same value using the same password. The random salt changes each time you encrypt it; this is by design, and the intent is to ensure that the final encrypted output is never the same (even when using the same content).

3. Now that you have it encrypted, you can replace the `ansible_password` value in your host file with the name of the variable that references the password (in this case, `admin_password`):

```
# hosts
[host1]
192.168.2.70
[host1:vars]
ansible_user=admin
ansible_password={{ admin_password }}
ansible_connection=ssh
ansible_shell_type=powershell
```

```
[host2]
192.168.2.71
[host2:vars]
ansible_user=admin
ansible_password={{ admin_password }}
ansible_connection=ssh
ansible_shell_type=powershell
```

> **Note**
>
> The advantage of **variable-level encryption** is that files can still easily be read and understood because there will be a mixture of plaintext alongside the encrypted variables.

The source code for this recipe can be found at `https://github.com/PacktPublishing/Oracle-Linux-Cookbook/tree/main/ch8/ansible-vault`.

## Cooking up the perfect lab environment with Vagrant

Recently at work, I was tasked with preparing a demo of **Oracle Linux Manager** and showcasing several features of the software. This is an easy enough thing to do, but there are several barriers to entry that stand in the way before you can access the web GUI for Oracle Linux Manager.

For starters, Oracle Linux Manager requires Oracle Linux 7; it's not yet certified on Oracle Linux 8. So, I set out to download the ISO for Oracle Linux 7 and proceeded to create a VM in VirtualBox and installed the OS. I then wanted to SSH into the box, so I had to go into the settings menu for that VM and configure port forwarding from the host to the guest. At this point, I was able to SSH in, and then followed the installation instructions for Oracle Linux Manager. It's not that bad setting things up, but there were several speed-bumps along the way. For instance, I needed to decide on a database to use. Oracle supports only Oracle Database for use with Oracle Linux Manager, but for the sake of brevity (and since this was only ever intended as a lab demonstration of Oracle Linux Manager), I decided to use **PostgreSQL**.

With so many manual steps, I'd be inclined to keep my newly created virtual machine and take care of it like a pet. They say containers are like cattle, and virtual machines are like pets. That is, until you've started using tools like Vagrant. Vagrant does a good job making your virtual machines blend in with the cattle – thanks to how easy it is to recreate your virtual machines using Vagrant, you no longer need to care for them the way you had to previously if you weren't using Vagrant.

This recipe will walk you through the process of creating a lab environment using **Vagrant**.

## Getting ready

You will need the following for this recipe:

- Oracle Linux

- Oracle VM VirtualBox

- Vagrant

Refer to the *Technical requirements* section at the beginning of this chapter if you need help installing Oracle VM VirtualBox and Vagrant.

## How to do it...

Vagrant is a tool used for managing the lifecycle of virtual machines. In this recipe, we're going to create a Vagrant box that automatically installs and configures Oracle Linux Manager. Oracle Linux Manager requires Oracle Linux 7. In this case, we can use the official **Oracle Linux 7 Vagrant Box** as our base:

```
$ vagrant init oraclelinux/7 https://oracle.github.io/vagrant-
projects/boxes/oraclelinux/7.json
```

Great, that has pulled in a nice base file for us to start with. Let's look at the `Vagrantfile` file to see what's inside:

```
# Vagrantfile
Vagrant.configure("2") do |config|
  config.vm.box = "oraclelinux/7"
  config.vm.box_url = "https://oracle.github.io/vagrant-projects/
boxes/oraclelinux/7.json"
end
```

The actual `Vagrantfile` generated by the `init` command contains 69 lines of code, but 65 of those lines are comments, hence I removed them to help make this recipe more easily comprehensible.

As we can see from this `Vagrantfile`, all we need is those four lines to launch an Oracle Linux 7 instance in **VM VirtualBox**. If you want to test it, enter the `vagrant up` command and when it's up and running, you can simply enter the `vagrant ssh` command to access the VM and see how it works. Once finished, type `vagrant destroy` to bring down the VM. Now, let's dive into ways to make this more useful; because I want to be able to type `vagrant up` and have not only an Oracle Linux VM, but also want that same command to result in a working copy of Oracle Linux Manager.

First things first, let's review the installation and configuration instructions for Oracle Linux Manager – this can be found at `https://docs.oracle.com/en/operating-systems/oracle-linux-manager/2.10/install/#Oracle-Linux-Manager`. Since we aren't using an Oracle database, we will divert slightly from the instructions outlined – this means we'll skip anything related to Oracle databases (for example, we won't need the Oracle Instant Client and *SQL\*Plus* packages).

To illustrate what we're going to do, I'll list all the steps from the guide, applying **bold** style to the steps we want to keep. The ones that are not bold will be skipped:

- `sudo yum install oracle-instantclient18.5-basic-18.5.0.0.0-3.x86_64.rpm oracle-instantclient18.5-sqlplus-18.5.0.0.0-3.x86_64.rpm`

- `echo "/usr/lib/oracle/18.5/client64/lib" | sudo tee /etc/ld.so.conf.d/oracle-instantclient18.5.conf`

- `sudo ldconfig`

- **`sudo yum list installed | grep jta`**

- **`sudo yum remove jta`**

- **`echo «exclude=jta*» >> /etc/yum.conf`**

- **`sudo yum-config-manager -disable ol7_addons`**

- `sudo firewall-cmd --permanent --add-port=69/udp`

- `sudo firewall-cmd --permanent --add-port=80/tcp`

- `sudo firewall-cmd --permanent --add-port=443/tcp`

- `sudo firewall-cmd --permanent --add-port=5222/tcp`

- `sudo firewall-cmd --permanent --add-port=5269/tcp`

- `sudo systemctl reload firewalld`

- **`sudo yum install oracle-release-el7`**

- **`sudo yum install oracle-linux-manager-server-release-el7`**

- **`sudo yum-config-manager --enable ol7_optional_latest`**

- **`sudo yum install`** `spacewalk-oracle` **`spacecmd spacewalk-utils`**

- `sudo spacewalk-setup --external-oracle`

And that's basically it. The following is for additional changes that we need to make to use Oracle Linux Manager with PostgreSQL:

```
sudo yum install spacewalk-setup-postgresql spacewalk-postgresql
```

Finally, we'll need to provide an answer file since the automation we're doing in Vagrant cannot be interactive:

```
sudo spacewalk-setup --non-interactive --answer-file=/tmp/answer-file.txt
```

Create a file named `answer-file.txt` and place the following content into the file:

```
admin-email = root@localhost
ssl-set-cnames = spacewalk
ssl-set-org = Oracle
ssl-set-org-unit = OLM
ssl-set-city = Raleigh
ssl-set-state = NC
ssl-set-country = US
ssl-password = Password1
ssl-set-email = root@localhost
ssl-config-sslvhost = Y
db-backend = postgresql
db-name = spaceschema
db-user = spaceuser
db-password = Password1
db-host = localhost
db-port = 5432
enable-tftp = Y
```

This summarizes the bulk of the installation and configuration steps. Next, in order to make all of this work so that we can deploy and provision Oracle Linux Manager automatically using Vagrant, we need to make some very simple changes. All we really need to do is paste those steps into a *Bash shell script* file and tell Vagrant to use a provisioner to run these commands on the box. Also, again, since automation cannot be interactive, we just need to add `-y` to all the `yum` commands.

Therefore, to clean things up and prepare them for Vagrant, our Bash script will look something like this:

```
#!/bin/bash

yum remove jta -y
echo "exclude=jta*" >> /etc/yum.conf
yum-config-manager --disable ol7_addons

yum install oracle-release-el7 -y

yum install oracle-linux-manager-server-release-el7 -y
yum-config-manager --enable ol7_optional_latest -y

yum install spacewalk-schema-2.10.14-1.el7 spacewalk-setup-postgresql
spacewalk-postgresql spacecmd spacewalk-utils -y

spacewalk-setup --non-interactive --answer-file=/tmp/answer-file.txt
```

> **Note**
>
> At some point while authoring this recipe, an update was made to the spacewalk-schema package making it no longer compatible with PostgreSQL. This can be fixed by pinning the spacewalk-schema package to `spacewalk-schema-2.10.14-1.el7` as shown in the preceding snippet.

I removed the call to `sudo` for each step since everything runs as root during the provisioning phase of Vagrant.

Now for the `Vagrantfile`, add a few lines so that Vagrant can copy the `answer-file.txt` file to the guest machine, then tell Vagrant to execute the script we just wrote. We'll also create a private network, which allows host-only access to the machine using a specific IP (this will allow us to easily access Oracle Linux Manager via our web browser):

```ruby
# -*- mode: ruby -*-
# vi: set ft=ruby :

# All Vagrant configuration is done below. The "2" in Vagrant.configure
# configures the configuration version (we support older styles for
# backwards compatibility). Please don't change it unless you know what
# you're doing.
Vagrant.configure("2") do |config|
  config.vm.box = "oraclelinux/7"
  config.vm.box_url = "https://oracle.github.io/vagrant-projects/boxes/oraclelinux/7.json"
  config.vm.network "private_network", ip: "192.168.56.10"
  config.vm.provision "file", source: "answer-file.txt", destination: "/tmp/answer-file.txt"
  config.vm.provision "shell", path: "provision.sh"
  config.vm.provision "shell", inline: "echo Access Oracle Linux Manager at https://192.168.56.10"
end
```

Figure 8.25 – Vagrant file for deploying OLM

> **Note**
>
> On Linux/Unix-based systems, VirtualBox will only allow IP addresses in `192.168.56.0/21` range to be assigned to host-only adapters. This allows for IP addresses starting at `192.168.56.1` and ending at `192.168.63.254`.

Now we can review what our directory should look like:

```
└── oracle-linux-manager
    ├── answer-file.txt
    ├── provision.sh
    └── Vagrantfile
```

We're ready to fire things up:

```
$ vagrant up
...

...

...
--> default: Running provisioner: shell...
    default: Running: inline script
    default: Access Oracle Linux Manager at https://192.168.56.10
```

You'll watch as the provisioning script installs and configures Oracle Linux Manager, and within a matter of minutes, you'll be able to point your browser to the IP address defined for the virtual machine to access Oracle Linux Manager. The best part about this is everything is **defined as code**. Everything we created in this recipe amounts to just 6 KB in size! Vagrant does an amazing job at solving the classic "*it works on my machine*" problem. You can take these 6 KB of code and deploy your work on any machine (Mac, Windows, Linux, etc.) – all you need is Vagrant and Oracle VM VirtualBox.

We could take this automation a few steps further to make it even more useful. For example, we could automate the creation of the first user for Oracle Linux Manager, automatically create the channels, repositories, and activation keys, then create clients for OLM and connect to them automatically. Getting into the details for all that is beyond the scope of this recipe, but if you're interested in seeing how this is done, I've got the solution published on GitHub – you can find that here: `https://github.com/PacktPublishing/Oracle-Linux-Cookbook/tree/main/ch8/vagrant`.

# Using Packer to modify source images

Packer is a tool used for automating the creation of machine images. In this recipe, we're going to use Packer to reference an **Oracle Linux 8** platform image as its source, install something using a provisioner, and push up a new OCID image with these changes onto OCI.

> **Note**
> Although OCI features a free tier that contains "Always Free" resources, this does not include the ability to store images. If you wish to follow along with this recipe, you will need to use a paid account.

## Getting ready

For this recipe, you will need the following:

- Oracle Linux
- Packer

Refer to the *Technical requirements* section at the beginning of this chapter if you need help installing Packer.

## How to do it...

Packer is often overlooked because it seems so simple on the surface; however, don't let this simplicity fool you – Packer is incredibly powerful and useful. In this recipe, we're going to use Packer to reference some release of Oracle Linux 8 as its base image, install something using a provisioner, and push up a new OCID image with these changes onto the OCI:

1. First, we will specify a Packer plugin that provides a builder called `oracle-oci`, which enables Packer to create machine images for OCI. We can do that in a file named `oracle-oci.pkr.hcl`. Input the following at the beginning of the file:

```
packer {
  required_plugins {
    oracle-oci = {
      version = ">= 1.0.4"
      source  = "github.com/hashicorp/oracle"
    }
  }
}
```

Figure 8.26 – Packer OCI builder plugin

2. Next, we will configure our authentication to OCI using the configuration options specified by the `oracle-oci` builder. Details on configuring the `oracle-oci` builder can be reviewed at `https://developer.hashicorp.com/packer/plugins/builders/oracle/oci`:

   - There are numerous ways to do this. One way is to reference variables for the authentication details directly in your `*.pkr.hcl` file, like this:

```
...
...
...
source "oracle-oci" "example" {
  tenancy_ocid        = "${var.tenancy_ocid}"
  compartment_ocid    = "${var.compartment_ocid}"
  user_ocid           = "${var.user_ocid}"
  fingerprint         = "${var.fingerprint}"
  key_file            = "${var.key_file}"
  subnet_ocid         = "${var.subnet_ocid}"
  availability_domain = "${var.availability_domain}"
  region              = "${var.region}"
```

Figure 8.27 – Referencing variables in Packer

- Then, we need to declare all of those variables in a file named `variables.pkr.hcl`. In this file, we declare the variable and specify the type, as well as providing a description to explain the purpose of the variable. Input the following into your `variables.pkr.hcl` file:

```
variable "tenancy_ocid" {
  type        = string
  description = "OCID of your tenancy"
}
variable "compartment_ocid" {
  type        = string
  description = "The OCID for your compartment"
}
variable "user_ocid" {
  type        = string
  description = "OCID of the user calling the API"
}
variable "subnet_ocid" {
  type        = string
  description = "The OCID of the subnet to create the VNIC in"
}
variable "availability_domain" {
  type        = string
  description = "The tenancy-specific prefix and availability domain. Example: Xebt:US-ASHBURN-AD-3"
}
variable "region" {
  type        = string
  description = "An OCI region"
}
variable "fingerprint" {
  type        = string
  description = "Fingerprint for the key pair being used"
}
variable "key_file" {
  type        = string
  description = "The path to the private key file"
}
```

Figure 8.28 – Declaration of variables in Packer

- Finally, we want to assign values to the variables. We place them in a file named `variables.auto.pkrvars.hcl`. It should look something like this:

```
tenancy_ocid        = "ocid1.tenancy.oc1..aaaaaaaa******"
compartment_ocid    = "ocid1.compartment.oc1..aaaaaaaa******"
user_ocid           = "ocid1.user.oc1..aaaaaaaa******"
subnet_ocid         = "ocid1.subnet.oc1.iad.aaaaaaaa******"
availability_domain = "Xebt:US-ASHBURN-AD-3"
region              = "us-ashburn-1"
key_file            = "./.oci/oci_api_key.pem"
fingerprint         = "12:34:56:78:90:ab:cd:ef:12:34:56:78:90:ab:cd:ef"
```

Figure 8.29 – Assigning variables in Packer

- Another way is to configure your OCI CLI in `~/.oci/config`. That would look something like this:

```
[DEFAULT]
user=ocid1.user.oc1..<unique_ID>
fingerprint=<your_fingerprint>
key_file=~/.oci/oci_api_key.pem
tenancy=ocid1.tenancy.oc1..<unique_ID>
region=us-ashburn-1

[ADMIN_USER]
user=ocid1.user.oc1..<unique_ID>
fingerprint=<your_fingerprint>
key_file=keys/admin_key.pem
pass_phrase=<your_passphrase>
```

> **Note**
>
> Full details on configuring your OCI CLI can be found here: `https://docs.oracle.com/en-us/iaas/Content/API/Concepts/sdkconfig.htm`

3. Once you have the authentication configured, you can start by defining the base image. This should look something like the following:

```
source "oracle-oci" "example" {
  ...
  ...

  ...
  base_image_ocid     = "ocid1.image.oc1.iad.aaaaaaaa******"
  image_name          = "Oracle Linux 8.8"
  shape               = "VM.Standard.E4.Flex"
  shape_config {
    ocpus         = 2
    memory_in_gbs = 4
  }
  ssh_username = "opc"
}
```

Figure 8.30 – Defining the base image in Packer

> **Note**
>
> To get the OCID for Oracle Linux 8, visit the following URL: `https://docs.oracle.com/en-us/iaas/images/oracle-linux-8x/`. This is region specific as well as architecture specific, so you'll want to find the latest Oracle Linux 8 image for x86 (or in other words, look for one without `aarch64` mentioned in the image name).

4.   Once you've defined the source, you can move on to instructing Packer on what to do during the build process. In this case, we'll call a provisioner so we can run a shell command to install Git:

```
  ...
  ...

  ...
build {
  name    = "Oracle Linux 8.8 with Git"
  sources = ["source.oracle-oci.example"]
  provisioner "shell" {
    inline = ["sudo dnf install -y git"]
  }
}
```

Figure 8.31 – Packer provisioners

5.   At this point, we've told Packer about what we want to use for our source and described what we want to do for our build. Your entire file should look something like this:

```
packer {
  required_plugins {
    oracle-oci = {
      version = ">= 1.0.4"
      source  = "github.com/hashicorp/oracle"
    }
  }
}

source "oracle-oci" "ol8u8" {
  tenancy_ocid        = "${var.tenancy_ocid}"
  compartment_ocid    = "${var.compartment_ocid}"
  user_ocid           = "${var.user_ocid}"
  fingerprint         = "${var.fingerprint}"
  key_file            = "${var.key_file}"
  subnet_ocid         = "${var.subnet_ocid}"
  availability_domain = "${var.availability_domain}"
  region              = "${var.region}"
  base_image_ocid     = "ocid1.image.oc1.iad.aaaaaaaa******"
  image_name          = "Oracle Linux 8.8"
  shape               = "VM.Standard.E4.Flex"
  shape_config {
    ocpus         = 2
    memory_in_gbs = 4
  }
  ssh_username = "opc"
}

build {
  name    = "Oracle Linux 8.8 with Git"
  sources = ["source.oracle-oci.ol8u8"]
  provisioner "shell" {
    inline = ["sudo dnf install -y git"]
  }
}
```

Figure 8.32 – Complete Packer file for modifying base images

---

**Note**

In the final file, I replaced the word `example` with `ol8u8` throughout to be a bit more descriptive about what I'm working with. This is simply a good form of self-documentation.

---

6. Next, we're going to run `packer init` to download the external plugin:

   ```
   $ packer init .
   ```

7. Finally, let's go ahead and build the OCID image:

   ```
   $ packer build .
   ```

Packer will spin up a new Oracle Linux 8.8 instance in the Oracle Cloud. Once the machine is running, it will run `sudo dnf install -y git` to install Git on the instance.

```
> packer build
Oracle Linux 8.8 with Git.oracle-oci.v8u8: output will be in this color.

==> Oracle Linux 8.8 with Git.oracle-oci.v8u8: Creating temporary ssh key for instance...
==> Oracle Linux 8.8 with Git.oracle-oci.v8u8: Creating instance...
==> Oracle Linux 8.8 with Git.oracle-oci.v8u8: Created instance (ocid1.instance.oc1.iad.anuwcljtgpczwcqccipyvlqqeujlypllzxp4fGesdqdwtpmtzj3ammfccovq).
==> Oracle Linux 8.8 with Git.oracle-oci.v8u8: Waiting for instance to enter 'RUNNING' state...
==> Oracle Linux 8.8 with Git.oracle-oci.v8u8: Instance 'RUNNING'.
==> Oracle Linux 8.8 with Git.oracle-oci.v8u8: Instance has IP: 129.158.247.254.
==> Oracle Linux 8.8 with Git.oracle-oci.v8u8: Using SSH communicator to connect: 129.158.247.254
==> Oracle Linux 8.8 with Git.oracle-oci.v8u8: Waiting for SSH to become available...
==> Oracle Linux 8.8 with Git.oracle-oci.v8u8: Connected to SSH!
==> Oracle Linux 8.8 with Git.oracle-oci.v8u8: Provisioning with shell script: /tmp/packer-shell790793282
    Oracle Linux 8.8 with Git.oracle-oci.v8u8: Ksplice for Oracle Linux 8 (x86_64)              12 MB/s | 3.9 MB    00:00
    Oracle Linux 8.8 with Git.oracle-oci.v8u8: MySQL 8.0 for Oracle Linux 8 (x86_64)            12 MB/s | 3.0 MB    00:00
    Oracle Linux 8.8 with Git.oracle-oci.v8u8: MySQL 8.8 Tools Community for Oracle Linux 8 (x 2.8 MB/s | 491 kB    00:00
    Oracle Linux 8.8 with Git.oracle-oci.v8u8: MySQL 8.0 Connectors Community for Oracle Linux 141 kB/s |  30 kB    00:00
    Oracle Linux 8.8 with Git.oracle-oci.v8u8: Oracle Software for OCI users on Oracle Linux 8  25 MB/s |  99 MB    00:04
    Oracle Linux 8.8 with Git.oracle-oci.v8u8: Oracle Linux 8 BaseOS Latest (x86_64)            45 MB/s |  64 MB    00:01
    Oracle Linux 8.8 with Git.oracle-oci.v8u8: Oracle Linux 8 Application Stream (x86_64)       44 MB/s |  49 MB    00:01
    Oracle Linux 8.8 with Git.oracle-oci.v8u8: Oracle Linux 8 Addons (x86_64)                   32 MB/s | 6.9 MB    00:00
    Oracle Linux 8.8 with Git.oracle-oci.v8u8: Latest Unbreakable Enterprise Kernel Release 7   42 MB/s |  23 MB    00:00
    Oracle Linux 8.8 with Git.oracle-oci.v8u8: Dependencies resolved.
    Oracle Linux 8.8 with Git.oracle-oci.v8u8: ==============================================================================
    Oracle Linux 8.8 with Git.oracle-oci.v8u8:  Package        Arch      Version           Repository      Size
    Oracle Linux 8.8 with Git.oracle-oci.v8u8: ==============================================================================
    Oracle Linux 8.8 with Git.oracle-oci.v8u8: Installing:
    Oracle Linux 8.8 with Git.oracle-oci.v8u8:  git            x86_64    2.39.3-1.el8_8    ol8_appstream   104 k
    Oracle Linux 8.8 with Git.oracle-oci.v8u8: Installing dependencies:
    Oracle Linux 8.8 with Git.oracle-oci.v8u8:  git-core       x86_64    2.39.3-1.el8_8    ol8_appstream    11 M
    Oracle Linux 8.8 with Git.oracle-oci.v8u8:  git-core-doc   noarch    2.39.3-1.el8_8    ol8_appstream   3.0 M
    Oracle Linux 8.8 with Git.oracle-oci.v8u8:  perl-Error     noarch    1:0.17025-2.el8   ol8_appstream    46 k
    Oracle Linux 8.8 with Git.oracle-oci.v8u8:  perl-Git       noarch    2.39.3-1.el8_8    ol8_appstream    79 k
    Oracle Linux 8.8 with Git.oracle-oci.v8u8:  perl-TermReadKey x86_64  2.37-7.el8        ol8_appstream    40 k
    Oracle Linux 8.8 with Git.oracle-oci.v8u8:
    Oracle Linux 8.8 with Git.oracle-oci.v8u8: Transaction Summary
    Oracle Linux 8.8 with Git.oracle-oci.v8u8: ==============================================================================
    Oracle Linux 8.8 with Git.oracle-oci.v8u8: Install  6 Packages
```

Figure 8.33 – Initial output after running packer build

Once Git is installed, it will take a snapshot of the instance and export this as a new OCID image, giving us a new starting point for all future instances.

```
    Oracle Linux 8.8 with Git.oracle-oci.v8u8: ------------------------------------------------------------------------------
    Oracle Linux 8.8 with Git.oracle-oci.v8u8: Total                                           37 MB/s |  14 MB    00:00
    Oracle Linux 8.8 with Git.oracle-oci.v8u8: Running transaction check
    Oracle Linux 8.8 with Git.oracle-oci.v8u8: Transaction check succeeded.
    Oracle Linux 8.8 with Git.oracle-oci.v8u8: Running transaction test
    Oracle Linux 8.8 with Git.oracle-oci.v8u8: Transaction test succeeded.
    Oracle Linux 8.8 with Git.oracle-oci.v8u8: Running transaction
    Oracle Linux 8.8 with Git.oracle-oci.v8u8:  Preparing       :                                                  1/1
    Oracle Linux 8.8 with Git.oracle-oci.v8u8:  Installing      : git-core-2.39.3-1.el8_8.x86_64                   1/6
    Oracle Linux 8.8 with Git.oracle-oci.v8u8:  Installing      : git-core-doc-2.39.3-1.el8_8.noarch               2/6
    Oracle Linux 8.8 with Git.oracle-oci.v8u8:  Installing      : perl-TermReadKey-2.37-7.el8.x86_64               3/6
    Oracle Linux 8.8 with Git.oracle-oci.v8u8:  Installing      : perl-Error-1:0.17025-2.el8.noarch                4/6
    Oracle Linux 8.8 with Git.oracle-oci.v8u8:  Installing      : perl-Git-2.39.3-1.el8_8.noarch                   5/6
    Oracle Linux 8.8 with Git.oracle-oci.v8u8:  Installing      : git-2.39.3-1.el8_8.x86_64                        6/6
    Oracle Linux 8.8 with Git.oracle-oci.v8u8:  Running scriptlet: git-2.39.3-1.el8_8.x86_64                       6/6
    Oracle Linux 8.8 with Git.oracle-oci.v8u8:  Verifying       : git-2.39.3-1.el8_8.x86_64                        1/6
    Oracle Linux 8.8 with Git.oracle-oci.v8u8:  Verifying       : git-core-2.39.3-1.el8_8.x86_64                   2/6
    Oracle Linux 8.8 with Git.oracle-oci.v8u8:  Verifying       : git-core-doc-2.39.3-1.el8_8.noarch               3/6
    Oracle Linux 8.8 with Git.oracle-oci.v8u8:  Verifying       : perl-Error-1:0.17025-2.el8.noarch                4/6
    Oracle Linux 8.8 with Git.oracle-oci.v8u8:  Verifying       : perl-Git-2.39.3-1.el8_8.noarch                   5/6
    Oracle Linux 8.8 with Git.oracle-oci.v8u8:  Verifying       : perl-TermReadKey-2.37-7.el8.x86_64               6/6
    Oracle Linux 8.8 with Git.oracle-oci.v8u8:
    Oracle Linux 8.8 with Git.oracle-oci.v8u8: Installed:
    Oracle Linux 8.8 with Git.oracle-oci.v8u8:  git-2.39.3-1.el8_8.x86_64              git-core-2.39.3-1.el8_8.x86_64
    Oracle Linux 8.8 with Git.oracle-oci.v8u8:  git-core-doc-2.39.3-1.el8_8.noarch     perl-Error-1:0.17025-2.el8.noarch
    Oracle Linux 8.8 with Git.oracle-oci.v8u8:  perl-Git-2.39.3-1.el8_8.noarch         perl-TermReadKey-2.37-7.el8.x86_64
    Oracle Linux 8.8 with Git.oracle-oci.v8u8:
    Oracle Linux 8.8 with Git.oracle-oci.v8u8: Complete!
==> Oracle Linux 8.8 with Git.oracle-oci.v8u8: Creating image from instance...
```

Figure 8.34 – Output as Packer completes the build process

When Packer is finished, you can view the newly published image by navigating to the **Compute | Custom Images** on the OCI Console. Here's an example of what that looks like:

Figure 8.35 – Viewing the recently published custom image on OCI

The source code for this recipe can be found at `https://github.com/PacktPublishing/Oracle-Linux-Cookbook/tree/main/ch8/packer-cloud`.

# Pack it up, pack it in, let me begin, err, umm… build

In this recipe, we're going to use Packer to start from source media (such as an ISO) to create our very own Vagrant box from scratch.

## Getting started

You will need the following for this recipe:

- Oracle Linux
- Oracle VM VirtualBox
- Packer

Refer to the *Technical requirements* section at the beginning of this chapter if you need help installing Oracle VM VirtualBox and Packer.

## How to do it...

More often than not, you can search the Vagrant catalog and find pre-made **Vagrantfiles** containing the operating system you're looking for. But what happens if what you need is not there? Or maybe you don't trust the author of the Vagrantfile and/or you simply prefer to create your own. You can do this manually, or you can do this entirely with code, by leveraging Packer. In this recipe, we'll use Packer to bake up a fresh Vagrant box from the Oracle Linux 8.8 source ISO. At a high level, Packer will download the ISO image for the operating system we wish to use, it will then spin up a VM using Oracle VM VirtualBox and install the VM. Afterward, it will export the VM in **Open Virtualization Format (OVF)**. Finally, it will compress this file and convert it into a Vagrant box file.

### *Oracle Linux 8 kickstart file*

1.  For this magic to work, you'll need to provide a kickstart file to automate the installation of the ISO. You can create your own, or use one from the Oracle Linux Image Tools found in the official Oracle Linux repository on GitHub. For this recipe, I'll be using one from the Oracle Linux Image Tools:

    ```
    https://github.com/oracle/oracle-linux/blob/main/oracle-linux-
    image-tools/distr/ol8-slim/ol8-ks.cfg
    ```

2.  Now, to get started with this recipe, we'll create a new directory called `ol8-vagrant`. In this directory, create a Packer file and name it `vagrant-ol8.pkr.hcl`, and go ahead and create a folder called `http` and place the kickstart file there. Once this is done, your file structure should look like this:

    ```
    └── vagrant-ol8
        ├── http
        │   └── ol8-ks.cfg
        └── vagrant-ol8.pkr.hcl
    ```

3.  In our kickstart file, we just need to set the password for the root user. So, in this case, we'll change the line that reads `rootpw --lock` to `rootpw --plaintext vagrant`.

4.  Next, we'll go ahead and work on the `vagrant-ol8.pkr.hcl` file. The first thing we'll need to do here is specify the plugins we'll need. Let's use the VirtualBox Builder since we want to create a VM from an ISO image, and the Vagrant Builder since we're going to convert our OVF file into a Vagrant box file. These can be added by placing the following code into your Packer configuration file:

```
packer {
  required_plugins {
    virtualbox = {
      source  = "github.com/hashicorp/virtualbox"
      version = "~> 1"
    }
    vagrant = {
      source  = "github.com/hashicorp/vagrant"
      version = "~> 1"
    }
  }
}
```

Figure 8.36 – Packer VirtualBox and Vagrant builder plugins

**Info:**

More info on the Packer VirtualBox plugin can be found here: `https://www.packer.io/plugins/builders/virtualbox`.

5.  Now we need to define a source. In this case, we want to use the Oracle Linux 8.8 ISO. Add the following to your `vagrant-ol8.pkr.hcl` file:

```
...
...
...
source "virtualbox-iso" "ol8u8" {
  guest_os_type    = "Oracle_64"
  iso_url          = "https://yum.oracle.com/ISOS/OracleLinux/OL8/u8/x86_64/OracleLinux-R8-U8-x86_64-dvd.iso"
  iso_checksum     = "sha256:cae39116245ff7c3c86d5305d9c11430ce5c4e512987563435ac59c37a082d7e"
  ssh_username     = "root"
  ssh_password     = "vagrant"
  headless         = "true"
  ssh_wait_timeout = "30m"
  http_directory   = "http"
  nic_type         = "virtio"
  boot_command = [
    "<up><tab> inst.text inst.ks=http://{{ .HTTPIP }}:{{ .HTTPPort }}/ol8-ks.cfg setup_swap=yes <enter>"
  ]
  vboxmanage = [
    ["modifyvm", "{{.Name}}", "--memory", "2048"],
    ["modifyvm", "{{.Name}}", "--cpus", "2"],
    ["modifyvm", "{{.Name}}", "--nat-localhostreachable1", "on"] # Fix for VBox 7. Remove this line if using VBox 6
  ]
  shutdown_command = "shutdown -P now"
}
```

Figure 8.37 – Packer file for building Vagrant boxes

**Important note**

Notice the `modifyvm` command, which sets `--nat-localhostreachable1` to on. This is a new setting that is `off` by default in Oracle VM VirtualBox 7. Setting this value to on fixes a networking issue that prevents Packer from sending the kickstart file to the VM. In other words, it's important to include this if you're using VirtualBox 7 to build your VM, but if you're on VirtualBox 6, you'll need to remove this line or your build will fail.

6. So, in the preceding code, we specified the `guest_os_type` as `"Oracle_64"` because we're building from an Oracle Linux ISO. Next, we input the URL for the ISO as well as the checksum. For `ssh_username`, we'll use `"root"` and for `ssh_password`, we'll use `"vagrant"` because these are the defaults that Vagrant expects in order to make things easy – especially if you plan to distribute your box publicly. If you intend to keep your box for private use only, it is best to use different values, as this will keep the box more secure.

**Info**

For more information on Vagrant usernames and passwords, visit `https://www.vagrantup.com/docs/boxes/base#vagrant-user`.

7. We'll set `headless` to `"true"` in order to prevent the virtual machine from starting the VirtualBox GUI. We increase the time for `ssh_wait_timeout` to give the operating system sufficient time to install and to get up and running. All of this is self-explanatory; that is, until we get to the `http_directory` setting.

8. All you really need to know is that we'll leverage the `http_directory` option as a convenient way to serve a directory using an HTTP server. It does this so that the boot command can point to a kickstart file – which we've placed in the `http` directory. `http://{{ .HTTPIP }}:{{ .HTTPPort }}/ol8-ks.cfg` tells the operating system exactly what it needs to reach the kickstart file. You don't really need to worry about the syntax of `{{ .HTTPIP }}` and `{{ .HTTPPort }}`; these are just template variables that are processed by the Packer templating engine.

9. For `nic_type`, the default value is `82540EM`, which equates to Intel PRO/1000 MT Desktop. That's a safe choice and is great when running old operating systems, but Oracle Linux 8 is a modern operating system so we're setting this to `virtio`. VirtIO is a para-virtualized driver and will give us better networking performance in the VM.

10. Now, on to the `boot_command`. Basically, we need to figure out what sequence of key presses are required in order to send a boot command to the operating system at boot time. In the case of Oracle Linux 8, we send key presses of *up* and *Tab*, and then we send instructions on where to find the kickstart file, and finally we tell it to press *Enter* to begin installing the OS.

11. For `vboxmanage`, I found that, by default, Packer tried to launch my VM with only 512 MB of memory, and that resulted in an error during the installation of the OS. In order to resolve this issue, I increased the memory to `2048`. I also gave it two CPUs just for good measure.

12. Finally, with the `shutdown_command`, we simply tell Packer how to shut down the system gracefully once all the provisioning is done. If we leave this blank Packer would forcefully shut down the machine.

> **Info**
>
> For a complete overview of available configuration options, see `https://www.packer.io/plugins/builders/virtualbox/iso`.

13. At this point, we have enough to install the OS automatically, but we need to do a few more things to prepare the virtual machine for Vagrant. To be specific, we need to add a user called `vagrant`, populate that user's authorized keys with a known public key for that user, and finally we'll want to install VirtualBox Guest Additions.

For these tasks, we'll leverage a provisioner to execute a shell script. This task takes place after the operating system is installed and while the virtual machine is still running. It's the last thing we'll do before we shut down the system and convert it to a Vagrant box.

Go ahead and add the following to the `vagrant-ol8.pkr.hcl` file:

```
...
  ...
  ...
build {
  sources = ["sources.virtualbox-iso.ol8u8"]

  provisioner "shell" {
    script = "scripts/vagrant-base-box.sh"
  }

  post-processor "vagrant" {
    output = "ol8-x64-virtualbox.box"
  }
}
```

Figure 8.38 – Packer file for building Vagrant boxes (continued)

> **Info**
>
> More info on post-processors can be found here: `https://www.packer.io/plugins/post-processors/vagrant/vagrant#virtualbox`.

14.  As you can see from the preceding screenshot, we're going to create a new folder called `scripts` and place the shell script in there:

```
└── ol8-vagrant
    ├── http
    │   └── ol8-ks.ks
    ├── scripts
    │   └── vagrant-base-box.sh
    └── vagrant-ol8.pkr.hcl
```

15.  Now, in the `vagrant-base-box.sh` script, we'll add this:

```bash
#!/bin/bash

# Prepare vagrant user
useradd vagrant
usermod -aG wheel vagrant
echo vagrant:vagrant | chpasswd
echo "vagrant ALL=(ALL) NOPASSWD: ALL" >> /etc/sudoers.d/vagrant
mkdir -m 0700 -p /home/vagrant/.ssh
curl https://raw.githubusercontent.com/hashicorp/vagrant/main/keys/vagrant.pub >> /home/vagrant/.ssh/authorized_keys
chmod 600 /home/vagrant/.ssh/authorized_keys
chown -R vagrant:vagrant /home/vagrant/.ssh

# Keep SSH speedy even when not connected to the internet
echo "UseDNS no" >> /etc/ssh/sshd_config

# Install packages required for VirtualBox Guest Additions
dnf install -y tar bzip2 kernel-uek-devel gcc make perl

# Install VirtualBox Guest Additions
mkdir -p /mnt/iso
mount -o loop,ro /root/VBoxGuestAdditions.iso /mnt/iso
/mnt/iso/VBoxLinuxAdditions.run
umount /mnt/iso
rm -rf /mnt/iso /root/VBoxGuestAdditions.iso

# Clean up to reduce size of Vagrant box
dnf remove -y kernel-uek-devel
dnf clean all
cat /dev/zero &>/dev/null > /tmp/zero.fill
rm -f /tmp/zero.fill
```

Figure 8.39 – Contents of the vagrant-base-box.sh script

16.  Next, we're going to run `packer init` to download the external plugin:

```
$ packer init .
```

17.  Now we're ready to build the Vagrant box. This part is simple, just run the following:

```
$ packer build .
```

After entering the command, you will see something like the following:

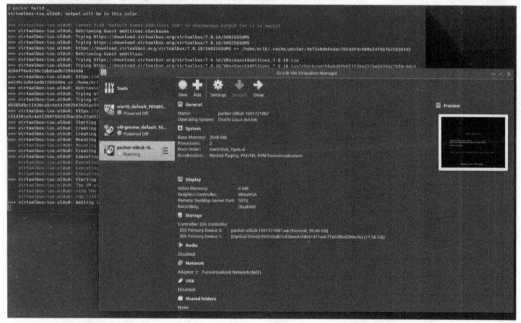

```
) packer build .
virtualbox-iso.ol8u8: output will be in this color.

==> virtualbox-iso.ol8u8: Cannot find "Default Guest Additions ISO" in vboxmanage output (or it is empty)
==> virtualbox-iso.ol8u8: Retrieving Guest additions checksums
==> virtualbox-iso.ol8u8: Trying https://download.virtualbox.org/virtualbox/7.0.10/SHA256SUMS
==> virtualbox-iso.ol8u8: Trying https://download.virtualbox.org/virtualbox/7.0.10/SHA256SUMS
==> virtualbox-iso.ol8u8: https://download.virtualbox.org/virtualbox/7.0.10/SHA256SUMS => /home/erik/.cache/packer/4ef3e0da8edac785d
8f4c608e54f8b7b25836495
==> virtualbox-iso.ol8u8: Retrieving Guest additions
==> virtualbox-iso.ol8u8: Trying https://download.virtualbox.org/virtualbox/7.0.10/VBoxGuestAdditions_7.0.10.iso
==> virtualbox-iso.ol8u8: Trying https://download.virtualbox.org/virtualbox/7.0.10/VBoxGuestAdditions_7.0.10.iso?checksum=bbabd89b8f
ff38a257bab039a278f0c4dc4426eff6e4238c1db01edb7284186a
==> virtualbox-iso.ol8u8: https://download.virtualbox.org/virtualbox/7.0.10/VBoxGuestAdditions_7.0.10.iso?checksum=bbabd89b8fff38a25
7bab039a278f0c4dc4426eff6e4238c1db01edb7284186a => /home/erik/.cache/packer/ddd94c771c4eadfb5704361dda9ffcbc79454341.iso
==> virtualbox-iso.ol8u8: Retrieving ISO
==> virtualbox-iso.ol8u8: Trying https://yum.oracle.com/ISOS/OracleLinux/OL8/u8/x86_64/OracleLinux-R8-U8-x86_64-dvd.iso
==> virtualbox-iso.ol8u8: Trying https://yum.oracle.com/ISOS/OracleLinux/OL8/u8/x86_64/OracleLinux-R8-U8-x86_64-dvd.iso?checksum=sha
256%3Acae39116245ff7c3c86d5305d9c11430ce5c4e512987563435ac59c37a082d7e
    virtualbox-iso.ol8u8: OracleLinux-R8-U8-x86_64-dvd.iso 2.31 GiB / 11.56 GiB [=====>-----------------------]  19.95% 04m33s
```

Figure 8.40 – Output of the "packer build" command

This will take a while, because it's actually doing quite a bit here. Remember what we talked about from a high level: Packer is going to download the ISO, create a VM, and install the OS, and afterward it will run everything in the script you just defined, but once all of this is done, you will be left with a nice neat .box file (which is exactly what we need to for use with Vagrant).

If you switch over to VirtualBox, you'll eventually see a new VM that was created by Packer. You can just leave it be and let Packer do its thing, but knowing this detail gives you the ability to know what's going on behind the scenes.

Figure 8.41 – Screenshot of VM being built and configured with Packer

Once the build is complete, you should see output similar to the following:

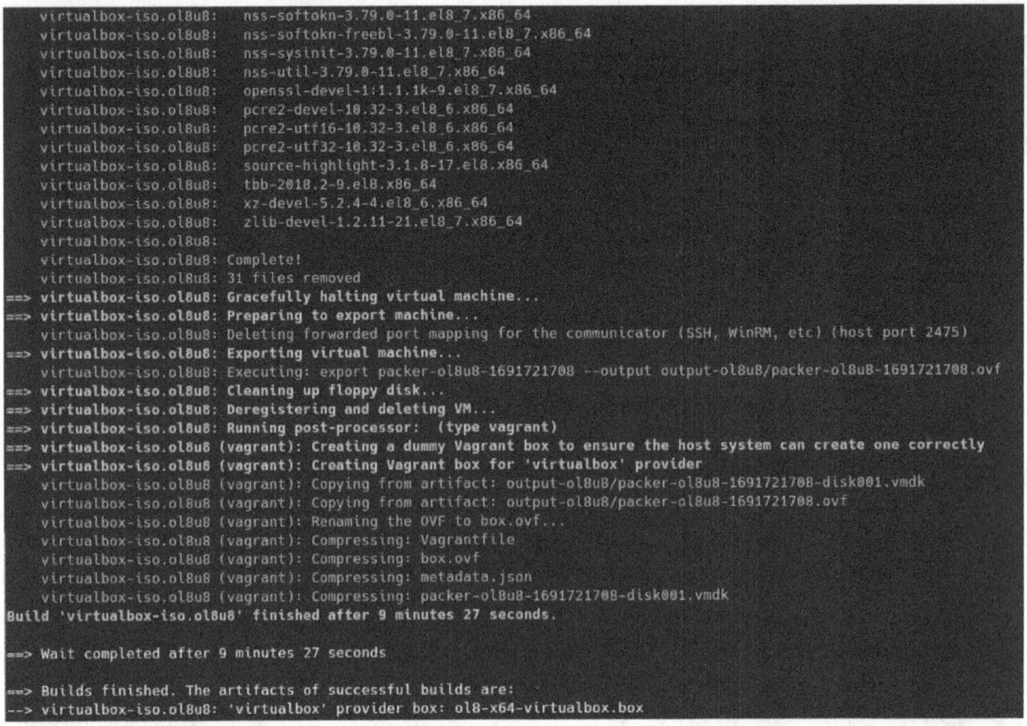

```
virtualbox-iso.ol8u8:    nss-softokn-3.79.0-11.el8_7.x86_64
virtualbox-iso.ol8u8:    nss-softokn-freebl-3.79.0-11.el8_7.x86_64
virtualbox-iso.ol8u8:    nss-sysinit-3.79.0-11.el8_7.x86_64
virtualbox-iso.ol8u8:    nss-util-3.79.0-11.el8_7.x86_64
virtualbox-iso.ol8u8:    openssl-devel-1:1.1.1k-9.el8_7.x86_64
virtualbox-iso.ol8u8:    pcre2-devel-10.32-3.el8_6.x86_64
virtualbox-iso.ol8u8:    pcre2-utf16-10.32-3.el8_6.x86_64
virtualbox-iso.ol8u8:    pcre2-utf32-10.32-3.el8_6.x86_64
virtualbox-iso.ol8u8:    source-highlight-3.1.8-17.el8.x86_64
virtualbox-iso.ol8u8:    tbb-2018.2-9.el8.x86_64
virtualbox-iso.ol8u8:    xz-devel-5.2.4-4.el8_6.x86_64
virtualbox-iso.ol8u8:    zlib-devel-1.2.11-21.el8_7.x86_64
virtualbox-iso.ol8u8:
virtualbox-iso.ol8u8: Complete!
virtualbox-iso.ol8u8: 31 files removed
==> virtualbox-iso.ol8u8: Gracefully halting virtual machine...
==> virtualbox-iso.ol8u8: Preparing to export machine...
    virtualbox-iso.ol8u8: Deleting forwarded port mapping for the communicator (SSH, WinRM, etc) (host port 2475)
==> virtualbox-iso.ol8u8: Exporting virtual machine...
    virtualbox-iso.ol8u8: Executing: export packer-ol8u8-1691721708 --output output-ol8u8/packer-ol8u8-1691721708.ovf
==> virtualbox-iso.ol8u8: Cleaning up floppy disk...
==> virtualbox-iso.ol8u8: Deregistering and deleting VM...
==> virtualbox-iso.ol8u8: Running post-processor: (type vagrant)
==> virtualbox-iso.ol8u8 (vagrant): Creating a dummy Vagrant box to ensure the host system can create one correctly
==> virtualbox-iso.ol8u8 (vagrant): Creating Vagrant box for 'virtualbox' provider
    virtualbox-iso.ol8u8 (vagrant): Copying from artifact: output-ol8u8/packer-ol8u8-1691721708-disk001.vmdk
    virtualbox-iso.ol8u8 (vagrant): Copying from artifact: output-ol8u8/packer-ol8u8-1691721708.ovf
    virtualbox-iso.ol8u8 (vagrant): Renaming the OVF to box.ovf...
    virtualbox-iso.ol8u8 (vagrant): Compressing: Vagrantfile
    virtualbox-iso.ol8u8 (vagrant): Compressing: box.ovf
    virtualbox-iso.ol8u8 (vagrant): Compressing: metadata.json
    virtualbox-iso.ol8u8 (vagrant): Compressing: packer-ol8u8-1691721708-disk001.vmdk
Build 'virtualbox-iso.ol8u8' finished after 9 minutes 27 seconds.

==> Wait completed after 9 minutes 27 seconds

==> Builds finished. The artifacts of successful builds are:
--> virtualbox-iso.ol8u8: 'virtualbox' provider box: ol8-x64-virtualbox.box
```

Figure 8.42 – Screenshot of completed build of Vagrant box

> **Note**
>
> The Oracle Linux ISO file is several gigabytes, so this really could take a while. Now may be the perfect time to take a break and have a coffee. ☕

18. Now it's time to prepare our box for use with Vagrant. We'll just run `vagrant init` to build our Vagrantfile:

```
$ vagrant init ol8-x64-virtualbox.box
```

The output is as follows:

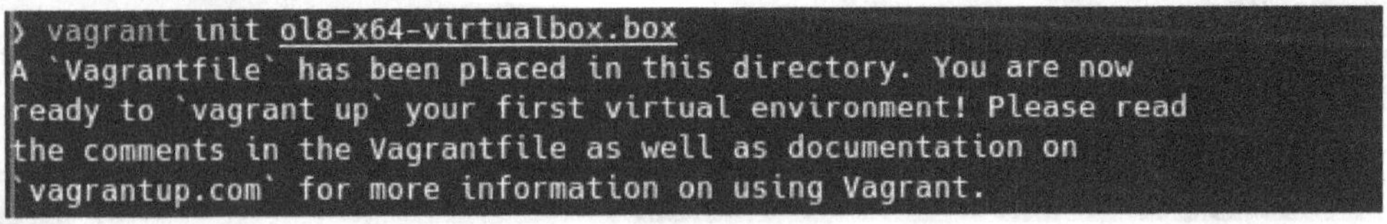

```
> vagrant init ol8-x64-virtualbox.box
A `Vagrantfile` has been placed in this directory. You are now
ready to `vagrant up` your first virtual environment! Please read
the comments in the Vagrantfile as well as documentation on
`vagrantup.com` for more information on using Vagrant.
```

Figure 8.43 – Initializing Vagrant box

---

**Helpful tip**

You could run `vagrant init` and `vagrant init .`, but it's best to specify the filename of the box. This way, Vagrant will automatically specify the proper value of the box inside the Vagrantfile. That's why for this recipe, we are running `vagrant init ol8-x64-virtualbox.box`.

---

19. Finally, it's time to test out our new Vagrant box by running `vagrant up`:

```
$ vagrant up
```

The output of this command is shown in the following screenshot:

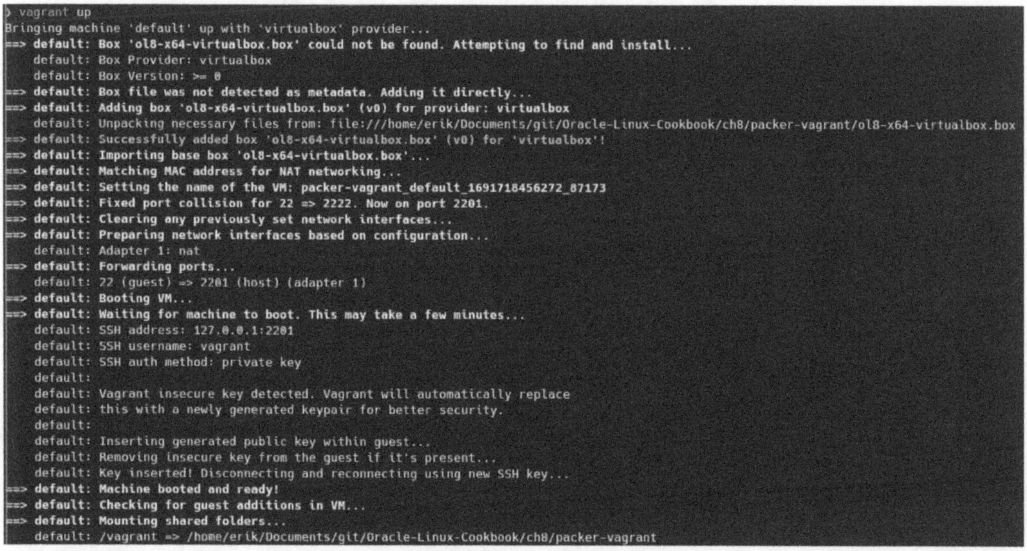

Figure 8.44 – Output of the "vagrant up" command

And there you have it. After a few short moments, your virtual machine will be up and running, and you can interact with it using the convenient commands made possible by Vagrant.

The source code for this recipe can be found at `https://github.com/PacktPublishing/Oracle-Linux-Cookbook/tree/main/ch8/packer-vagrant`.

---

**Important note**

If you're still developing your Vagrant box and need to test after each build, you'll want to make sure you're testing the latest box that you've built. I actually ran into an issue thinking that my changes weren't persisting until I realized Vagrant was using a cached box from a previous build. You can remove old boxes with `vagrant box remove ol8-x64-virtualbox.box`.

---

# 9

# Keeping the Data Safe – Securing a System

No one wants to be the headline news story, especially when their data is stolen. One of the best ways to help protect your data is to secure the operating system and its services. Securing is often compared to an onion, as there are multiple layers that are difficult to peel open, each providing some defense against bad actors. When bad actors attack your data, it's not always to steal it; it's often to change it as well. To make matters worse, when you move to the cloud, you will have to protect not only against internal threats, such as rogue contractors or employees, and external threats, such as hackers attacking the systems, but you also have to protect your data against your cloud provider as well. In security, you never know who is the bad actor!

It is not just protecting your systems against bad actors; many industries also require a strong security stance. This is common with healthcare, which often requires security controls for compliance with the **Health Insurance Portability and Accountability Act (HIPAA)**. Businesses that process credit cards must meet the **Payment Card Industry Data Security Standard (PCI-DSS)** principles, and many governmental organizations must implement security standards to be compliant with the **Federal Risk and Authorization Management Program (FedRAMP)** for their cloud workloads.

> **Note**
> Security teams have their own language! The term "bad actors" refers to hackers — the folks trying to modify or steal the data. They do this by attacking the systems against attack surfaces, basic system components, and services that are reachable by the bad guys.

When you secure systems, you must cover more than just one attack surface. These attack surfaces can be data at rest, data in motion, services such as HTTP, or even the Linux kernel. You also need to use tools that can help identify how the system is configured to best protect the data. In this chapter, the goal is to give you several recipes to help you identify risks and protect your data.

We will cover the following main recipes in this chapter:

- Signing Git commits with GPG
- Encrypting all web traffic
- Encrypting all data at rest
- Validating adherence to a compliance policy
- Port protection and restricting network access
- Keeping SELinux active

# Technical requirements

For this recipe, you will need an Oracle Linux 8 system. As with most of these recipes, a VM on your desktop using a desktop virtualization product such as Oracle VirtualBox is recommended. A small VM with 2 cores, 2 GB RAM, and a few free gigabytes of disk space is fine. Ideally, before you start, you should update your system to the latest packages available. This only takes a few minutes and can save you a ton of time when troubleshooting issues caused by a bug.

Many of the recipes in this book have their related configuration files available in GitHub at `https://github.com/PacktPublishing/Oracle-Linux-Cookbook`.

# Signing Git commits with GPG

This recipe will show you how to digitally sign Git commits and RPM packages using a **GNU Privacy Guard** (**GPG**) keypair. A GPG keypair consists of two parts: the public key and the private key.

This is done by creating a GPG keypair and using it to sign Git commits and RPM packages.

## Getting ready

In order to work with GPG and Git, you first need to install a few packages. Normally GPG is installed by default when the package `gnupg2` is installed.

Git should be installed using `dnf install git -y`.

## How to do it...

The first step is to create a GPG key if you do not already have one. This key will be used to sign both your Git commits and RPM packages. To work with the GPG key, you can use the `gpg` or `gpg2` commands; both are the same thing, as `gpg` links to `gpg2`.

The GPG key is created via the command line:

```
[erik@ol8 ~]$ gpg2 --gen-key
```

The command will ask for some information, mainly your real name and email address. After you enter the information and continue, it will ask you to set a passphrase to use the key. Do not forget the passphrase! If you do, the key will become unusable and you will lose all data encrypted with the key. You can choose not to use a passphrase, but if you do this, you will be asked to verify this several times. The output of the key creation should be similar to the following screenshot:

```
[erik@ol8 ~]$ gpg2 --gen-key
gpg (GnuPG) 2.2.20; Copyright (C) 2020 Free Software Foundation, Inc.
This is free software: you are free to change and redistribute it.
There is NO WARRANTY, to the extent permitted by law.

Note: Use "gpg --full-generate-key" for a full featured key generation dialog.

GnuPG needs to construct a user ID to identify your key.

Real name: Erik Benner
Email address: erik@talesfromthedatacenter.com
You selected this USER-ID:
    "Erik Benner <erik@talesfromthedatacenter.com>"

Change (N)ame, (E)mail, or (O)kay/(Q)uit? o
We need to generate a lot of random bytes. It is a good idea to perform
some other action (type on the keyboard, move the mouse, utilize the
disks) during the prime generation; this gives the random number
generator a better chance to gain enough entropy.
We need to generate a lot of random bytes. It is a good idea to perform
some other action (type on the keyboard, move the mouse, utilize the
disks) during the prime generation; this gives the random number
generator a better chance to gain enough entropy.
gpg: key BF1143507C71FD74 marked as ultimately trusted
gpg: revocation certificate stored as '/home/erik/.gnupg/openpgp-revocs.d/735C115F1970DCF89D8DE1DCBF1143507C71FD74.rev'
public and secret key created and signed.

pub   rsa2048 2022-10-02 [SC] [expires: 2024-10-01]
      735C115F1970DCF89D8DE1DCBF1143507C71FD74
uid                      Erik Benner <erik@talesfromthedatacenter.com>
sub   rsa2048 2022-10-02 [E] [expires: 2024-10-01]

[erik@ol8 ~]$
```

Figure 9.1 – GPG keys created

Optionally, you can use the `--full-generate-key` option, which can be used to create keys stored on hardware devices, among other uses.

Once the key is created, it is put in your keyring, the `pubring.kbx` file in the `.gnupg` directory in your home directory. To see all the keys in the file, run the `gpg2 --list-keys --keyid-format=long` command.

The `gpg --list-secret-keys` command is used to list the secret keys (i.e., private keys) stored in your GPG keyring. Running the command will show output similar to the following figure for GPG keys:

```
[erik@ol8 ~]$ gpg --list-secret-keys --keyid-format=long
/home/erik/.gnupg/pubring.kbx
----------------------------
sec    rsa2048/E921BF9E922221B6 2022-10-02 [SC] [expires: 2024-10-01]
       6510F084DBB33055BBF98562E921BF9E922221B6
uid                    [ultimate] Erik Benner <erik@talesfromthedatacenter.com>
ssb    rsa2048/51C3D2520DC1419E 2022-10-02 [E] [expires: 2024-10-01]

sec    rsa2048/9547D88673951178 2022-10-02 [SC] [expires: 2024-10-01]
       728FB7E4C6712661953BFB049547D88673951178
uid                    [ultimate] Erik Benner <erik@xyzzy.net>
ssb    rsa2048/B73A4C2EE1E88DFF 2022-10-02 [E] [expires: 2024-10-01]

sec    rsa2048/BF1143507C71FD74 2022-10-02 [SC] [expires: 2024-10-01]
       735C115F1970DCF89D8DE1DCBF1143507C71FD74
uid                    [ultimate] Erik Benner <erik@talesfromthedatacenter.com>
ssb    rsa2048/3EB671BAE72D1A47 2022-10-02 [E] [expires: 2024-10-01]
```

Figure 9.2 – GPG keys

The output gives several columns of information for each key:

- sec: This column indicates that the key is a secret key.

- rsa2048/4096/...: This column shows the algorithm and key length used by the key. For example, rsa2048 indicates that the key uses the RSA algorithm with a key length of 2,048 bits. If the long format is used, this will also contain the key fingerprint after the key length.

- [creation date]: This column shows the date on which the key was created.

- [expiration date]: If the key has an expiration date set, it will be shown in this column. If not, this column will be empty.

- [uid]: This column shows the user ID associated with the key. This is usually the name and email address of the key's owner.

- [ssb]: This column indicates that the key has a corresponding subkey (i.e., a separate key used for encryption, signing, or authentication).

- [expires]: If the subkey has an expiration date set, it will be shown in this column. If not, this column will be empty.

The key fingerprint is a shortened digital representation of the key. It allows other people to validate that your public key was sent with no tampering. The long key ID format for the GPG command is a 16-character hexadecimal string that uniquely identifies a public or private key in GPG. It is often used to refer to a specific key when working with GPG.

The long key ID is derived from the full 40-character fingerprint of the key. The fingerprint is a cryptographic hash of the key's public key material, and it is used to verify the authenticity of the key. The long key ID is the last 16 characters of the fingerprint.

Now that you have a key, we need to import it into Git. In the following example, we will use the key E921BF9E922221B6. To import the key, we will use the following command:

```
git config --global user.signingkey E921BF9E922221B6
```

Then, we can set Git to sign all commits by default using the following command:

```
git config --global commit.gpgsign true
```

## How it works...

Git can sign both commits and tags using the GPG key. Be careful with Git though, as it isn't consistent. `git tag` uses `-s` to sign tags, but `git commit` uses `-s` to add the **developers certificate of origin (DCO)** signed-off line to the commit text and `-S` actually signs the commit using GPG.

To set up a new tag, we will use the Git tag `-s $TAG -m $TAG_DESCRIPTION`:

```
$ git tag -s v1.0 -m 'Version 1.0 tag'

You need a passphrase to unlock the secret key for
user: "Erik Benner <erik@talesfromthedatacenter.com>"
2048-bit RSA key, ID 922221B6, created 2024-04-01
```

> **Note**
>
> You can also set `tag.gpgsign` either globally or per-repo to ensure all tags are automatically signed.

Next, we can show the tag with `git show v1.0`:

```
$ git show v1.0
tag v1.0
Tagger: Erik Benner <erik@talesformthedatacenter.com >
Date:    Sun April 2 215:24:41 2023 -2300

Version 1.0 tag
-----BEGIN PGP SIGNATURE-----
Version: GnuPG v1

JHGSksdhj847yskKJHSnd874t1KJAHGS32674GJHSAD784ghsjkd7*&^ADDXGFdgj3kjj
hde018GDKjskhdh8737ybdhajkjkjhsadfs7892987812mmxnbcbsd8JASJ74845jfhHA
SHDepkjahZXkjs83828732ZMKDjh92yaskjagZKDSJHGHHD&=7213kj4ha,,jhsad10al
qpdif9839928hdkask
=EFTF
-----END PGP SIGNATURE-----
```

```
commit 7fhs49185hflvmsgd742825hhabzb182ufnc8
Author: Erik Benner <erik@talesformthedatcenter.com>
Date:    Sun Apr 2 12:52:11 2023 -2300

    Change version number
```

After this, when we check code using Git, add a `-S` option to the command to automatically sign the commit with the tag:

```
git comit -a -S -m "comment goes here"
```

> **Note**
>
> This is not needed if `commit.gpgsign=true` is set either globally or in the active Git repo.

## Encrypting all web traffic

It's important to encrypt the communication to and from your web servers. Even a simple blog or company website with no login has several advantages of being encrypted:

- **Maintaining user trust**: Encrypting your web pages with HTTPS helps establish trust between your website and your users. When a user sees the padlock icon in their web browser indicating that the connection is secure, they can be more confident that their data is being transmitted securely. Browsers will show sites that are not encrypted. Chrome and Edge browsers will show text as *not secure* next to the URL or as Mozilla's red slashed padlock.

- **SEO benefits**: Google has stated that HTTPS is a ranking factor in their search algorithm. This means that websites that use HTTPS may rank higher in search results than those that do not.

- **Browser warnings**: Modern web browsers such as Chrome and Firefox now display warning messages when a user visits a non-HTTPS website that collects sensitive information. This can discourage users from using your website and negatively impact your business.

- **Compliance**: If your website is subject to certain regulations or standards, such as PCI DSS or HIPAA, encrypting your web pages with HTTPS may be required to comply with those regulations.

> **Note**
>
> While SSL is a term that is commonly used, modern systems actually use **Transport Layer Security (TLS)** as the encryption technology. SSL, being an older technology, has some security flaws, which is why TLS was developed as an upgraded version of SSL. TLS addresses the existing vulnerabilities of SSL, making it a much safer option.

Overall, encrypting web pages with HTTPS is important for protecting sensitive data, maintaining user trust, and complying with regulations and standards. It is also becoming increasingly important for SEO and avoiding browser warnings that may negatively impact your website's reputation. It's also easy to do and free with services such as Let's Encrypt (https://letsencrypt.org/) and ZeroSSL (https://zerossl.com/).

Both Let's Encrypt and ZeroSSL provide free security certificates, including SSL/TLS certificates, that are used to encrypt HTTP traffic. SSL/TLS certificates are used to encrypt web traffic, allowing for encrypted communication between web servers and web browsers. Let's Encrypt was created to make it easier for website owners to obtain SSL/TLS certificates and enable HTTPS on their websites. Prior to Let's Encrypt, obtaining SSL/TLS certificates was often a complicated and expensive process involving manual verification and payment to certificate authorities. Let's Encrypt streamlines this process by automating the verification process and providing certificates for free.

Let's Encrypt certificates are trusted by all major web browsers and operating systems. They are issued for a period of 90 days and can be renewed automatically using an automated client software. Let's Encrypt also provides an **Automated Certificate Management Environment** (**ACME**) protocol that allows web servers to automate the process of obtaining, renewing, and revoking certificates.

## Getting ready

For this example, you will need a web server running Oracle Linux. The server needs to be accessible over the internet so that the Let's Encrypt system can verify the URL. In this example, I will be using a VM on Oracle Cloud, using their free tier of service. This VM is running on an Arm-based CPU with 2 cores and 12 GB RAM. Both ports 80 and 443 are opened up to this server. This process works the same regardless of processor type or cloud. The system is running Oracle Linux 8 with the latest patches.

## How to do it...

To do this, we need to do a few things:

1. Install Apache with mod_ssl and all its requirements.
2. Get acme.sh from Git.
3. Create a cert using the webroot mode. Webroot mode requires that the site is accessible from the internet on both ports 80 and 443. While it is easy to implement, there is another verification method using DNS. For more information about different challenge types, refer to https://letsencrypt.org/docs/challenge-types/.
4. Conduct testing.

### Installing Apache with mod_ssl and all its requirements

1.  So let's get started as the root user. First, we need to add some packages:

    -   `httpd` – Apache web server
    -   `mod_ssl` – enables SSL on Apache

    You can do this with the following command:

    ```
    dnf install -y httpd mod_ssl
    ```

2.  Next, let's add both ports 80 and 443 to the firewall. This is done as the root with the following commands:

    ```
    firewall-cmd --zone=public --permanent --add-service=http
    firewall-cmd --zone=public --permanent --add-service=https
    firewall-cmd --reload apache
    ```

3.  Now, let's set up a virtual server for `ssltest.talesfromthedatacenter.com`. This way, we can later add the SSL certs just for this virtual server. As the root, let's make a directory for the files and `chown` them to the `apache` user:

    ```
    mkdir -p /var/www/ssltest
    chown apache:apache /var/www/ssltest
    ```

4.  Next, we will add a config file `ssltest.conf` in `/etc/httpd/conf.d`:

    ```
    <VirtualHost *:80>
        # Put this in /etc/httpd/conf.d/ssltest.conf
        Alias /.well-known/acme-challenge/ /var/www/ssltest/.well-
    known/acme-challenge/
        <Directory "/var/www/ssltest/.well-known/acme-challenge/">
            Options None
            AllowOverride None
            ForceType text/plain
            RedirectMatch 404 "^(?!/\.well-known/acme-challenge/
    [\w-]{43}$)"
        </Directory>
        RewriteEngine On
        RewriteCond %{REQUEST_URI} !^/.well-known/acme-challenge
    [NC]
        RewriteCond %{HTTPS} off
        RewriteRule (.*) https://%{HTTP_HOST}%{REQUEST_URI}
    [R=301,L]
    </VirtualHost>
    ```

5. After you save the file, run an `apachctl configtest`. It is good practice to always run this test when you modify the config files.

```
apachectl configtest
Syntax OK
```

6. Next, let's start Apache and make sure we can get to the default page. The `enable` option will restart the web server when the system starts. The `--now` option will start the server now:

```
systemctl enable --now httpd
```

7. Now, point your browser to the site on port 80. You should see the default Apache page. Notice, the **Not secure** flag in the upper-left corner! The site is *not* using SSL:

This page is used to test the proper operation of the Apache HTTP server after it has been installed. If you can read this page it means that the Apache HTTP server installed at this site is working properly.

**If you are a member of the general public:**

The fact that you are seeing this page indicates that the website you just visited is either experiencing problems or is undergoing routine maintenance.

If you would like to let the administrators of this website know that you've seen this page instead of the page you expected, you should send them e-mail. In general, mail sent to the name "webmaster" and directed to the website's domain should reach the appropriate person.

For example, if you experienced problems while visiting www.example.com, you should send e-mail to "webmaster@example.com".

**If you are the website administrator:**

You may now add content to the directory /var/www/html/. Note that until you do so, people visiting your website will see this page and not your content. To prevent this page from ever being used, follow the instructions in the file /etc/httpd/conf.d/welcome.conf.

You are free to use the images below on Apache Linux powered HTTP servers. Thanks for using Apache!

Figure 9.3 – Apache test page with no SSL

### Getting acme.sh from Git

Now, we need to grab the `acme.sh` script from Git:

1. First, we need to install Git with the following command:

```
dnf install -y git
```

2.  Next, let's make a directory called acme:

    ```
    mkdir acme
    ```

3.  Now, we can clone from the official Git site (https://github.com/acmesh-official/
    acme.sh) with the following command:

    ```
    git clone https://github.com/acmesh-official/acme.sh.git
    ```

And then run the installer, updating your direcotry and email address as needed.

```
/root/acme/acme.sh --install -m my@email.com
```

### *Creating a cert using the webroot mode*

1.  Next, let's register for an account, passing an email address as the variable:

    ```
    /root/acme/acme.sh/acme.sh --register-account -m erik@
    talesfromthedatacenter.com
    [Sun Apr  2 22:02:01 GMT 2023] No EAB credentials found for
    ZeroSSL, let's get one
    [Sun Apr  2 22:02:02 GMT 2023] Registering account: https://
    acme.zerossl.com/v2/DV90
    [Sun Apr  2 22:02:03 GMT 2023] Registered
    [Sun Apr  2 22:02:03 GMT 2023] ACCOUNT_
    THUMBPRINT='QPU6rxYiTHrRkweBPKtAhUqnflvlBSdl0Xu4N89JhyY'
    ```

    Save the ACCOUNT_THUMBPRINT for future use. This is also saved in ./ca/acme.zerossl.
    com/v2/DV90/ca.conf.

2.  Now, we can run the script, passing the URL and the apache home directory for the site:

    ```
    ./acme.sh --issue  -d ssltest.talesfromthedatacenter.com --log
    ```

The following figure shows the command running with the new certificate being installed by
the script.

```
[root@lets-encrypt acme]# /root/acme.sh/acme.sh --issue  -d ssltest.talesfromthedatacenter.com --log
[Sun Apr  2 22:56:24 GMT 2023] Using CA: https://acme.zerossl.com/v2/DV90
[Sun Apr  2 22:56:24 GMT 2023] Single domain='ssltest.talesfromthedatacenter.com'
[Sun Apr  2 22:56:24 GMT 2023] Getting domain auth token for each domain
[Sun Apr  2 22:56:27 GMT 2023] Getting webroot for domain='ssltest.talesfromthedatacenter.com'
[Sun Apr  2 22:56:27 GMT 2023] Verifying: ssltest.talesfromthedatacenter.com
[Sun Apr  2 22:56:27 GMT 2023] Processing, The CA is processing your order, please just wait. (1/30)
[Sun Apr  2 22:56:31 GMT 2023]
[Sun Apr  2 22:56:31 GMT 2023] Verify finished, start to sign.
[Sun Apr  2 22:56:31 GMT 2023] Lets finalize the order.
[Sun Apr  2 22:56:31 GMT 2023] Le_OrderFinalize='https://acme.zerossl.com/v2/DV90/order/Na6isKcdgR84PtqHFCg3XQ/finalize'
[Sun Apr  2 22:56:32 GMT 2023] Order status is processing, lets sleep and retry.
[Sun Apr  2 22:56:32 GMT 2023] Retry after: 15
[Sun Apr  2 22:56:48 GMT 2023] Polling order status: https://acme.zerossl.com/v2/DV90/order/Na6isKcdgR84PtqHFCg3XQ
[Sun Apr  2 22:56:48 GMT 2023] Downloading cert.
[Sun Apr  2 22:56:48 GMT 2023] Le_LinkCert='https://acme.zerossl.com/v2/DV90/cert/z7l8GHTCJb_P7bgMYao8yw'
[Sun Apr  2 22:56:49 GMT 2023]
-----BEGIN CERTIFICATE-----
MIIEKDCCA62gAwIBAgIQcvtRKarM9ySrwDJpUSnQBDAKBggqhkjOPQQDAzBLMQsw
CQYDVQQGEwJBVDEQMA4GA1UEChMHWmVyb1NTTDEqMCgGA1UEAxMhWmVyb1NTTCBF
Q0MgRG9tYWluIFNlY3VyZSBTaXRlIENBMB4XDTIzMDQwMjAwMDAwMFoXDTIzMDcw
MTIzNTk1OVowLTErMCkGA1UEAxMic3NsdGVzdC50YWxlc2Zyb21oaGVkYXRhY2Vu
dGVyLmNvbTBZMBMGByqGSM49AgEGCCqGSM49AwEHA0IABKvmVqlxNH4VvYKKxhYC
0fBDTXG/WgjaMJ6woJk/cSAJ9Uefy7b5OkkJrmPExo723xB65CSRZrVxoPrti4QR
uB+jggKPMIICizAfBgNVHSMEGDAWgBQPa+ZLzjlHrvZ+kB558DCRkshfozAdBgNV
HQ4EFgQUYcT9Mwim/gyVm3t13D+2LPtzlfkwDgYDVR0PAQH/BAQDAgeAMAwGA1Ud
EwEB/wQCMAAwHQYDVR01BBYwFAYIKwYBBQUHAwEGCCsGAQUFBwMCMEkGA1UdIARC
MEAwNAYLKwYBBAGyMQECAk4wJTAjBggrBgEFBQcCARYXaHR0cHM6Ly9zZWN0aW9u
LmNvbvbS9DUFMwCAYG24EMAQIBMIGIBggrBgEFBQcBAQR8MHowSwYIKwYBBQUHMAKG
P2h0dHA6Ly96ZXJvc3NsLmNydC5zZWN0aWdvLmNvbS9aZXJvU1NMRUNDRG9tYWlu
U2VjdXJlU2l0ZUNBLmNydDArBggrBgEFBQcwAYYfaHR0cDovL3plcm9zc2l3ub2Nz
cC5zZWN0aWdvLmNvbTCCAQUGCisGAQQB1nkCBAIEgfYEgfMA8QB3AK33vvp8/xDI
i509nB4+GGq0Zyldz7EMJMqFhjTr3IKKAAABh0QvwTsAAAQDAEgwRgIhAL5piIL8
65gvBzReOlS9YmpQwVYsg0k8O2DrqCAnod4fAiEA4AB3BFuVY4+t/qC396YR/mTo
8Bbgdnm9XB/54EoEL94AdgB6MoxU2LcttiDqOOBSHumEFnAyE4VNO9IrwTpXolLr
UgAAAYdEL8GaAAAEAwBHMEUCIQDf1UNwdmeOi2IyKnk99uccio3FbYvFvfhPAkq8
GvR4bwIgRamWqxSq/2cS4/v8gQzHXwhHB96jKNuPW93Sf/fMe1cwLQYDVR0RBCYw
JIIic3NsdGVzdC50YWxlc2Zyb210aGVkYXRhY2VudGVyLmNvbTAKBggqhkjOPQQD
AwNpADBmAjEAwEEP3TukmrYwSTiZp+p5I2A9i3hRSEyX+Klw87yn6QYrvDLAhWFB
DeKZM36dyt68AjEAt8eRhT6yTOOAa68yQGlidaM+WPLm90fsiK4YaTgBeTwyoWIE
```

Figure 9.4 – Certificate to be installed

The script will restart Apache.

## Testing

1.  You can now go to the site with an HTTPS. You will see a padlock in the left side of the address bar. The site is now secure. This is seen in the following figure:

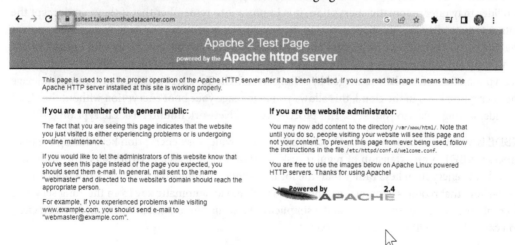

Figure 9.5 – SSL keys installed

## How it works...

The way this works is the `acme.sh` script generates a temporary key file and places it in the `.well-know/acme-challenge` directory. The system then queries from the internet to the server to get the file. If it can get to the file, the test passes and new keys are issued. It is important to monitor this, as third-party security software or SELinux can impact your ability to get to the temporary key file.

Now that the certificate is set up, there is one task left to do to make this a refresh. You can easily have the system check daily for a new certificate by adding in the following cron job. As a note, you will need to adjust the location of the script based on where you installed it. In this case, it was installed in `/home/acme/.acme.sh`:

```
0 0 * * * /home/acme/.acme.sh/acme.sh --cron --home /home/acme/.acme.
sh > /dev/null
```

> **Note**
>
> When using keys that automatically update, it is highly recommended to monitor your sites consistently for SSL errors. Ideally, you are checking for SSL errors once an hour just in case things break. Look in the web server's SSL logs and also run a check with a tool such as wget or curl to verify that the site is running. Both wget and curl will fail with an error if the SSL key is invalid.

# Encrypting all data at rest

Encrypting your data in motion is great, but you also need to encrypt the data at rest. This is especially important in the cloud, where you are sharing storage with many other users. While your cloud provider may offer automatic encryption, it is important to remember that if they can decrypt the data automatically, they also have access to the keys. To truly protect your data, you need to encrypt the data with keys that your cloud does not have access to. This can be done easily with **Linux Unified Key Setup** (**LUKS**). Large organizations will also want to use **Clevis**, which enables the automatic decryption of data from keys managed by a Tang server. The Tang server is used to store and manage the encryption keys. In the cloud, this allows you to manage your boot encryption without the cloud provider having access to your keys. This process is called **Network Bound Disk Encryption** (**NBDE**).

NBDE is a security feature used in Oracle Linux that provides disk encryption keys during the boot process. NBDE is an extension of regular disk encryption and uses a network server to store and provide the encryption keys rather than the local machine. Combined with NUKS, this allows both a local key (that requires a manual passphrase to use) and an automatic key from the Tang server to decrypt the boot drive. This gives you the simplicity of a secure automated boot, but in an emergency, you can still boot without the Tang server.

## Getting ready

Unlike other recipes, this one will need a minimum of two VMs: one to act as the Tang server and the other to act as a client. Both systems should be updated to the latest software.

## How to do it...

In this recipe, we will do the following:

- Create a server named `tang`:
  - Install and configure a Tang server
- Build another server named `clevis`:
  - Install and configure Clevis
  - Configure LUKS to work with Clevis to encrypt a data volume

### Configuring a Tang server

The Tang server is used by Oracle Linux to provide encryption keys during the boot process. Here's a basic overview of how it operates:

- During the boot process, the remote system contacts the Tang server and requests an encryption key
- The Tang server generates a random encryption key and sends it back to the remote system
- The remote system uses the encryption key to unlock its encrypted drive, allowing it to boot
- The Tang server discards the encryption key so it cannot be used again

One of the key benefits of using a Tang server is that it can provide encryption keys to remote systems even if the main encryption key is compromised. This can improve the security of the system by limiting the amount of damage that can be done if the main encryption key is compromised.

1.  To install the Tang server as the root, we will simply install the software with `dnf`, open up the firewall ports, and set the server to run. This is all done as the root user.

    Installing via `dnf` is easy; just run the following command:

    ```
    dnf install -y tang
    ```

2.  We will add ports to the firewall. The trusted network will be the subnet that you are booting from. In this case, `192.168.56.0/24` is my boot subnet. Don't forget to update the subnet to your subnet when running the following firewall commands:

```
firewall-cmd --zone=trusted --add-source=192.168.56.0/24
firewall-cmd --zone=trusted --add-service=http
firewall-cmd --runtime-to-permanent
```

3.  Configure the service to start upon booting and also start now with the following command:

```
systemctl enable --now tangd.socket
```

You can verify that the service is running with the following command:

```
systeemctl status tangd command;
# systemctl status tangd.socket
☒ tangd.socket - Tang Server socket
   Loaded: loaded (/usr/lib/systemd/system/tangd.socket;
enabled; vendor preset: disabled)
   Active: active (listening) since Mon 2023-07-17 13:52:58 EDT;
2min 46s ago
   Listen: [::]:80 (Stream)
 Accepted: 0; Connected: 0;
    Tasks: 0 (limit: 48611)
   Memory: 0B
   CGroup: /system.slice/tangd.socket

Jul 17 13:52:58 tang.m57.local systemd[1]: Listening on Tang
Server socket.
```

4.  Once Tang is running, there should be key files in `/var/db/tang`. You can also run the command `tang-show-keys`. This will show all of the thumbprints of the keys in the system:

```
[root@tang ~]# tang-show-keys
RxdbjAY7_N19UEYBO6XIUVosv0s
[root@tang ~]#
```

Next, let's set up the client system with LUKS to encrypt the data drive.

### Setting up LUKS

1.  First, install the required packages with the following `dnf` command:

```
dnf -y install cryptsetup clevis clevis-luks clevis-dracut
```

2.  Now, we will encrypt the entire raw data device. By encrypting the entire device, all meta data about the volume is encrypted, along with the actual data itself. In this example, we

have /dev/sdb, which is a small 20 GB device. You can see by checking all the block devices with the lsblk command:

```
[root@clevis ~]# lsblk
NAME            MAJ:MIN RM   SIZE RO TYPE MOUNTPOINT
sda               8:0    0  100G  0 disk
├─sda1            8:1    0    1G  0 part /boot
└─sda2            8:2    0 72.9G  0 part
  ├─ol-root     252:0    0   50G  0 lvm  /
  ├─ol-swap     252:1    0  7.9G  0 lvm  [SWAP]
  ├─ol-var      252:2    0    5G  0 lvm  /var
  ├─ol-home     252:3    0    5G  0 lvm  /home
  └─ol-var_log  252:4    0    5G  0 lvm  /var/log
sdb               8:16   0   20G  0 disk
sr0              11:0    1 1024M  0 rom
```

3.  Encrypt /dev/sdb with the following command:

```
cryptsetup luksFormat --type luks2 --cipher aes-xts-plain64 \
  --key-size 512 --hash sha256 --use-random --force-password /
dev/sdb
```

**WARNING: Doing this will delete ALL DATA on the device**, including any partitions:

```
[root@clevis ~]# cryptsetup luksFormat --type luks2 --cipher aes-xts-plain64 \
> --key-size 512 --hash sha256 --use-random --force-password /dev/sdb
WARNING: Device /dev/sdb already contains a 'crypto_LUKS' superblock signature.

WARNING!
========
This will overwrite data on /dev/sdb irrevocably.

Are you sure? (Type 'yes' in capital letters): YES
Enter passphrase for /dev/sdb:
Verify passphrase:
[root@clevis ~]#
```

Figure 9.6 – Encrypting the drive

When running the command, you will also be prompted for a passphrase. **DO NOT LOSE THIS** or you will be unable to decrypt the drive manually.

4.  Next, let's manually unlock the drive using the previously saved passphrase with the following command:

```
cryptsetup --verbose luksOpen /dev/sdb datadisk1
```

Once unlocked, you should see the disk in /dev/mapper:

```
[root@clevis ~]# ls /dev/mapper/datadisk1
/dev/mapper/datadisk1
```

5.  Now we can use /dev/mapper/datadisk1 like any normal disk. In the example, let's create a xfs filesystem on /dev/mapper/datadisk1:

    ```
    mkfs.xfs /dev/mapper/datadisk1
    ```

    We will also make a mount point /data:

    ```
    mkdir /data
    ```

6.  To use the disk, we need to pull the UUID of the disk. This is done with the following blkid command. The UUID will be used to identify the disk to decrypt it later:

    ```
    [root@clevis ~]# blkid -s UUID  /dev/mapper/datadisk1
    /dev/mapper/datadisk1: UUID="58c9f051-f243-4c42-af4f-
    62d2e3e3b90f"
    ```

7.  Mounting the filesystem on reboot required us to add the fstab entry with the following command:

    ```
    echo "UUID=58c9f051-f243-4c42-af4f-62d2e3e3b90f /data xfs
    defaults 0 0" | sudo tee -a /etc/fstab
    ```

8.  Now we can mount the disk with the following command:

    ```
    mount /data
    ```

9.  Next, we need to bind a Tang key to the device using Clevis with the following command. We will pass the device and Tang server information via the following command line. You will need to use the existing LUKS password to add the keys to Tang:

    ```
    [root@clevis ~]# clevis luks bind -d /dev/sdb tang
    '{"url":"http://tang.m57.local"}'
    Warning: Value 512 is outside of the allowed entropy range,
    adjusting it.
    The advertisement contains the following signing keys:

    RxdbjAY7_N19UEYBO6XIUVosv0s

    Do you wish to trust these keys? [ynYN] Y
    Enter existing LUKS password:
    ```

    We can now look at the LUKS key slots. You should see the key in the second slot now.

    As seen in the following screenshot, slot 1: is populated with a key:

```
[root@clevis ~]# cryptsetup luksDump /dev/sdb
LUKS header information
Version:         2
Epoch:           5
Metadata area:   16384 [bytes]
Keyslots area:   16744448 [bytes]
UUID:            218ec8bc-2508-4e34-a569-1e8d3783874e
Label:           (no label)
Subsystem:       (no subsystem)
Flags:           (no flags)

Data segments:
  0: crypt
        offset: 16777216 [bytes]
        length: (whole device)
        cipher: aes-xts-plain64
        sector: 512 [bytes]

Keyslots:
  0: luks2
        Key:         512 bits
        Priority:    normal
        Cipher:      aes-xts-plain64
        Cipher key:  512 bits
        PBKDF:       argon2i
        Time cost:   8
        Memory:      1048576
        Threads:     4
        Salt:        49 d8 90 9e b0 28 0e 3f 23 af f8 f5 4f 56 53 39
                     6f 03 42 1f e6 d9 5e b6 fa 87 e8 c7 8e 19 30 81
        AF stripes:  4000
        AF hash:     sha256
        Area offset:32768 [bytes]
        Area length:258048 [bytes]
        Digest ID:   0
  1: luks2
        Key:         512 bits
        Priority:    normal
        Cipher:      aes-xts-plain64
        Cipher key:  512 bits
        PBKDF:       pbkdf2
        Hash:        sha256
        Iterations:  1000
        Salt:        7b 50 80 17 64 f9 77 2d 9f c8 5b 93 ea ed 1d f3
                     76 bc 7b a1 3d 78 bc ab 03 4b 08 4e ec 51 20 e8
        AF stripes:  4000
        AF hash:     sha256
        Area offset:290816 [bytes]
        Area length:258048 [bytes]
        Digest ID:   0
Tokens:
  0: clevis
        Keyslot:   1
Digests:
  0: pbkdf2
        Hash:        sha256
        Iterations:  158108
        Salt:        55 90 39 de 70 3f 5e 31 5c c7 0f 0b 0c 8a c1 47
                     c8 ea b8 d2 b0 e9 2c a0 6d a1 d7 1f 8f f9 cd 6b
        Digest:      7b b7 ea cc d1 2e 53 a7 bf 26 b0 d0 a2 3c 13 2d
                     57 cc 26 97 c7 0e 45 27 07 64 4e 51 bb aa fd ba
[root@clevis ~]# █
```

Figure 9.7 – LUKS with the second slot used

10. Next, we need to configure the disk to decrypt the drive on boot. We first need to pull the new UUID of the encrypted drive:

```
[root@clevis ~]# blkid -s UUID  /dev/sdb
/dev/sdb: UUID="218ec8bc-2508-4e34-a569-1e8d3783874e"
```

11. Next, let's enable the Clevis service:

```
systemctl enable clevis-luks-askpass.path
```

12. Now, we need to add the device to the /etc/crypttab file. The crypttab file contains a list of all encrypted drives:

```
echo "encrypteddisk UUID=218ec8bc-2508-4e34-a569-1e8d3783874e -
_netdev" | sudo tee -a /etc/crypttab
```

13. Next, we will update the /etc/fstab file for the filesystem, changing the default to _netdev. This will allow the device to mount after the other non-encrypted filesystems.

14. The /etc/fstab should look similar to the following screenshot, with the UUID of the encrypted drive mounting as a _netdev:

```
[root@clevis ~]# more /etc/fstab

#
# /etc/fstab
# Created by anaconda on Tue Apr  4 15:07:11 2023
#
# Accessible filesystems, by reference, are maintained under '/dev/disk/'.
# See man pages fstab(5), findfs(8), mount(8) and/or blkid(8) for more info.
#
# After editing this file, run 'systemctl daemon-reload' to update systemd
# units generated from this file.
#
/dev/mapper/ol-root         /                        xfs      defaults       0 0
UUID=801861e9-c364-4c1c-9966-1906901fe222 /boot              xfs      defaults         0 0
/dev/mapper/ol-home     /home        xfs      defaults      0 0
/dev/mapper/ol-var      /var         xfs      defaults      0 0
/dev/mapper/ol-var_log  /var/log     xfs      defaults      0 0
/dev/mapper/ol-swap     none         swap     defaults      0 0
UUID=58c9f051-f243-4c42-af4f-62d2e3e3b90f /data xfs _netdev 0 0
[root@clevis ~]# █
```

Figure 9.8 – fstab

## How it works...

Clevis and Tang are both software tools that are used to unlock and decrypt disks automatically during the boot process of a Linux system.

Here is a brief overview of how they work:

1. During the boot process, the system prompts the user for a passphrase to unlock and decrypt the disk.

2.  With Clevis and Tang, this prompt is replaced with an automated process that unlocks and decrypts the disk using a network-based key server.

3.  Clevis and Tang work together to create a *binding* between the encrypted disk and the key server. This binding is based on a *policy* that specifies the conditions under which the disk can be unlocked.

4.  When the system boots up, it contacts the key server and requests the decryption key for the encrypted disk. The key server checks the policy to determine whether the conditions for unlocking the disk have been met.

5.  If the policy conditions are met, the key server sends the decryption key to the system, which then uses it to unlock and decrypt the disk.

6.  If the policy conditions are not met, the key server denies the request for the decryption key, and the disk remains locked.

## There's more...

Optionally, you can also modify the system to allow an admin to manually enter the initial password when the system boots. To do this, install `clevis-dracut`:

```
dnf install -y clevis-dracut
```

Then, rebuild the boot files:

```
dracut -fv
```

When the system boots, you will have the opportunity to enter the passphrase manually:

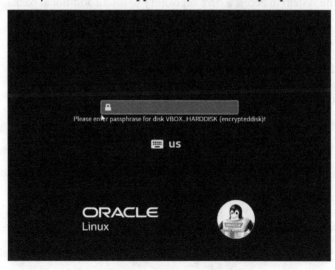

Figure 9.9 – Manual passphrase entry

Now you have an encrypted filesystem with an automatic way to decrypt it, as well as a manual method for use in emergencies.

# Validating adherence to a compliance policy

Securing systems is much more than encrypting data at rest or in motion. Many configuration files should be checked, along with other common security settings. This can be done automatically using **Security Content Automation Protocol** (**SCAP**) files. SCAP is a standardized framework that is used to automate the process of maintaining the security of computer systems. It is a suite of specifications that provide a standardized approach to security automation, enabling organizations to implement consistent and repeatable security practices across their IT infrastructure.

SCAP defines a common language for communicating security-related information, which allows security tools and products from different vendors to work together seamlessly. It includes a set of standards and guidelines for creating and sharing security content, such as vulnerability data, security checklists, and configuration baselines. Some of the key components of SCAP include the **Common Vulnerabilities and Exposures** (**CVE**) database, which is used to identify and track known security vulnerabilities, and the **Common Configuration Enumeration** (**CCE**) database, which provides a standardized method for identifying configuration settings that are relevant to security.

The easiest way to do this is to use a tool called OpenSCAP, which comes with Oracle Linux.

## Getting ready

As with the other test, we will need an Oracle Linux system to play with. Nothing else is required other than the ability for the system to access a `dnf` repository to install additional packages.

## How to do it...

The first step is to install OpenSCAP, usually by installing the entire suite of tools:

- `scap-workbench`: A GUI
- `openscap-scanner`: Scans systems
- `openscap`: The OpenSCAP core
- `openscap-utils`: Several command-line tools for scanning systems and containers
- `scap-security-guide`: Commonly used SCAP files

This is done via `dnf` with the following command:

```
dnf install -y scap-workbench
```

Once OpenSCAP is installed, you have two ways to run the tool: via a GUI or by using the command line. To start the GUI, run `scap-workbench`. This launches an easy-to-use GUI that will let you run scans.

> **Note**
>
> If you install `scap-workbench` and X11 is not installed, `dnf` will install it. If you are not using X11 on your servers, consider installing the `scap-workbench` on a WSL Oracle Linux system or a system with X11. You can also install SCAP Workbench on a Windows desktop. Downloads for Windows can be found on the Open SCAP website, `https://www.open-scap.org/`.

## How it works...

While many users run the GUI, you can also use a command line.

When the GUI Launches, you need to pick the type of systems you wish to scan. Here, OL8 is being used:

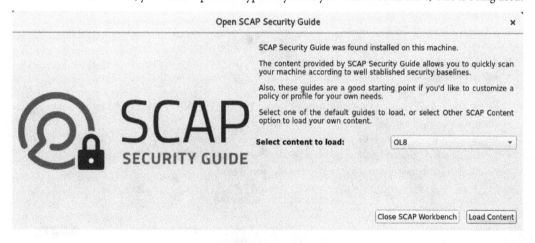

Figure 9.10 – Workbench launch

Next, select the profile you wish to use for the scan. The profile is the standard that you are comparing to. You must pick one of the profiles to continue:

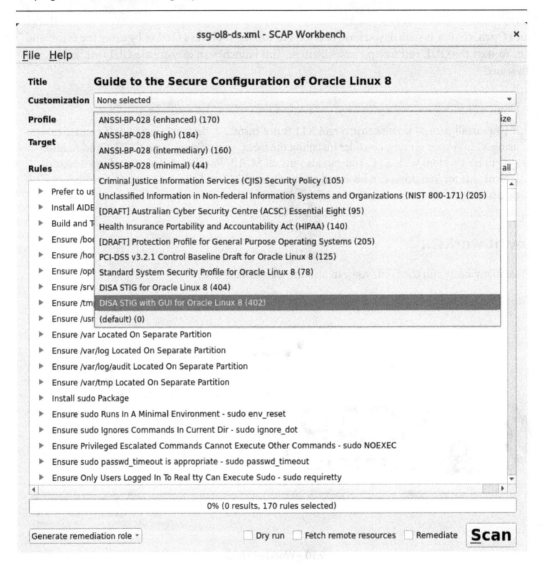

Figure 9.11 – SCAP profiles

The families of profiles included are as follows:

- **ANSSI-BP**: ANSSI-BP is a set of security recommendations developed by the **French National Agency for the Security of Information Systems** (**ANSSI**) to provide guidance on securing information systems. The ANSSI-BP recommendations cover a wide range of topics, including network security, secure software development, access control, cryptography, incident response, and security monitoring.

- **CJIS**: The **Criminal Justice Information Services (CJIS)** are a division of the **Federal Bureau of Investigation (FBI)** in the United States. The CJIS division is responsible for providing law enforcement agencies with access to criminal justice information systems, which includes databases of criminal records, fingerprints, and other related information. The CJIS division was established in 1992 and provides services to more than 18,000 law enforcement agencies across the United States. Its mission is to provide accurate and timely information to law enforcement officials to help them solve and prevent crimes, while also ensuring the privacy and security of the information.

- **NIST-800**: NIST-800 refers to a series of guidelines and standards for information security developed by the **National Institute of Standards and Technology (NIST)** in the United States. The NIST-800 series includes a set of publications that provide guidance on various aspects of information security, such as risk management, security controls, and incident response. The NIST-800 series is widely used by government agencies, private sector organizations, and other entities to improve the security of their information systems. The publications in the series are regularly updated to reflect changes in the threat landscape and advancements in security technology.

- **ACSC**: The **Australian Cyber Security Centre (ACSC)** is a government agency that is responsible for enhancing the cyber security capabilities and resilience of the Australian government, businesses, and the community. The ACSC was established in 2014 and is a part of the **Australian Signals Directorate (ASD)**.

- **HIPAA**: The **Health Insurance Portability and Accountability Act (HIPAA)** is a federal law in the United States that protects healthcare information. This law establishes standards for protecting the privacy and security of individuals' health-related information. HIPAA includes specific requirements for securing **electronic protected health information (ePHI)**, which is health information that is stored or transmitted electronically.

- **PCS-DSS**: The **Payment Card Industry Data Security Standard (PCI-DSS)** is a set of security standards established by major credit card companies that ensure that organizations that have access to credit card details protect the confidentiality and integrity of cardholder data. PCI-DSS is designed to reduce the risk of data breaches and credit card fraud.

- **STIG**: STIG stands for **Security Technical Implementation Guide**, which is a set of guidelines developed by the **Defense Information Systems Agency (DISA)** in the United States for securing information systems and software used by the **Department of Defense (DoD)**. STIG provides detailed information on how to configure and maintain various technologies to meet DoD security requirements and ensure that systems are hardened against cyberattacks.

When picking a standard, you can use the default generic standards (such as the *Standard System Security Profile for Oracle Linux 8* found at `https://static.open-scap.org/ssg-guides/ssg-ol8-guide-standard.html`) or a standard that aligns with the workload. For example, for healthcare, HIPAA is likely the appropriate standard. If you are in the US Federal Government ecosystem, the STIG standard is widely used even outside of the DoD. Once you pick the standard, you have several additional options, as seen in the following screenshot. You can pick a local or remote machine, as well as a remediation role. The remediation role allows the system to automatically resolve issues if possible, but any admin should be careful using this. This is because many of the standards can break system functionality. Always be careful when automatically remediating issues, especially with the more stringent standards, such as STIG and CJIS.

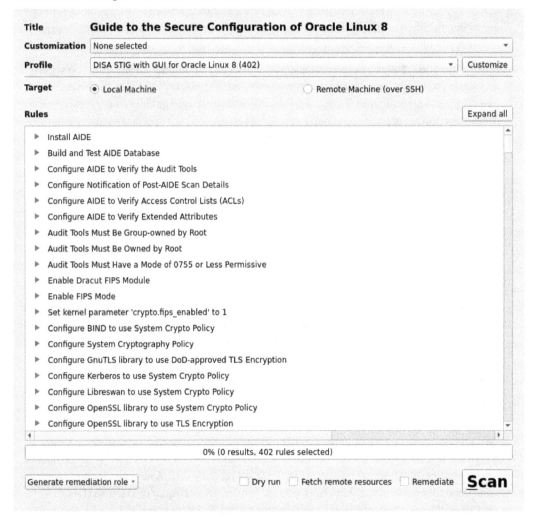

| Title | **Guide to the Secure Configuration of Oracle Linux 8** |
|---|---|
| Customization | None selected |
| Profile | DISA STIG with GUI for Oracle Linux 8 (402)    Customize |
| Target | ● Local Machine        ○ Remote Machine (over SSH) |
| Rules | Expand all |

▶  Install AIDE
▶  Build and Test AIDE Database
▶  Configure AIDE to Verify the Audit Tools
▶  Configure Notification of Post-AIDE Scan Details
▶  Configure AIDE to Verify Access Control Lists (ACLs)
▶  Configure AIDE to Verify Extended Attributes
▶  Audit Tools Must Be Group-owned by Root
▶  Audit Tools Must Be Owned by Root
▶  Audit Tools Must Have a Mode of 0755 or Less Permissive
▶  Enable Dracut FIPS Module
▶  Enable FIPS Mode
▶  Set kernel parameter 'crypto.fips_enabled' to 1
▶  Configure BIND to use System Crypto Policy
▶  Configure System Cryptography Policy
▶  Configure GnuTLS library to use DoD-approved TLS Encryption
▶  Configure Kerberos to use System Crypto Policy
▶  Configure Libreswan to use System Crypto Policy
▶  Configure OpenSSL library to use System Crypto Policy
▶  Configure OpenSSL library to use TLS Encryption

0% (0 results, 402 rules selected)

Generate remediation role ▾        ☐ Dry run  ☐ Fetch remote resources  ☐ Remediate    **Scan**

Figure 9.12 – Scan settings

Once you have made your choices, select **Scan**.

Depending on the standard used, the scan can run in as fast as a few seconds or take over 20 minutes. When the scan is complete, you can use the GUI to review the results:

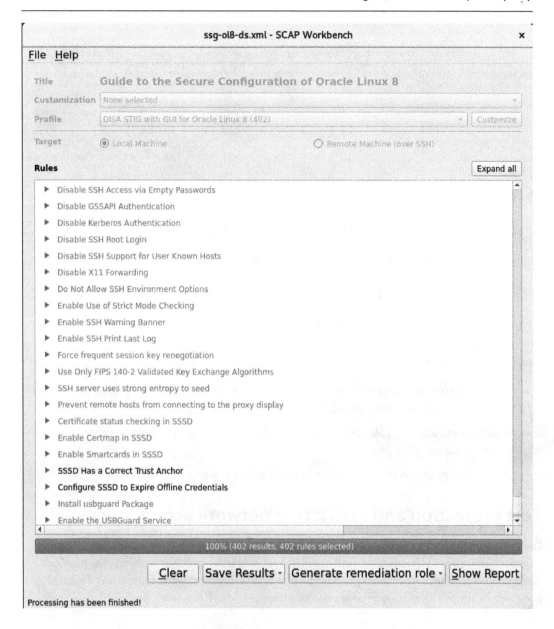

Figure 9.13 – Scan results

Not all fixes involve changing a simple setting. Some may require additional filesystems or kernel settings. To see the details of a finding, simply expand the results as seen in the following screenshot:

▼  Disable X11 Forwarding

The X11Forwarding parameter provides the ability to tunnel X11 traffic through the connection to enable remote grapl
connections when SSH's X11Forwarding option is enabled. The default SSH configuration disables X11Forwarding. The
X11Forwarding. To explicitly disable X11 Forwarding, add or correct the following line in /etc/ssh/sshd_config: X11Forw

▼  Do Not Allow SSH Environment Options

Ensure that users are not able to override environment variables of the SSH daemon. The default SSH configuration di
used if no value is set for PermitUserEnvironment. To explicitly disable Environment options, add or correct the followi

▶  Enable Use of Strict Mode Checking

▶  Enable SSH Warning Banner

▶  Enable SSH Print Last Log

▶  Force frequent session key renegotiation

Figure 9.14 – Result details

At the bottom of the summary, you have several options:

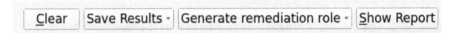

Figure 9.15 – Report options

These options are as follows:

- **Save Results**: Saves the results as a HTML file, an **Asset Reporting File** (**ARF**) file, or an **Extensible Configuration Checklist Description Format** (**XCDDF**) file

- **Generate remediation role**: Generates a script in bash, Ansible, or Puppet format to automate the remediation of the server

- **Show Report**: Opens up the HTML-formatted report in a browser

# Port protection and restricting network access

Oracle Linux has a firewall built into the distribution. This firewall is called **firewalld**, short for **firewall daemon**. firewalld is a dynamic firewall management tool used on Linux systems that provides a simple and consistent way to manage firewall rules across different distributions. It is designed to allow administrators to manage firewall rules in a flexible and efficient way.

## Getting ready

As with the other test, we will need an Oracle Linux system to play with. Nothing else is required. The system is enabled by default on most installations. To check the status of the daemon, you can use the `systemctl` command as follows:

```
systemctl status firewalld
```

The output is displayed in the following screenshot:

```
[root@ol8 ~]# systemctl status firewalld
 firewalld.service - firewalld - dynamic firewall daemon
   Loaded: loaded (/usr/lib/systemd/system/firewalld.service; enabled; vendor preset: enabled)
   Active: active (running)     since Tue 2023-04-04 22:23:14 EDT; 1min 10s ago
     Docs: man:firewalld(1)
 Main PID: 841 (firewalld)
    Tasks: 2 (limit: 4020)
   Memory: 748.0K
   CGroup: /system.slice/firewalld.service
           └─841 /usr/libexec/platform-python -s /usr/sbin/firewalld --nofork --nopid

Apr 04 22:23:13 ol8.m57.local systemd[1]: Starting firewalld - dynamic firewall daemon...
```

Figure 9.16 – firewalld status

## How to do it...

You can see the current configuration using the `firewall-cmd` with the `--list-all` option:

```
[root@ol8 ~]# firewall-cmd --list-all
```

This will show the following information:

```
[root@ol8 ~]# firewall-cmd --list-all
public (active)
  target: default
  icmp-block-inversion: no
  interfaces: enp0s3 enp0s8
  sources:
  services: cockpit dhcpv6-client ssh
  ports:
  protocols:
  forward: no
  masquerade: no
  forward-ports:
  source-ports:
  icmp-blocks:
  rich rules:
```

Figure 9.17 – firewall-cmd --list-all

The output of the preceding command displays a comprehensive summary of the active firewall rules and configurations managed by firewalld on a Linux system. The output is organized into several sections:

- `public` (active): This line displays the name of the active firewall zone, which in this example is the public zone. When `Target:default` is present, this indicates that this is the default zone and that it is currently active.

- `interfaces: enp0s3 enp0s8`: This line shows the network interface(s) that is assigned to the active firewall zone. In this example, both the `enp0s3` and `enp0s8` interfaces are assigned to the public zone.

- `sources`: This line displays the IP addresses or network ranges that are allowed to access the firewall zone. If no sources are defined, this line will be blank.

- `services: cockpit dhcpv6-client ssh`: This line lists the services that are allowed to access the firewall zone. In this example, incoming traffic for the cockpit, `dhcpv6-client`, and `ssh` services are allowed.

- `ports`: This line shows the TCP and UDP ports that are allowed to access the firewall zone. If no ports are defined, this line will be blank.

- `protocols`: This line shows protocols, such as TCP/UDP/ICMP, that are managed at a protocol level.

- `forward`: This shows whether zone forwarding is enabled.

- `masquerade: no`: This line indicates whether masquerading is enabled or disabled for the firewall zone. Masquerading allows packets from one network to appear as if they are coming from another network.

- `forward-ports`: This line shows any forwarded ports that are defined for the firewall zone. Forwarded ports allow incoming traffic on a specific port to be redirected to a different port or IP address.

- `source-ports`: This line shows any source ports that are defined for the firewall zone. Source ports allow incoming traffic from a specific port to be redirected to a different port or IP address.

- `icmp-blocks`: This line displays any **Internet Control Message Protocol** (**ICMP**) packets that are blocked by the firewall. ICMP packets are used for network diagnostics and troubleshooting.

- `rich rules`: This line shows any rich rules that are defined for the firewall zone. Rich rules allow more complex rules to be defined using a syntax that is similar to the `iptables` syntax.

Adding new rules is easy to do. A rule can be added using the service name (found in the `/etc/services` file) or the port number. The most common task is to add a common user service, such as `http` or `mysql`. This is done by adding the `--add-service` option to the command. When the service is added, the configuration will not survive a reboot unless the `--permanent` option is added. Some common examples are as follows:

```
firewall-cmd --permanent --add-service=http
firewall-cmd --permanent --add-service=imap
firewall-cmd --permanent --add-service=pop
firewall-cmd --permanent --add-service=mysql
```

Optionally, you can specify the protocol and port to allow the service. The following are examples of adding TCP or UDP ports:

```
firewall-cmd --permanent --add-port=1521/TCP
firewall-cmd --permanent --add-port=6900/UDP
```

You can also remove a port or service by using the --remove-port or --remove-service options:

```
firewall-cmd --permanent --remove-service=pop
firewall-cmd --permanent --remove-port=6900/UDP
```

When you are done making changes, you will need to reload the firewall rules. This is done with the --reload option:

```
firewall-cmd --reload
```

## How it works...

firewalld is based on the netfilter framework, which is a set of hooks that allows network packets to be filtered by the kernel. This framework is used to implement the iptables firewall on many Linux systems. firewalld provides a higher-level abstraction of the netfilter framework, allowing administrators to define rules in terms of services, ports, and protocols rather than directly manipulating iptables rules. One of the key advantages of firewalld is its ability to define firewall rules that match on multiple attributes. For example, administrators can define a rule that matches on both the source and destination IP address, as well as the protocol and port number. This allows more granular control over network traffic and makes it easier to define complex firewall policies.

firewalld also allows administrators to define firewall rules in terms of network zones. A zone is a set of network interfaces that are assigned a specific level of trust. For example, an administrator might define a public zone for network interfaces that are exposed to the internet and a trusted zone for network interfaces that are only accessible from trusted internal networks. Each zone can have its own set of firewall rules, allowing administrators to apply different policies to different network interfaces.

## Keeping SELinux active

**SELinux**, or **Security-Enhanced Linux**, is a security module that provides **mandatory access control (MAC)** policies in the Linux kernel. It is needed because it offers a higher level of security for Linux systems by enforcing strict rules on what processes and users can do on the system. By default, Linux uses **discretionary access control (DAC)**, which means that any user or process can access any file or resource, as long as they have the appropriate permissions. This can lead to security vulnerabilities, as any compromised process or user can potentially access and modify sensitive data or system files.

SELinux adds an extra layer of security by enforcing mandatory access control policies that restrict access to files and resources based on the security context of the process or user. This means that even if a process or user has the appropriate permissions, they will only be able to access resources that are explicitly allowed by the SELinux policy.

This recipe will cover how to create a custom SELinux policy instead of disabling it and how to allow services to do things such as bind to low ports (<1024).

## Getting ready

As with the other test, we will need an Oracle Linux system to play with. Nothing else is required. The system is enabled by default on most installations. To see the status of SELinux, you can use the command getenforce. The command will return the current active state. There are three states:

- enforcing – SELinux is active and blocking activity that is not allowed
- permissive – SELinux is enabled, but will not block any activity
- disabled – SELinux is disabled

Addition commands are available if you install the setools using dnf:

```
dnf install -y setools-console
```

You can also use the command sestatus to get more information about SELinux:

```
[root@ol8 ~]# sestatus
SELinux status:                 enabled
SELinuxfs mount:                /sys/fs/selinux
SELinux root directory:         /etc/selinux
Loaded policy name:             targeted
Current mode:                   enforcing
Mode from config file:          enforcing
Policy MLS status:              enabled
Policy deny_unknown status:     allowed
Memory protection checking:     actual (secure)
Max kernel policy version:      31
```

You can also use the SELinux type to manage resources. SELinux types are labels used to classify various resources in a Linux system, such as processes, files, directories, and network ports. SELinux types are an important part of SELinux security policies, as they determine which processes and users can access specific resources on the system.

There are several types of SELinux types, including the following:

- **User types**: User types are used to define the security context of a user. They are also used to confine the actions of a user to a specific set of resources on the system.

- **Role types**: Role types are used to define the security context of a role. They are also used to confine the actions of a user to a specific set of resources on the system.

- **Domain types**: Domain types are used to define the security context of a process. Each process on the system is assigned a unique domain type, which determines which resources the process can access.

- **Type enforcement types**: Type enforcement types are used to define the security context of a file or directory and confine the actions of a process to a specific set of resources on the system.

- **Network port types**: Network port types are used to define the security context of a network port. Network port types are used to restrict network access to specific ports or services on the system.

In addition to these types, there are also several special types used by SELinux, such as the `unconfined_t` type, which is used for processes that are not confined by SELinux, and the `system_u` and `root_t` types, which are used for system resources and processes.

## How to do it...

The state of SELinux can be changed on the fly using the command `setenforce` with the parameters 1 or 0. Using 1 puts SELinux into `enforcing` mode, while 0 puts it into `permissive` mode.

Additionally, you can edit the configuration file, `/etc/selinux/config`, and set the field SELinux to any one of the three states. This is also the only way to disable SELinux.

While disabling SELinux is tempting for many admins, it can easily be updated to allow the required behavior.

SELinux also logs to the `/var/log/audit/audit.log` file by default.

## How it works...

SELinux has several layers of security managing files, ports, and kernel modules. They are all managed by the `semanage` command.

### semanage

`semanage` is a command-line tool used that's to manage SELinux policies in Linux systems. It is used to create, modify, or delete SELinux policies, as well as manage file contexts and network ports. Here are some common uses of the `semanage` command:

- `semanage` can be used to create, modify, or delete policy modules. For example, you can create a new policy module with the following command:

```
semanage module -a kernelmodule.pp
```

This will add the policy module `kernelmodule.pp` to the SELinux policy.

- `semanage` can be used to manage file contexts, including adding or modifying contexts for specific files or directories. For example, you can add a new file context with the following command:

```
semanage fcontext -a -t httpd_sys_content_t '/var/www/
html(/.*)?'
```

This will add a new file context that allows the HTTPd process to access files and directories under `/var/www/html`.

- `semanage` can be used to manage network ports and services, including adding or modifying port types and policies. For example, you can define a new port type with the following command:

```
semanage port -a -t www2 -p tcp 8080
```

This will add a new port type www2 for TCP port `8080`.

- `setsebool`: SELinux has Boolean variables that can be either enabled or disabled to control specific security policies. To change the value of these variables, you can use the `setsebool` command to enable or disable certain SELinux policies. A useful example is when you set `httpd_can_network_connect` to true for a web server:

```
setsebool -P httpd_can_netowork_connect on
```

- `getsebool`: To view the status of SELinux policies, you can use the `getsebool` command. This command displays Boolean variables that can enable or disable certain policies. To view all values, use the `-a` option. Alternatively, you can pass a specific value to check, as shown in this example:

```
getsebool httpd_can_network_connect
httpd_can_network_connect --> off
```

### SELinux fixfiles

SELinux `fixfiles` is a command-line tool that's used to restore the SELinux file contexts of files and directories. SELinux uses file contexts to determine which processes and users can access specific files or directories on the system. When file contexts are changed or corrupted, it can cause issues with system functionality or security. The `fixfiles` command is used to restore the SELinux file contexts to their default values. This can be useful when you encounter issues with file access or SELinux-related errors. Here are some common ways to use the `fixfiles` command:

- **Restore default file contexts for a directory**: To restore the default file contexts for a specific directory, you can use the following command:

```
fixfiles restore /directory_to_fix
```

This will recursively restore the default file contexts for all files and directories within the specified directory.

- **Restore default file contexts for the entire system**: To restore the default file contexts for the entire system, run the following command:

```
fixfiles restore
```

This will restore the default file contexts for all files and directories on the system. Note that this can take some time to complete and may cause temporary disruptions to system functionality.

- **Verify file contexts**: You can use the following command to verify the file contexts for a specific file or directory:

```
matchpathcon /file_to_verify
```

This will display the expected file context for the specified file or directory. If the displayed context does not match the actual context, you can use the `fixfiles` command to restore the default context.

> **Note**
>
> If SELinux was disabled for any amount of time, these contexts would not have been set while it was not running. There is a shortcut to get SELinux to re-label the entire filesystem hierarchy:
> `# touch /.autorelabel`
>
> Now reboot the machine. As SELinux starts, it will set all file and security contexts to the default for each type and location.

## SELinux users

SELinux users are labels used to classify different types of users in a Linux system. SELinux users are an important part of SELinux security policies, as they are used to confine the actions of a user to a specific set of resources on the system.

There are several types of SELinux users:

- **System users**: System users are users that are defined by the system and are used to run system services or daemons. These users are typically assigned a unique SELinux user label, which is used to confine the actions of the user to a specific set of resources on the system.

- **Login users**: Login users are users that are defined by the system and are used to log into the system. These users are typically assigned a unique SELinux user label, which is used to confine the actions of the user to a specific set of resources on the system.

- **Staff users**: Staff users are users that are defined by the system and are used by staff members to perform their work. These users are typically assigned a unique SELinux user label, which is used to confine the actions of the user to a specific set of resources on the system.

- **User-defined users**: User-defined users are users that are defined by the system administrator. These users are typically assigned a unique SELinux user label, which is used to confine the actions of the user to a specific set of resources on the system.

Here are some of the commonly used SELinux user commands:

- `semanage user`: This command is used to manage SELinux users and their properties. For example, to create a new SELinux user, you can use the command `semanage user -a -R "s0-s0:c0.c1023" -r s0 -L s0:c0.c1023 -P user -n username`.

- `semanage login`: This command is used to manage SELinux login mappings, which map system users to SELinux users. For example, to create a new login mapping, you can use the command `semanage login -a -s user_u -r s0 username`.

- `semanage staff`: This command is used to manage SELinux staff mappings, which map staff users to SELinux users. For example, to create a new staff mapping, you can use the command `semanage staff -a -s user_u -r s0 username`.

- `semanage sudo`: This command is used to manage SELinux sudo mappings, which map sudoers to SELinux users. For example, to create a new sudo mapping, you can use the command `semanage sudo -a -r s0 -R "s0-s0:c0.c1023" -L s0:c0.c1023 -U username`.

- `semanage port`: This command is used to manage SELinux port mappings, which map ports to SELinux types. For example, to create a new port mapping, you can use the command `semanage port -a -t http_port_t -p tcp 80`.

# 10
# Revisiting Modules and AppStreams

In this chapter, we're going to learn more about **modules** and **application streams** (**AppStreams**). We went over the new organization of repositories and the concept of modularity in *Chapter 5, Software Management with DNF*, but now we're going to be tapping into the true power of AppStreams with the following recipes:

- Searching and listing AppStream modules

- Installing applications and development tools via AppStream

- Using AppStreams to install different versions of software

- Removing packages via AppStream

## Technical requirements

The concept of AppStreams is new and was introduced in Oracle Linux 8. With that being said, as long as you are running Oracle Linux 8, you will have all that's needed to follow along in this chapter.

## Searching and listing AppStream modules

First things first, let's review the list of commands that pertain to modules:

- `disable`: Disable a module with all its streams

- `enable`: Enable a module stream

- `info`: Print detailed information about a module

- `install`: Install a module profile, including its packages

- `list`: List all module streams, profiles, and states

- `provides`: List modular packages

- `remove`: Remove installed module profiles and their packages

- `repoquery`: List packages belonging to a module

- `reset`: Reset a module

- `switch-to`: Switch a module to a stream and *distrosync* RPM packages

- `update`: Update packages associated with an active stream

## How to do it...

AppStreams are easy to use. To get started, it's generally best to check for a list of available modules. This can be done by entering one simple command, `dnf module list`, into the Terminal/console:

```
[vagrant@localhost ~]$ dnf module list
Last metadata expiration check: 0:10:24 ago on Mon 05 Dec 2022 05:18:04 AM UTC.
Oracle Linux 8 Application Stream (x86_64)
Name                      Stream                Profiles
389-ds                    1.4
ant                       1.10 [d]              common [d]
container-tools           ol8 [d]               common [d]
container-tools           1.0                   common [d]
container-tools           2.0                   common [d]
container-tools           3.0                   common [d]
container-tools           4.0                   common [d]
eclipse                   ol8                   java [d]
freeradius                3.0 [d]               server [d]
gimp                      2.8 [d]               common [d], devel
go-toolset                ol8 [d]               common [d]
httpd                     2.4 [d]               common [d], devel, minimal
idm                       DL1                   adtrust, client, common [d], dns, server
idm                       client [d]            common [d]
inkscape                  0.92.3 [d]            common [d]
javapackages-runtime      201801 [d]            common [d]
jmc                       ol8 [d]               common [d], core
libselinux-python         2.8                   common
llvm-toolset              ol8 [d]               common [d]
log4j                     2 [d]                 common [d]
mailman                   2.1 [d]               common [d]
mariadb                   10.3 [d]              client, galera, server [d]
mariadb                   10.5                  client, galera, server [d]
```

Figure 10.1 – Output of dnf module list

The output continues with a rather long list of modules, and at the end, you will see a keymap of what the different letters mean:

```
ruby                  2.5 [d]           common [d]           An interpreter of object-oriented scripting language
ruby                  2.6               common [d]           An interpreter of object-oriented scripting language
ruby                  2.7               common [d]           An interpreter of object-oriented scripting language
ruby                  3.0               common [d]           An interpreter of object-oriented scripting language
ruby                  3.1               common [d]           An interpreter of object-oriented scripting language
rust-toolset          ol8 [d]           common [d]           Rust
satellite-5-client    1.0 [d]           common [d], gui      ULN client packages
scala                 2.10 [d]          common [d]           A hybrid functional/object-oriented language for the JVM
squid                 4 [d]             common [d]           Squid - Optimising Web Delivery
subversion            1.10 [d]          common [d], server   Apache Subversion
subversion            1.14              common [d], server   Apache Subversion
swig                  3.0 [d]           common [d], complete Connects C/C++/Objective C to some high-level programming languages
swig                  4.0               common [d], complete Connects C/C++/Objective C to some high-level programming languages
varnish               6 [d]             common [d]           Varnish HTTP cache
virt                  ol [d]            common [d]           Virtualization module

Hint: [d]efault, [e]nabled, [x]disabled, [i]nstalled
[vagrant@localhost ~]$
```

Figure 10.2 – Module keymap via hints

Here are several modules that immediately caught my eye: `container-tools`, `gimp`, `go-tools`, `inkscape`, `mariadb`, `mysql`, `nginx`, `nodejs`, `python`, and `php`. These are modules, but you will notice that each module has a stream, and each stream contains a profile. If we were to visualize this in a chart, it might look a bit like this:

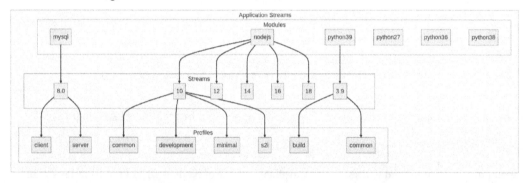

Figure 10.3 – Visualizing AppStreams

Now, let's say we want to get more information on a particular module. In this case, let's take a look at `nodejs`. First, we're going to want to specify `nodejs` when we ask for the list. We can do this by adding the name of the module after the `list` command, like so:

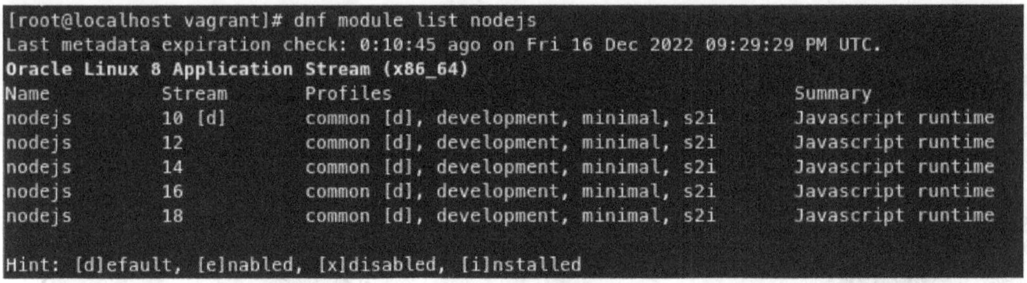

```
[root@localhost vagrant]# dnf module list nodejs
Last metadata expiration check: 0:10:45 ago on Fri 16 Dec 2022 09:29:29 PM UTC.
Oracle Linux 8 Application Stream (x86_64)
Name            Stream          Profiles                                    Summary
nodejs          10 [d]          common [d], development, minimal, s2i       Javascript runtime
nodejs          12              common [d], development, minimal, s2i       Javascript runtime
nodejs          14              common [d], development, minimal, s2i       Javascript runtime
nodejs          16              common [d], development, minimal, s2i       Javascript runtime
nodejs          18              common [d], development, minimal, s2i       Javascript runtime

Hint: [d]efault, [e]nabled, [x]disabled, [i]nstalled
```

Figure 10.4 – Output of dnf module list nodejs

At the bottom of the list, you will see the following:

```
Hint: [d]efault, [e]nabled, [x]disabled, [i]nstalled
```

From this, we can see that stream 10 is labeled as default (d) for nodejs. What does this mean, exactly? Basically, if we were to run dnf module install nodejs, we would end up with the latest version of Node.js in stream 10 (and yes, stream 10 correlates to Node.js 10).

> **Note**
>
> At the time of writing, the latest version of Node.js in the 10 series stream is nodejs-1:10.24.0-1.module+el8.3.0+9671+154373c8.x86_64.

We can dig deeper and learn more about this specific AppStream by typing the following:

```
# dnf module info nodejs:10
```

The output of that command will show every available release of Node.js within the 10 series stream. There are several but, for the sake of brevity, I have pasted the last two from the list:

```
Name              : nodejs
Stream            : 10 [d][a]
Version           : 8030020210118191659
Context           : 229f0a1c
Architecture      : x86_64
Profiles          : common [d], development, minimal, s2i
Default profiles  : common
Repo              : ol8_appstream
Summary           : Javascript runtime
Description       : Node.js is a platform built on Chrome's JavaScript runtime for easily
hat makes it lightweight and efficient, perfect for data-intensive real-time application
Requires          : platform:[el8]
Artifacts         : nodejs-1:10.23.1-1.module+el8.3.0+9642+87902f83.x86_64
                  : nodejs-devel-1:10.23.1-1.module+el8.3.0+9642+87902f83.x86_64
                  : nodejs-docs-1:10.23.1-1.module+el8.3.0+9642+87902f83.noarch
                  : nodejs-full-i18n-1:10.23.1-1.module+el8.3.0+9642+87902f83.x86_64
                  : nodejs-nodemon-0:1.18.3-1.module+el8.1.0+5392+4d6b561f.noarch
                  : nodejs-packaging-0:17-3.module+el8.1.0+5392+4d6b561f.noarch
                  : npm-1:6.14.10-1.10.23.1.1.module+el8.3.0+9642+87902f83.x86_64

Name              : nodejs
Stream            : 10 [d][a]
Version           : 8030020210225164533
Context           : 229f0a1c
Architecture      : x86_64
Profiles          : common [d], development, minimal, s2i
Default profiles  : common
Repo              : ol8_appstream
Summary           : Javascript runtime
Description       : Node.js is a platform built on Chrome's JavaScript runtime for easily
hat makes it lightweight and efficient, perfect for data-intensive real-time application
Requires          : platform:[el8]
Artifacts         : nodejs-1:10.24.0-1.module+el8.3.0+9671+154373c8.x86_64
                  : nodejs-devel-1:10.24.0-1.module+el8.3.0+9671+154373c8.x86_64
                  : nodejs-docs-1:10.24.0-1.module+el8.3.0+9671+154373c8.noarch
                  : nodejs-full-i18n-1:10.24.0-1.module+el8.3.0+9671+154373c8.x86_64
                  : nodejs-nodemon-0:1.18.3-1.module+el8.1.0+5392+4d6b561f.noarch
                  : nodejs-packaging-0:17-3.module+el8.1.0+5392+4d6b561f.noarch
                  : npm-1:6.14.11-1.10.24.0.1.module+el8.3.0+9671+154373c8.x86_64

Hint: [d]efault, [e]nabled, [x]disabled, [i]nstalled, [a]ctive
```

Figure 10.5 – Output of dnf module info nodejs:10

The interesting thing here is that every stream within the 10 series is labeled `[d]` `[a]` (default and active); that's because the `Stream` entry is referring to the stream itself, and not any specific release within the stream.

# Installing applications and development tools via AppStream

From the previous recipe, we're familiar with how to search for and list applications in AppStreams; let's now dive into installing applications and development tools via AppStream.

## How to do it...

Building from the last recipe, in which we examined `nodejs`, let's go ahead and install it. There's more than one way to do this. You can enable the module and then use the standard `dnf install [package(s)]` command to install the packages:

```
# dnf module enable nodejs
# dnf install nodejs npm
```

You can also use the standard `dnf` commands without specifying modules and the default module will get enabled as part of the transaction:

```
# dnf install nodejs npm
```

Or, the preferred way is to tap directly into the new set of `dnf module` commands and simply run `dnf module install [module name(s)]`:

```
# dnf module install nodejs
```

The output is shown in the following screenshot:

```
[root@localhost vagrant]# dnf module install nodejs:10:8030020210118191659
Last metadata expiration check: 0:49:43 ago on Fri 16 Dec 2022 07:04:33 PM UTC.
Dependencies resolved.
================================================================================
 Package Arch    Version                                  Repository      Size
================================================================================
Installing group/module packages:
 nodejs  x86_64  1:10.23.1-1.module+el8.3.0+9642+87902f83  ol8_appstream  8.9 M
 npm     x86_64  1:6.14.10-1.10.23.1.1.module+el8.3.0+9642+87902f83  ol8_appstream  3.7 M
Installing module profiles:
 nodejs/common

Enabling module streams:
 nodejs           10

Transaction Summary
================================================================================
Install  2 Packages

Total download size: 13 M
Installed size: 45 M
Is this ok [y/N]: 
```

Figure 10.6 – Output of dnf module install nodejs

What you get is the latest in the default AppStream (if nothing is enabled), but if for some reason you wanted an older version in the stream, you can select that by appending a colon and the version to the end of the command. For example, if I didn't want the latest and, instead, wanted the version before it, I would type the following:

```
# dnf module install nodejs:10:8030020210118191659
```

The output is shown in the following screenshot:

```
[root@localhost vagrant]# dnf module install nodejs:10:8030020210118191659
Last metadata expiration check: 0:49:43 ago on Fri 16 Dec 2022 07:04:33 PM UTC.
Dependencies resolved.
================================================================================
 Package Arch    Version                                    Repository    Size
================================================================================
Installing group/module packages:
 nodejs x86_64  1:10.23.1-1.module+el8.3.0+9642+87902f83    ol8_appstream 8.9 M
 npm    x86_64  1:6.14.10-1.10.23.1.1.module+el8.3.0+9642+87902f83 ol8_appstream 3.7 M
Installing module profiles:
 nodejs/common

Enabling module streams:
 nodejs          10

Transaction Summary
================================================================================
Install  2 Packages

Total download size: 13 M
Installed size: 45 M
Is this ok [y/N]: █
```

Figure 10.7 – Output of dnf module install nodejs:10:8030020210118191659

This would instruct DNF to install the releases of Node.js (and related artifacts) that correlate to the version specified.

Another thing to notice is that, by default, only the common profile will be installed. We can specify a different profile (for example, the development profile), by appending a forward slash and a profile name:

```
# dnf module install nodejs:10/development
```

The output is shown in the following screenshot:

```
[root@localhost vagrant]# dnf module install nodejs:10/development
Last metadata expiration check: 0:51:12 ago on Fri 16 Dec 2022 07:04:33 PM UTC.
Dependencies resolved.
================================================================================
 Package           Arch    Version                         Repository      Size
================================================================================
Installing group/module packages:
 nodejs            x86_64  1:10.24.0-1.module+el8.3.0+9671+154373c8  ol8_appstream   8.8 M
 nodejs-devel      x86_64  1:10.24.0-1.module+el8.3.0+9671+154373c8  ol8_appstream   164 k
 npm               x86_64  1:6.14.11-1.10.24.0.1.module+el8.3.0+9671+154373c8
                                                            ol8_appstream   3.7 M
Installing dependencies:
Installing dependencies:
 annobin           x86_64  10.67-3.0.1.el8                 ol8_appstream   955 k
 dwz               x86_64  0.12-10.el8                     ol8_appstream   109 k
 efi-srpm-macros   noarch  3-3.0.1.el8                     ol8_appstream    22 k
 ghc-srpm-macros   noarch  1.4.2-7.el8                     ol8_appstream   9.3 k
 go-srpm-macros    noarch  2-17.el8                        ol8_appstream    13 k
 keyutils-libs-devel x86_64 1.5.10-9.el8                   ol8_baseos_latest  48 k
 krb5-devel        x86_64  1.18.2-14.0.1.el8               ol8_baseos_latest 560 k
 libcom_err-devel  x86_64  1.45.6-4.el8                    ol8_baseos_latest  38 k
 libkadm5          x86_64  1.18.2-14.0.1.el8               ol8_baseos_latest 187 k
 libselinux-devel  x86_64  2.9-5.el8                       ol8_baseos_latest 200 k
 libsepol-devel    x86_64  2.9-3.el8                       ol8_baseos_latest  87 k
 libverto-devel    x86_64  0.3.0-5.el8                     ol8_baseos_latest  18 k
 nodejs-packaging  noarch  17-3.module+el8.1.0+5392+4d6b561f  ol8_appstream    20 k
 ocaml-srpm-macros noarch  5-4.el8                         ol8_appstream   9.3 k
 openblas-srpm-macros noarch 2-2.el8                       ol8_appstream   7.9 k
 openssl-devel     x86_64  1:1.1.1k-6.el8_5                ol8_baseos_latest 2.3 M
 pcre2-devel       x86_64  10.32-2.el8                     ol8_baseos_latest 605 k
 pcre2-utf16       x86_64  10.32-2.el8                     ol8_baseos_latest 229 k
 pcre2-utf32       x86_64  10.32-2.el8                     ol8_baseos_latest 220 k
 perl-srpm-macros  noarch  1-25.el8                        ol8_appstream    11 k
 python-rpm-macros noarch  3-43.el8                        ol8_appstream    16 k
 python-srpm-macros noarch 3-43.el8                        ol8_appstream    15 k
 python3-rpm-macros noarch 3-43.el8                        ol8_appstream    15 k
 qt5-srpm-macros   noarch  5.15.3-1.el8                    ol8_appstream    11 k
 redhat-rpm-config noarch  129-1.0.1.el8                   ol8_appstream    89 k
 rust-srpm-macros  noarch  5-2.el8                         ol8_appstream   9.2 k
 unzip             x86_64  6.0-46.0.1.el8                  ol8_baseos_latest 196 k
 zip               x86_64  3.0-23.el8                      ol8_baseos_latest 270 k
Installing module profiles:
 nodejs/development
Enabling module streams:
 nodejs                      10

Transaction Summary
================================================================================
Install  31 Packages

Total download size: 19 M
Installed size: 56 M
Is this ok [y/N]:
```

Figure 10.8 – Output of dnf module install nodejs:10/development

You can even specify more than one profile, like so:

```
# dnf module install nodejs:10/development nodejs:10/s2i
```

The output is shown in the following screenshot:

```
[root@localhost vagrant]# dnf module install nodejs:10/development nodejs:10/s2i
Last metadata expiration check: 0:52:40 ago on Fri 16 Dec 2022 07:04:33 PM UTC.
Dependencies resolved.
================================================================================
 Package              Arch    Version                          Repository   Size
================================================================================
Installing group/module packages:
 nodejs               x86_64  1:10.24.0-1.module+el8.3.0+9671+154373c8  ol8_appstream  8.8 M
 nodejs-devel         x86_64  1:10.24.0-1.module+el8.3.0+9671+154373c8  ol8_appstream  164 k
 nodejs-nodemon       noarch  1.18.3-1.module+el8+5141+5528e502         ol8_appstream  964 k
 npm                  x86_64  1:6.14.11-1.10.24.0.1.module+el8.3.0+9671+154373c8
                                                               ol8_appstream  3.7 M
Installing dependencies:
 annobin              x86_64  10.67-3.0.1.el8                  ol8_appstream  955 k
 dwz                  x86_64  0.12-10.el8                      ol8_appstream  109 k
 efi-srpm-macros      noarch  3-3.0.1.el8                      ol8_appstream   22 k
 ghc-srpm-macros      noarch  1.4.2-7.el8                      ol8_appstream  9.3 k
 go-srpm-macros       noarch  2-17.el8                         ol8_appstream   13 k
 keyutils-libs-devel  x86_64  1.5.10-9.el8                     ol8_baseos_latest   48 k
 krb5-devel           x86_64  1.18.2-14.0.1.el8                ol8_baseos_latest  560 k
 libcom_err-devel     x86_64  1.45.6-4.el8                     ol8_baseos_latest   38 k
 libkadm5             x86_64  1.18.2-14.0.1.el8                ol8_baseos_latest  187 k
 libselinux-devel     x86_64  2.9-5.el8                        ol8_baseos_latest  200 k
 libsepol-devel       x86_64  2.9-3.el8                        ol8_baseos_latest   87 k
 libverto-devel       x86_64  0.3.0-5.el8                      ol8_baseos_latest   18 k
 nodejs-packaging     noarch  17-3.module+el8.1.0+5392+4d6b561f ol8_appstream   20 k
 ocaml-srpm-macros    noarch  5-4.el8                          ol8_appstream  9.3 k
 openblas-srpm-macros noarch  2-2.el8                          ol8_appstream  7.9 k
 openssl-devel        x86_64  1:1.1.1k-6.el8_5                 ol8_baseos_latest  2.3 M
 pcre2-devel          x86_64  10.32-2.el8                      ol8_baseos_latest  605 k
 pcre2-utf16          x86_64  10.32-2.el8                      ol8_baseos_latest  229 k
 pcre2-utf32          x86_64  10.32-2.el8                      ol8_baseos_latest  220 k
 perl-srpm-macros     noarch  1-25.el8                         ol8_appstream   11 k
 python-rpm-macros    noarch  3-43.el8                         ol8_appstream   16 k
 python-srpm-macros   noarch  3-43.el8                         ol8_appstream   15 k
 python3-rpm-macros   noarch  3-43.el8                         ol8_appstream   15 k
 qt5-srpm-macros      noarch  5.15.3-1.el8                     ol8_appstream   11 k
 redhat-rpm-config    noarch  129-1.0.1.el8                    ol8_appstream   89 k
 rust-srpm-macros     noarch  5-2.el8                          ol8_appstream  9.2 k
 unzip                x86_64  6.0-46.0.1.el8                   ol8_baseos_latest  196 k
 zip                  x86_64  3.0-23.el8                       ol8_baseos_latest  270 k
Installing module profiles:
 nodejs/development
 nodejs/s2i
Enabling module streams:
 nodejs                       10

Transaction Summary
================================================================================
Install  32 Packages

Total download size: 20 M
Installed size: 60 M
Is this ok [y/N]:
```

Figure 10.9 – Output of dnf module install nodejs:10/development nodejs:10/s2i

Or, if you wish to install all the profiles, simply use an asterisk to indicate a wildcard selection:

```
# dnf module install nodejs:10/*
```

The output is shown in the following screenshot:

```
[root@localhost vagrant]# dnf module install nodejs:10/*
Last metadata expiration check: 0:53:59 ago on Fri 16 Dec 2022 07:04:33 PM UTC.
Dependencies resolved.
================================================================================
 Package              Arch    Version                          Repository   Size
================================================================================
Installing group/module packages:
 nodejs               x86_64  1:10.24.0-1.module+el8.3.0+9671+154373c8  ol8_appstream  8.8 M
 nodejs-devel         x86_64  1:10.24.0-1.module+el8.3.0+9671+154373c8  ol8_appstream  164 k
 nodejs-nodemon       noarch  1.18.3-1.module+el8+5141+5528e502  ol8_appstream  964 k
 npm                  x86_64  1:6.14.11-1.10.24.0.1.module+el8.3.0+9671+154373c8
                                                               ol8_appstream  3.7 M
Installing dependencies:
 annobin              x86_64  10.67-3.0.1.el8                  ol8_appstream  955 k
 dwz                  x86_64  0.12-10.el8                      ol8_appstream  109 k
 efi-srpm-macros      noarch  3-3.0.1.el8                      ol8_appstream   22 k
 ghc-srpm-macros      noarch  1.4.2-7.el8                      ol8_appstream  9.3 k
 go-srpm-macros       noarch  2-17.el8                         ol8_appstream   13 k
 keyutils-libs-devel  x86_64  1.5.10-9.el8                     ol8_baseos_latest  48 k
 krb5-devel           x86_64  1.18.2-14.0.1.el8                ol8_baseos_latest 560 k
 libcom_err-devel     x86_64  1.45.6-4.el8                     ol8_baseos_latest  38 k
 libkadm5             x86_64  1.18.2-14.0.1.el8                ol8_baseos_latest 187 k
 libselinux-devel     x86_64  2.9-5.el8                        ol8_baseos_latest 200 k
 libsepol-devel       x86_64  2.9-3.el8                        ol8_baseos_latest  87 k
 libverto-devel       x86_64  0.3.0-5.el8                      ol8_baseos_latest  18 k
 nodejs-packaging     noarch  17-3.module+el8.1.0+5392+4d6b561f  ol8_appstream   20 k
 ocaml-srpm-macros    noarch  5-4.el8                          ol8_appstream  9.3 k
 openblas-srpm-macros noarch  2-2.el8                          ol8_appstream  7.9 k
 openssl-devel        x86_64  1:1.1.1k-6.el8_5                 ol8_baseos_latest 2.3 M
 pcre2-devel          x86_64  10.32-2.el8                      ol8_baseos_latest 605 k
 pcre2-utf16          x86_64  10.32-2.el8                      ol8_baseos_latest 229 k
 pcre2-utf32          x86_64  10.32-2.el8                      ol8_baseos_latest 220 k
 perl-srpm-macros     noarch  1-25.el8                         ol8_appstream   11 k
 python-rpm-macros    noarch  3-43.el8                         ol8_appstream   16 k
 python-srpm-macros   noarch  3-43.el8                         ol8_appstream   15 k
 python3-rpm-macros   noarch  3-43.el8                         ol8_appstream   15 k
 qt5-srpm-macros      noarch  5.15.3-1.el8                     ol8_appstream   11 k
 redhat-rpm-config    noarch  129-1.0.1.el8                    ol8_appstream   89 k
 rust-srpm-macros     noarch  5-2.el8                          ol8_appstream  9.2 k
 unzip                x86_64  6.0-46.0.1.el8                   ol8_baseos_latest 196 k
 zip                  x86_64  3.0-23.el8                       ol8_baseos_latest 270 k
Installing module profiles:
 nodejs/common
 nodejs/development
 nodejs/minimal
 nodejs/s2i
Enabling module streams:
 nodejs                        10

Transaction Summary
================================================================================
Install  32 Packages

Total download size: 20 M
Installed size: 60 M
Is this ok [y/N]:
```

Figure 10.10 – Output of dnf module install nodejs:10/*

# Using AppStreams to install different versions of software

Now, we're going to expand on what we know about AppStreams, and instead of installing an application from the default module stream, we're going to specify a different stream.

## How to do it...

There are multiple ways to do this: simply specifying the installation of a different stream will get the job done, or you can first manually enable a different version. My preference is to specify the version as I install it because, in that case, the AppStream will automatically enable that version:

```
# dnf module install nodejs:16
```

> **Note**
>
> If you already installed some version of an AppStream, it is best to remove the old one before resetting and installing a different version. This will be covered later.

The output is shown in the following screenshot:

```
[root@localhost vagrant]# dnf module install nodejs:16
Last metadata expiration check: 0:00:32 ago on Fri 16 Dec 2022 09:05:16 PM UTC.
Dependencies resolved.
================================================================================
 Package    Arch     Version                                 Repository     Size
================================================================================
Installing group/module packages:
 nodejs     x86_64   1:16.18.1-3.module+el8.7.0+20893+df13f383   ol8_appstream   12 M
 npm        x86_64   1:8.19.2-1.16.18.1.3.module+el8.7.0+20893+df13f383   ol8_appstream   2.0 M
Installing module profiles:
 nodejs/common

Enabling module streams:
 nodejs              16

Transaction Summary
================================================================================
Install  2 Packages

Total download size: 14 M
Installed size: 49 M
Is this ok [y/N]: y
Downloading Packages:
(1/2): npm-8.19.2-1.16.18.1.3.module+el8.7.0+20893+df13f383.x8 7.4 MB/s | 2.0 MB   00:00
(2/2): nodejs-16.18.1-3.module+el8.7.0+20893+df13f383.x86_64.r 20 MB/s |  12 MB    00:00
--------------------------------------------------------------------------------
Total                                          23 MB/s |  14 MB    00:00
Running transaction check
Transaction check succeeded.
Running transaction test
Transaction test succeeded.
Running transaction
  Running scriptlet: npm-1:8.19.2-1.16.18.1.3.module+el8.7.0+20893+df13f383.x86_64    1/1
  Preparing        :                                                                 1/1
  Installing       : npm-1:8.19.2-1.16.18.1.3.module+el8.7.0+20893+df13f383.x86_64    1/2
  Installing       : nodejs-1:16.18.1-3.module+el8.7.0+20893+df13f383.x86_64          2/2
  Running scriptlet: nodejs-1:16.18.1-3.module+el8.7.0+20893+df13f383.x86_64          2/2
  Verifying        : nodejs-1:16.18.1-3.module+el8.7.0+20893+df13f383.x86_64          1/2
  Verifying        : npm-1:8.19.2-1.16.18.1.3.module+el8.7.0+20893+df13f383.x86_64    2/2

Installed:
  nodejs-1:16.18.1-3.module+el8.7.0+20893+df13f383.x86_64
  npm-1:8.19.2-1.16.18.1.3.module+el8.7.0+20893+df13f383.x86_64

Complete!
```

Figure 10.11 – Output of dnf module install nodejs:16

You'll see from the printout that the module stream for nodejs 16 will be enabled. Now, if we list out the module stream for nodejs, we'll see the following:

```
[root@localhost vagrant]# dnf module list nodejs
Last metadata expiration check: 0:03:03 ago on Fri 16 Dec 2022 09:05:16 PM UTC.
Oracle Linux 8 Application Stream (x86_64)
Name        Stream      Profiles                                    Summary
nodejs      10 [d]      common [d], development, minimal, s2i       Javascript runtime
nodejs      12          common [d], development, minimal, s2i       Javascript runtime
nodejs      14          common [d], development, minimal, s2i       Javascript runtime
nodejs      16 [e]      common [d] [i], development, minimal, s2i   Javascript runtime
nodejs      18          common [d], development, minimal, s2i       Javascript runtime

Hint: [d]efault, [e]nabled, [x]disabled, [i]nstalled
```

Figure 10.12 – Output of dnf module list nodejs

As you can see, 10 is still the default, but 16 is enabled (e). AppStreams maintains a default stream to allow normal usage of dnf to function without requiring the user to know anything about AppStreams. Additionally, if we were to reset the module, it would revert back to the original settings – that is, it would make 10 the only default and enabled version, and version 16 would no longer be enabled. Furthermore, it's important to note that only one stream can be enabled at a time. To recap, a default stream is inherently enabled when no other stream is enabled. If you enable a different stream, it is the only one that can be installed from, but it's easy to reset and switch to another. To do so, simply do the following:

```
# dnf module remove nodejs
# dnf module reset nodejs
```

You will see confirmation about the module being reset:

```
Disabling module profiles:
  nodejs/common
Resetting modules:
  nodejs
```

At this point, we are cleared to install a different version. Let's go with Node.js 14 this time around:

```
# dnf module install nodejs:14
```

You will see a confirmation about what the package manager plans to do:

```
[root@localhost vagrant]# dnf module install nodejs:14
Last metadata expiration check: 0:04:57 ago on Fri 16 Dec 2022 09:05:16 PM UTC.
Dependencies resolved.
================================================================================
 Package   Arch     Version                                    Repository    Size
================================================================================
Downgrading:
 nodejs    x86_64   1:14.20.1-2.module+el8.6.0+20874+338992dc   ol8_appstream  11 M
 npm       x86_64   1:6.14.17-1.14.20.1.2.module+el8.6.0+20874+338992dc  ol8_appstream  3.7 M
Installing module profiles:
 nodejs/common

Enabling module streams:
 nodejs              14

Transaction Summary
================================================================================
Downgrade  2 Packages

Total download size: 15 M
Is this ok [y/N]: y
Downloading Packages:
(1/2): npm-6.14.17-1.14.20.1.2.module+el8.6.0+20874+338992dc.x 7.8 MB/s | 3.7 MB    00:00
(2/2): nodejs-14.20.1-2.module+el8.6.0+20874+338992dc.x86_64.r  18 MB/s | 11 MB    00:00
--------------------------------------------------------------------------------
Total                                          23 MB/s | 15 MB    00:00
Running transaction check
Transaction check succeeded.
Running transaction test
Transaction test succeeded.
Running transaction
  Running scriptlet: npm-1:6.14.17-1.14.20.1.2.module+el8.6.0+20874+338992dc.x86_64         1/1
  Preparing        :                                                                        1/1
  Downgrading      : npm-1:6.14.17-1.14.20.1.2.module+el8.6.0+20874+338992dc.x86_64         1/4
  Downgrading      : nodejs-1:14.20.1-2.module+el8.6.0+20874+338992dc.x86_64                2/4
  Cleanup          : nodejs-1:16.18.1-3.module+el8.7.0+20893+df13f383.x86_64                3/4
  Cleanup          : npm-1:8.19.2-1.16.18.1.3.module+el8.7.0+20893+df13f383.x86_64          4/4
  Running scriptlet: npm-1:8.19.2-1.16.18.1.3.module+el8.7.0+20893+df13f383.x86_64          4/4
  Verifying        : nodejs-1:14.20.1-2.module+el8.6.0+20874+338992dc.x86_64                1/4
  Verifying        : nodejs-1:16.18.1-3.module+el8.7.0+20893+df13f383.x86_64                2/4
  Verifying        : npm-1:6.14.17-1.14.20.1.2.module+el8.6.0+20874+338992dc.x86_64         3/4
  Verifying        : npm-1:8.19.2-1.16.18.1.3.module+el8.7.0+20893+df13f383.x86_64          4/4

Downgraded:
  nodejs-1:14.20.1-2.module+el8.6.0+20874+338992dc.x86_64
  npm-1:6.14.17-1.14.20.1.2.module+el8.6.0+20874+338992dc.x86_64

Complete!
```

Figure 10.13 – Output of dnf module install nodejs:14

You may notice that you are downgrading. Just as you might suspect, if no module is installed, it will say Installing; if installing a number that is greater than the currently installed version, it will say Upgrading; and if installing a number that is less than the currently installed version, it will say Downgrading. Regardless of what the package manager says it is doing, you will be left with the version you requested – it's as simple as that.

You should be aware there is another way to switch to a different stream. Rather than using remove, reset, and then install, you can achieve this with one step by using switch-to:

```
[root@localhost vagrant]# dnf module switch-to nodejs:16
Last metadata expiration check: 0:07:00 ago on Fri 16 Dec 2022 09:05:16 PM UTC.
Dependencies resolved.
================================================================================
 Package   Arch       Version                                Repository     Size
================================================================================
Upgrading:
 nodejs    x86_64     1:16.18.1-3.module+el8.7.0+20893+df13f383    ol8_appstream   12 M
 npm       x86_64     1:8.19.2-1.16.18.1.3.module+el8.7.0+20893+df13f383   ol8_appstream   2.0 M
Switching module streams:
 nodejs               14 -> 16

Transaction Summary
================================================================================
Upgrade  2 Packages

Total download size: 14 M
Is this ok [y/N]:
```

Figure 10.14 – Output of dnf module switch-to nodejs:16

This is the recommended method of changing stream versions because it accomplishes the change in just one step, and it provides a very clear printout of the action taking place. Its status is Upgrading, and it is going from 14 -> 16.

> **Note**
>
> There is actually another way to switch modules on the fly. If you set module_stream_switch to True in /etc/dnf/dnf.conf, then you can install a different module without using the switch-to syntax.
>
> Here is an example:
>
> echo "module_stream_switch=True" >> /etc/dnf/dnf.conf

### What about Python?

If you review the list of modules, you may notice that Python consists of multiple modules rather than a single module with multiple AppStreams:

```
# dnf module list python*
```

The output can be seen in the following screenshot:

```
[root@localhost vagrant]# dnf module list python*
Last metadata expiration check: 0:09:33 ago on Sun 23 Jul 2023 02:11:14 AM UTC.
Oracle Linux 8 Application Stream (x86_64)
Name       Stream       Profiles              Summary
python27   2.7 [d]      common [d]            Python programming language, version 2.7
python36   3.6 [d]      build, common [d]     Python programming language, version 3.6
python38   3.8 [d]      build, common [d]     Python programming language, version 3.8
python39   3.9 [d]      build, common [d]     Python programming language, version 3.9

Hint: [d]efault, [e]nabled, [x]disabled, [i]nstalled
```

Figure 10.15 – Output of dnf module list python*

This seems weird at first, but consider that Python is an integral part of the Oracle Linux operating system and that each Oracle Linux release comes with a platform Python version. The specific platform Python version may differ for each Oracle Linux release, and the respective platform Python version will be supported for the full lifespan of that version of Oracle Linux. For Oracle Linux 7, the platform Python version is 2.7 and is always installed, and for Oracle Linux 8, the platform Python version is 3.6. In other words, Python 2.7 is supported for the full lifespan of Oracle Linux 7, and Python 3.6 is supported for the full lifespan of Oracle Linux 8. On Oracle Linux 8, the platform Python is exclusively intended for use by system utilities such as Yum and DNF. Python for general purpose is not installed by default on Oracle Linux 8, and so this is where AppStream modules come into play.

You can install multiple versions of Python on Oracle Linux 8 by specifying the module correlating to the desired version of Python. All of the Python modules can be installed and used simultaneously on the same machine, and you can specify which installation you wish to use by typing out the version – for example, `python3.6 --version`, `python3.8 --version`, and so on.

By default, the `python3` command is always aliased to Python 3.6 if it is installed on the system, and that is because Python 3.6 is the platform Python version on Oracle Linux 8.

# Removing packages via AppStream

Removing packages via AppStream is straightforward. In general, all you need to do is instruct the package manager to remove instead of install. If the package manager finds a module that matches, it will proceed to remove the related packages.

## How to do it...

Building off the examples in the previous recipe, let's remove the Node.js module by running the `dnf module remove nodejs` command:

```
[root@localhost vagrant]# dnf module remove nodejs
Last metadata expiration check: 0:09:52 ago on Fri 16 Dec 2022 09:05:16 PM UTC.
Dependencies resolved.
================================================================================
 Package Arch     Version                                      Repository     Size
================================================================================
Removing:
 nodejs  x86_64   1:14.20.1-2.module+el8.6.0+20874+338992dc     @ol8_appstream  37 M
 npm     x86_64   1:6.14.17-1.14.20.1.2.module+el8.6.0+20874+338992dc  @ol8_appstream  15 M
Disabling module profiles:
 nodejs/common

Transaction Summary
================================================================================
Remove  2 Packages

Freed space: 52 M
Is this ok [y/N]:
```

Figure 10.16 – Output of dnf module remove nodejs

From this message, you can see that NPM will be uninstalled, but that isn't quite what you would expect considering that the Node.js module installed more than just NPM. If you want to remove everything related to the module, you'll need to pass in the `--all` flag, like so:

```
# dnf module remove nodejs --all
```

This time, you will see that all associated packages are queued for removal:

```
[root@localhost vagrant]# dnf module remove nodejs --all
Last metadata expiration check: 0:07:49 ago on Fri 16 Dec 2022 09:29:29 PM UTC.
Dependencies resolved.
==================================================================================
 Package              Arch    Version                              Repository          Size
==================================================================================
Removing:
 nodejs               x86_64  1:14.20.1-2.module+el8.6.0+20874+338992dc @ol8_appstream   37 M
 nodejs-devel         x86_64  1:14.20.1-2.module+el8.6.0+20874+338992dc @ol8_appstream  967 k
 nodejs-packaging     noarch  23-3.module+el8.3.0+7818+6cd30d85    @ol8_appstream      41 k
 npm                  x86_64  1:6.14.17-1.14.20.1.2.module+el8.6.0+20874+338992dc
                                                                   @ol8_appstream      15 M
Removing unused dependencies:
 annobin              x86_64  10.67-3.0.1.el8                      @ol8_appstream     968 k
 brotli-devel         x86_64  1.0.6-3.el8                          @ol8_appstream      53 k
 dwz                  x86_64  0.12-10.el8                          @ol8_appstream     225 k
 efi-srpm-macros      noarch  3-3.0.1.el8                          @ol8_appstream      38 k
 ghc-srpm-macros      noarch  1.4.2-7.el8                          @ol8_appstream     414
 go-srpm-macros       noarch  2-17.el8                             @ol8_appstream     7.2 k
 keyutils-libs-devel  x86_64  1.5.10-9.el8                         @ol8_baseos_latest  33 k
 krb5-devel           x86_64  1.18.2-14.0.1.el8                    @ol8_baseos_latest 1.1 M
 libcom_err-devel     x86_64  1.45.6-4.el8                         @ol8_baseos_latest  17 k
 libkadm5             x86_64  1.18.2-14.0.1.el8                    @ol8_baseos_latest 219 k
 libselinux-devel     x86_64  2.9-5.el8                            @ol8_baseos_latest 188 k
 libsepol-devel       x86_64  2.9-3.el8                            @ol8_baseos_latest 127 k
 libverto-devel       x86_64  0.3.0-5.el8                          @ol8_baseos_latest  26 k
 ocaml-srpm-macros    noarch  5-4.el8                              @ol8_appstream     737
 openblas-srpm-macros
                      noarch  2-2.el8                              @ol8_appstream     104
 openssl-devel        x86_64  1:1.1.1k-6.el8_5                     @ol8_baseos_latest 3.4 M
 pcre2-devel          x86_64  10.32-2.el8                          @ol8_baseos_latest 1.8 M
 pcre2-utf16          x86_64  10.32-2.el8                          @ol8_baseos_latest 586 k
 pcre2-utf32          x86_64  10.32-2.el8                          @ol8_baseos_latest 570 k
 perl-srpm-macros     noarch  1-25.el8                             @ol8_appstream     794
 python-rpm-macros    noarch  3-43.el8                             @ol8_appstream     4.2 k
 python-srpm-macros   noarch  3-43.el8                             @ol8_appstream     5.1 k
 python3-rpm-macros   noarch  3-43.el8                             @ol8_appstream     3.6 k
 qt5-srpm-macros      noarch  5.15.3-1.el8                         @ol8_appstream       0
 redhat-rpm-config    noarch  129-1.0.1.el8                        @ol8_appstream     149 k
 rust-srpm-macros     noarch  5-2.el8                              @ol8_appstream     1.1 k
 unzip                x86_64  6.0-46.0.1.el8                       @ol8_baseos_latest 414 k
 zip                  x86_64  3.0-23.el8                           @ol8_baseos_latest 822 k
Disabling module profiles:
 nodejs/common
 nodejs/development

Transaction Summary
==================================================================================
Remove  32 Packages

Freed space: 63 M
Is this ok [y/N]: 
```

Figure 10.17 – Output of dnf module remove nodejs --all

Now that's more like it. Type y and press *Enter*, and the module will be removed.

## There's more...

So, now that we've gone over the usage of AppStreams, you might be asking yourself, "*Didn't we already have a similar capability with Software Collections?*" The answer is yes, but there is a big difference between Software Collections and AppStreams.

Where Software Collections provides Parallel Availability and Parallel Installability, AppStreams provides only Parallel Availability.

According to the Fedora docs, "*Parallel Availability means that more than one major release of a popular software project is available for installation.*" And "*Parallel Installability means that more than one major release of a software project can be installed on the same userspace.*"

Now you might be asking, "*Wait, so you're telling me that AppStreams is not as good as what we had before?*" Well, not exactly. It turns out that Parallel Installability isn't all it's cracked up to be. Although it seems nice on the surface to have the ability to install multiple versions of software on the same system, in reality, it is plagued with complications of requiring users to know they need to do something extra in order to actually make use of the installed software and/or alternate version. For example, if you wanted to install multiple versions of Node.js, you would first need to enable the desired Software Collection for Node.js, and then you would also need to know where to look for and activate the specific version you want to use. In other words, you cannot simply use the alternate version of the software in the normal way because the packages would get installed in non-standard locations.

AppStreams solves this because it does not allow for Parallel Installability; instead, it provides the capability of Parallel Availability. In other words, you install one and only one package at a time, and you use it like you normally would. If you want a different version, well, you simply enable a different stream.

As a bonus, AppStreams is particularly useful when creating containers that are single-use by design. Having AppStreams means each container image is configured with the right version of the module, which is then globally available within the container. If you need multiple versions, just run multiple containers.

AppStreams makes it much easier to install different versions of software, and the best thing is, even if you know nothing about AppStreams, you can still use DNF the old-fashioned way and get your basic applications installed.

# Lions, Tigers, and Containers – Oh My! Podman and Friends

These days, it's all about containers. Docker made containers cool and brought them into the mainstream, and Podman is here to come to the rescue as an open source container runtime that is open and available to all. Oracle Linux 7 includes Oracle Container Runtime for Docker, whereas Oracle Linux 8 and beyond include Podman, Buildah, and Skopeo.

With every new release, Podman closes the gap between it and Docker. With Podman v2.0, it began offering a fully compliant build that enables technologies such as `docker-compose` to work interchangeably with Podman. With Podman v4.1.0, you are now able to seamlessly mount the host machine's home directory into the Podman machine VM, making it available within container volume mounts. This chapter is largely intended for users who have some basic experience with Docker, and will help users understand the differences between Docker and Podman so that they can successfully migrate their workloads to this so-called "drop-in replacement." If you're not familiar with Docker or are new to the concept of containers, it may be helpful to peruse the Get Started guide from Docker, which can be found here: `https://docs.docker.com/get-started/`.

In this chapter, we're going to cover the following recipes:

- Ridding yourself of demons – err um – daemons, with Podman
- Giving your containers a root canal
- Creating handy-dandy utility containers
- Docker Compose with Podman
- Managing stacks with pods
- Containerized databases
- Buildah and Skopeo – Podman's friends with benefits

# Technical requirements

Podman, Buildah, and Skopeo are all included in the `container-tools` module from application streams:

```
$ sudo dnf module install container-tools
```

The source code for the recipes in this chapter can be found at `https://github.com/PacktPublishing/Oracle-Linux-Cookbook`.

# Ridding yourself of demons – err um – daemons, with Podman

Docker and Podman are both tools that aim to make it easier to run and manage containers on a host machine. Since Podman is the new kid on the block, you may be wondering how you can switch from Docker to Podman. While technically it is possible to run both Docker and Podman together on the same system, there are very few practical reasons to do this. Since both tools provide the same core capabilities, I would advise you to choose one or the other.

One of the key benefits of switching to Podman is you will inherently lose the daemon that lurked behind the scenes of Docker. You see, Docker relies on a daemon that does all the heavy lifting of managing containers. This may not seem so bad on the surface, but there are some things to be aware of when it comes to this architecture.

For starters, having an extra daemon running in the background means there is one more point of failure. If that dedicated daemon for Docker crashes, you lose all your containers. The additional daemon also increases your attack surface, and because the Docker daemon has root access to the system, any compromise made to the Docker daemon puts your system at greater risk.

This recipe aims to exorcise those demons – err, um – discontinue the use of the Docker daemon. The best thing is, if you aren't using Docker and you only ever installed Podman, you don't need to worry about anything – that's because Podman is rootless by default, and it leverages **systemd** to manage your containers. **systemd** is a tried-and-tested system-level daemon that provides an array of system components, including a system and service manager, parallelization capabilities, logging, and utilities to manage and maintain system configuration.

On the other hand, if you were previously using Docker, we're going to show you how to switch. It's really quite simple – all you need to do is remove Docker and install Podman.

## Getting ready

I'm running on x86-64 bit architecture, but Oracle Linux and Podman also work on Arm. However, it's important to know that not all containers are compiled in Arm, or vice versa. With that being said, it may be easier to follow this guide using an x86-64 bit CPU:

- Oracle Linux

- Podman

## How to do it...

1.  Remove Docker by running the following command:

    ```
    $ sudo dnf remove -y docker-ce docker-ce-cli containerd.io
    docker-compose-plugin
    ```

2.  After this, you will be able to install Podman with the following:

    ```
    $ sudo dnf module install container-tools
    ```

3.  If you previously added your user to the `docker` group, you may go ahead and delete that group because it is no longer needed:

    ```
    $ sudo groupdel docker
    ```

Now you're running containers without the Docker daemon, and by default with Podman, you're rootless.

# Giving your containers a root canal

Straight from the Docker documentation, you will find that "*The Docker daemon binds to a Unix socket instead of a TCP port. By default that Unix socket is owned by the user root and other users can only access it using sudo. The Docker daemon always runs as the root user.*"

The documentation then proceeds to instruct you to add your user to the `docker` group in order to use Docker without using `sudo`. That sounds great, right? Well, the thing is, the `docker` group grants privileges equivalent to the `root` user. This can have dire consequences. For instance, any location on your host filesystem can be mounted into the container – and I do mean any! This even includes the / (root) directory and the container can then alter your host filesystem without any restrictions. There are several other security vulnerabilities that are a direct result of this architecture, but you get the picture.

What's different about Podman is that by default, it runs rootless; in other words, you can run containers using Podman without root privileges. When I first heard this, I thought it meant the user in the container was not root, but that's not really the case. Rootless containers simply mean that the user instantiating the containers does not have root privileges. There are a few things to know about running a container without root privileges, and this recipe aims to instruct you how to run rootless containers, while at the same time explaining the differences between rootless and rootful.

## Getting ready

- Oracle Linux
- Podman

## How to do it...

To run rootless containers with Podman, all you need to do is use Podman as a user without root privileges. Also, do not append sudo to any Podman commands, because if you do, you would then be running the container as the root user.

What's different about rootless containers?

### Network modes

There are three common network modes supported by Podman:

- Bridged
- macvlan
- slirp4netns

First, there's a **bridged** network, which is the default used by rootful Podman. Bridged networking creates a network interface on the host and dedicates this interface to the container. Another network mode is **macvlan**, which is a virtual LAN that basically forwards an entire network interface from the host into the container. Finally, there is **slirp4netns**, which enables you to connect a network namespace to the internet in a completely unprivileged way. Rootless Podman leverages **slirp4netns** because unprivileged users lack the ability to create network interfaces on the host. In order to bypass this limitation, **slirp4netns** instead creates a tunnel from the host and into the container in order to forward traffic.

### Network ports

When you run your containers without root access, you may run into issues exposing certain network ports. For example, it is common for users to expose ports 80 and/or 443 when running containers; however, if you try to do this while running a rootless container, you will see a message like the following:

```
Error response from daemon: rootlessport cannot expose privileged
port 80, you can add 'net.ipv4.ip_unprivileged_port_start=80' to /
etc/sysctl.conf (currently 1024), or choose a larger port number (>=
1024): listen tcp 0.0.0.0:80: bind: permission denied
```

Rootless Podman is limited to exposing ports 1024 and above. If you wanted to expose a lower port, you would need to first configure this as root in order to allow unprivileged users to expose lower port numbers.

Let's say you wanted to allow rootless Podman to expose the standard HTTP web port (port 80). In this case, you can run this command:

```
sudo sysctl net.ipv4.ip_unprivileged_port_start=80
```

If you want these settings to persist, simply follow the guidance of the error message received earlier. That is, edit the /etc/sysctl.conf file and append net.ipv4.ip_unprivileged_port_start=80.

# Creating handy-dandy utility containers

This recipe shows how to use Podman to quickly spin up a container to complete useful tasks.

This recipe will walk you through the process of creating super useful utilities leveraging containers. The basic principle of containers encourages us to formulate our containers to do only one thing – that is, to provide some form of utility and nothing more. You should not create a container that does too much. With that being said, most container images already exist to provide a useful utility. In this recipe, we are going to look at examples of containers that serve a useful purpose, and we're going to explore how to make use of this.

## Getting ready

We will require the following:

- Oracle Linux
- Podman

## How to do it...

The main intention of this recipe is to show how we can use containers to achieve a function without installing additional packages on our local machine. Once you have Podman installed on your local machine, you can tap into an entire ecosystem of useful packages and utilities without installing more packages – instead, you simply run a container image that contains those packages, or, alternatively, you create a new container and install the desired packages there.

Why would anyone prefer to do this? For starters, it allows you to minimize the number of packages and dependencies you're installing on your host machine. With fewer packages, you reduce your attack surface in terms of security. Additionally, your operating system's repositories might be limited to access to certain packages, or it might not have access to the latest versions. Instead of going through the effort of adding potentially untrusted repositories to install the packages you need, why not simply launch a container that contains everything you need for the specific function you're trying to achieve?

Before we try to tap into the true potential of containers, we first need to discuss a few important concepts that will make this process a bit easier.

## Entrypoint

The entrypoint of a container defines what command the container will run by default. You can find the entrypoint of a container by specifying the `inspect` command and piping that to `jq` to extract only the entrypoint.

First, pull the image if you don't already have it on your system:

```
$ podman pull docker.io/pandoc/core
```

Now let's inspect the image and run `jq` to query for the entrypoint:

```
$ podman image inspect pandoc/core | jq -r '.[].Config.Entrypoint[0]'
```

**Bonus**: Let's assume we do not have `jq` installed on our computer. In this case, we can pipe the output of `inspect` to a container that contains `jq`:

```
$ podman image inspect pandoc/core | podman run -i --rm stedolan/jq -r
'.[].Config.Entrypoint[]'
```

In either case, the output of this command will be `/usr/local/bin/pandoc`.

This tells us that when we run the `pandoc/core` container, the default command that gets executed will be `/usr/local/bin/pandoc`.

Sometimes, a container's entrypoint might be a script. For example, you might check for the entrypoint and learn that the entrypoint is `docker-entrypoint.sh`. You can reveal more about this file by overriding the entrypoint and using `cat` to see the contents of the file. For example, let's say we were to inspect the `node` container image:

```
$ podman image inspect node | jq -r '.[].Config.Entrypoint[]'
```

We would find that the entrypoint is `docker-entrypoint.sh`.

Now, let's override the entrypoint to examine the contents of this file:

```
$ podman run --rm --entrypoint=/bin/bash node -c 'cat docker-
entrypoint.sh'
```

In this case, the output is the following:

```
cat: docker-entrypoint.sh: No such file or directory
```

This is because in the case of the `node` image, the `docker-entrypoint.sh` file is not in the working directory; instead, it is found in the path. So, we'll try another way to examine this file:

```
$ podman run --rm --entrypoint=/bin/bash node -c 'cat $(which docker-
entrypoint.sh)'
```

The output will be as follows:

```
#!/bin/sh
set -e

if [ "${1#-}" != "${1}" ] || [ -z "$(command -v "${1}")" ]; then
  set -- node "$@"
fi

exec "$@"
```

Figure 11.1 – Output of docker-entrypoint.sh

Now that we know about the default entrypoint, we can use this as we determine what we're going to do with the container. Sometimes we might want to use the default entry point as intended, whereas other times we might benefit from overriding the default entrypoint to use some other available packages within the container – it all depends on what we're trying to do.

### Working directory

You'll often want to specify the working directory inside the container, because that's where the container is configured by default to perform its work. To get the working directory of a container, you can run the following:

```
$ podman image inspect pandoc/core | jq -r '.[].Config.WorkingDir'
```

Again, you get bonus points if you do this without installing `jq` by running this:

```
$ podman image inspect pandoc/core | podman run -i --rm stedolan/jq -r
'.[].Config.WorkingDir'
```

In either case, the output of this command will be `/data`.

This tells us that when we run the `pandoc/core` container, the default working directory inside the container is `/data`.

### Volume mounting

In order to make use of a container that performs a task against files on your local machine, you'll first need to mount a volume into the container. An easy way to do this is to specify your present working directory by specifying $ (pwd). Another method might be to specify ./. The order in which this is done is by declaring the host machine's directory first, and the container's directory second.

For example, if you wanted to mount the present working directory of the host machine into the working directory of the container, you would run `-v $(pwd):/data`. In this example, we are saying we want our present working directory on the host machine to be accessible inside the container at the `/data` path. Remember, we found the working directory of the container when we used the `podman inspect` command.

### Super useful utility containers

Now that we've discussed some of the important concepts, I am going to list examples of useful utilities I've found in containers and then will expand on the practicality of leveraging containers for these functions.

### Converting a Markdown file to docx using pandoc

In this example, let's imagine we have a document that we want to convert to another type. There are many tools we can leverage to do this, but one such tool that comes to mind is pandoc. Rather than installing pandoc on my local machine, I'll simply run the `pandoc/core` container, which has pandoc preinstalled. The entrypoint in the `pandoc` container is `/bash/pandoc`. This means that anything after the specification of the container image will automatically append to the `pandoc` command inside the container.

We can run `--help` after the `pandoc/core` command to learn how to use the utility, for example:

```
$ podman run --rm pandoc/core --help
```

From that (you can also view the man page maintained here: `https://linux.die.net/man/1/pandoc`), I now have some insight into how to use pandoc. In this case, I can use the `pandoc` command within the container by mounting my present working directory into the container and specifying my source document and what I want the output to be, for example:

```
$ podman run --rm -v $(pwd)/:/data pandoc/core -s input.md -o output.docx
```

Since the working directory inside the container is `/data`, and since I have that mounted to my host system, if the container creates a new file inside that directory, I will be able to find the output on my host system. Cool!

### Making a change to an image or video file using FFMPEG

In this example, we will leverage FFMPEG within a container in the same way we leveraged pandoc in the previous container. Using the FFMPEG container is especially handy because FFMPEG tends to rely on lots and lots of dependencies that I'd prefer not to install on my local machine. Additionally, it's nice that the official FFMPEG container comes packaged with the latest version, and it works great!

Just like in the previous example, we can run `--help` after the `ghcr.io/linuxserver/ffmpeg` command to learn how to use FFMPEG, for example:

```
$ podman run --rm ghcr.io/linuxserver/ffmpeg --help
```

From the output (you can also view the man page maintained here: `https://linux.die.net/man/1/ffmpeg`), I can see a plethora of options, but for the sake of brevity, I will simply show how you can use `ffmpeg` from a container to convert video within a container, for example:

```
$ podman run --rm -it -v $(pwd):/config \
ghcr.io/linuxserver/ffmpeg \
-ss 00:00:30 -t 5 -i /config/input.mkv \
-vcodec libx265 -crf 30 /config/output.mp4
```

This command will start at 00 hours, 00 minutes, and 30 seconds (specified by `-ss`) into the video, and will record 5 seconds (specified by `-t`). It will then convert the video, and the output can be found in `./config/output.mp4`.

## Using Node.js within a container

Let's say we need to build a Node.js application. To do this, we'll want to use Node and npm. In *Chapter 10*, we discussed the usefulness of application streams and how you can leverage application streams to install different versions of Node.js. Well, just like anything else in life, there is *more than one way to skin a cat*.

Rather than installing Node.js on your host system, why not leverage Node.js within a container instead? The `node` container includes Node and npm. By default, when you run the `node` container, you are executing the `node` command, as this is the default entrypoint (as you may recall from earlier when we discussed entrypoints).

Let's say we want to use the `npm` command instead – we can do this by overriding the entrypoint. At this point, we know we can override the entrypoint by leveraging bash and appending a command at the end, but we also need to know where to mount our host system:

```
$ podman image inspect node | podman run -i --rm stedolan/jq -r '.[].
Config.WorkingDir'
```

From this, we can see that the default working directory within the container is null. Does that mean we can't use the container the way we want? Of course not, because we can simply override the entrypoint and take matters into our own hands. In this scenario, I will mount the present working directory from my host system into an `/app` directory, and I'll override the entry point to bash so I can instruct the container to change directory to `/app` before I run the npm command to build my Node.js application. Here's how that can be done:

```
$ podman run --rm -v $(pwd):/app --entrypoint bash node -c 'cd /app &&
npm run build'
```

Once NPM completes the build, you'll find your application binaries inside a directory called `./build` on your host machine

But wait, just as I mentioned earlier, there is *more than one way to skin a cat*. A more elegant way to achieve the same thing might be to instead tell Podman where you want the working directory to be. If we do this, we don't even need to set bash as our entry point – instead, we can jump straight into npm. This can be done with the `-w` (or `--workdir`) command, like so:

```
$ podman run --rm -v $(pwd):/app --workdir /app --entrypoint npm node
run build
```

In my opinion, the second approach is cleaner, but the end result is the same.

### Running a lightweight NGINX web server to preview a web page locally

In this example, we might as well continue from the last exercise, where we built a Node.js application. Now that we have our Node .js application built/compiled, let's host it inside an NGINX container. We can do this by simply mounting the build directory into the `/user/share/nginx/html` directory inside the NGINX container.

How did I know to host it inside this specific directory? In this case, I had to read up on the NGINX documentation for the NGINX container. You can usually find this type of documentation on any container registry that hosts the container you're looking to run.

The command to host our build directory locally is the following:

```
$ podman run --rm --name ol8cookbook -p 80:80 -v ${pwd}/build:/usr/
share/nginx/html:ro -d nginx
```

With Podman, the default setting for rootless ports cannot expose privileged port 80. If you have not changed this setting, you will see a message such as this:

```
Error: rootlessport cannot expose privileged port 80, you can
add 'net.ipv4.ip_unprivileged_port_start=80' to /etc/sysctl.conf
(currently 1024), or choose a larger port number (>= 1024): listen tcp
0.0.0.0:80: bind: permission denied
```

You can override this setting if you have root privileges, with the following:

```
$ sudo sysctl net.ipv4.ip_unprivileged_port_start=80
```

Alternatively, you can simply choose to use a port number of 1024 or higher. Once you have the container running, you can preview the local website by navigating to `http://localhost` (if you're using port 80) or `http://localhost:8080` (or whatever port that you assigned if you did not go with port 80).

# Docker Compose with Podman

Podman is a powerful container engine that is typically accessed via a **command-line interface (CLI)** to facilitate the configuration and running of containers. It's very handy to use the CLI to quickly launch a new container instance or to directly access existing containers, but what if you need to run multiple containers all at once? You could still use the CLI, but then you'll probably get into the habit of copying and pasting long commands, which is not exactly the most ideal way of having a repeatable way of launching and deploying containers. Instead, why not use something such as Docker Compose? Docker Compose allows you to configure your container applications as code, in the popular **Yet Another Markup Language (YAML)** format. YAML is designed to be declarative and human-readable. With Docker Compose, you can define your multiple containers' attributes, including volumes, environment variables, networking information, and more, all in a single `docker-compose.yml` file.

While Docker Compose is a great utility for configuring your containers as code, it's important to know that Docker Compose was designed to be used with Docker. With that being said, there are a few things to be aware of when using Docker Compose with Podman.

## Getting ready

We will require the following:

- Oracle Linux
- Podman
- Docker Compose

## How to do it...

In this recipe, we're going to talk about how you can use Docker Compose with Podman.

Since Compose files typically involve multiple containers and applications communicating with one another, I recommend the use of the Netavark- and Aardvark-based network stack rather than the CNI-based stack. Netavark and Aardvark are new in Podman 4.0 and offer reduced overhead and significant performance enhancements. Additionally, I experienced issues with the default CNI-based stack, whereas switching to Netavark and Aardvark enabled my containers to communicate with each other as expected:

1.  To switch out your network stack, simply specify `netavark` as the network backend in the `/usr/share/containers/containers.conf` file. You can do this quickly by running the following `sed` command:

    ```
    sudo sed -i 's/network_backend = "cni"/network_backend =
    "netavark"/g' /usr/share/containers/containers.conf
    sudo podman info | grep networkBackend
    ```

> **Note**
>
> If you already running containers on your system, you will need to run `sudo podman system reset` in order to fully switch to the Netavark- and Aardvark-based network stack, but just be aware that this command will remove all your existing images, containers, pods, networks, and volumes.

2. Now that is out of the way, let's start by installing Docker Compose:

```
sudo curl -SL https://github.com/docker/compose/releases/
download/v2.20.3/docker-compose-linux-x86_64 -o /usr/local/bin/
docker-compose
sudo chmod +x /usr/local/bin/docker-compose
```

3. While we're at it, since Docker Compose expects to make calls to Docker (rather than Podman), it might be a good idea to install the `podman-docker` package to ensure Podman is called anytime a reference to Docker is being made:

```
sudo dnf install podman-docker
```

4. Next, we need to enable the Podman socket:

   - To use Docker Compose in a rootless manner, use this command:

```
systemctl --user enable --now podman.socket
export DOCKER_HOST=unix://$XDG_RUNTIME_DIR/podman/podman.sock
echo 'export DOCKER_HOST=unix://$XDG_RUNTIME_DIR/podman/podman.
sock' >> ~/.bash_profile
```

   - To use Docker Compose in a rootful manner, use this command:

```
sudo systemctl enable --now podman.socket
sudo export DOCKER_HOST=unix:///run/podman/podman.sock
sudo echo 'export DOCKER_HOST=unix:///run/podman/podman.sock' >>
/root/.bash_profile
```

5. Now that Docker Compose is ready to go, we'll need a Compose file to test things with. Let's first examine a Compose file:

```
services:
  portainer:
    image: portainer/portainer-ce
    container_name: portainer
    volumes:
      - $XDG_RUNTIME_DIR/podman/podman.sock:/var/run/docker.sock
      - portainer:/data
    ports:
      - "9000:9000"
    restart: unless-stopped

volumes:
  portainer:
    name: portainer
```

Figure 11.2 – Compose file for Portainer

In a `docker-compose.yml` file, we define how we want Docker (or Podman in this case) to run multi-container applications. In the case of this `docker-compose.yml` file, we define the services and the volumes we want Podman to create, and we configure various parameters of the service to our liking.

> **Info**
>
> For a comprehensive overview of the entire Compose specification, see `https://docs.docker.com/compose/compose-file/`.

6.  Now, let's test things and see if Docker Compose will work. Save the contents of the Compose file in a file named `docker-compose.yml`.

7.  Using the terminal, change directory to the same directory you saved the `docker-compose.yml` file in and run the following:

    ```
    docker-compose up -d
    ```

    If all goes well, you should see some activity in the terminal indicating that Podman is downloading the container image, creating the volume, and finally, it will start to run the container just as we defined in the Compose file.

8.  Once the container is running, navigate to the port we specified to see if it's working as expected. To do this, simply point your browser to `http://127.0.0.1:9000`.

Congratulations, you are now using Docker Compose with Podman.

# Managing stacks with pods

Keeping everything organized with stacks and prepping for Kubernetes.

Podman supports concepts that do not exist in Docker. One of the big ones is pods – so I guess that's where the name *Podman* derives from... *Podman = Pod Manager*. In this recipe, you will learn how to keep things organized by managing stacks with Podman. We'll achieve this functionality through the use of pods. Pods consist of one or more containers. Because pods are the smallest deployable units that you can create and manage in Kubernetes, familiarizing yourself with pods will help you bridge the gap between containers and Kubernetes.

## Getting ready

We will require the following:

- Oracle Linux
- Podman
- Docker Compose

## How to do it...

Before we jump into the recipe, we should first discuss a little more about pods. As mentioned previously, pods consist of one or more containers. Pods will always contain an `infra` container, which, by default is based on the `k8s.gcr.io/pause` image. The `infra` container basically does nothing but sleep – this ensures that the container continues to run even while idle, and it holds the port bindings, namespaces, and cgroups from the kernel. Once the pod is created, the attributes assigned to the `infra` container cannot be changed. It's important to remember that any ports that need to be exposed will need to be done during the initial creation of the pod.

Outside of the pod exists a **conmon** (**container monitor**) instance that watches the primary process of the container. Each container has its own instance of conmon.

The following diagram provides an architectural overview of what makes up a pod.

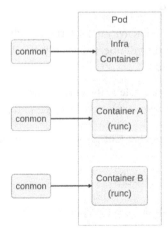

Figure 11.3 – Architectural overview of a pod

Here are the Podman commands that relate to pods:

```
Manage pods

Description:
  Pods are a group of one or more containers sharing the same network,
pid and ipc namespaces.

Usage:
  podman pod [command]

Available Commands:
  clone       Clone an existing pod
  create      Create a new empty pod
  exists      Check if a pod exists in local storage
  inspect     Displays a pod configuration
  kill        Send the specified signal or SIGKILL to containers in
pod
  logs        Fetch logs for pod with one or more containers
  pause       Pause one or more pods
  prune       Remove all stopped pods and their containers
  ps          List pods
  restart     Restart one or more pods
  rm          Remove one or more pods
  start       Start one or more pods
  stats       Display a live stream of resource usage statistics for
the containers in one or more pods
  stop        Stop one or more pods
  top         Display the running processes of containers in a pod
  unpause     Unpause one or more pods
```

As can be seen from the preceding commands, you can use the Podman CLI to create a pod and run your containers within the pod.

## Manual pod creation

Let's say we wanted to deploy Wiki.js inside a pod. Wiki.js is open source Wiki software built on Node.js and relies on a database backend. In other words, we want a pod that looks like this:

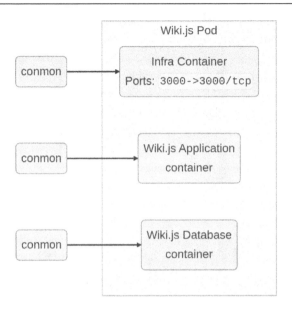

Figure 11.4 – Architecture of a Wiki.js pod

We can construct this pod manually by following these steps:

1.  The first step is to create a pod. As we do this, we need to ensure we configure the port mappings to allow ingress into port 3000. We will do this using the podman pod command:

    ```
    podman pod create -p 3000:3000 wikijs-pod
    ```

2.  Next, we need to create our database container inside the pod. We can do this through the use of the --pod tag:

    ```
    podman run -td --pod wikijs-pod --name wikijs-db --env POSTGRES_
    DB=postgres --env POSTGRES_PASSWORD=wikijsrocks --env POSTGRES_
    USER=postgres -v wikijs-db-data:/var/lib/postgresql/data
    postgres
    ```

3.  Now that the database is up and running, we'll need to create our application container inside the pod. Again, we'll use the --pod tag to ensure this container runs inside the same pod as the database:

    ```
    podman run -td --pod wikijs-pod --name wikijs --env DB_
    TYPE=postgres --env DB_HOST=wikijs-db --env DB_PORT=5432
    --env DB_USER=postgres --env DB_PASS=wikijsrocks --env DB_
    NAME=postgres ghcr.io/requarks/wiki
    ```

4.  Now that the application is running, point your browser to http://127.0.0.1:3000/.

## Automatic pod creation

Podman allows you to create pods manually using the command-line interface, but another cool feature of Podman is that it natively supports Kubernetes manifests. Since pods are the smallest deployable units that you can create and manage in Kubernetes, this means that deploying Kubernetes manifests in Podman will result in the creation of pods by default.

Writing a full Kubernetes manifest is outside the scope of this recipe, but I'm going to show you how you can generate a Kubernetes manifest automatically using Podman, and subsequently use that manifest to deploy your containers into pods. Since we just learned about using Compose files in the previous recipe, we're going to leverage them again here, and then we'll supercharge them by converting them into Kubernetes manifests:

1.  The first thing to do is to deploy your containers from a Compose file. For this recipe, we'll start with a Compose file for Wiki.js.

```
services:

  wikijs-db:
    image: postgres
    container_name: wikijs-db
    environment:
      POSTGRES_DB: postgres
      POSTGRES_PASSWORD: wikijsrocks
      POSTGRES_USER: postgres
    restart: unless-stopped
    volumes:
      - wikijs-db-data:/var/lib/postgresql/data
    healthcheck:
      test: pg_isready
      start_period: 5s
      interval: 5s
      timeout: 5s
      retries: 55

  wikijs:
    image: ghcr.io/requarks/wiki:2
    container_name: wikijs
    depends_on:
      wikijs-db:
        condition: service_healthy
    environment:
      DB_TYPE: postgres
      DB_HOST: wikijs-db
      DB_PORT: 5432
      DB_USER: postgres
      DB_PASS: wikijsrocks
      DB_NAME: postgres
    restart: unless-stopped
    ports:
      - "3000:3000"

volumes:
  wikijs-db-data:
```

Figure 11.5 – Compose file for Wiki.js

Wiki.js requires two containers, one for the application itself, and the other is a PostgreSQL database.

2.  Now that we have our Compose file, let's use Docker Compose to deploy the containers:

    ```
    docker-compose up -d
    ```

    Wait as the container images are pulled in, and for the status of `wikijs` to change to `Started`.

3.  Once the containers are running, verify that everything works by pointing your browser to `http://127.0.0.1:3000`.

4.  If you see the Wiki.js setup screen, you're good to go. At this point, we're going to generate a Kubernetes manifest (called `wikijs.yaml`) from the two containers we just launched:

    ```
    Podman generate kube -s -f wikijs.yaml wikijs wikijs-db
    ```

5.  Now that the Kubernetes manifest is generated, let's bring down the containers we just launched:

    ```
    Docker-compose down
    podman volume prune
    ```

6.  The next step is to use `podman play kube` to bring up the containers in a pod using the Kubernetes manifest, but before we do that, we need to fix one of the hostnames specified in the environment variables.

    The reason we need to do that is the name of the pod is appended to the name of every container running within the pod. So instead of our database container being called `wikijs-db`, it will be called `wikijs-pod-wikijs-db`. If you look at the manifest, you'll see that `wikijs` is configured to hook up to a database container called `wikijs-db`, so we need to update the value of `DB_HOST` and change it to `wikijs-pod-wikijs-db`.

    You can do this reliably using the `yq` command. If you don't have `yq` installed on your computer, no worries, just use a `yq` container:

    ```
    Podman run –rm -v ${PWD}:/workdir docker.io/mikefarah/yq e -i
    '(select(.kind == "Pod").spec.containers[] | select(.name ==
    "wikijs" ).env[] | select(.name == "DB_HOST")).value = "wikijs-
    pod-wikijs-db"' wikijs.yaml
    ```

    > **Note**
    >
    > Refer to the *Creating handy-dandy utility containers* recipe for more information on how to use a container as a utility.

7.  Once you've corrected the `DB_HOST` value, run the following command:

    ```
    podman play kube wikijs.yaml
    ```

8. Verify that the pod is running:

```
podman pod ls
podman ps -ap
```

Finally, go ahead and navigate to `http://127.0.0.1:3000`.

# Containerized databases

This recipe discusses best practices regarding the use of containerized databases.

## Getting ready

We will require the following:

- Oracle Linux
- Podman

## How to do it...

Containers make databases a much easier pill to swallow for your everyday application deployments. There's not a lot to discuss in this recipe, but there are a few best practices with containerized databases that will definitely be useful to know about.

### Do one thing and one thing only

Just as a core principle of containers is to do one thing and one thing only, the same principle applies to containerized databases. What do I mean by that? Well, for starters, you might be inclined to launch a containerized database and subsequently create multiple schemas within that database and/or multiple databases within that single container. Let's say you have several applications that require a MySQL database, then it probably seems like a good idea to have a single MySQL database container with separate database schemas for each containerized application… something that looks a bit like this:

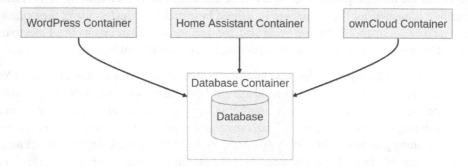

Figure 11.6 – What not to do with containerized databases

The problem with this architecture is that it does not adhere well to the principle of doing one thing and one thing only. Instead, I recommend spinning up a separate container for each database an application needs. Name that container so that it is complementary to the application it's paired with – something like this:

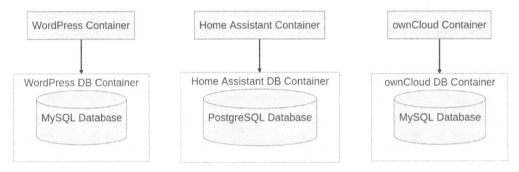

Figure 11.7 – A better way to use containerized databases

For example, let's say you have a WordPress container that requires a database. In this scenario, if you named your WordPress container wordpress01, then you should name your MySQL container wordpress01-db. Having a separate container for every database you want to run will make it easier to troubleshoot issues and will additionally serve as a more reliable architectural model for your deployed applications. If you need to take one containerized database down, you're then only affecting one application, rather than all of them if you chose to run multiple databases within one container.

## Data storage

Persistent data is something you'll need to address when running databases in containers. With Podman, you have two primary options: volumes and bind mounts. With volumes, Podman will manage the storage of your database by writing the data to disk using its own internal volume management system. With bind mounts, you will need to specify a location on the host system and mount that into the container. Either option is fine, and typically volumes are easier because it requires less configuration by the user, but the downside is that the data can be more difficult to locate on the host system. Additionally, it is possible for the volumes to be deleted by mistake via careless use of the podman volume prune command. With that being said, for demonstrations or quick tests, I like to use volumes, but for persistent data that is truly important, I prefer to use bind mounts.

Creating volumes is simple. There are a few ways in which Podman allows for the creation of volumes. You can create a volume manually from the command line via the podman volume create [NAME] command. You can also let Podman do the heavy lifting for you, as it is capable of creating volumes automatically during container creation. Podman can create a named volume if you specify the name; for example, running podman run -v my_data:/var/lib/mysql mysql:8-oracle will create a volume called my_data. Podman can also create an anonymous volume if you leave out the -v my_data:/data specification and instead run podman run -it oraclelinux:8.

If you want to use a bind mount instead, all you need to do is specify the location of where that mount should reside on the host system. For example, if you want to store your data in `/mnt/hdd/podman/volumes/`, you would simply need to specify this location as the source location. I prefer to set my volume location as an environment variable called `VOLUME_DIR` so that I can reference it with `${VOLUME_DIR}`. Then, when I specify creating a bind mount in the container, I simply use `podman run -v ${VOLUME_DIR}/wordpress:/var/lib/mysql mysql:8-oracle`. This will ensure that all my data is stored in a predictable location on my system, and each container gets its dedicated folder within that path.

## Initialization scripts

Most containerized databases feature a way to facilitate the running of scripts after initial setup, which can be very handy. This is typically done by allowing the user to mount a directory from the host machine that contains `.sql` and/or `.sh` files into the `/docker-entrypoint-initdb.d` directory of the container. The scripts are generally executed in alphabetical order and thus can be easily controlled by adding a prefix with a number, for example, `01_users.sql`, `02_permissions.sql`, `03_hostname.sh`, and so forth:

- The MySQL database:

  The MySQL database supports `*.sh` and `*.sql` scripts in the following mount points:

  **`/docker-entrypoint-initdb.d`**

- The PostgreSQL database:

  The PostgreSQL database supports `*.sh`, `*.sql`, and `*.sql.gz` scripts in the following mount points:

  **`/docker-entrypoint-initdb.d`**

- The MongoDB database:

  MongoDB supports `*.sh` and `*.js` scripts in the following mount points:

  **`/docker-entrypoint-initdb.d`**

- The Oracle database:

  The Oracle database supports `*.sh` and `*.sql` scripts in the following mount points:

  - `/opt/oracle/scripts/setup`: Post-setup scripts

  - `/opt/oracle/scripts/startup`: Post-startup scripts

  - `/docker-entrypoint-initdb.d`: Symbolic link representing the aforementioned directories

### Controlling the startup order

Using a Compose file, you are able to control the startup order of your containers by using condition attributes. A nice way to ensure your database is up and running (and ready to accept connections) is to configure a health check against the database. Once the health check succeeds, the database container will become healthy. The application that requires the database can be configured not to start until the database container enters a healthy state. This can be done using the depends_on option.

If you wanted to add a health check to a PostgreSQL database, you could configure that with the following:

```
healthcheck:
    test: pg_isready
    start_period: 5s
    interval: 5s
    timeout: 5s
    retries: 55
```

Then, for the application, you would simply specify the service name (in this example, wikijs-db):

```
depends_on:
    wikijs-db:
        condition: service_healthy
```

When these options are configured properly, you will no longer see repeated connection failures as the application tries to connect to a database that isn't ready, because the application container won't even start until the database container is healthy.

### Tying it all together

Now that we've discussed these database best practices, it's time to tie it all together with a Compose file to deploy a WordPress website. WordPress requires a MySQL database, so in the Compose file, we're deploying two services: wordpress01 (WordPress content management system) and wordpress01-db (MySQL database).

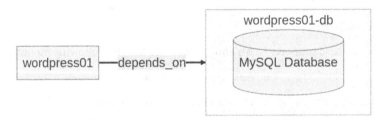

Figure 11.8 – Visual topology of an application and its database

In the `wordpress01` service, we can easily reference the database host by the name label assigned to the service of the database – this is all thanks to the awesome name resolution capabilities supported by Podman `dns` plugins. You'll also see that we are leveraging a health check on the `wordpress01-db` service so that it doesn't become healthy until `mysqladmin` is able to get a response from pinging the database service, and `wordpress01` is configured with `depends_on` so that it will not try to start until `wordpress01-db` is in a healthy state. Since this example is intended to be a quick proof-of-concept deployment, I chose to use a named volume rather than a bind mount for the data, but you can also see the use of a bind mount for the initialization scripts. Last but not least, notice that we're using a dedicated database container (`wordpress01-db`) that is complementary to the application container (`wordpress01`). The contents of the Compose file for this WordPress website might look something like this:

```
services:
  wordpress01:
    image: wordpress
    container_name: wordpress01
    depends_on:
      wordpress01-db:
        condition: service_healthy
    restart: always
    ports:
      - 8080:80
    environment:
      WORDPRESS_DB_HOST: wordpress01-db
      WORDPRESS_DB_USER: myuser
      WORDPRESS_DB_PASSWORD: mysqlpw
      WORDPRESS_DB_NAME: mysqldb

  wordpress01-db:
    image: mysql:8-oracle
    container_name: wordpress01-db
    restart: always
    environment:
      MYSQL_ROOT_PASSWORD: myqlrootpw
      MYSQL_USER: myuser
      MYSQL_PASSWORD: mysqlpw
      MYSQL_DATABASE: mysqldb
    volumes:
      - ./data/init:/docker-entrypoint-initdb.d # Initialization scripts
      - wordpress01-db-data:/var/lib/mysql #Data directory
    healthcheck:
      test: mysqladmin ping -h 127.0.0.1 -u $$MYSQL_USER --password=$$MYSQL_PASSWORD
      start_period: 5s
      interval: 5s
      timeout: 5s
      retries: 55

volumes:
  wordpress01-db-data:
```

Figure 11.9 – Compose file for WordPress

Go ahead and try to deploy this setup for yourself. You can view the logs of the application with `podman logs -f wordpress01` to see that it connects to the database successfully on the first attempt. Let's use Docker Compose to create and start the containers. You can do that just as we described in the earlier recipe on Docker Compose, by navigating to the directory where your `docker-compose.yml` file lives and running the following command:

```
docker-compose up -d
```

# Buildah and Skopeo – Podman's friends with benefits

The title of this chapter mentions *Podman and Friends*. Well, up until this point, you have probably noticed we didn't talk much about Podman's friends. Podman brings along a couple of companions to facilitate all your container management needs. These buddies of Podman are otherwise known as Buildah and Skopeo.

Where Podman is primarily focused on running containers, Buildah focuses on building them, and Skopeo focuses on handling images and transferring them to/from remote container registries.

## Getting ready

We will require the following:

- Oracle Linux
- Podman
- Buildah
- Skopeo

## How to do it...

In this recipe, we'll explore the basic usage of Buildah and Skopeo to reveal how these two friends of Podman can enhance your experience and workflow when dealing with containers.

### Building container images with Buildah

While Podman can be used for basic container image builds, Buildah is a utility that is fully focused on building OCI-compliant images. Not only can Buildah be used to build images from a Containerfile or Dockerfile, but it can also very neatly change existing container images.

First things first, let's see how Buildah can be used to build images from a Containerfile. With Podman, we build images using the `podman build -t <image_name>.` command. When we call on Podman to perform a build, it is actually using a subset of Buildah's functionality to build the image. To use Buildah directly, we only need to use a slightly different command. For example, let's say we have a file named `Containerfile` with the following content:

```
FROM oraclelinux:8
RUN dnf install -y rhn-setup yum-utils && dnf clean all
ENTRYPOINT ["/bin/bash"]
```

In order to build it with Buildah. You'll enter `buildah bud -t <image_name>`. In this example, I'm going to name the image `ol-repo-sync`. Let's do this now:

```
buildah bud -t ol-repo-sync .
```

The results in this scenario are the same as if you were to do this with Podman. Where Buildah really shines, is its ability to make changes to working containers, and it can also create new images from working containers.

In order to keep things simple for this recipe, we're going to replicate what was specified in `Containerfile`, except instead of using `Containerfile` directly, we're going to do things ad hoc with Buildah. So let's make some changes to a pre-existing Oracle Linux 8 image and store it as a new image. First, we're going to run `buildah from` to load up a working container in Buildah:

```
buildah from oraclelinux:8
```

That's going to return the following output:

```
oraclelinux-working-container
```

This tells us the name of the newly created working container. Now that we have a Buildah container ready to work with, let's add some packages to it. In this example, we're going to add the same packages that `Containerfile` specified earlier. Enter the following commands:

```
buildah run oraclelinux-working-container dnf -y install rhn-setup
yum-utils
buildah run oraclelinux-working-container dnf clean all
```

You will see the DNF package manager do its thing, and afterward, you will be left with an Oracle Linux base image plus the new packages we installed as a result of the `buildah run` command.

Finally, we need to define the `entrypoint` into this container. We can do this by leveraging the `buildah config` command:

```
buildah config --cmd '' oraclelinux-working-container
buildah config --entrypoint '["/bin/bash"]' oraclelinux-working-
container
```

> **Note**
>
> At the time of writing, there appears to be a bug in Buildah that populates the cmd value unless we explicitly give it an empty value first. This can lead to unexpected behavior of the resulting image. According to the documentation for Buildah, setting `entrypoint` without defining a value for cmd should clear out any assigned value for cmd, but that was not the case in my testing of Buildah version `1.29.1`. To circumvent this, I found it best to explicitly set cmd to an empty value before defining the entry point for the image.

In order to create a new image from this working container, all we need to do is run the `buildah commit` command. In this example, we're going to name it `ol-repo-sync-buildah` so we can compare it with the image built from the aforementioned `Containerfile`:

```
buildah commit --rm oraclelinux-working-container ol-repo-sync-buildah
```

Now that we've created the image using Buildah, we can run `podman inspect` against both `ol-repo-sync` and `ol-repo-sync-buildah` and we'll see that the two are more or less identical. Also, take note of the size of the two images. We can check that by using the `buildah images` command:

```
$ buildah images
```

The output will look something like this:

```
REPOSITORY                                  TAG      IMAGE ID       CREATED          SIZE
localhost/ol-repo-sync-buildah-mount        latest   31e796a1d235   11 seconds ago   279 MB
localhost/ol-repo-sync-buildah              latest   af5fd13ae420   2 minutes ago    285 MB
localhost/ol-repo-sync                      latest   fbe8b199737c   3 minutes ago    285 MB
```

Figure 11.10 – Listing of Buildah images

This time around, we can see that the size is a bit smaller because we leveraged the DNF package manager from the host system to install packages in the container via the `buildah mount` command. This is obviously not a huge difference in size, but it begins to show the benefits that Buildah brings to the table with containers.

As you can see, Buildah grants us fine-tuned control of our container images and it can be a very powerful ally because it allows us to temporarily mount files and packages from the host system in the container to perform actions without ever actually installing said files and packages in the container. Ultimately, you're able to achieve a leaner container image. Furthermore, Buildah provides the ability to script out your container image builds as it's all done from the command line. This can prove to be very powerful when combined with things such as automation and/or CI/CD pipelines. It may take some time to get the hang of building your container images with Buildah, but the results can be rewarding if you stick with it.

## Inspecting remote images using Skopeo

Do you remember when we talked about the need to pull an image before you can inspect it? This was covered in the *Creating handy-dandy utility containers* recipe. Well, what if I told you that we can leverage Skopeo to inspect images that are in remote repositories without needing to first pull them to our local machine? That is exactly what we're going to do here.

In the *Creating handy-dandy utility containers* recipe, you were instructed to run the following:

```
podman pull docker.io/pandoc/core
podman image inspect pandoc/core | podman run -i --rm stedolan/jq -r
'.[].Config.Entrypoint[]'
```

That's because if you tried to run `podman image inspect` without first pulling the container to your local machine, you would see the following error:

`Error: inspecting object: pandoc/core: image not known`Skopeo allows us to work directly with container images living in remote repositories. To illustrate how this works, let's first get rid of our local `pandoc/core` container image:

```
podman image rm pandoc/core
```

Now that the image is removed from our local machine, let's use Skopeo to inspect the image directly from its remote repository:

```
skopeo inspect --config docker://docker.io/pandoc/core:latest | podman
run -i --rm stedolan/jq -r '.config.Entrypoint[]'
```

Pretty nifty, right? I did notice there were some minor changes to the JSON paths that affected how I needed to structure my `jq` command to properly extract the entry point I was looking for, but all in all, leveraging Skopeo to inspect remote images yields the same information that you would get if you first pulled it in with Podman. I can definitely see advantages to using Skopeo, especially when working with larger images and/or when needing to inspect images in an automated CICD pipeline.

## Handling remote images with Skopeo

Skopeo can also be used to transfer container images from one remote container repository to another, without needing to pull/download it locally first. The syntax is similar to the standard Linux `cp` command. In `cp`, we use `cp <source> <destination>`, and with Skopeo we use `skopeo copy <source> <destination>`. As an example, if we want to copy the `pandoc/core` image from one registry to another, all we need to do is run this:

```
skopeo copy docker://docker.io/pandoc/core:latest docker://example.
com/pandoc/core:latest
```

Likewise, we can also transfer it to our local Podman container storage through the use of the `containers-storage` prefix, for example:

```
skopeo copy docker://docker.io/pandoc/core:latest containers-
storage:pandoc/core:latest
```

Additionally, if we wanted to specify some other location, we could simply use the `dir` prefix followed by the path. But in this case, be sure the path exists prior and omit any characters that are incompatible with the Linux filesystem, for example:

```
mkdir -p $(pwd)/pandoc/core
skopeo copy docker://docker.io/pandoc/core:latest dir:$(pwd)/pandoc/
core
```

Lastly, Skopeo can also be used to delete images from remote repositories or from local container storage. To do this, simply run the following:

```
skopeo delete containers-storage:pandoc/core:latest
```

# 12

# Navigating Ansible Waters

In this chapter, we'll walk through several recipes that will expand your knowledge on installing **Oracle Linux Automation Manager** (**OLAM**), managing its foundation, creating playbooks, maximizing those playbooks, and helping you understand the capabilities of OLAM. Each recipe will open your eyes to the full scope of what automation can accomplish; from patching to deploying fully functional hybrid cloud environments, OLAM can change the direction in which you think of computing and open your mind to a new world of rinse and repeat. The following are the touch points of a small subsection of what automation can simplify.

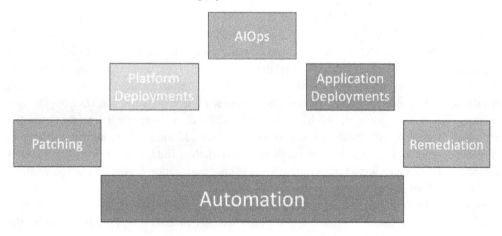

Figure 12.1 – Automation touch points

In this chapter, the following recipes will cover the installation, configuration, and usability of the OLAM platform:

- Installing OLAM
- Zip through configuring and managing OLAM from the foundation up
- OLAM isn't fantasy football, but they both use playbooks

- Controlling the patching chaos

- Look beyond automation

- Set it and forget it

## Installing OLAM

Since the dawn of time we, as the human race, have tried to make things easier, quicker, and more efficient. However, I'm sure most of us have heard from our parents, "*Never take shortcuts*," or "*When I was a kid, I had to walk to and from school uphill, in the snow, with one leg, both ways.*" These anecdotes really never change; they evolve as we get to our parent's age, and we try to pass on our wisdom to the next generation. Well, what if I told you that you could have your cake and eat it too? Automation is the evolution of computing and the automation of repeatable tasks. Now, of course, we can't automate everything, and there are certain tasks that aren't worth the effort to automate, because they're not repeatable or the factors change to the point that automation would break the process.

The dictionary definition of automation is "*the application of technology, programs, robotics, or process to achieve outcomes with minimal human input.*" Note *process* – the process in which we change, execute, or alter the outcome of a result. Automation is that process change. We can automate the installation of an application, such as the installation of Microsoft Office, or an antivirus; we've been automating these processes since the beginning of the world of computing. Now, we carry automation to the next level. Take, for instance, Ansible Tower, Red Hat's version of automation. Both Ansible and OLAM are built on AWX, which is a powerful and modern web UI and API that allows you to easily manage your organization's Ansible playbook, inventories, vault, and credentials. With AWX, you can streamline your automation processes and simplify your infrastructure management tasks, all from a single, user-friendly interface. For instance, say that a university computer science professor has a lab to prepare every week; the lab has 50 students, and each one requires a separate virtual lab to participate. The professor wouldn't want to sit there and rebuild the lab environment every week. With Ansible, a playbook (not the football playbook, but an outline and functional requirements) can be put together to execute a subset of commands automating the creation of that lab environment. By creating that playbook, an engineer can alter a few variables to change the number of virtual machines, memory, vCPU, or any other resource or application being used. Essentially, Ansible and the Ansible playbook shorten the process of creating that lab exponentially, making it repeatable and saving the professor from recreating it every week.

OLAM is an automation suite and comes bundled as an open source Linux distribution (Oracle Linux), based on AWX and Ansible Tower. OLAM is a configurable automation platform, much like Ansible, with the ability to create, manage and change playbooks. OLAM is installed with a UI, as you'll see later in this recipe, as well as a CLI. Both the UI and CLI are fully functional and have all the granularity of Ansible Tower, available at no cost, with a premier support subscription. OLAM can be used, as shown in the following figure, to create playbooks that can automate processes within multiple arenas, from on-premise virtualization farms and HCI environments to application deployments, reaching into multiple cloud platforms and hybrid cloud distributions.

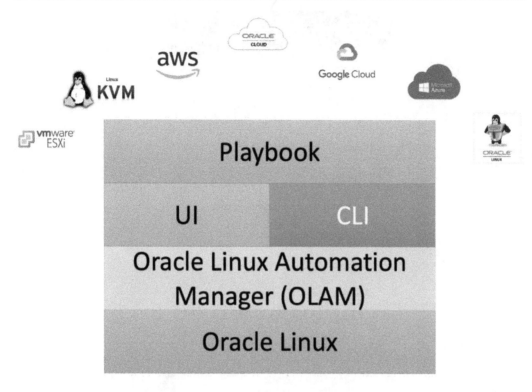

Figure 12.2 – The playbook hierarchy

In this recipe, we'll be installing OLAM. As with any application installation, we need to prepare a base environment to install the application on – in this case, Oracle Linux 8 of course. We'll need to prepare and configure that OS, which we will not be walking through in detail, as that was covered in a previous recipe in this book. However, it is advisable that you install the OS with a GUI.

## Getting ready

We'll be installing OLAM in **Oracle Cloud Infrastructure** (**OCI**) as a virtual machine. Refer to *Chapters 3* and *4* on navigating and configuring OCI virtual machines. We'll briefly walk through the creation of the VM in the following steps:

1.  Navigate to OCI **Instances**, to create a host instance for OLAM:

Figure 12.3 – Instances for VM Creation

2.  You'll want to create an instance, by clicking on **Create instance**:

Figure 12.4 – Instance Creation

3.  You can name your instance, and select a compartment to host the VM:

## Create compute instance

Create an instance to deploy and run applications, or save as a reusable Terraform stack for creating an instance with Resource Manager.

Name

instance-20231213-2350

Create in compartment

benneraced2022 (root)

Figure 12.5 – Name your instance

4. After naming the VM, you can select the location, or **Availability Domain (AD)** you want to host the VM. The AD we're using is the default AD for OCI:

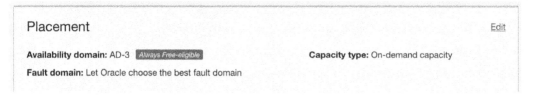

Figure 12.6 – Availability Domain

5. We're giving our VM 8 GB of RAM and 2 vCPUs, so we'll want to select the correct host configuration. You'll want to edit and change the shape as shown in the following screenshot:

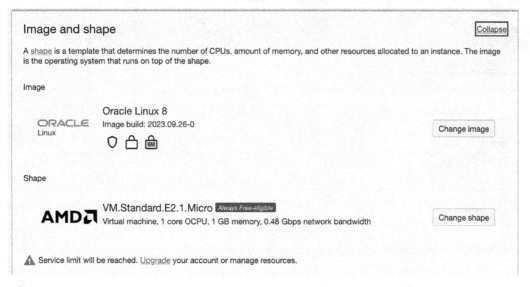

Figure 12.7 – Image Size and Shape

6.  Edit the shape by clicking on **Change shape** and select your shape as shown under **Shape name**:

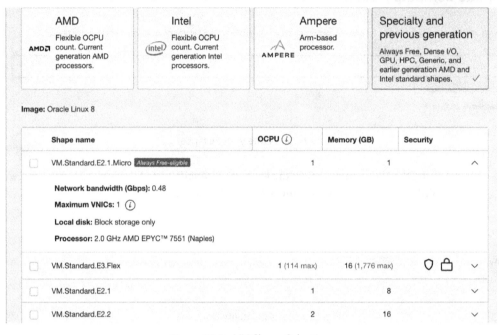

Figure 12.8 – VM Shape Selection

7.  The **VM.Standard.E3.FLEX** shape allows you to specify your resources:

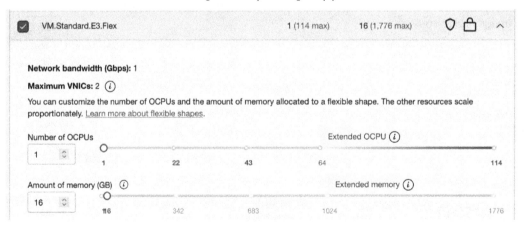

Figure 12.9 – VM Resource Configuration

8.  We're going to select 8 GB of RAM (memory) and 2 vCPUs. The minimal requirements for OLAM are 2 vCPU's and 4 GB of RAM:

Figure 12.10 – VM Resource Selections

9.  After configuring your VM resources, you'll have to configure your access keys (public key):

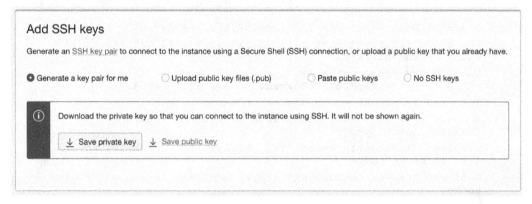

Figure 12.11 – SSH Key choices

10. You can either create, upload, paste, or continue without a key. We're going to paste our key, by selecting the key, and copying the pasted key:

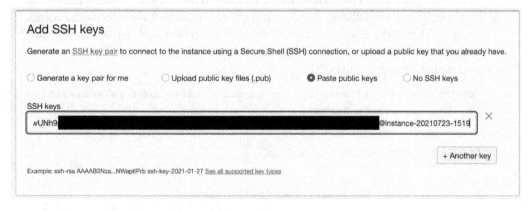

Figure 12.12 – SSH Key Pasting

11. After configuring your key, scroll down to the end of the instance screen, and click on **Create**:

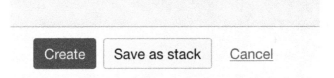

Figure 12.13 – VM Creation

12. Once you've created your instance, access the VM using SSH with the `opc` user and your key:

```
% ssh -i sshkey_private_lab opc@193.122.148.147
The authenticity of host '193.122.148.147 (193.122.148.147)'
can't be established.
ED25519 key fingerprint is
SHA256:nF+ilxdx0SpWZZxiFZOJFvektZc8YhBI76j1Qm64w3A.
This key is not known by any other names
Are you sure you want to continue connecting (yes/no/
[fingerprint])? yes
Warning: Permanently added '193.122.148.147' (ED25519) to the
list of known hosts.
Activate the web console with: systemctl enable --now cockpit.
socket

[opc@instance-20231213-2350 ~]$
```

13. Adding a YUM repository isn't difficult at all, and it enables you to update, install, deinstall, or patch certain aspects at the OS and kernel levels, including applications. As mentioned earlier in the chapter, you can add these repositories, via DNF to the OS, while walking through the GUI, or later after the installation. Either way, you'll have to either have access to the outside, meaning we'll have to be able to reach out of the environment to Oracle repositories or a local mirror set up. We're not going to walk through setting up a local mirror, but we will walk through adding the repos using DNF:

```
[opc@olam-test ~]$ sudo DNF -y install oraclelinux-release-el8
Ksplice for Oracle Linux 8
(x86_64)                                                39 MB/s
| 3.2 MB       00:00
MySQL 8.0 for Oracle Linux 8
(x86_64)                                                38 MB/s |
3.0 MB       00:00
MySQL 8.0 Tools Community for Oracle Linux 8
(x86_64)                            7.3 MB/s | 491 kB      00:00
MySQL 8.0 Connectors Community for Oracle Linux 8
(x86_64)                            600 kB/s |  30 kB      00:00
```

```
Oracle Software for OCI users on Oracle Linux 8
(x86_64)                              96 MB/s |  93 MB     00:00
Oracle Linux 8 BaseOS Latest
(x86_64)                                            118 MB/s
|   62 MB      00:00
Oracle Linux 8 Application Stream
(x86_64)                                      114 MB/s |   48
MB      00:00
Oracle Linux 8 Addons
(x86_64)                                                    56
MB/s |  6.9 MB       00:00
Latest Unbreakable Enterprise Kernel Release 7 for Oracle Linux
8 (x86_64)           95 MB/s |   18 MB      00:00
Package oraclelinux-release-el8-1.0-32.el8.x86_64 is already
installed.
Dependencies resolved.
Nothing to do.
Complete!
```

As shown in the preceding code, we're adding several repos; most of these are required for either OS-level patches or installing OLAM.

14. One of the most important aspects of all the prerequisites is the ability for an application to see outside of the internal system into the ecosystem; in order to do this, we need to open up a portal outside of the internal system – in other words, we open firewall ports, as shown here:

```
[opc@olam-test ~]$ sudo firewall-cmd --add-port=27199/tcp
--permanent
success
[opc@olam-test ~]$ sudo firewall-cmd --add-service=http
--permanent
success
[opc@olam-test ~]$ sudo firewall-cmd --add-service=https
--permanent
success
[opc@olam-test ~]$ sudo firewall-cmd --reload
success
[opc@olam-test ~]$
```

15. After we open those ports, we're going to have to enable the repo we just installed with DNF. This can be done before configuring the firewall as well:

```
[opc@olam-test ~]$ sudo DNF config-manager --enable ol8_baseos_
latest
[opc@olam-test ~]$
```

16. After enabling that repo, we need to install and configure the OLAM repo, as shown here:

```
[opc@olam-test ~]$ sudo DNF install oraclelinux-automation-
manager-release-el8
Oracle Linux 8 BaseOS Latest Oracle Linux 8
 Application Stream Oracle
Linux 8 Addons
Truncated for size
Complete!
```

17. As we did with the base repo, we need to enable the OLAM repo as well:

```
[opc@olam-test ~]$ sudo DNF config-manager --enable ol8_
automation2 ol8_addons ol8_UEKR7 ol8_appstream
```

18. After enabling the newer OLAM repository, we need to disable the old one:

```
[opc@olam-test ~]$ sudo DNF config-manager --disable ol8_
automation
```

19. Once that is done, we've completed the prerequisites for the OLAM installation from an application perspective. However, we need to prepare the database for OLAM now. In order to do this, we need to install and configure the database module. OLAM uses a Postgres database, which is SQL-based. The following is the command to install that module:

```
[opc@olam-test ~]$ sudo DNF module reset postgresql
Oracle Linux 8 BaseOS Latest
(x86_64)                                          157 kB/s | 3.6
kB      00:00
Oracle Linux 8 Application Stream
(x86_64)                                          233 kB/s | 3.9
kB      00:00
Oracle Linux 8 Addons
(x86_64)                                          153 kB/s |
3.0 kB      00:00
Oracle Linux Automation Manager 2.0 based on the open source
projects Ansib 3.1 MB/s | 644 kB      00:00
Latest Unbreakable Enterprise Kernel Release 7 for Oracle Linux
8 (x86_64)    147 kB/s | 3.0 kB      00:00
Dependencies resolved.
Nothing to do.
Complete!
```

20. Once we install the module, it needs to be enabled:

```
[opc@olam-test ~]$ sudo DNF module enable postgresql:13
Last metadata expiration check: 0:00:54 ago on Tue 22 Aug 2023
07:12:29 PM GMT.
Dependencies resolved.
================================================================
=========================================
 Package                   Architecture          Version
                   Repository          Size
================================================================
=========================================
Enabling module streams:
 postgresql                                       13

Transaction Summary
================================================================
=========================================

Is this ok [y/N]: y
Complete!
```

21. Now that we've installed and enabled the Postgres module, we can install the database:

```
[opc@olam-test ~]$ sudo DNF install postgresql-server
Last metadata expiration check: 0:02:35 ago on Tue 22 Aug 2023
07:12:29 PM GMT.
Dependencies resolved.
================================================================
=========================================
 Package                   Arch          Version
                                 Repository          Size
================================================================
=========================================
Installing:
 postgresql-server        x86_64        13.11-1.0.1.module+el8.8.0+2
1141+00b1aed9        ol8_appstream        5.6 M
Installing dependencies:
 libpq                    x86_64        13.5-1.
el8                                      ol8_appstream        198 k
 postgresql               x86_64        13.11-1.0.1.module+el8.8.0+2
1141+00b1aed9        ol8_appstream        1.5 M

Transaction Summary
================================================================
=========================================
Install  3 Packages
```

```
The output has been truncated...
Installed:
  libpq-13.5-1.el8.x86_64
  postgresql-13.11-1.0.1.module+el8.8.0+21141+00b1aed9.x86_64
  postgresql-server-13.11-1.0.1.module+el8.8.0+21141+00b1aed9.
x86_64

Complete!
```

22. Initiating the database is next. This prepares it for use and allows data to be overwritten if already present:

```
[opc@olam-test ~]$ sudo postgresql-setup --initdb
 * Initializing database in '/var/lib/pgsql/data'
 * Initialized, logs are in /var/lib/pgsql/initdb_postgresql.log
```

23. After the initiation, you'll want to change the password schema to match requirements:

```
[opc@olam-test ~]$ sudo sed -i "s/#password_encryption.*/
password_encryption = scram-sha-256/" /var/lib/pgsql/data/
postgresql.conf
```

24. Now, we will enable the database, as shown here:

```
[opc@olam-test ~]$ sudo systemctl enable --now postgresql
Created symlink /etc/systemd/system/multi-user.target.wants/
postgresql.service → /usr/lib/systemd/system/postgresql.service.
```

25. After enabling the database, we want to make sure everything is prepared for the OLAM installation, so we'll want to get the status of the database. The following is the command to display the status:

```
[opc@olam-test ~]$ sudo systemctl status postgresql
⊠ postgresql.service - PostgreSQL database server
   Loaded: loaded (/usr/lib/systemd/system/postgresql.service;
enabled; vendor preset: disabled)
   Active: active (running) since Tue 2023-08-22 19:18:44 GMT;
23s ago
  Process: 46810 ExecStartPre=/usr/libexec/postgresql-check-db-
dir postgresql (code=exited, status=0/SUCCES>
 Main PID: 46813 (postmaster)
    Tasks: 8 (limit: 22519)
   Memory: 16.9M
   CGroup: /system.slice/postgresql.service
           ├─46813 /usr/bin/postmaster -D /var/lib/pgsql/data
           ├─46814 postgres: logger
           ├─46816 postgres: checkpointer
```

```
├─46817 postgres: background writer
├─46818 postgres: walwriter
├─46819 postgres: autovacuum launcher
├─46820 postgres: stats collector
└─46821 postgres: logical replication launcher


Aug 22 19:18:44 olam-test systemd[1]: Starting PostgreSQL
database server...
Aug 22 19:18:44 olam-test postmaster[46813]: 2023-08-22
19:18:44.097 GMT [46813] LOG:  redirecting log outp>
Aug 22 19:18:44 olam-test postmaster[46813]: 2023-08-22
19:18:44.097 GMT [46813] HINT:  Future log output w>
Aug 22 19:18:44 olam-test systemd[1]: Started PostgreSQL
database server.
```

As you see in the preceding code, `active (running)` tells you that the database is active and running, and you're ready to start the installation of OLAM.

Once this is done, we're ready to get into the meat and potatoes – installing OLAM.

## How to do it...

After we've completed the prerequisites, we're ready to move on to the installation. Remember that the firewall ports, installing the YUM repositories and Postgres, and enabling them are important. Without these prerequisites, you will not be able to move forward and the installation will fail:

1. The first step to install OLAM is the creation of the AWX user. Remember that AWX is the foundation that OLAM is built on, so this is really important:

```
[opc@olam-test ~]$ sudo su - postgres -c "createuser -S -P awx"
Enter password for new role: welcome1
Enter it again: welcome1
```

2. Now, that we've installed the database engine, we're going to install the database, as shown here:

```
[opc@olam-test ~]$ sudo su - postgres -c "createdb -O awx awx"
```

3. After we install the database, we want to edit the config file:

```
[root@olam-test ~]# vi /var/lib/pgsql/data/pg_hba.conf
```

4. Do you remember when we defined the password variables? Here, we're noting that in the host-based authentication config file, highlighted in the following snippet. After we're finished, we'll want to make sure to save and exit the configuration:

```
# TYPE  DATABASE        USER            ADDRESS
                METHOD
```

```
# "local" is for Unix domain socket connections only
local    all              all
                                        peer
# IPv4 local connections:
host     all              all          127.0.0.1/32
            ident
# IPv6 local connections:
host     all              all          ::1/128
              ident
# Allow replication connections from localhost, by a user with
the
# replication privilege.
local    replication      all
                                        peer
host     replication      all          127.0.0.1/32
            ident
host     replication      all          ::1/128
              ident
host all all 0.0.0.0/0 scram-sha-256
```

5. Now, we're going to edit the Postgres config file; this further defines the database and how it's accessed. You'll want to annotate this with the NAT (mapping private addresses to a public IP in the simplest of terms) address of the host – that is, your virtual machine. The editable section is between the quotation marks – 'OCI NAT Address':

```
[root@olam-test ~]# vi /var/lib/pgsql/data/postgresql.conf
#----------------------------------------------------------------
----------------
# CONNECTIONS AND AUTHENTICATION
#----------------------------------------------------------------
----------------

# - Connection Settings -

listen_addresses = 'OCI NAT Address' - IP address in ifconfig
#listen_addresses = 'localhost'          # what IP address(es) to
listen on;
```

6. After editing that file, again, make sure to save and exit that configuration. After you have saved the file, you'll want to restart Postgres to make sure all of your changes have been committed:

```
[root@olam-test ~]# systemctl restart postgresql
```

7.  After all these changes have been committed, I always like to update all the YUM repos and make sure we have all the updates loaded. In order to do this, we have to update our system. The following is the DNF command to update the repositories:

```
[root@olam-test ~]# DNF update -y
Last metadata expiration check: 1:43:57 ago on Tue 22 Aug 2023
10:48:21 PM GMT.
Dependencies resolved.
================================================================
================================================================
============
 Package                                 Architecture
         Version
                                     Repository
               Size
================================================================
================================================================
============
The output has been truncated for length.
```

8.  After you've updated all of the YUM repositories, take a quick look at the preceding code, and note all of the repos we added and enabled in the previous section. You'll want to restart your virtual machine to make sure all the changes are reflected:

```
[root@olam-test ~]# reboot
```

9.  The following is the command and the output to install OLAM:

```
[root@olam-test ~]# DNF -y install ol-automation-manager
Last metadata expiration check: 1:52:46 ago on Tue 22 Aug 2023
10:48:21 PM GMT.
Dependencies resolved.
================================================================
================================================================
============
 Package                                 Architecture    Version
                                     Repository
               Size
================================================================
================================================================
============
Installing:
 ol-automation-manager                   x86_64          2.0.1-3.
 el8                                      ol8_
 automation2              41 M
Installing dependencies:
The output has been truncated for length
[root@olam-test ~]# vi /etc/redis.conf
```

10. Now, you'll want to exit root, which is very important; you cannot continue as root for AWX:

```
[root@olam-test ~]# exit
```

11. Here's where we'll be changing our user to awx to continue the installation:

```
[opc@olam-test ~]# su -l awx -s /bin/bash
```

12. Since OLAM runs in a cloud-native environment, we're using Podman to orchestrate the tuning and creation of that fabric. The following is the command to use the latest version of Podman to migrate to and create that environment within your virtual machine:

```
[awx@olam-test ~]$ podman system migrate
```

13. Now, we're going to pull down the latest version of OLAM from the Oracle Docker registry, by running the following command:

```
[awx@olam-test ~]$ podman pull container-registry.oracle.com/
oracle_linux_automation_manager/olam-ee:latest
Trying to pull container-registry.oracle.com/oracle_linux_
automation_manager/olam-ee:latest...
Getting image source signatures
Copying blob 1ca7c848b9e5 done
Copying blob a2cd216732a7 done
Copying blob 13ec27f79a4b done
Copying blob 0b5aff3da93f done
Copying config b764e737f4 done
Writing manifest to image destination
Storing signatures
```

14. Now, we want to migrate our environment to the containers:

```
[awx@olam-test ~]$ awx-manage migrate
Operations to perform:
  Apply all migrations: auth, conf, contenttypes, main, oauth2_
provider, sessions, sites, social_django, sso, taggit
Running migrations:
The output has been truncated for length.
```

15. Now, we want to create our user:

```
[awx@olam-test ~]$ awx-manage createsuperuser --username admin
--email bubba@nobody.com
Password:
Password (again)
```

16. After we've created our environment and user, we need to configure that environment. This will write the encryption key and annotate the location, address, hostname, and other identifiers. However, the VM-specific data is necessary:

```
[awx@olam-test ~]$ openssl req -x509 -nodes -days 365 -newkey
rsa:2048 -keyout /etc/tower/tower.key -out /etc/tower/tower.crt
Generating a RSA private key
.....................................+++++
.......................................................................
...............+++++
writing new private key to '/etc/tower/tower.key'
-----
You are about to be asked to enter information that will be
incorporated
into your certificate request.
What you are about to enter is what is called a Distinguished
Name or a DN.
There are quite a few fields but you can leave some blank
For some fields there will be a default value,
If you enter '.', the field will be left blank.
-----
Country Name (2 letter code) [XX]:01
State or Province Name (full name) []:Florida
Locality Name (eg, city) [Default City]:Miami
Organization Name (eg, company) [Default Company Ltd]:
Organizational Unit Name (eg, section) []:
Common Name (eg, your name or your server's hostname) []:olam-
test
Email Address []:email@email.com
```

17. We want to exit the `awx` user now and `su` to root:

```
[awx@olam-test ~]$ exit
[awx@olam-test ~]$ sudo su - root
```

18. Now, we want to set up our web server. This is done with a typical, widely distributed, canned configuration, as shown here:

```
cat << EOF | sudo tee /etc/nginx/nginx.conf > /dev/null
> user nginx;
> worker_processes auto;
> error_log /var/log/nginx/error.log;
> pid /run/nginx.pid;
>
> # Load dynamic modules. See /usr/share/doc/nginx/README.
dynamic.
```

```
> include /usr/share/nginx/modules/*.conf;
>
> events {
>     worker_connections 1024;
> }
>
> http {
>     log_format  main  '$remote_addr - $remote_user [$time_
local] "$request" '
>                       '$status $body_bytes_sent "$http_
referer" '
>                       '"$http_user_agent" "$http_x_forwarded_
for"';
>
>     access_log  /var/log/nginx/access.log  main;
>
>     sendfile            on;
>     tcp_nopush          on;
>     tcp_nodelay         on;
>     keepalive_timeout   65;
>     types_hash_max_size 2048;
>
>     include             /etc/nginx/mime.types;
>     default_type        application/octet-stream;
>
>     # Load modular configuration files from the /etc/nginx/
conf.d directory.
>     # See http://nginx.org/en/docs/ngx_core_module.
html#include
>     # for more information.
>     include /etc/nginx/conf.d/*.conf;
> }
> EOF
```

19. Now, we want to provision our instance, which we define in the following code. First, we have to switch the awx user:

```
[root@olam-test ~]# sudo su -l awx -s /bin/bash
[awx@olam-test ~]$ awx-manage provision_instance
--hostname=10.0.0.193 --node_type=hybrid
Successfully registered instance 10.0.0.193
(changed: True)
```

20. We'll register the default environments by running the following command:

```
[awx@olam-test ~]$ awx-manage register_default_execution_
environments
'OLAM EE (latest)' Default Execution Environment registered.
'OLAM EE (latest)' Default Execution Environment updated.
Control Plane Execution Environment registered.
(changed: True)
[awx@olam-test ~]$ awx-manage register_queue
--queuename=controlplane --hostnames=10.0.0.193
Creating instance group controlplane
Added instance 10.0.0.193 to controlplane
(changed: True)
controlplane
(changed: True)
```

21. Now, we need to edit the receptor configuration file, which provides address information so that our OLAM landing page's address is identified. We're going to need to switch user to root, if you're not already root, again here:

```
[root@olam-test ~]# vi /etc/receptor/receptor.conf
---
- node:
    id: 10.0.0.44

- log-level: debug

- tcp-listener:
    port: 27199

#- work-signing:
#    privatekey: /etc/receptor/work_private_key.pem
#    tokenexpiration: 1m

#- work-verification:
#    publickey: /etc/receptor/work_public_key.pem

#- tcp-peer:
#    address: 100.100.253.53:27199
#    redial: true

#- tls-server:
#    name: mutual-tls
#    cert: /etc/receptor/certs/awx.crt
```

```
#       key: /etc/receptor/certs/awx.key
#       requireclientcert: true
#       clientcas: /etc/receptor/certs/ca.crt


- control-service:
    service: control
    filename: /var/run/receptor/receptor.sock


- work-command:
    worktype: local
    command: /var/lib/ol-automation-manager/venv/awx/bin/
ansible-runner
    params: worker
    allowruntimeparams: true
#       verifysignature: true
```

22. Now, we're going to enable the OLAM service by running the following command; this begins the process of accessing OLAM:

```
[root@olam-test ~]# systemctl enable --now ol-automation-
manager.service
Created symlink /etc/systemd/system/multi-user.target.wants/
ol-automation-manager.service → /usr/lib/systemd/system/
ol-automation-manager.service.
```

23. Now, we want to preload our data by running the following command. Once this is done, we'll be ready to log in to our OLAM instance, and our installation will be complete:

```
[awx@olam-test ~]$ awx-manage create_preload_data
```

24. Here, you'll want to enter your OCI public IP address – `https://'public_IP'`. You can find this in your OCI console, within your VM configuration. You will be asked to enter your password twice. Once this is done, your OLAM installation is complete and your console is configured.

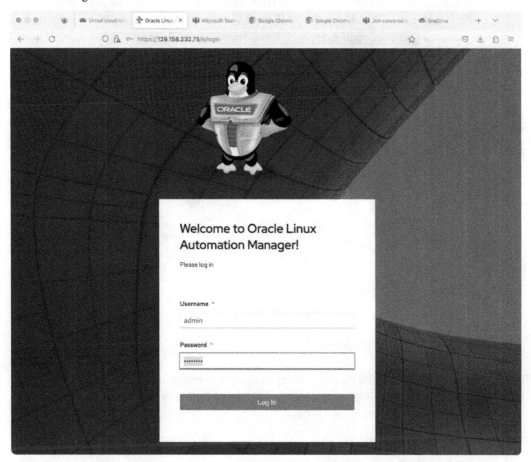

Figure 12.14 – OLAM password creation

# Zip through configuring and managing OLAM from the foundation up

Managing OLAM can be done either through the UI or via the CLI. Here, we'll be working through the UI. Think of it this way – OLAM is the platform on which you'll be managing your projects, inventories, playbooks, and automation through either your UI or CLI. Projects are at the top layer, and the hierarchy descends from there to playbooks and, eventually, triggering automations. Whether you use the UI or CLI, you'll have granular control over your key environments.

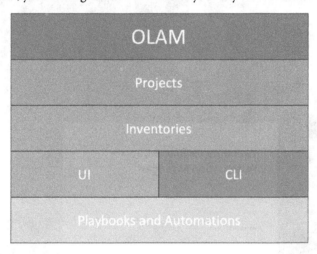

Figure 12.15 – The OLAM hierarchy

This recipe will walk you through viewing, understanding, and executing basic commands in your OLAM environment, creating projects, managing groups, and adding to inventories.

## Getting ready

As shown in the following figure, and in the previous recipe, you'll want to log in to your OLAM environment:

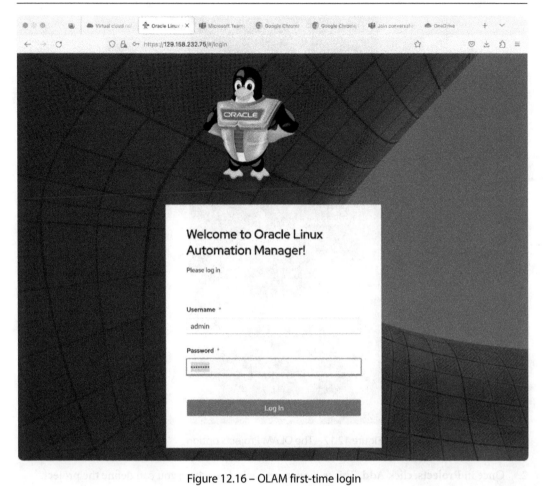

Figure 12.16 – OLAM first-time login

The first and highest level in the OLAM hierarchy is the project. You must create a project, and that will be the host to all the playbooks and automation in that hierarchy. You can have multiple projects that are assigned to different assets and inventories. Let's see how to do that in the following steps:

1.    In order to create a project, you'll want to go to the **Resources** tab and navigate to **Projects**:

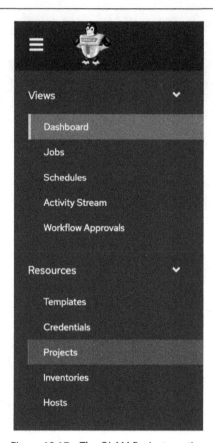

Figure 12.17 – The OLAM Projects option

2.  Once in **Projects**, click **Add**. This will open up a window where you can define the project.

Figure 12.18 – Adding a project

3.  Once you've opened up your project configuration page, you'll want to strategize how you want your project to look. In this case, we're creating a test environment, and we have set up two separate test nodes for lab purposes.  Defaults are used for the playbook directory as well as the project path.

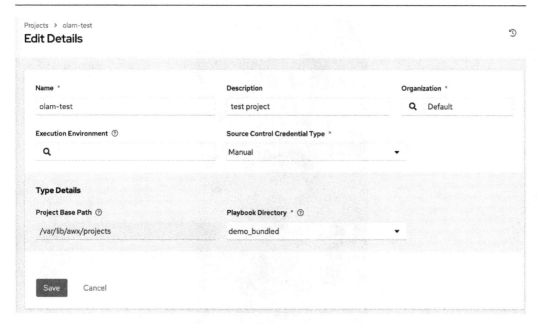

Figure 12.19 – The project variables

4.   After you've configured your project, you will want to save that information, which will bring you to a screen showing your fully configured project.

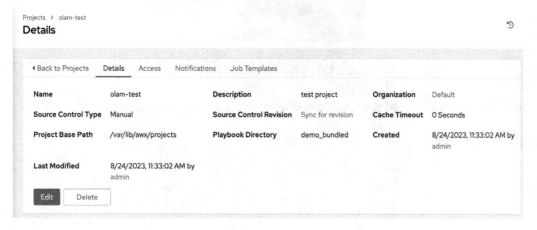

Figure 12.20 – The project configuration page

5.   Once you've configured your project, you'll want to configure your credentials, much like your project, as shown here:

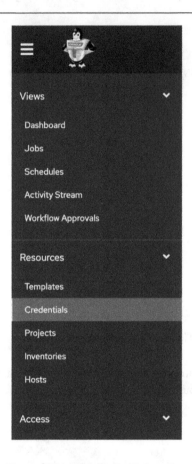

Figure 12.21 – The Credentials option

6.   The next step is to add your credential data for your opc user and machine.

## Credentials

Figure 12.22 – Credential addition

7.   You'll want to either copy or create a key, which you'll use to access machines. Paste it into the **SSH Private Key** section, and enter the names of your key and user.

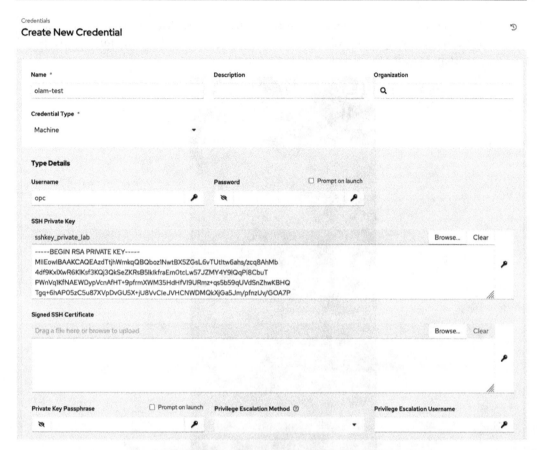

Figure 12.23 – Credential variables and the SSH private key

8.   After you save the credential, the configured credential will be displayed, as shown here:

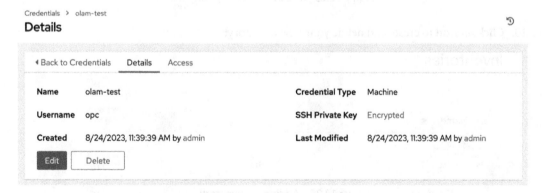

Figure 12.24 – Credential configuration page

9.  Next, you'll need to add an inventory. Remember that two test virtual machines were created for this, and in this recipe, they will be used as test environments. Select **Inventories**, and follow the next steps to define the inventory after selecting.

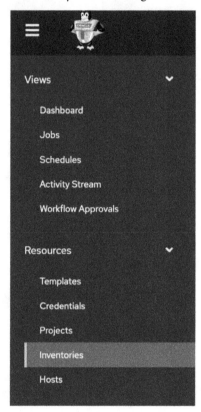

Figure 12.25 – The Inventories option

10. Click on **Add** to create and define your new inventory:

## Inventories

Figure 12.26 – Adding an inventory

11. You'll define your inventory with a name, using the default organization:

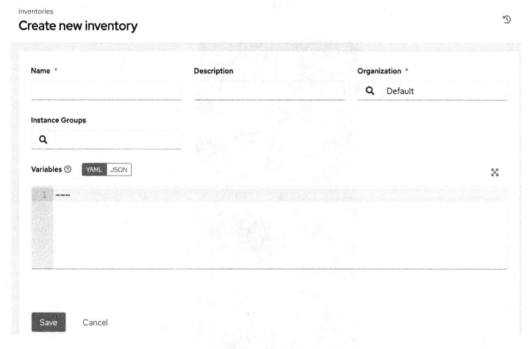

Figure 12.27 – Inventory variables

12. The configured test inventory is shown here:

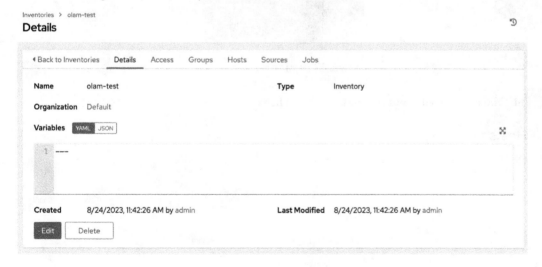

Figure 12.28 – The inventory configuration page

13. After creating an inventory, we have to add hosts to it. This will involve adding machines that we can test automation on. Select **Hosts** in the menu selection, and then the host from the list, as shown here:

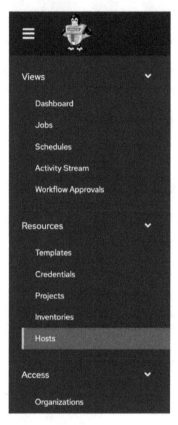

Figure 12.29 – The Hosts option

14. You can then add your new host, as shown here:

Figure 12.30 – Adding a host

15. The following is the configuration page to create your new host; make sure to select the inventory you just created:

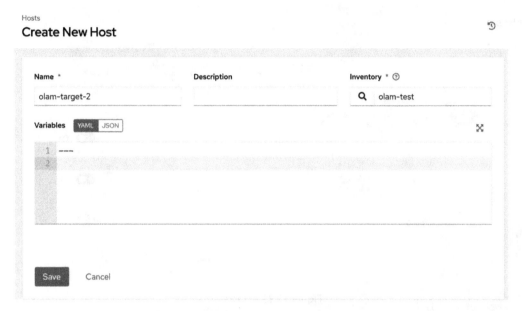

Figure 12.31 – The host variables

16. Make sure to save your configuration. Once you have done so, the host configuration will be displayed.

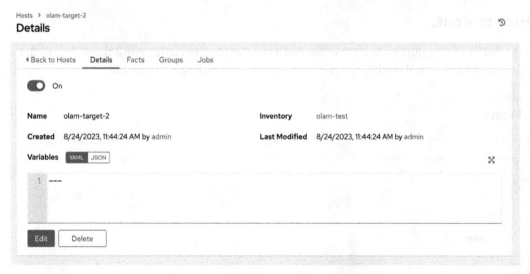

Figure 12.32 – The host configuration page

17. You'll have to repeat this, as only one host was created here; to show multiplicity, two hosts need to be created to mimic a working environment.

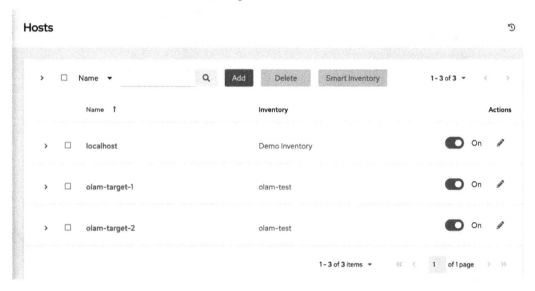

Figure 12.33 – Hosts

The setup and basic configuration of OLAM are complete. In the following recipes, we'll review how to run playbooks and further advanced configurations of OLAM. In the next recipe, we'll test our final configuration by running a command against the two test servers created.

## How to do it...

1. After adding the two hosts, you can test-run a set of commands against them. To run the commands, you'll need to navigate back to **Hosts** and click **Run Command**:

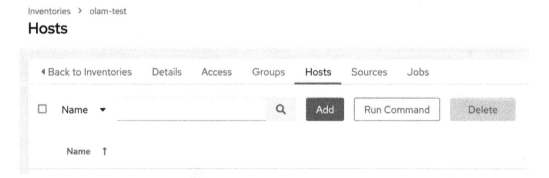

Figure 12.34 – Running simple commands on hosts

2.  You'll choose the module(s) you'll want to run – in this case, **shell** (which runs a shell script) – and **Forks** will be the number of times that the shell script will be executed – in this case, twice because we have two nodes. Here, we're using uptime as the variable argument. This runs in a shell environment, much like you would run it in any Linux environment.

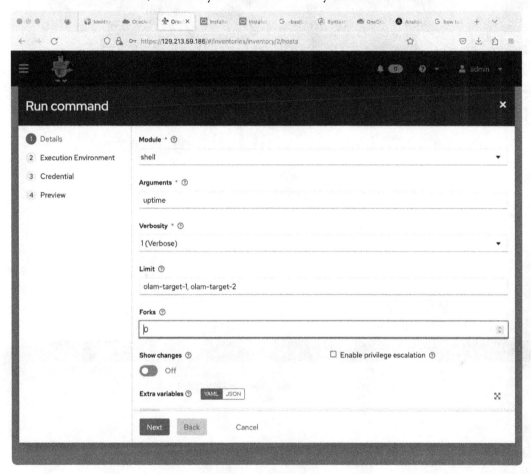

Figure 12.35 – The command variables

3.    We'll have to define the environment we want to run in, which is **OLAM EE (latest)**.

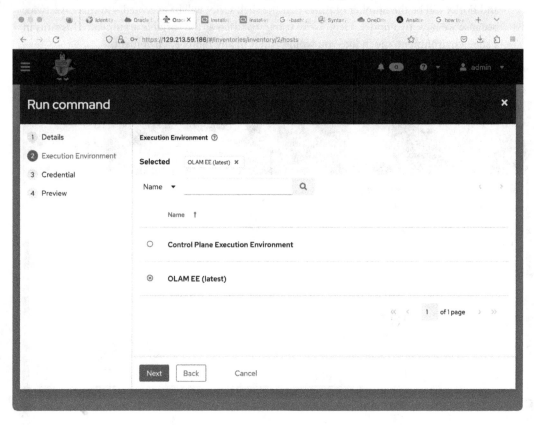

Figure 12.36 – The execution environment

4.  These are the credentials we used before on the two test nodes we created:

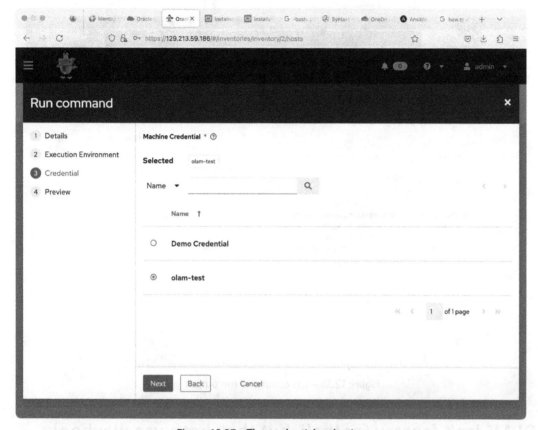

Figure 12.37 – The credentials selection

5.  The following is the output to the test; as you can see, the uptime is listed for each environment, `olam-target-1` and `olam-target-2`.

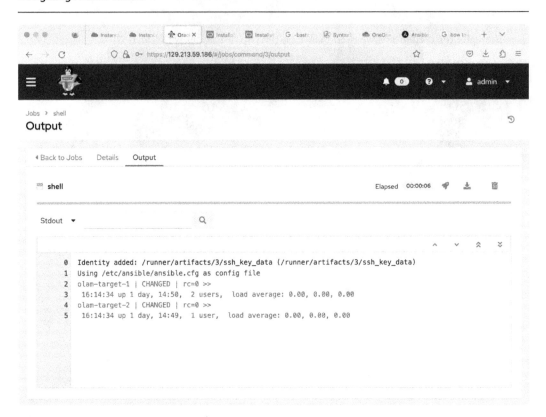

Figure 12.38 – The command run output

## OLAM isn't fantasy football, but they both use playbooks

Most of us know about fantasy football, where we follow teams, draft players, and bet on winners and losers. Well, we're not betting anything here, other than whether our environment will work, but we are using something called a **playbook**. Consider a playbook much like that used by a football coach to train their team; it's the same concept. We're predefining an environment or event, and programmatically architecting it to behave in the way we tell it, creating or changing the environment we are defining, or even reclaiming resources (taking back CPU, RAM, and disk space from decommissioned environments). Whatever we define within the constraints of OLAM, we can execute.

In order to create our playbook, we need to figure out who, what, where, when, and maybe even why:

- Who – What resources groups are we targeting?

- What – What kind of resources are we targeting? A VM? A physical machine?

- Where – Where are these resources located? In a CSP, VM farm, or physical server?

- When – When are we going to execute on the environment? Is it event-based (meaning do we clear disk space when a log fills up /tmp)?

- Why – Why are we targeting this environment? Is it a database server and logs are maxing out disk space, a web server is over utilized, or an event is having a repeat affect?

A playbook can be triggered in many different ways, In AIOps, we focus on triggers; these can be an SNMP trap, agent-based triggers (such as a full disk, as shown previously), or a directed event from a platform. Let's return to the other four variables – who, what, where, and when; *who* is which environment, *what* is what machines are used, *where* is the location of the environment(s), and *when* is when this playbook will run, and whether it will be triggered or run at a certain time. All or any of these are plausible and can be gradually defined.

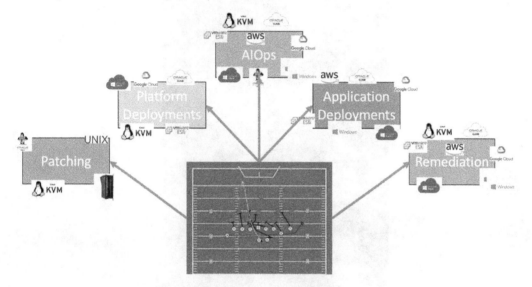

Figure 12.39 – Playbooks and their touch points

## Getting ready

Getting ready to build your own playbooks and/or utilize existing ones isn't the monumental task it seems. In this recipe, we'll explore adding a Git repository to your OLAM instance. This is done for a few reasons:

- Version control – control your code, who edits it, and the versions you're on. Remember that things change, including infrastructure and OS versions. You want to keep track of what changes in your playbooks so that you can adjust to the changes.

- Keeping track of your playbooks – save them, collaborate, and share. You can share your templates and reuse them. Remember that one of the most important reasons why automation is so useful is repetition, limiting the need for human interaction in repetitive steps.

- Git gives you a pipeline into your templates and allows you to easily add playbooks you've written to templates that you've written and created.

In order to add a Git repository to OLAM, you'll need to first create it and add it to your OLAM project:

1. First, go to the **Projects** tab, as shown here.

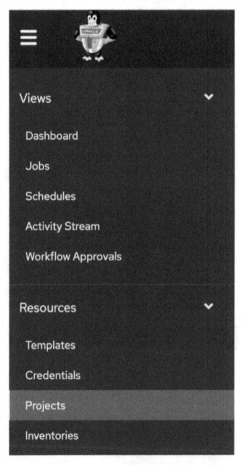

Figure 12.40 – Projects menu

2. Navigate to the test project we created, or create a new one – in this case, Oracle was created, since we're going to add the Oracle sample playbooks to OLAM.

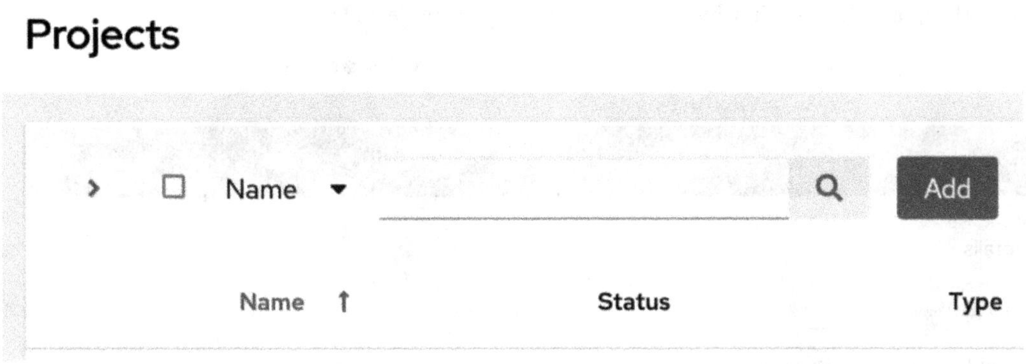

# Projects

Figure 12.41 – Adding a project

3.    Enter the information for the project, including your Git data:

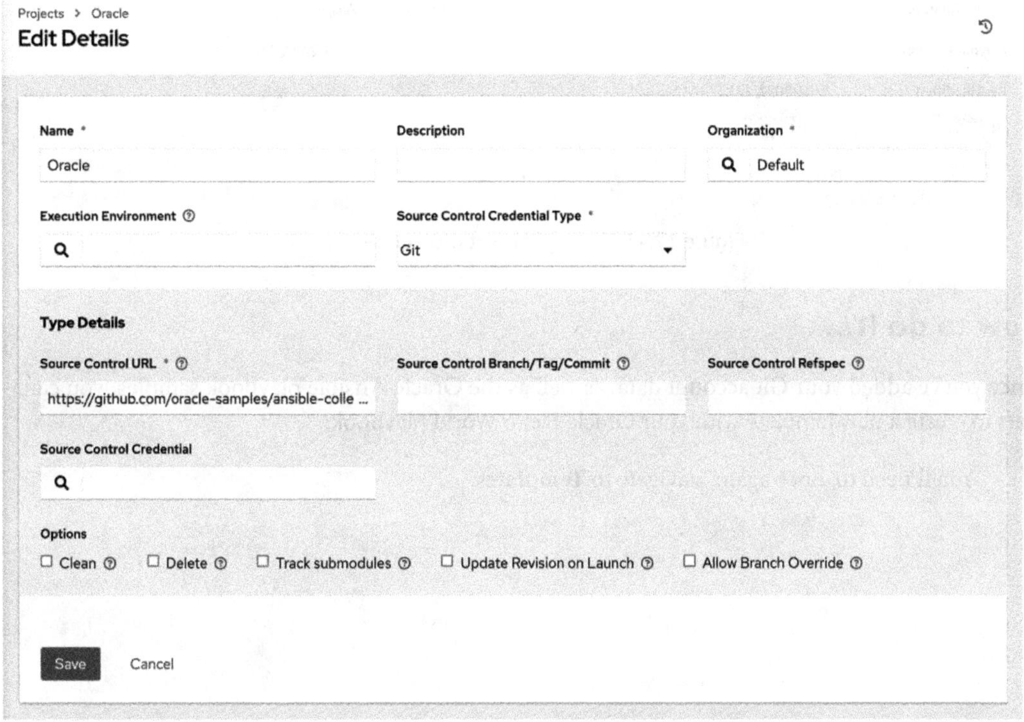

Figure 12.42 – Project configuration and variables for the Oracle Git repository

4.   Then, save the project, which will bring you to your project's **Details** screen.

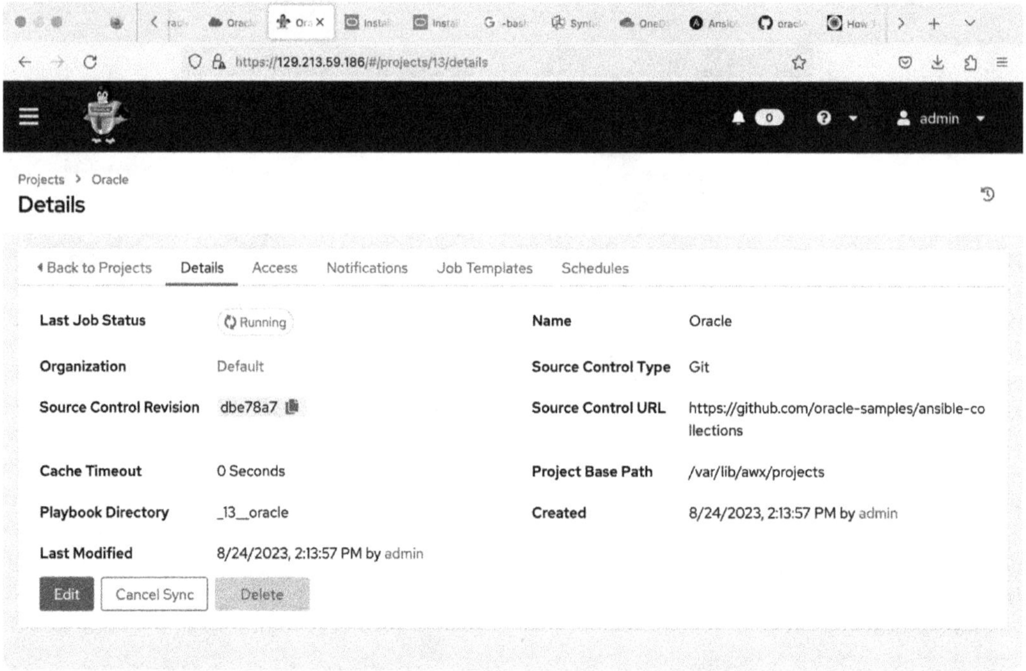

Figure 12.43 – The Oracle Git project details

## How to do it...

Once you've added your Git account data, as well as the Oracle Ansible playbook samples, you can start to create a new template with your Oracle Hello World playbook:

1.   You'll need to, once again, navigate to **Templates**:

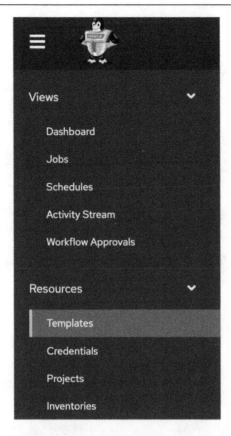

Figure 12.44 – The Templates option

2.  Click **Add** to create a new template.

# Templates

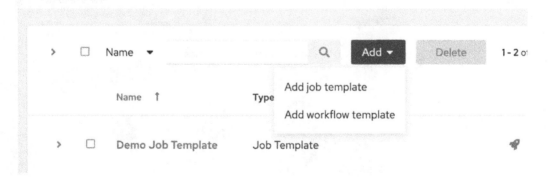

Figure 12.45 – Adding a job template

3. Complete the worksheet with the correct variable, as we did in the previous recipe.

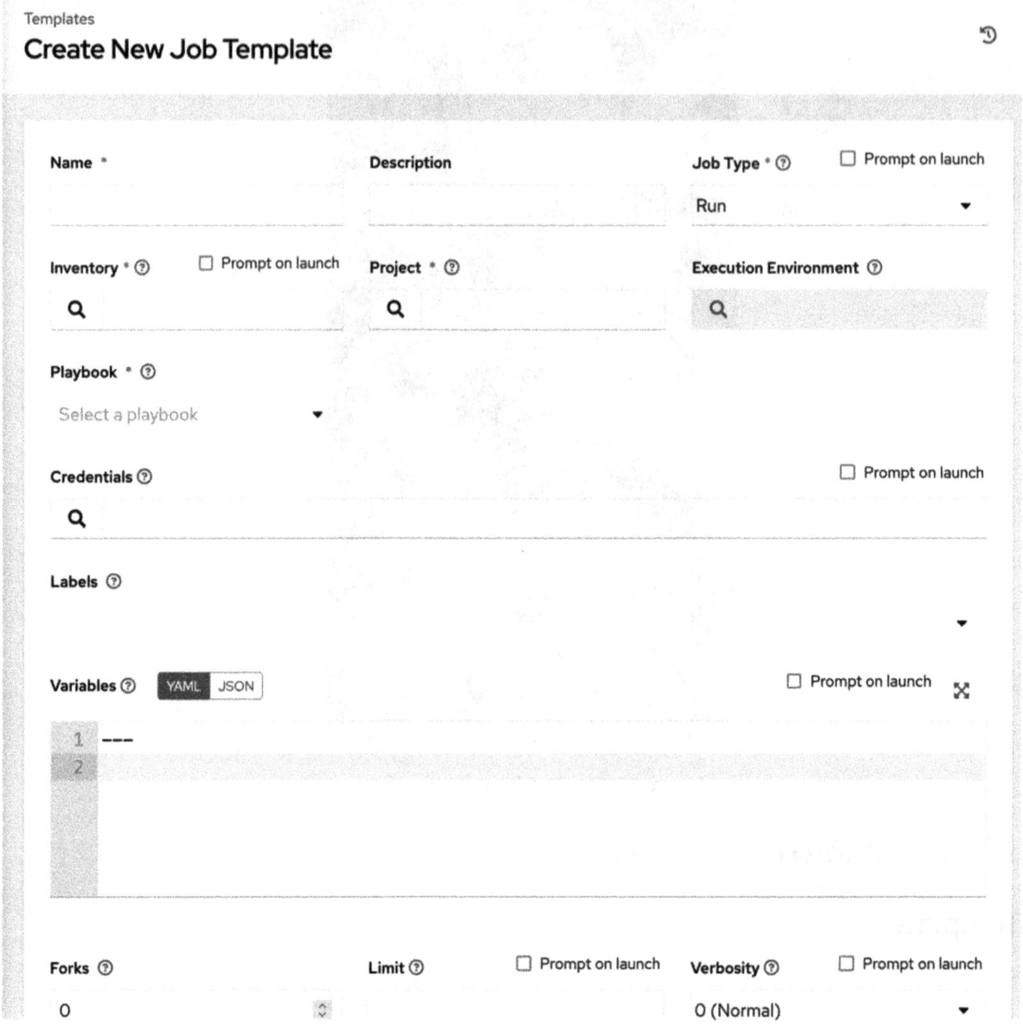

Templates
## Create New Job Template

| Name * | | Description | | Job Type * ⑦ | ☐ Prompt on launch |
|---|---|---|---|---|---|
| | | | | Run | ▾ |

| Inventory * ⑦ | ☐ Prompt on launch | Project * ⑦ | | Execution Environment ⑦ | |
|---|---|---|---|---|---|
| 🔍 | | 🔍 | | 🔍 | |

Playbook * ⑦

Select a playbook    ▾

Credentials ⑦                                                                    ☐ Prompt on launch

🔍

Labels ⑦

▾

Variables ⑦  [YAML] [JSON]                                            ☐ Prompt on launch    ⤨

```
1  ---
2
```

| Forks ⑦ | | Limit ⑦ | ☐ Prompt on launch | Verbosity ⑦ | ☐ Prompt on launch |
|---|---|---|---|---|---|
| 0 | | ⇕ | | 0 (Normal) | ▾ |

Figure 12.46 – The job template variables

4.  This time, we're going to select a playbook from the Oracle samples we selected.

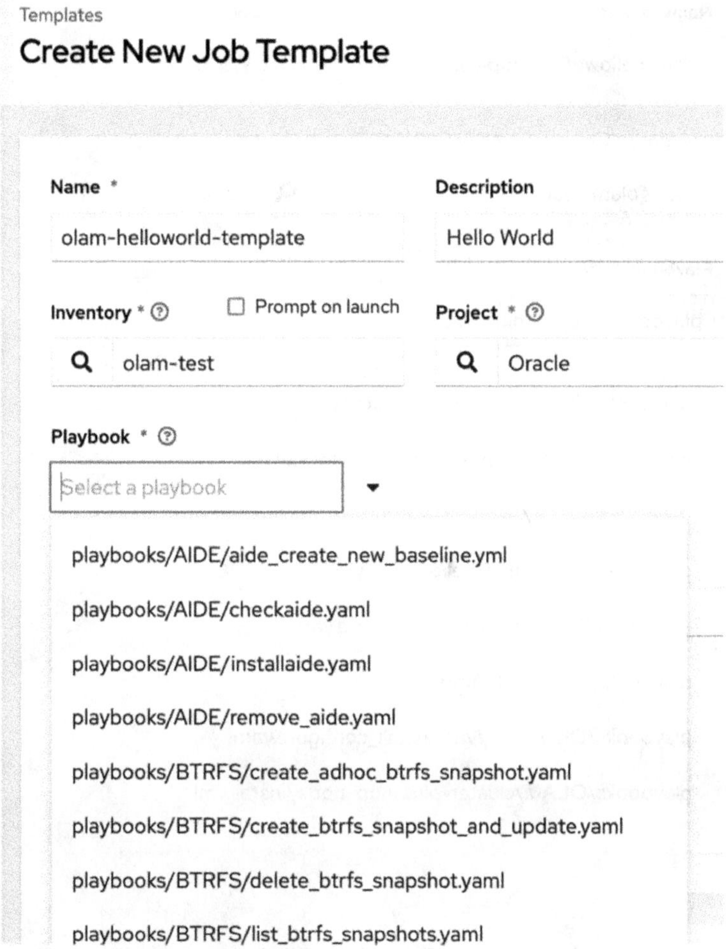

Templates

# Create New Job Template

**Name** *

olam-helloworld-template

**Description**

Hello World

**Inventory** * ⑦     ☐ Prompt on launch

Q   olam-test

**Project** * ⑦

Q   Oracle

**Playbook** * ⑦

Select a playbook     ▼

playbooks/AIDE/aide_create_new_baseline.yml

playbooks/AIDE/checkaide.yaml

playbooks/AIDE/installaide.yaml

playbooks/AIDE/remove_aide.yaml

playbooks/BTRFS/create_adhoc_btrfs_snapshot.yaml

playbooks/BTRFS/create_btrfs_snapshot_and_update.yaml

playbooks/BTRFS/delete_btrfs_snapshot.yaml

playbooks/BTRFS/list_btrfs_snapshots.yaml

Figure 12.47 – The Oracle Git sample playbook selection

5.    We want to select the Oracle Hello World playbook:

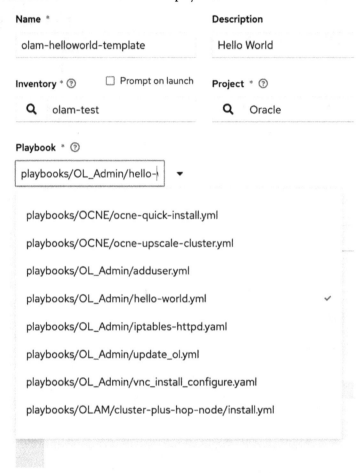

**Name** *

olam-helloworld-template

**Description**

Hello World

**Inventory** * ⑦          ☐ Prompt on launch

Q    olam-test

**Project** * ⑦

Q    Oracle

**Playbook** * ⑦

playbooks/OL_Admin/hello-    ▼

playbooks/OCNE/ocne-quick-install.yml

playbooks/OCNE/ocne-upscale-cluster.yml

playbooks/OL_Admin/adduser.yml

playbooks/OL_Admin/hello-world.yml                    ✓

playbooks/OL_Admin/iptables-httpd.yaml

playbooks/OL_Admin/update_ol.yml

playbooks/OL_Admin/vnc_install_configure.yaml

playbooks/OLAM/cluster-plus-hop-node/install.yml

Figure 12.48 – The Hello World playbook

6.   Make sure to assign **Privileged Escalation** access to the template.

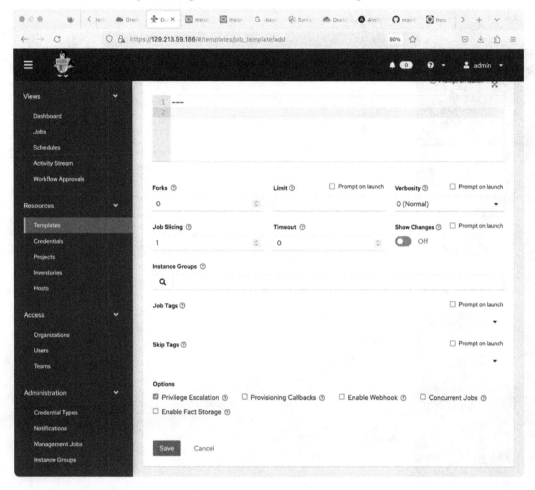

Figure 12.49 – Job privilege credentials

7.    Save your template, which will bring you to the **Details** page.

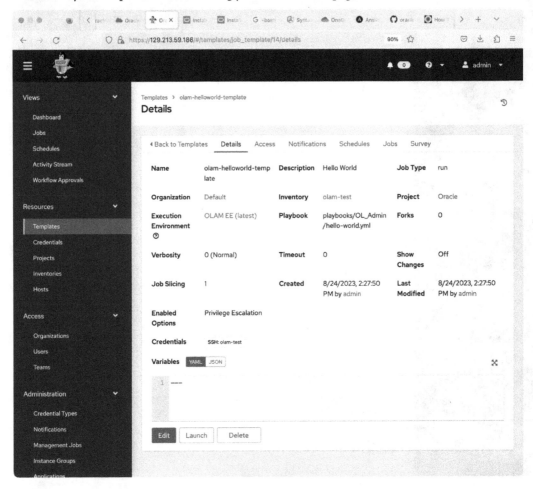

Figure 12.50 – The job configuration details

8.  You can launch the template to see the results.

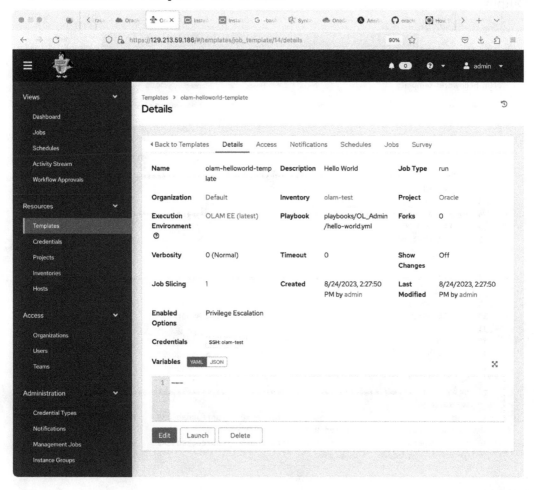

Figure 12.51 – The job launch

9.  Remember that your results will appear under the **Output** tab.

Figure 12.52 – The job output and results

## Controlling the patching chaos

Patching is a curse word to many, a comfort to some, and necessary to all. There is certainly a rational fear regarding patching on when to patch, how to patch, and what to patch. The who, what, where, when, and how words apply here too. These concerns are legitimate; I mean who wants to patch? It can be messy, and it's time-consuming. We may not be able to mitigate the concerns, but we can shorten the time taken to automate. This is one aspect where automation helps to speed up operations, and it eases the frustration of having to patch multiple environments.

A common automation question is, "What can we do to minimize what we can, and what do we have to do manually?" The concept that we'll be able to create a playbook for anything and automate everything is simply not realistic. Firstly, there are some things we wouldn't want to automate, and that depends on who you work for, or your organization's policies and **standard operating procedures (SOPs)** toward automation. I've worked with certain defense contractors and agencies that have multiple boards voting on what automations are allowed, and they were very particular on what was and wasn't approved. However, overall, automation is a great equalizer in saving us time and energy.

This recipe will walk through patching at a high level and help you understand how automation can go beyond, saving time and energy by automating repeatable steps.

## Getting ready

Before we institute any playbooks, we have to make sure we have all the prerequisites in place, including writing the playbook itself. In this case, we will write a basic playbook, update the YUM repository on two servers, and reboot those servers after the update is complete. This can be expanded into multiple OSs, kernels, and/or application patching – the sky's the limit.

## How to do it...

1. As mentioned previously, we need to first examine and create a new playbook for our patching effort here. In order to do that, we will navigate to our template (playbook):

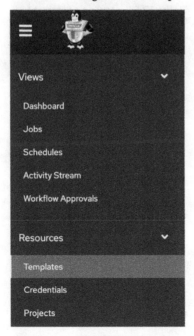

Figure 12.53 – The Templates option

2.  As mentioned previously, we have the template we wrote earlier. However, we're going to click on **Add** to create another.

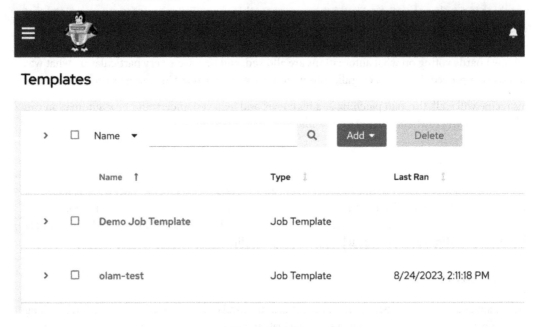

Figure 12.54 – Adding a template

3.  Select **Add job template**.

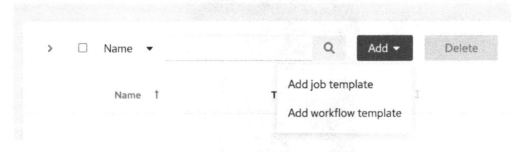

Figure 12.55 – Adding a job template

4. You'll want to follow the same flow that we used for the initial template we created. However, this time, we're going to select a different playbook:

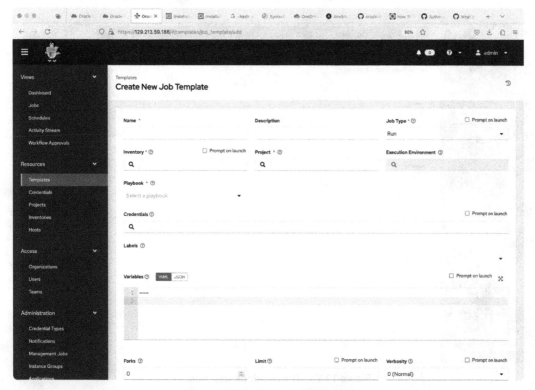

Figure 12.56 – Adding job variables

5.  We'll name this one `Patching`, and we'll select the updated YUM playbook.

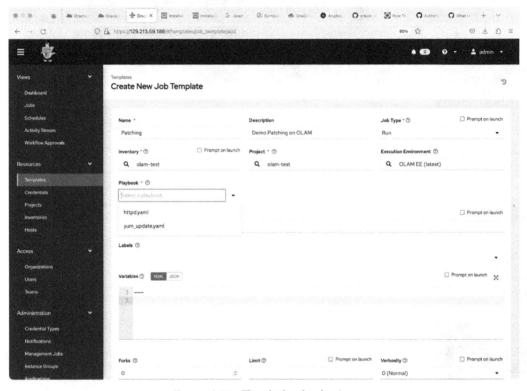

Figure 12.57 – The playbook selection

6.  As shown in the following screenshot, the template is fully populated.

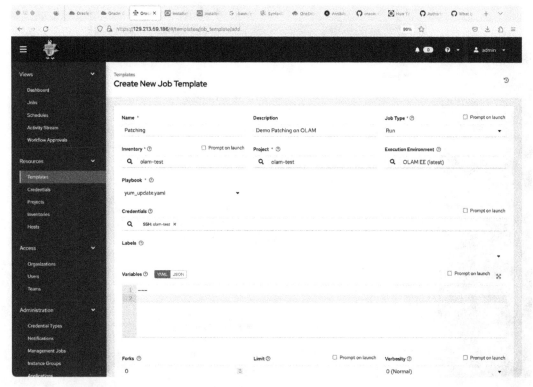

Figure 12.58 – Job variables

7.  Make sure to give your template **Privileged Escalation** access, meaning admin access.

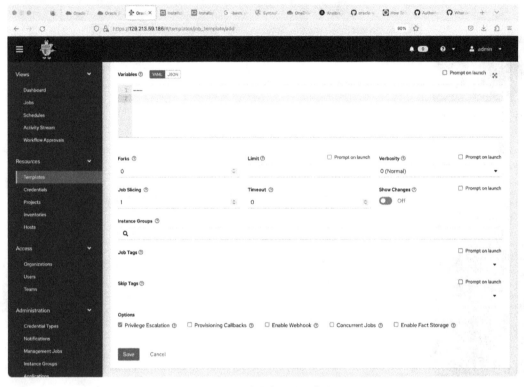

Figure 12.59 – Privilege Escalation

8. Save your template, which will bring you to your template's **Details** screen.

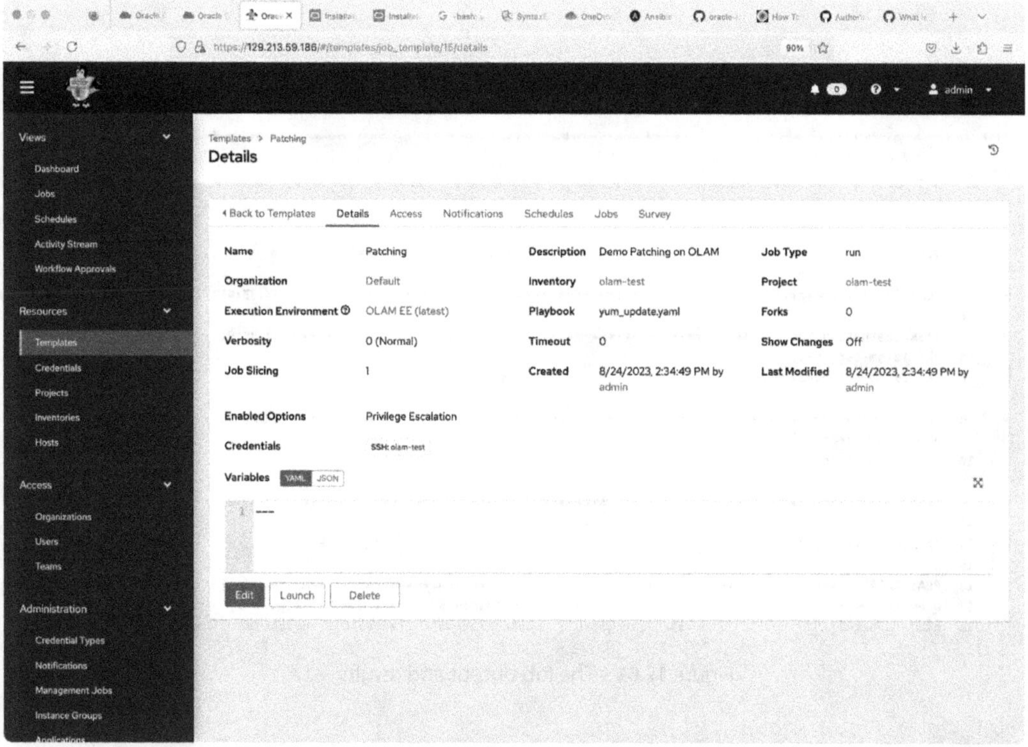

Figure 12.60 – The job configuration details and launch

9. Execute your template and playbook by clicking on **Launch**. The output of your template will be under the **Output** tab and will show any errors, omissions, and/or success. Remember to read through the output because you can have successful output with errors and/or skipped/missed steps.

Figure 12.61 – The job output and results

# Look beyond automation

Before we can create any resources, we need to have a place to create those resources. In this case, we're using OCI as our incubator, so obviously, we need to add OCI to our OLAM instance. In order to do this, we need to create credentials to allow OLAM to access OCI. This doesn't stop at OCI. OLAM is your doorway into hybrid cloud solutions. You can deploy on-premises solutions through virtualization fabrics and HCI solutions such as VxRail, VMware, and OpenStack. We won't be covering hybrid cloud solutions in this recipe, although we did cover hybrid cloud in past recipes, such as migrating a virtual machine as a template into OCI or uploading an image to create an AMI image in AWS. These techniques can also be used in hybrid cloud scenarios, working with and moving workloads' ingress and egress to **cloud service providers (CSPs)**. As you can see, the possibilities are there, and they are endless.

To delve a little further into **IaC** (**Infrastructure as Code**), we have to look at the definition of infrastructure as a service. Take a step back and reframe the way you think about infrastructure, and then reconstitute that in your head as moving numbers, fields, and landscapes. That's what IaC is; it's an ever-evolving landscape that keeps on changing its definition to match what the end state is. Have you ever played the game *Tetris*? IaC looks and feels like *Tetris*, although, in this case, we win every time; we're just fitting pieces next to one another, creating an environment that matches what we need it to look like. There are so many different variables we can use to transform our everyday tasks into IaC – for example, expanding compute, storage, and/or network.  For example, imagine we have virtual machine A, an image for web servers. We have two web servers deployed for a small university. That university has challenges during general admissions periods and needs to expand seamlessly. We can use autoscaling or workload expansion to implement new web servers, supplementing the university's needs until the requirement expires. These examples are a little more intensive than the example in this recipe, but it's essential to see the value of code as we move along this freeway of change in an evolving IT landscape.

## Getting ready

Ansible provides building blocks for platform configuration and managing compute instances. In this recipe, we're going to take a different look at Ansible, and we'll see how to use it to write a playbook to instantiate a new virtual machine in OCI. We're going to learn the basics of playbooks, beyond using the predefined Oracle basics we explored a couple of recipes ago, to discover the benefits of IaC through Ansible, and we'll also learn how to create a foundation for Ansible to be used in the form of playbooks. Lastly, you'll learn how to create playbooks and configure and manage resources on OCI.

To start, we need to configure our environment. This includes connecting our OLAM instance to OCI. This will allow us to execute our playbook in our OCI tenancy.

1.  First, we need to go to **Credentials**.

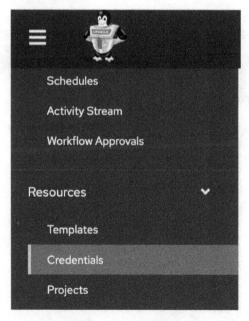

Figure 12.62 – The Credentials option

2.   You'll want to add a credential for OCI.

## Credentials

Figure 12.63 – Adding credentials

3.   You'll have to collect the following information from your OCI tenancy – the user **Oracle Cloud Identifier** (**OCID**), fingerprint, tenant OCID, and region. All these can be found under **User** | **User settings** | **API Keys**.

Navigate and log in to your OCI console, and go to the user (the person icon on the right-hand side):

Figure 12.64 – The user icon on the right-hand side

Then, navigate to **User settings**:

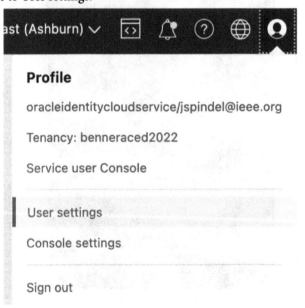

Figure 12.65 – The OCI User settings option

All the data will be under **API Keys**:

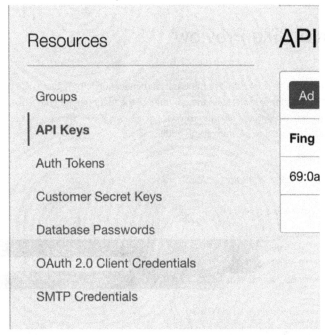

Figure 12.66 – The OCI API Keys menu

4. Make sure to select the **View Configuration file** option:

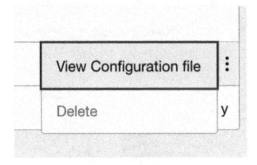

Figure 12.67 – Configuration file

5.    All the data you need for the OCI setting in OLAM will be in this configuration file:

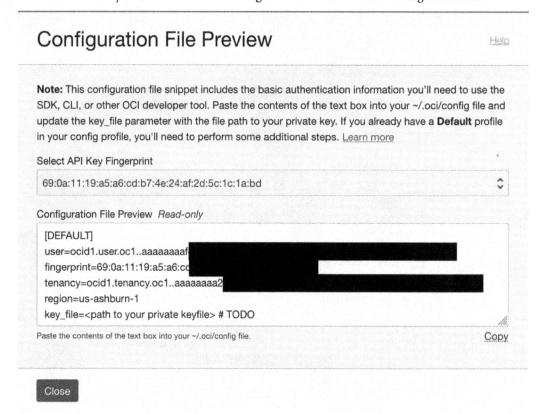

Figure 12.68 – The configuration file details

6.   Enter all the collected information.

Figure 12.69 – The credential variables for the OCI user OCID, fingerprint, and tenant OCID

7.   Don't forget to cut and paste in the private user key used to access your OCI account. This is the key you have on your system that you use to log in to OCI.

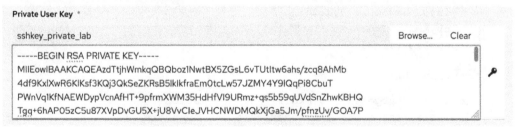

Figure 12.70 – The OCI private key

8.  Save the credential, which will bring you to the **Details** page, showing you a summary of the credential you just configured.

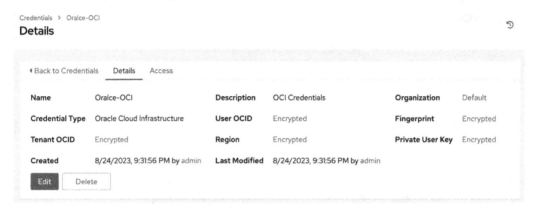

Figure 12.71 – The OCI OLAM credential configuration details

## How to do it...

1.  Check the version of Ansible core:

```
[opc@olam-target-1 ~]$ ansible --version
ansible [core 2.14.2]
   config file = /etc/ansible/ansible.cfg
   configured module search path = ['/home/opc/.ansible/plugins/
modules', '/usr/share/ansible/plugins/modules']
   ansible python module location = /usr/lib/python3.11/site-
packages/ansible
   ansible collection location = /home/opc/.ansible/collections:/
usr/share/ansible/collections
   executable location = /usr/bin/ansible
   python version = 3.11.2 (main, Jun 14 2023, 13:00:29) [GCC
8.5.0 20210514 (Red Hat 8.5.0-18.0.2)] (/usr/bin/python3.11)
   jinja version = 3.1.2
   libyaml = True
[opc@olam-target-1 ~]$
```

2.  Create an inventory:

```
[opc@olam-target-1 ~]$ mkdir ~/ol-automation
[opc@olam-target-1 ol-automation]$ vi inventory
130.61.100.96
~
~
```

```
~
~
```

3.  View and confirm the inventory list:

```
[opc@olam-target-1 ol-automation]$ ansible-inventory -i
inventory --list
{
    "_meta": {
        "hostvars": {}
    },
    "all": {
        "children": [
            "ungrouped"
        ]
    },
    "ungrouped": {
        "hosts": [
            "130.61.100.96"
        ]
    }
}
[opc@olam-target-1 ol-automation]$
```

4.  Add a group to the inventory:

```
[opc@olam-target-1 ol-automation]$ vi inventory

[preproduction]
130.61.100.96
~
~
~
~
```

5.  Run the inventory list again, as shown here:

```
[opc@olam-target-1 ol-automation]$ ansible-inventory -i
inventory --list
{
    "_meta": {
        "hostvars": {}
    },
    "all": {
        "children": [
            "ungrouped",
```

```
                "preproduction"
            ]
        },
        "preproduction": {
            "hosts": [
                "130.61.100.96"
            ]
        }
    }
}
```

6.  Run `ping` to verify your inventory:

```
[opc@olam-target-1 ol-automation]$ ansible all -i inventory -m
ping
olam-target-1 | SUCCESS => {
    "ansible_facts": {
        "discovered_interpreter_python": "/usr/bin/python"
    },
    "changed": false,
    "ping": "pong"
}
```

7.  Create your playbook:

```
[opc@olam-target-1 ansible]$ sudo vi packt.yml
---
- hosts: olam-target-2
  tasks:
    - name: Print message
      debug:
        msg: Hello from Packt Oracle Linux 8 Cookbook
~
~
~
~
```

8.  Run your playbook:

```
[opc@olam-target-1 ansible]$ ansible-playbook -i inventory
packt.yml

PLAY [all] **********************************************************
***************
TASK [Gathering Facts] *********************************************
***************
```

```
[WARNING]: Platform linux on host olam-target-2 is using the
discovered Python
interpreter at /usr/bin/python, but future installation of
another Python
interpreter could change this. See https://docs.ansible.com/
ansible/2.14.2/referen
ce_appendices/interpreter_discovery.html for more information.
ok: [olam-target-2]
TASK [Print message] ********************************************
****************
ok: [olam-target-2] => {
    "msg": "Hello from Packt Oracle Linux 8 Cookbook"
}
PLAY RECAP ******************************************************
****************
olam-target-2:
ok=2      changed=0      unreachable=0      failed=0      skipped=0
       rescued=0      ignored=0
```

# Set it and forget it

In Ansible playbooks, loops provide flexibility and efficiency to automate Oracle Linux environments or any Linux environment through OLAM. Users can define dictionaries in their playbooks and use loop statements. Dictionaries are like books, with all your infrastructure or applications in lists, and they can be used to describe variables in an automation. This allows a set of tasks to be executed for each item in the loop, reducing the need for repetitive coding and making playbooks more concise and manageable.

For instance, if you want to install multiple packages on a group of Oracle Linux servers without loops, you would need to write separate tasks for each package and server. However, by using loops in OLAM with Ansible, you can define a list of packages and a list of servers and iterate over them, installing the packages on each server in a single task.

## Getting ready

In the previous recipe, we've shown that OLAM has additional features and capabilities that enhance automation capabilities, through either the web-based UI or the command line. Users can granularly and visually define and manage their automation workflows, simplifying the process of creating and managing complex automation tasks. Furthermore, this provides a centralized platform to manage and monitor the execution of Ansible playbooks.

In the following example, we have two sample servers, the same target-1 and target-2 servers from the previous recipe, and we need to change the permissions of a specific user on both servers. Without using loops, we would need to write separate tasks for each server, resulting in redundant code. However, by utilizing loops, we can simplify the playbook and make it more efficient.

In this example, we will start by defining the playbook's name and the target hosts, using the `hosts` directive. We will also set `become` as `true`, indicating that the playbook should run with administrative privileges:

```yaml
---
- name: Change User Permissions
  hosts: server_group
  become: true

  vars:
    target_users:
      - user1
      - user2

  tasks:
    - name: Change user permissions
      file:
        path: /home/{{ item }}/documents
        owner: {{ item }}
        group: {{ item }}
        mode: "0755"
      with_items: "{{ target_users }}"
```

Next, we define a variable, `target_users`, that contains a list of users for whom we want to change permissions. In this case, we have `user1` and `user2` as our target users.

The `tasks` section contains a single task named `Change user permissions`. This task uses the `file` module to change the ownership, group, and mode of the specified directory.

The `with_items` loop is used to iterate over the `target_users` list. Each iteration of the loop sets the `item` variable to the current user from the list. This variable is then used in the `path`, `owner`, and `group` parameters of the `file` module.

By using this loop, the playbook will execute the task for each user in the `target_users` list, effectively changing the permissions for both user and folder permissions:

```yaml
- name: Change user permissions
  hosts: all
  tasks:
    - name: Change permissions for users
      file:
        path: /path/to/directory
```

```
      owner: "{{ item }}"
      state: directory
    loop: "{{ users }}"
```

In the preceding example, `file` is used to change the ownership of the specified directory to each user in the `users` list. The `item` variable represents the current user in the loop.

By following these steps, you can write and execute an Ansible loop in OLAM to change user permissions in different servers and the described directories. This will allow you to automate the process and ensure consistent permissions across multiple systems, among many other aspects of administering multiple environments.

## How to do it...

1.  You'll need to write the playbook first; I have used the demo project for simplicity purposes:

```
[opc@olam-test /]$ cd /var/lib/awx/
[opc@olam-test awx]$ ls
awxfifo  projects  rsyslog  uwsgi.stats  venv
[opc@olam-test awx]$ cd projects/
[opc@olam-test projects]$ cd demo_bundled/
[opc@olam-test demo_bundled]$ ls
httpd.yaml  permissions.yaml  yum_update.yaml
[opc@olam-test demo_bundled]$
[opc@olam-test demo_bundled]$ sudo vi change_permissions.yaml
---
- name: Change file permissions
  hosts: olam-test-1, olam-test-2
  become: true
  tasks:
    - name: Change permissions for /tmp/changedir
      file:
        path: /tmp/changedir
        owner: root
        group: root
        mode: "0755"
...
[opc@olam-target-2 tmp]$ ls -ltr
total 0
drwxr-xr-x. 2 root root 6 Oct 18 11:53 unified-monitoring-agent
drwxrwxr-x. 2 opc  opc  6 Oct 26 15:27 changedir
[opc@olam-target-2 tmp]$
```

2.  Each component of the playbook is separated into its own section to simplify the loop topology. The following components are included:

    - `name`: This is the name of the playbook.

    - `hosts`: This specifies the target servers where the playbook will be executed. You can define the hosts directly in the playbook or use an inventory file.

    - `become: true`: This allows the playbook to run with elevated privileges, which might be required to change user permissions.

    - `tasks`: This section contains the list of tasks to be executed.

    - `name`: This is a description of the task.

    - `file`: This module is used to change the permissions of a directory.

    - `path`: This is the path to the directory where you want to change permissions.

    - `owner`: This parameter specifies the username that the ownership should be changed to. In this example, we used the `item` variable, which represents the current user in the loop.

    - `state: directory`: This ensures that the path is a directory.

3.  OLAM will execute the playbook on the specified servers, changing the user permissions for the specified directory to users `user1` and `user2` in this example.

4.  Make sure to replace `/path/to/directory` with the actual path of the directory you want to change permissions for, and update the list of users as per your requirements.

5.  Ensure that you have proper SSH connectivity and the necessary privileges to change permissions on the target servers. The following code snippet is a simple, canned YAML file depicting file permissions:

```yaml
---
- name: Change file permissions
  hosts: olam-test-1, olam-test-2
  become: true
  tasks:
    - name: Change permissions for /tmp/changedir
      file:
        path: /tmp/changedir
        owner: root
        group: root
        mode: "0755"
```

6.  OLAM will run the playbook on the specified servers, changing the permissions of `/tmp/changedir` to `root:root`, with a mode of `0755`.

7.  Save the playbook file.

8.  Ensure you have proper SSH connectivity to the target servers.

9.  Open the OLAM web-based user interface.

10. Create a new playbook in OLAM, or open an existing one.

11. Copy the content of the `change_permissions.yaml` playbook file into the playbook editor in OLAM.

12. Save the playbook in OLAM.

13. Execute the playbook by selecting the target servers (`olam-test-1` and `olam-test-2`) from the inventory, or by manually specifying their IP addresses.

14. Click on the **Run** button in OLAM to execute the playbook.

15. OLAM will run the playbook on the specified servers, changing the permissions of `/tmp/changedir` to `root:root`, with port `0755`.

# 13
# Let's All Go to the Cloud

We've come a long way when it comes to virtualization. From segmenting virtual slices and striping (precursor to virtualization) DNA sequencers across hundreds of university campuses to the most sophisticated virtual farms capable of hosting thousands of **virtual machines** (**VMs**) and petabytes of storage, they all have one thing in common: complexity. But does it really have to be complex? When I think about virtualization, I think of four resources: compute, memory, storage, and network. They all intertwine with one another to create that fabric. Without compute or memory, you can't host a workload. Without storage, you can't host or store application or workload components, and without a network, your workload can't go anywhere. Imagine your car is your workload, the highway is your network, the passengers are your compute and memory, and the trunk is storage.

In this chapter, we will run through how to find, maximize, and use Oracle Linux to its full potential in a local environment as well as a public cloud, such as **Oracle Cloud Infrastructure** (**OCI**) or **Amazon Web Services** (**AWS**). We'll run through exercises in building out a custom local Oracle Linux 8.x environment and walk through the process of moving that VM to OCI as an image, as well as to other **cloud service providers** (**CSPs**) including AWS as an AMI. *Cloud native* is a huge buzzword and a disruptive technology. The *Making Docker Desktop more manageable with Portainer* recipe will walk through creating a Portainer environment that can manage your container ecosystem around one application.

We will cover the following recipes in this chapter:

- Oracle Linux in the cloud
- Making Docker Desktop more manageable with Portainer
- Using VirtualBox to springboard VMs to OCI
- For everyone else, let's make custom images for AWS

# Technical requirements

Generally, and in this case, it's easier to build the OS being used with a **graphical user interface** (GUI). With this being said, you can still install a GUI if you didn't build the server with a GUI originally. The following is a list of steps detailing how to add and configure a GUI:

1. Install the GUI packages:

   ```
   $ (sudo if not root) dnf groupinstall "Server with GUI"
   ```

2. Set the GUI as the default target:

   ```
   $ (sudo if not root) systemctl set-default graphical.target
   ```

3. Set the GUI as the default startup source:

   ```
   $ (sudo if not root) ln -sf /lib/systemd/system/runlevel5.target
   /etc/systemd/system/default.target
   ```

4. Restart the server:

   ```
   $ (sudo if not root) reboot (or shutdown -r now)
   ```

# Oracle Linux in the cloud

We could list all the CSPs here and break apart their pros and cons, but ultimately, every CSP has a main competency. What Oracle Linux does is add to that competency, making the product stronger and more versatile. Much like any other (open source) Linux distribution, Oracle Linux is a versatile and powerful OS. In the case of Oracle Linux, the OS was designed with elements that are compatible with RHEL, not to compete, but to add functionality as well as a portal into Oracle functionality beyond RHEL.

The fluidity of Oracle Linux, much like RHEL, allows it to go beyond just being an OS. Oracle Linux extends the playing field, maximizing the Linux toolsets surrounding virtualization into VM management through **Oracle Linux Virtualization Manager** (**OLVM**), cross-functionality into cloud platforms, and automation, just to name a few. What Oracle aims to do is to offer the functionality of an RHEL OS but go beyond that and tie that OS into a global business network of toolsets to drive business success. Now, after all the fluff comes the real power and versatility of Oracle Linux, some of which was mentioned at the beginning of this chapter. This recipe is about which CSPs are most compatible with Oracle Linux; however, understanding what and how the OS operates is integral to understanding which CSPs are more compatible with Oracle Linux and thus maximizing its capability.

Oracle supports and promotes open source technologies for business-critical environments. Oracle is a founding member of the Linux Foundation, Eclipse Foundation, and Java Community Process, and contributes significantly to open source projects. Oracle software combined with open source technologies offers high performance, reliability, and data security while reducing computing costs.

The following diagram provides a cost-benefit analysis of Oracle Linux "Free" (the only paid component is support) versus RHEL with the extended features added on, as mentioned previously.

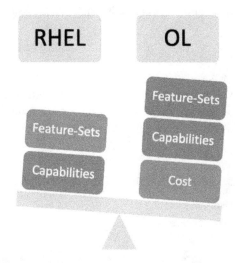

Figure 13.1 – RHEL versus Oracle Linux

As with any Linux distribution, each CSP has its own flavor or choice of Linux platform. For instance, AWS has **Amazon Linux 2 (AL2)**, Azure offers compatibility with anything RHEL or Ubuntu based, and Oracle has Oracle Linux, of course. There are so many differences between Ubuntu and Oracle Linux, AL2, and so on, but we're not here to discuss the differences. Ultimately, all CSPs can run Linux distributions, but not all are optimized for Oracle Linux. With AWS and Azure, you have the option of **Buying Your Own Support (BYOS)** from Oracle (support includes access to patching, upgrades, and OS support) or using these services for free without tech support. With OCI Premier, support is included for free. The following diagram shows the main CSPs and their differing adoptions of Oracle Linux.

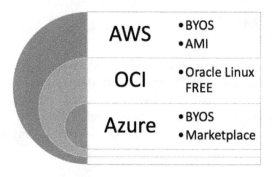

Figure 13.2 – Cloud options

Who's the fairest of them all? Let's walk through what Linux distributions are offered within AWS. We'll briefly touch on AWS EC2 Image Builder to visualize the versatility of Linux within any environment on AWS and beyond. This will come into use later in this chapter, in the *Using VirtualBox to springboard VMs to OCI* recipe.

## Getting ready

You'll first have to have an AWS account, be it personal or through your organization; it doesn't really matter so long as you have the correct authorization to access the account and build out the infrastructure. In this case, I selected **Root user**, as this is my personal account, and I have those rights.

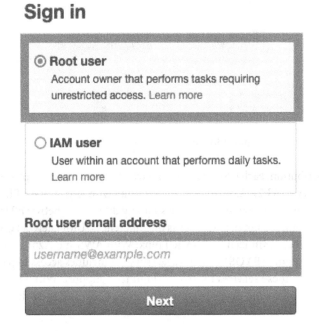

Figure 13.3 – Root sign-in

After entering your user type, you'll want to provide your password and continue through the authentication options. I've enabled **Multi-Factor Authentication** (**MFA**) and would strongly suggest using this method to protect your account. If MFA is enabled, you next walk through capturing that code, as shown in the following figure. Note that there are other two-factor authentication options, but using Google Authenticator is best practice. However, one could use any app, such as Microsoft, RSA, and so on.

Figure 13.4 – MFA

Once you're past the login and MFA sections, you'll find yourself on the AWS landing page. You'll want to navigate to EC2, AWS Compute Resources in AWS speech (CPU, RAM), to understand the flavors of Linux available and what your options are beyond the default choices that come as standard Linux images (AMIs). Note that just because a flavor isn't listed doesn't mean it isn't available: there are other options through the Marketplace or via custom images.

Figure 13.5 – Compute

Once you've entered the world of AWS EC2, the easiest way to see what's on offer is **EC2 Image Builder**. Image Builder translates the complex image world into easier-to-understand concepts that help transcribe your technical requirements into executions:

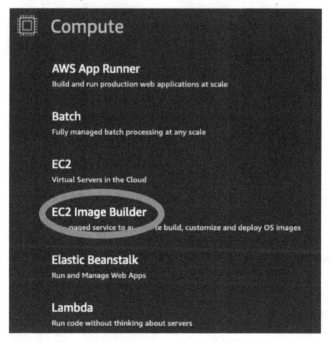

Figure 13.6 – Image Builder

After entering **Image Builder**, you'll want to navigate to **Image products**, under **Amazon Marketplace**. This is the portal to everything else offered under the AWS umbrella and will take you directly to the image products.

Figure 13.7 – Image products

> **Note**
>
> Be careful when selecting Oracle AMIs. There are third parties that will charge you to use AMIs but will not provide Oracle tech support. Some of them can get very expensive, costing you hundreds of dollars per year.

As mentioned in the preceding note, you will not find official Oracle Linux images on the **AWS Marketplace** tab. Follow the instructions in this recipe in the *How to do it...* section to access the official Oracle Linux images.

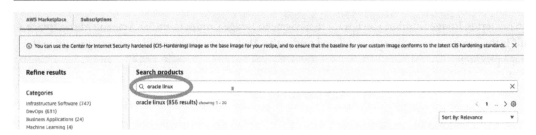

Figure 13.8 – Search in Marketplace for Oracle Linux

If you search for `oracle linux` on AWS Marketplace as in the preceding screenshot, you will only see offerings of Oracle Linux distributions built by other organizations and offered to the public through AWS Marketplace. *These are not official Oracle Linux images.* Later in this chapter, we'll walk through building a VM in Oracle VirtualBox and converting that image, through AWS, into an AMI.

## How to do it...

Here are the steps you need to follow to find Oracle AMIs:

1.   Point your browser to `https://console.aws.amazon.com/ec2/`.

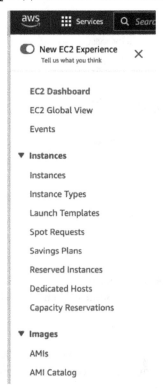

Figure 13.9 – Find AMIs under the Images dropdown

2.  In the left navigation panel, select **AMIs**, then **Public images** from the window that appears:

Figure 13.10 – Public images

3.  Filter by owner using the ID 131827586825. The ID is related to official Oracle images, and will only show official Oracle Linux AMIs created by Oracle:

| Name | | AMI name | Source | Owner |
|---|---|---|---|---|
| | AMI ID | | | |
| | AMI name | OL7.9-x86_64-HVM-2023-01-05 | 131827586825/OL7.9-x86_64-HVM-20... | 131827586825 |
| | Architecture | OL8.5-x86_64-HVM-2021-11-24 | 131827586825/OL8.5-x86_64-HVM-20... | 131827586825 |
| | Creation date | OL8.6-x86_64-HVM-2022-05-19 | 131827586825/OL8.6-x86_64-HVM-20... | 131827586825 |
| | Description | OL8.7-x86_64-HVM-2023-03-07 | 131827586825/OL8.7-x86_64-HVM-20... | 131827586825 |
| | Image size | OL8.8-arm64-HVM-2023-06-23 | 131827586825/OL8.8-arm64-HVM-20... | 131827586825 |
| | Image type | OL8.8-x86_64-HVM-2023-06-21 | 131827586825/OL8.8-x86_64-HVM-20... | 131827586825 |
| | Kernel ID | OL9.0-x86_64-HVM-2022-07-28 | 131827586825/OL9.0-x86_64-HVM-20... | 131827586825 |
| | Owner | | | |

Figure 13.11 – Oracle AMIs

4.  Select the official Oracle AMI you wish to use. After choosing the AMI, simply launch the AMI to continue the configuration of resources and the OS:

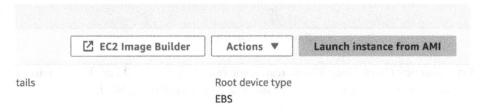

Figure 13.12 – Instance launch

5.  After launching, this will bring you to the OS image and VM buildout page (see the following figure). Here, you add a suitable name for your VM and choose the OS and network keypair for your VM, as shown in the following instance launch window.

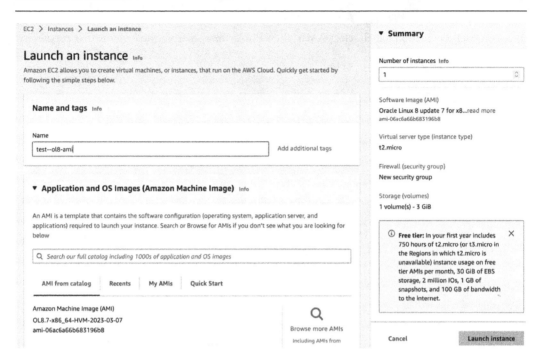

Figure 13.13 – Instance configuration

6.    Once you've launched your new VM from the chosen AMI, you'll see the launch status:

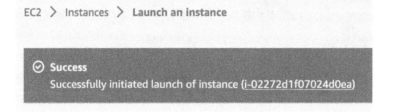

Figure 13.14 – Launch status

7.    Once your new Oracle Linux VM is created, you can visualize that VM on the **Compute | EC2 | Images** tab in OCI. Then, click on the instance ID and copy the public IP address.

Figure 13.15 – Public IP

8.  Open either PuTTY or a terminal, depending on whether you're on a Windows machine or a Mac, and ssh to your machine using OPC as the user (this is the default Oracle user; these terms are changeable, but we won't go into this here). The first time, running the ssh command will add the key pair permanently for authentication to the list of known hosts:

```
% ssh opc@18.116.203.168
The authenticity of host '18.116.203.168 (18.116.203.168)' can't
be established.
ED25519 key fingerprint is
SHA256:HS1eSJOOs3s1MxDU41nYfDkxMQ7uocISC211xLnQJTk.
This key is not known by any other names
Are you sure you want to continue connecting (yes/no/
[fingerprint])? yes
Warning: Permanently added '18.116.203.168' (ED25519) to the
list of known hosts.
```

# Making Docker Desktop more manageable with Portainer

Portainer is a container management platform, as mentioned in the introduction to this chapter. Portainer was originally designed as a UI for Docker, but now it supports several other container environments as well. With over 1 million users and a significant presence on GitHub, Portainer offers two versions: the free and open source **Community Edition** (CE) and a paid **Enterprise Edition** (EE). In this recipe, we will be working with the free and open source version.

If you prefer managing your containers through a GUI, Portainer is an excellent option. While CLI commands and API endpoints are great for development, a GUI is often more user-friendly for managing production applications. With Portainer, you can easily monitor multiple endpoints and grant team members access to a shared deployment environment. The following figure shows how Portainer and the container images align with Docker, and how Portainer makes managing images simpler. Portainer offers a UI over the Docker CLI, making it easier for the layman and seasoned engineer alike to navigate container management.

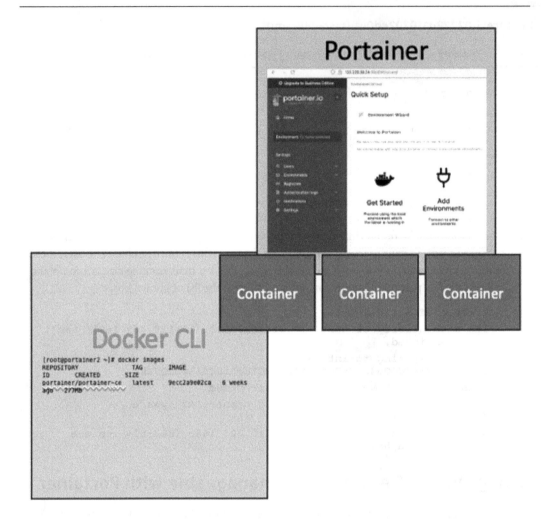

Figure 13.16 – Portainer container management

Portainer is usually deployed within its own container. If you are using Docker, this guide will help you get Portainer up and running. However, if you prefer to use Kubernetes, you can also run Portainer directly using the official Helm chart. Here's a brief overview of the steps you need to take to set up Portainer:

1. Install Docker.

2. Create and configure a container for Portainer.

3. Open the necessary ports and configure OCI accordingly.

4. Log in to the Portainer interface and set up the UI.

The following sections will provide a detailed explanation of each step. Before proceeding, make sure you have installed Docker. If you're using a Windows or Mac computer, you can download and install the latest version of the Docker Desktop installer. Linux users can experiment with the beta version of Docker Desktop for Linux or use the following instructions to install Docker Engine. For this guide, we'll be creating an Oracle Linux VM in the OCI cloud and installing Portainer on that VM, rather than in a local environment.

## Getting ready

There's some initial work to carry out. As mentioned previously, Docker is a container management environment. Portainer, in this recipe, will reside in a Docker container, so we will need to install and configure Docker. You'll reuse some of these skills again later on in this chapter when it comes to creating images. Indeed, this foundational work we're doing here will help you throughout this chapter, as these skills lay the groundwork for managing Oracle Linux environments, whether they're in the cloud or on-premises.

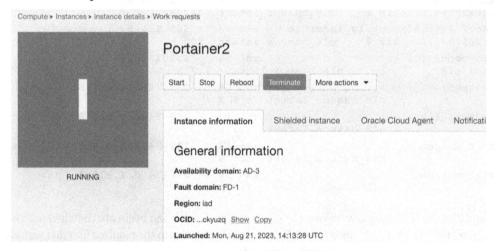

Figure 13.17 – Portainer VM creation

The information required to log in to the Portainer VM is located in the image data, as shown previously. Remember, just like in the previous chapters related to creating VMs in OCI, to create and add the public key. As we saw previously, this is the only way you'll be able to log in to this environment.

Log in to the VM as shown, using the default OPC user:

```
% ssh opc@132.226.58.24
Activate the web console with: systemctl enable --now cockpit.socket

Last login: Mon Aug 21 14:15:13 2023 from 107.200.172.229
[opc@portainer2 ~]$
```

After logging in, you'll want to update the repositories. To do this, as in the other recipes in this cookbook, you'll need superuser privileges. The following output from the update was truncated for length:

```
[opc@portainer2 ~]$ sudo su -
Last login: Mon Aug 21 15:28:41 GMT 2023 on pts/0
[root@portainer2 ~]# yum upgrade -y && yum update -y
=======================================================================
=================================
Package                          Arch        Version
Repository             Size
=======================================================================
=================================
Upgrading:
 cloud-init                       noarch      22.1-
8.0.4.el8_8.1               o18_appstream       1.1 M
 iscsi-initiator-utils            x86_64      6.2.1.4-8.
git095f59c.0.1.el8_8    o18_baseos_latest  382 k
 iscsi-initiator-utils-iscsiuio   x86_64      6.2.1.4-8.
git095f59c.0.1.el8_8    o18_baseos_latest  102 k
 microcode_ctl                    x86_64      4:20230214-
2.0.3.el8               o18_baseos_latest  7.7 M
 systemd                          x86_64      239-74.0.4.el8_8.
3                    o18_baseos_latest  3.6 M
 systemd-libs                     x86_64      239-74.0.4.el8_8.
3                    o18_baseos_latest  1.1 M
 systemd-pam                      x86_64      239-74.0.4.el8_8.
3                    o18_baseos_latest  506 k
 systemd-udev                     x86_64      239-74.0.4.el8_8.
3                    o18_baseos_latest  1.6 M
```

After updating the repositories, we're ready to start installing Docker and begin our container journey. In order to install Docker, we'll need to install the ZIP utilities to unzip the required files that we have downloaded. To do this, we'll use the dnf command:

```
[root@portainer2 ~]# dnf install -y dnf-utils zip unzip
```

After installing the ZIP utilities, we'll have to enable the Docker repository in order to download Docker. The following is the command to enable the repo and add it to the repo list:

```
[root@portainer2 ~]# dnf config-manager --add-repo=https://download.
docker.com/linux/centos/docker-ce.repo
Adding repo from: https://download.docker.com/linux/centos/docker-ce.
repo
```

> **Note**
>
> We need to eliminate a vulnerability that allows attackers to overwrite the host `runc` binary by executing a root command with any type of container. Attackers can exploit this vulnerability to use a new container with an attacker-controlled image or infiltrate an existing container if they have previous write access:
>
> ```
> [root@portainer2 ~]# dnf remove -y runc
> ```

Install Docker using the following `dnf` command. The following output has been truncated for length:

```
[root@portainer2 ~]# dnf install -y docker-ce --nobest
Docker CE Stable -
x86_64                                                          1.3 MB/s
|  49 kB     00:00
Dependencies resolved.
 Package                         Arch      Version
          Repository                 Size
Installing:
 docker-ce                       x86_64    3:24.0.5-1.
el8                                docker-ce-stable    24 M
...
[Truncated due to length]
...
Complete!
```

Once Docker is installed, we can move on to enabling the Docker service and starting Docker Engine. In order to enable the Docker service, we need to use `systemctl`, as shown in the following snippet:

```
[root@portainer2 ~]# systemctl enable docker.service
Created symlink /etc/systemd/system/multi-user.target.wants/docker.
service → /usr/lib/systemd/system/docker.service.
```

Once the service is enabled, we can move to start the Docker service/Docker Engine. We'll once again be using `systemctl` to call Docker Engine to start:

```
[root@portainer2 ~]# systemctl start docker.service
```

After starting the service, we'll want to ascertain the status of the service to be assured that Docker has started properly and the service is running and healthy:

```
[root@portainer2 ~]# systemctl status docker.service
● docker.service - Docker Application Container Engine
   Loaded: loaded (/usr/lib/systemd/system/docker.service; enabled;
vendor preset: disabled)
   Active: active (running) since Mon 2023-08-21 15:50:49 GMT; 1min
19s ago
     Docs: https://docs.docker.com
```

```
  Main PID: 76180 (dockerd)
     Tasks: 9
    Memory: 28.2M
    CGroup: /system.slice/docker.service
            └─76180 /usr/bin/dockerd -H fd:// --containerd=/run/
containerd/containerd.sock

Aug 21 15:50:48 portainer2 systemd[1]: Starting Docker Application
Container Engine...
...
Truncated due to length lines 1-20/20 (END)
...
```

Now that our Docker Engine is up and running, we want to see what Docker version is running, as well as its health and all other Docker Engine-related data:

```
[root@portainer2 ~]# docker info
Client: Docker Engine - Community
 Version:    24.0.5
 Context:    default
 Debug Mode: false
 Plugins:
  buildx: Docker Buildx (Docker Inc.)
    Version:  v0.11.2
    Path:     /usr/libexec/docker/cli-plugins/docker-buildx
  compose: Docker Compose (Docker Inc.)
    Version:  v2.20.2
    Path:     /usr/libexec/docker/cli-plugins/docker-compose

Server:
 Containers: 0
  Running: 0
  Paused: 0
  Stopped: 0
 Images: 0
 Server Version: 24.0.5
 Storage Driver: overlay2
  Backing Filesystem: xfs
  Supports d_type: true
  Using metacopy: false
  Native Overlay Diff: false
  userxattr: false
 Logging Driver: json-file
 Cgroup Driver: cgroupfs
```

```
Cgroup Version: 1
Plugins:
 Volume: local
 Network: bridge host ipvlan macvlan null overlay
 Log: awslogs fluentd gcplogs gelf journald json-file local
logentries splunk syslog
 Swarm: inactive
 Runtimes: runc io.containerd.runc.v2
 Default Runtime: runc
 Init Binary: docker-init
 containerd version: 8165feabfdfe38c65b599c4993d227328c231fca
 runc version: v1.1.8-0-g82f18fe
 init version: de40ad0
 Security Options:
  seccomp
   Profile: builtin
 Kernel Version: 5.15.0-103.114.4.el8uek.x86_64
 Operating System: Oracle Linux Server 8.8
 OSType: linux
 Architecture: x86_64
 CPUs: 2
 Total Memory: 15.32GiB
 Name: portainer2
 ID: 597d584f-bf1c-4cda-aa22-8ca2c28f33c0
 Docker Root Dir: /var/lib/docker
 Debug Mode: false
 Experimental: false
 Insecure Registries:
  127.0.0.0/8
 Live Restore Enabled: false
```

Since Portainer requires a later Python environment, we'll want to be sure that the correct version is installed. Python is a prerequisite to the installation. The following command output has been truncated for length:

```
yum install -y libffi libffi-devel openssl-devel python3 python3-pip
python3-devel
Last metadata expiration check: 0:13:58 ago on Mon 21 Aug 2023
03:43:32 PM GMT.
Package libffi-3.1-24.el8.x86_64 is already installed.
Package openssl-devel-1:1.1.1k-9.el8_7.x86_64 is already installed.
Package python36-3.6.8-38.module+el8.5.0+20329+5c5719bc.x86_64 is
already installed.
Package python3-pip-9.0.3-22.el8.noarch is already installed.
Dependencies resolved.
```

```
========================================================================
=======================================
 Package              Arch      Version
                                Repository           Size
========================================================================
=======================================
Installing:

Complete!
```

To install Python, we use PIP, which is the standard package manager for Python. PIP allows you to manage and install all packages that aren't typically part of the standard Python library. Installing Python is an underlying requirement for the Portainer installation.

You'll want to exit out of root to install this version of Python:

```
[opc@portainer2 ~]$ pip install --upgrade --ignore-installed pip
setuptools
Defaulting to user installation because normal site-packages is not
writeable
Collecting pip
  Downloading pip-21.3.1-py3-none-any.whl (1.7 MB)
     |████████████████████████████████| 1.7 MB 38.3 MB/s
Collecting setuptools
  Downloading setuptools-59.6.0-py3-none-any.whl (952 kB)
     |████████████████████████████████| 952 kB 78.6 MB/s
Installing collected packages: setuptools, pip
Successfully installed pip-21.3.1 setuptools-59.6.0
```

You'll want to be root again here to install and update yum packages. Yum requires root privileges to execute, so you'll want to `sudo` or `su` to root.

After we've updated the Python installation, we need to install and update the Python library requirements for Docker and Portainer:

```
[opc@portainer2 ~]$ sudo su -
Last login: Mon Aug 21 15:33:33 GMT 2023 on pts/0
[root@portainer2 ~]# yum install -y libffi libffi-devel openssl-devel
python3 python3-pip python3-devel
```

You'll want to exit out of root here to install `docker-compose`, using Python pip to execute. Python pip is the standard for installing any Python package and is the go-to method for installing those packages in a secure manner:

```
[root@portainer2 ~]# exit
logout
[opc@portainer2 ~]$ pip3 install docker-compose
```

## How to do it...

1.  Now we're ready to start installing and configuring our Portainer environment. We'll have to first create a volume for Portainer. We do this by telling Docker to create that volume:

    ```
    [opc@portainer2 ~]$ sudo docker volume create portainer_data
    portainer_data
    ```

2.  After creating the volume, we install the Portainer container and expose the port that the Portainer UI will use, and through which we will access that UI:

    ```
    [opc@portainer2 ~]$ sudo docker run -d -p 9000:9000 --name
    portainer --restart always -v /var/run/docker.sock:/var/
    run/docker.sock -v portainer_data:/data portainer/portainer-
    ce:latest
    Unable to find image 'portainer/portainer-ce:latest' locally
    latest: Pulling from portainer/portainer-ce
    772227786281: Pull complete
    96fd13befc87: Pull complete
    5171176db7f2: Pull complete
    a143fdc4fa02: Pull complete
    b622730c7bdc: Pull complete
    c1cad9f5200f: Pull complete
    d8a77b01f2cb: Pull complete
    0d4d8543f764: Pull complete
    c6fd0bcf10c9: Pull complete
    889200668c1c: Pull complete
    4f4fb700ef54: Pull complete
    Digest: sha256:94c3056dbe879f3a3df06b427713392a0962924914f5c2fc
    557de3797f59f926
    Status: Downloaded newer image for portainer/portainer-ce:latest
    8893b79c137ab4f63bf621180a39fbfed744731a5f9c038218a54a8b05422c2c
    ```

3.  Once Portainer is installed, next run `docker ps` to ascertain which containers are running and their health, within Docker Engine.

```
[opc@portainer2 ~]$ sudo docker ps
CONTAINER ID   IMAGE                         COMMAND        CREATED       STATUS        PORTS                                                                  NAMES
8893b79c137a   portainer/portainer-ce:latest "/portainer"   2 weeks ago   Up 2 minutes  8000/tcp, 9443/tcp, 0.0.0.0:9000->9000/tcp, :::9000->9000/tcp          portainer
```

Figure 13.18 – Docker containers running

4.  Once Portainer is installed, and `docker ps` shows Portainer is up and running, we'll have to make sure OCI is configured to allow port `9000` to be visible. In order to expose this port, we'll have to inform OCI of the **Virtual Cloud Network (VCN)** we're working in to allow that port to open.

Networking » Virtual cloud networks » vb-oci-test » Security List Details

Figure 13.19 – Security list navigation

After we have navigated to the relevant security list, we'll want to create a rule like that shown in the following screenshot.

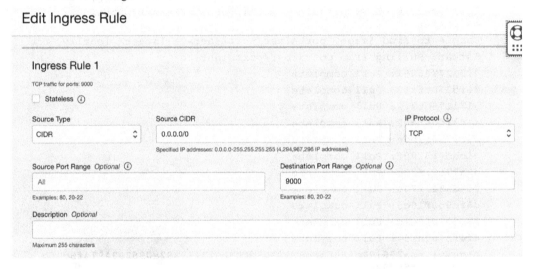

Figure 13.20 – VCN security list rule creation

Once the rule is created, we can see the port exposed outside of OCI.

Figure 13.21 – Security list rule

We're able to open a browser and access the Portainer UI. In order to reach the UI, we need two items, the VM's public IP and the port. The following screenshot shows the port, `9000`, and the IP is the same IP we used to access the VM when we used `ssh` to log in to the VM.

You can also find the IP on the OCI console. Navigate to your VM from the **Compute** menu, then go to **Instance**, which will take you to all your created VMs in the OCI console menu. Then, copy the IP address of the VM, as shown in the following screenshot.

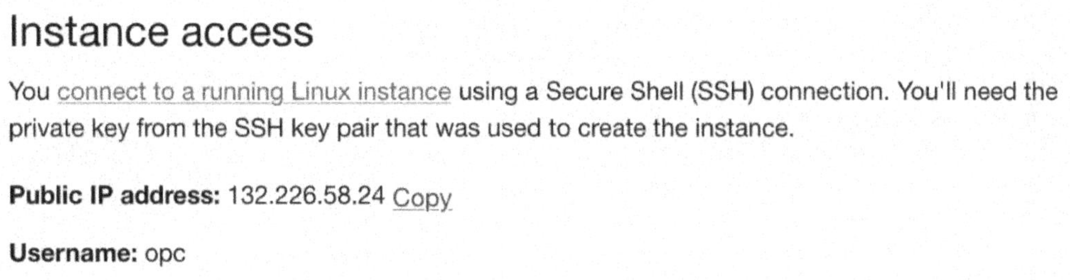

## Instance access

You connect to a running Linux instance using a Secure Shell (SSH) connection. You'll need the private key from the SSH key pair that was used to create the instance.

**Public IP address:** 132.226.58.24 Copy

**Username:** opc

Figure 13.22 – IP of the VM

5.  Once you have the address, open your browser and enter that information in the form of `https://<IP>:9000`. In our case, this is `https://132.226.58.24:9000`.

    Note: You may have to refresh the Portainer environment if you get a stale page like the following:

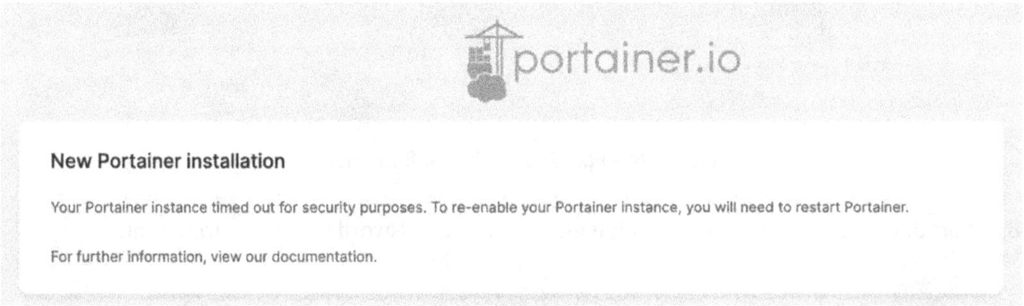

**New Portainer installation**

Your Portainer instance timed out for security purposes. To re-enable your Portainer instance, you will need to restart Portainer.

For further information, view our documentation.

Figure 13.23 – Portainer landing page

6.  In order to refresh, you'll need to restart the Portainer environment by running the `docker restart` command:

```
[opc@portainer2 ~]$ sudo docker restart portainer
portainer
```

7.  After you've restarted Portainer, you can go back to the browser and refresh the page. You should be able to hit the Portainer welcome page now.

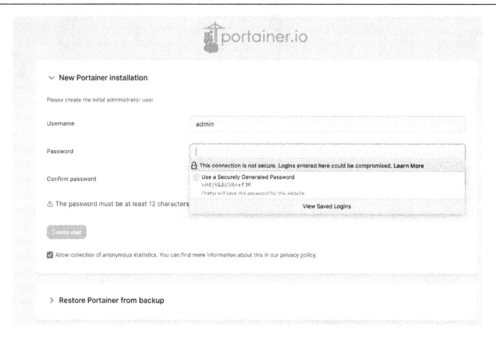

Figure 13.24 – Portainer initial configuration

8.    Portainer will make you set a 12-digit alphanumeric password for the environment.

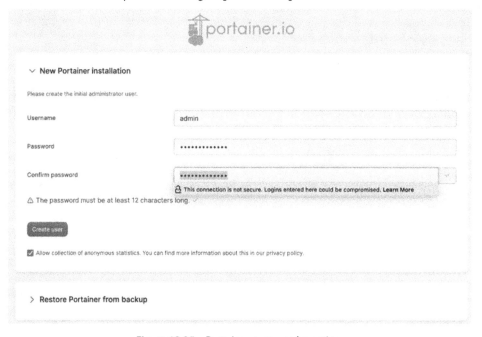

Figure 13.25 – Portainer password creation

You now have a working Portainer environment running inside a container in Docker, hosted by a VM in OCI.

## Using VirtualBox to springboard VMs to OCI

Working 9 to 5 with workloads?

One common factor in a number of these recipes is moving workloads from one environment to another. Working between different hypervisor types (e.g., VMware, KVM, and Xen) is done using common formats, such as the **Open Virtualization Format/Open Virtualization Appliance (OVF/OVA)**. Essentially, this puts components into a centrally understandable format that most virtualization host environments can understand. Images are transferable and interchangeable between virtualization formats. In this case, there are a few more puzzle pieces that need to be in place, such as network, storage, and a limitation on the number of attached drives.

Imagine a world where any workload (be it application- or database-based) can stay with you throughout the project life cycle, and be transferable between different virtualization farms, or CSPs. You can carry these created environments with you throughout your environments.

VirtualBox resides on your system as a host and is classified as a "type 2" hypervisor, allowing you to host multiple guest machines on your host environment. Your host environment, VirtualBox, has every aspect of a virtual farm that one would expect from a larger enterprise product, just broken down into much smaller and simpler parts. The compute and memory aspects are carved out from your host environment (your computer). The storage components are comprised of parts of your local hard drive, or external storage environments such as an externally attached NVMe drives. Lastly, the network is made up of bridge components, which are virtual networks that sit above your physical interfaces.

What comes first, the VM or the OS?

Every evolution begins with a foundation. Before we can even consider migrating a VM from VirtualBox to OCI, we must prepare that VM for migration. In the case of VirtualBox, there are just a couple of prework items to complete before you build a VM to migrate to a cloud environment, such as OCI. We'll walk through these prerequisites throughout this recipe. The following diagram describes the stages of configuring, installing, and migrating a VM to a CSP.

Figure 13.26 – VM configuration stages

## Getting ready

Preparing the OS isn't any different from setting the foundation before building a house. I find it easier to initially configure the OS on the VirtualBox user interface configuration, then ssh after you bring up networking and have established communication, meaning you have connectivity into the virtual machine.

There are five stages in preparing a VM image to be imported into OCI as an image. These are as follows:

1. **Interface names**: This involves standardization to ensure interface names are recognized by the host environment. This is translatable to how the host system implements networking.

2. **Interface configuration**: Here, we confirm there are no MAC addresses shown, among other pre-configuration tasks. Duplicate MAC addresses lead to extra complexity, making this a key point in configuration.

3. **GRUB(2) configuration**: This involves preparing the kernel.

4. **Serial console configuration**: This step is pretty much the number-one error on import and use. Without it, your OCI environment will fail on import, or the VM will not boot.

5. **Rebooting the OS**; that is, restarting your machine.

The following diagram walks through the configuration stages of the OS from boot to reboot:

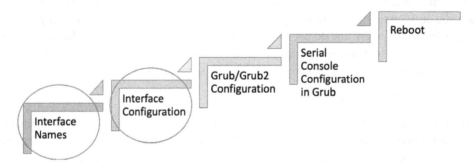

Figure 13.27 – OS configuration stages

Notice the interface names after the change:

```
[root@small-ol8 ~]# dmesg | grep -i eth
[    4.702620] e1000 0000:00:03.0 eth0: (PCI:33MHz:32-bit)
08:00:27:8d:0f:64
[    4.702628] e1000 0000:00:03.0 eth0: Intel(R) PRO/1000 Network
Connection
[    5.371103] e1000 0000:00:08.0 eth1: (PCI:33MHz:32-bit)
08:00:27:89:87:98
[    5.371132] e1000 0000:00:08.0 eth1: Intel(R) PRO/1000 Network
Connection
```

```
[     5.373296] e1000 0000:00:08.0 enp0s8: renamed from eth1
[     5.374971] e1000 0000:00:03.0 enp0s3: renamed from eth0
```

We'll need to execute the change on the kernel with the changes shown in the following code block, renaming the interface to match. This will require GRUB(2), as GRUB is the middleman between the kernel and the OS. We have the current interface names now, so where do we go from here? What we're doing here is renaming the interfaces to reflect a more acceptable name, such as net0 or Eth0. So, we have to move (mv) or rename the interface filenames:

```
[root@small-ol8 network-scripts]# mv /etc/sysconfig/network-scripts/
ifcfg-enp0s3 /etc/sysconfig/network-scripts/ifcfg-net0
[root@small-ol8 network-scripts]# mv /etc/sysconfig/network-scripts/
ifcfg-enp0s8 /etc/sysconfig/network-scripts/ifcfg-net1
```

After we rename the interfaces, we need to change the entries in the configuration files themselves to match the filename. In the following code, we're renaming the configuration of net0:

```
[root@small-ol8 network-scripts]# vi /etc/sysconfig/network-scripts/
ifcfg-net0

TYPE=Ethernet
PROXY_METHOD=none
BROWSER_ONLY=no
BOOTPROTO=dhcp
DEFROUTE=yes
IPV4_FAILURE_FATAL=no
IPV6INIT=yes
IPV6_AUTOCONF=yes
IPV6_DEFROUTE=yes
IPV6_FAILURE_FATAL=no
IPV6_ADDR_GEN_MODE=eui64
NAME=enp0s3
UUID=e9e58f08-3fcc-4a43-b605-797a6bc9998f
DEVICE=enp0s3
ONBOOT=yes

TYPE=Ethernet
PROXY_METHOD=none
BROWSER_ONLY=no
BOOTPROTO=dhcp
DEFROUTE=yes
IPV4_FAILURE_FATAL=no
IPV6INIT=yes
IPV6_AUTOCONF=yes
IPV6_DEFROUTE=yes
```

```
IPV6_FAILURE_FATAL=no
IPV6_ADDR_GEN_MODE=eui64
NAME=net0
#UUID=e9e58f08-3fcc-4a43-b605-797a6bc9998f
DEVICE=net0
ONBOOT=yes
```

We're doing the same thing here as previously, but in this case, we're changing net1:

```
[root@small-ol8 network-scripts]# vi /etc/sysconfig/network-scripts/
ifcfg-net1

TYPE=Ethernet
PROXY_METHOD=none
BROWSER_ONLY=no
BOOTPROTO=dhcp
DEFROUTE=yes
IPV4_FAILURE_FATAL=no
IPV6INIT=yes
IPV6_AUTOCONF=yes
IPV6_DEFROUTE=yes
IPV6_FAILURE_FATAL=no
IPV6_ADDR_GEN_MODE=eui64
NAME=enp0s8
UUID=eb2e5ed7-ec13-4f76-a0bf-48e7bcf45e84
DEVICE=enp0s8
ONBOOT=yes

TYPE=Ethernet
PROXY_METHOD=none
BROWSER_ONLY=no
BOOTPROTO=dhcp
DEFROUTE=yes
IPV4_FAILURE_FATAL=no
IPV6INIT=yes
IPV6_AUTOCONF=yes
IPV6_DEFROUTE=yes
IPV6_FAILURE_FATAL=no
IPV6_ADDR_GEN_MODE=eui64
NAME=net1
#UUID=eb2e5ed7-ec13-4f76-a0bf-48e7bcf45e84
DEVICE=net1
ONBOOT=yes
```

In the following code block, we're using `ip  a` to identify the interfaces and make sure our changes have taken effect:

```
[root@small-ol8 ~]# ip a
1: lo: <LOOPBACK,UP,LOWER_UP> mtu 65536 qdisc noqueue state UNKNOWN
group default qlen 1000
    link/loopback 00:00:00:00:00:00 brd 00:00:00:00:00:00
    inet 127.0.0.1/8 scope host lo
      valid_lft forever preferred_lft forever
    inet6 ::1/128 scope host
      valid_lft forever preferred_lft forever
2: net0: <BROADCAST,MULTICAST,UP,LOWER_UP> mtu 1500 qdisc fq_codel
state UP group default qlen 1000
    link/ether 08:00:27:8d:0f:64 brd ff:ff:ff:ff:ff:ff
    inet 10.0.2.5/24 brd 10.0.2.255 scope global dynamic noprefixroute
net0
      valid_lft 459sec preferred_lft 459sec
    inet6 fe80::a00:27ff:fe8d:f64/64 scope link noprefixroute
      valid_lft forever preferred_lft forever
3: net1: <BROADCAST,MULTICAST,UP,LOWER_UP> mtu 1500 qdisc fq_codel
state UP group default qlen 1000
    link/ether 08:00:27:89:87:98 brd ff:ff:ff:ff:ff:ff
    inet 192.168.56.5/24 brd 192.168.56.255 scope global dynamic
noprefixroute net0
      valid_lft 85059sec preferred_lft 85059sec
    inet6 fe80::a00:27ff:fe89:8798/64 scope link noprefixroute
      valid_lft forever preferred_lft forever
4: virbr0: <NO-CARRIER,BROADCAST,MULTICAST,UP> mtu 1500 qdisc noqueue
state DOWN group default qlen 1000
    link/ether 52:54:00:9a:de:c3 brd ff:ff:ff:ff:ff:ff
    inet 192.168.122.1/24 brd 192.168.122.255 scope global virbr0
      valid_lft forever preferred_lft forever
[root@small-ol8 ~]#
```

What does GRUB configuration do? It alters the way the OS boots and loads kernels. For example, let's look at what changing the serial connection details accomplishes. (We're getting a little off-subject here; however, it's important to understand how OCI works in worse-case scenarios.) Imagine you can't reach your server; the network is down, but the server is green and up. You can use a serial connection as a back door. The following `console` edit instructs the OS to allow an out-of-band connection to the VM:

```
GRUB_TIMEOUT=5
GRUB_DISTRIBUTOR="$(sed 's, release .*$,,g' /etc/system-release)"
GRUB_DEFAULT=saved
GRUB_DISABLE_SUBMENU=true
```

```
GRUB_TERMINAL_OUTPUT="console"
GRUB_DISABLE_RECOVERY="true"
GRUB_ENABLE_BLSCFG=true
~
~
~


GRUB_TIMEOUT=5
GRUB_DISTRIBUTOR="$(sed 's, release .*$,,g' /etc/system-release)"
GRUB_DEFAULT=saved
GRUB_DISABLE_SUBMENU=true
GRUB_TERMINAL="serial console"
GRUB_TERMINAL_OUTPUT="console"
GRUB_CMDLINE_LINUX="console=tty1 console=ttyS0,115200"
GRUB_DISABLE_RECOVERY="true"
GRUB_ENABLE_BLSCFG=true
GRUB_SERIAL_COMMAND="serial --unit=0 -speed=115200"
~
~
~
```

The following command reloads GRUB. As we can't edit GRUB directly, we edit it through a configuration file, and use this to execute edits on GRUB. This tells the OS that we're ready to reload and have entered new data:

```
[root@small-ol8 ~]# grub2-mkconfig -o /boot/grub2/grub.cfg
```

Since we edited GRUB and made a couple of other OS changes, it's good to get a fresh start with things:

```
[root@small-ol8 network-scripts]# reboot
```

Going through these configuration changes can be confusing. When it comes down to it, we're narrowing the differences between OCI-born instances and the instance we're configuring in this recipe. The GRUB changes are getting the environment ready to operate within the OCI tenancy.

There are a few more steps you'll have to configure on your host machine for connectivity between VirtualBox and OCI. The way VirtualBox communicates with OCI is through an **Application Programming Interface** (**API**). This connectivity requires public and private API keys to be created, and that public key to be uploaded to OCI.

There are several steps in the authentication between VirtualBox and OCI. The following are the components, and their OCID/outputs are what will be needed for connectivity to OCI:

- OCI account:

  - Tenancy

- Compartment

- VCN

- Storage bucket

- API keys

- VirtualBox – make sure to create and capture the required keys, as shown after this list:

  - API keys

- Host OS (your computer) – make sure to create and capture the required keys, as detailed after this list:

  - API keys

Private and public keys are the gateway components to sharing information from one environment with another. A public key can be shared and is used as an encryption method to keep a packet. The private key is kept local, is not shared beyond that user, and is used to decrypt the packet. When placed together, the private and public keys create a lockbox, keeping the packets flowing between two systems secret while in transit. `openssl` is used to generate the keys, both public and private.

```
█████████████████████████$ openssl genrsa -out oci-api-key.pem 2048
Generating RSA private key, 2048 bit long modulus
.............................+++
........................+++
e is 65537 (0x10001)
█████████████████████████$ ls
oci-api-key.pem
█████████████████████████$ ▯
```

Figure 13.28 – OpenSSL key creation

After creating the preceding key, you need to change the permissions so the key can be used only by you. We'll use `chmod` to configure those permissions and allow the key to be used by the user.

```
█████████████████████████$ chmod 600 oci-api-key.pem
█$ ▮
```

Figure 13.29 – OpenSSL key permissions

After creating the private key, we need to create the public key. This is the key you'll be uploading to OCI so VirtualBox and OCI can communicate with one another. We use the private key to create a public key so the two environments can communicate with one another.

```
                            1$ openssl rsa -pubout -in oci-api-key.pem -out oci-
api-key-public.pem
writing RSA key
                            1$ ▮
```

Figure 13.30 – Public key creation

The next steps are to collect the required data from your OCI cloud account to enter the VirtualBox configuration. The information entered will help VirtualBox integrate, through the OCI API, your OCI tenancy and compartments through your VCN. Imagine this as building a highway between VirtualBox and OCI. The keys, both public and private, are the keys to the kingdom, allowing packets to traverse that highway.

## How to do it...

The following steps walk through uploading the key and configuring VirtualBox to communicate with OCI:

1.  First, just as with any other CSP, we need to log in to our account.

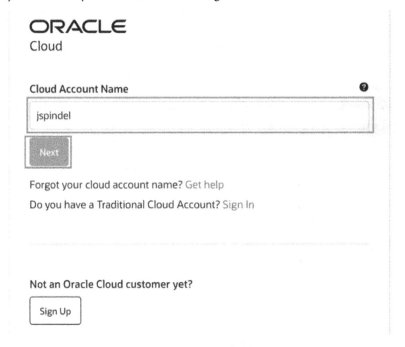

Figure 13.31 – Log in to your account

And this is where we wait for OCI to log us in…

Figure 13.32 – Logging in

2. Once you've logged in to your account, you're ready to log in to the tenancy itself. This is where the action begins, and you'll start to see your efforts pay off. We start by identifying our tenancy and continue from there.

Figure 13.33 – Choose and log in to verify your identity provider

3.   Once you're logged in and inside the tenancy, most of the data needed will be in the user settings and is linked to the public key upload. The keys themselves generate a fingerprint, which is the pathway between OCI and VirtualBox.

You'll see your user icon on the right-hand side of the OCI portal. This will take you into the area with all your account, tenancy, and personal data. This is also where you'll configure your key access.

Figure 13.34 – OCI profile

Once you expand that menu, you'll see **User settings**. This is the access point for all your user access to OCI.

Figure 13.35 – User settings

4.   The **API Keys** section will allow you to enter key values for access.

Figure 13.36 – Administrators' privileges and API keys

5.  In the following screenshot, you can see all the keys currently uploaded to OCI, reflecting your specific user. If you click **Add API Key**, this will bring up the options for adding a key.

Figure 13.37 – API keys

6.  Select **Choose Public Key File** and then select the file from your local environment. Remember we created a public key in the last section. We're going to select that public key here.

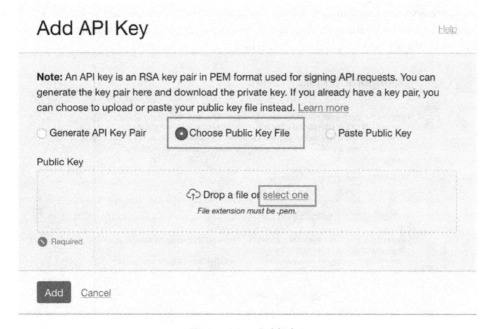

Figure 13.38 – Public key

7.  Once you've chosen the key and it's uploaded to OCI, you'll see that key on screen. Click **Add**:

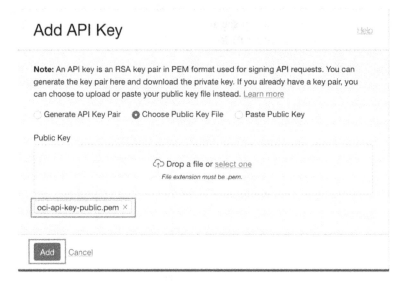

Figure 13.39 – Added key committed

8.  Now that we've got past the key imports, we've arrived at a point where we can start to configure access. A configuration screen will appear after you've officially added the key. This configuration file is all that you need, aside from a compartment OCID, which we'll talk about later, to configure the VirtualBox/OCI interface.

Figure 13.40 – Configuration displayed

Copy the information under **Configuration File Preview**. You'll need it to configure VirtualBox to communicate with OCI.

9.  We're heading back to VirtualBox now. Near the thumbtack icon will be a menu bar. This menu is the heart of VirtualBox and allows you to alter everything from vdisks, as shown in the following screenshot, to network configurations and, of course, settings relating to the cloud. Expand the **Cloud** menu item to access the OCI settings:

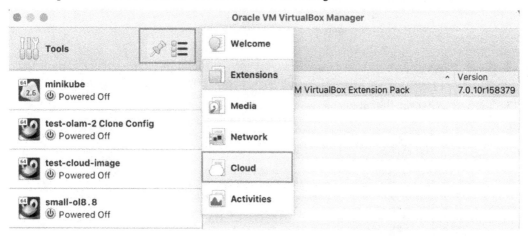

Figure 13.41 – VirtualBox OCI cloud configuration settings

10. Once you've selected this option, you'll have to enter a name. I will enter OCI, since we are using OCI.

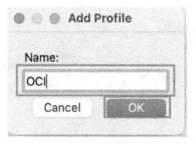

Figure 13.42 – Configuration name

11. Now, under **Oracle Cloud Infrastructure**, you'll see your new profile, **OCI**. You can click on **Properties**, which will allow you to configure that OCI profile.

Figure 13.43 – Name committed

12. This is where it's handy to have the OCI portal open in another window, or cut and paste the variables in a notepad. You'll need all the info we went over a couple of sections ago in *Figure 13.40*.

13. The first OCID you'll want to copy is that of `user`:

Figure 13.44 – User OCID

14. Paste that OCID into the **user** property on the OCI profile, shown in the preceding screenshot, into VirtualBox. Hopefully, you'll now see where we're going with this.

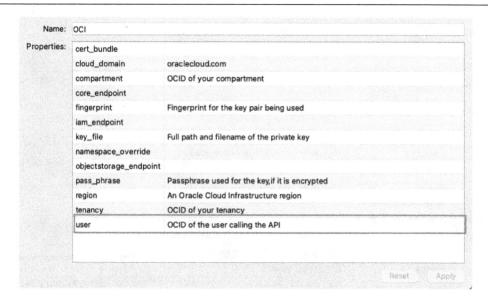

Figure 13.45 – Configuring the user OCID

15. As previously, but this time with `tenancy`, copy the OCID and go back to VirtualBox.

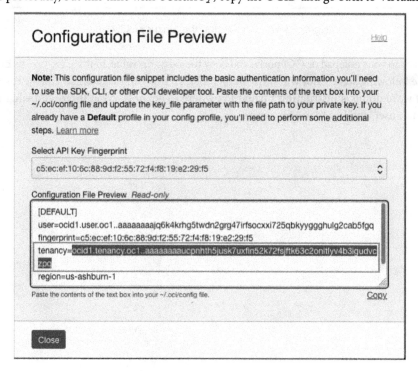

Figure 13.46 – Tenancy OCID

16. Again, as previously, paste the tenancy OCID in the **tenancy** field.

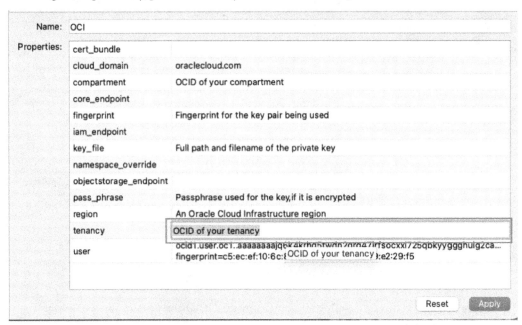

| Name: | OCI | |
|---|---|---|
| Properties: | cert_bundle | |
| | cloud_domain | oraclecloud.com |
| | compartment | OCID of your compartment |
| | core_endpoint | |
| | fingerprint | Fingerprint for the key pair being used |
| | iam_endpoint | |
| | key_file | Full path and filename of the private key |
| | namespace_override | |
| | objectstorage_endpoint | |
| | pass_phrase | Passphrase used for the key, if it is encrypted |
| | region | An Oracle Cloud Infrastructure region |
| | tenancy | OCID of your tenancy |
| | user | ocid1.user.oc1..aaaaaaaajq6k4krhqbtwdn2nrna7irfsocxxi725qbkyyggghuig2ca...<br>fingerprint=c5:ec:ef:10:6c:{ OCID of your tenancy }:e2:29:f5 |

Reset    Apply

Figure 13.47 – Configuring the tenancy OCID

17. Go back to your notepad or OCI portal and copy the `region` value, in this case, `us-asburn-1`, as the following screenshot will show. Remember, all this will make sense shortly. Essentially, what we're doing is instructing VirtualBox where to go, how to get there, and what region, tenancy, user, and key to use for access.

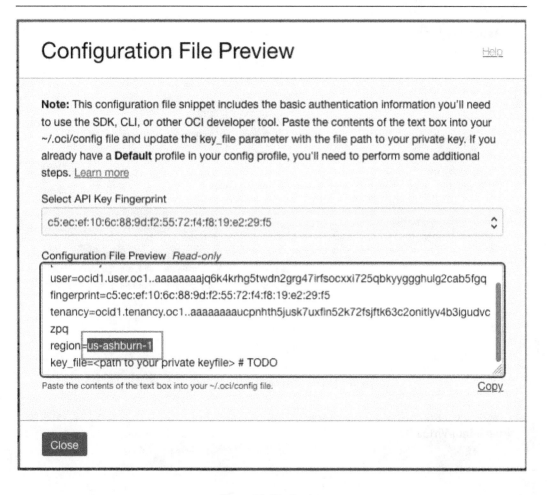

Figure 13.48 – Region

18. As previously, paste the region in the correct field.

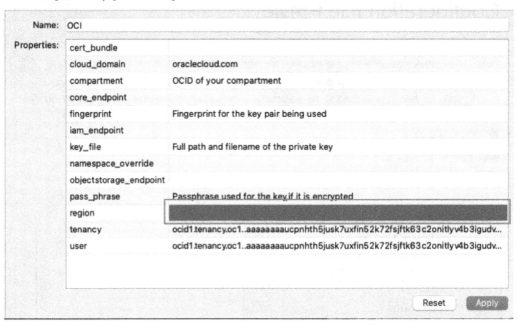

| Name: | OCI | |
|---|---|---|
| Properties: | cert_bundle | |
| | cloud_domain | oraclecloud.com |
| | compartment | OCID of your compartment |
| | core_endpoint | |
| | fingerprint | Fingerprint for the key pair being used |
| | iam_endpoint | |
| | key_file | Full path and filename of the private key |
| | namespace_override | |
| | objectstorage_endpoint | |
| | pass_phrase | Passphrase used for the key, if it is encrypted |
| | region | |
| | tenancy | ocid1.tenancy.oc1..aaaaaaaaucpnhth5jusk7uxfin52k72fsjftk63c2onitlyv4b3igudv... |
| | user | ocid1.tenancy.oc1..aaaaaaaaucpnhth5jusk7uxfin52k72fsjftk63c2onitlyv4b3igudv... |

Reset    Apply

Figure 13.49 – Configuring the region

19. Next, you'll need to go to the OCI console or notepad and copy the `fingerprint` value to input into VirtualBox.

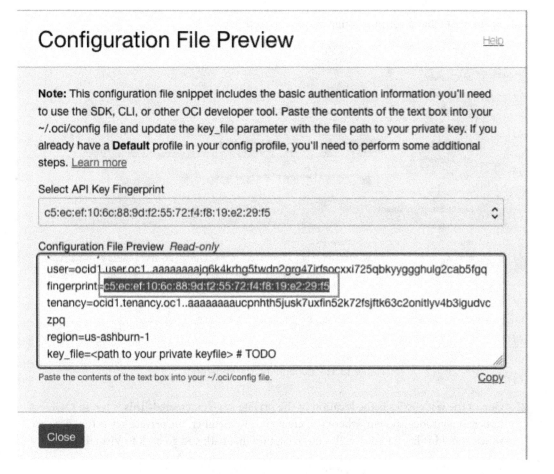

Figure 13.50 – Fingerprint

20. Again, paste that fingerprint value into the appropriate field.

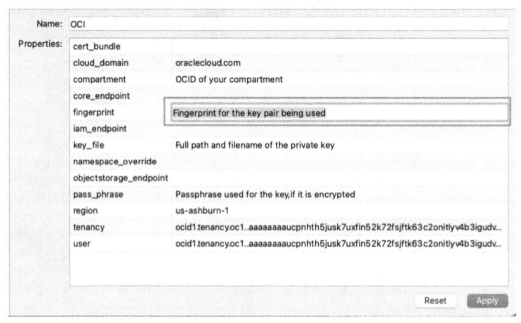

Figure 13.51 – Configuring the fingerprint

21. One of the last entries is the location of the private key you created. This is not in OCI, but rather in your local system, where you created it. Remember, the private key is the local key, which shouldn't be shared. You'll want to capture that path and go back to VirtualBox.

```
[jspindel-MBP2:apikey jspindel$ ls
oci-api-key-public.pem  oci-api-key.pem
jspindel-MBP2:apikey jspindel$ pwd
/Users/jspindel/Desktop/apikey
jspindel-MBP2:apikey jspindel$
```

Figure 13.52 – API key location

22. As shown previously, paste the path into the appropriate field.

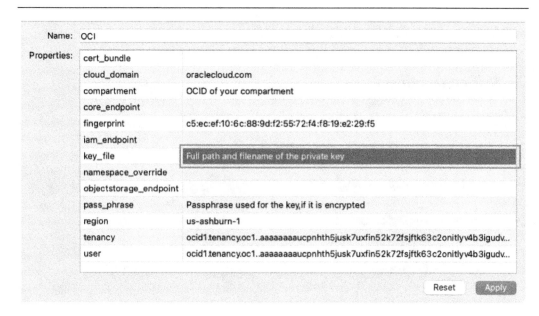

Figure 13.53 – Configuration key location

23. Last but not least, you'll want to go back to your OCI portal and find the **Compartments** menu. I find a simple search to be the easiest way of locating this option, but if you want to go directly to it, you'll find it under **Identity**.

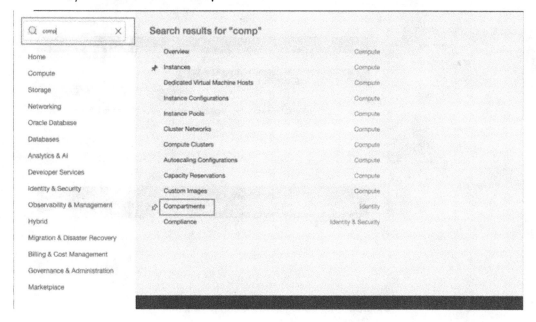

Figure 13.54 – Compartments

24. Expand the compartment you want to use and copy the OCID to enter it into the VirtualBox OCI configuration.

Figure 13.55 – Compartment selection

25. As shown previously, paste that OCID into the appropriate field.

Figure 13.56 – Configuring the compartment

26. After all the data is entered, you should see that OCID's region, user, tenancy, key file location, compartment, and fingerprint properties are all populated.

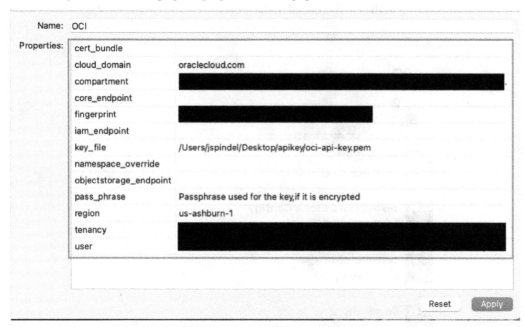

Figure 13.57 – Completed configuration

27. Once you've confirmed that everything is complete, apply the settings. You'll see the new profile show up; we named it **OCI**.

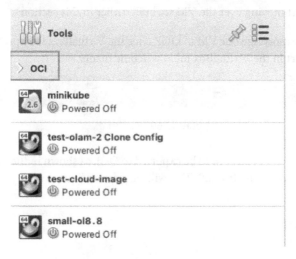

Figure 13.58 – VirtualBox OCI

28. If you expand that profile, you'll see the tenancy is now empty. If you already had infrastructure deployed there, you would see those resources show up here, provided they are running in the same compartment as the OCID entered in the profile.

Figure 13.59 – Expanded OCI

You're now ready to start moving over the VM we built earlier in this section:

1. The first step in exporting your VM to OCI, once the VirtualBox OCI profile is configured, is to click on **Export** in the VirtualBox main welcome menu.

Figure 13.60 – Export

2. You'll next need to select the VM to be exported to OCI, as shown in the following screenshot – in this case, it's called **small-ol8.8**. This will vary depending on what you named your VM.

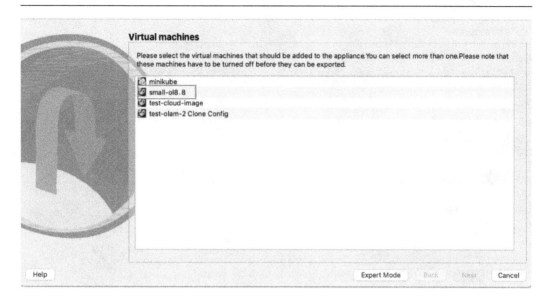

Figure 13.61 – Image selection

3.  After you choose your VM, you must configure the format in which to export the VM. We're going to expand the **Format** dropdown, as shown in the following screenshot. The format being chosen is Oracle Cloud Infrastructure, as we're migrating this VM to OCI. As a side note, exports aren't only for OCI. You can export a VM as an OVF to a myriad of platforms, for example, Vmware, OLVM, KVM, HyperV, or AWS. As mentioned at the beginning of this recipe, OVF and OVA both reflect somewhat the same concept: they say, "here's an exported environment and here's how to put it back together." There are, however, some differences between OVF and OVA. OVF can be viewed as a group of files making up an environment, with an attached manifest identifying the files and how they are used. OVA is a single file; consider it a server in a box, an already-built environment ready to be imported. Both can be used outside of OCI, but in this case, we're going to concentrate on an OCI export using .ova as the file extension.

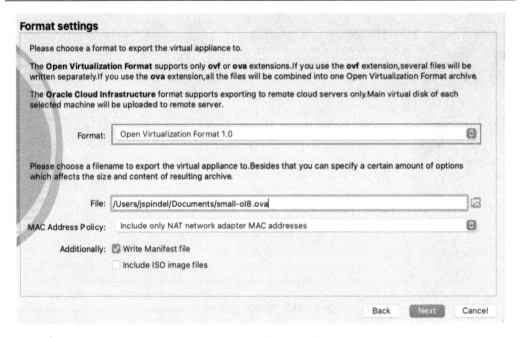

Figure 13.62 – Image format configuration

4.  As shown previously, choose **Oracle Cloud Infrastructure** for the format and **OCI** as the VirtualBox profile, as highlighted in red in the following screenshot.

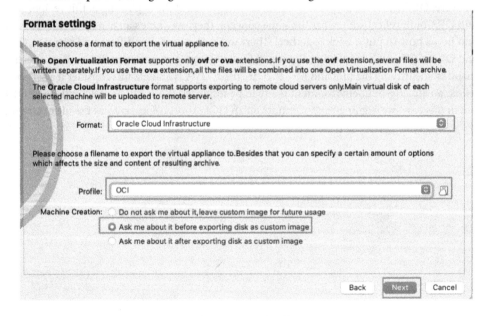

Figure 13.63 – Profile

5.  You'll want to make sure all your variables are correct, as shown in the following screenshot, as well as confirming you have an available storage bucket:

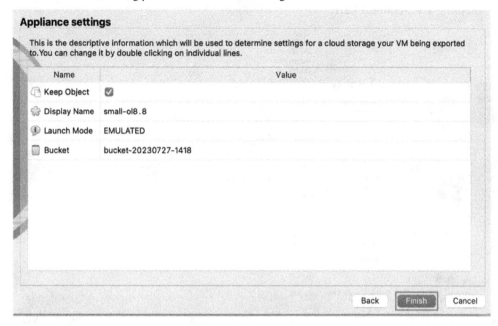

Figure 13.64 – Image output

6.  You'll want to expand the **Shape** section and choose another shape, as VM.Optimized.Flex will not be recognized by OCI. I identified a usable shape, as shown in the following figure, that is available and lightweight. Follow the following image for shape selection:

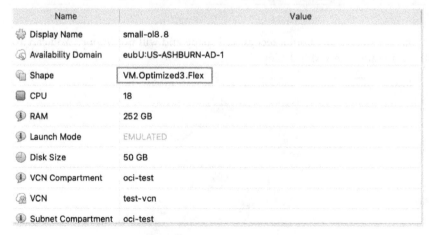

Figure 13.65 – Shape selection

7.  As shown previously, expanding this section will give you several shape choices. As a note, a shape is a predetermined size, reflecting a set number of resources. In this case, we're choosing **VM.Standard.E2.1**:

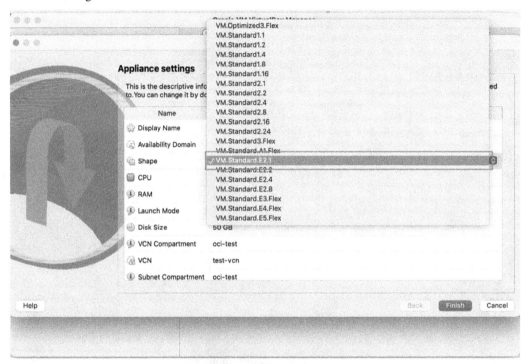

Figure 13.66 – Image shape

> **Note**
>
> VM.Optimized3.Flex is not a recognized shape and will not import. You can always change the shape after the VM is deployed.

8.    Once you've chosen the appropriate shape, finish configuring the export, then click **Finish** to execute the migration to OCI.

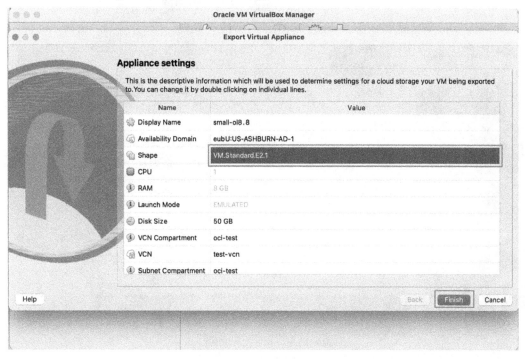

Figure 13.67 – Image shape committed

9.   Make sure your image shape is identified and the correct shape was selected:

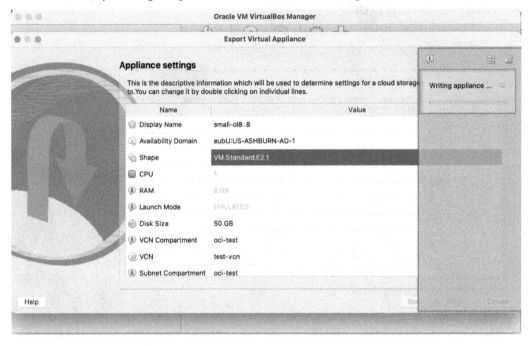

Figure 13.68 – Image writing

10.  Once the export is completed, you'll see your VM running in OCI, and you'll be able to log in to your portal and see that same VM running within your OCI tenancy as well.

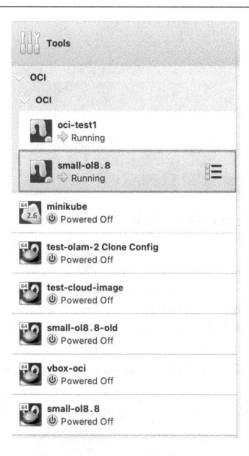

Figure 13.69 – Image running

As shown in the preceding screenshot, the image is now running as a VM in OCI.

## For everyone else, let's make custom images for AWS

It seems very simple: build an image, export the image, and import the image (wash, rinse, and repeat). The concept isn't much more complicated than that. However, there are steps to go through, and some of those steps have catches.

You'll first have to walk through the steps of setting up and configuring the AWS CLI. Much like the OCI CLI, AWS's CLI is a direct command line executing against the AWS API. After the CLI is installed and configured, we'll walk through setting up an S3 bucket, configuring that bucket, and changing access to allow upload. The following figure shows the stages and their touchpoints throughout this recipe. The AWS CLI is the common thread in staging and executing, along with the GUI. The storage factors in AWS are managed by access control and authentication, which allow us to create, store, and manipulate stored objects and buckets.

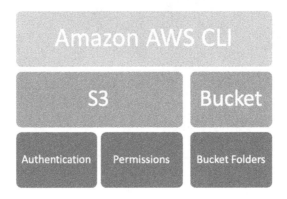

Figure 13.70 – AWS CLI storage connections

## Getting ready

Before we can start using the CLI, we must download and install the requisite package. For this recipe, I am using a Mac. You can easily navigate to AWS and download the CLI for Windows or Linux. Regardless, once the CLI is installed, the commands do not differ other than the locations and some other OS-specific changes, which really only apply to Windows:

```
root# curl "https://awscli.amazonaws.com/AWSCLIV2.pkg" -o "AWSCLIV2.
pkg"
```

After downloading the package, you'll have to install the CLI. This is done by executing the install package, as shown:

```
root# installer -pkg ./AWSCLIV2.pkg -target /
```

In this case, we upgraded the Python version to match what the AWS CLI requires. You can check this by running a `which` command at the end, which will show the location of the AWS CLI install, and `--version`, which will list the version of the AWS CLI, as well as Python:

```
root# which aws
/usr/local/bin/aws
root# aws --version
aws-cli/2.7.28 Python/3.9.11 Darwin/21.6.0 exe/x86_64
```

After you've installed the AWS CLI, we'll move on to configuring the Oracle Linux OS. We'll later configure the AWS CLI with the details of our AWS account and data center location:

Figure 13.71 – Create a new VM

You'll want to fill in all the fields as we did in previous sections. Make sure to name your VM by referencing the disk you created (`/Users/USER/Desktop/<NAME>`). This will help keep things in place later. You can always go back to the VM in VirtualBox and find the associated media, but it's easier to name the disk now, while creating the VM.

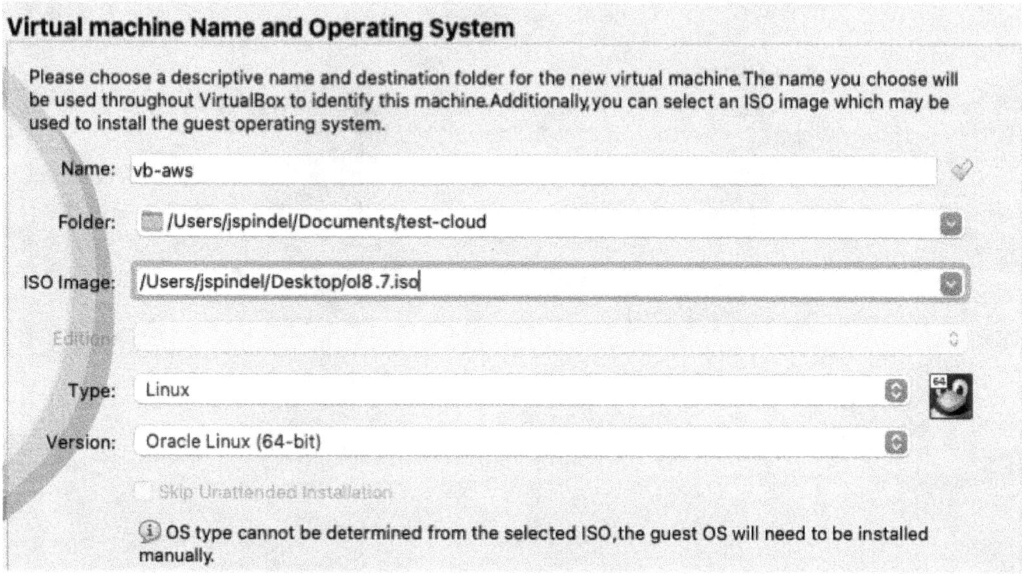

**Virtual machine Name and Operating System**

Please choose a descriptive name and destination folder for the new virtual machine. The name you choose will be used throughout VirtualBox to identify this machine. Additionally, you can select an ISO image which may be used to install the guest operating system.

Name:     vb-aws

Folder:     /Users/jspindel/Documents/test-cloud

ISO Image:     /Users/jspindel/Desktop/ol8.7.iso

Edition:

Type:     Linux

Version:     Oracle Linux (64-bit)

Skip Unattended Installation

ⓘ OS type cannot be determined from the selected ISO, the guest OS will need to be installed manually.

Figure 13.72 – ISO selection

If you remember, in the previous section, we allocated CPU and memory. Just like in any other build environment, we need to specify, install, and configure resources. Whether they are virtual or physical, we're still installing resources. In this case, we're configuring this VM with 4 GB of RAM and two vCPUs. Remember, a vCPU is the equivalent of a processor thread. So, here we're installing two vCPUs, which is the equivalent of one physical core (two threads (vCPUs) = one processor core).

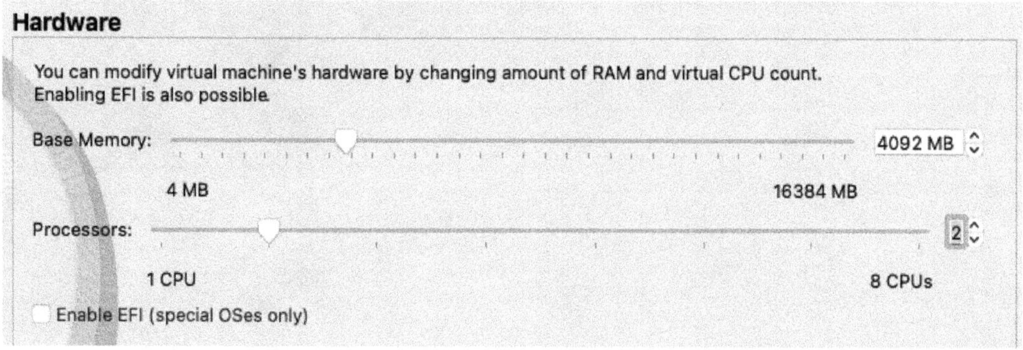

**Hardware**

You can modify virtual machine's hardware by changing amount of RAM and virtual CPU count. Enabling EFI is also possible.

Base Memory:                                                          4092 MB

4 MB                                                    16384 MB

Processors:                                                          2

1 CPU                                                    8 CPUs

Enable EFI (special OSes only)

Figure 13.73 – Resources

After we've configured the CPU and memory resources, we're ready to move on to choosing the media (disk) we're attaching to our VM. In this case, we're not going to choose the default of creating a disk, instead using an existing one. Remember, we created our own drive in .vmdk format, so let's select to use an existing virtual hard disk file here.

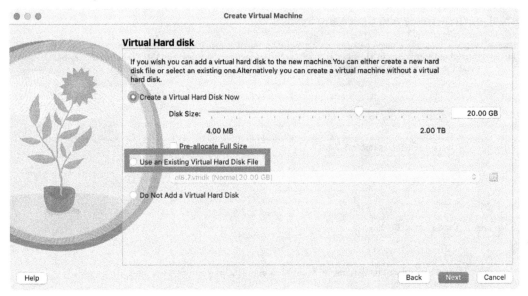

Figure 13.74 – Options to create or use an existing disk

Remember to select the drive (assuming you created one before) that matches the name of the VM, or create a new one. Note that the .vmdk extension should be used again in order for it to be recognized.

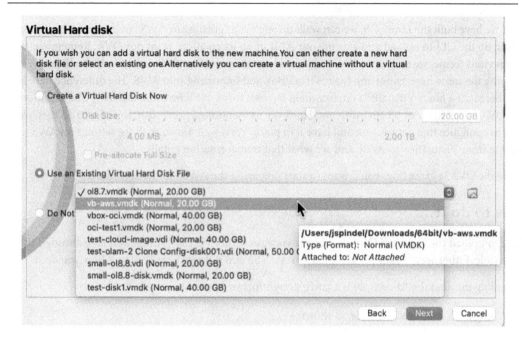

Figure 13.75 – Disk selection

As in past recipes, we confirm our selections on the **Summary** screen and execute the configuration by selecting **Finish**. We won't be walking through the build, as we have other recipes that take you through configuring OSs.

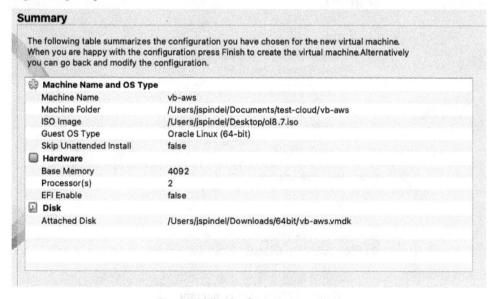

Figure 13.76 – Configuration summary

Once we have built the Linux OS, we can walk through configuring our AWS environment, including setting up the CLI to upload and execute our AMI upon its creation, from our OVA. Remember, in the previous recipe, we built out a VM and created an OCI from that OVA image in VirtualBox. We'll be doing the same here, exporting from VirtualBox and importing into AWS. The difference here is that there isn't a fancy VirtualBox environment to work from. We'll be using the AWS CLI to import that OVA image into our S3 environment. However, as mentioned previously, in order to do that, we need to configure that connection and have it in place. We'll walk through those settings on AWS to migrate from VirtualBox to AWS, and see what that transformation entails.

While the OVA is exporting, you'll want to start preparing the AWS CLI configuration.

## How to do it...

You can upload the exported OVA in one of two ways, either via the command line or through the S3 console. Either way, it's simply an upload to AWS S3 and it doesn't really matter how you do it.

Uploading through the S3 console is a fairly straightforward process:

1.   Log in to your AWS console, as shown:

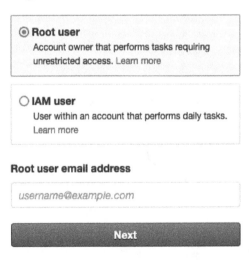

Figure 13.77 – Sign in as root user

2.  After signing in, navigate to S3.

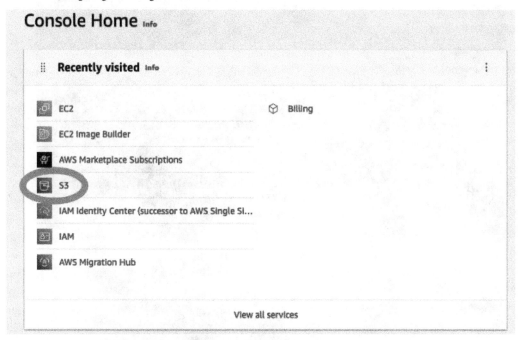

Figure 13.78 – AWS menu

If S3 isn't on your most recently visited list, navigate to **Storage** and select **S3**, or just type S3 in the search bar.

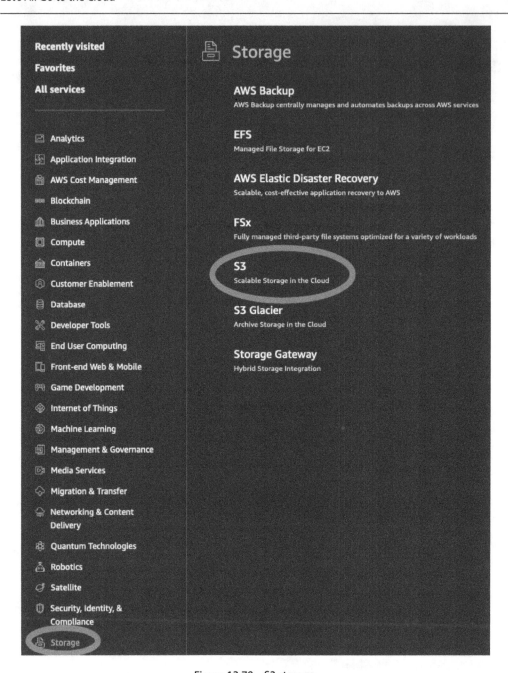

Figure 13.79 – S3 storage

3.  After navigating to S3, you'll want to create a bucket for your OVA to be uploaded to. A bucket is essentially object storage and a great place to store images and the like.

Figure 13.80 – S3 bucket

4. After selecting **Create bucket**, you'll want to name that bucket and configure other aspects of it.

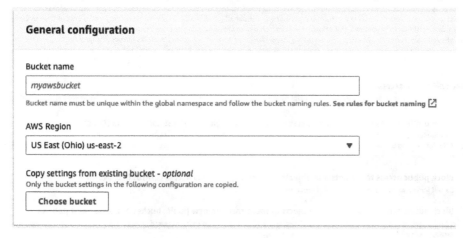

Figure 13.81 – Bucket name and region

5. After naming, choose which region, as per the AWS docs, the bucket should be created under. Remember to create the bucket in the same region you're operating in and will be using for this exercise. In this case, we'll be deploying into US East 2 - Ohio.

6. We won't be enabling any ACLs here:

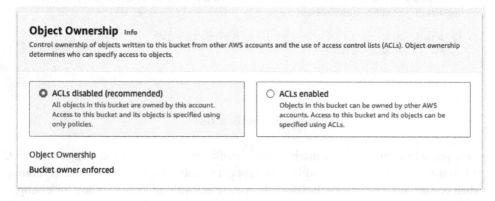

Figure 13.82 – ACLs

7.  As mentioned previously concerning AWS access control, we're going to uncheck **Block all public access** and open the S3 bucket up to direct public (i.e., external) access.

> **Note**
>
> This is not generally a best practice; we are just doing this for testing purposes.

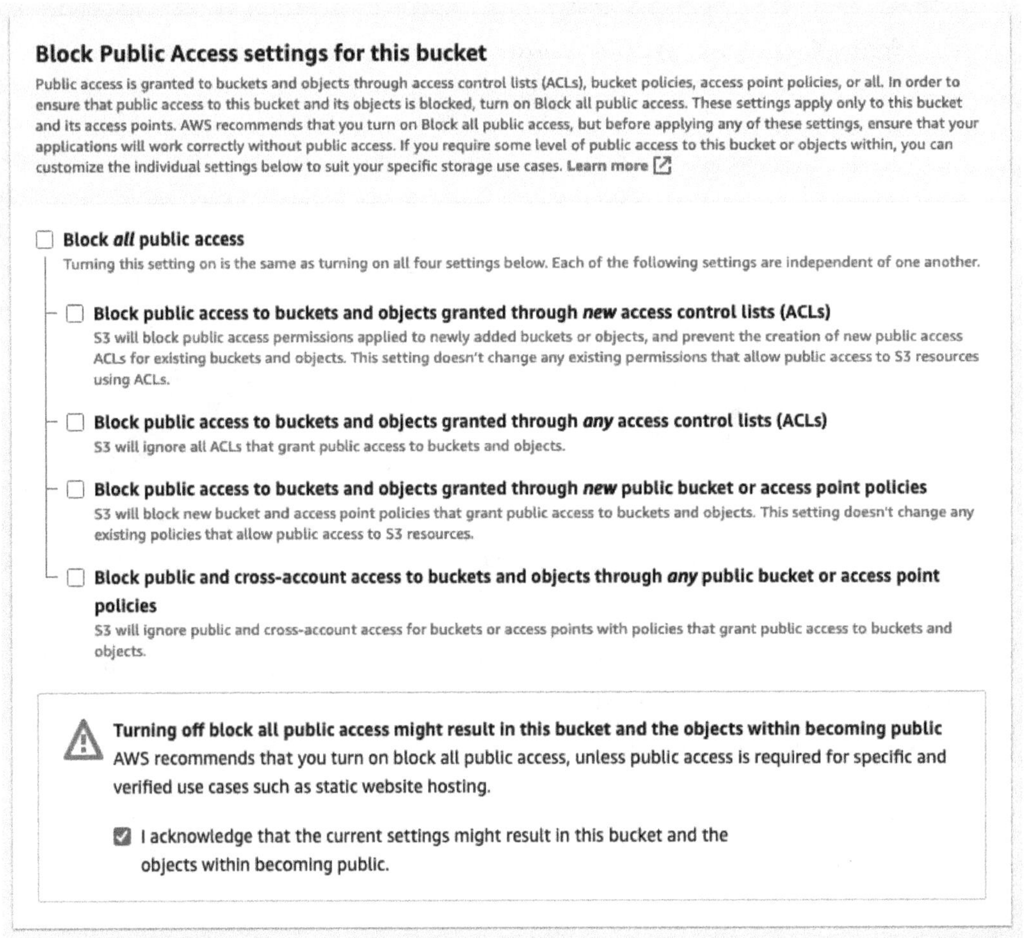

**Block Public Access settings for this bucket**

Public access is granted to buckets and objects through access control lists (ACLs), bucket policies, access point policies, or all. In order to ensure that public access to this bucket and its objects is blocked, turn on Block all public access. These settings apply only to this bucket and its access points. AWS recommends that you turn on Block all public access, but before applying any of these settings, ensure that your applications will work correctly without public access. If you require some level of public access to this bucket or objects within, you can customize the individual settings below to suit your specific storage use cases. Learn more [↗]

☐ **Block *all* public access**
Turning this setting on is the same as turning on all four settings below. Each of the following settings are independent of one another.

  ☐ **Block public access to buckets and objects granted through *new* access control lists (ACLs)**
  S3 will block public access permissions applied to newly added buckets or objects, and prevent the creation of new public access ACLs for existing buckets and objects. This setting doesn't change any existing permissions that allow public access to S3 resources using ACLs.

  ☐ **Block public access to buckets and objects granted through *any* access control lists (ACLs)**
  S3 will ignore all ACLs that grant public access to buckets and objects.

  ☐ **Block public access to buckets and objects granted through *new* public bucket or access point policies**
  S3 will block new bucket and access point policies that grant public access to buckets and objects. This setting doesn't change any existing policies that allow public access to S3 resources.

  ☐ **Block public and cross-account access to buckets and objects through *any* public bucket or access point policies**
  S3 will ignore public and cross-account access for buckets or access points with policies that grant public access to buckets and objects.

  ⚠ **Turning off block all public access might result in this bucket and the objects within becoming public**
  AWS recommends that you turn on block all public access, unless public access is required for specific and verified use cases such as static website hosting.

  ☑ I acknowledge that the current settings might result in this bucket and the objects within becoming public.

Figure 13.83 – Public access

8.  We're going to keep versioning disabled (the default), as shown in the following screenshot, as this is a one-time bucket and will not be kept perpetually. You'll want to enable versioning when you're working through the life cycle of a project with multiple versions, for example, multiple iterations of an image.

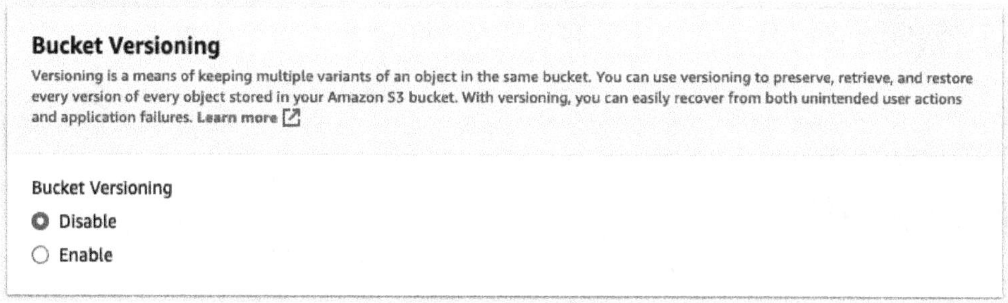

**Bucket Versioning**

Versioning is a means of keeping multiple variants of an object in the same bucket. You can use versioning to preserve, retrieve, and restore every version of every object stored in your Amazon S3 bucket. With versioning, you can easily recover from both unintended user actions and application failures. **Learn more** [↗]

Bucket Versioning

◉ Disable

◯ Enable

Figure 13.84 – Versioning

9.  Again, since we're keeping this basic, we will not be associating any tags either.

**Tags** (0) - *optional*

You can use bucket tags to track storage costs and organize buckets. **Learn more** [↗]

No tags associated with this bucket.

Add tag

Figure 13.85 – Tags

10.  We're going to use standard server-side encryption with S3-managed keys.

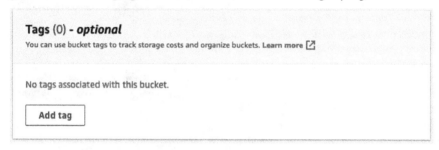

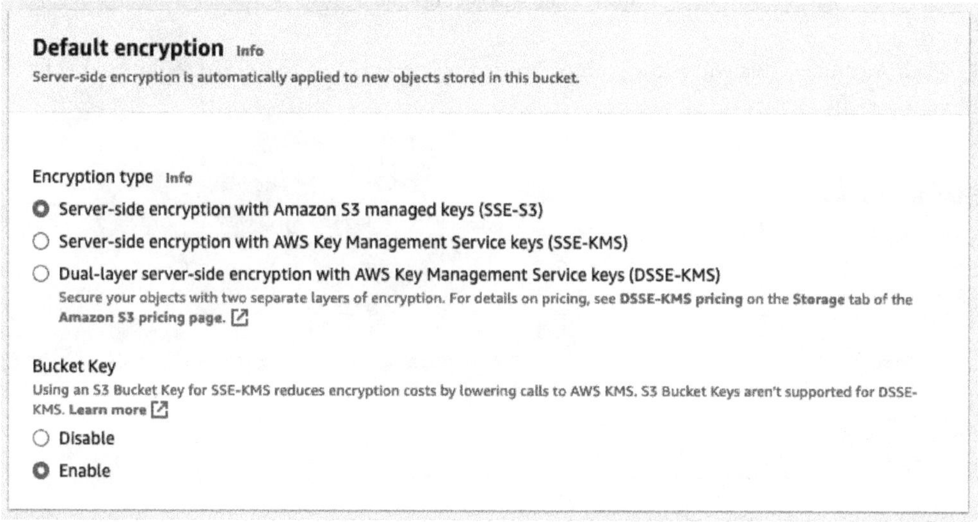

**Default encryption** Info

Server-side encryption is automatically applied to new objects stored in this bucket.

Encryption type Info

◉ Server-side encryption with Amazon S3 managed keys (SSE-S3)

◯ Server-side encryption with AWS Key Management Service keys (SSE-KMS)

◯ Dual-layer server-side encryption with AWS Key Management Service keys (DSSE-KMS)
   Secure your objects with two separate layers of encryption. For details on pricing, see **DSSE-KMS pricing** on the **Storage** tab of the **Amazon S3 pricing page.** [↗]

Bucket Key

Using an S3 Bucket Key for SSE-KMS reduces encryption costs by lowering calls to AWS KMS. S3 Bucket Keys aren't supported for DSSE-KMS. **Learn more** [↗]

◯ Disable

◉ Enable

Figure 13.86 – Encryption

11.  Ignore the advanced options as well and go ahead with creating the bucket.

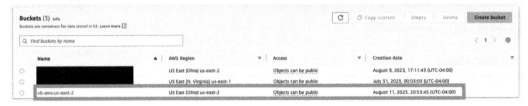

Figure 13.87 – Bucket display

12.  Navigate to the newly created `vb-aws-us-east-2` bucket and click on **Upload**.

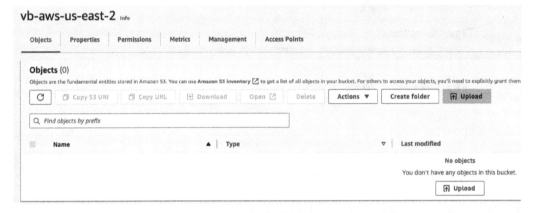

Figure 13.88 – Object upload

13.  Click **Add files**. This will allow you to choose the correct OVA to upload to the bucket from your own filesystem.

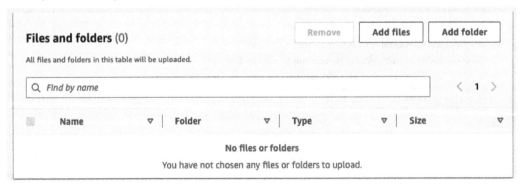

Figure 13.89 – Add files

14. We're going to choose the OVA we created at the beginning of this recipe.

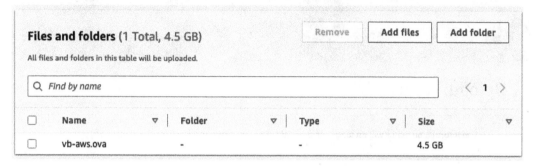

Figure 13.90 – File selection

15. Once you've added the file, carry out the upload.

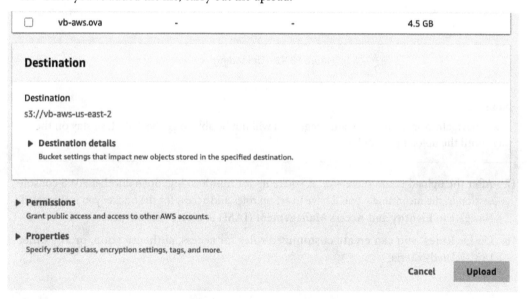

Figure 13.91 – File destination

16. The status bar will show the progress and the **Summary** section will show the destination in S3, as shown in the following screenshot.

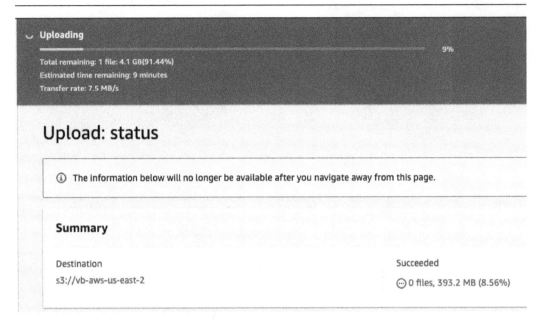

Figure 13.92 – Uploading

> **Note**
>
> If you navigate away from this status page, you will not be able to get back to it, so stay on the
> page until the upload is complete.

17. After the upload is complete – or, if you're up for multitasking, open another AWS console
    session in the meantime – you'll have to set up roles and access for the bucket you just created.
    Navigate to **Identity and Access Management (IAM)** to access the role data.

18. Under **Roles**, you can create customized roles for access, authentication, or any other
    IAM-related criteria.

Figure 13.93 – AWS Roles

We'll be configuring roles and permissions from the command line. We must create an IAM user and secret as without access or authentication, the CLI won't operate. Then we can configure the CLI to be connected to our account.

To configure and associate the user with that access key, you have to navigate back to IAM, as the following steps will walk through.

Figure 13.94 – Security, Identity, & Compliance menu

19. Once you've expanded **Security, Identity, & Compliance**, you will see the option to navigate to the IAM console. Alternatively, you can type IAM in the search bar. As we're trying to help you become familiar with the console, we will detail the specific steps to get to this option.

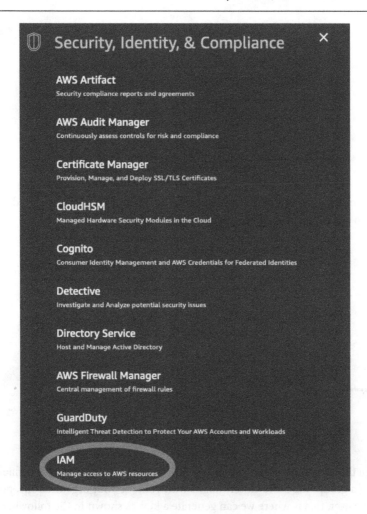

Figure 13.95 – IAM

20. In order to access and create keys, we must understand what a key is for, and how it related to a user. So, let's navigate to **Users**. We'll walk through key creation as follows.

Figure 13.96 – Users

21. You'll want to create the user as shown in the following screenshot, which you can do by navigating to **Add users**. We'll name our user user-admin:

Figure 13.97 – User name

22. Now that we've named our user, just like with any other system, we need to define the user, add them to a group, and assign privileges.

Figure 13.98 – User definition

23. We'll assign this user to the admin group and click **Next** to continue. You can define permissions by creating a group that more closely aligns with your, or your organization's, policies. After creating the user, this is where we can generate a key, as shown in the following screenshot, with the secret attached. The following steps walk through how to do this.

Figure 13.99 – Credentials

24. The **Security credentials** tab is where you create the access key.

## Access key best practices & alternatives Info

Avoid using long-term credentials like access keys to improve your security. Consider the following use cases and alternatives.

Use case

○ **Command Line Interface (CLI)**
You plan to use this access key to enable the AWS CLI to access your AWS account.

○ **Local code**
You plan to use this access key to enable application code in a local development environment to access your AWS account.

○ **Application running on an AWS compute service**
You plan to use this access key to enable application code running on an AWS compute service like Amazon EC2, Amazon ECS, or AWS Lambda to access your AWS account.

○ **Third-party service**
You plan to use this access key to enable access for a third-party application or service that monitors or manages your AWS resources.

○ **Application running outside AWS**
You plan to use this access key to enable an application running on an on-premises host, or to use a local AWS client or third-party AWS plugin.

○ **Other**
Your use case is not listed here.

⚠ **Alternatives recommended**
  • Use AWS CloudShell, a browser-based CLI, to run commands. Learn more ☑
  • Use the AWS CLI V2 and enable authentication through a user in IAM Identity Center. Learn more ☑

Confirmation
☐ I understand the above recommendation and want to proceed to create an access key.

Cancel    **Next**

Figure 13.100 – CLI access control and credentials creation

This access key is specifically for the CLI, so that's the option we'll want to select, as shown in the preceding screenshot, and then click **Next**. We're not creating any tags in this recipe, so feel free to skip that step and create the access key.

> **Note**
>
> Download the `.csv` file (the credential document), or show and copy the secret access key by clicking on the two squares next to the secret access key. This is the only place where you can copy these keys, whether you write them down or paste them into a notepad. **Once you close this page, you won't be able to recover this information.** You could create and reconfigure the CLI without losing the data, but that would be a lot of unnecessary work, so just make sure to write down the secret.

## Retrieve access keys <sub>Info</sub>

### Access key

If you lose or forget your secret access key, you cannot retrieve it. Instead, create a new access key and make the old key inactive.

| Access key | Secret access key |
|---|---|
| 🗗 AKIA3HX45UYOK7HIAZHA | 🗗 eZ5mZxzGhEYM0AfyBznLDqIT6TMsUz//AO2DMQst   Hide |

### Access key best practices

- Never store your access key in plain text, in a code repository, or in code.
- Disable or delete access key when no longer needed.
- Enable least-privilege permissions.
- Rotate access keys regularly.

For more details about managing access keys, see the best practices for managing AWS access keys.

[ Download .csv file ]    [ **Done** ]

Figure 13.101 – Secret

Make sure to copy the secret access key, which in our case is shown below – yours will differ from the one we have here: `eZ5mZxzGhEYM0AfyBznLDqIT6TMsUz//AO2DMQst`.

25. Once you've created the key and noted down the secret access key, the access key will be active.

Figure 13.102 – Access key

26. After you've added the access key, you'll be able to run `aws configure` in the CLI:

```
root# aws configure
AWS Access Key ID [****************AZHA]: AKIA3HX45UYOK7HIAZHA
AWS Secret Access Key [****************MQst]:
Default region name [us-east-2]: us-east-2
Default output format [json]: json
```

> **Note**
>
> If you put JSON in all caps, this will fail. It will not report a failure, but your command will fail when run against the API.

27. After you've configured the CLI, you can execute the following to convert your image from an OVA to an AMI:

```
root# aws ec2 import-image --description "VM Image" --disk-
containers Format=ova,UserBucket="{S3Bucket=vb-aws-us-east-
2,S3Key=vb-aws.ova}"
{
    "Description": "VM Image",
    "ImportTaskId": "import-ami-0908bf8d72b678cdf",
    "Progress": "1",
    "SnapshotDetails": [
        {
            "DiskImageSize": 0.0,
            "Format": "OVA",
            "UserBucket": {
                "S3Bucket": "vb-aws-us-east-2",
                "S3Key": "vb-aws.ova"
            }
        }
    ],
    "Status": "active",
    "StatusMessage": "pending"
}
```

28. The following command will ascertain the status of the conversion:

> **Note**
> `import-ami-xxxxxxxx` will change every time you execute a conversion.

```
aws ec2 describe-import-image-tasks --import-task-ids import-
ami-<AMI-ID>
```

I've executed the command and run it several times to show each step of the process. After the following steps, you'll be able to use your newly created AMI in your AWS tenancy. When walking through the import tasks, I refreshed here to show all the versions of the updates.

29. Run the following command to show the status of the import:

```
root# aws ec2 describe-import-image-tasks --import-task-ids
import-ami-0908bf8d72b678cdf
{
    "ImportImageTasks": [
        {
            "Description": "VM Image",
            "ImportTaskId": "import-ami-0908bf8d72b678cdf",
```

```
            "Progress": "19",
            "SnapshotDetails": [
                {
                    "DiskImageSize": 8211946496.0,
                    "Format": "VMDK",
                    "Status": "active",
                    "UserBucket": {
                        "S3Bucket": "vb-aws-us-east-2",
                        "S3Key": "vb-aws.ova"
                    }
                }
            ],
            "Status": "active",
            "StatusMessage": "converting",
            "Tags": []
        }
    ]
}
```

After a couple of minutes, you can run this command throughout the import process to show the status. Keep on running this command every few minutes to check the current status. The valid statuses are the following:

- `active`: The import task has started

- `converting`: The image is being converted into an AMI

- `updating`: The AMI import is being updated

- `validating`: The import is being validated

- `validated`: Validation is completed

- `completed`: The AMI is ready to use

- `deleted`: The import task has been canceled

When the AMI is complete, the following will be the end status:

```
{
    "ImportImageTasks": [
        {
            "Architecture": "x86_64",
            "Description": "VM Image",
            "ImageId": "ami-055ce6a1f65862de6",
            "ImportTaskId": "import-ami-0908bf8d72b678cdf",
            "LicenseType": "BYOL",
            "Platform": "Linux",
```

```
            "SnapshotDetails": [
                {
                    "DeviceName": "/dev/sda1",
                    "DiskImageSize": 8211946496.0,
                    "Format": "VMDK",
                    "SnapshotId": "snap-08a2c2a985caf8a6c",
                    "Status": "completed",
                    "UserBucket": {
                        "S3Bucket": "vb-aws-us-east-2",
                        "S3Key": "vb-aws.ova"
                    }
                }
            ],
            "Status": "completed",
            "Tags": [],
            "BootMode": "legacy_bios"
        }
    ]
}
```

30. After the process has completed, you will be able to log back in to the AWS console and navigate to your EC2 environment. In order to launch a new VM with the ability to select your AMI as the template, click **Launch instance**.

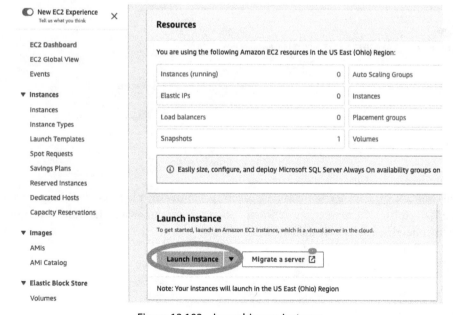

Figure 13.103 – Launching an instance

31. Once you're in the launch menu, you can drill down into other AMIs available.

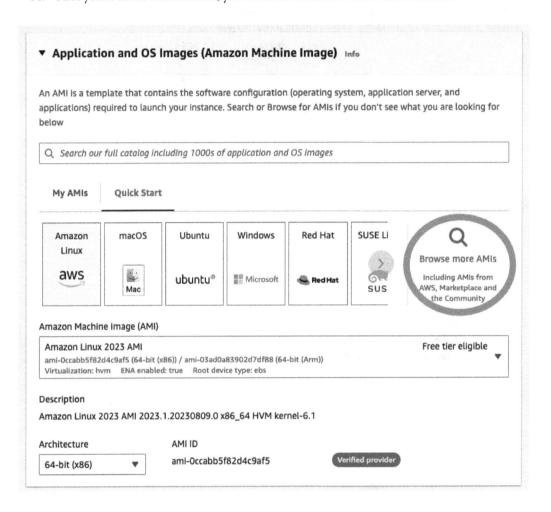

Figure 13.104 – Browse AMIs

32. This will take you to your customized AMIs and (as shown earlier in *Figure 13.7, Image products*), the Marketplace. The Marketplace is where you can share your own AMIs with the community or use ones that others have uploaded.

Figure 13.105 – Created AMI

33. As shown previously, you'll see the available AMI, created in this recipe, reflected. Also as an aside, besides the AMIs on offer in the Marketplace, you can also find a number of OSs, including Oracle Linux.

34. If you navigate to the newly created AMI, you'll see that you can select that image as your AMI to execute and create a VM.

Figure 13.106 – AMI selection

By selecting the AMI, you're attaching that AMI as your image and executing the creation of a VM from the selected image (the AMI).

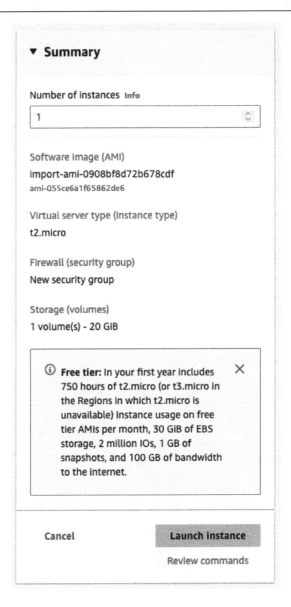

Figure 13.107 – Instance launch configuration

35. After selecting the AMI and executing the launch, you'll enter into the standard launch protocols for creating an AWS VM, including creating a key pair, naming the pair, and downloading the key. You can pre-create these keys as well.

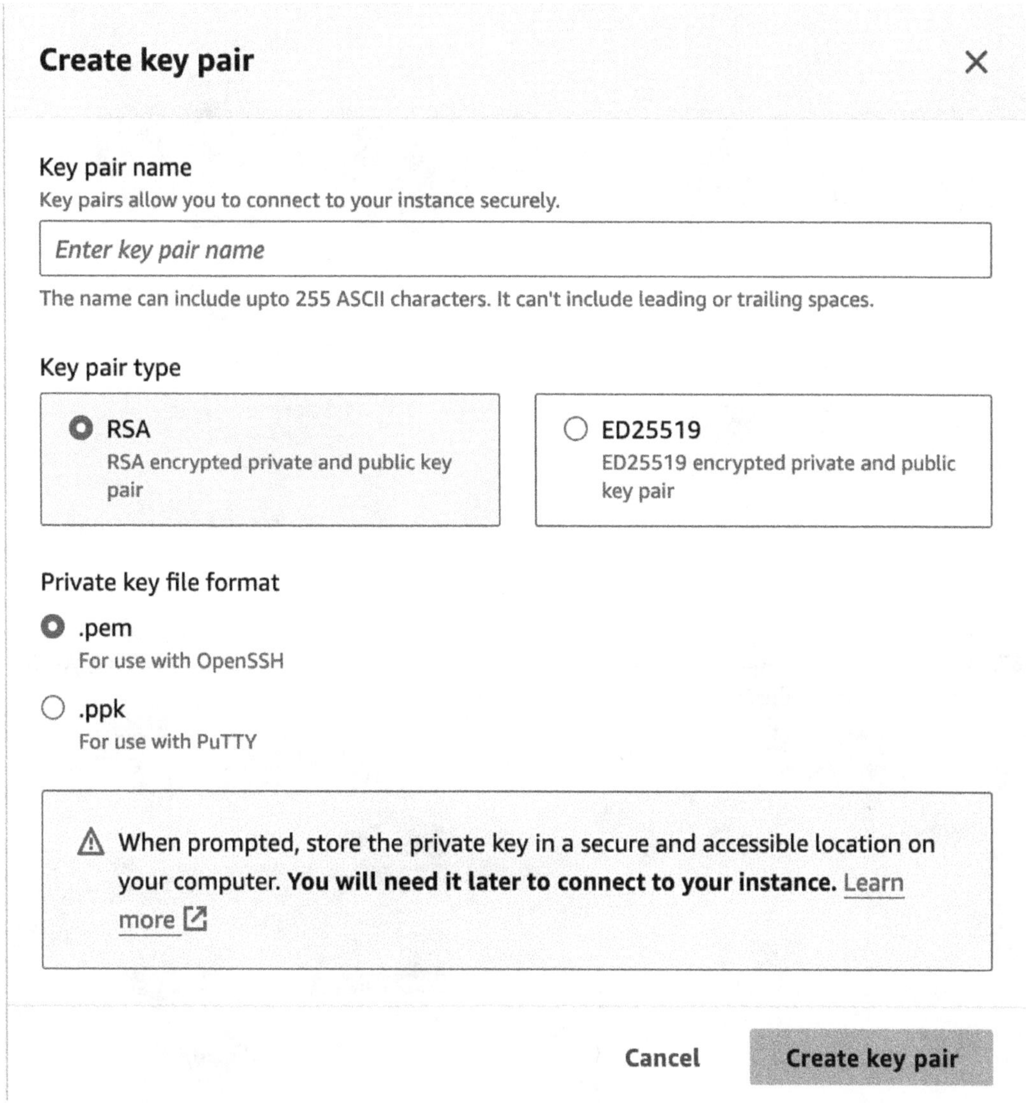

# Create key pair                                                  ✕

## Key pair name

Key pairs allow you to connect to your instance securely.

```
Enter key pair name
```

The name can include upto 255 ASCII characters. It can't include leading or trailing spaces.

## Key pair type

○ **RSA**
  RSA encrypted private and public key pair

○ **ED25519**
  ED25519 encrypted private and public key pair

## Private key file format

● **.pem**
  For use with OpenSSH

○ **.ppk**
  For use with PuTTY

> ⚠ When prompted, store the private key in a secure and accessible location on your computer. **You will need it later to connect to your instance.** Learn more 🗗

Cancel          **Create key pair**

Figure 13.108 – Key pair

36. Once you create the key pair, the private key will download to your local machine and you can go ahead and launch your VM.

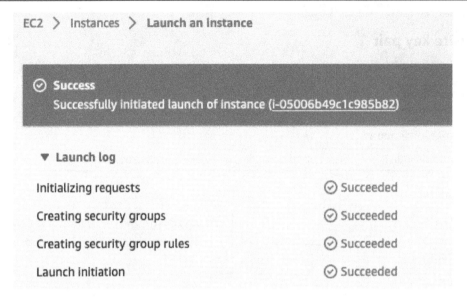

Figure 13.109 – Success status

37. You can navigate to your VM by clicking on the instance ID. Once you're in the instance, you'll be able to capture the IP and log in to your new VM.

Figure 13.110 – Public IP

38. To log in to the machine, you can use the key pair or the passwords created when you built the machine; either will work:

```
root# ssh oracle@3.135.211.36
oracle@3.135.211.36's password:
Activate the web console with: systemctl enable --now cockpit.
socket

Last login: Sat Aug 12 01:45:46 2023 from 107.200.172.229
```

# Index

## A

# P

**Pacemaker 161**
features 182
used, for HA clustering 181-189
**packages**
removing, via AppStream 327-329
**Packer 232**
used, for creating Vagrant box from Oracle
   Linux 8.8 source ISO 269-277
using, to modify source images 262-269
**Packer VirtualBox plugin**
reference link 271
**Parallel Availability 329**
**Parallel Installability 329**
**patching chaos**
controlling 406-413
**Payment Card Industry Data Security
   Standard (PCI-DSS) 279, 301**
**playbook creation**
reference link 246
**playbooks 394**
creating 422
running 422
using 394-405
**Podman 331, 332**
benefits 332
Docker Compose, using with 341-343
installing 333
rootless containers, running with 333, 334
utility containers, creating with 335
**pods 344**
automatic pod creation 347, 348
manual pod creation 345, 346
stacks, managing with 344, 345
**portable roles**
creating, for Ansible 246, 247

**Portainer**
used, for making Docker Desktop
   manageable 439-451
**port protection 304-307**
**port scanning tool 37**
**PostgreSQL 257**
**power-on self-test (POST) 68**
**Preboot Execution Environment
   (PXE) 2, 8, 29**
**Process ID (PID) 229**
**public key, adding to OCI console**
reference link 245
**PXE boot 29**
**PXE client 30**
**PXE server 30**
**Python 326, 327**

# Q

**quality assurance (QA) 24**

# R

**rack unit (RU) 14**
**RAIDed Btrfs volume**
creating 100-108
monitoring 100-108
resizing 100-108
**Raspberry Pi**
Oracle Linux, installing on 15-17
**Real Application Clusters (RAC) 165**
**reconnaissance 210**
**Red Hat Compatible Kernel
   (RHCK) 4, 66, 97**
removing 88-93
working 72-74
**Red Hat Enterprise Linux (RHEL) 127**
**Red Hat Package Manager (RPM) 2, 30, 127**

www.packtpub.com

Subscribe to our online digital library for full access to over 7,000 books and videos, as well as industry leading tools to help you plan your personal development and advance your career. For more information, please visit our website.

## Why subscribe?

- Spend less time learning and more time coding with practical eBooks and Videos from over 4,000 industry professionals

- Improve your learning with Skill Plans built especially for you

- Get a free eBook or video every month

- Fully searchable for easy access to vital information

- Copy and paste, print, and bookmark content

Did you know that Packt offers eBook versions of every book published, with PDF and ePub files available? You can upgrade to the eBook version at packtpub.com and as a print book customer, you are entitled to a discount on the eBook copy. Get in touch with us at customercare@packtpub.com for more details.

At www.packtpub.com, you can also read a collection of free technical articles, sign up for a range of free newsletters, and receive exclusive discounts and offers on Packt books and eBooks.

# Other Books You May Enjoy

If you enjoyed this book, you may be interested in these other books by Packt:

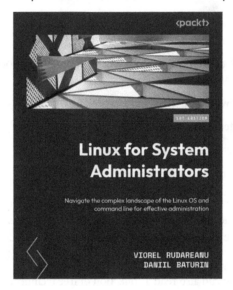

**Fedora Linux System Administration**

Alex Callejas

ISBN: 978-1-80461-840-0

- Discover how to configure a Linux environment from scratch
- Review the basics of Linux resources and components
- Familiarize yourself with enhancements and updates made to common Linux desktop tools
- Optimize the resources of the Linux operating system
- Find out how to bolster security with the SELinux module
- Improve system administration using the tools provided by Fedora
- Get up and running with open container creation using Podman

**Linux for System Administrators**

Viorel Rudareanu, Daniil Baturin

ISBN: 978-1-80324-794-6

- Master the use of the command line and adeptly manage software packages
- Manage users and groups locally or by using centralized authentication
- Set up, diagnose, and troubleshoot Linux networks
- Understand how to choose and manage storage devices and filesystems
- Implement enterprise features such as high availability and automation tools
- Pick up the skills to keep your Linux system secure

## Packt is searching for authors like you

If you're interested in becoming an author for Packt, please visit `authors.packtpub.com` and apply today. We have worked with thousands of developers and tech professionals, just like you, to help them share their insight with the global tech community. You can make a general application, apply for a specific hot topic that we are recruiting an author for, or submit your own idea.

## Share Your Thoughts

Now you've finished *Oracle Linux Cookbook*, we'd love to hear your thoughts! Scan the QR code below to go straight to the Amazon review page for this book and share your feedback or leave a review on the site that you purchased it from.

`https://packt.link/r/1803249285`

Your review is important to us and the tech community and will help us make sure we're delivering excellent quality content.

# Download a free PDF copy of this book

Thanks for purchasing this book!

Do you like to read on the go but are unable to carry your print books everywhere?

Is your eBook purchase not compatible with the device of your choice?

Don't worry, now with every Packt book you get a DRM-free PDF version of that book at no cost.

Read anywhere, any place, on any device. Search, copy, and paste code from your favorite technical books directly into your application.

The perks don't stop there, you can get exclusive access to discounts, newsletters, and great free content in your inbox daily

Follow these simple steps to get the benefits:

1.  Scan the QR code or visit the link below

https://packt.link/free-ebook/978-1-80324-928-5

2.  Submit your proof of purchase
3.  That's it! We'll send your free PDF and other benefits to your email directly